CORPORATE GOVERNANCE

The *Robert W. Kolb Series in Finance* provides a comprehensive view of the field of finance in all of its variety and complexity. The series is projected to include approximately 65 volumes covering all major topics and specializations in finance, ranging from investments, to corporate finance, to financial institutions. Each volume in the *Kolb Series in Finance* consists of new articles especially written for the volume.

Each *Kolb Series* volume is edited by a specialist in a particular area of finance, who develops the volume outline and commissions articles by the world's experts in that particular field of finance. Each volume includes an editor's introduction and approximately thirty articles to fully describe the current state of financial research and practice in a particular area of finance.

The essays in each volume are intended for practicing finance professionals, graduate students, and advanced undergraduate students. The goal of each volume is to encapsulate the current state of knowledge in a particular area of finance so that the reader can quickly achieve a mastery of that special area of finance.

CORPORATE GOVERNANCE

A Synthesis of Theory, Research, and Practice

Editors
H. Kent Baker
Ronald Anderson

The Robert W. Kolb Series in Finance

WILEY
John Wiley & Sons, Inc.

Published by John Wiley & Sons, Inc., Hoboken, New Jersey.
Published simultaneously in Canada.

Library of Congress Cataloging-in-Publication Data:

Corporate governance : a synthesis of theory, research, and practice / H. Kent Baker and Ronald Anderson, editors.
p. cm. – (The Robert W. Kolb series in finance)
Includes index.
ISBN 978-0-470-49913-9 (cloth)
1. Corporate governance. 2. Industrial management. I. Baker, H. Kent (Harold Kent), 1944– II. Anderson, Ronald.
HD2741.C77468 2010
338.6–dc22

2010010864

Printed in the United States of America

10 9 8 7 6 5 4 3 2 1

Contents

Acknowledgments

This book represents an ensemble of players, each providing unique contributions. *Corporate Governance* would not have been possible without the outstanding work of dozens of scholars and practitioners who wrote the chapters. We particularly and gratefully acknowledge their diligent work in providing multiple revisions of each chapter. The book benefited substantially from the capable editorial assistance of Meghan Nesmith, who painstakingly reviewed the chapters and made many substantive suggestions. We thank our talented publishing team at John Wiley & Sons, including Laura Walsh, Jennifer MacDonald, Michael Lisk, and many others. We appreciate the support provided by Bob Kolb, the series editor, throughout the process of producing this book. We also want to recognize the support provided by the Kogod School of Business Administration at American University, especially Dean Richard Durand and Senior Associate Dean Kathy Getz. Finally, we are indebted to our friends and families, who have been silent partners in this effort and have helped to make this project possible. Linda Baker deserves special thanks for her patience, support, and editing.

PART ONE

Background and Perspectives on Corporate Governance

History, Systems, Best Practices, and Empirical Evidence

Separation of Ownership and Control

CHAPTER 1

An Overview of Corporate Governance

H. KENT BAKER
University Professor of Finance and Kogod Research Professor, American University

RONALD ANDERSON
Professor of Finance and Gary Cohn Endowed Research Professor, American University

INTRODUCTION

The importance of corporate governance became dramatically clear at the beginning of the twenty-first century as a series of corporate meltdowns arising from managerial fraud, misconduct, and negligence caused a massive loss of shareholder wealth. The firm's owners (shareholders) asked who, if anybody, is responsible for protecting and promoting the value of their investment. Yet governance issues and problems have a long and sometimes shocking history. Adam Smith (1776/1904, V.1.107) wrote in *Wealth of Nations*:

> *Being the managers of other people's money rather than their own, it cannot be expected that they [managers] should watch over it with the same anxious vigilance which [they would] watch over their own. Negligence and profusion, therefore, must always prevail, more or less, in the management of the affairs of such a company.*

Based on their seminal work, Jensen and Meckling (1976) can perhaps be credited with bringing governance issues to the forefront in the field of finance. In scholarly finance research, agency theory provides the general framework for analyzing managerial behavior. Agency theory in its simplest form proposes that the firm's owners (principals) hire managers (agents) and then delegate the firm's day-to-day operating decisions to these managers. The theory further assumes that both parties—owners and managers—seek to maximize their personal utility. In the case of shareholders, this translates into stock price (wealth) maximization. For managers, utility maximization does not necessarily translate into maximizing shareholder wealth. Managers, for instance, may prefer to focus on short-term earnings that correspond with their remaining tenure in the firm rather than long-term earnings growth that leads to shareholder wealth maximization. Similarly, managers may seek to adopt low-risk projects that impose little personal risk on their future employment prospects or wealth, even if these projects do not maximize the wealth of diversified shareholders.

Obfuscating or manipulating accounting reports appeared to be a particularly prevalent form of the agency problem during the first decade of this century. Managers of large and well-known companies such as Enron, WorldCom, and Tyco engaged in illegal reporting activities that led to a massive loss of shareholder wealth. Because shareholders in many countries are largely absentee owners and managers control firm operating decisions, managers can place their own interests before those of the shareholders, thus generating a principal-agent conflict. Shleifer and Vishny (1997) refer to the agency problem as the issues that financiers face in ensuring that managers do not expropriate or waste funds on unattractive projects but rather provide an appropriate rate of return on invested funds.

Academics and practitioners sometimes question the adequacy of the principal-agent model in describing and prescribing the manager-shareholder relationship. Agency theory focuses squarely on managers and shareholders and assumes these parties work toward their own best economic self-interest. Yet other models depict different managerial motivations and/or different parties to the relationship. Stewardship theory, for instance, contends that managers possess sufficient self-motivation to act in the best interests of all firm stakeholders (Davis, Schoorman, and Donaldson 1997). Stewards of corporate assets eschew purely self-serving behavior that harms the firm and instead focus on promoting group interests because they inherently seek to do a good job (Donaldson and Davis 1991). Stakeholder theory argues that many firm constituents, such as employees, customers, and suppliers, have important stakes in the firm and as a consequence, their interests should be considered along with those of shareholders (Freeman 1984). Critics of agency theory further argue that the model only considers economic outcomes and ignores the ethical dimensions of managerial decision making. Yet, despite the alternative models and criticisms, agency theory remains the central paradigm in the finance literature when examining managerial decision making and the relationship that managers hold with the firm.

How do shareholders control and monitor managers who seek to maximize their personal utility? The fraction or portion of the firm's outstanding equity held by managers constitutes an important control mechanism. Jensen and Meckling (1976) note that as managers hold an increasingly larger share of the firm's equity, they are less likely to pursue self-serving actions as they bear a larger fraction of the cost. Consequently, in firms where managers hold large equity stakes, managers' and shareholders' interests may be well aligned, thus providing strong incentives to maximize shareholder wealth.

Building upon Jensen and Meckling's (1976) notion that managerial equity stakes alleviate the principal-agent problem, scholars of agency theory developed various incentive systems to align the interests of managers and shareholders. These systems or devices include stock option grants, restricted stock grants, long-term incentive payouts—generally, any monetary mechanism that provides managers with incentives to increase shareholder wealth. Via these wealth-sharing mechanisms, shareholders bear a cost but the cost may be justified if managers create more wealth than they receive. Yet recent history suggests that in many instances, the share of wealth received was insufficient to resolve the principal-agent conflict.

Beyond systems seeking to align managers' interests with those of the firm's owners, shareholders seek to control managerial behavior and actions through monitoring. Boards of directors arguably represent shareholders' most important monitoring device (Fama 1980; Fama and Jensen 1983). Boards have a fiduciary responsibility to represent the best interests of shareholders. In carrying out their function, boards undertake the duties of hiring, firing, and compensating top-level managers. Further, directors review and in many cases have final approval rights before managers can proceed with corporate actions. Understanding the importance of boards of directors in protecting shareholder interests, business scholars provide various prescriptions on board composition. Directors, for instance, should not simply be cronies of the top management team. Rather, board members should be independent of managers, bring knowledge and business acumen to discussions, and pursue actions that increase shareholder wealth.

Managers also confront monitoring and oversight from other firm constituents. Bondholders, an important provider of firm capital, seek to directly control managerial actions through covenants in lending contracts. Bondholders can indirectly control managers by varying the rate charged to firms for the use of their capital. Corporate charters, bylaws, and internal control procedures affect managers' behavior by explicitly defining permissible actions. Federal and state legislative bodies influence managerial actions by establishing legal strictures. Federal oversight also comes through regulatory bodies such as the Securities and Exchange Commission (SEC) and the Commodities Future Trading Commission (CFTC). Accounting procedures established through the Financial Accounting Standards Board (FASB) and other regulatory bodies seek to ensure that managers provide timely and relevant firm-level information, thereby allowing shareholders and other investors to make informed decisions. All of these strictures, regulations, and regulatory bodies affect managerial behavior and actions and influence the principal-agent conflict. However, the interests of some of these constituents may not necessarily be aligned with those of shareholders, thereby creating another level of conflict within the firm.

Corporate governance covers the broad array of systems, processes, and procedures that seek to regulate the relationship between managers and shareholders in particular and among all firm stakeholders in general. The chapters in this volume focus primarily on the relationship between managers and shareholders and, in some instances, between controlling shareholders and minority shareholders. Many classifications exist to describe corporate governance. Governance can be defined as internal or external to the firm. It can be described as being international or domestic. Governance can also be defined as to whether it seeks to provide appropriate managerial incentives or managerial oversight or monitoring. These classifications, among others, accurately and aptly define the multiple and varying dimensions of the subject.

Despite the growing interest in corporate governance, many questions still exist. The goal of this book is to provide a comprehensive view of the shareholder-manager relationship and to examine the current state of governance mechanisms in mitigating the principal-agent conflict. As a result, the book may help to improve public understanding about corporate governance and may contribute to the continuing debate surrounding this topic. Although the concepts and principles of governance apply to a broad range of organizations, the focus of the book is narrowed to address the governing of for-profit, publicly owned businesses whose main concern is to improve shareholder welfare and value. The sheer volume of work written on the subject makes the prospect of surveying corporate governance a daunting task. Consequently, the book primarily focuses on research conducted since Jensen and Meckling's (1976) treatise on the theory of the firm.

This book should be of interest to academics, managers, business students, regulators, and others interested in corporate governance. In fact, anyone wanting to gain a better understanding of the multiple facets of corporate governance for academic or applied purposes should find this book to be useful given its scope and currency. In particular, this volume should provide useful insights in educating business students and training current managers. For example, the book is appropriate as a stand-alone or supplementary book for undergraduate or graduate level courses in corporate governance. To this end, each chapter contains a series of discussion questions and guideline answers to help reinforce key concepts.

STRUCTURE OF THE BOOK

The book consists of 30 chapters divided into four main parts. These chapters are written by recognized scholars in the field of corporate governance who offer multiple perspectives. A brief synopsis of each part and chapter follows.

Part One: Background and Perspectives on Corporate Governance

The remaining nine chapters of Part One consist of two parts. The first part comprises Chapters 2 through 7, which provide an overview of corporate governance. These chapters offer a brief history of corporate governance, explore corporate governance systems, discuss corporate best practices, and review the relationship between corporate governance and firm performance in both a domestic and an international context. The second part consists of Chapters 8 through 10, which examine the separation of ownership and control. These chapters emphasize the role of agency theory and other approaches to corporate governance.

History, Systems, Best Practices, and Empirical Evidence

Chapter 2: The Financial Determinants of American Corporate Governance: A Brief History (Lawrence E. Mitchell and Dalia T. Mitchell) This chapter is a preliminary exploration of the interdependence of finance and the rules of corporate governance. It argues that the surviving rules and norms of corporate governance, among many that jurists articulated throughout the twentieth century, were primarily those that reflected the financial realities of their times. Finance drove the reconceptualization of New Jersey corporate law at the turn of the twentieth century, which in turn facilitated the great merger wave that catalyzed the intertwined movements for federal incorporation and antitrust reform. Finance made the attempts of the 1920s and 1930s to restrain corporate power ineffective and shaped public understanding of the form and function of the board of directors during the mid-century age of managerialism. Finance led to the broad acceptance of the monitoring board and the norm of shareholder value in the last decades of the twentieth century. The current financial crisis illustrates some of the consequences of the law's deference to finance.

Chapter 3: Corporate Governance Systems (Christian Andres, Andre Betzer, Marc Goergen, and Daniel Metzger) Hicks (1969) and Chandler (1977, 1984) were the first to propose a typology of capitalist systems. Their typologies are based on the world's largest economies and the ways these economies finance and govern their companies. Since then, more general typologies have been advanced that propose particular factors to explain the differences in corporate governance across the world and ultimately the differences in economic growth. These typologies can be classed into two broad schools: (1) hierarchies of institutional settings, and (2) the "varieties of capitalism" literature, which is centered on the notion of complementarity. The former school includes several theories arguing that differences in corporate governance are due to differences in the quality of law, politics, and electoral systems, and the ways companies are financed. This chapter reviews these classifications and examines how they fit with the empirical evidence on national corporate governance characteristics.

Chapter 4: Corporate Governance Best Practices (Alex Todd) Chapter 4 introduces the concept of *aspirational corporate governance* (ACG). ACG proves a context and formal framework that boards might employ to guide corporate governance improvements for any organization regardless of its business objectives, control structure, or legal context. The ACG framework can be used to diagnose and design corporate governance principles, systems, and practices appropriate for the complexities of sustaining a self-regulating governance structure. ACG allows organizations to adapt through innovation to create new possibilities for delivering value in a complex, uncertain world.

Chapter 5: What's Wrong with Corporate Governance Best Practices? (Christopher Søren Shann Turnbull) This chapter critiques corporate governance practices widely promoted as being *best* for publicly traded corporations. The criteria used to identify good governance are those that minimize the involvement of regulators or lawmakers with such corporations. The different drivers of corporate evolution in Europe and the United States explain the development of some of the counterproductive practices in Anglophone countries. These include directors obtaining inappropriate powers, and conflicts of interest for directors and auditors. These intrinsically flawed practices have become enshrined as best practices in governance codes, governance metrics, regulations, securities exchanges, and the law. This chapter uses the natural laws of requisite variety, identified by mathematicians who founded the science of governance in the 1940s, to explain why current practices are not best. Natural laws explain why the communication and control architecture of corporations and corporate regulators do not permit executives, directors, or regulators to directly monitor or control on a reliable basis the complex workings of modern firms without co-regulators.

Chapter 6: The Effect of Corporate Governance on Performance (Sanjai Bhagat, Brian Bolton, and Roberta Romano) Corporate governance is the set of processes that provides an assurance to outside investors of a fair return on their investment.

This chapter focuses on the empirical evidence of the relationship between corporate governance and performance. While the findings in the earlier literature are mixed, the recent literature documents that better governance is sometimes related to certain measures of performance. First, better governance as measured by several academic indexes and stock ownership of board members is positively correlated with accounting measures of operating performance. Second, none of the widely used governance measures—indexes or individual board characteristics—are correlated with future stock market performance. Third, given poor firm performance, the probability of disciplinary management turnover is positively correlated with stock ownership of board members. Better-governed firms, as measured by the academic and commercial indexes, are less likely to experience disciplinary management turnover in spite of their poor performance. The evidence provides a strong argument for considering dollar ownership of the board members as a corporate governance measure.

Chapter 7: International Corporate Governance Research (Diane K. Denis) Research in international corporate governance establishes that legal systems and corporate ownership structures vary systematically across countries. Such differences have important implications for countries and for the individual firms within them. Country-level governance systems impact the development of financial markets and, therefore, the ability of individual firms to raise the financial capital needed to undertake profitable investment opportunities. Firms can partially overcome weak country governance through firm-level governance mechanisms and access to an increasingly globalized financial system, but should do so only if the benefits exceed the costs. Governance reforms have been common during the past 10 years. The goal of future reform should be systems of laws that provide for vibrant markets in which countries and firms can choose governance systems that maximize value.

Separation of Ownership and Control

Chapter 8: Agency Theory: Incomplete Contracting and Ownership Structure (Iain Clacher, David Hillier, and Patrick McColgan) This chapter discusses and highlights some of the key issues concerning agency relationships and the costs that arise from them. The two main agency relationships considered are those between professional managers and outside shareholders and between controlling and minority shareholders. Depending on a corporation's ownership structure and the institutional environment in which it operates, one of two agency relationships will dominate. The goal of corporate governance is to mitigate the costs arising from agency relationships. Thus, an understanding of agency theory and the factors that exacerbate agency relationships is important for the efficient allocation of corporate resources.

Chapter 9: Theories and Models of Corporate Governance (Thomas W. Joo) Chapter 9 is a brief historical survey of American legal theory's leading models of the corporation, with emphasis on the contemporary theory of contractarianism. Legal theory must be understood within the historical context that shapes its normative goals and underlying normative assumptions. Theorists should not simply apply this insight retrospectively to others' work, but should expressly consider and discuss it in formulating and presenting their own future theories.

Chapter 10: Unfettered Agents: The Role of Ethics in Corporate Governance (Donald Nordberg) The theory and practice of corporate governance potentially point to substantial and even catastrophic risk if the agents of shareholders (senior management) are left unfettered and free to choose their own direction. From the 1930s to the present day, corporate collapses point to the need for mechanisms to control managers. Critics of the principal-agent approach argue that agency theory and its solutions do not singularly hold the answer because the theory takes an economic rather than ethical view of behavior. This chapter explores the main theoretical perspectives that have contributed to knowledge of corporate governance: agency, stewardship, and stakeholder. The chapter sets these perspectives against three competing views of ethics, pitting utilitarian against deontological views, and then shows how the renewed interest among philosophers in virtue ethics in recent years might help better explain boardroom decisions.

Part Two: Internal Governance

Part Two consists of seven chapters, which review and investigate governance systems that work internally to the firm. This section also contains two parts. The first part includes Chapters 11 to 13, which examine the boards of directors, while the second part consists of Chapters 14 to 17, which review the role of compensation, equity ownership structure, and turnover as internal control mechanisms.

Boards of Directors

Chapter 11: Board Composition and Organization Issues (Matteo Tonello) This chapter examines the composition of boards of directors in today's U.S. public companies. The topics covered include size and diversity, professional backgrounds, independence and affiliations, age restrictions and retirement policies, and limits to serving on multiple boards. The chapter describes practical organizational issues, including the formation of standing and special committees, the adoption of classification structures, leadership assignments, attendance policies, executive sessions for outside directors, and other operational matters. The discussion of major legal standards and best practices is accompanied by current statistical data based on proxy statement analyses and a survey of corporate members of The Conference Board, the New York-based independent research organization.

Chapter 12: Board Diversity (Daniel Ferreira) This chapter discusses some of the research findings concerning board composition with an emphasis on the demographic characteristics of board members. The chapter starts with a discussion of how economics and management scholars differ in their theoretical analyses of board diversity. These theoretical perspectives are then used to uncover the costs and benefits of board diversity. After a brief overview of the empirical literature, the case of gender diversity in the boardroom is discussed in greater detail. Implications for research, business practice, and policy are briefly summarized.

Chapter 13: Board Subcommittees for Corporate Governance (Zabihollah Rezaee) Boards of directors often delegate their oversight responsibilities to board subcommittees. The three most common subcommittees are audit, compensation, and nominating committees. An audit committee, consisting of at least three independent directors, assists the entire board in overseeing corporate governance, internal controls, risk management, financial reporting, audit activities, and other oversight functions. The compensation committee, also comprising at least three independent directors, reviews, designs, and implements directors' and executives' evaluation and compensation plans. The nominating committee, consisting of at least three independent directors, commonly assists the full board in identifying and recommending candidates for nomination to the board of directors and to ensure a fair election process. The board of directors may also establish special committees for assistance in carrying out its advisory and strategic functions. Examples of special committees are corporate governance, financing, budgeting, investment, risk management, executive, litigation or investigative, and mergers and acquisitions.

Compensation, Ownership, and Turnover

Chapter 14: Executive Compensation: Incentives and Externalities (Phillip Geiler and Luc Renneboog) The classical framework on executive pay (including principal-agent, stewardship, and stakeholder theories) claims that remuneration contracts result from a market mechanism that is further corrected by several corporate governance mechanisms, such as good corporate governance rules, shareholder activism, shareholder coalitions, and top-management turnover. This chapter casts serious doubt on the effectiveness of this market mechanism. The available empirical evidence indicates that managerial self-dealing, the skimming of corporate profits by managers through compensation packages, and the existence of hidden compensation create a serious agency problem. In short, executive compensation often seems to be a mismatch with shareholder value creation.

Chapter 15: Compensation Consultants and Executive Pay (Martin J. Conyon) This chapter provides a review of the recent literature on compensation consultants and executive pay. Six major pay consulting firms dominate the market. These firms advise client firms about executive pay and frequently supply other services such as actuarial work. Some evidence indicates that chief executive officer (CEO) pay is higher in firms using compensation consultants. The hypothesis that CEO pay is higher in firms whose consultants face potential conflict of interests, such as cross-selling of other services, is not as empirically robust.

Chapter 16: Corporate Governance and Ownership Structure (John J. McConnell, Stephen B. McKeon, and Wei Xu) Concerns about corporate governance arise because of the principal-agent conflict that can occur when control of the firm is separated from ownership. This chapter reviews the literature, both theoretical and empirical, that investigates whether ownership of a firm's shares influences the firm's performance and value, where the "who" of ownership refers to classes of shareholders including managers, atomistic outside shareholders, institutional investors, nonmanagement blockholders, and families. There appears to be consensus that there is likely to be an optimal allocation of shares among the various classes of shareholders (i.e., an optimal ownership structure exists), but there is no consensus as to what that allocation is or whether it can be identified empirically.

Chapter 17: The Effects of Management Turnover on Firm Performance (Mark R. Huson and Robert Parrino) This chapter summarizes the theory and evidence from the academic literature on the effects of management turnover on firm performance. This literature, which had its origins in the sociology and management literatures of the 1950s, has also received considerable attention in the accounting and finance literature in recent years. Overall, the evidence suggests that management turnover can affect performance. However, the potential magnitude of this effect varies with the circumstances surrounding the turnover, such as whether it is forced or voluntary, the characteristics of the new manager (including whether that manager is an insider or an outsider), and the opportunities for value-enhancing change. The effect of turnover on firm performance ultimately depends on the condition of the firm at the time of turnover, as well as the ability of the board to identify a high-quality replacement manager and its willingness to support changes in the real activities of the business.

Part Three: External Governance

Part Three examines external governance devices and is divided into four segments. The first part consists of Chapters 18 to 21, which examine nonexecutive shareholders such as blockholders, families, institutional shareholders, and other owners, as well as shareholder activism. The second part comprises Chapters 22 to 24 and focuses on nonequity stakeholders such as creditors, banks, and others. In the third part, Chapters 25 to 27 deal with the role of proxy contests and corporate takeovers. The fourth part, which consists of Chapters 28 to 30, examines the role that accounting, legal, and regulatory intervention play in corporate governance.

Nonexecutive Shareholders

Chapter 18: Corporate Monitoring by Blockholders (Isabelle Dherment-Férère and Luc Renneboog) This chapter compares the ability of different corporate governance regimes to discipline poorly performing management. The analysis suggests that the German corporate governance system best assumes this disciplinary role. German corporations, as large shareholders and as new blockholders, remove underperforming management. Pyramid ownership structures do not hinder the exertion of control power by the ultimate blockholders. In addition, when a firm has contracted a substantial amount of debt with the German universal banks, managerial disciplining occurs more frequently. Although poor performance is correlated with higher managerial turnover, no evidence exists that disciplining is taking place by large blockholders in the United Kingdom. Executive directors who own large stakes seem to be entrenched in the firm even in the wake of poor performance. In the Belgian corporate governance system, corporations and nonexecutive directors assume the monitoring and disciplinary role. In contrast, the French system does not seem to be adept at removing poorly performing executive directors. The CEO dominates the board and little evidence suggests that board structure and composition are related to disciplining underperforming management. Furthermore, control by holding companies and the government entrenches the management of poorly performing French firms.

Chapter 19: The Governance of Family Firms (Morten Bennedsen, Francisco Pérez-González, and Daniel Wolfenzon) In the past decade, corporate governance research has documented that families control most publicly traded firms around the world. This finding has triggered a considerable body of research that seeks to understand the governance of family firms and their impact on firm performance. This chapter critically examines this literature. The chapter highlights the fact that the main governance issue facing family firms is balancing the benefits associated with having a controlling family with the challenges this structure imposes on minority shareholders. Common governance mechanisms are less likely to be effective whenever control and decision rights are concentrated around a family. The chapter emphasizes the crucial role of family governance in the allocation of resources and reviews recent studies that seek to understand the impact of family characteristics on firm decisions and performance. The chapter also discusses some of the most important topics for future research.

Chapter 20: Institutional and Other Shareholders (Chris Mallin) The global financial crisis has placed increased emphasis on the role of institutional shareholders such as pension funds, insurance companies, and mutual funds. In addition, the spotlight has fallen on other shareholders including hedge funds, private equity, sovereign wealth funds, and banks. In response to the increasing expectation for institutional shareholders to act as owners rather than simply holders of shares, they are becoming more engaged with the companies in which they invest. Institutional shareholders' engagement is facilitated by the various tools of governance: constructive dialogue, (proxy) voting, shareholder proposals (resolutions), and focus lists. The effectiveness of shareholder engagement is still open to discussion. Yet there have been notable victories such as *say on pay*, whereby investors can vote on remuneration committee reports, resulting in various companies amending their executive remuneration packages.

Chapter 21: The Politics of Shareholder Activism (Donald Nordberg) Shareholder activism is an exercise of power that may be benign or threatening to the interests of corporate management, boards, and other shareholders. The complexity of the relationships among management, boards, and others helps explain the difficulties directors face in pursuing shareholders' interest. What arises, particularly in relation to the growth of hedge fund activism, is greater dispersion of shareholder interests and growing questions about the legitimacy of how those interests are acted out in the political landscape of corporation governance. This chapter offers a framework to examine the stance that shareholders take when exercising or not exercising their power. Anticipating the expression of shareholder power involves assessing their intentions along three dimensions: (1) their attitude toward an individual stock (buy, hold, or sell), (2) their approach to activism (docile, walkers, or activist), and (3) their investment horizons (long-term, short-term, or *perverse*—where shareholders' economic interests do not coincide with their holdings).

Nonequity Stakeholders

Chapter 22: Executive Behavior: A Creditor Perspective on Managerial Ownership (Ronald Anderson, Sattar Mansi, and David Reeb) Using relational and adversarial models of managerial behavior, this chapter examines how creditors, an important corporate stakeholder, regard executive ownership. Based on creditors' unique claims on firm assets, the chapter argues that agency and stewardship models of managerial behavior offer differing predictions on the role of executive stock holdings. Using a sample of S&P 500 firms, the analysis indicates that creditors are particularly concerned with executive ownership, suggesting these important stakeholders view executive equity stakes as an important governance device. Further analysis reveals that during the late 1990s and early 2000s (a period of heightened governance interests), creditors placed incrementally greater emphasis on managerial ownership as a mechanism to protect their investments in the firm. These findings suggest that creditors perceive managerial ownership as an agency-theoretic governance device rather than a stewardship mechanism that fosters managerial commitment and promotes group interests. Overall, the analysis indicates that managerial ownership influences executive behavior.

Chapter 23: Governance of Banking Institutions (Renée Birgit Adams) This chapter documents some little-known features of bank governance involving bank boards and describes regulation and laws that are likely to influence bank governance. It also describes how organizational form and activities of banks may influence bank boards and provides some new evidence on these influences. The chapter points out some potential problems with the measurement of CEO compensation and ownership structures in banking. A main conclusion is that applying governance standards developed from the study of nonfinancial firms to banks is unlikely to improve bank governance.

Chapter 24: Corporate Governance: Nonequity Stakeholders (Marc Goergen, Chris Brewster, and Geoffrey Wood) Shareholders are not the only stakeholders in an organization. This chapter examines the influence of other stakeholders in a range of contexts, focusing particularly on employees. An influential strand of the finance literature focuses on the nature and extent of shareholder rights vis-à-vis employees. Unlike most of the current literature on the topic, which relies on a limited number of case studies and/or broad macroeconomic data, this chapter draws on evidence from a large-scale survey of organizations to highlight the complex nature of corporate governance regimes and how they are affected by the relative strength of unions and collective representation at the organizational level. The chapter looks at employment security and training and development across regimes. It also notes differences between societal institutions, legal traditions, political parties, and electoral systems across countries and indicates some limitations of the mainstream finance and economics literature along with the value of alternative socioeconomic approaches.

Proxy Contests and Markets

Chapter 25: Proxy Contests (Peter G. Szilagyi) Chapter 25 provides an overview of the role and effectiveness of proxy contests in corporate governance. Proxy contests have traditionally been viewed as an expensive and inefficient alternative to takeovers in forcing changes in corporate control. Indeed, until recently, proxy contests were relatively infrequent, waged mostly by individuals, and generally failed to improve corporate performance. However, a new wave of successful contests emerged in the 2000s, dominated by hedge funds seeking governance arbitrage and using innovative campaign strategies. Whether this new wave will be sustained in the long run depends on the SEC's new voting and proxy access rules that favor shareholders but are likely to reduce dissident incentives to initiate proxy contests.

Chapter 26: Corporate Takeovers and Restructurings (Mike Stegemoller) An important component of a well-functioning corporate governance system is the indirect external governance of takeovers and restructuring activities. Alongside the motives of creating synergies and taking advantage of market mispricing, takeovers act as a market for corporate control in which managers risk being replaced if they underperform, thereby mitigating the principal-agent conflict. Restructuring events such as subsidiary sales, spin-offs, equity carve-outs, and targeted stock issuances reduce agency problems by revealing information about the performance of subsidiary managers and relieving information asymmetries about the parent firm. Consequently, while there are different motives for takeovers and restructurings, both lead to massive changes in internal governance. Thus, examining these changes provides information about governance.

Chapter 27: Corporate Takeovers and Wealth Creation (Marina Martynova and Luc Renneboog) This chapter analyzes the expected synergies of mergers and acquisitions as reflected in the short-term wealth effects around the takeover announcement. Takeovers are expected to create synergies as their announcements trigger statistically significant abnormal returns of 9.13 percent for the targets and 0.53 percent for bidding firms. The characteristics of the targets and bidding firms and of the bid itself are able to explain a significant part of these returns: (1) *deal* hostility increases the target's return but decreases the bidder's returns; (2) the private status of the target is associated with higher bidder's returns; and (3) an equity payment leads to a decrease in both bidder and target returns. A comparison of the UK and continental European M&A markets reveals that the takeover returns of UK targets substantially exceed those of continental European firms, while UK bidders earn significantly lower announcement returns than continental European ones.

Accounting, Legal, and Regulatory Intervention

Chapter 28: Corporate Governance and Accountability (Renee M. Jones) This chapter describes the sources of corporate governance standards for American corporations and analyzes the accountability mechanisms designed to ensure that corporate officials act faithfully in the management of corporate affairs. The chapter focuses on the financial reporting system, under the U.S. securities laws, that forms the foundation of the accountability system, and discusses structures and rules designed to ensure the integrity of financial reporting. The roles of the SEC, accounting and auditing regulators, and the board of directors are examined. Special emphasis is given to the Sarbanes-Oxley Act of 2002, which aimed to correct perceived weaknesses within the system. The chapter concludes that U.S. corporate governance systems are sound in design but that problems in enforcement prevent the regime from effectively constraining abuses and excesses of corporate leaders.

Chapter 29: Corporate Governance Rules and Guidelines (Zabihollah Rezaee) The past decade has witnessed a move toward global financial markets and the cross-border flow of capital. Public companies worldwide form the basis of the global economy. Recent financial crises and the resulting global economic meltdown are rooted in a variety of factors including failure of market correction mechanisms and ineffective corporate governance. General perception is that subsidizing or bailing out troubled companies and their executives does not serve the economy, whereas better accountability and more effective and efficient corporate governance rules and guidelines should improve the global economy. Corporate governance rules and guidelines presented in this chapter are intended to promote a corporate culture and environment within which companies can operate to generate sustainable performance while protecting the interests of all stakeholders.

Chapter 30: Economics Aspects of Corporate Governance and Regulation (Valentina Bruno and Stijn Claessens) Country-level investor protection and other corporate governance rules can help alleviate agency problems and overcome contract incompleteness, encouraging better firm performance. However, firms already adopt governance practices voluntarily and, as such, the implicit and explicit costs of any rule may exceed its benefits. This chapter provides a survey of the relevant theoretical and empirical literature on this issue. Not surprisingly, in light of the complex interactions between corporate governance rules and firm practices with various externality effects, the literature argues for both positive and negative aspects of existing and new country rules. This review also makes clear that many issues remain unanswered due to methodological and data limitations. Nevertheless, a key finding of this survey is that corporate governance and related rules cannot be considered in isolation from other country-specific economic and institutional factors.

Part Four: Answers to Chapter Discussion Questions

Part Four gives readers answers to the discussion questions presented at the end of each chapter.

SUMMARY AND CONCLUSIONS

As this book suggests, corporate governance is a multifaceted subject. In broad terms, corporate governance refers to the way in which a corporation is directed, administered, and controlled. Corporate governance also concerns the relationships among the various internal and external stakeholders involved as well as the governance processes designed to help a corporation achieve its goals. Of prime importance are those mechanisms and controls that are designed to reduce or eliminate the principal-agent problem. Good corporate governance is important because it not only provides the cornerstone for the integrity of corporations, financial institutions, and markets, but also is central to the health and stability of world economies.

The current financial crisis has highlighted many corporate governance failures. As a consequence of high-profile collapses of corporations since 2001, heightened attention has focused on the corporate governance practices of modern corporations. As Kirkpatrick (2009, 1) notes:

> *. . . the financial crisis can be to an important extent attributed to failures and weaknesses in corporate governance arrangements which did not serve their purpose to safeguard against excessive risk taking in a number of financial services companies. Accounting standards and regulatory requirements have also proved insufficient in some areas. Last but not least, remuneration systems have in a number of cases not been closely related to the strategy and risk appetite of the company and its longer-term interests.*

The financial crisis required governments to make massive interventions in their financial systems. For example, the U.S. federal government passed the Sarbanes-Oxley Act in 2002 as a means of restoring public confidence in corporate governance. The financial crisis also led the Organization for Economic Co-operation and Development (OECD), which consists of the governments of 30 democracies, to update the *OECD Principles of Corporate Governance* (OECD 2004) and to provide an analysis of the role of corporate governance in the financial crisis (OECD 2009). The current turmoil in economies throughout the world suggests a need to reexamine the adequacy of corporate governance. This book provides a challenging and comprehensive synthesis of the myriad of theoretical and practical issues that arise from the debate on how to create effective corporate governance.

REFERENCES

Chandler, Alfred D. Jr. 1977. *The visible hand: The managerial revolution in American business.* Cambridge, MA: Belknap Press of Harvard University Press.

———. 1984. The emergence of managerial capitalism. *Business History Review* 58 (4): 473–503.

Davis, James H., F. David Schoorman, and Lex Donaldson. 1997. Toward a stewardship theory of management. *Academy of Management Review* 22 (1): 20–47.

Donaldson, Lex, and James H. Davis. 1991. Stewardship theory or agency theory: CEO governance and shareholder returns. *Australian Journal of Management* 16 (1): 49–64.

Fama, Eugene F. 1980. Agency problems and the theory of the firm. *Journal of Political Economy* 88 (2): 288–307.

Fama, Eugene F., and Michael C. Jensen. 1983. Separation of ownership and control. *Journal of Law and Economics* 26 (2): 301–325.

Freeman, R. Edward. 1984. *Strategic management: A stakeholder approach.* Boston: Pitman Publishing.

Hicks, John. 1969. *A theory of economic history.* Oxford: Clarendon Press.

Jensen, Michael C., and William H. Meckling. 1976. Theory of the firm: Managerial behavior, agency costs and ownership structure. *Journal of Financial Economics* 3 (4): 305–360.

Kirkpatrick, Grant. 2009. *The corporate governance lessons from the financial crisis.* Financial Market Trends. Paris: OECD. http://www.oecd.org/dataoecd/32/1/42229620.pdf.

OECD. 2004. *OECD Principles of corporate governance.* Paris: OECD. http://www.oecd.org/dataoecd/32/18/31557724.pdf.

———. 2009. *Corporate governance and the financial crisis—Key findings and main messages.* Paris: OECD. http://www.oecd.org/dataoecd/3/10/43056196.pdf.

Shleifer, Andrei, and Robert W. Vishny. 1997. A survey of corporate governance. *Journal of Finance* 52 (2): 737–783.

Smith, Adam. 1776/1904. The wealth of nations. London: Methuen & Co. http://www.econlib.org/library/Smith/smWNCover.html.

ABOUT THE AUTHORS

H. Kent Baker is a university professor of finance and a Kogod Research Professor in the Kogod School of Business at American University. He has held faculty and administrative positions at Georgetown University and the University of Maryland. Professor Baker has written or edited 10 books including *Survey Research in Corporate Finance: Bridging the Gap between Theory and Practice* (Oxford University Press, 2010); *Behavioral Finance: Investors, Corporations, and Markets* (John Wiley & Sons, 2010); *Dividends and Dividend Policy* (John Wiley & Sons, 2009), and *Understanding Financial Management: A Practical Guide* (Wiley-Blackwell, 2005). He has more than 230 publications in academic and practitioner outlets, including in the *Journal of Finance, Journal of Financial and Quantitative Analysis, Financial Management, Financial Analysts Journal,* and *Harvard Business Review*. Professor Baker ranks among the most prolific authors in finance during the past half century. He has consulting and training experience with more than 100 organizations and has presented more than 700 training programs in the United States, Canada, and Europe. Professor Baker holds a BSBA from Georgetown University; MEd, MBA, and DBA degrees from the University of Maryland; and two PhDs, an MA, and an MS from American University. He also holds CFA and CMA designations.

Ronald Anderson is a professor of finance and real estate and the Gary Cohn Endowed Research Professor in the Kogod School of Business at American University. He currently serves as the chair of the Department of Finance and Real Estate. He worked as corporate executive and engineer for Schlumberger Limited for over 11 years in the United States, Europe, Africa, and South America. Professor Anderson's research focuses on the relation between managers and shareholders, and also upon the firm's other investors and their interaction with firm managers and shareholders. He is perhaps best known for his work that examines the relationship between founding-family ownership and firm attributes in publicly traded companies. His research has appeared in such journals as the *Journal of Finance, Journal of Financial Economics, Administrative Science Quarterly, Journal of Financial and Quantitative Analysis,* and *Journal of Accounting and Economics*. Professor Anderson's consulting focuses on helping founding families improve corporate governance practices and assisting families in corporate matters such as succession, acquisitions, and project valuation. He received his BS in engineering and an MBA from the University of Pittsburgh, and a PhD in finance from Texas A&M University.

CHAPTER 2

The Financial Determinants of American Corporate Governance: A Brief History

LAWRENCE E. MITCHELL
Theodore Rinehart Professor of Business Law, The George Washington University

DALIA T. MITCHELL
Professor of Law and History, The George Washington University

INTRODUCTION

To understand the historical development of the rules of American corporate governance, one must understand the financial history of the modern public corporation, for that history contains the principal determinants of the roles of the corporation's directors, officers, and shareholders. While intellectual trends, responses to business crises, politics, and social pressures have all contributed to the development of American corporate governance rules, the rules that survived were those that reflected the financial realities of the time. Finance, in short, drove law.

This chapter begins with the dramatic growth in the scale of private business organizations at the turn of the twentieth century and developments in state corporate law that supported this growth. The first part focuses on New Jersey's revision of its general incorporation statute that took place between 1889 and 1896. Drafted in a manner that alleviated businessmen's concerns that competition among corporations in new industries would threaten the success of industrialization, this new corporation law provided tools to rationalize competition through combination. It was the first major legislation to permit corporate combination by loosening historically tight restrictions on capital structure and corporate purpose and offering means to evade increasingly confusing antitrust laws. Corporations could now incorporate for any lawful purpose and exist as holding companies solely to own other corporations. The statute gave investment bankers and trust promoters, acting through the board, the power to print corporate stock and use it to buy up corporations at inflated prices. Taking their fees in stock, these promoters, along with the original shareholders, then sold their stock to a burgeoning middle class eager to invest while continuing to control their corporations through a variety of legal devices. From 1896 to 1903 the new financiers combined between 2,600 and 8,600 corporations (the differential is based upon different technical but not substantive definitions) and created, by one estimate, $20 billion in new corporate capital. The financiers were now in control. The modern stock market—with its negligible shareholder protection and its embrace of an omnipotent board—was born.

The second part of the chapter covers the mid-century years, from the late 1920s through the 1960s, starting with efforts to use state corporate law to restrain corporate power exercised by the control group. It suggests that the financial structure of American corporations undermined such efforts. From the beginning of American industrialization, retained earnings and debt played by far the largest part in financing productive enterprise. During the Great Depression and for the three decades that followed, retained earnings continued to supply the majority of America's investment capital, protecting management from capital market pressures. Public shareholders were relatively unimportant and their numbers had plummeted following the Great Crash of 1929. This situation doomed the mid-century attempts to restrain corporate power by encouraging shareholder participation or by imposing stricter fiduciary duties on the board, especially toward their minority shareholders. Public corporations did not especially need their shareholders to fund operations, and courts increasingly retreated into a posture that allowed wide discretion to directors. Thus the age of managerialism was born at a time when self-financing, combined with relationship bank financing, protected boards from the pressures of their public shareholders and the capital markets.

An aggressive campaign undertaken by the New York Stock Exchange (NYSE) to broaden stock ownership among Americans in the 1950s and 1960s helped lead to an explosion in public stock ownership. Still, public stock did not finance production. Throughout the 1950s and 1960s, retained earnings and debt still dominated, and the law continued to defer to the reality of managerialism. But the 1970s brought change. The third part of the chapter shows the general breakdown of the public market in the 1970s which, along with political turmoil, brought increasingly radical demands for reform. Corporate boards were a principal target for those who challenged the establishment, leading boards to realize that their choice was either to provide a solution or to face tougher regulation. The result, firmly in place by the early 1980s, was the modern independent monitoring board.

Coming as it did on the heels of challenges to the existing managerial order, the monitoring model allowed courts to treat directors as agents of the shareholders. Moreover, with directors having limited time and knowledge, stock prices became the most accessible metric for a corporation's (and a board's) success. The contemporary norm of shareholder valuism was born. Takeovers, stock buybacks, and leverage became the principal techniques to achieve stock price appreciation, and shareholders—especially the now-powerful institutional shareholders—demanded it. Retained earnings disappeared as corporations used equity in order to return money to their shareholders, and corporate debt skyrocketed. Accommodating agents as the courts allowed, if not encouraged, them to be, corporate boards have since led American industry into financial disaster.

CORPORATE GOVERNANCE IN THE AGE OF TRUSTS

By 1890, monsters roamed the earth. Although only seven businesses were organized in the trust form, these businesses gave their name to an entire species of large manufacturing corporations that had sprung out of America's early nineteenth-century efforts at industrialization. Standard Oil controlled almost 90 percent of the United States petroleum market by 1878, and the Sugar Trust controlled 75 percent of the sugar refining industry by the 1880s. Other industrial businesses dominated local, regional, and national markets. J. P. Morgan, assembling U.S. Steel in 1901, recognized that unless he persuaded Andrew Carnegie to sell into the combination, he would have a competitor so formidable as to threaten the success of the already huge project. From New York to St. Louis, from Baltimore to Cleveland and Chicago, and beyond to the west in San Francisco, American industrial businesses, whether organized in the trust form or not, were becoming very large (Chernow 1998; Mitchell 2007).

Only a few industrial concerns achieved national dominance. Much more common were medium to large businesses that competed within their regions to capture enough revenue to pay high fixed costs. The railroads, with steady demand for rolling stock, new track, repairs, and the high cost of debt financing, suffered from overcompetition with a vengeance, but other new industries did as well. Attempts at cooperation to control competition and sustain production characterized many of these industries, beginning with the railroads and moving to petroleum, cotton oil, lead, beef, flour, and steel. So in addition to large and growing businesses, Americans of the last quarter of the nineteenth century were confronted with an accelerating, if not yet entirely effective, movement to combine businesses into far more massive concerns. This was a worrisome development. Businesses that dominated their industries precluded competition and, more importantly, controlled pricing (Kolko 1965; Wiebe 1977).

By 1890, a number of states had passed strong antitrust measures, encouraged by a rural population that feared the power these large companies had over the prices of farming and living necessities. In 1890 Congress passed the Sherman Anti-Trust Act. But these efforts had little significant direct effect. Just as small farmers, manufacturers, and shopkeepers feared the flour trust, the sugar trust, and Sears Roebuck, so larger industrialists needed to create trusts to eliminate ruinous price competition that drove prices below fixed costs and threatened bankruptcy. In a world driven by finance, the industrialists' concerns won (Mitchell 2007).

Changes in state corporate law were crucial in undermining federal antitrust regulation by accommodating the industrialists' needs. Nineteenth-century corporate law imposed tight limits on what corporations could do. They could not own stock in other corporations, merge without the unanimous consent of the shareholders, or capitalize their businesses at valuations of their own determination. These limitations, along with traditional common law restraint of trade doctrines, stymied business cooperation as the century drew to a close. Several states including Maine, West Virginia, and Delaware modified their corporate laws to give boards more power to order the affairs of their corporations. No law was as comprehensive or as aggressively marketed as that of New Jersey (Horwitz 1992; Grandy 1993; Mitchell 2007).

In 1888 (effective 1889), New Jersey amended its corporate law to permit one corporation to own stock in another. In slightly (but economically immaterial) different form, this revision effectively legalized the outlawed trust form of business combination. By the time trust lawyer James B. Dill comprehensively rewrote what became the New Jersey Corporation Law of 1896, all of the transformative pieces were in place. New Jersey corporations could own and vote the stock of other corporations, incorporate for any lawful purpose (including simply to own stock in other companies), operate entirely out of state as long as they maintained a registered office in New Jersey (which meant a plaque on the wall of the newly formed Corporation Trust Company of New Jersey), and, most important, use their own stock to buy assets, including the stock of other companies (Report of Commissioners 1896; Mitchell 2007). This last provision appeared in other state corporation laws by 1896, but New Jersey went a step further. In the absence of actual fraud, its statute gave the directors the sole power to determine the value of the assets to be purchased (and thus the stock to be issued). Most of the giant business combinations of the turn of the century were formed and financed by virtue of this new law. Before long, most states had adopted laws similar to New Jersey's (Mitchell 2007).

American industrialization might well have continued on the nineteenth-century trajectory it had set for itself had its structure not been changed by New Jersey's liberation of boards. New Jersey's statute allowed directors to buy corporations for inflated prices and to use stock instead of cash for these purchases. Given the incentives of trust promoters who took their fees in stock, the stock was promptly sold to a newly rising and financially ambitious middle class (Mitchell 2007).

Finance drove the liberalization of corporate law. The great merger wave that followed America's emergence from a four-year depression in 1897, just as the New Jersey legislature had fortuitously perfected its corporate law, brought an aggregate of $20 billion in new capitalization into the American business economy, primarily in the form of common and preferred stock and, to a lesser extent, bonds (Conant 1904; Moody 1904). The sell-off would, in fits and starts, continue through the middle of the nineteen-teens, catalyzed then by tax changes. By the end of the first decade of the century, a class of public stockholders had been established as an important characteristic of the American economy (Mitchell 2007).

This new class had little role in corporate affairs. The new corporate statutes ended the individual shareholder's ability to participate in corporate management. The erosion of the traditional *ultra vires* doctrine and the reintroduction of the idea that the board's power was original and undelegated helped minimize shareholder control. So did changing voting rules. Proxy voting, which was banned in the early nineteenth century, became the norm and an instrument to strip meaningful voice from the shareholders. The shareholders' right to remove directors at will was eliminated. In addition, states gradually adopted statutes allowing a simple majority of the shareholders to approve the sale of corporate assets, abolishing the nineteenth-century rule of unanimity. By 1926, the common law rule had disappeared in almost every state (Horwitz 1992; Tsuk Mitchell 2006).

Other legal devices further weakened shareholders. The newly legalized holding company allowed pyramiding, where one corporation controlled the majority of stock of many direct and indirect subsidiaries, leaving control with the shareholders at the parent level. This control technique soon became common (Bonbright and Means 1932). Outright restrictions on the voting rights of certain classes of shareholders, including nonvoting stock and conditional voting stock, also became common around 1910 (Stevens 1926: Tsuk Mitchell 2006).

Most important, the new statutes allowed the board to capitalize the corporation as it saw fit. This permitted financiers to use inflated stock to buy companies at inflated prices and dump the stock on the market. At first, overcapitalization was relatively transparent because common stock was issued at large par values, typically $100. But in 1912 New York became the first state to authorize no-par stock. The nominal justification was that the growing group of small, middle-class stockholders had been misled into buying speculative common stock because of a widely held and false belief that par value was the real economic value of the stock (Report of the Railroad Securities Commission 1911; Dodd 1930; Mitchell 2007).

No-par stock eliminated the problem of overcapitalization by permitting boards to avoid any notional amount of share capital. With this tool in hand, corporations could avoid the charges of financial fraud and corporate mismanagement that had been levied at them from virtually all corners of the nation. Overcapitalization continued to be an issue well into the 1930s, but mostly in the context of regulated industries in which rates of return were administratively determined. Industrial corporations were, for the most part, off the hook, and shareholders were left to rely for protection on questionable securities markets, the reputations of investment banking houses, and the arcane and still quite primitive science of valuation. Deprived of their voice, shareholders were also dependent more than ever on the goodwill of corporate boards and control groups for the integrity of their investments (Mitchell 2007).

Federal lawmakers tried to displace New Jersey and its imitators with a federal corporation law that restricted boards' almost unrestrained abilities to capitalize and combine corporations. While the principal corporate governance concern was to prevent the control group from engaging in fraudulent finance, the first serious calls for minority shareholder protection also began to be heard. These efforts continued following the Panic of 1907 and through the end of the First World War, culminating in failed attempts to pass federal disclosure laws to protect securities holders. In 1918 shareholder-protective disclosure legislation first received serious congressional attention, backed by President Wilson. But these early efforts fizzled by the beginning of the next decade (Seligman 2003; Mitchell 2007).

Finance triumphed with a vengeance, offering the new class of shareholders seemingly more valuable gains than protective legislation. The laws that were drawn to serve finance, and a business movement that was financially driven, transformed the character of American business from industrial production to financial manipulation. Where the industrialists of the nineteenth century lived very well on their dividends, the financiers of the twentieth century and their clients demanded large multiples of earnings for the opportunity to share in the future profits of industry. Manufacturing was simply a means to that end.

The well-known banker domination of the boards of industrial corporations was firmly in place in the early decades of the twentieth century, accomplished by such devices as voting trusts and pyramided holding companies (Berle and Means 1932). These investment-banking houses that put together the combinations and controlled the boards had made their reputations selling bonds, and it appears to have been for the sake of bondholders that they ruled. But the principal goal of industry had become not only to pay interest on the bonds but also, and perhaps more important, to pay dividends on the stock.

The bubble that collapsed in 1903 showed just how difficult it was to support the new financial superstructure and how hard corporations tried. U.S. Steel is exemplary. Following the collapse of its stock price (after it had passed a dividend), Charles Schwab, consummate steel man and Carnegie's carefully groomed successor, was fired as president of U.S. Steel and replaced by trust promoter Judge Elbert Gary (McCraw and Reinhardt 1989). By 1908, the power of U.S. Steel's executive committee had been completely usurped by its finance committee.

The stock frenzy of the early part of the century left the new combinations with ravaged stock prices and unhappy shareholders. Stock prices could only be grown and supported in the long term by real earnings, not financial fads. U.S. Steel began retaining earnings to support its securities prices but it was not until 1929 that its book value reached its 1901 capitalization (Mitchell 2007). Other corporations bought their stock back from the market to achieve the same result. The consequence was that by the 1930s industrial corporations no longer needed their stockholders (who had largely deserted them following the crash anyway), but instead could and did live off their retained earnings. This practice persisted largely until the late 1960s and created the conditions for mid-century managerialism and its accompanying modes of corporate governance. These developments are examined in the next section.

FROM CRASH TO CRASH: INTERNAL FINANCE AND THE AGE OF MANAGERIALISM

The seeds of managerialism had begun to take root even as the aftereffects of the merger wave were still being addressed. For ordinary shareholders, having an interest in an enterprise no longer meant having power over the enterprise. This separation of ownership from control allowed corporations and, more seriously, the control group—an investment bank, a wealthy individual, or management—to amass tremendous power over individuals, groups, and even the state (Tsuk Mitchell 2006). The practice of retaining earnings to support stock prices kept corporations from returning to the public market and allowed them to finance primarily from within, protecting first control groups and later management from external scrutiny. For more than two decades after the Great Crash of 1929, public stockholding dropped to a tiny proportion of the population and active trading was desultory, leaving the potential pressure of the market so dissolute that control groups and management-controlled corporate boards had little to fear from their shareholders (Sobel 1975).

Reformers and corporate law scholars were concerned about these developments. With concentrated and seemingly unrestrained power dominating American corporate behavior, attention shifted from the capitalization concerns of the first two decades to the perennial issue of corporate power. In the 1920s, reformers focused on empowering minority shareholders to counter the control group and help channel corporate power toward socially beneficial goals. Some sought to achieve these goals by imposing on corporations mandatory voting rights while other reformers called for establishing permanent shareholder representative organizations to communicate with management (Tsuk Mitchell 2006). Ultimately, corporate law scholars converged on a different solution. In a series of early to mid-1930s books and articles, legal scholars such as Adolf A. Berle Jr. and William O. Douglas attempted to define a distinct role for the board of directors (as distinguished from management) in restraining the control group from abusing corporate power. They described corporate powers as powers in trust and directors as trustees for the corporation, its shareholders, and the community (Tsuk Mitchell 2009).

Berle, who viewed directors as trustees for the shareholders, wanted the board to protect the public shareholders from fraud and other manipulative practices that plagued the securities markets in the early decades of the twentieth century. He believed that in so doing, directors would also help channel corporate power toward socially beneficial goals (Berle 1931 and 1932). Douglas was especially concerned about corporate internal hierarchies and wanted directors to protect public shareholders from management. He called for the creation of an independent board of directors, the task of which would be to set the corporation's policies and monitor the executives lest they abuse their managerial power to benefit themselves or the control group (Douglas 1934).

Neither Berle nor Douglas saw any contradiction between the directors' role as trustees for the community and their role as the shareholders' fiduciaries. Both wanted to constrain those in control, whether investment bankers, minority owners, or management. Demanding that directors act as trustees for the community and that they represent the interests of public shareholders were thus complementary requirements. Theirs was nonetheless a position that the courts did not find easy to embrace. More broadly, the courts never fully endorsed the trusteeship idea. Instead, courts preferred to view the directors' role as analogous to the position of elected officials in a representative democracy (Tsuk Mitchell 2009). Combined with a financial structure that shielded corporations (and their boards) from the public markets, describing directors as representatives helped severely dilute directors' (and managers') duties.

By the early 1940s, as more shareholders attempted to use the derivative suit to challenge directors' actions, courts (with New York courts at the helm) drew on the model of representative democracy to limit the shareholders' ability to challenge directors' actions. The courts' tool was an exemption from liability for honest mistakes (that is, mistakes that even a prudent person might make) from which directors benefited throughout the nineteenth century. Expanding the scope of this exemption to encompass any and all directors' mistakes, courts created the modern business judgment rule as a rule of complete deference to directors' expert opinion. In the absence of fraud, conflict of interest, or bad faith, courts refrained from evaluating directors' actions in matters entrusted to their discretion even when the directors' errors were gross. Shareholders, who were already precluded from instructing directors as to how the corporation should be managed (even in closely held corporations), were now also mostly prevented from challenging directors' decisions that harmed the corporation (Tsuk Mitchell 2009).

At the same time, courts also used the concept of fairness to replace earlier notions of trust as the foundation of the duty of loyalty. Trust required corporate directors and managers to work in their corporation's best interests and prohibited them from considering their interests while dealing with matters within the scope of their fiduciary obligations. In turn, fairness, a concept of balance and proportionality, allowed directors and managers to take their own interests into account in their examination of self-dealing transactions. Within a few decades, the courts' fairness test became fixated on process rather than substance. By the end of the twentieth century, the circumstances in which a fiduciary could be found to violate this fairness standard were relatively few (Mitchell 1993).

Federal regulation also did little to protect the shareholders' role in corporate affairs. In 1943, the Securities and Exchange Commission (SEC) attempted to help disenfranchised shareholders by passing Rule 14a-8, which required the board of directors to include certain proposals from shareholders in its annual proxy solicitation. The SEC staff saw the small, long-term shareholder as the principal beneficiary of the rule. Presumably, the rule was designed to protect the individual shareholder against the corporation's management. The directors, viewed as the shareholders' representatives (or fiduciaries), were entrusted with the task of mediating potential conflicts between management and shareholders (Committee on Interstate and Foreign Commerce, House of Representatives, Hearings 1943; Nicholas 2002; Tsuk Mitchell 2006).

By the time Rule 14a-8 was enacted, though, the SEC had lapsed into a period of dormancy and ineffectiveness following significant attempts at market reform, first by Chairman William Douglas and then by his less-effective successor, Jerome Frank. After Frank's relatively brief term as chairman and a very short interval in which Edward Eicher served in the position, Roosevelt appointed the conciliatory Ganson Purcell as chairman, ushering in a period of SEC complacency that lasted until Kennedy's appointment of William C. Cary in 1961. At the time of Purcell's appointment, business groups, their patience exhausted by the regulatory flowering of the New Deal and the aggressive stock exchange reforms hammered out between Douglas and NYSE president William McChesney Martin, were adamantly opposed to any attempt to promote shareholder activism (Sobel 1975; Seligman 2003). And the SEC staff saw merit in their opposition. While insisting on enacting Rule 14a-8, the SEC staff was tentative about the appropriate scope of shareholder participation. Purportedly seeking to promote shareholder democracy, the SEC staff also hoped that the ideal of shareholder democracy would legitimize management's power to run the corporation (Tsuk Mitchell 2006).

Subsequent developments brought that latter aspect to the fore as American industry performed well during the Truman administration. Beginning shortly after its adoption (and continuing well into the 1980s), the shareholder proposal rule, especially the definition of proper subjects for shareholder proposals and the qualifications of the submitting shareholders, underwent cycles of interpretation and amendment by the SEC and the courts. These changes corresponded to and helped shape changing visions of the relationship between shareholders, executives, and directors in the large public corporation. Ultimately, these changes destroyed any possibility of effective shareholder participation.

The first set of changes to Rule 14a-8, adopted in 1947, formalized the role of the SEC's Division of Corporation Finance in reviewing shareholder proposals that corporations wanted to omit from their proxy statements. A year later, the SEC made additional changes, expanding the conditions under which a corporation was allowed to exclude proposals addressing proper subjects. In 1952, the SEC went further, excluding from the scope of permissible shareholder proposals those addressing "general economic, political, racial, religious, social or similar causes" (SEC Release No. 4775). Two years later, the SEC excluded proposals referring to ordinary business from the appropriate scope of shareholders action. Corporations could omit both those proposals having to do with too general (economic, political, racial, religious, or social) matters and those dealing with too narrow issues—that is, ordinary business (Emerson and Latcham 1954; Nicholas 2002; Tsuk Mitchell 2006).

The 1954 amendments left little of the original purpose of the shareholder proposal rule. The only power that shareholders still had, other than the ability to sell their stock, was the often-impractical power to launch a proxy contest. Instead of seeking to foster communication and cooperation between individual shareholders and managers, the 1954 amendments helped legitimate representative democracy as the model of corporate governance. The idea that public shareholders were merely investors, as distinguished from participants, prevailed. By the 1990s, this market-centered vision would dominate not only the SEC's and courts' interpretation of the shareholder proposal rule but also corporate law more generally (Tsuk Mitchell 2006).

There are different explanations for the rise and demise of the shareholder proposal rule and the erosion of directors' duties. The best, though not exclusive, explanation lies in the financial reality of mid-century public corporations. Heavy reliance on internal finance insulated the control group, which had begun to pass from large shareholders and investment bankers to management-dominated boards, from the discipline of the stock market and public shareholders. Corporations obtained necessary external financing largely from banks, with whom corporate management developed close relationships and whose representatives often sat on corporate boards. And politicians were in no mood to disturb American business during one of its greatest periods of expansion. With public shareholders largely irrelevant to business, the law could do little to invigorate them. Exhibit 2.1 illustrates the degree to which American corporations relied on their own earnings

Exhibit 2.1 Ratios of Internal to Total Sources of Nonfinancial Corporations, 1901–1962

Years	Ratio
1901–1912	0.55
1913–1922	0.60
1923–1929	0.55
1930–1933	—
1934–1939	0.98
1940–1945	0.80
1946–1949	0.64
1946–1956	0.61
1957–1962	0.61

Sources: Kuznets (1961, 248, Table 39) for 1901–1956; Sametz (1964, 455, Table 4) for 1957–1962.

to finance operations, showing the ratios of internal to total sources of funding of nonfinancial corporations from 1901 to 1962. The table shows that internal funding sources provided a majority of all corporate funding well through the middle of the twentieth century, peaking in the Depression years when external funding was unavailable but otherwise remaining substantial.

IRS records confirm the extent to which retained earnings formed the majority of corporate finance through the middle of the century. The remaining funds were supplied about one-third by long-term debt, roughly 10 percent by short-term debt, and the balance by accounts receivable. New equity capital was largely irrelevant (Mitchell 2010).

As late as 1952, only 6.5 million individuals—4.2 percent of the American population—owned any stock, and institutional ownership was insignificant, although the latter would start to rise substantially by the end of the decade. Taken by itself, the small number of public investors does not speak directly to stock's relative importance, or lack thereof, in corporate financing. But combined with the empirical data demonstrating the importance of internal financing, the conclusion that external stockholders were financially insignificant to corporate finance is hard to dispute.

Under these circumstances, the laws of corporate governance could only have minimal effect upon directors' conduct even if the courts or the SEC had chosen to be aggressive. Shareholders continued to receive dividends as the primary form of return on their investments at the discretion of the boards, and a continuous stream of dividends served a protective function against widespread shareholder activism or shareholder suits.

Reformers could also easily assume that there was no need to protect public shareholders as public shareholders' interests were not, in fact, ignored. Studies found that between the late 1930s and the 1960s, a plurality to a majority of public corporations had control blocks of stock; 27 percent of directors by the late 1950s were substantial shareholders or representatives of financial institutions; and, on average, boards owned just less than 10 percent of their corporations' stock. Moreover, executive stock compensation had reached at least 36 percent of total executive compensation in the late 1950s and early 1960s (Mitchell 2007). If one accepted, as many had come to do, that shareholders were only investors, there seemed to be little need further to protect the public shareholders' ability to affect the management of their corporations. The road for the market-centered vision of the corporation was paved.

TO MARKET

Even as internal finance helped to sustain the managerial era, developments were taking place that laid the groundwork for a massive change in corporate governance from the management board to the independent monitoring board. With this change came an almost absolute shield from liability, a shift in the description of directors from trustees or representatives of the shareholders to agents of the shareholders, and a turn from managerial concern with business growth to shareholder valuism. Corporate boards' focus shifted from managing for growth to managing for stock price. As had been true at the turn of the century, the fulcrum of change was the stock market. The monitoring board that emerged from the turbulent 1970s saw stock price as its metric of corporate performance and the enhancement of shareholder value as its mandate.

As noted earlier, stock ownership was not widespread among the American population during the middle of the century, and the market was neither active nor deep. This caused particular concern for the members of the New York Stock Exchange (NYSE), especially among commission brokers who made their living by selling stock to outsiders. Average annual turnover on the NYSE between 1945 and 1955 was 15.72 percent, with a high of 24 percent in 1945 and a low of 13 percent in 1952 (NYSEData.com Factbook). As NYSE historian Robert Sobel (1975) notes, many exchange members could no longer even afford to lunch at the NYSE's exclusive club.

The NYSE decided to address the problem by mass marketing stock—or the idea of investing in stock—much in the same way that consumer industries throughout the country had long been doing. Under its new president, G. Keith Funston, the NYSE embarked upon a campaign called "Own Your Share of American Business." So focused was Funston on trading volume that his speeches admitted his lack of concern over who issued stock, as long as there was stock to bring investors' dollars to the floor of the NYSE. Advertising was sophisticated and targeted various potential groups of stock buyers based on extensive market research. Reviving, after a fashion, the early-century brokerage houses' "buy on time" plans, the NYSE initiated a successful Monthly Investment Plan to facilitate stock buying by Americans of modest means. And, partly ignoring the more aggressive advice of its advertising agency, the NYSE emphasized dividends and carefully worded the risks of stock ownership in a manner that was both truthful and comforting (Mitchell 2010).

The NYSE emphasized dividends because it explicitly hoped not only to increase its members' income with widespread share ownership but also to establish a broader political base with which to lobby against double taxation. At the same time, the "Own Your Share of American Business" campaign bore the origins of the modern speculative market for capital gains. The NYSE was perfectly honest with its members that stimulating broader stock holdings could create a more speculative market (and therefore higher turnover and higher commissions). Low turnover meant low commissions and lower profits for the specialists who controlled the NYSE. Hence, in its 1955 Annual Report (NYSE 1955), the NYSE also complained that the Federal Reserve Board, through a lack of understanding of the importance of securities credit, had raised margin requirements twice that year. While buying stock on margin could be consistent with the desire for dividends, it was considerably more clearly related to investing for capital appreciation.

Explosive market development in the succeeding years, with a marked turn to investing for capital gains, demonstrated the success of the NYSE's programs. Turnover remained at pre-campaign levels throughout the 1960s. But by the early 1970s, turnover had begun a more or less steady upward trend through 40 percent and 50 percent and climbing higher to annual turnovers more like 54 percent in 1993. It soared into the 80 to 90 percent range and beyond later that decade, reaching a high of 123 percent in 2007 (NYSEdata.com Factbook). Similarly, while dividends were the currency of investing in the 1950s, they became less important to investors in the 1960s and have continued along this path since. The NYSE had succeeded in its goals, and shareholders' desires for dividends gave way to the demand for capital appreciation. Greater volatility and higher brokers' profits were the result (Sobel 1975; Mitchell 2010).

Stock ownership also increased rapidly in the 1960s. By 1965 more than 20 million individuals—10 percent of the population—owned stock, and in 2002 slightly more than 84 million Americans, or 29 percent of the total population, directly owned stock. Additionally, a major difference occurred in the form of ownership. Although indirect ownership through institutions was practically nonexistent in 1952 and modest in 1965, a significant majority owned stock through institutions in 2002 (Mitchell 2009b).

This rapidly growing market hit some significant snags leading to important changes in corporate governance rules and norms. The back-office crisis of the late 1960s and the market collapse of 1971 caused extreme disruptions that, together with other crises like Watergate, the foreign bribery scandals, the 1970 bankruptcy of Penn Central, the dual oil crises, and growing inflation, as well as increasing popular discontent with the war in Vietnam, generated a search for culprits. The insular, secretive, privileged, and increasingly defensive managerial board provided a target. Major reform efforts resulted in the reconceptualization of the board, most completely articulated by Melvin Eisenberg in 1976 and enshrined by the American Law Institute in its *Principles of Corporate Governance*, which was received with great fanfare in 1979 (although it would not reach completion until 1994). The new board—an independent monitoring rather than a managing board—achieved consensus approval just in time for the takeover decade of the 1980s, by the middle of which a particular version of it had been firmly accepted by the Delaware courts (Mitchell 2009a).

Eisenberg (1976) wanted to use the monitoring model substantially to redefine directors' duties, but the Delaware courts saw matters differently. Responding to the demands of the legal and business communities, the Delaware courts focused on the structural aspect of the monitoring model, stressing the monitoring role of independent directors (independence narrowly defined as lack of control or domination by an individual interested in the transaction). This, in turn, allowed the courts to shield directors from liability. If a majority of independent, disinterested directors, following the courts' procedural requirements, approved the board's actions (including conflict-of-interest transactions), the courts declared such actions to be shielded from further judicial inquiry (Mitchell 2009a).

The Delaware courts' analyses of the 1980s' hostile takeover cases ensured that the inside directors were the true beneficiaries of the monitoring model's liability shielding function. Because successful hostile bidders typically replaced the board, any decision of a target corporation's directors to adopt a defensive tactic was tainted by conflict of interest. But because inside directors derived their livelihoods from their positions with the target corporation, they faced potentially more serious conflict than did the independent directors. Given the potential conflict of interest, a decision by a board to engage in a defensive tactic should have been analyzed under the fairness test, as was any other form of self-dealing. However, beginning with *Unocal Corp. v. Mesa Petroleum Co.* (1985, 955), the Delaware courts adopted a more lenient test—a two-prong test that assessed, first, whether the directors "had reasonable grounds for believing that a danger to corporate policy and effectiveness existed" and, second, whether the defensive tactic the board adopted was "reasonable in relation to the threat posed." More important, the Delaware courts emphasized that if a majority of the independent directors endorsed the defensive tactic under review, then the board's action would likely meet the burden of the *Unocal* test (Tsuk Mitchell 2009; Mitchell 2009a).

Delaware courts did more to shield the insiders from liability. Seeking to protect and encourage directors' discretion to say no to hostile bidders, Delaware courts turned their attention, generally, to the business judgment rule and its relationship to the duty of care. In *Aronson v. Lewis* (1984, 812), the Delaware Supreme Court declared that the rule, "an acknowledgment of the managerial prerogatives of Delaware directors," was a presumption "that in making a business decision the directors of a corporation acted on an informed basis, in good faith and in the honest belief that the action taken was in the best interests of the company." Placing the burden of rebutting the presumption on the party challenging the decision, the Delaware Supreme Court held that "absent an abuse of discretion, [directors'] judgment will be respected by the courts" (*Aronson* 1984, 812).

The informed requirement was not part of the business judgment rule before *Aronson* (Johnson 2000). However, in *Aronson* (1984, 812), the Court stressed that "to invoke the rule's protection directors have a duty to inform themselves, prior to making a business decision, of all material information reasonably available to them." Moreover, without precedent to support its claim, the Court also announced that "while the Delaware cases use a variety of terms to describe the applicable standard of care, our analysis satisfies us that under the business judgment rule director liability is predicated upon concepts of gross negligence" (*Aronson* 1984, 812).

Aronson radically changed the contours of the business judgment rule and duty of care. A year later, in *Smith v. Van Gorkom* (1985, 873), a case that shocked the business and legal communities by finding directors liable for breach of the duty of care, the Supreme Court of Delaware reasserted that "under the business judgment rule director liability is predicated upon concepts of gross negligence" and further concluded that "the concept of gross negligence is also the proper standard for determining whether a business judgment reached by a board of directors was an informed one." Unless a plaintiff arguing a breach of the duty of care demonstrated that the directors were grossly negligent (that is, grossly negligent with respect to the requirement to be informed), the directors would have the presumption of the business judgment rule and the court would not second-guess their actions. In short, a rule that originated in an understanding of human fallibility and transformed into a rule of deference to expert opinion had become, by century's end, a defense precluding judicial inquiry into the directors' challenged actions (Tsuk Mitchell 2009).

Delaware's legislature obliged in 1986 by enacting section 102(b)(7), which allowed corporations to include in their charters provisions that limited, or even eliminated, the personal liability of directors for almost all breaches of the duty of care. Other jurisdictions followed suit. Moreover, the Delaware courts, using *Aronson* as their precedent, reduced the duty of care to a bare minimum. Not only was the bar of gross negligence difficult to meet, but the courts also shrank the duty of care to the requirement that directors be informed, a duty that the directors could easily fulfill by following the script provided in *Van Gorkom* (Johnson 2000; Tsuk Mitchell 2009).

By the mid-1980s, the Delaware courts made it patently clear that the power of the monitoring board was absolute and unquestionable, including the power to prevent shareholders from exercising their right to exit the corporation by selling their stock to a hostile bidder. The Delaware courts legitimated their grant of such absolute power by protecting the shareholder vote—a meaningless ritual at best—from impediment by directorial action (Tsuk Mitchell 2006). As Delaware's Chancellor William Allen explained in *Blasius Industries Inc. v. Atlas Corp.* (1988, 659), the "shareholder franchise" is "the ideological underpinning upon which the legitimacy of directorial power rests." Whether the vote is "seen functionally as an unimportant formalism, or as an important tool of discipline," it "legitimates the exercise of power by some (directors and officers) over vast aggregations of property that they do not own."

Directors, in short, were neither trustees nor representatives but agents of the shareholders. Yet the obligations derived from their status as agents were limited to allowing shareholders to exercise their typically ineffective voting power. The monitoring model rested on the twin assumptions that the directors' actual function was to monitor the executives and that independent directors could best perform this function. While the courts did not explicitly make the connection, the independent directors, presumably without other ties to the corporation, made less fictitious the ideas that the shareholders elected directors and thus that the directors were their agents (Tsuk Mitchell 2009). The rhetoric of agency legitimated the independent directors' power while the courts' reliance on the independent directors' opinions helped limit the liability imposed on the board as a whole.

Why did the Delaware courts embrace the interpretation of the monitoring model that emasculated directors' liability? Again, the reasons lie in finance. The monitoring model was established on a financial background very different from that of the middle of the century. The stock market was rapidly growing, and corporations were using their retained earnings (and replacing them with debt) in order to be able to return value to shareholders, to avoid being taken over, or to finance those takeovers that succeeded. From its highs of the mid-century, internal finance dropped steadily and consistently through 40 percent in the 1960s, 30 percent in the 1970s, 20 percent in the 1980s, and the teens in the 1990s, to reach a low of 3.23 percent of corporate financing in 2002 following the events of 9/11 before recovering slightly to a little over 11 percent in 2005.

The idea that directors were representatives of the shareholders was suitable for a time when internal finance was the norm and public shareholdings modest and correlated well with a rule of deference to the directors' expert judgment. The notion that directors were agents seemed a better fit for a time when public stock ownership, and especially institutional ownership, had skyrocketed. But as agents, directors could not be presumed to be experts. They could only be described as performing the tasks assigned to them by their principals, the shareholders. In such a context, the business judgment rule could only be a means of protecting directors from their principals when the latter challenged how the task was performed; it could only be a rule shielding directors from liability (Tsuk Mitchell 2009).

The influence of finance reached deeper. With internal finance at record lows, the stock market became the principal governor of corporate behavior and stock price appreciation became an end in and of itself. While debt replaced retained earnings as corporate America's main means of finance, demands on American corporations to demonstrate elevated stock prices were multiple and growing. Apathetic individual investors and institutional investors alike came to see stock price as the best measure of corporate success, or at least as the best whip against corporate directors, their agents. And the courts made investors' wishes real. Viewing the independent directors as best suited for the task of guaranteeing continued stock price appreciation, the decisions of the Delaware courts simply advised directors as the shareholders' agents to maximize shareholder profit so as not to trigger the ire of their principals.

SUMMARY AND CONCLUSIONS

The corporate governance rules that have survived are those that reflected the financial imperatives of corporations over time. Little question exists today that the shareholder value norm dominates. Legal responsiveness to finance continues to develop as North Dakota has enacted a public corporations statute (the Publicly Traded Corporations Act of 2007) that embraces shareholder valuism by giving shareholders dramatically greater access to, and participation in, corporate decision making than they have thus far enjoyed. The SEC has proposed rules to facilitate greater proxy access (Rule 14a-11), a similar proposal is pending in the Senate, and even Delaware has modified its laws to permit corporations to provide greater participation rights to shareholders (8 Del. Gen. Corp. L., 2009). As history shows, continuation of this trend will depend upon the sources and needs of corporate finance.

This preliminary analysis demonstrates only correlation between finance and corporate governance rules, not causation, and proving the latter is doubtful even in an expanded study. But the correlation is sufficiently strong to suggest that those who study corporate law must study it not as an abstract body of rules but rather in the context of the business and financial realities that underlie those rules and to which they appear to respond.

DISCUSSION QUESTIONS

1. What were businessmen's concerns at the end of the nineteenth century and what is the relationship between law's response to these concerns and the emergence of the modern stock market?
2. How did the turn-of-the-twentieth-century changes to corporate law affect the role of the individual shareholder and her expectations? What were the financial and governance consequences of these expectations?
3. What were the 1930s and 1940s attempts to control corporate power and why did they fail?
4. What is the relationship between the rise of the monitoring model of the board and changes in corporate finance in the second half of the twentieth century?

REFERENCES

American Law Institute. 1994. *Principles of corporate governance: Analysis and recommendations.* St. Paul, MN: American Law Institute Publishers.

Berle, Adolf A., Jr. 1931. Corporate powers as powers in trust. *Harvard Law Review* 44 (7): 1049–1074.

———. 1932. For whom corporate managers are trustees: A note. *Harvard Law Review* 45 (8): 1365–1372.

Berle, Adolf A., Jr., and Gardiner C. Means. 1932. *The modern corporation and private property.* New York: Macmillan Co.

Bonbright, James C., and Gardiner C. Means. 1932. *The holding company, its public significance and its regulation*. New York: McGraw-Hill.

Chernow, Ron. 1998. *Titan: The life of John D. Rockefeller, Sr*. New York, NY: Random House.

Conant, Charles A. 1904. *Wall Street and the country: A study of recent financial tendencies*. New York: G. P. Putnam's Sons.

Dodd, David L. 1930. *Stock watering: The judicial valuation of property for stock-issue purposes.* New York: Columbia University Press.

Douglas, William O. 1934. Directors who do not direct. *Harvard Law Review* 47 (8): 1305–1334.

Eisenberg, Melvin A. 1976. *The structure of the corporation: A legal analysis*. Boston: Little, Brown.

Emerson, Frank D., and Franklin C. Latcham. 1954. *Shareholder democracy: A broader outlook for corporations*. Cleveland: Press of Western Reserve University.

Grandy, Christopher. 1993. *New Jersey and the fiscal origins of the modern American corporation law*. New York: Garland.

Horwitz, Morton J. 1992. *The transformation of American law, 1870–1960: The crisis of legal orthodoxy*. New York: Oxford University Press.

Johnson, Lyman. 2000. The modest business judgment rule. *Business Lawyer* 55 (2): 625–652.

Kolko, Gabriel. 1965. *Railroads and regulation*. Princeton: Princeton University Press.

Kuznets, Simon. 1961. *Capital in the American economy: Its formation and financing*. Princeton: Princeton University Press.

McCraw, Thomas K., and Forest Reinhardt. 1989. Losing to win: U.S. Steel's pricing, investment decisions, and market share, 1901–1938. *Journal of Economic History* 49 (3): 593–619.

Mitchell, Lawrence E. 1993. Fairness and trust in corporate law. *Duke Law Journal* 43 (3): 425–491.

———. 2007. *The speculation economy: How finance triumphed over industry*. San Francisco: Berrett-Koehler.

———. 2009a. The trouble with boards. In *The new corporate governance*, ed. Troy A. Paredes and F. Scott Kieff, forthcoming. New York: Cambridge University Press.

———. 2009b. Who needs the stock market? Part I: The empirical evidence. http://papers.ssrn.com/sol3/papers.cfm?abstract_id=1292403

———. 2010. The legitimate rights of public shareholders. *Washington and Lee Law Review, forthcoming.* http://papers.ssrn.com/ sol3/papers.cfm?abstract_id=1352025

Moody, John. 1904. *The truth about the trusts.* New York: Moody.

New York Stock Exchange and Affiliated Companies. 1955. Annual Report.

NYSEData.com Factbook.

Nicholas, Phillip A., Jr. 2002. *The Securities and Exchange Commission and the Shareholder Proposal Rule: Agency, administration, corporate influence, and shareholder power, 1942–1988.* PhD dissertation. State University of New York at Albany.

Sametz, Arnold W. 1964. Trends in the volume and composition of equity finance. *Journal of Finance* 19 (3) 450–469.

Seligman, Joel. 2003. *The transformation of Wall Street: A history of the Securities and Exchange Commission and modern corporate finance*. 3rd ed. New York: Aspen Publishers.
Sobel, Robert. 1975. *NYSE: A history of the New York Stock Exchange, 1935–1975*. New York: Weybright and Talley.
Stevens, W. H. S. 1926. Stockholders' voting rights and the centralization of voting control. *Quarterly Journal of Economics* 40 (3) 353–392.
Tsuk Mitchell, Dalia. 2006. Shareholders as proxies: The contours of shareholder democracy. *Washington and Lee Law Review* 63 (4): 1503–1578.
———. 2009. Status bound: The twentieth-century evolution of directors' liability. *NYU Journal of Law and Business* 5 (1): 63–151.
Wiebe, Robert H. 1977. *The search for order, 1877–1920*. New York: Hill and Wang.

CASES

Aronson v. Lewis, 473 A.2d 805 (Del. 1984).
Blasius Industries Inc. v. Atlas Corp., 564 A.2d 651 (Del. 1988).
Smith v. Van Gorkom, 488 A.2d 858 (Del. 1985).
Unocal Corp. v. Mesa Petroleum Co., 493 A.2d 946 (Del. 1985).

GOVERNMENTAL AND LEGISLATIVE MATERIAL

Committee on Interstate and Foreign Commerce, House of Representatives. 78th Congress, 1943. Hearings regarding H.R. 1493, H.R. 1821, and H.R. 2019 (bills to suspend the authority of the Securities and Exchange Commission under section 14[a] and section 14[b] of the Securities Exchange Act to issue rules relating to the solicitation of proxies, consents, and authorizations during the period of war emergency).
8 Delaware General Corporation Law 102(b)(7), 112, 113.
New Jersey Public Laws 385–386. 1888.
Publicly Traded Corporations Act, North Dakota 10-35-01 – 33. 2007.
Report of Commissioners Appointed to Revise the General Acts of the State of New Jersey Relating to Corporations. 1896. Jersey City: Jersey City Printing.
Report of the Railroad Securities Commission to the President and Letter of the President Transmitting the Report to Congress, House of Representatives, doc. no. 256, 62 Congress, 2d Session, December 11, 1911.
Securities Exchange Act, Release No. 4775. 1952.

ABOUT THE AUTHORS

Lawrence E. Mitchell has taught for almost 20 years at The George Washington University Law School where he holds the Theodore Rinehart chair in business law and serves as executive director of the Center for Law, Economics and Finance. His books include *The Speculation Economy: How Finance Triumphed over Industry* (Berrett-Koehler, 2007) (winner of the 2007 Foreword Magazine Gold Medal and the 2008 IPPY Award Silver Medal), and *Corporate Irresponsibility: America's Newest Export* (Yale University Press, 2001). Professor Mitchell has written widely on issues of corporate law, governance, history, and finance, among other subjects, and is a founder of the Progressive Corporate Law school of scholarship, named after his 1995 anthology. He is an alumnus of Williams College and Columbia University Law School.

Dalia T. Mitchell's writings focus on the history of U.S. legal thought. Her book, *Architect of Justice: Felix S. Cohen and the Founding of American Legal Pluralism* (Cornell University Press, 2007), won the 2007 American Historical Association's Littleton-Griswold Prize for the best book in any subject on the history of American law and society. She is currently working on a book exploring the relationship between corporate law and theory and the rise of the modern American state. Professor Mitchell is an alumna of Tel Aviv University, Harvard Law School, and the History Department at Yale University. She was a senior fellow at the graduate program at Harvard Law School, a Samuel I. Golieb fellow in legal history at NYU School of Law, and a fellow at the inaugural J. Willard Hurst Summer Institute in Legal History at the University of Wisconsin.

CHAPTER 3

Corporate Governance Systems

CHRISTIAN ANDRES
Assistant Professor of Finance, University of Mannheim

ANDRÉ BETZER
Assistant Professor of Finance, University of Mannheim

MARC GOERGEN
Professor of Finance, Cardiff Business School and European Corporate Governance Institute (ECGI)

DANIEL METZGER
Financial Markets Group, London School of Economics

INTRODUCTION

This chapter reviews the main taxonomies of corporate governance systems. The review not only covers the taxonomies developed by financial economists and legal scholars, but also discusses the so-called "varieties of capitalism" (VOC) literature, which has been ignored by most of the former two groups of scholars. Contrary to most of the finance and law literature, the VOC literature does not claim that one system or model of corporate governance is superior to all others. Rather, it is based on the notion of complementarity whereby a specific set of institutions, via their interactions, are more efficient than if each institution were to work in isolation. In contrast, the mainstream finance literature advocates the key role of stock and debt markets for financial development and considers all other institutional arrangements aiming at providing finance to corporations as inferior.

The remainder of the chapter has the following organization. The next section reviews the various taxonomies of corporate governance systems by focusing on the rationale underlying each taxonomy as well as its theoretical predictions. The following section then discusses the empirical evidence on cross-country differences in corporate governance and how the observed differences fit with the various taxonomies of corporate governance systems. The chapter then provides a summary and conclusions.

TAXONOMIES OF CORPORATE GOVERNANCE SYSTEMS

This section reviews the different taxonomies of corporate governance systems. The classifications presented in this section all lead to empirically testable hypotheses. While this section focuses on the underlying rationale behind each classification and therefore presents only very limited empirical evidence as to the validity of each classification, the next section provides a direct answer to the question of how well these taxonomies fit with the stylized facts known about the different corporate governance systems. The taxonomies reviewed in this section include the market-based versus bank-based systems, the insider versus the outsider system, legal families, political determinants, and the VOC literature.

Market-Based versus Bank-Based Systems

The first attempts to categorize different systems of capitalism go back to the seminal work of Hicks (1969) and Chandler (1977 and 1984). Hicks distinguished between market-based economies and bank-based economies. Market economies are characterized by their strong reliance on public equity and debt markets whereas bank economies rely on banks to finance corporations. Recently, Allen and Gale (2000) revived this classification. They distinguish between market-based and bank-based (or, alternatively, intermediary-based) systems of corporate control. Their analysis focuses on a comparatively small number of countries (the United Kingdom and the United States as examples of market-based systems and France, Germany, and Japan as examples of bank-based systems). Yet their main insights can be generalized to a large extent.

Following in the footsteps of Roe (1994), Allen and Gale (2000) point out that the differences in the history and regulation of the banking industry have had a large influence on the development of national corporate governance systems. In market-based systems, banks and insurance companies act mainly as financial intermediaries and only rarely hold equity interests in commercial and manufacturing firms. In the United States, regulation (mainly via the Glass-Steagall Act of 1933) has prevented banks from holding direct equity stakes in companies. Further, insurance companies as well as mutual and pension funds are restricted to a maximum equity ownership in a single firm to prevent them from having control over the firm.

Even though financial firms face less formal regulation in the United Kingdom, insurance companies follow self-imposed limitations with regard to their holdings in nonfinancial corporations. Conversely, regulation on corporate ownership by banks is far less restrictive in the bank-based system. In France, Germany, and Japan, banks are allowed to hold directly equity in other companies. Franks and Mayer (2001) show that German banks play an important role as providers of equity finance to corporations. In addition, the influence of banks is not just limited to their direct equity holdings but is further amplified by the proxy votes that they receive from small shareholders who frequently give the banks with whom they deposit their shares the right to vote on their behalf.

On the positive side, the strong role of banks potentially mitigates the free-rider problem associated with dispersed ownership (Holmstrom 1982). On the negative side, powerful financial intermediaries also come at a cost because they limit the development of public equity and debt markets by establishing close bank-firm ties. Allen and Gale (2000) argue that this not only has an effect on firm financing but also has consequences for private households. In market-based systems, equity is an important proportion of households' investment assets, whereas cash and bond equivalents make up the majority of households' assets in bank-based systems.

Insider versus Outsider Systems

The classification of corporate governance systems into insider systems and outsider systems can be traced to Franks and Mayer (1996 and 2001). According to their taxonomy, well-developed equity and debt markets, dispersed ownership, and an active takeover market are the characteristics of the outsider system. Conversely, the role of financial intermediaries such as commercial banks and insurance companies as financiers to firms and potential monitors of market-listed corporations is limited in this system. Managers of widely held corporations are primarily disciplined through the active takeover market—in other words, via hostile takeovers. Managers therefore act mainly in the interests of shareholders. Examples of the outsider system of corporate control are the United Kingdom and the United States.

In contrast to the outsider system, firms in the insider system are mainly governed by insiders who have privileged access to information. Corporate ownership is highly concentrated and forms complex webs via cross-holdings and pyramids. In many cases, founding families and other dominant shareholders hold seats on the board of directors and/or are directly involved in the management. Ownership is also very stable over time. The stable ownership, together with legal barriers to hostile takeovers (in particular for foreign investors), inhibits the development of an active market for corporate control. In this system, firms not only take the interests of shareholders into account but also consider the interests of various other stakeholders. For example, employees are granted control rights via seats they hold on the board of directors or other corporate committees. Most of Continental Europe can be classified as insider systems.

Legal Families—Civil Law versus Common Law

La Porta, Lopez-de-Silanes, Shleifer, and Vishny (1998) started a new strand of literature on corporate governance, which is based upon the premise that investors are willing to pay more for financial assets if their rights are better protected by the law. As managers tend to act in their own interest if left to their own devices, shareholders rely on legal means to ensure themselves an adequate return on their investment. Better legal protection guarantees that a larger part of the company's profits will be paid out to investors—in the form of dividends or share repurchases—as opposed to being spent on investment projects that primarily benefit entrenched managers. Shareholders will then be more willing to invest and entrepreneurs will be able to finance their investment projects with external funds more easily. As a consequence, law and the degree of its enforcement are important determinants of the development of financial markets and economic growth.

La Porta et al. (1998) examine how the legal protection of shareholders and creditors differs across 49 countries and analyze whether these variations can help explain the observed differences in corporate ownership patterns. Based on the idea that company law of different countries generally originates from only a few legal traditions (Watson 1974), they classify countries as either civil law or common law countries. Civil law derives from the Romano-Germanic legal tradition and mainly uses statutes and codes as the means of ordering legal rules. Among civil law countries, La Porta et al. further differentiate between the French, German, and Scandinavian legal families. Outside Continental Europe, the legal systems of countries such as China, Japan, South Korea, and Taiwan are also based on civil law. In contrast, common law, which is English in origin, is shaped by judges who make judgments in court which then act as precedents for similar future judicial disputes. Common law prevails in the former British colonies such as Australia, Canada, India, and the United States.

For each of 49 countries, La Porta et al. (1998) analyze the company and bankruptcy laws that govern the dealings between directors and shareholders as well as the dealings between the corporation and its creditors. Their analysis shows that laws vary substantially across countries, mostly along the lines of legal origin. Generally speaking, common law countries have the strongest and civil law countries the weakest protection of investors' rights and interests. Both shareholders and creditors are best protected in common law countries, while French civil law countries offer the weakest protection. German and Scandinavian civil law offers intermediate levels of investor protection. The authors find that the quality of law enforcement is highest in German and Scandinavian civil law countries, slightly lower in common law countries, and the lowest in French civil law countries.

La Porta et al. (1998) also argue that corporate governance mechanisms, such as concentrated ownership, have emerged to compensate for weak law. Large shareholders need less legal protection to enforce their claims and only rely on minimal support from the judiciary. Indeed, if managers repeatedly act against the wishes of the large investor, they are likely to be replaced swiftly by the latter. Therefore, large blockholders differ from small shareholders in the sense that they have not only the incentive to monitor the managers effectively, but also the power to do so. In line with these arguments, La Porta et al. find a negative correlation between ownership concentration and the quality of legal protection. Their evidence shows that the highest ownership concentration is in French civil law countries.

In sum, the influential paper by La Porta et al. (1998) provides strong evidence that the legal origin of a country's law is an important determinant of investor rights and the level of enforcement of these rights. Strong investor rights enable a separation of ownership from control whereas weak investor rights will prevent such a separation and maintain concentrated control.

Electoral Systems—Proportional versus Majoritarian

Pagano and Volpin (2005) propose a taxonomy that also takes into account the degree of investor protection. They argue, however, that ultimately the characteristics of political systems, rather than legal origins, explain differences in regulation across countries. They directly challenge the view of La Porta et al. (1998) that law, and hence the body of rules protecting shareholders, is exogenous to a country.

Pagano and Volpin believe that the recent reforms in corporate law and corporate governance regulation constitute strong reasons in favor of an endogenous relation: Politicians cater to the (economic) preferences of their voters and adjust company law accordingly.

Pagano and Volpin (2005) develop a model that deals with the setting of company law (i.e., shareholder protection) and labor law (i.e., employee protection). Two parties compete for votes by (credibly) committing to a political agenda before the elections. Voters consist of entrepreneurs, rentiers, and workers. *Rentiers* are people who do not need to work as they can comfortably live off the revenues from their wealth. Pagano and Volpin assume that entrepreneurs who prefer weak shareholder protection and employees who prefer safe jobs have comparatively homogeneous political preferences and favor one party over the other. Conversely, rentiers have more dispersed preferences and have a less pronounced bias for either party.

According to Pagano and Volpin (2005), the outcome of the political process hinges on the electoral system. Under a proportional system, political parties will try to cater to groups with homogeneous preferences—that is, entrepreneurs and employees. Such behavior is entirely rational because the number of extra voters who can be won over by changing the political agenda is greater if the shift is in the direction of a more homogeneous group. Hence, Pagano and Volpin (2005) predict that for countries whose electoral system puts a stronger emphasis on the proportional election rule (e.g., Austria, Ireland, Italy, and Scandinavia), shareholder protection will be weak and employment protection will be strong. Under a majoritarian system, which prevails in countries such as Canada, Japan, the United Kingdom, and the United States, the consequences are reversed; that is, such a system causes strong shareholder protection and weak employment protection. Under the majoritarian system, the party that wins more districts will win the election, creating a strong incentive to compete for the pivotal district. This district consists of the ideologically uncommitted group of residual voters (the rentiers). Because these groups prefer strong shareholder protection and weak employment protection, their political preferences will be the ones to which the parties will cater.

Pagano and Volpin (2005) test their predictions on a panel of 47 countries. In line with their predictions, they find that the proportionality of the electoral system is negatively correlated with the level of shareholder protection and positively correlated with employee rights. In their analysis, the authors also control for differences in legal origin and find only limited support for the predictions of La Porta et al. (1998) once the model specification controls for the type of voting system.

Political Determinants—Social Democracy

Roe (2003) argues that politics ultimately determines the choice of the corporate governance system in industrialized economies. He attributes the differences between the corporate governance model of the United States and that of Continental European countries to the opposing ideological views with regard to the question of how societies achieve social stability. He contends that the social democracies of Continental Europe have reached social peace by favoring employees over shareholders. This implies that layoffs, which potentially increase efficiency, are comparatively hard, unemployment benefits high, and managers are pushed to forgo profit maximization. Moreover, social democracies tend not to focus on the means by which equity owners align the interests of managers to ownership interests contrary to less socially responsive nations: high incentive compensation (due to the resulting envy, which could weaken the motivation of workers), hostile takeovers (because efficiency and productivity might be increased at the cost of employees), and shareholder wealth maximization in general (because companies are not supposed purely to promote shareholder values). In other words, social democracies aim for greater social equality at the cost of reduced corporate efficiency. Roe further argues that concentrated ownership is the logical consequence of these social preferences. As market forces such as the managerial labor market and the market for corporate control are underdeveloped, large blockholdings remain as they are shareholders' best way of keeping managers in check.

Roe (2003) tests his predictions on a sample of Organisation of Economic Co-operation and Development (OECD) countries and finds evidence in support of a positive relation between ownership concentration and measures of social democratic power. In addition, he finds that labor protection is stronger in countries with more diffuse ownership.

The "Varieties of Capitalism" Literature

The "varieties of capitalism" (VOC) literature (e.g., Hall and Soskice 2001) offers a broad conceptual framework that tries to answer a wide variety of questions on the distributional outcomes of political economies. It is based on the premise that firms and individuals do not only invest in fixed assets and technologies but also in competencies and skills that are developed via relationships with others. These relationships entail coordination problems that are resolved differently in coordinated market economies (CMEs) than in liberal market economies (LMEs). Hall and Soskice analyze how firms in these two systems resolve coordination problems in five distinct areas: (1) the market for corporate control, (2) the internal structure of the firm, (3) industrial relations including wage bargaining, (4) education and training systems for employees, and (5) intercompany relations.

The authors argue that firms in CMEs use strategic interactions to resolve many of these problems. Firms, trade unions, business associations, and investors interact with each other via a dense long-term network. The network generates private information to insiders, which reduces the need for active outside monitoring through capital markets. Hall and Soskice (2001) give the Continental European countries as examples of CMEs.

Conversely, firms from LMEs rely more heavily on markets to resolve the coordination problems. Relations between economic agents are weakly regulated and governmental intervention is very limited. For example, while in CMEs, wages are the outcome of industry-level bargaining between unions and business associations, in LMEs they are the result of direct negotiations between individual workers and their employers. Hall and Soskice (2001) consider the United Kingdom, the United States, and Australia to be examples of LMEs.

Contrary to the finance literature, the VOC literature does not argue that one system is superior to another one (e.g., Goergen, Brewster, and Wood 2009). Rather, it argues that complementarities between various institutions are important. An institution acts as a complement to another one if it improves the efficiency and/or the functioning of that latter institution. Ultimately, this implies that institutional arrangements from one country can only be exported to other countries and implemented in a different institutional context with great difficulty (Goergen, Martynova, and Renneboog 2005). Hence, the VOC literature does not argue that setting investor rights and employee rights consists of a zero-sum game whereby the rights of one group can only be improved by reducing the rights of the other. It rather claims that strong shareholder rights may coexist with strong workers' rights and complement each other.

EMPIRICAL EVIDENCE ON CORPORATE GOVERNANCE SYSTEMS

This section reviews the empirical evidence on how well the various classifications of corporate governance systems fit with the stylized facts uncovered by empirical research.

Ownership Structure

Since Berle and Means' (1932) seminal work, a stylized fact in the literature is that the ownership structure of U.S. public corporations is widely held (e.g., La Porta et al. 1998; Becht 2001; Denis and McConnell 2003; Enriques and Volpin 2007; Franks, Mayer, and Rossi 2007). Although several empirical papers such as Eisenberg (1976), Demsetz and Lehn (1985), Holderness and Sheehan (1988), and Morck, Shleifer, and Vishny (1988) have raised doubts about the atomistic shareholder structure in the United States, La Porta et al.'s (1998) influential cross-country study reinforced this view. Their analysis of the ownership structure of the 10 largest nonfinancial public corporations in 45 countries concludes that the United States has uncommonly diffuse ownership. Another stylized fact is that ownership in the bank-based economies of Japan and Germany is highly concentrated due to the substantial cross holdings among companies in the same keiretsu (e.g., Prowse 1992) and "complex webs of holdings and pyramids of intercorporate holdings" (Franks and Mayer 2001, 944), respectively.

Holderness (2009) challenges the current thinking about ownership concentration around the world, particularly in the United States. He emphasizes that former studies suffer from several limitations. First, most empirical studies focus on large companies and ignore medium and small companies. For example, La Porta et al. (1998) and Enriques and Volpin (2007) focus on the 10 or 20 largest firms, which are clearly not representative of the whole U.S. market. Second, there are substantial issues with the quality of electronic databases used in former empirical studies such as Becht (2001). Third, Holderness (2009, 1384) notes that even empirical studies using hand-collected data sets "understate block ownership [in the United States] by 15–20 percent" because they do not account for severe disclosure inconsistencies in the directors' and officers' proxy statements. Holderness provides a detailed discussion of these issues.

Given these limitations, Holderness (2009), apart from his own study, recognizes Faccio and Lang (2002) and Claessens, Djankov, and Lang (2000) as empirical cross-country studies with reliable ownership data. These studies use hand-collected data on shareholders who own at least 5 percent of the votes in public corporations and trace the ownership of each company to its ultimate owners. As Holderness (p. 1386) notes, robustness checks on all three data sets reveal that "differences between . . . [all] . . . sources are trivial." He argues that this supports the superior quality of these studies.

Holderness (2009) documents that, for a representative sample of 375 U.S. public firms and against conventional wisdom, 96 percent of all firms have at least one large blockholder who owns 5 percent or more of the votes. Even among the largest U.S. firms (the S&P 500 firms), 89 percent have at least one blockholder. In sum, blockholders own 39 percent of a firm's common stock. Furthermore, after controlling for the size of the company in multivariate regressions, the ownership concentration in U.S. firms is no different from that of firms from other countries. These findings contradict the conventional wisdom that U.S. public corporations are predominantly widely held and, more generally, that ownership of public firms is less concentrated in countries with stronger investor protection.

Holderness (2009, 1406) concludes that "the pervasiveness of large shareholders in the United States, a country with strong investor protection laws, raises doubts about the empirical foundation and hence the validity of [the key theory from the law and finance literature promoted predominantly by La Porta et al. 1998]." In addition, his findings partially contradict Franks and Mayer's (1996 and 2001) characterization of the U.S. corporate governance system as an outsider system with dispersed ownership.

Claessens et al. (2000) investigate the ownership of 2,980 firms in nine East Asian countries: Hong Kong, Indonesia, Japan, South Korea, Malaysia, the Philippines, Singapore, Taiwan, and Thailand. Overall, the concentration of control rights in these countries decreases with the level of economic development. The largest blockholder in Thai, Indonesian, and Malaysian firms owns on average 35 percent, 34 percent, and 28 percent, respectively. By contrast, the largest shareholder in Japan, Korea, and Taiwan only owns 10 percent, 18 percent, and 19 percent of the control rights, respectively. In particular, the finding of diffuse ownership in Japan is astonishing as earlier research such as Hoshi, Kashyap, and Scharfstein (1991), Prowse (1992), and Kaplan (1994) emphasize the importance of *keiretsu* groups and their interlocking shareholdings and hence have shaped the view of Japan as being a country with concentrated ownership. However, Holderness (2009) and Miwa and Ramseyer (2002) confirm Claessens et al.'s (2000) finding of a dominance of widely-held firms in Japan. Miwa and Ramseyer believe that in the United States there is a widespread misconception about ownership concentration in Japan. Miwa and Ramseyer (p. 212) argue that keiretsus are "creatures of the academic and journalistic imagination, from the start they existed only because we collectively willed it thus." However overall, the East Asian evidence on ownership concentration corroborates La Porta et al.'s (1998) and Franks and Mayer's (1996 and 2001) classification of corporate governance system.

Faccio and Lang (2002) provide evidence on the concentration of ownership in 5,232 companies in 13 Western European countries. Consistent with La Porta et al. (1998) and Franks and Mayer (1996 and 2001), they find predominantly widely held ownership in Ireland (62 percent of all firms are widely held) and the United Kingdom (63 percent), and concentrated ownership in Continental Europe.

In Continental Europe, Scandinavia has the highest percentage of widely held firms (Sweden 39 percent, Norway 37 percent, and Finland 29 percent) whereas Germany (10 percent), Austria (11 percent), and Italy (13 percent) have the lowest percentages. These patterns perfectly fit with La Porta et al. (1998) as countries with weaker minority shareholder protection exhibit higher ownership concentration.

Claessens et al. (2000), Faccio and Lang (2002), and Holderness (2009) also investigate the identity of the largest shareholder. Holderness distinguishes between (1) families, (2) financial institutions, (3) corporations, (4) the government, and (5) miscellaneous. He does not find significant differences between the United States and the rest of the world. For example, in 53 percent of all U.S. firms and 59 percent of firms from the rest of the world, the largest shareholder is a family. The only significant difference is in terms of government ownership, which is absent in the United States. In contrast, in 6 percent of all non-U.S. firms, the largest shareholder is the government. Again, there seems to be little justification for classing the United States as an outsider system given, among other things, the substantial family ownership in its corporations.

Claessens et al. (2000) provide evidence that families are the predominant blockholder in eight of the nine East Asian countries in their analysis. Only Japan clearly stands out with 39 percent of the companies dominated by a financial institution and 42 percent of all companies being widely held. This confirms the view that Japan is a bank-based system. Furthermore, the government is an important shareholder in many East Asian countries such as Singapore, Malaysia, and Indonesia. Claessens et al. (p. 109) argue that this finding confirms that corporate governance systems in East Asia exhibit an "increased dependence of politicians and tycoons." Further, they provide support for the ways that La Porta et al. (1998) and Franks and Mayer (1996 and 2001) qualify these corporate governance systems.

With regard to Western Europe, Faccio and Lang's (2002) findings are consistent with La Porta et al. (1998) as well as Franks and Mayer (1996 and 2001). They find that ownership of companies in the United Kingdom and Ireland is diffuse with about two-thirds of all companies having no dominant shareholder with a stake larger than 20 percent. In contrast, Continental Europe (Austria, Belgium, France, Germany, Italy, Portugal, and Spain) is mainly family controlled, which is typical of the insider system. Further, financial institutions in Continental Europe—Belgium, Italy, France, and Germany—own more than 20 percent of the voting stock in 13 percent, 12 percent, 11 percent, and 9 percent of all companies, respectively. According to Franks and Mayer (2001, 953–954), their influence, in particular that of banks, is further strengthened in Germany as they "derive their influence not only from their direct holdings of equity, but also from their holdings of proxy votes. . . . In total, the average size of bank proxies in [their German] sample of 49 firms was 17.6 percent." These facts support the view that Germany, alongside Japan, is a bank-centered system as discussed in Goergen, Manjon, and Renneboog (2008).

Private benefits of control are another frequently cited feature of some corporate governance systems. Bebchuk (1999) argues that private benefits of control are particularly high in the insider system as ownership is concentrated. Furthermore, La Porta et al. (1998) predict that in countries with low shareholder protection, insiders extract private benefits from their companies to the detriment of the minority shareholders. Support for this assertion comes from several studies investigating the premium on voting shares compared to nonvoting shares. This premium can be seen as a proxy for the size of private benefits. For countries with strong shareholder protection such as the United States and the United Kingdom, Lease, McConnell, and Mikkelson (1983) and Megginson (1990) report a low voting premium of 5 percent and 13 percent, respectively. In contrast, the voting premium for countries with weak shareholder protection is typically much larger, for example, 82 percent for Italy (Zingales 1994), 29 percent for Germany (Muus and Tyrell 1999), 51 percent for France (Muus 1998), and 27 percent for Switzerland (Horner 1988). This pattern is largely confirmed by the extensive cross-country studies of Nenova (2003) and Dyck and Zingales (2004). Dyck and Zingales (pp. 589–590) show via various multivariate regressions that "in countries where private benefits of control are large, ownership is more concentrated . . . and capital markets are less developed." Both studies confirm that the level of private benefits in each country can be explained by the legal system and the quality of law enforcement. As Dyck and Zingales show, the exception is again Japan, the country which is commonly classed as having an insider system where there is no evidence of substantial private benefits of control.

Besides nonvoting stock, the largest blockholder can also enhance his control via pyramids and cross-holdings. Consistent with La Porta et al. (1998) and Franks and Mayer (1996 and 2001), the discrepancy between voting rights and cash flow rights is found to be more substantial in insider systems with a weak protection of minority shareholder interests. Indeed, Masulis, Wang, and Xie (2009) and Holderness (2009) find that in only 6 percent of all U.S. publicly listed firms, the largest blockholder owns more voting rights than cash flow rights. Faccio and Lang (2002) report that the equivalent figure for Europe is 32 percent (with the lowest discrepancy of cash flow and voting rights in the United Kingdom and Ireland, as expected). Claessens et al. (2000) find that the equivalent figure for East Asian firms is as high as 47 percent. Claessens et al., Faccio and Lang, and Lins (2003) suggest that control rights in excess of ownership rights through dual class stock, pyramids, and cross-holdings are common in countries with low minority shareholder protection and large block holdings. This evidence supports La Porta et al.'s and Franks and Mayer's classifications of corporate governance systems.

Market for Corporate Control

The different classifications of corporate governance systems have clear predictions as to which countries have a well-developed market for corporate control and which ones do not. According to La Porta et al. (1998), Franks and Mayer (1996 and 2001), and Allen and Gale (2000), the expectation is for an active market for corporate control in the outsider system or the market-based system. The empirical evidence reviewed in this section largely confirms this prediction.

Several papers such as Jensen and Ruback (1983), Andrade, Mitchell, and Stafford (2001), and Holmstrom and Kaplan (2001) provide evidence that the market for corporate control is very active in the United States. In fact, Denis and McConnell (2003, 19) note that the market for corporate control is "an important corporate governance mechanism, a 'court of last resort' for assets that are not being utilized to their full potential." Firth (1997) and Franks and Mayer (1996) document an active market for corporate control in New Zealand and the United

Kingdom, two examples of the outsider system. Conversely, Franks and Mayer (2001), Kabir, Cantrijn, and Jeunink (1997), and Xu and Wang (1997) show that the market for corporate control is virtually nonexistent in Germany, the Netherlands, and China. Denis and McConnell (2003, 20) argue that "[t]his general lack of importance of takeovers is perhaps not surprising given the relatively high ownership concentration in most other (non-Anglo Saxon) countries." However, due to the change in takeover regulation in EU countries, Goergen and Renneboog (2004, 10) show that the European market for corporate control has become "almost as large as the U.S. market." This recent development in the market for corporate control is further supported by recent events hitting the global banking industry. Indeed, banks from countries with weak investor protection such as France, Spain, and China are now taking over failing banks from countries believed to provide high levels of investor protection such as the United Kingdom and the United States.

Board of Directors

In most countries, boards of directors are to ensure that managers maximize shareholder value. Their main duties are the hiring and firing of managers and monitoring and compensating management. As Adams and Ferreira (2007) note, the board may also act as an adviser to the management. Empirical studies have looked at differences in terms of board characteristics across countries and how these differences affect corporate decisions and performance. Board characteristics that have been studied include the size of the board, its independence from the management, the background of the directors, and busyness as measured by the number of seats the members hold on the boards of other companies.

A huge challenge that scholars face when studying boards is the possible endogeneity of their structure. Hermalin and Weisbach (1998) present a model where board effectiveness is a function of its independence. The independence of the board is the outcome of bargaining between the existing CEO and the board of directors. As this bargaining process can typically not be observed by outsiders, including scholars, any regression analysis attempting to explain the board structure is likely to suffer from biases given the existence of these unobservable variables that are correlated with the error term.

Despite this issue, many studies have attempted to analyze board structure and its impact on corporate performance. The results of earlier studies on the United States, surveyed by Hermalin and Weisbach (2003), can be summarized as follows. First, more independent boards (where independence is measured by the fraction of outside directors) are not associated with superior firm performance. Again, the reason for the absence of a positive link may be the endogeneity of board structure. In other words, firms that have performed badly in the past may have boards with more independent directors. Second, the size of the board is negatively related to performance. The following section reviews more recent studies investigating the consistency of these findings over time and across countries as well as those adding further dimensions to the analysis. Moreover, the findings are reconciled with the different taxonomies of corporate governance systems.

Recent studies include Lehn, Patro, and Zhao (2004); Boone, Field, Karpoff, and Raheja (2007); Coles, Daniel, and Naveen (2008); and Linck, Netter, and Yang (2008). The latter study analyzes the board structure of 7,000 U.S. firms. Based on data from 1990 to 2004, Linck et al. document how board structure has changed over time and how it varies across large and small firms. The determinants of board structure are different for small and large firms. Outside director ownership is significantly related to board structure for medium and large firms, but not for small firms.

Although most of the empirical work is on U.S. boards, a reasonable number of studies of other countries now exists. Similar to the United States, most of Europe has one-tiered boards. Still, some countries such as Germany and Austria have two-tiered boards. In other countries including France and Finland, companies can choose between a one-tiered and two-tiered board structure. Moreover, in Germany, employees have the right to be represented on the board (the Codetermination Law or *Mitbestimmungsgesetz*). This is consistent with Franks and Mayer's (2001) description of the insider system where insiders who have privileged access to information mainly hold positions on the board of directors.

Dahya, McConnell, and Travlos (2002) study the effectiveness of UK boards analyzing the effect of the "Code of Best Practice" published by the Cadbury Committee, appointed by the UK government in 1992. The Code recommends that publicly listed companies should have at least three outside directors and that the position of the chairman of the board and chief executive officer (CEO) should not be held by the same person. They find that CEO turnover increased after the publication of the code and that the relationship between CEO turnover and performance was strengthened. Carline, Linn, and Yadav (2002) study the influence of the governance structure on the financial performance of mergers and acquisitions. Based on 81 UK transactions between 1985 and 1994, they find some evidence that performance changes are worse when bidders have large boards of directors.

Kaplan and Minton (1994) analyze the appointments of outsiders (defined as former directors of banks or nonfinancial corporations) to the boards of Japanese nonfinancial corporations between 1980 and 1988. They find that generally appointments of both bank and nonfinancial directors increase with poor stock performance. Bank directors are also more frequently appointed when earnings losses are high. When comparing their results for Japan with those for the United States, they find significant differences. The sensitivity of appointments of outside directors to firm performance is less strong in Japan. Appointments of blockholder directors are relatively infrequent, though they are sensitive to both performance and top executive turnover. Linking this evidence to the market-based versus bank-based taxonomy of Allen and Gale, Kaplan and Minton (p. 257) conclude that the results are "also consistent with the view that the relationship-oriented system of corporate governance in Japan substitutes for the more market-oriented system in the United States."

Blasi and Shleifer (1996) and McCarthy and Puffer (2002) examine Russian boards during 1992 and 1994. They document that boards are generally controlled by insiders and that managers resist outsiders. Outsiders on the board are typically blockholders. McCarthy and Puffer confirm these results. Most boards contain almost exclusively insiders. Some Russian companies have adopted two-tiered boards similar to those in Germany and some French companies. Russian law allows for members to sit on both boards. However, the law restricts the percentage of management board members that can sit on the board of directors to 25 percent of the seats.

Dahya, Dimitrov, and McConnell (2008) analyze the relationship between corporate value and board composition in 22 countries. After controlling for the country-level, legal shareholder protection, they find that performance is positively correlated with the fraction of independent directors on the board and that this relationship is stronger in countries with weaker legal shareholder protection. This is consistent with La Porta et al. (1997a), who argue that in countries with weak law some corporate governance mechanisms adapt to act as substitutes for legal rules.

Franks and Mayer (2001) show that banks hold 11 percent of the seats and 26 percent of the chairmanships in German companies. They interpret this as evidence in favor of their classification of insider-outsider systems with Germany being an example of the insider system where banks' influence and control are strong. Kroszner and Strahan (2001) compare the presence of bankers on boards across Germany, Japan, and the United States. They find that 75 percent of German firms have at least one banker on the board compared to 53 percent of Japanese firms, and only 32 percent of U.S. firms. This is consistent with Franks and Mayer's classification based on insider-outsider systems, but also with La Porta et al.'s (1997a, 1998) classification based on legal families. While banks may be beneficial via the monitoring of the firms in which they invest, they may also create their own agency problem. Indeed, while one duty of the bankers sitting on the board is to promote shareholders' interests at large, this duty may be in direct conflict with their role as a lender or a potential lender. As a conclusion, Franks and Mayer argue that high shareholder protection can discourage active involvements by banks. They interpret their empirical findings as being consistent with this hypothesis.

Legal Families

To test their hypothesis that in countries with better legal protection investors require lower expected rates of return and hence firms are more likely to use external finance, La Porta, Lopez-de-Silanes, Shleifer, and Vishny (1997a) measure the use of external finance across the different legal families. Their results show that the use of external finance is highest in common law countries with strong investor protection and lowest in countries with weak investor protection (i.e., the French civil law countries). Since the seminal work by La Porta et al., a large literature on the economic consequences of legal origins has developed. The key question is whether these more recent studies confirm the earlier stylized facts reported by La Porta et al. and more generally whether their findings can be reconciled with the various taxonomies of corporate governance systems.

The main strand of this recent literature is concerned with the effects of legal systems on investor protection and ultimately financial development. Recent work has extended and/or revised La Porta et al.'s (1997a, 1998) original measures of investor protection. For example, Djankov, La Porta, Lopez-de-Silanes, and Shleifer (2008) present a new measure of legal protection of minority shareholders measuring the risk of expropriation by corporate insiders. Based on interviews with law firms from 72 countries, they compute an anti-self-dealing index. They then study the link between the index and several measures of stock market development. Consistent with their theory, Djankov et al. find that common law countries have the most developed stock markets while French civil law countries have the least developed. German and Scandinavian law countries are in between common law and civil law countries.

La Porta, Lopez-de-Silanes, and Shleifer (2006) analyze how securities laws of 49 countries regulate the issuance of new equity to the public. Based on the responses to questionnaires sent to legal experts, they obtain proxies for the strength of specific disclosure requirements which reduce the cost to investors of claiming damage payments when information has been wrong or omitted. Moreover, they construct several indexes measuring the efficiency of public enforcers such as securities commissions and central banks. They find that the disclosure requirements are positively correlated with the size of stock markets while the indexes for public enforcement do not seem to matter.

Djankov, Hart, McLiesh, and Shleifer (2006) measure the efficiency of debt enforcement for 88 countries. They find that the efficiency of debt enforcement is strongly correlated with per capita income and correlates positively with debt market development across countries. Moreover, the efficiency of debt enforcement varies strongly across legal origins. While the French legal origin countries have the lowest level of efficiency, common law countries are much more efficient when enforcing debt. Further, Djankov, McLiesh, and Shleifer (2007) investigate the development of private credit markets across countries. Employing data on legal creditor rights and private and public credit registries, they construct a creditor rights index for 129 countries. These authors observe that common law countries have higher creditor rights scores than French civil law countries, confirming their earlier findings. In sum, there is strong evidence that the legal origin shapes legal investor protection and ultimately financial development.

The law and finance literature face two types of criticisms. First, scholars have questioned how to measure investor and creditor protection. Second, there is criticism that legal origins are merely proxies for other factors that affect legal rules, but are not the true drivers for the observed differences across corporate governance systems.

Graff (2008) voices the first type of criticism. He challenges the validity of the original data underlying the taxonomy of legal families. Graff (p. 67) argues that "practically irrelevant" proxies for shareholder protection, namely "proxy by mail" and "shares not blocked before meeting," are included in the anti-director rights index, whereas "two relevant and valid indicators, 'one share–one vote' and 'mandatory dividends,' are excluded for unconvincing reasons." According to Graff, addressing these criticisms invalidates the theory's key finding of a link between legal tradition and shareholder protection.

Spamann (2008) makes a similar criticism. A reexamination of the anti-director rights index (ADRI) calls for changes for 33 out of the 46 countries covered by La Porta et al. (1997a, 1998). Spamann consults primary legal sources and local lawyers, contrary to La Porta et al. who use mainly secondary sources. He finds that the correlation between the corrected measure and the original one is only 0.53. Spamann (p. 3) comments that "[t]he corrected [measure] does not differ systematically between common and civil law countries. One of La Porta et al.'s (1998) two key findings had been that common law countries offer greater legal investor protection than civil law countries. The corrected data do not bear this out." Using the corrected measure, Spamann cannot replicate the results of several former studies.

The second type of criticism states that legal origin is only a proxy for other factors such as religion, culture, and politics, which ultimately affect the rules and outcomes. For example, Licht, Goldschmidt, and Schwartz (2005) use data from different sociological surveys to construct measures of cultural attitude. They note that their study reveals correlations, predicted on the basis of theory, between national scores on cultural value dimensions and indexes of shareholder voting rights and of creditor rights. These findings suggest that a national culture that promotes assertiveness in reconciling conflicting interests and that promotes tolerance for the uncertainty this creates is consistent with using litigation to deal with economic conflicts. The correlations between national culture and legal rules hold regardless of other major characteristics of countries.

Moreover, comparing the countries in each legal family with each cultural region, they find only partial overlapping. Licht et al. (p. 232) conclude that a classification on the basis of legal families

> *provides only a partial depiction of the universe of corporate governance regimes. Shareholder rights are higher in countries belonging to the English-speaking cultural region. However, these countries fare no better than others in protecting creditors. This casts doubt on the alleged general superiority of statutes in common law countries for protecting investors.*

Interestingly, La Porta, Lopez-de-Silanes, Shleifer, and Vishny (1997b) find a strong link between trust and economic outcomes.

Stulz and Williamson (2003) measure differences in culture by differences in religion and language for 49 countries. They find that the cross-country variations in terms of the shareholder rights index cannot be explained by the culture index. However, when controlling for the legal origin of a country, culture helps explain these cross-country variations. The relation between culture and investor rights is especially strong for creditor rights. Catholic countries protect the rights of creditors less well than Protestant countries. Moreover, a country's principal religion predicts the cross-sectional variation in creditor rights better than the origin of its legal system. Yet Haber and Perotti (2007) argue that because legal origin and cultural characteristics are time invariant, they cannot explain changes over time. Conversely, changes in political institutions are potential candidates to explain these time variations. The theoretical model by Pagano and Volpin (2005) and the empirical evidence they provide for the predictions of their model give some credence to Haber and Perotti's argument.

The "Varieties of Capitalism"

While the simple form of the "varieties of capitalism" (VOC) literature distinguishes between two polar systems, the liberal market economies (LMEs) and the coordinated market economies (CMEs), some (e.g., Amable 2003; Harcourt and Wood 2007) argue that this dichotomous approach is difficult to reconcile with the distinct character of the economies of Southern Europe, the Nordic social democracies, and the Rhineland economies of Continental Europe.

For example, Amable (2003) identifies four different types of capitalism. These are the market-based or liberal market economies (LMEs) such as the United

Kingdom and the United States; the social democratic economies of Denmark, Finland, and Sweden; the Southern European economies of Greece, Italy, Portugal, and Spain; and Continental European capitalism found in Austria, Belgium, France, and Germany. Others such as Deeg and Jackson (2007), Hancké, Rhodes, and Thatcher (2006), and Harcourt and Wood (2003) also point out the marked differences between Continental European and (Nordic) social democratic countries. These differences relate to national politics, the nature of neo-corporatist arrangements, and the role of trade unions.

SUMMARY AND CONCLUSIONS

Taxonomies of corporate governance systems developed by legal and finance scholars typically advocate the superiority of one system over all the others. In contrast, the "varieties of capitalism" literature does not claim that one system dominates all the others. Instead, it argues that, as institutions tend to be complementary to each other, different sets of institutional arrangements and practices may lead to similar economic outcomes. This is confirmed by similar standards of living across the industrialized world, despite marked difference in terms of corporate governance.

Further, the current economic crisis calls for a rethinking of taxonomies that are based on hierarchies of systems. Indeed, banks and other financial institutions from the United Kingdom and the United States, two countries deemed to have the highest levels of shareholder protection, seem to have expropriated their shareholders while banks from countries believed to provide weak shareholder protection seem to have been left relatively unscathed by the crisis. In some cases, the latter have even come to the rescue of the former.

DISCUSSION QUESTIONS

1. In what major way does the "varieties of capitalism" (VOC) literature differ from the other recent classifications of corporate governance systems?
2. A study by Holderness (2009) raises doubts about the traditional portrayal of corporate ownership and control in the United States. What are the reasons for questioning the traditional view?
3. The law and finance literature, which argues that the main driver of corporate governance is the quality of law and its enforcement, have recently faced two types of criticism. What are these criticisms?
4. Have the recent bank failures caused by the credit crunch proved false some of the classifications of corporate governance systems and/or their premises? Explain why or why not.

REFERENCES

Adams, Rene, and Daniel Ferreira. 2007. A theory of friendly boards. *Journal of Finance* 62 (1): 217–250.

Allen, Franklin, and Douglas Gale. 2000. *Comparing financial systems*. Cambridge, MA: MIT Press.

Amable, Bruno. 2003. *The diversity of modern capitalism*. Oxford: Oxford University Press.

Andrade, Gregor, Mark Mitchell, and Erik Stafford. 2001. New evidence and perspectives on mergers. *Journal of Economic Perspectives* 15 (2): 103–120.
Bebchuk, Lucian A. 1999. A rent-protection theory of corporate ownership and control. Working paper, Harvard University.
Becht, Marco. 2001. Beneficial ownership in the United States. In *The control of corporate Europe*, ed. Marco Becht and Colin P. Mayer, 285–299. Oxford: Oxford University Press.
Berle, Adolfus A., and Gardine C. Means. 1932. *The modern corporation and private property*. New York: Macmillan.
Blasi, Joseph, and Andrei Shleifer. 1996. Corporate overnance in Russia: An initial look. In *Corporate governance in Central Europe and Russia: Volume 2—Insiders and the state*, ed. Roman Frydman, Cheryl W. Gray, and Andrzej Rapaczynski, 78–108. Budapest: Central European University Press.
Boone, Audra L., Laura Casares Field, Jonathan L. Karpoff, and Charu G. Raheja. 2007. The determinants of corporate board size and composition: An empirical analysis. *Journal of Financial Economics* 85 (1): 66–101.
Carline, Nicholas F., Scott C. Linn, and Pradeep K. Yadav. 2002. The influence of managerial ownership on the real gains in corporate mergers and market revaluation of merger partners: Empirical evidence. Working paper, Lancaster University and University of Oklahoma.
Chandler, Alfred D., Jr. 1977. *The visible hand: The managerial tevolution in American business*. Cambridge, MA: Belknap Press of Harvard University Press.
———. 1984. The emergence of managerial capitalism. *Business History Review* 58 (4): 473–503.
Claessens, Stijn, Simeon Djankov, and Larry H. P. Lang. 2000. The separation of ownership and control in East Asian corporations. *Journal of Financial Economics* 58 (1): 81–112.
Coles, Jeffrey L., Naveen D. Daniel, and Lalitha Naveen. 2008. Boards: Does one size fit all? *Journal of Financial Economics* 87 (2): 329–356.
Dahya, Jay, Orlin Dimitrov, and John J. McConnell. 2008. Dominant shareholders, corporate boards, and corporate value: A cross-country analysis. *Journal of Financial Economics* 87 (1): 73–100.
Dahya, Jay, John J. McConnell, and Nickolaos G. Travlos. 2002. The Cadbury Committee, corporate performance, and top management turnover. *Journal of Finance* 57 (1): 461–483.
Deeg, Richard, and Gregory Jackson. 2007. Towards a more dynamic theory of capitalist variety. *Socio-Economic Review* 5 (1): 149–79.
Demsetz, Harold, and Kenneth Lehn. 1985. The structure of corporate ownership: Causes and consequences. *Journal of Political Economy* 93 (6): 1155–1177.
Denis, Diane K., and John J. McConnell. 2003. International corporate governance. *Journal of Financial and Quantitative Analysis* 38 (1): 1–36.
Djankov, Simeon, Oliver Hart, Caralee McLiesh, and Andrei Shleifer. 2006. *Debt enforcement around the world*. Cambridge, MA: NBER Working paper 12807.
Djankov, Simeon, Rafael La Porta, Florencio Lopez-de-Silanes, and Andrei Shleifer. 2008. The law and economics of self-dealing. *Journal of Financial Economics* 88 (3): 430–465.
Djankov, Simeon, Caralee McLiesh, and Andrei Shleifer. 2007. Private credit in 129 countries. *Journal of Financial Economics* 84 (2): 299–329.
Dyck, Alexander, and Luigi Zingales. 2004. Private benefits of control: An international comparison. *Journal of Finance* 59 (2): 537–600.
Eisenberg, Melvin A. 1976. *The structure of the corporation*. Boston: Little, Brown & Company.
Enriques, Luca, and Paolo Volpin. 2007. Corporate governance reforms in continental Europe. *Journal of Economic Perspective* 21 (1): 117–140.
Faccio, Mara, and Larry H. P. Lang. 2002. The ultimate ownership of Western European countries. *Journal of Financial Economics* 65 (3): 365–395.

Firth, Michael. 1997. Takeovers in New Zealand: Motives, stockholder returns, and executive share ownership. *Pacific-Basin Finance Journal* 5 (4): 419–440.

Franks, Julian, and Colin Mayer. 1996. Hostile takeovers and the correction of managerial failure. *Journal of Financial Economics* 40 (1): 163–181.

———. 2001. Ownership and control of German corporations. *Review of Financial Studies* 14 (4): 943–977.

Franks, Julian, Colin Mayer, and Stefano Rossi. 2007. Ownership: Evolution and regulation. Working paper, London Business School.

Goergen, Marc, Chris Brewster, and Geoffrey Wood. 2009. Corporate governance and training. *Journal of Industrial Relations* 51 (4): 461–489.

Goergen, Marc, Marina Martynova, and Luc Renneboog. 2005. Corporate governance convergence: Evidence from takeover regulation reforms in Europe. *Oxford Review of Economic Policy* 21 (2): 243–268.

Goergen, Marc, Miguel C. Manjon, and Luc Renneboog. 2008. Is the German system of corporate governance converging towards the Anglo-American model? *Journal of Management and Governance* 12 (1): 37–71.

Goergen, Marc, and Luc Renneboog. 2004. Shareholder wealth effects of European domestic and cross-border takeover bids. *European Financial Management* 10 (1): 9–45.

Graff, Michael. 2008. Law and finance: Common law and civil law countries compared: An empirical critique. *Economica* 75 (297): 60–83.

Haber, Stephen, and Enrico Perotti. 2007. The political economy of finance. Working paper, Stanford University and University of Amsterdam.

Hall, Peter A., and David Soskice. 2001. *Varieties of capitalism: The institutional foundations of comparative advantage*. Oxford: Oxford University Press.

Hancké, Bob, Martin Rhodes, and Mark Thatcher. 2006. Introduction: Beyond varieties of capitalism. In *Beyond varieties of capitalism: Conflict, contradictions and complementarities*, ed. Bob Hancké, Martin Rhodes, and Martin Thatcher (eds.), 3–38. Oxford: Oxford University Press.

Harcourt, Mark, and Geoffrey Wood. 2003. Under what circumstances do social accords work? *Journal of Economic Issues* 37 (3): 747–767.

———. 2007. The importance of employment protection for skill development in coordinated market economies. *European Journal of Industrial Relations* 13 (2): 141–159.

Hermalin, Benjamin E., and Michael S. Weisbach. 1998. Endogenously chosen boards of directors and their monitoring of the CEO. *American Economic Review* 88 (1): 96–118.

———. 2003. Boards of directors as an endogenously determined institution: A survey of the economic literature. *Economic Policy Review* 9 (1): 7–26, Federal Reserve Bank of New York.

Hicks, John. 1969. *A theory of economic history*. Oxford: Clarendon Press.

Holderness, Clifford G. 2009. The myth of the new ownership in the United States. *Review of Financial Studies* 22 (4): 1377–1408.

Holderness, Clifford G. C., and Dennis P. Sheehan. 1988. The role of majority shareholders in publicly held corporations. *Journal of Financial Economics* 20 (1–2): 317–46.

Holmstrom, Bengt. 1982. Moral hazard in teams. *Bell Journal of Economics* 13 (2): 324–340.

Holmstrom, Bengt, and Steven N. Kaplan. 2001. Corporate governance and merger activity in the U.S.: Making sense of the 1980s and 1990s. *Journal of Economic Perspectives* 15 (2): 121–144.

Horner, Melchior R. 1988. The value of the corporate voting right: Evidence from Switzerland. *Journal of Banking and Finance* 12 (1): 69–84.

Hoshi, Takeo, Anil Kashyap, and David Scharfstein. 1991. Corporate structure, liquidity, and investment: Evidence from Japanese industrial groups. *Quarterly Journal of Economics* 106 (1): 33–60.

Jensen, Michael C., and Richard S. Ruback. 1983. The market for corporate control: The scientific evidence. *Journal of Financial Economics* 11 (1–4): 5–50.
Kabir, Rezaul, Dolph Cantrijn, and Andreas Jeunink. 1997. Takeover defenses, ownership structure and stock returns in the Netherlands: An empirical analysis. *Strategic Management Journal* 18 (2): 97–109.
Kaplan, Steven. 1994. Top executive rewards and firm performance: A comparison of Japan and the United States. *Journal of Political Economy* 102 (3): 510–546.
Kaplan, Steven, and Bernadette Minton. 1994. Appointments of outsiders to Japanese boards: Determinants and implications for managers. *Journal of Financial Economics* 36 (2): 225–257.
Kroszner, Randall S., and Philip E. Strahan. 2001. Bankers on boards: Monitoring, conflicts of interest, and lender liability. *Journal of Financial Economics* 62 (3): 415–452.
La Porta, Rafael, Florencio Lopez-de-Silanes, and Andrei Shleifer. 2006. What works in securities laws? *Journal of Finance* 61 (1): 1–32.
La Porta, Rafael, Florencio Lopez-de-Silanes, Andrei Shleifer, and Robert Vishny. 1997a. Legal determinants of external finance. *Journal of Finance* 52 (3): 1131–1150.
———. 1997b. Trust in large organizations. *American Economic Review* 87 (2): 333–338.
———. 1998. Law and finance. *Journal of Political Economy* 106 (6): 1113–1155.
Lease, Ronald C., John J. McConnell, and Wayne H. Mikkelson. 1983. The market value of control in publicly traded corporations. *Journal of Financial Economics* 11 (1–4): 439–471.
Lehn, Kenneth, Sukesh Patro, and Mengxin Zhao. 2004. Determinants of the size and structure of corporate boards. Working paper, University of Pittsburgh, Kansas State University, and University of Alberta.
Licht, Amir, Chanan Goldschmidt, and Shalom Schwartz. 2005. Culture, law, and corporate governance. *International Review of Law and Economics* 25 (2): 229–255.
Linck, James S., Jeffry M. Netter, and Tina Yang. 2008. The determinants of board structure. *Journal of Financial Economics* 87 (2): 308–387.
Lins, Karl V. 2003. Equity ownership and firm value in emerging markets. *Journal of Financial and Quantitative Analysis* 38 (1): 159–184.
Masulis, Ronald W., Cong Wang, and Fei Xie. 2009. Agency problems at dual-class companies. *Journal of Finance* 64 (4): 1697–1727.
McCarthy, Daniel, and Sheila Puffer. 2002. Corporate governance in Russia: Towards a European, US, or Russian model? *European Management Journal* 20 (6): 630–640.
Megginson, William. 1990. Restricted voting stock, acquisition premiums, and the market value of corporate control. *Financial Review* 25 (2): 175–198.
Miwa, Yoshiro, and J. Mark Ramseyer. 2002. The fable of the keiretsu. *Journal of Economics and Management Strategy* 11 (1): 69–224.
Morck, Randall, Andrei Shleifer, and Robert W. Vishny. 1988. Management ownership and market valuation: An empirical analysis. *Journal of Financial Economics* 20 (1–2): 293–315.
Muus, Christian. 1998. Non-voting shares in France: An empirical analysis of the voting premium. Working paper, Johann Wolfgang Goethe-Universitaet, Frankfurt am Main.
Muus, Christian, and Marcell Tyrell. 1999. An empirical analysis of the voting premium in Germany. Working paper, Johann Wolfgang Goethe-Universitaet, Frankfurt am Main.
Nenova, Tatiana. 2003. The value of corporate voting rights and control: A cross-country analysis. *Journal of Financial Economics* 68 (3): 325–351.
Pagano, Marco, and Paolo Volpin. 2005. The political economy of corporate governance. *American Economic Review* 95 (4): 1005–1030.
Prowse, Stephen D. 1992. The structure of corporate ownership in Japan. *Journal of Finance* 47 (3): 1121–1141.
Roe, Mark J. 1994. *Strong managers. Weak owners. The political roots of American corporate finance.* Princeton: Princeton University Press.
———. 2003. *The political determinants of corporate governance.* Oxford: Oxford University Press.

Spamann, Holger. 2008. " Law and Finance" revisited. Working paper, Harvard Law School.
Stulz, Rene, and Rohan Williamson. 2003. Culture, openness, and finance. *Journal of Financial Economics* 70 (3): 313–49.
Watson, Alan. 1974. *Legal transplants: An approach to comparative law*. Charlottesville, VA: University of Virginia Press.
Xu, Xiaonian, and Yan Wang. 1997. Ownership structure, corporate governance, and firms' performance: The case of Chinese stock companies. Working paper, World Bank.
Zingales, Luigi. 1994. The value of the voting right: A study of the Milan stock exchange. *Review of Financial Studies* 7 (1): 125–148.

ABOUT THE AUTHORS

Christian Andres is assistant professor of finance at the University of Mannheim, Germany. He holds a master's degree and a PhD from the University of Bonn. During his doctoral studies, he spent several months as a visiting scholar at the University of Sheffield and at the University of Florida. His primary research interests are in the areas of empirical corporate finance and corporate governance. He has published in academic journals such as the *Journal of Corporate Finance* and the *Journal of Empirical Finance*.

André Betzer holds a bachelor's degree in economics from the University of Toulouse. He earned his master's and PhD degree in economics from the University of Bonn. He is an assistant professor of finance at the University of Mannheim. His research focuses mainly on issues of corporate finance and corporate governance. He has published in academic journals such as *European Financial Management*, *Journal of Business Finance and Accounting*, and *Journal of Empirical Finance*.

Marc Goergen holds a BA in economics from the Free University of Brussels, an MBA from Solvay Business School in Brussels, and a DPhil in economics from Oxford University. Professor Goergen holds a chair in finance at Cardiff Business School, Cardiff University. His previous appointments have been at UMIST, the University of Manchester, Reading University, and the University of Sheffield. His research interests are in corporate finance, specifically in initial public offerings (IPOs), corporate governance, mergers and acquisitions, managerial compensation, private equity, and insider trading. His research has been published in various academic journals including *European Financial Management*, *Journal of Corporate Finance*, *Journal of Finance*, and *Journal of Law, Economics and Organization*. He is also a research associate of the European Corporate Governance Institute (www.ecgi.org).

Daniel Metzger holds a master's degree in mathematics from the University of Warwick and a diploma in economics from the University of Bonn. He is currently undertaking his graduate studies at the London School of Economics (LSE). Since September 2007, he has been affiliated with the Financial Markets Group (FMG) at the LSE. His research focuses mainly on issues of corporate finance, corporate governance, and personnel economics.

CHAPTER 4

Corporate Governance Best Practices

ALEX TODD
Founder and President, Trust Enablement Incorporated

INTRODUCTION

The relative merits of corporate governance best practices only become apparent when set against the contextual background of the role of corporate governance and the purpose of best practices. This chapter begins with an overview of corporate governance concepts to provide a perspective for the ensuing discussion about current and evolving practices. The discussion challenges conventional wisdom by examining the foundations of corporate governance for context, before introducing new criteria that can help guide the evolution of future corporate governance regulations, principles, models, and practices.

The chapter contains five sections. The first section explains how corporate governance is being overwhelmed by the complexity of its surrounding issues. It provides context for the evolving role of corporate governance and emergent issues burdening corporate directors. The second section introduces a framework for *aspirational corporate governance* (ACG) as a generalized approach to diagnosing current and designing future corporate governance best practices. The third section uses the ACG framework to analyze current corporate governance guidance. It examines and compares Organisation for Co-operation and Economic Development (OECD) and National Association of Corporate Directors (NACD) principles, and generally accepted best practices. The fourth section provides examples of leaders in corporate governance who embody many ACG characteristics. The final section concludes by suggesting that governance committees lead the transformation of corporate governance systems based on ACG.

PURPOSE OF CORPORATE GOVERNANCE

The purpose of corporate governance is to direct and control the activities of an organization by establishing structures, rules, and procedures for decision making. The most contentious aspects of governance revolve around answers to the questions "On whose behalf?" and "To what end?" Corporate law of most common law jurisdictions indicates that corporate directors have the fiduciary duty to be loyal to the best interests of the corporation (Black 1999). According to Tarantino (2008, 4), a corporation is a legal person that "requires the actions of real people to operate" in order to properly serve the interests of society. This view is supported not only by the Companies Act of 2006 in the United Kingdom that requires corporate directors to consider social interests but also by the 2008 Supreme Court of Canada's ruling suggesting that corporations fairly balance the interests of all stakeholders commensurate with "the corporation's duties as a responsible citizen" (Tory and Cameron, 2009, 3).

The literal legal interpretation of a director's duties to the corporation views the corporation as a person, subject to public laws that govern the relationship between individuals and society. Governments therefore grant every corporation a legal license to operate by way of a corporate charter. By contrast, the inferred legal interpretation that directors owe duties to shareholders (because shareholders bear the greatest risk due to their residual claim of corporate profits) views corporations as private property. This view subjects corporations to private law that governs relationships between individuals, which include contract law and property law. If corporations are not property but legal persons (Bakan 2004), ownership of a person, even a legal person, could be considered slavery and therefore illegal. Ironically, corporations won the right to be legal persons by successfully claiming rights to the Fourteenth Amendment to the United States Constitution, which was enacted to end slavery (Nicholls 2005).

Whether directors primarily serve society or the owners of their company is unclear. If they primarily serve owners, then what value do corporate boards add in owner-managed corporations or those with active, controlling shareholders? What about not-for-profit and government organizations without equity owners? Conversely, if directors primarily serve a broader constituency of stakeholders (or society at large), is it possible to determine which groups are being served and how directors can prioritize between divergent stakeholder interests? Moreover, if directors are to serve stakeholders' interests beyond those of their shareholders, why should shareholders solely determine the election of directors? This ambiguity about the underlying context within which corporate boards operate makes the job of the director more nuanced and complex.

Leblanc and Gillies (2005, 5) provide the following observation about directors, quoting Anderson and Antony (1986):

> *The director walks a tightrope. His responsibility is to be supportive to management, but not a rubber stamp. He directs, but he does not manage. Legally he has the ultimate responsibility for both the formulation of strategy and its implementation, but as a practical matter in most circumstances he relies on the CEO. He and his fellow directors elected the CEO, but he may later have to remove him. He is responsible for the long run health of the company, but most of the information he receives on performance relates to the short run. He has a legal responsibility to the shareowners, but he has a moral responsibility to the employees, customers, vendors, and society as a whole. He is responsible for keeping the shareholders informed, but at the same time he should not disclose information that would be adverse to the company's best interest. He has personal goals, as does the CEO. However, the director must ensure that neither his goals nor those of the CEO overshadow their obligation to the corporation and its goals.*

When balancing competing interests, directors are expected to rely on good business judgment and board procedures, without objective criteria to help them make substantive contributions to governance and business decisions. In fact, NACD (2009, 7) contains the following observation about the modern corporation.

> *The corporation today faces pressures and scrutiny from a variety of stakeholders (for example, employees, customers, suppliers, special interest groups, communities, politicians, and regulators) having diverse interests in its operation and success ... the board must understand the diverse interests of stakeholders and investors, and consider competing demands and pressures as necessary and appropriate while ensuring that the corporation is positioned to create the long-term value.... Serving as a director is demanding and ... requires integrity, objectivity, judgment, diplomacy, and courage.*

Controlling and directing corporations is a complex responsibility. Thus, the task to design meaningful corporate governance best practices seems impossible when answers to even the most fundamental questions about the role and purpose of corporate governance are ambiguous and the decision criteria directors are expected to use are subjective.

Principal-Agent Conflict

Agency theory presumes that self-interested managers are agents of the company's owners (principals) who need to be monitored and controlled in order to effectively align their behavior with the interests of the owners. Corporate boards of directors preside over management on the premise of mistrust. The outcome has been an increase in regulation and controls that restrict board and management activity, such as growing demand for director independence and alignment of executive compensation to performance. As Turnbull (2000, 24) notes, "A basic conclusion of agency theory is that the value of a firm cannot be maximised because managers possess discretions, which allow them to expropriate value to themselves."

In contrast, *stewardship theory* presumes that managers are inherently good stewards of corporations and can be trusted to work diligently to attain high levels of corporate profit and shareholder returns. Ironically, this presumption leads to the ultimate conclusion that boards of directors are reduntant and that stakeholder advisory boards are sufficient.

Both theories are valid in understanding the relation between boards and managers. In many cases, such as in family or government controlled companies, boards are simply "advisers devoid of real power" (Leblanc and Gillies 2005). In other cases, the inherent limitations of blindly following corporate governance best practices adopted by boards that do not go far enough have backfired (Tarantino 2008). The corporate scandals at Enron, WorldCom, Parmalat, and the U.S. subprime mortgage crisis that precipitated the global economic recession of 2008 are examples of instances where boards with complete corporate governance best practices checklists were misguided by the lack of perspective and appreciation for overriding principles to guide their activities.

Stout (2003, 667) offers another point of view: "shareholders also seek to 'tie their own hands' by ceding control to directors." In other words, shareholders of public companies generally prefer to trust rather than control their boards. Paradoxically, in jurisdictions where directors' fiduciary duties to the corporation have been interpreted to extend to shareholders (beyond the corporation), executive and independent directors' duties are based on the higher standard suggested by stewardship theory, because directors are expected to be good stewards of shareholder interests. As Turnbull (2000, 28) notes, a fiduciary duty "is higher than that of an agent as the person must act as if he or she was the principal rather than a representative." These examples do not invalidate the prinicipal-agent conflict, but serve to demonstrate its inadequacy as a sufficient theory for corporate governance.

Both agency theory and stweardship theory lead to self-fulfilling prophecies. Agency theory, founded on a presumption of mistrust, propels a downward spiral of increased regulation. In contrast, stewardship theory, founded on a presumption of trust, fuels an increasing trust that leads to boards without independent directors, or even to boards that have no monitoring function but rather serve only as advisers (Turnbull 2000). As Turnbull notes, both theories are valid but contingent upon the institutional and cultural context. He explains that individuals sometimes behave competitively, sometimes collaboratively, but usually both. To coexist, both agency and stewardship theories must form part of a broader dialectic theory. For example, the *political theory* for corporate governance, proposed by Gomez and Korine (2008), is consistent with the OECD's (2004, 17) first principle of corporate governance: "Ensuring the Basis for an Effective Corporate Governance Framework."

The *stakeholder model* provides another perspective that puts the corporation's self-interest ahead of shareholders and other stakeholders. According to the stakeholder model, the corporation is entirely dependent on its stakeholders' resources to create value, and considers stakeholders' interests as critical for sustaining itself and its value-creation activities. This model is consistent with Adam Smith's notion of capitalism based on enlightened self-interest. Smith (2009, 11) wrote, "It is not from the benevolence of the butcher, the brewer, or the baker that we expect our dinner, but from their regard to their own interest." Institutions such as the OECD now recognize this inherent interdependence between a firm and its stakeholders (OECD 2004). As Reiter (2006, 59) notes, literal interpretation of the law that "directors owe their fiduciary duty of loyalty exclusively to the corporation, not to its shareholders nor its creditors, even where the corporation is in distress" is consistent with the stakeholder model. This is because the stakeholder model views the firm as incomplete. The firm is seen as entirely dependent on and vulnerable to the board of directors. This is a critical test for a fiduciary relationship.

Finally, the political model offers a macro framework to provide context for corporate governace. Under the political model, governments use corporate governance as a mechanism to allocate corporate power, privilege, and profits between corporations and their stakeholders. In other words, corporate governance is an instrument of public policy (Turnbull 2000).

This review of theories and models suggests that corporate governance is about more than resolving the *principal-agent conflict*. In fact, corporate governance is highly complex as it must consider and adapt to numerous important relationships with uncertain cause-effect influences on matters that range from survival to sustainability.

Best Practices

The quest for corporate governance best practices that seek to generalize may be misguided. A best practice suggests that there is a cause-effect relationship between specified repeated procedures and desired outcomes. Complex systems by definition do not lend themselves easily to predefined best practices. Instead, less prescriptive guiding principles may be better suited to promoting judgment and adaptation within more broadly defined aspirational criteria. Nevertheless, even principle-based guidance must direct decision makers toward desired outcomes. The United Kingdom, Canada, Australia, and Hong Kong have opted in favor of a principles-based approach to reforming corporate governance, while the United States has relied increasingly on a rules-based approach based on legislation emanating from the Sarbanes-Oxley Act. Regulations mandate compliance to a minimum standard, which makes them effective as an expedient intervention. However, they are inflexible and drive behavior toward a minimum acceptable standard, rather than promoting objectives that yield superior results. Moreover, regulations encourage opportunistic behavior that seeks competitive advantage by finding loopholes in the practices or the law.

Another issue with prescriptive practices is their tendency to maximize a specific outcome that effectively outweighs other valid objectives. As Lipman and Lipman (2006, 3) note, proponents of a specific set of corporate governance best practices may primarily seek "to prevent corporate scandals, fraud and potential civil and criminal liability to an organization," while exponents of distinctly different and possibly conflicting practices may seek to optimize for specific business objectives, such as maximizing share value. Todd (2008, 84) offers the following view about diverse priorities for corporate governance:

> *While improved compliance is necessary for the protection and enhancement of public and shareholder confidence, it has led to the prevailing assumption that a more independent and engaged board is the prescription for all that ails today's corporations. While this may be true in some cases, new research reveals that corporate governance standards cannot be consistently applied to different structures; one size does not "fit all." The research suggests that the appropriate style of corporate governance in any business is a strategic consideration directly influenced by its relative position in the corporate lifecycle. Simply stated, different sets of governance practices are associated with distinct measures of business performance. Corporations need to actively consider their strategic priorities before adopting corporate governance reforms and corporate strategies that enhance both business performance and governance effectiveness.*

The proliferation of best practices by prominent organizations, such as Institutional Shareholder Services' (part of RiskMetrics Group) Corporate Governance Quotient (CGQ) and those of many other national and institutional rating and benchmarking services, has prompted the National Association of Corporate Directors (NACD) in the United States and other corporate governance organizations to caution directors against slavishly following corporate governance best practices. According to NACD (2009, 2):

> *Concerns arise . . . about the overly prescriptive use of best practice recommendations by some proponents, without recognition that different practices may make sense for different boards and at different times given the circumstances and culture of a board and the needs of the company. . . . It has often been said that "one size does not fit all" when it comes to corporate governance. The Principles are intended to assist boards and shareholders to avoid rote "box ticking" in favor of a more thoughtful and studied approach.*

If a simplified best practices approach to improving corporate governance is inadequate for the inherent complexities of a corporate governance system, then how should policy makers and governance committees define and apply guiding principles? In other words, are there valid assumptions about the context and desired outcomes for corporate governance effectiveness, and what are the performance levers that can shape desirable corporate governance structures and practices?

NEW CONTEXT FOR CORPORATE GOVERNANCE

According to Zaffron and Logan (2009), the starting point for transforming corporate governance is becoming aware of the collective view of the nature of corporate governance. If people were to perceive corporate governance as a necessary evil, designed to protect shareowners from self-interested managers, corporate governance would continue to be defined by regulations, oversight, and restrictions regarding business conduct. This perspective and its resulting actions would perpetuate a cycle of mistrust and motivate opportunism. If, by contrast, people were to perceive corporate governance as being a vital public policy instrument for sustaining the prosperity engine of capitalism, then the future of corporate governance would become defined by openness to new possibilities.

Likewise, by limiting the discussion of corporate governance by using the familiar language (Zaffron and Logan 2009) of *shareholder value* and *management oversight*, transformation will be impossible. If people are willing to recognize the complexity of corporate governance but refuse to accept the possibility that governing complexity is feasible, current consideration and response patterns will remain recursive and self-fulfilling. People will continue to believe that directors cannot realistically be expected to take on a broader mandate and that shareholders would not allow them to do so, even if boards were so inclined.

A closer inspection of the prior statement reveals several dangerous assumptions. In the situation just described, nothing substantively new is possible. Complaints regarding director independence and management compensation will continue, based on the self-fulfilling assumption that management cannot be trusted to fully represent shareholder interests. Although existing complaints may be valid, they represent neither the complete truth nor the breadth of possible truths. A narrow focus on popular complaints may overlook broader, more transformative governance issues; the causes rather than the symptoms. In fact, concentration on alleviating symptoms may be an example of a preference to avoid complexity. Maintaining this view will lead to one trajectory toward a "default future" (Zaffron and Logan 2009). Interrupting this pattern of escalating regulations and opportunistic behavior requires acknowledging the possibility that many best practices and even guiding principles approaches to corporate governance may be misguided.

Is there openness to the possibility of a collectively valued, sustainable system of corporate self-governance? If so, because the currently accepted view of corporate governance does not allow for this possibility, the following section proposes a new approach.

Aspirational Corporate Governance (ACG)

Aspirational corporate governance (ACG) provides guidance on good corporate governance. Turnbull (2004, 9) notes, "Good corporate governance needs to be defined in terms of the ability of corporations to become self-governing on a reliable, sustainable and socially desirable basis." ACG is based on Turnbull's *network governance* approach for attaining good corporate governance. Turnbull (2002b) argues that recent corporate scandals and financial crises are symptoms of deficient corporate governance based on outdated top-down command-and-control hierarchies that are unable to cope with complexity. Firms cannot regulate themselves and are vulnerable to corruption. He advocates for a new breed of ecological organization based on nature's ability to manage complexity by distributing decision making among members of nonhierarchical organizations (analogous to ant colonies) and evolving sustainable levels of complexity that exceed the cognitive capacity of any controlling individual or group.

Turnbull applies the Law of Requisite Variety to address uncertainties in complex governance systems. Turnbull (2002b, 30) bases his recommendations on cybernetics, the *science* of governance that has deep theoretical roots in complexity science, a field of study that attempts to describe how complex systems work. As Turnbull (2004, 10) notes, academics in the field of systems science (study of the nature of complex systems) widely recognize that "regulation of complexity can only be achieved indirectly by establishing a requisite variety of co-regulators."

Network governance imposes new burdens on corporate directors. Although requisite variety more aptly reflects the environment within which the firm operates than Anglo-style unitary board governance structures, it also introduces a whole new level of complexity and ambiguity into the governance system. Tory and Cameron (2009, 1) comment that a broader governance mandate may impose "a nebulous duty [on directors] to treat all affected stakeholders fairly, commensurate with 'the corporation's duties as a responsible citizen.'" According to Mohammed and Schwall (2009), institutional systems are generally averse to such ambiguity inherent in novel, complex, and insoluble situations. Tory and Cameron claim that this aversion to ambiguity results from the difficulty of assigning accountability within such systems. Embracing complexity represents a major challenge for corporate governance stakeholders that ACG may help resolve.

ACG adds a human dimension to network governance by introducing Elliott Jaques' requisite organization system model for matching capability to job complexity. Requisite organization considers the cognitive capacity of governing parties to deliberate at appropriate levels of abstraction and conceptualization. A key objective of requisite organization is to appropriately match the required cognitive levels of work with the levels of management capability. Levels of work are based on principles of complexity and their relation to value creation. ACG's requisite organization plays a critical role in supporting network governance, by including people in corporate governance who are more comfortable with complexity and less likely to perceive ambiguous or inconsistent situations as threatening.

Darwin (1859, 490) wrote about "the Extinction of less-improved forms" 150 years ago. According to O'Riley, Harreld, and Tushman (2009, 3), "[Darwin's] logic applies to organizations today." O'Riley et al. (p. 18) advocate for a "deliberate approach to variation-selection-retention that uses existing firm assets and capabilities and reconfigures them to address new opportunities." Although feedback mechanisms are an explicit consideration of network governance, network governance deals more with the structure than the attributes of self-adjustment. ACG also contributes an adaptive capacity dimension as a "deliberate approach" to satisfy stakeholder requirements for empowerment and risk transference (Todd 2007a and 2007b) that allows strategic stakeholders to engage in the governance process.

In summary, ACG provides a diagnostic and design framework to account for the complexities of good corporate governance by considering requisite organization, requisite variety, and adaptive capacity parameters. This approach helps guide the evolution of corporate governance practices through the complexities of conflicting organizational, stakeholder, and societal objectives. ACG also provides critical conceptual tools that can empower designers to accept aspirational corporate governance challenges they may otherwise have avoided.

Requisite Organization

Management layers of an organizational hierarchy need to operate at different levels of work complexity depending on various factors. According to Van Clieaf and Kelly (2005, 5), these factors include "the level of innovation complexity; the planning horizon; the level of complexity of assets/capital managed; and the level of complexity of stakeholder groups to be managed given the number of different businesses and countries in which the enterprise may operate." CEOs need to have the appropriate level of cognitive capacity to fully consider the impact of their decisions. More complex organizations are best served by CEOs who possess a higher level of cognitive capacity.

Similarly, to add business value beyond that of lower level management, managers at every incremental level in an organizational hierarchy need to possess a cognitive capacity greater than that of their subordinates, which allows them to "see further than the individuals they are leading" (King, King, Solomon, and Cason, 1997, 2). Following the same logic, corporate directors need to collectively possess a cognitive capacity that is at least one level higher than the CEO. Depending on the complexity of governance considerations the business warrants, a cognitive hierarchy of two or more levels above that of the CEO might be required.

For example, in a mining company, the CEO's required level of work may be relatively low, perhaps with a five-year business planning horizon. However, a broader set of noncommercial sustainability considerations may require the directors and other governance participants to direct the activities of the business with a 25-year horizon—several work levels higher than that of the CEO. Requisite organization principles help organizations embrace complexity. Requisite organization measures can be a valuable indicator of a corporate governance system's capacity to manage complexity.

Requisite Variety

Complex systems exhibit complex cause-effect dynamics that breed uncertainty. Organizations that shun uncertainty in favor of simplified, familiar solutions become rigid. Conversely, those that embrace uncertainty by being open to new possibilities become dynamic. As Clampitt and Williams (2005, 13) note, "the randomness associated with uncertainty makes it difficult to develop strategies that appropriately adapt to present and future circumstances."

Requisite variety is the science of minimizing the number of choices required to resolve uncertainty. Requisite variety also recognizes that an autonomous system needs to acquire an internal model of its environment to persist and achieve dynamic equilibrium. This suggests that aspirational governance practices should embrace uncertainty by adopting network governance. Network governance provides inputs from a sufficient variety of sources and through distinct channels to manage high levels of uncertainty. These inputs might include multiple boards, advisory councils, and/or watchdog organizations that involve "strategic stakeholders through employee assemblies, customers forums and supplier panels" (Turnbull 2002a, 11) as part of the corporate governance system. As Turnbull (p. 1) states, "The design rules used to establish stakeholder controlled network organizations such as VISA International and the Mondragón Corporación Cooperativa are shown to follow deeper criteria identified by the science of governance that is also known as cybernetics." Thus, complex organizations that need to consider the interests and feedback from a large number of constituents are better served by adopting a network governance structure. Requisite variety measures can be a strong indicator of the ability of a corporate governance system to deal with uncertainty.

Adaptive Capacity

Analogous to weather patterns, complex systems are generally in a state of dynamic disequilibrium. Successfully balancing the number and the variety of stakeholders' influences on a corporation is not simply a matter of gaining a sufficiently abstracted understanding of their relationship dynamics and managing uncertainty. Balance also requires that appropriate corporate governance mechanisms become activated to respond to internal and external forces. Adaptive capacity provides two complementary means by which ACG systems can respond to empower stakeholders to reduce their uncertainty, or to transfer risks away from stakeholders in order to make uncertainty acceptable (Todd 2007a). For example, boards could empower more shareholders and/or stakeholders with voting rights, or choose instead to voluntarily tie their own hands in order to appease stakeholders without relinquishing control. A self-regulating system needs to be able to respond dynamically to its environment. Adaptive capacity measures could be an important indicator of the sustainability of a corporate governance system.

ACG Framework

The ACG framework specifies three aspirational conditions for good corporate governance:

1. *Requisite organization* handles information complexity.
2. *Requisite variety* in information from stakeholders reduces uncertainty.
3. *Adaptive capacity* provides response mechanisms to compensate for stakeholder uncertainty.

Exhibit 4.1 shows a hypothetical measure of ACG, based on these three parameters.

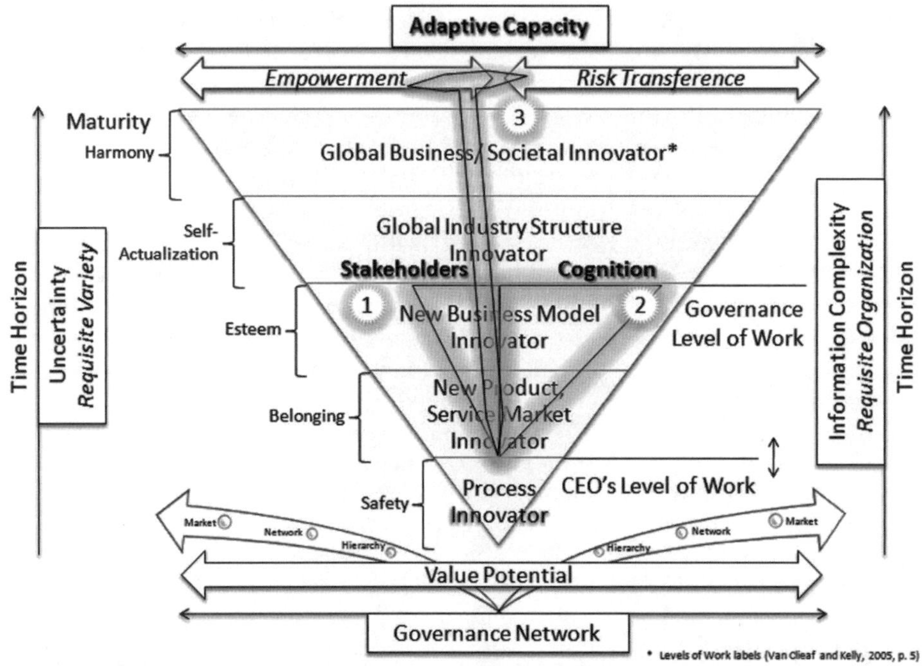

Exhibit 4.1 Aspirational Corporate Governance (ACG) Framework

The framework in Exhibit 4.1 provides a perspective on the context and the dynamic relationship between these three elements. Context is represented by an aspirational maturity hierarchy that depicts "levels of innovation and risk" (Van Clieaf and Kelly 2005) and is conceptually consistent with Maslow's hierarchy of needs to correspond with the evolutionary maturity of a firm. Two of the three elements that represent *requisite variety* and *requisite organization* are depicted as triangular bubble charts set against the hierarchy context. The area occupied by each triangular bubble shows the extent to which the condition it represents is being satisfied or the measured value for the condition. The vertical dimension (height) of the triangular bubbles depicts the value added by the corporate governance system beyond that of the CEO.

A pendulum is used to illustrate *adaptive capacity*, the third element of the framework. It indicates the types of response mechanisms being employed within the empowerment–risk transference continuum of possibilities. The horizontal span of all elements reflects the number of participants in the governance network contributing to each condition. The thickness of the head of the pendulum can be used to visually represent the number of adaptive capacity mechanisms being employed to engage stakeholders.

For example, a shareholder-controlled unitary board, composed primarily of controlling shareholders and CEOs of similar companies, might look like two short vertical lines (collapsed triangles, lacking the horizontal dimension that quantifies participants) that stop short of the first Level of Work category above the CEO (to indicate that the governance Level of Work is similar to the CEO's). The pendulum, representing adaptive capacity, might tilt to the extreme left (on the Empowerment side) with a virtually imperceptible head (indicating few adaptive mechanisms). By contrast, VISA's multi-stakeholder governance structure might show up as two very wide triangular bubble charts that come close to the horizontal edges of the context image in the background, and their vertical height might extend up two or more Level of Work categories. The adaptive capacity pendulum, in this case, might tilt midway to the left (in the Empowerment space) with a wide head that reaches into the Risk Transference space on the right. In other words, larger spaces occupied by the three elements of the ACG framework would indicate more aspirational governance systems.

Implications

The ACG framework provides general principles for good corporate governance of any organization. To date, most of the work on corporate governance best practices focuses on large, publicly traded companies. Many in the business community generally accept that best practices should simply protect the interests of shareholders seeking to maximize the long-term value of their shares. Although numerous attempts have been made to connect corporate governance best practices to business performance, such as Brown and Caylor's (2004) study, the results of such studies have been mixed. Today's best practices recommendations and rankings do not claim to directly improve business performance, only to protect shareholders' interests, which may or may not be aligned with the strategic priorities of the corporation. The governance-performance dynamic of privately held and not-for-profit companies is even less understood.

As is often the case, the solution to one problem creates another. ACG provides a scheme for embracing bigger and more worthy problems. It seeks to protect the sustainable self-governance interests of any organization. It does so not only by providing a self-regulating sense-and-respond system of governance, but also by adapting its structure and processes to support the strategic objectives of the business. ACG intrinsically encompasses parameters that directly affect business performance by allowing for strategic stakeholders in the governance system.

As Todd (2008, 87) reports, an analysis by Brown and Caylor (2004) showing a positive correlation between corporate governance best practices and business performance reveals that "governance styles (beyond discrete governance practices) are associated with business performance." The analysis concludes that corporations pursuing a share valuation strategy should consider adopting formal governance practices that establish higher levels of trust with investors and analysts. Similarly, corporations pursuing a sales growth strategy should adopt corporate governance practices that cede more control to management—in other words, have fewer independent directors. Todd also reports that truly independent boards presided over companies that were more profitable, and that management-influenced boards distributed more cash to shareholders. The study further infers a possible connection between governance styles and the natural life cycle of a company, suggesting that early stage companies are more likely to prioritize in favor of revenue growth while more mature ones seek to maximize profits.

The implications of this analysis are even more profound because they provide empirical evidence that supports strategic-stakeholder corporate governance networks as a valid aspirational objective. Clearly, corporate governance practices that directly contribute to business performance can add more value to the corporation than those whose mandate is simply to protect shareholder interests. For example, firms pursuing a revenue growth strategy may be well advised to network their management-controlled board style of corporate governance with a customer advisory council. Similarly, those pursuing a share valuation strategy may want to network their trusted board style with a broader investor constituency. Mature corporations seeking to optimize for profitability might consider augmenting their independent director style of governance with a broader stakeholder advisory governance network.

Although boards already seek to manage information effectively to varying degrees, ACG provides a formal framework that they might employ to focus and guide their activities in a more deliberate way. It creates a new space for conversations among boards, management, and other key stakeholders, and solidifies the basis for collaboration. ACG also gives executives a credible voice on how governance structures and practices might be refined to support strategic business objectives. More generally, ACG provides analysts and policy makers with universally applicable, measurable, and comparable criteria for guiding the evolution of corporate governance structures and practices.

ANALYSIS

This section puts the ACG framework into action by examining how the three criteria of requisite organization, requisite variety, and adaptive capacity map to today's corporate governance landscape. The section first diagnoses international and national guidance on corporate governance principles, and proceeds to examine a specific set of best practices found to improve business performance.

OECD Principles

The Organisation for Economic Co-operation and Development (OECD) provides international guidance on corporate governance in the form of recommended principles. According to the OECD (2004, 2), foremost among its objectives is "to achieve the highest sustainable economic growth and employment and a rising standard of living in member countries, while maintaining financial stability, and thus to contribute to the development of the world economy." As ACG aspires to help organizations contribute to the same objectives, a diagnosis of the OECD Principles of Corporate Governance may be the most telling indicator of the completeness of the ACG framework and how it corresponds to an international benchmark.

Exhibit 4.2 categorizes the six OECD principles (OECD 2004) based on the elements of the ACG framework: requisite organization, requisite variety, and adaptive capacity. The principles are equally balanced across the three ACG parameters.

Principle I (Ensuring the Basis for an Effective Corporate Governance Framework) and Principle VI (The Responsibilities of the Board) satisfy the criteria of the ACG framework for contributing to requisite organization. They deal with the structure and the mandate of the board (a level of abstraction above the principles that address board function), and therefore these principles address complexity.

Exhibit 4.2 Diagnosis of OECD Principles of Corporate Governance

	ACG Parameters		
Principles	**Requisite Organization (Complexity)**	**Requisite Variety (Uncertainty)**	**Adaptive Capacity (Self-adjustment)**
Principle I Ensuring the Basis for an Effective Corporate Governance Framework	√		
Principle II The Rights of Shareholders and Key Ownership Functions			√
Principle III The Equitable Treatment of Shareholders			√
Principle IV The Role of Stakeholders in Corporate Governance		√	
Principle V Disclosure and Transparency		√	
Principle VI The Responsibilities of the Board	√		
	2	2	2

Principles IV (The Role of Stakeholders in Corporate Governance) and V (Disclosure and Transparency) satisfy the criteria for contributing to requisite variety because they handle information reliance, and therefore tackle uncertainty. Principle II (The Rights of Shareholders and Key Ownership Functions) and Principle III (The Equitable Treatment of Shareholders) satisfy the criteria for contributing to adaptive capacity because they contend with affecting change, and thereby self-adjustment.

Each principle not only contributes to one of the ACG criteria but also does so in a balanced manner. These findings reciprocally reinforce the ACG framework and the OECD Principles.

NACD Principles

The diagnosis of the National Association of Corporate Directors (NACD) Key Agreed Principles to Strengthen Corporate Governance for U.S. Publicly Traded Companies reveals somewhat different ACG indications (Daly 2009). See Exhibit 4.3.

In contrast with OECD's role as a guidance provider to countries, the NACD directly guides corporate directors. NACD principles begin at a lower level of abstraction and provide more detailed guidance with 10 principles. Nevertheless, the following sections of Daly (2009) discuss these principles. "Board Responsibility for Governance," "Director Competency and Commitment," and "Integrity,

Exhibit 4.3 Diagnosis of NACD Principles to Strengthen Corporate Governance

	ACG Parameters		
Principles	**Requisite Organization (Complexity)**	**Requisite Variety (Uncertainty)**	**Adaptive Capacity (Self-adjustment)**
I. Board Responsibility for Governance	√		
II. Corporate Governance Transparency		√	
III. Director Competency and Commitment	√		
IV. Board Accountability and Objectivity		√	
V. Independent Board Leadership		√	
VI. Integrity, Ethics, and Responsibility	√		
VII. Attention to Information, Agenda, and Strategy		√	
VIII. Protection Against Board Entrenchment			√
IX. Shareholder Input in Director Selection			√
X. Shareholder Communications		√	
	3	5	2

Ethics, and Responsibility" deal with structure and the mandate of the board, and therefore satisfy the requisite organization criteria of the ACG framework. Other principles concern uncertainty, and contribute to satisfying requisite variety criteria; "Corporate Governance Transparency," "Board Accountability and Objectivity," "Independent Board Leadership," "Attention to Information, Agenda, and Strategy," and "Shareholder Communications." Finally, "Protection Against Board Entrenchment," and "Shareholder Input in Director Selection" deal with affecting change, and satisfy the adaptive capacity criteria.

Compared to OECD principles, NACD principles are more skewed toward addressing requisite variety. This is likely due to an emphasis on director independence, which is consistent with an agency-theory-based view of corporate governance for publicly traded companies. In contrast, the adaptive capacity column amassed the fewest NACD principles. This scarcity could suggest reluctance to reform corporate governance practices.

Best Practices

The skewing effect of the distribution of NACD principles between the columns of the ACG framework is magnified when applying the same analysis to generally accepted best practices. Of the 46 corporate governance best practices found by Brown and Caylor (2004) to be associated with an aspect of business performance, only 4 concern requisite organization, while 33 fall into the requisite variety category and 9 address adaptive capacity. With more than 70 percent of best practices belonging to requisite variety, the focus of best practices overwhelmingly deals with the principal-agent conflict. In fact, best practices virtually ignore the NACD principles associated with improving the quality and effectiveness of corporate governance structures and practices, namely those that satisfy requisite organization criteria. Representing about 20 percent of all best practices, the adaptive capacity category is proportional with NACD principles (see Exhibit 4.4).

A simple count of principles and practices only serves as a rough indicator of the state of corporate governance practices. Counting the number of principles or practices trivializes the aspirational nature of each of the three factors specified by the ACG framework. A truer representation of the three ACG parameters would measure the level to which each principle or practice contributes to enhancing a board's willingness and ability to engage on matters of governance complexity, stakeholder uncertainty, and self-correction. This kind of analysis of the same corporate governance best practices, when overlaid diagrammatically over the ACG framework, would look more like a short vertical bar chart instead of a triangular bubble chart, depicting a unitary-board hierarchical governance structure. Even to boards following the agency theory for corporate governance, ACG presents a road map for improving their practices by innovating on the requisite organization parameter. Progress in requisite organization by unitary boards (i.e., by expanding the scope of the governance committee) would appear as taller bar charts in the ACG framework diagram (still lacking the horizontal dimension of requisite variety).

EXAMPLES OF CORPORATE GOVERNANCE INNOVATIONS

As Dimma (2006, 53) notes, "Increasingly boards are expected to be more demanding, more aggressive, more indefatigable, and more unsparing." However, new expectations of corporate governance go far beyond addressing the so-called principal-agent conflict. The Conference Board of Canada (2009, vi) comments that it is "crucial that governance 'make a difference' to organizational success and sustainability" and "innovations of boards of directors and governing bodies . . . is a dynamic and critical element of their organizations' success." The Conference Board of Canada encourages boards to tackle important challenges. These challenges include operating in an anticipatory mode, providing leadership for organizations to be effective globally, and leading transformation initiatives that improve organizational effectiveness and sustainability by being creative and embracing unique new approaches. The board's call for a new approach to corporate governance is aspirational. Current best practices fall short of these expectations. Aspirational corporate governance offers a universal approach to evaluating and innovating corporate governance practices to meet ever-changing societal expectations.

As Turnbull (2002b, 16) comments, network governance structures are most evident in public sector enterprises that "are subject to external checks and balances that do not exist in the private sector." There are also numerous examples of network governance in the private sector but not all satisfy ACG and good corporate governance objectives. In many cases, these governance systems are based on

Exhibit 4.4 Diagnosis of Corporate Governance Best Practices

	ACG Parameters		
Best Practices	**Requisite Organization (Complexity)**	**Requisite Variety (Uncertainty)**	**Adaptive Capacity (Self-Adjustment)**
1. Do all directors attend at least 75 percent of board meetings or have a valid excuse for nonattendance?		√	
2. Is the board controlled by more than 50 percent independent directors?		√	
3. Is the compensation committee composed solely of independent outside directors?		√	
4. Is the nominating committee composed solely of independent outside directors?		√	
5. Does a policy exist requiring outside directors to serve on no more than five additional boards?	√		
6. Is the size of the board of directors at least 6 but not more than 15 members?		√	
7. Does a former CEO serve on the board?		√	
8. Does the governance committee meet at least once during the year?	√		
9. Are board guidelines in each proxy statement?		√	
10. Does management respond to shareholder proposals within 12 months?		√	
11. Are board members elected annually?			√
12. Are the CEO and chairman's duties separated or is a lead director specified?		√	
13. Is the CEO listed as having a "related-party transaction" in a proxy statement?		√	
14. Does the CEO serve on more than two additional boards of other public companies?	√		
15. Do shareholders vote on directors selected to fill a vacancy?			√

Exhibit 4.4 (*Continued*)

	ACG Parameters		
Best Practices	**Requisite Organization (Complexity)**	**Requisite Variety (Uncertainty)**	**Adaptive Capacity (Self-Adjustment)**
Executive and Director Compensation			
16. Did option repricing occur within past three years?		√	
17. Did the average options granted in the past three years as a percentage of basic shares outstanding exceed 3 percent (option burn rate)?		√	
18. Is option repricing prohibited?		√	
19. The last time shareholders voted on a pay plan, did ISS (or equivalent organization) deem its cost to be excessive?		√	
20. Does the company provide any loans to executives for exercising options?		√	
21. Did directors receive all or a portion of their fees in stock?		√	
22. Were stock incentive plans adopted with shareholder approval?			√
23. Do interlocks exist among directors on the compensation committee?		√	
24. Do nonemployees participate in company pension plans?		√	
Progressive Practices			
25. Is the performance of the board reviewed regularly?		√	
26. Do outside directors meet without the CEO and disclose the number of times they met?		√	
27. Is there a mandatory retirement age for directors?			√
28. Is there a board-approved CEO succession plan in place?		√	
29. Are directors required to submit their resignation upon a change in job status?		√	
30. Do director term limits exist?		√	
31. Does the board have outside advisers?		√	

(*Continued*)

Exhibit 4.4 (*Continued*)

	ACG Parameters		
Best Practices	**Requisite Organization (Complexity)**	**Requisite Variety (Uncertainty)**	**Adaptive Capacity (Self-Adjustment)**
Charter/Bylaws			
32. Is the company authorized to issue blank check preferred stock?		√	
33. Is a simple majority vote required to approve a merger (not a supermajority)?			√
34. Does the company either have no poison pill or have a pill that was shareholder approved?			√
35. Are shareholders allowed to call special meetings?		√	
36. Is a majority vote required to amend charter/bylaws (not a supermajority)?			√
37. May shareholders act by written consent, even if the consent is non-unanimous?			√
Ownership			
38. Is officers' and directors' ownership at least 1 percent but not more than 30 percent of total shares outstanding?		√	
39. Are executives subject to stock ownership guidelines?		√	
40. Are directors subject to stock ownership guidelines?		√	
41. Do all directors with more than one year of service own stock?		√	
Director Education			
42. Has at least one member of the board participated in an accredited director education program?	√		
Audit			
43. Is there a formal policy on auditor rotation?		√	
44. Are fees being paid to the auditor less for consulting than for audit services?		√	
45. Does the audit committee consist solely of independent outside directors?		√	
Jurisdiction of Incorporation			
46. Is the company incorporated in a jurisdiction without any antitakeover provisions?			√
	4	33	9

influential ownership and control networks designed to preserve existing power structures rather than facilitate operational feedback for organic self-correction to improve competitiveness and sustainability (Turnbull 2002a).

According to Turnbull (2002a, 5), Mondragón Corporación Cooperativa (MCC) in Spain, the Japanese keiretsu system, VISA International in the United States, and John Lewis Partnership and the Scott Bader Commonwealth in the United Kingdom provide "compelling evidence for the value of compound boards ... even in cultures where unitary boards are dominant." Turnbull's (p. 11) rationale is that they "introduce a division of power to provide checks and balances to facilitate self-governance." For example, John Lewis Partnership, an employee-owned retail conglomerate, incorporates a Partnership Council to hold the executive to account with the power to discuss any matter and even dismiss the chairman. The Partnership Board consists of the chairman, five partner (employee) directors elected by the Partnership Council, five executive directors appointed by the chairman, and two outside nonexecutive directors. This governance structure is said to provide a balance between commercial acumen and corporate conscience. From an ACG perspective, requisite organization is addressed by the Partnership Council (or Supervisory Board) that is concerned with more than commercial considerations; requisite variety is achieved by having three governing authorities (Partnership Board, Partnership Council, and chairman); and adaptive capacity is assured by appointing directors from multiple authorities and empowering the Partnership Council to remove the chairman.

Aspirational corporate governance explicitly addresses a complexity consideration that is implicit in Turnbull's network governance model. Supervisory boards, stakeholder congresses and councils, review boards, senates, and watchdog boards serve to broaden the governance network with diverse perspectives and thereby reduce uncertainty. In addition, they add value by addressing complexity at higher levels of abstraction, providing views from elevated vantage points. They increase the cognitive capacity of corporate governance by presenting a bigger picture of the intricate tangle of strategic and systemic considerations over a longer time horizon, and equip them to handle dilemmas, ambiguities, inconsistencies, and novelties. ACG allows organizations to thrive in a complex and uncertain world by advancing governance systems that are open to a broad spectrum of possibilities.

SUMMARY AND CONCLUSIONS

This chapter introduces a new context for corporate governance best practices in which corporate governance is the mechanism that naturally connects organizations to their environment. Aspirational corporate governance (ACG) might help organizations achieve this objective. The ACG framework defines the critical corporate governance factors needed to direct organizations toward value-creating opportunities that are increasingly obscured by complexity and concealed within labyrinths of uncertainty. ACG systems are designed for requisite organization, requisite variety, and adaptive capacity to sustain firms in ever-changing business environments. Conditions for ACG apply universally to all organizations and can enhance the effectiveness of any existing governance model or structure. Rather than replacing previous governance principles and practices, ACG is a universal diagnostic tool for measuring and analyzing these (existing and prospective) principles and practices as well as a blueprint for improving the design of any governance system.

An ACG analysis of prominent corporate governance principles and practices reveals remarkable congruence with international guidelines, but increasing divergence in national and institutional approaches. Nevertheless, some outstanding examples of corporate governance systems that direct the business of highly successful corporations, such as VISA International, serve as beacons for what is possible.

The power to transform corporate governance systems resides with boards of directors and shareholders. According to Darazsdi and Stobaugh (2003, 2), governance committees have the mandate to oversee "the board's governance processes and effectiveness." While most of the recent attention for corporate governance reform has been directed toward strengthening audit and compensation committees, the work of governance committees remains largely a formality. They often serve a dual function as also the nominating committee, which consumes most of their attention. Governance process and effectiveness considerations are relegated to infrequent review, often annually. Corporate governance reform needs to begin in governance committee meetings. Members of governance committees should strive for the appropriate level of cognitive capacity to wisely lead boards through the complexities of evolving their organization's corporate governance system. While engaged in this process, they may find using the ACG framework instructive for assuming an expanded role, perhaps even constituting a Supervisory or Corporate Governance Board (Turnbull 2000) that deliberately creates a corporate environment for sustainable business performance and adaptability to changes in the business context.

DISCUSSION QUESTIONS

1. On whose behalf should corporate boards direct and control the activities of the organization?
2. Why do corporate directors need to be concerned about more than the principal-agent conflict?
3. Why do corporate governance best practices limit possibilities to improve corporate governance effectiveness?
4. How does aspirational corporate governance (ACG) make improving existing corporate governance best practices possible?
5. What does the ACG diagnosis of guiding corporate governance principles and practices reveal?
6. How could governance committees apply ACG to create a corporate environment that delivers sustainable business performance and adapts to changing conditions for business?

REFERENCES

Anderson, Charles A., and Robert N. Antony. 1986. *The new corporate directors.* New York: John Wiley & Sons.

Bakan, Joel. 2004. *The corporation: The pathological pursuit of profit and power.* Toronto, Ontario: Penguin Group.

Black, Bernard. 1999. *Corporate law and residual claimants*. eScholarship Repository, University of California, http://repositories.cdlib.org/blewp/27/.

Brown, Lawrence D., and Marcus L. Caylor. 2004. *SSRN—Corporate governance and firm performance*. http://papers.ssrn.com/sol3/papers.cfm?abstract_id=586423.

Clampitt, Phillip G., and Williams M. Lee. 2005. *Managing organizational uncertainty: Conceptualization and measurement*. http://www.imetacomm.com/otherpubs/research/manorguncertain.pdf.

Conference Board of Canada. 2009. *The Conference Board of Canada/Spencer Stuart 2009 National Awards in Governance: Recognizing governance innovation in the private, public, and not-for-profit sectors*. http://www.conferenceboard.ca/Libraries/GOV_AWARDS_PUBLIC/NatAwdsGov_WinnersCircle2009_booklet.sflb.

Daly, Kenneth. 2009. *Key agreed principles to strengthen corporate governance for U.S. publicly traded companies*. https://secure.nacdonline.org/source/Orders/index.cfm?section=&task=3&CATEGORY=GOV&PRODUCT_TYPE=SALES&SKU=GOV-001&DESCRIPTION=&FindSpec=&CFTOKEN=82848916&continue=1&SEARCH_TYPE=.

Darazsdi, James J., and Robart B. Stobaugh. 2003. *The corporate governance committee—Director's handbook series*. Washington, DC: National Association of Corporate Directors.

Darwin, Charles R. 1859. *On the origin of species by means of natural selection, or the preservation of favoured races in the struggle for life*. London: John Murray.

Dimma, William A. 2006. *Tougher boards for tougher times: Corporate governance in the post-Enron era*. Mississauga, Ontario: John Wiley & Sons Canada, Ltd.

Gomez, Pierre-Yves., and Harry Korine. 2008. *Entrepreneurs and democracy: A political theory of corporate governance*. Cambridge, MA: Cambridge Univesity Press.

King, Sandra W., Ra W. King, George T. Solomon, and Kathryn Cason. 1997. *Potential capability and organizational transition: An application of Elliott Jaques' stratified systems theory in a family-owned business*. http://citeseerx.ist.psu.edu/viewdoc/summary?doi=10.1.1.31.9412.

Leblanc, Richard., and James Gillies. 2005. *Inside the boardroom: How boards really work and the coming revolution in corporate governance*. Mississauga, Ontario: John Wiley & Sons Canada, Ltd.

Lipman, Frederick D., and L. Keith Lipman. 2006. *Corporate governance best practices: Strategies for public, private, and not-for-profit organizations*. Hoboken, NJ: John Wiley & Sons.

Mohammed, Susan, and Alexander Schwall. 2009. Individual differences and decision making: What we know and where we go from here. In *International Review of Industrial and Organizational Psychology*, Volume 24, ed. Gerard P. Hodgkinson and J. Kevin Ford. Hoboken, NJ: John Wiley & Sons.

NACD. 2009. *Key principles to strengthen corporate governance for U.S. publicly traded companies*. https://secure.nacdonline.org/StaticContent/StaticPages/DM/NACDKeyAgreedPrinciples.pdf.

Nicholls, Christopher C. 2005. *Corporate law*. Toronto: Emond Montgomery Publication.

Organisation for Co-operation and Economic Development (OECD). 2004. *OECD principles of corporate governance*. http://www.oecd.org/dataoecd/32/18/31557724.pdf.

O'Riley, Charles, J. Bruce Harreld, and Michael Tushman. 2009. Organizational ambidexterity: IBM and emerging business opportunities. Research paper 2025, Stanford University Graduate School of Business; Working paper 53, Rock Center for Corporate Governance at Stanford University. http://ssrn.com/abstract=1418194.

Reiter, Barry. 2006. *Directors' duties in Canada*. Toronto, Ontario: CCH Canada Limited.

Smith, Adam. 2009. *The wealth of nations: Books 1–3: Complete and unabridged*. New York: Classic House Books.

Stout, Lynn. A. 2003. The shareholder as Ulysses: Some empirical evidence on why investors in public corporations tolerate board governance. *University of Pennsylvania Law Review* 152 (2): 667–712.

Tarantino, Anthony. 2008. *Governance, risk and compliance handbook*. Hoboken, NJ: John Wiley & Sons.

Todd, Alex. 2007a. *Trust measures and indicators for customers and investors—part 1: Measuring trust indicators for customers*. http://trustenablement.com/local/Trust_Measures_and_Indicators_for_Customers.pdf.

———. 2007b. *Trust measures and indicators for customers and investors—part 2: Measuring trust indicators for investors*. http://trustenablement.com/local/Trust_Measures_and_Indicators_for_Investors.pdf.

———. 2008. Corporate governance best practices: One size does not fit all. *ICSA International* 2 (March): 84–88.

Tory, James C., and John Cameron. 2009. *Directors' duties after BCE: Supreme Court of Canada decides*. http://www.torys.com/Publications/Documents/Publication%20PDFs/MA 2009-2.pdf.

Turnbull, Shann. 2000. Corporate governance: Theories, challenges and paradigms. http://ssrn.com/abstract=221350.

———. 2002a. *A new way to govern*. Working paper 5. London: New Economics Foundation. http://ssrn.com/abstract=310263 or DOI: 10.2139/ssrn.310263.

———. 2002b. *A new way to govern organizations and society after Enron*. London: NEF Pocketbooks.

———. 2004. *Agendas for reforming corporate governance, capitalism and democracy*. http://ssrn.com/abstract=546942 or DOI: 10.2139/ssrn.546942.

Van Clieaf, Mark., and Janet Langford Kelly. 2005. The new DNA of corporate governance. *Directorship* 31 (3): 1, 4–11.

Zaffron, Steve, and Dave Logan. 2009. *The three laws of performance: Rewriting the future of your organization and your life*. San Francisco: Jossey-Bass.

ABOUT THE AUTHOR

Alex Todd is a serial innovator and entrepreneur. He is a thought leader in rebuilding trust for business and architect of the Trust Enablement Framework, a universal scheme for diagnosing and designing conditions for trust. He used this Framework to derive the Governance Lifecycle Model for identifying corporate governance styles and the Aspirational Corporate Governance Framework being introduced in this volume. The Framework is founded on information theory and was inspired by his work with public key infrastructure (PKI) at IBM. It has also helped him share valuable insights about various areas of business that include leadership, collaboration, sales and marketing, public relations, online social networks, electronic commerce, supply chain management, risk management, and business strategy. His work has been published by McMaster University, the Conference Board of Canada, the Institute of Chartered Secretaries and Administrators (ICSA), The Institute of Certified Public Accountants of Singapore, Institutional Shareholder Services (ISS), and John Wiley & Sons. His firm, Trust Enablement Inc., helps business leaders and policy makers design new approaches for enabling stakeholder trust.

CHAPTER 5

What's Wrong with Corporate Governance Best Practices?

CHRISTOPHER SØREN SHANN TURNBULL
Principal, International Institute for Self-governance

INTRODUCTION

Corporate governance describes how power is exercised in corporations whether their purpose is for profit or not for profit. This chapter critiques practices widely promoted as being "best" for publicly traded corporations (hereafter simply "corporations"). Corporations attract investors on the expectation of providing economic gains. Economic results can provide one basis for evaluating the efficacy of the exercise of corporate power. But both investors and governments can have other concerns such as the diligence, good faith, honesty, transparency, and accountability of those who exercise power. Corporate power can be exercised by directors, officers, dominant shareholders, and in some situations stakeholders such as unions, bankers, major suppliers, and/or customers.

The basic determinants of the exercise of corporate power are country and state (or local) laws, corporate charters, security exchange listing requirements, regulators, and influential stakeholders. This chapter critiques these determinants as well as codes of best practices. This analysis is based on identifying the conflicts of interest between those who exercise corporate power and other corporate stakeholders. The chapter also focuses on how conflicts are identified, managed, mediated, and/or communicated to parties with the will and capacity to hold those involved to account and/or take corrective measures.

Defining Good Corporate Governance

Good governance is typically defined in terms of practices, processes, or economic performance. In this chapter, *good governance* is defined as the ability of corporations to efficaciously achieve their purpose while minimizing the involvement of the law or regulators in protecting and furthering the interests of corporate stakeholders and society in general. Implicit in this definition is the need to recognize companies' multiple concerns and objectives, as is mostly recognized by law. The definition also offers a criterion by which good governance is judged. In other words, good governance becomes dependent upon firms furthering their self-governance.

Good corporate governance becomes a way to enrich the governance of society by allowing firm stakeholders to obtain the information, will, and power to protect and further their interests while minimizing reliance on the law and regulators. This definition recognizes that firms are part of the political system of how power is distributed and exercised in society.

Criteria for Good Governance from the Natural Sciences

The preceding definition is also consistent with the control and communication systems of living things. The natural science of control and communication was identified only in the previous century when Wiener (1948, 11) named it *cybernetics*, which he described as "control and communication in the animal and the machine."

Stafford Beer pioneered the application of cybernetic insights into the design and management of social organizations in the 1960s and 1970s. Some described his prolific publications as *management cybernetics*, *operations research*, *management science*, or *system science*. At that time, most management systems were organized as command and control hierarchies. Later, Tricker (1984) promoted the phrase *corporate governance* to describe the governance of management hierarchies.

Technology now allows grounding organization design in the natural sciences to permit cybernetics to be described as the science of governance (Turnbull 2002b). This allows physical laws to provide the criteria for determining how corporations can become self-governing on the most reliable basis. It also means that the self-regulating strategies found in biota can inspire how to design the communication and control architecture of corporations to further their self-governance.

The three most relevant natural laws are those that specify how to improve the reliability of (1) communications (Shannon and Weaver 1949); (2) control (Ashby 1957); and (3) decision making (Neumann 1947). The gist of these laws is that communications, control, and decision making can be made as reliable as desired by increasing, respectively, the number of communication channels, control agents, and decision-making centers for each. Of particular importance is a corollary of Ashby's (p. 206) law that requires a *requisite variety* of control agents to regulate complexity. This means that the regulation of complexity only becomes physically possible indirectly through the use of co-regulators. The use of co-regulators to control complexity has not been widely recognized. Auditors and credit rating agents could act as co-regulators if they became subject to the power of the investors seeking protection rather than the firms being regulated.

In the 1990s, scholars began describing, identifying, and developing theories of nonhierarchical organizations (Nohira and Eccles 1992; Mathews 1996; Craven, Piercy, and Shipp 1996; Jones, Hesterly, and Borgatti 1997; Podolny and Page 1998; Turnbull 2000a and 2002b). Radner (1992, 1384) states, "I know no theoretical research to date that compares the relative efficiency of hierarchical and nonhierarchical organizations within a common model." In the following year, Jensen (1993, 873) observed that "we're facing the problem of developing a viable theory of organizations." This problem has also been identified by other leading workers in the field. Zingales (2000, 4) states that "[existing theories] seem to be quite ineffective in helping us cope with the new type of firms that are emerging." The new types of nonhierarchical firms include those with *network governance*. Jones et al. report that network governance emerged by competitive necessity in the more dynamic and complex industries such as electronics and biotechnology. This phenomenon can be explained by the laws of requisite variety as network governance introduces a variety of communication channels, control centers, and controllers. However, Jones et al. did not identify firms with more than one board and so their research was only based on network governance between firms whereas this author uses the term to also include networks of boards within firms (Turnbull 2010).

A framework for analyzing and comparing nonhierarchical organizations with network-governed firms arose from technological advances in the 1990s. Cochrane (1997 and 2000), the head scientist at the British Telecom Research Laboratories, measured the maximum rate at which humans can receive and transmit data in terms of bits and bytes used to described the capabilities of electronic networks. Likewise, Kurzweil (1999), an MIT voice recognition scientist, reported the limited ability of humans to process and store data measured in the bytes used to define the operating capabilities of computers.

Cochrane and Kurzweil identified the physiological and neurological limits of humans to receive, store, retrieve, manipulate, and use or transmit data on a reliable basis. These human limitations restrict the ability of more complex organizations to operate efficiently, effectively, or on a sustainable self-governing basis. The limited ability of humans to transact bytes is independent of the technology that they may employ to receive or transmit data and its higher-order derivatives of information, knowledge, and wisdom. While identifying the number of bytes associated with these higher-order social constructs is impossible, their transmission is dependent upon bytes being transacted. Transaction Byte Analysis (TBA) provides a way to explain *bounded rationality* (Williamson 1975, 4) and the need for multidivisional ("M-Form") corporations (Williamson 1975, 136) to minimize information overload (Turnbull 2000c, 106). M-Form corporations reduce information overload of senior managers by decomposing decision-making labor into various specialized divisions such as production, marketing, finance, and human resources.

TBA provides a basis for explaining why firms exist and how to create the most effective and sustainable structure (Turnbull 2001). The Williamson framework described as transaction cost economics (TCE) is based on socially constructed *transaction costs* that are difficult to identify and impossible to measure without making assumptions about relative contributions of fixed and variable costs.

Framework for Evaluating Good Governance

TBA provides the framework sought by Radner (1992, 1384) to compare "the relative efficiency of hierarchical and non-hierarchical organizations." It provides a basis for the efficacy of the communication and control architecture between humans to be evaluated by its ability to economize the transaction of bytes while achieving the desired integrity of communications, control, and decision making. Economizing the transaction of bytes is necessary to keep communication, control, and decision making in social organizations within "human constraints in transacting bytes" compiled by Turnbull (2000c, 111). As the transaction of bytes involves perturbations in energy or matter, economizing bytes also economizes the social construct of cost. Indeed, in knowledge-intensive organizations, transaction costs can represent a proxy for bytes. In this way TBA can subsume TCE.

TBA has been used to demonstrate the competitive advantages of network governance as found in the stakeholder-controlled cooperatives with multiple boards (Turnbull 2000c, 243–247). With an appropriate communication and control architecture, multiple boards can introduce distributed intelligence, control, and communications. They also introduce the decomposition of decision-making labor to minimize information overload by chief executive officers (CEOs) and directors of firms governed by a unitary board. In this way, internal network governance can introduce a requisite variety of communication, control, and decision making to meet the natural science criteria for furthering reliable or *best* practices. A condition precedent for enhancing self-governance and *good governance* as defined in this chapter is the division of power and the checks and balances that network governance can introduce to introduce *A New Way to Govern* (Turnbull 2002a). A corollary is that complex corporations without appropriately designed multiple boards are less able to be self-governing and thus less able to represent best practice.

A related problem of firms governed by a single board is the manifold conflicts of interest for the directors (Turnbull 2000c). As Monks and Sykes (2002, 9) note, directors obtain "major inappropriate powers of corporate management." In particular, directors obtain absolute power to identify and manage their own conflicts of interest, providing a basis for corruption of the directors and the company.

As discussed in the following section, the historical origins of corporations explain the evolution of corporate governance concepts and their subsequent degradation. The chapter then proceeds to review currently accepted best practices. A closing section follows with a summary and conclusions.

EVOLUTION OF CORPORATE CONCEPTS

This section reviews the origins of the corporate concept in England, Continental Europe, and the United States. It explains how earlier practices provided better governance and how these were lost or how their use created problems as new institutional structures and relationships evolved.

Political Origins of Corporate Concepts

The English concept of a corporation evolved as means for the sovereign with absolute powers to delegate some powers of self-governance to towns, guilds, abbeys, and universities. The continental European concept of a company developed later for commercial reasons through common law. The Corporation of London has its origins in a charter granted by King William the Conqueror in 1067 that allowed Londoners to obtain some powers of self-governance. For similar reasons, the sovereign granted charters to monasteries, other local government bodies, and universities at a time when Parliament did not have such discretions for the nation.

When the Pope gave his blessing in 1594 to divide international trade between the Spanish and the Portuguese, English sovereigns countered by issuing charters granting monopoly rights for their citizens to trade and/or colonize specified foreign lands. The history of the East India Company illustrates how empire building could be privatized while simultaneously raising revenues for the Crown from taxes collected on imported goods. English sovereigns also granted a number of corporate charters for the colonization of America to become a contributing cause for the war of independence. To negate the political power of English corporations after the war, state governments in the United States initially placed limits on the life of corporate charters and the nature of their ownership. As Grossman and Adams (1993) explain, this limited the ability of corporations being used again as instruments of colonization.

Unlike English civil law corporations with unlimited life, Continental European corporations were created by a common law deed of association for commercial purposes that placed a time limit on their existence. This allowed investors to liquidate their holdings without the need for a stock exchange. Continuity of operations was dependent upon shareholder reinvestment in a successor entity. This made managers dependent upon investors for their rehiring and created a compelling incentive for managers to look after investors.

The deed of association created limited liability for managers by requiring that the company be liquidated if it did not maintain adequate capital to cover the debts for which managers were responsible under common law. This also provided an incentive for managers to avoid the risk of losses. Lead investors formed what is now described as a supervisory board to appoint managers. In this way they avoided personal liability by not incurring debts. Limited liability for investors was achieved by not recording the identity of shareholders on bearer shares that could be exchanged like currency notes. Corporations became a society of anonymous investors and hence the term *Société Anonyme* and the letters *S.A.* located after the names of some European corporations.

Best Practice Auditing

The Joint Stock Companies Act of 1844 first established the ability of a group of investors to form a corporation without a special act of the English Parliament. The Act made provisions for one or more shareholders (not necessarily an accountant) to carry out an annual statutory audit. The auditors were appointed by and reported to shareholders but were paid by the government through the Commissioners of the Treasury (O'Connor 2004). The company was required to reimburse the government for the cost of the audit.

This arrangement avoids the untenable conflicts of interest for both directors and auditors imposed by the so-called best practice of the Combined Code on Corporate Governance (2003) in the United Kingdom and the Sarbanes Oxley Act (SOX) in the United States. The nature of these conflicts is best explained by considering the ethical standards of a modern court of law. For example, allowing those being judged to select and pay a judge would be unacceptable. But the Combined Code and SOX prescribe just this relationship with directors selecting and paying those judging their financial statements. It also creates a conflict for the auditors who are being selected and paid by the directors whose statements they are judging.

The 1845 UK Companies Clauses Act authorized elected shareholder auditors to hire accountants (O'Connor 2004). This act required the audited accounts and balance sheet to be filed for public inspection at a government registrar. A model constitution was attached to the UK 1862 Companies Act. This provided for the formation of a shareholder audit committee (discussed later in this chapter).

However, because the model constitution was not required by law, it was not widely implemented.

Independence of Auditors Misleading

Even with the conflicts identified thus far, regulators around the world allow auditors to attest that they are independent. The use of the word *independent* in this context is misleading to the general investing public who are unfamiliar with the ability of lawyers to prostitute the accepted understanding of words. The fact that auditors can attest to their independence reveals the extent to which their profession has captured lawmakers and regulators. Some Continental European jurisdictions avoid the conflict by allowing shareholders to elect a second board that is constituted independently from the directors being held to account. The second board became a shareholders' audit committee to avoid conflicts between directors and auditors.

However, the Italian statutory shareholder audit committee for Parmalat was elected on the same plutocratic basis as directors of one vote per share (Melis 2004 and 2005). As the CEO was also the major shareholder, he could control both the board and the independently elected audit committee in a way similar to many Anglo corporations with only a single board. Parmalat failed in 2003.

Turnbull (2000a) introduced a shareholder audit committee for an Australian start-up company in 1988. This was achieved by shareholders approving a change in the constitution of the company, which can be done without altering Australian law. The shareholder audit committee was described as a *corporate senate*. Its three members were democratically elected on a one-vote-per-investor basis instead of the plutocratic basis of electing directors on one-vote-per-share. Minority investors obtained the power to protect themselves in ways unavailable in the case of Parmalat.

Best Practice Avoids a Dictatorship of the Majority

As an additional safeguard to protect shareholders with a corporate senate, Turnbull arranged for directors to be elected by a form of preferential voting described as *cumulative voting* (Bhagat and Brickley 1984). Each share still had one vote but each shareholder obtained as many votes as there were vacancies on the board with the option of cumulating all their votes for one or more nominees. In this way, minority interests can appoint directors to avoid a dictatorship of the majority. For directors representing a minority interest, the incentive then exists to become whistle blowers on a private basis in advising the corporate senate of any board conflicts that could be subject to a senate veto.

Although the notion of a shareholder audit committee had been around since at least 1862 in the United Kingdom, the idea resurfaced 133 years later when Hatherly (1995) suggested such a committee. Hatherly was once the director of accounting and auditing research at the Institute of Chartered Accountants of Scotland and Wales, a member of the UK Auditing Practices Board, and chairman of the Audit Practice Board's Auditing Research Group. As reported by *AccountancyAge* (2004), the National Association of Pension Funds recommended a shareholder audit committee to the UK government in 2004 but the government ignored this recommendation. Earlier in Australia, Senator Andrew Murray (1998) recommended in his minority report to the Australian Parliament the adoption of a more robust version of the corporate senate. Murray more aptly described it as a *corporate governance board* (CGB). Unlike a corporate senate that only had veto powers over director conflicts, the CGB obtained the additional power to make decisions on audits, director remuneration, and nomination.

The only proactive powers of a corporate senate were to provide the chairman for shareholder meetings and manage the voting process for directors. The purpose of holding an annual general meeting of shareholders in the United Kingdom and many of its former colonies is to hold the directors accountable, vote for their election, and determine their pay. An untenable conflict of interest is created if a director controls these processes by chairing the meeting. However, these unethical conflicts are so ubiquitously accepted that they are commonly ignored in considering best corporate governance practices. Likewise, the belief that share markets are transparent and informed is inconsistent with the practice of stock exchanges concealing from investors the identity of those buying or selling their shares. This practice developed to allow stockbrokers to exploit their clients by secretly trading ahead of them or with them.

Covert share trading practice exposes another myth: Directors should only trade shares after a meeting of shareholders when the public is supposed to be equally informed. Best practice would be for directors and any other insiders to inform the market and their counterparties before trading rather than after the event. A prior-warning approach described as *sunlight trading* would allow insiders to trade at any time during the year to create a more informed and liquid market.

How Audit Practices Degraded

Until the mid-nineteenth century, U.S. corporations were, in effect, audited directly by citizens and regulated by state legislatures (Grossman and Adams 1993). This was at a time when shareholders elected directors on a democratic one-vote-per-investor basis rather than by a plutocratic one vote per share. The New Jersey Supreme Court ruled in 1834 that corporate constitutions with one vote per share were illegal (Dunlavy 1998). However, wealthy and influential interests later persuaded judges to reverse this decision. Today, giant corporations such as News Corporation Limited and Google can issue common shares without voting rights.

The intense local democratic supervision and regulation of U.S. corporations was cast aside by the growth and influence of giant enterprises that emerged at the end of the nineteenth century. Powerful shareholders, according to Friedman (1973, 456), "bought and sold governments" as well as judges. States competed with each other to introduce more liberal conditions for corporations to obtain charters and to operate. As O'Connor (2004, 30) notes, this created a "race to the bottom" in corporate deregulation. As a result, by the beginning of the twentieth century few states required corporations to present accounts or to appoint auditors. Consequently, more than 30 percent of companies quoted on the New York Stock Exchange during the 1925–1929 economic boom did not provide accounts.

Even when corporations did not publish accounts, some nonexecutive directors (NEDs) would still establish what today would be described as a board audit committee (Guthrie and Turnbull 1995). Their motivation had nothing to do with the presentation of accounts or accountability to investors. Instead, NEDs were entirely motivated by self-interest to avoid becoming personally liable for loans obtained by the firm that were supported by negative pledges by the directors. An external auditor was required to check that management had not breached any loan covenants.

To ensure that management complied with the loan covenants, NEDs would meet separately from the executives and hire a public accountant to follow the money trail. There was no need for the accountant to make judgments on the timing of recognizing income or expenses, or on the value of liabilities and assets or which accounting policies to adopt. In this way, external auditing was established in the United States to carry out an internal audit function for the directors. This played a role in adoption by the United States of confused and conflicting audit practices (Turnbull 2005).

The Confusion of U.S. and UK Audit Practices

In 1933, the U.S. Congress established the Securities and Exchange Commission (SEC) with an Act that also required corporations to audit accounts when issuing shares interstate. The U.S. audit requirements were modeled on the prospectus provisions of the 1929 UK Companies Act. The UK Act did not require a balance sheet, only a "certified profit and loss statement" for the previous three years (O'Connor 2004). UK prospectus information is concerned with the economic performance of the company to protect investors. This is different from the legal role for UK statutory audits. The House of Lords determined in the Caparo case of 1990 that the purpose of a statutory audit was to carry out a governance role. This purpose is consistent with the requirement that audits are also required for nonprofit corporations that do not issue shares, such as professional associations and charities.

Directors in the United Kingdom appoint the auditor for a prospectus and the audit report is addressed to the directors. However, statutory auditors in the United Kingdom are appointed by shareholders/members and the audit report is addressed to them, not the directors. Under some circumstances, members may not be shareholders, such as when a corporation has its liabilities limited by a guarantee and not by shares.

The requirements in the U.S. 1933 Act for audited accounts regarding newly issued shares were carried over into the U.S. 1934 Act for the interstate sale of existing shares. O'Connor (2004, 61) reports that as the U.S. 1933 Act "left it open as to who would hire and set compensation for the auditors, this responsibility fell to management and/or the board of directors—the very parties whom the auditors were supposed to be checking up on!" O'Connor (p. 59) points out that the SEC then had to find a way

> *to make sure the accountant-as-auditor was independent of the client, so as to be able to render an objective and accurate opinion. . . . The result was a labyrinth compendium of principles, rules, interpretations, and no-action letters whose sole constant feature seemed to be change. The most recent revision to this bramble bush is the auditor independence provisions of the Sarbanes-Oxley Act of 2002.*

O'Connor (2004, 60) states that "the problem of auditor independence was created by the federal securities laws: initially, through the statutory audit provision for prospectuses in the 1933 Act, and then exacerbated by the de facto extension of this audit to an annual requirement under the 1934 Act." O'Connor (p. 62) observes:

> *Thus, the American accountant/auditor is placed in the untenable position of the agent serving many masters with conflicting interests. In such an imbroglio, is it any wonder that the group who hires, fires, and sets compensation for the auditor becomes the* de facto *client? Over time, laudable efforts to establish protections such as audit committees of company boards that would insulate auditors from the direct influence of management have been instituted. But these still fail to take the simple step of pushing control of the audit relationship back to shareholders where it belongs.*

Rather than remove the conflicts of interest for auditors and directors created by the SEC mandated rules, SOX has exacerbated the problem by enshrining them in statute. As Romano (2004, 16) notes, "The learning of the literature, which was available when Congress was legislating, is that SOX's corporate governance provisions were ill-conceived. The political environment explains why Congress would enact legislation with such mismatched means and ends." Companies registered in other countries who are seeking to have their securities traded in the United States are adopting the intrinsically flawed U.S. auditing architecture.

There are many reasons other countries are encouraged to enshrine the conflicted U.S. audit practices in their own economies. First, other countries see the United States as the prime role model for a market-based economy. Second, the Organisation of Economic Co-operation and Development (OECD) Corporate Governance Principles follow U.S. practice. Third, corporate governance rating agencies typically base their metrics on OECD-like principles, creating market forces for corporations outside the United States to adopt U.S. practices. Fourth, the size and influence of U.S. markets provide practical incentives. Fifth, the World Bank, International Monetary Fund, and other international and bilateral finance and aid agencies proselytize and encourage so called good governance using the U.S. and/or OECD principles.

The sixth and most insidious influence on other countries is the presence and actions of the big international accounting firms. The United States remains their most important client base. The fact that some other countries assume the U.S. approach represents the most creditable, relevant, and advanced example of audit practices is understandable. Indeed, as Hatherly (1995, 504) notes, the belief that existing practices "represent the natural order of things" provides a basis for insinuating U.S. practices around the globe.

Many governance commentators are surprised that U.S. laws, regulations, and stock exchange listing rules provide less protection for minority shareholders and investors than in other much less influential countries. The management-friendly U.S. jurisdictions provide an incentive for foreign multinational corporations to move their domicile to the United States in the same way that U.S. companies raced to the bottom to change their domicile to Delaware. According to Bush (2004, 5) "the State of Delaware 'has no framework for public financial reporting.'" The ability of corporations registered in Delaware to facilitate continued family control and/or allow a family control block to be disposed of, without providing adequate protection for minority shareholders, provides one explanation of why the formerly Australian-registered News Corporations Limited moved its registered domicile to Delaware in 2004.

Delaware's system of *plurality* voting allows any director who obtains one vote to be elected regardless of how many negative votes are cast against him. This self-perpetuating practice is unacceptable in many non-U.S. jurisdictions. Also unacceptable elsewhere is the U.S. practice of allowing brokers and advisers to vote shares when shareholders themselves fail to vote. This practice provides another way for directors to obtain support for their tenure, pay, and other actions.

Shareholders of corporations incorporated in the United Kingdom and its other former colonies have more powers than those incorporated in the United States. However, notwithstanding the suggestion by O'Connor (2004) that the UK system has advantages over the U.S. audit regime, governance practices in the United Kingdom create conflicts of interest for auditors and directors, which are considered next.

Conflicted UK Audit Committees

The U.S. audit conflict created by directors appointing the auditor is prima facie avoided in the United Kingdom where the law requires members/shareholders to approve the appointment. In practice this means that the directors nominate and remunerate the auditor, so identical conflicts arise. However, the audit report is prepared for members but not for directors as in the United States. Another difference is that in the United Kingdom, the accounts are audited, not just the financial statements as in the United States. This allows the U.S. audit to be more superficial in its scope, especially when materiality becomes a criterion.

In his House of Lords judgment, Lord Justice Oliver (Caparo 1990, 16) posed the following rhetorical question: What is the purpose of holding an annual meeting and what is the purpose of the directors presenting accounts to be audited? He answered these questions by pointing out the following:

> *This is the only occasion in each year upon which the general body of shareholders is given the opportunity to consider, to criticise, and to comment upon the conduct by the board of the company's affairs, to vote upon the directors' recommendation as to dividends, to approve or disapprove the directors' remuneration and, if thought desirable, to remove and replace all or any of the directors. It is the auditors' function to ensure, so far as possible, that the financial information as to the company's affairs prepared by the directors accurately reflects the company's position in order, first, to protect the company itself from the consequences of undetected errors or, possibly, wrongdoing (by, for instance, declaring dividends out of capital) and, secondly, to provide shareholders with reliable intelligence for the purpose of enabling them to scrutinise the conduct of the company's affairs and to exercise their collective powers to reward or control or remove those to whom that conduct has been confided.*

To counter the argument that the purpose of the audit was to inform investors of the economic value of the company, Lord Oliver (Caparo 1990, 17) went on to express his disbelief that "the legislature, in enacting provisions clearly aimed primarily at the protection of the company and its informed control by the body of its proprietors, can have been inspired also by consideration for the public at large and investors in the market in particular."

Lord Bridge supported the view of Lord Oliver (Caparo 1990, 11) of the need for audits to provide shareholders with "reliable intelligence for the purpose of enabling them to scrutinize the conduct of the company's affairs." Bridge quoted an 1896 judgment in affirming that there is "No doubt [the auditor] is acting antagonistically to the directors in the sense that he is appointed by the shareholders to be a check upon them." Because Anglophone corporations do not established a shareholder audit committee, auditors now treat the directors and the company as their client, rather than the shareholders. Lord Bridge noted this and stated: "In carrying out his investigation and in forming his opinion the auditor necessarily works very closely with the directors and officers of the company. He receives his remuneration from the company. He naturally, and rightly, regards the company as his client" (Caparo 1990, 12).

This explains how UK audit practices became muddled. For the existing flawed system of so-called best audit practice to have any creditability, it becomes crucial to support the myth that auditors can be independent. As considered next, empirical evidence shows this independence to be impossible.

IMPOSSIBILITY OF AUDIT INDEPENDENCE

As Shapiro (2005) notes, auditors cannot be independent of the directors they judge because the legal architecture of Anglophone corporations makes this impossible. This practice cannot be changed by describing some directors as independent and using them to control the auditor, because the financial statements hold all directors responsible. The very process of establishing a director audit committee in either the United States or the United Kingdom exacerbates the conflicts. Audit committees provide a more intimate and frequent basis for bonding the external auditor to the directors rather than to the shareholders who use the information. The FACG (1992, 27) report recommends greater interaction between the auditor and the directors when stating that "the external auditor should normally attend audit committee meetings, as should the finance director." The UK Combined Code (2003) follows these provisions.

Bazerman, Morgan, and Loewenstein (1997) identify five reasons external audits fail that are relevant to either the United States or the United Kingdom. Experiments reported by Bazerman, Loewenstein, and Moore (2002) validate their analysis. The results are consistent with earlier experiments by Milgram (2004) that explain how good people can do bad things, as occurred in Nazi Germany and with the My Lai massacre.

In the context of corporations governed by single or *unitary* boards with dispersed shareholders, as found in the United Kingdom and the United States, having shareholders manage and pay the auditor is impractical. Therefore, directors in the United Kingdom are forced to act as the agent for shareholders in this regard. As the role of the auditor is to act antagonistically, this creates a fundamental conflict of interest for the auditor. Even the most ethical and conscientious director is placed in the position of exerting power over the auditor and so perceived to be in a conflict of interest situation that corporate constitutions and the law generally require directors to avoid.

While many people including some scholars view directors as acting as agents for the shareholders, this is not their normal legal relationship. Directors are principals of the company, not its agents. The confusion arises because directors are elected by and are accountable to shareholders. Yet the fiduciary duty of directors is to the company as a whole. The company is a different legal entity from any one shareholder or even all shareholders as a whole.

Technically, managers become the agents of the company and, thus, agents of the directors. When corporations have widely dispersed shareholders, managers form *power coalitions*, as described by Dallas (1988, 28), to co-opt directors and make them their agents.

Bazerman et al. (1997 and 2002) point out that auditors unconsciously become agents of the directors as they are employed by them. Directors in turn become a tool of an internal coalition in which management is the "dominant coalition member" (Dallas 1988, 29). Auditors then become agents of management to subrogate the very purpose of appointing auditors.

In an effort to deny the conflicts of interest current arrangements create, the big audit firms and directors have developed a self-serving myth that the role of the external auditor is not to check the company and directors, but rather to check management. This has led to what Rodrigues (2007) describes as the *fetishization* of appointing so-called independent directors.

The Role of So-Called Independent Directors

As Rodrigues (2007, 1) states, "According to conventional wisdom, a supermajority independent board of directors is the ideal corporate governance structure. Debate nevertheless continues: empirical evidence suggests that independent boards do not improve firm performance." Baghat and Black (2002) provide one such source of empirical evidence. Rodrigues (p. 1) points out that the SOX concept of director independence represents "fundamentally different conceptions of independence" than that set out by Delaware Law. Clarke (2007, 73) identifies three types of independence and states that "the whole purpose of having independent directors is surprisingly under theorized, leading to inconsistent rules." Page (2009) identifies the "unconscious bias" of "independent" NEDs. Monks and Sykes (2002, 16) ask why "refine definitions of 'independence' which everyone knows to be untrue?" As Hayward (2003, 3) notes, a former audit partner of one of the big four audit firms in the United Kingdom confirms this view by stating:

> *There are two fundamental problems with independent audit. The first is that it isn't independent at all. It is in reality—and, as things stand, inevitably—closely aligned with the company management. The second problem is that it is an uncompetitive market, dominated by four large firms.*

SUMMARY AND CONCLUSIONS

Monks and Sykes (2002, 37) state that "Corporations are ultimately a system of power." In spite of continuous inquiries, reviews, and law reforms, the power of corporations continues to increase. An important source of increased power is changes in the nature of corporate shareholders. Instead of shareholders being individuals representing their own interests and that of society, shareholders are increasingly becoming faceless investment institutions that can have interests that conflict with and/or are irresponsible with the interests of personal investors and society.

The conflicts can arise from many sources. The investment institution may be owned by the corporation and so is not in a position to make corporate directors accountable. Alternatively, the directors of the investment institution could be directors of the corporation of their business associates, which will also inhibit making corporate directors accountable. The investment institution could be seeking to sell insurance or other financial services to the corporation and so inhibit it from making corporate directors accountable. Even if a fiduciary agent such as an investment institution can make directors accountable, the agent does this for its own corporate agenda. The conflicts arise from the increasing trend of capitalism to be managed by faceless and conflicted fiduciary agents. Fiduciary capitalism inhibits good corporate governance and debases democracy. A cure would be for the ownership of corporations to become vested in voting citizens after the time horizon of fiduciary equity investors, which is around 10 years. This outcome could be achieved on a voluntary basis from a tax incentive. The incentive would transfer the corporate tax base to investors so more revenue could be raised than lost (Turnbull 2000b).

Governments typically commission powerful and influential businesspeople to lead inquiries into how to reduce abuses. Using such individuals for this purpose has allowed the powerful and commercial vested interests to perpetuate the current system and only make token changes. Definitions of *best* practices become self-serving rhetoric to preserve the status of the powerful. Monks (2008) describes how CEOs used their power through the Business Roundtable to persuade accounting practices to accept their self-serving agenda. The professional integrity of other service providers to CEOs like auditors, consultants, and rating agencies are likewise compromised. As a result of this and the muddled thinking explained in this chapter, regulators and lawmakers have been captured by existing accepted so-called best practices and politically cannot consider fundamental changes. In some cases, good people have promoted counterproductive practices, as when the United States adopted the UK prospectus arrangements for annual audits and the United Kingdom adopted the U.S. practice of audit committees made up of directors instead of investors.

Widely accepted best practices involve such matters as having so-called independent directors as a board majority to monitor and direct executives. Best practice is then to form board committees with a majority of directors classified as independent to manage the conflicts that arise from determining the accountability of directors through their audited accountants. Best practice also requires transparency in publishing information on the terms of reference of these committees with their composition and operating procedures. The separation of the role of CEO and board chair is also seen as a best practice.

However, the classification of a director as independent may not be relevant to the decisions being made. Board conflicts of interest cannot be avoided by delegation to subcommittees. Unitary boards are inherently conflicted no matter how a director may be classified. The more independent a director is of colleagues, the business, and its industry, the less information and authority a director possesses to carry out his core fiduciary duty to monitor and direct management without relying on management reports with their inbuilt incentive to be self-serving. This makes current best practices uncompetitive as well as unethical (Turnbull 2011).

Corporate power as exercised by Anglophone countries has been a highly influential model for the rest of the world. It is promoted globally by prestigious and influential institutions such as the World Bank and many other well-meaning agencies. Financial aid has been tied to the fundamentally flawed governance system and practices of Anglophone countries. As Monks and Sykes (2002, 19) note, "When the overall system is flawed, 'best practice' comparisons have no place." Convincing the existing keepers of the currently accepted best practices—especially government regulators, professional advisers, and those with corporate power—to change their minds is difficult.

Reversing current views may require a new generation of influential leaders educated in governance science. At present the relevancy of the natural governance laws to social organizations has not gained traction in scholarly discourse, let alone among regulators and lawmakers. One exception was former U.S. Vice President Al Gore, who saw the need for changing the role of government for it to become consistent with the science of governance. Specifically, recognizing that regulating the complexities of society required an indirect approach (Ashby 1957), Gore (1996) believed that the role of government should be "more on imprinting the DNA" of social institutions to make them self-regulating like biota.

The DNA of social institutions is represented by their constitutions (Turnbull 2000c). The role of government is therefore to license organizations to operate provided that they adopt constitutions to protect and further the interests of their stakeholders. This would require corporations to establish their own firm-specific system of co-regulators to provide the requisite variety of control to match the variety of interests and concerns of their stakeholders. The role, cost, and intrusion of government into corporate activities would be displaced by corporations acting as co-regulators to further and protect the interests of citizens. Corporations in turn would need to distribute and share powers with their stakeholders and other citizens so these constituents could obtain the power to protect themselves directly and/or through others to safeguard their interests (Turnbull 2008).

The objective of reducing the role of government while increasing the public good in protecting and furthering the interests of citizens necessitates corporations adopting network governance (Turnbull 2002a). Network governance by nature distributes power and so is not likely to be voluntarily introduced by command and control hierarchies in the government or private sector. The introduction of network governance is thus likely to evolve from the bottom up with the development of ever more complex and dynamic industries, as described by Jones et al. (1997).

Another possible way in which current flawed corporate governance systems could be replaced is that they will become sufficiently discredited and/or broken.

A breakdown of an existing system facilitates a breakthrough. The global financial crisis of 2008 has instigated some minor changes that were not possible to consider or implement previously. Proposals in 1977 to give U.S. shareholders more power to nominate directors and make them accountable were reintroduced in May 2009 (Shapiro 2009). Yet correcting the current flawed practices apparently requires a much more serious breakdown and/or a much longer time period to allow the insights of governance science to be applied. In this way democracy could be enriched by reducing the role, size, and cost of government.

DISCUSSION QUESTIONS

1. What are the implications of defining *good corporate governance* in terms of the ability of firms to be self-governing on a sustainable basis?
2. What are the inherent limitations and problems arising from firms governed by a single board?
3. Identify how auditing in the United Kingdom and the United States differs and the conflicts created by accepted practices.
4. Identify the problems that arise from boards appointing directors who are classified as independent.
5. Identify how network governance can reduce business risks and provide competitive advantages.
6. What are the reasons for considering that corporate law and regulators are irresponsible?

REFERENCES

AccountancyAge. 2004. NAPF urges auditor shake-up. December 13, London.

Ashby, W. Ross. 1957. *An introduction to cybernetics*. London: Chapman & Hall Limited.

Bazerman, Max H., George Loewenstein, and Don A. Moore. 2002. Why good accountants do bad audits. *Harvard Business Review*. 80 (11): 95–98.

Bazerman, Max H., Kimberly P. Morgan, and George F. Loewenstein. 1997. The impossibility of auditor independence. *Sloan Management Review* 38 (4): 89–94.

Bhagat, Sanjai, and Bernard S. Black. 2002. The non-correlation between board independence and long-term firm performance. *Journal of Corporation Law* 27 (2): 231–273.

Bhagat, Sanjai, and James A. Brickley. 1984. Cumulative voting: The value of minority shareholder voting rights. *Journal of Law and Economics* 27 (2): 339–365.

Bush, Tim. 2004. Where economics meets the law: The U.S. financial reporting system compared to that of other jurisdictions. *Mind the GAAPs*. Working paper. London: Hermes Focus Asset Management Limited.

Caparo. 1990. *House of Lords Judgment of Caparo Industries plc v. Dickman and Others*, 2 AC 650. London. http://www.bailii.org/uk/cases/UKHL/1990/2.html.

Clarke, Donald C. 2007. Three concepts of the independent director. *Delaware Journal of Corporate Law* 32 (1): 73–111.

Cochrane, Peter. 1997. Private e-mail communication, December 21. London: British Telecom.

———. 2000. Hard drive: Bandwidth and brandwidth. April 6. London: *Telegraph*.

Combined Code on Corporate Governance. 2003. London: Financial Service Authority.

Craven, David W., Nigel F. Piercy, and Shannon H. Shipp. 1996. New organizational forms for competing in highly dynamic environments: The network paradigm. *British Journal of Management* 7 (3): 203–218.

Dallas, Lynne L. 1988. Two models of corporate governance: Beyond Berle and Means. *Journal of Law Reform* 22 (1): 19–116.

Dunlavy, Colleen A. 1998. Corporate governance in late 19th-century Europe and the U.S.: The case of shareholder voting rights. In *Comparative Corporate Governance: The State of the Art and Emerging Research*, ed. Klaus J. Hopt, Hideki Kanda, Mark J. Roe, Eddy Wymeersch, and Stefan Prigge, 5–39. Oxford: Clarendon Press.

FACG. 1992. *The financial aspects of corporate governance*. London: Gee and Co. Ltd.

Friedman, Lawrence M. 1973. *A history of American law*. New York: Simon and Schuster.

Gore, Al. 1996. The technology challenge: What is the role of science in American society? Prepared remarks delivered to the American Association for the Advancement of Science, Baltimore, MD, February 12.

Grossman, Richard L., and Frank T. Adams. 1993. *Taking care of business: Citizenship and the charter of incorporation*. Cambridge, MA: Charter Ink.

Guthrie, James, and C. S. Shann Turnbull. 1995. Audit committees: Is there a role for corporate senates and/or stakeholders councils? *Corporate Governance: An International Review* 3 (2): 78–89.

Hatherly, David J. 1995. The case for the shareholder panel in the UK. *European Accounting Review* 4 (3): 535–553.

Hayward, Jonathan 2003. *Thinking not ticking: Bringing competition to the public interest audit*. London: Centre for the Study of Financial Innovation (CSFI).

Jensen, Michael C. 1993. The modern industrial revolution: Exit and the failure of control systems. *Journal of Finance* 48 (3): 831–880.

Jones, Candace, William S. Hesterly, and Stephen P. Borgatti. 1997. A general theory of network governance: Exchange conditions and social mechanisms. *Academy of Management Review* 22 (4): 911–945.

Kurzweil, Ray. 1999. *The age of spiritual machines: When computers exceed human intelligence*. New York: Viking.

Mathews, John. 1996. Holonic organisational architectures. *Human System Management* 15 (1): 27–54.

Melis, Andrea. 2004. On the role of the board of statutory auditors in Italian listed companies. *Corporate Governance: An International Review* 12 (1): 74–84.

———. 2005. Corporate governance failures: To what extent is Parmalat a particularly Italian case? *Corporate Governance: An International Review* 13 (4): 478–488.

Milgram, Stanley. 2004. *Obedience to authority: An experimental view*. New York: HarperCollins.

Monks, Robert A. G. 2008. *Corpocracy: How CEOs and the Business Roundtable hijacked the world's greatest wealth machine—and how to get it back*. Hoboken, NJ: John Wiley & Sons.

Monks, Robert A. G., and Allen Sykes. 2002. *Capitalism without owners will fail: A policymaker's guide to reform*. New York: Centre for the Study of Financial Innovation (CSFI).

Murray, Andrew. 1998. *Minority report on the Company Law Review Bill 1997*. Canberra: Australian Parliamentary Joint Committee on Corporations and Securities.

Neumann, John von. 1947. *Theory of games and economic behaviour*. New Haven, CT: Yale University Press.

Nohira, Nitin, and Robert G. Eccles. 1992. *Networks and organizations: Structure, form and action*. Cambridge, MA: Harvard University.

O'Connor, Sean M. 2004. Be careful what you wish for: How accountants and Congress created the problem of auditor independence. *Boston College Law Review* 45 (5): 741–828.

Page, Antony. 2009. Unconscious bias and the limits of director independence. *University of Illinois Law Review* 2009 (1): 237–294.

Podolny, Joel M., and Karen L. Page. 1998. Network forms of organization. *Annual Review of Sociology* 24 (1): 57–76.

Radner, Roy. 1992. Hierarchy: The economics of managing. *Journal of Economic Literature* 30 (3): 1382–1415.

Rodrigues, Usha. 2007. "The fetishization of independence. *UGA Legal Studies Research Paper* 07–007.

Romano, Roberto. 2004, The Sarbanes-Oxley Act and the making of quack corporate governance. Yale ICF Working paper 04-37. ECGI, Finance.

Shannon, Claude E., and Warren Weaver. 1949. *The mathematical theory of communications*. Urbana, IL: University of Illinois Press.

Shapiro, Amy. 2005. Who pays the auditor calls the tune? Auditing regulation and clients' incentives. *Seton Hall Law Review* 35 (3): 1029–1095.

Shapiro, Mary L. 2009. Speech by SEC Chairman: Statement at SEC open meeting on facilitating shareholder director nominations.

Tricker, Robert I. 1984. *Corporate governance: Practices, procedures, and powers in British companies and their boards of directors*. England: Ashgate Publishing.

Turnbull, C. S. Shann. 2000a. Corporate charters with competitive advantages. *St. Johns Law Review* 74 (44): 101–159.

———. 2000b. Stakeholder governance: A cybernetic and property rights analysis. In *Corporate governance: The history of management thought*, ed. R. I. Tricker, 401–413. London: Ashgate Publishing.

———. 2000c. *The governance of firms controlled by more than one board: Theory development and examples*. PhD dissertation. Sydney: Macquarie University.

———. 2001. Grounding the theory of the firm in the natural sciences. *Presented to the 13th Annual Meeting of the Society for the Advancement of Socio-Economics, University of Amsterdam, June 30.*

———. 2002a. *A new way to govern: Organisations and society after Enron*. London: New Economics Foundation.

———. 2002b. The science of corporate governance. *Corporate Governance: An International Review* 10 (4): 256–272.

———. 2005. How US and UK auditing practices became muddled to muddle corporate governance principles. *The ICFAI Journal of Audit Practice* 2 (3): 49–68.

———. 2008. The theory and practice of government de-regulation. In *International Finance Review: Institutional Approach to Global Corporate Governance* 9, ed. Jongmoo Jay Choi and Sandra Dow, 117–139.

———. 2010. Design concepts for governance architects. Working Paper. 30 March. http://ssrn.com/abstract=1556831.

———. 2011. Why "best" corporate governance practices are unethical and less competitive In *Business ethics for personal integrity and social responsibility*, 2nd ed., ed. Laura Hartman and Joseph DesJardins, forthcoming Burr Ridge, IL: McGraw-Hill.

Wiener, Norbert. 1948. *Cybernetics: Or, control and communication in the animal and the machine*. New York: John Wiley & Sons, Inc.

Williamson, Oliver E. 1975. *Markets and hierarchies: Analysis and antitrust implications*. New York: Free Press.

Zingales, Luigi. 2000. *In search of new foundations*. CRSP Working paper 515.

ABOUT THE AUTHOR

Christopher Søren Shann Turnbull, Dip. Elec. Eng. (Hobart), BS (Melbourne), MBA (Harvard), and PhD (Macquarie), has been chairman and/or CEO of listed corporations and a serial entrepreneur establishing new firms, three of which became publicly traded. He was a founding author in 1975 of the first course to provide an educational qualification for company directors. His PhD thesis built on his engineering knowledge of communication and control systems to apply the natural science of governance to social organizations. Two core chapters of his PhD dissertation were republished with the seminal contributions of leading scholars in the *Corporate Governance* volume of *The History of Management Thought* (Ashgate Publishing 2000). He is a prolific author on reforming the theory and practices of capitalism with his academic contributions and books, archived at http://ssrn.com/author=26239. In 1991 he advised on reform in Czechoslovakia and the People's Republic of China. His clients have included other governments and multinational corporations.

CHAPTER 6

The Effect of Corporate Governance on Performance

SANJAI BHAGAT
Professor of Finance, University of Colorado at Boulder

BRIAN BOLTON
Professor of Finance, University of New Hampshire

ROBERTA ROMANO
Oscar M. Ruebhausen Professor of Law, Yale Law School, NBER and ECGI

INTRODUCTION

Corporate governance is the set of processes that provides an assurance to outside investors of a fair return on their investment. The focus of U.S. corporate governance systems is the agency problem: an organizational concern that arises when the owners (in a corporation, the shareholders) are not the managers who are in control. When owners and managers are not identical, the managers can take actions that benefit themselves at the owners' (shareholders') expense. For example, managers may not work as diligently as they are able because the increase in firm value that their hard work produces is shared with stockholders (in proportion to stockholders' equity investments), while managers bear the full cost of their greater exertion.

Corporate law seeks to mitigate the agency problem by providing an organizing framework to facilitate and support mechanisms of firms' corporate governance by which managers are incentivized and constrained to act in the shareholders' interest. The most elemental components of a corporate governance system are the board of directors, shareholder meetings and voting, and executive compensation.

The Board of Directors

Some commentators and many institutional investors consider directors who are not employees of the corporation (independent or outside directors) to be the crucial corporate governance mechanism for monitoring managers (Eisenberg 1976; CalPERS 2008). Congress and the stock exchanges, under the shadow of the Securities and Exchange Commission (SEC), have codified this notion of the directors' role by mandating, respectively, appointment of independent directors to all of the audit, compensation, and nominating committee positions, and a majority of the board.

The Shareholder Franchise and Block Ownership

Shareholder meetings, and more specifically the voting rights exercised at these meetings, provide the shareholder-owners with an opportunity to select and replace directors, to approve or reject management initiatives, and to present proposals for management's consideration while otherwise interacting directly with management. In recent years, institutional investor activism has focused on the voting governance mechanism by sponsoring proposals on a variety of governance issues such as takeover defenses and executive compensation as well as by negotiating with management over the proposals' substance (Romano 2001). Such activism is also connected to the governance mechanism of the board of directors, in that shareholder proposals often seek to increase the representation of independent directors on the board. However, the current emphasis of shareholder proposals has been directed at the right to nominate directors and the number of votes required in such elections.

Shareholders owning significant blocks of stock (blockholders) are often separately characterized in the academic literature as a mechanism of corporate governance (Shleifer and Vishny 1997). As the cost of a blockholder's activism is more likely to be recouped by the pro rata benefits obtained because it is spread over more shares, blockholders are more able than small shareholders to use their ownership to monitor managers. The most acute example of the working of this governance mechanism is the hostile takeover because a takeover results in a complete concentration of ownership and control that fully internalizes the costs and benefits of the agency problem. Concomitantly, even the threat of a takeover can function as a mechanism to discipline managers.

Executive Compensation

A final important component of firms' internal governance is executive compensation. There is a well-developed literature on the fashioning of incentives to achieve consonance between managers' actions and shareholders' interests through the use of stock and stock option compensation (Holmstrom 1979). Compensation in the form of stock and stock options has therefore often been emphasized as a key to improved corporate performance. Such compensation has been the most substantial component of executive pay for well over a decade. Congress implicitly accepted the governance function of equity-based executive incentive compensation when it eliminated the corporate income tax deduction for executive salaries in excess of $1 million, because the limitation was applicable only to non-incentive-based compensation (i.e., firms could still deduct compensation over $1 million paid in the form of bonus, stock, or stock options tied to market performance measures).

The tide of popular opinion turned against equity- and option-based compensation after Enron and other corporate accounting scandals came to light, fueled by repeated assertions in the media from journalists, commentators, and public and union pension funds that executive compensation was unreasonably high. This turn of events was not an altogether surprising development as executive compensation has long been a target of populist press attacks after market declines.

Managerial incentive alignment through equity ownership has not, however, been entirely discredited as an important mechanism of corporate governance by those who consider executive compensation to be excessive. Even the most severe critics of executive compensation have not advocated elimination of incentive pay. Instead, they have endorsed structural reforms that give shareholders greater control over director elections, under the assumption that the outcome will be lower total compensation and better incentivized equity pay packages (Council of Institutional Investors [CII], 2008).

This chapter focuses on the empirical evidence of the relationship between corporate governance and performance. The remainder of the chapter has the following organization. The next section summarizes the extant literature on governance mechanisms and firm performance. The following two sections discuss aggregated measures of corporate governance and the relationship of these measures to performance. The subsequent section focuses on the role of corporate governance in disciplining management subsequent to poor performance. The final section includes a summary and conclusions.

GOVERNANCE MECHANISMS AND FIRM PERFORMANCE

Despite widespread belief in the importance of governance mechanisms for resolving agency problems, the empirical literature investigating the effect of individual corporate governance mechanisms on corporate performance has not been able to consistently identify positive effects. There have been innumerable studies examining the impact of board composition on performance. The decisive balance of studies finds no relation between director independence and performance, whether measured by accounting or stock return measures (Romano 1996; Bhagat and Black 1999). Similarly, most studies seeking to measure the performance impact of shareholder activism through shareholder proposals find no significant stock price effect from that activity. When researchers study the negotiations over proposals that result in a proposal's withdrawal, the findings are inconsistent with respect to statistical significance and vary with proposal and proponent type among other factors. At the other end of the activism spectrum, proxy fights for board seats have significant positive price effects, regardless of whether challengers succeed. The incentive effect from having to spend substantial personal resources to engage in such challenges and the more important consequences that result from such costly efforts no doubt explain the differential performance effect of this activity.

The relation between voting rights and performance has not been as extensively studied as that of board composition, at least in part because most governance activists have focused their attention on the board. Not surprisingly, studies show that voting rights are economically quite valuable. While differential voting rights are not particularly prevalent among U.S. firms, studies of corporations issuing dual-class stock find significant premia accorded to the voting shares where both classes trade. Moreover, there is some evidence that the closer voting rights approximate one share, one vote—that is, the closer the fraction of insiders' voting rights to their fraction of economic ownership (dividend rights)—the higher the value of the firm (Gompers, Ishii, and Metrick 2010).

Because voting rights run in tandem with ownership, studies investigating the relation between ownership and performance can be viewed, at least in firms with only one class of stock, as equivalent to examining the relation between voting rights and performance. Morck, Shleifer, and Vishny (1988) and McConnell and Servaes (1990) find nonlinear relations between insider stock ownership and performance. For small-scale share blocks, there are positive valuation effects, presumably from monitoring. As control increases, the benefits from blockholding decrease, either because there are no economies of scale from blockholding or because the benefits are offset by potential expropriation (the thesis often advanced in the academic literature). In either scenario, lower firm values result.

A similar relation has not been consistently detected for outside block ownership. Bhagat, Black, and Blair's (2004) study of relational investing (outsiders holding large blocks for the long term) does not identify a systematic positive performance effect.

The literature on the performance effects of insider stock ownership, particularly in relation to executive compensation, is also less extensive than that regarding board composition. A few studies report a positive price effect from the announcement of adoption of stock-option compensation plans, and other studies find a positive relation between management compensation, particularly the equity component, and performance. Studies of the impact of director stock ownership have similarly ambiguous findings. Studies that calculate ownership as the percentage of shares owned by outside directors, such as Mehran (1995), report no significant relationship between performance and ownership.

Yet Bhagat and Bolton (2008) find a significant positive relation between performance and ownership, using the dollar value of the stock ownership of the median outside director as the governance measure. They provide two rationales for the merits of their ownership metric. First, it is theoretically consistent with the political economy literature that identifies the median voter as the key (marginal) decision maker. Second, the metric is a more plausible benchmark for measuring the incentive effects of ownership because directors, as economic agents, are more likely to focus on policies' impact on the dollar value of their holdings in the company rather than on the percentage owned. The following simple example illustrates the incentive effect. Suppose that Director A owns a 0.01 percent equity stake in a $10 billion company, while Director B owns a 0.1 percent equity stake in a $100 million company. A's stake equates to a $1 million equity ownership, whereas B's stake equates to a $100,000 equity ownership. All other things being equal, A is likely to devote more time and attention to board responsibilities than is B.

In sum, the empirical literature focusing on individual governance mechanisms has not consistently identified a relationship between governance and performance. Nevertheless, the appropriate conclusion to draw from this extensive line of research is not that efforts at improving corporate governance are a waste of time and effort. Rather, there are limitations with a research design that examines the effect on performance of only one dimension of a firm's governance when governance mechanisms are numerous and interaction effects are quite probable. That is undoubtedly a factor contributing to the contemporary attention directed at governance indexes, which combine multiple governance dimensions into one number. In all likelihood, the more compelling reason for the success of indexes is the elegant simplicity of having one summary number for capturing the multiple dimensionality of governance.

AGGREGATED MEASURES OF CORPORATE GOVERNANCE: GOVERNANCE INDEXES

The corporate governance indexes that are currently in use by academics and commercial vendors vary considerably with respect to which features of firms' corporate governance are deemed sufficiently important to be included. The initial foray into creating an index was an academic inquiry. However, that line of research rapidly generated commercial products marketed primarily to institutional investors seeking information about the quality of firms' corporate governance, as well as to firms wanting to signal governance quality to investors.

Gompers, Ishii, and Metrick's G-Index

The creation of firm-level corporate governance indexes began with Gompers, Ishii, and Metrick (2010). They constructed their index from data on the governance characteristics of more than 1,000 firms, including most large public corporations (the Fortune 500 and Standard & Poor's 500), compiled by the Investor Responsibility Research Center (IRRC), a nonprofit research group that served institutional investors. Because the IRRC's clients had become active in corporate governance in order to oppose takeover defenses in the 1980s, most of the governance features tracked by the IRRC are defensive tactics.

Relying on the IRRC's judgment as to which corporate governance mechanisms investors considered to be important, Gompers et al. added up the number of provisions of each firm. They then assigned one point for each provision that they viewed as restricting shareholder rights and one point for the absence of either of two provisions that they viewed as constraining manager power and thereby enhancing shareholder rights. Gompers et al. thus equally weighted the 24 governance features tracked by IRRC in fashioning their measure of corporate governance quality. The sum of the components is the *governance* or G-Index. According to Gompers et al., firms with the poorest corporate governance consistently underperformed those with the best corporate governance.

Bebchuk, Cohen, and Ferrell's E-Index

Bebchuk, Cohen, and Ferrell (2009) advanced a governance index, the E-Index, composed of a subset of just six of the G-Index factors. Examining the relationship between the E-Index and industry-adjusted Tobin's q and stock returns, Bebchuk et al. confirmed the correlation between governance and future performance found in Gomper et al.'s (2003) study.

Although Gompers et al.'s (2003) governance index has been used extensively in the academic literature while Bebchuk et al.'s (2009) index has not, the latter index has made some commercial inroads. Glass Lewis & Company, which provides research and advisory services to institutional investors, markets a governance ranking termed the *Board Accountability Index* that is derived from Bebchuk et al.'s research. The Board Accountability Index uses five of the six components of the E-Index, and Glass Lewis markets it as derived from the "fact" that "good governance can improve shareholder returns."

Brown and Caylor's Gov-Score Index

Brown and Caylor (2006) created a more extensive governance index than the G- and E-Indexes, using firm-level governance information obtained from Institutional Shareholders Services (ISS). ISS is the market leader of firms providing governance and proxy voting advisory services and is now known as RiskMetrics. Using 51 equally weighted firm-level characteristics, Brown and Caylor find that Gov-Score is significantly positively related to Tobin's q—in other words, that superior performance is associated with higher-quality governance.

Proprietary Governance Indexes

The commercial indexes ranking public corporations' governance quality, which are provided by proxy research and advisory services such as ISS, Egan-Jones Proxy Services, GovernanceMetrics International, and The Corporate Library (TCL), differ distinctly from the academic indexes in several important dimensions. First, firms' scores on the proprietary indexes do not consist of summations of equally weighted factors. Rather, commercial index providers vary the weights accorded different governance factors, using either their discretion regarding the importance of the factor or quantitative analyses to determine the appropriate weights. Second, commercial indexes deemphasize takeover defenses, in contrast to the indexes constructed by Gompers et al. (2010) and Bebchuk et al. (2009). For example, some providers do not even include defenses as a governance factor, while others place greater weights on the non-takeover-related factors (internal governance measures such as board and executive compensation attributes). Third, some commercial indexes are relative rankings of firms in relation to other firms in their industry, market, or geographic region, whereas the academic indexes are absolute rankings of governance quality independent of the practices of comparable firms. Finally, ISS, the leading provider by far of this type of service, updates the factors in its index to capture trends in corporate governance. For example, ISS recently incorporated two items that have become the focus of activist institutional investor attention—majority voting for directors and option backdating—while eliminating option expensing (as expensing is now required).

The difference in index construction across academic and commercial creators can be best explained as a function of both expertise, which commercial providers believe they possess, and a differing analytical approach to governance. The academic index constructors intentionally sought not to make choices regarding the weights assigned to governance attributes. The rationale for this choice is twofold. First, the academics who develop governance indexes do not hold themselves out to be experts in assessing governance quality, compared to the vendors from whom they acquired the data. Second, given the absence of a theoretical model relating attributes to performance, equally weighting attributes identified by third-party governance experts plausibly immunizes their work from charges of "stacking the deck." By contrast, commercial vendors are actively marketing governance expertise and exercise judgment regarding the weights accorded to the different components of an index as well as across firms.

IS THERE A RELATIONSHIP BETWEEN GOVERNANCE QUALITY AND PERFORMANCE?

Although the development of academic governance indexes has given vitality to, if not sparked, the flourishing of a commercial governance-index market, the academic literature that introduced indexes has not satisfactorily established a causal relation between governance and performance. Although Gompers et al. (2010), Brown and Caylor (2006), and Bebchuk et al. (2009) find positive associations between their indexes' rankings of governance quality and firm performance, correlations are obviously not causation. Subsequent work has even questioned whether a positive association truly exists (Cremers and Nair 2005; Lehn, Patro, and Zhao 2006; Core, Guay, and Rusticus 2006).

Might a Single Governance Mechanism Be Preferable to an Index?

Today, the dominant approach to evaluating the quality of a firm's corporate governance is to construct an index comprising multiple dimensions of a firm's governance structure. Yet some governance scholars still consider specific board characteristics to be the critical determinants of corporate governance (Hermalin and Weisbach 2003). Providers of commercial indexes also emphasize board factors over the takeover-related governance factors emphasized in most academic indexes. This raises the fundamental question of whether a single board characteristic can be as effective a measure of corporate governance as indexes that consider multiple measures of corporate charter provisions and board characteristics. While this is an empirical question, a single board characteristic can be as effective as or even superior to an index in evaluating corporate governance on both theoretical and methodological grounds. If a single board characteristic can dominate an index as a proxy for good governance, then it could be a more parsimonious proxy for predicting performance. Moreover, using a single board characteristic would diminish or eliminate the need for and/or attractiveness to institutional investors of using commercial services to measure a portfolio firm's governance quality. Therefore, setting out the rationale for why a single governance mechanism related to the board might fare at least as well as an index in evaluating a firm's overall governance quality is useful.

What is the theoretical rationale that would suggest one characteristic as reflecting a firm's quality of governance? Corporate law provides the board of directors with the authority to make, or at least ratify, all firm decisions including decisions about investment policy, management compensation policy, and board governance itself. The board's pivotal role suggests focusing on board attributes in order to identify a single governance variable that might serve as an alternative to an index. From both a theoretical and an intuitive perspective, an independent board, or board members with stock ownership, may have adequate incentives to oversee important corporate decisions and monitor management action implementing those decisions (Fama 1980; Fama and Jensen 1983; Bhagat, Carey, and Elson 1999). Accordingly, board independence and outside board members' stock ownership appear to be excellent candidates for the characteristic that could best serve as a proxy for overall good governance.

Evaluating the quality of a firm's governance from a single board characteristic rather than a multifactor index might also be justified on econometric grounds. The measurement error in computing a single variable such as a board's stock ownership, for instance, might well be lower than that of an index, which requires accurate identification of a multitude of board processes, executive compensation practices, and firm charter and bylaw provisions. The more numerous the attributes of governance that must be tracked to identify the quality of a firm's governance, the greater is the possibility of error in recording the value of any one component, and hence in measuring overall quality. Also, the greater the imprecision in the calculation of the proxy for firms' governance quality, the higher is the probability that the statistical analysis misspecifies the relation between governance and performance.

There are certainly analytical problems presented by single governance variables. For example, the independence of the board is conventionally identified by the proportion of directors who are neither employed by nor affiliated with (i.e., have no material relations with) a firm, but data indicate that not all such independent directors are equal with respect to monitoring effectiveness. Therefore, using board independence alone as a proxy for governance may result in misspecification of statistical analyses. However, the identification and measurement problems may be even more problematic with respect to indexes.

For instance, constructing an index requires weighting all of the variables in the index. The weights a particular index assigns to individual board characteristics and other governance features are critical. If the weights are not consistent with the weights used by market participants in assessing the relation between governance and firm performance, users may draw incorrect inferences about the relation between governance and firm performance even if the governance components in the index are correctly measured.

Another problem with a weighting system for an index of governance quality is that good governance features may well be substitutes to other governance mechanisms and the interactions among them may also be complex and subtle. Given these possibilities, treating governance devices simply as complements, which is the effect of assigning positive weights to all of the good governance attributes of an index (the approach of the academic indexes), would be incorrect. Such an index ranking will provide an inaccurate measure of the relative quality of firms' governance. Researchers have undertaken little modeling of corporate governance and no satisfactory theory exists of when or whether different aspects of good governance should be understood to be substitutes or complements. Yet empirical research indicates that the concern that good governance features may well be substitutes and the interactions among them may also be complex and subtle is not hypothetical (Gillan, Hartzell, and Starks 2007).

In addition to finding that high-quality governance on one dimension may offset a need for what are conventionally thought to be best practices on another governance dimension. Gillan et al. (2007) find that governance varies with specific characteristics of firms. Namely, the correlated sets of governance features between board independence and takeover defenses are also correlated with other characteristics of firms such as firm age, institutional ownership, research and development (R&D) expenditures, tangible assets, and capital expenditures. The combination of these two findings underscores the fact that firms choose their governance characteristics. If particular governance mechanisms or combinations thereof are best suited for specific operating environments, then the expectation is that systematic variation in governance choices exists across firms. Moreover, if firms optimize across governance choices, then there should be no systematic performance differences in the cross-section comparison of firms with different governance combinations. That is, firms with better governance index scores should not outperform those with lower rankings.

A firm's ability to select its governance regime presents a thorny technical issue of endogeneity for traditional statistical analyses. Virtually all studies of governance including those by Gompers et al. (2010), Brown and Caylor (2006), and Bebchuk et al. (2009) experience this limitation. This could explain, for instance, why research focused on single governance mechanisms does not identify a relation between governance and performance. It may also explain why Gompers et al.'s findings are not robust to alternate specifications, time periods, or estimation methods.

Econometric Issues: Performance and Governance Are Endogenous

A core and knotty econometric problem in the literature examining the relationship between governance quality and performance is that governance and performance are not independent of one another. The presence of some governance features may be motivated by incentive-based economic models of managerial behavior—models that also affect performance. Broadly speaking, these models fall into two categories: agency (also referred to as moral hazard) and adverse selection models.

In agency models, a divergence in the interests of managers and shareholders causes managers to act in ways that are costly to shareholders. Such actions are most often characterized as the consumption of perquisites on the job, such as lavish offices. Other means by which managers may exercise discretion for benefit at the shareholders' expense are shirking (lack of effort) or selecting inferior projects (i.e., projects with too little or too much risk). Contracts cannot preclude this activity if shareholders are unable to observe managerial behavior directly, but firms can use governance devices such as managerial ownership to induce managers to act in a manner consistent with shareholders' interest (Grossman and Hart 1983).

The basis of adverse selection models is the hypothesis that managers possess differing levels of ability, which shareholders cannot observe. In this setting, ownership may be used to induce revelation of the manager's private information, such as information about cash flow or the manager's ability to generate cash flow. Performance provides information to the principal about the ability of the manager and is therefore reflected in managerial payoffs, which may include dismissal for poor performance (Myerson 1979).

In both settings noted in the preceding two paragraphs, a manager has information that shareholders do not possess, although shareholders are aware of their informational disadvantage. Accordingly, the contracting problem is how to write a contract that mitigates the information asymmetry. In either of the two scenarios, some features of corporate governance may be interpreted as characteristics of the asymmetry-mitigating contract governing shareholder-manager relations. The same unobservable features of managerial behavior or ability that are linked to ownership and performance affect governance. In this sense, governance and performance are endogenous. Analyzing the relation between governance and performance requires different statistical techniques if the two variables are endogenously related than if they are exogenously related (that is, if the relation is bidirectional rather than one-way). An exogenous relationship is universally assumed in the literature on governance indexes, as well as in most of the studies of individual governance mechanisms.

In order to examine the alternative methodology, there needs to be more specification of the potential two-way relationships between different governance attributes, firm characteristics, and performance. At least since Berle and Means' (1932) classic work identifying the potential agency problem in U.S. public corporations, economists have emphasized the costs of diffused share ownership—that is, the impact of ownership structure on performance. But as Demsetz (1983) argues, because many successful public companies have diffused share ownership, there must be offsetting benefits—such as better risk bearing—to render it difficult to assert that concentrated ownership should be positively associated with performance. Moreover, performance could determine ownership for reasons related to performance-based compensation and insider information. For example, superior firm performance leads to an increase in the value of stock options owned by management, which, if exercised, would increase their share ownership. Further, if there are serious divergences between insider and market expectations of future firm performance, then insiders have an incentive to adjust their ownership in relation to the expected future performance. Finally, Himmelberg, Hubbard, and Palia (1999) contend that ownership structure may be endogenously determined by the firm's contracting environment, which differs across firms in both observable and unobservable ways. For example, if the scope for perquisite consumption in a firm is low, then a low level of management ownership may be the optimal incentive contract.

In addition to ownership, leverage (debt in the capital structure) is a firm characteristic related to governance—in the form of monitoring by creditors—that may be endogenously determined with performance. In a seminal paper, Grossman and Hart (1986) consider the ex ante efficiency perspective to derive predictions about a firm's financing decisions in an agency setting. An initial entrepreneur seeks to maximize firm value by employing a disciplinary mechanism that forces him to choose the value-maximizing level of debt. Extending that idea, Bhagat, Bolton, and Subramanian (2010) show that the optimal choice of debt differs from the shareholders' and the managers' perspective.

The conflict of interest between managers and shareholders over financing policy arises for three reasons. First, shareholders are much better diversified than managers who, besides having stock and stock options in the firm, have their human capital tied to the firm. Second, as Jensen (1986) suggests, a larger level of debt precommits the manager to working harder to generate and pay off the firm's cash flows to outside investors. Third, Stulz (1988) notes that managers may increase leverage beyond what might be implied by some "optimal capital structure" in order to increase the voting power of their equity stakes and thereby reduce the likelihood of a takeover and the resulting possible loss of employment.

While the aforementioned research focuses on capital structure and managerial entrenchment, a different strand of the literature focuses on the relation between ownership and capital structure. Separate works by Grossman and Hart (1986) and Hart and Moore (1990) consider an incomplete contracting environment characterized by the difficult task of specifying all possible future states of nature and relevant decisions in a contract that can be enforced in a court. In such an incomplete contracting environment, the firm can use the allocation of control rights to management through stock ownership, rather than the provision of contractual payments under compensation agreements, to provide incentives to the managers to make necessary investments (such as investing in firm-specific human capital) that maximize the value of the firm.

This brief overview of the interrelationships among corporate governance, including capital and ownership structure and corporate performance, suggests that studying the relationship between corporate governance and performance from an econometric viewpoint requires formulating a system of simultaneous equations that specifies the relationships among the aforementioned variables. In a recent work, Bhagat and Bolton (2008) specify and estimate the following system of four simultaneous equations, which captures the interrelationships among these variables:

$$\text{Performance} = f_1(\text{Ownership, Governance, Capital Structure}, Z_1, \varepsilon_1) \quad (6.1)$$

$$\text{Governance} = f_2(\text{Performance, Ownership, Capital Structure}, Z_2, \varepsilon_2) \quad (6.2)$$

$$\text{Ownership} = f_3(\text{Governance, Performance, Capital Structure}, Z_3, \varepsilon_3) \quad (6.3)$$

$$\text{Capital Structure} = f_4(\text{Governance, Performance, Ownership}, Z_4, \varepsilon_4) \quad (6.4)$$

The Z_i are vectors of control variables and instruments influencing the dependent variables, and the ε_i are the error terms associated with exogenous noise and the unobservable features of managerial behavior or ability that explain cross-sectional variation in performance, ownership, capital structure, and governance.

Most of the extant literature already discussed, such as Gompers et al.'s (2010) and Bebchuk et al.'s (2009) studies, analyzes the relation between governance and performance considering only the first equation in this system. This limited examination is equivalent to estimating this system using ordinary least squares (OLS), instead of two-stage least squares (2SLS) or three-stage least squares (3SLS), which are econometrically more appropriate for estimating a system of simultaneous equations.

What happens if one estimates a system of simultaneous equations using OLS? For the sake of exposition, assume there is no relationship between (a specific measure of) governance and (a specific measure of) performance. Under such an assumption, the OLS estimates of the relationship between governance and performance can be statistically insignificant, significantly positive, or significantly negative. Conversely, if the truth is that there is, say, a positive relationship between governance and performance, the OLS estimates of the relationship between governance and performance can also be statistically insignificant, significantly positive, or significantly negative. In other words, OLS estimates of this system of equations cannot permit making any econometrically defensible inferences about the relationship between governance and performance.

The example in the next subsection illustrates that this general econometric wisdom is correct in the context of estimating the relationship between governance and performance. Findings about the relationship between various governance measures and performance identified in the literature using OLS are not always robust when those relationships are estimated in a system of simultaneous equations. However, estimating a simultaneous equation system in order to handle endogeneity is not without its own technical issues. To estimate a system of simultaneous equations, the researcher must identify exogenous instrumental variables that explain one of the endogenous variables but not the other(s), and with multiple endogenous variables, as in the system of equations represented by equations (6.1) through (6.4), an instrumental variable is needed for each of the endogenous variables in an equation. Identification of such instruments can be exceedingly difficult because, when two variables' values are integrally connected, most explanatory variables affecting one will also most likely directly affect the other.

Corporate Governance and Future Performance

Bhagat and Bolton (2008) undertook a comprehensive, comparative analysis of the relationship between governance indexes, single attributes of governance, and performance. They used a sample of the largest 1,500 U.S. corporations over the period 1998–2002 and the simultaneous equation setup described earlier in equations (6.1) through (6.4). Exhibits 6.1 and 6.2 summarize their results regarding the relationship between governance and performance. Previous studies have used both stock market–based and accounting-based measures of performance, as do Bhagat and Bolton in their comparative analysis. However, Bhagat and Bolton emphasize accounting measures rather than stock returns as the appropriate performance measure for this analysis. If investors anticipate the effect of corporate governance on performance, then long-term stock returns will not be significantly correlated with governance even if a significant correlation between performance and governance indeed exists (Bhagat and Jefferis 2002). Accounting measures, by contrast, do not suffer from such an anticipation problem.

Neither Exhibit 6.1 nor Exhibit 6.2 includes Tobin's Q as a performance measure even though prior studies, notably those by Gompers et al. (2010) and Bebchuk et al. (2009), treated Tobin's Q as a key performance measure. This omission is justified because Tobin's Q has two serious shortcomings, even if it does not suffer from the anticipation problem of stock returns. The first shortcoming is identified as follows: If a firm has a high fraction of its assets as intangible assets rather than tangible assets and if monitoring intangible assets is difficult for shareholders, then shareholders will likely require a higher level of managerial ownership to

Exhibit 6.1 Performance-Governance Relationship: Performance Measured by Return on Assets

This table presents the coefficients on the governance variable from equation (6.1) estimated from the following system (p-values are in parentheses):

(1a) Performance = f_1 [Ownership, Governance, Leverage, Log(Assets), Industry Performance, (R&D and Advertising Expenses)/Assets, Board Size, Stock Volatility, Treasury Stock/Assets, ε_1]
(1b) Governance = f_2 [Performance, Ownership, Leverage, (R&D and Advertising Expenses)/Assets, Board Size, Stock Volatility, Median Director Ownership Percentage, Percentage Independent Directors, ε_2]
(1c) Ownership = f_3 [Performance, Governance, Log(Assets), Leverage, (R&D and Advertising Expenses)/Assets, Board Size, Stock Volatility, CEO Tenure/CEO Age, ε_3]
(1d) Leverage = f_4 [Performance, Governance, Ownership, Industry Leverage, Log(Assets), (R&D and Advertising Expenses)/Assets, Board Size, Stock Volatility, Altman's Z-Score, ε_4]

Operating performance (ROA) is considered for three time periods: contemporaneous (ROA_t), next year (ROA_{t+1}), and next two years ($ROA_{t+1 \text{ to } t+2}$). The following governance variables are considered: the Gompers, Ishii, and Metrick (2010) G-Index; the Bebchuk, Cohen, and Ferrell (2004) E-Index; The Corporate Library (TCL) Benchmark score; the Brown and Caylor (2004) Gov-Score (data are available only for 2002); the dollar value of the median director's stock holdings; a dummy variable equal to 1 if the CEO is also the chair of the board, 0 otherwise; and the percent of directors who are independent. The sample consists of about 1,500 of the largest U.S. corporations for the period 1998–2002. In some cases data constraints allow for consideration of only a shorter period.

	Governance Measure						
Performance Measure	**GIM G-Index**	**BCF E-Index**	**TCL Benchmark Score**	**Brown and Caylor Gov-Score**	**$ Value of Median Director's Holdings**	**CEO-Chair Duality (=1 if Dual)**	**% of Directors Independent**
ROA_t	−0.013	−0.034	−0.005	−0.004	0.006	−0.029	−0.131
	(0.01)	(0.01)	(0.05)	(0.60)	(0.01)	(0.00)	(0.00)
ROA_{t+1}	−0.011	−0.031	−0.003	−0.005	0.005	−0.029	−0.121
	(0.03)	(0.02)	(0.27)	(0.61)	(0.04)	(0.00)	(0.00)
$ROA_{t+1 \text{ to } t+2}$	−0.004	−0.015	−0.002	—	0.002	−0.017	−0.068
	(0.16)	(0.07)	(0.21)		(0.16)	(0.00)	(0.01)

align incentives properly. But, because the firm has a high fraction of its assets as intangibles, it will have a high Tobin's Q. The numerator of the Tobin's Q ratio (market price) will impound the present value of the cash flows generated by the intangible assets, while the denominator (book value) usually does not include investments the firm has made in its intangible assets. As a consequence, these intangible assets will generate a positive correlation between ownership and performance, but this relation is spurious, not causal, due to the calculation of Tobin's Q.

Second, a higher Tobin's Q might be reflective of a firm's greater market power, which is an intangible asset that affects the numerator and not the denominator of the ratio. Shareholders who are cognizant of the fact that this market power shields the management from the discipline of the product market will probably require managers of such a company to own more stock. This is because greater managerial ownership will be expected to better align managers' incentives with shareholder interests and to offset the effect of the reduced discipline of the product market. In that scenario, there would again be a spurious relationship between performance as measured by Tobin's Q and managerial ownership. Because ownership is inextricably related to governance, the problematic use of Tobin's Q to analyze the relation between performance and ownership cannot be avoided by analyzing the relation between performance and governance features that exclude ownership (e.g., analyses of Gompers et al. [2010] and Bebchuk et al. [2009]).

The results in Exhibit 6.1 indicate a significant negative correlation between the G-Index and next year's return on assets (ROA). Given that lower G-Index numbers reflect fewer defenses and thus more exposure to the external governance mechanism of the market for control, the findings in Exhibit 6.1 are consistent with a positive relationship between good governance, as measured by Gompers et al. (2010), and operating performance. Results using the contemporaneous operating performance are similar. However, this relationship is insignificant, although the sign is still negative, when considering operating performance over the next two years. These findings are consistent with Gompers et al.'s finding of a positive relation between good governance and performance for the period 1990–1999, and the results extend these findings to 2000–2002. However, Gompers et al.'s finding of a positive relation between good governance and performance is based on long-term stock returns as the measure of performance. In addition, their analysis does not take into account the endogeneity of the relationships among corporate governance, performance, capital structure, and corporate ownership structure. As previously noted, if investors anticipate the effect of corporate governance on performance, long-term stock returns will not be significantly correlated with governance even if a significant correlation between performance and governance exists. Indeed, as documented by Bhagat and Bolton (2008) and summarized in Exhibit 6.2, there is no significant or consistent relationship between Gompers et al.'s measure or any other measure of governance and stock returns.

Exhibit 6.1 also indicates that there is a significant negative correlation between the E-Index and next year's ROA. As with the G-Index, lower E-Index numbers reflect better governance; hence, these results are consistent with a positive relationship between operating performance and good governance (as measured by

Exhibit 6.2 Performance-Governance Relationship: Performance Measured by Stock Return

This table presents the coefficients on the governance variable from equation (6.1) estimated from the following system (p-values are in parentheses):

(1a) Performance = f_1 [Ownership, Governance, Leverage, Log(Assets), Industry Performance, (R&D and Advertising Expenses)/Assets, Board Size, Stock Volatility, Treasury Stock/Assets, ε_1]

(1b) Governance = f_2 [Performance, Ownership, Leverage, (R&D and Advertising Expenses)/Assets, Board Size, Stock Volatility, Median Director Ownership Percentage, Percentage Independent Directors, ε_2]

(1c) Ownership = f_3 [Performance, Governance, Log(Assets), Leverage, (R&D and Advertising Expenses)/Assets, Board Size, Stock Volatility, CEO Tenure/CEO Age, ε_3]

(1d) Leverage = f_4 [Performance, Governance, Ownership, Industry Leverage, Log(Assets), (R&D and Advertising Expenses)/Assets, Board Size, Stock Volatility, Altman's Z-Score, ε_4]

Stock return (RETURN) is considered for three time periods: contemporaneous ($RETURN_t$), next year ($RETURN_{t+1}$), and next two years ($RETURN_{t+1 \text{ to } t+2}$). The following governance variables are considered: the Gompers, Ishii, and Metrick (2010) G-Index; the Bebchuk, Cohen, and Ferrell (2004) E-Index; The Corporate Library (TCL) Benchmark score; the Brown and Caylor (2004) Gov-Score (data are available only for 2002); the dollar value of the median director's stock holdings; a dummy variable equal to 1 if the CEO is also the chair of the board, 0 otherwise; and the percent of directors who are independent. The sample consists of about 1,500 of the largest U.S. corporations for the period 1998–2002. In some cases data constraints allow for consideration of only a shorter period.

	Governance Measure						
Performance Measure	**GIM G-Index**	**BCF E-Index**	**TCL Benchmark Score**	**Brown and Caylor Gov-Score**	**$ Value of Median Director's Holdings**	**CEO-Chair Duality (=1 if Dual)**	**% of Directors Independent**
$RETURN_t$	−0.010	−0.044	−0.018	0.011	0.012	−.0024	−0.157
	(0.75)	(0.59)	(0.12)	(0.73)	(0.44)	(0.70)	(0.53)
$RETURN_{t+1}$	−0.013	−0.021	0.000	−0.049	0.008	−0.064	−0.250
	(0.71)	(0.81)	(0.97)	(0.41)	(0.64)	(0.29)	(0.33)
$RETURN_{t+1 \text{ to } t+2}$	−0.007	−0.001	0.003	—	0.003	−0.025	−0.092
	(0.64)	(0.97)	(0.64)		(0.72)	(0.30)	(0.40)

Bebchuk et al. [2009]). Results using the contemporaneous and next two years' operating performance are similar. But again, paralleling Gompers et al.'s (2010) analysis, Bebchuk et al.'s finding of a positive relationship between good governance and performance is based on long-term stock returns. As Exhibit 6.2 indicates, there is no significant relationship between Bebchuk et al.'s measure of governance and stock returns.

Single governance variables related to the board of directors also exhibit significant relationships with accounting performance. There is a significant and positive relationship between the dollar value of the median director's stock ownership and operating performance.

Similarly, the separation of the positions of CEO and board chairman (referred to in the literature as CEO-chair duality) is negatively and significantly related to contemporaneous, next year's, and next two years' operating performance. This finding, along with the results for the G- and E-Indexes, suggests that greater managerial control may lead to lower future operating performance. This result also sharply contrasts the previous literature that generally reports no significant relation between CEO-chair duality and future performance (e.g., Brickley, Coles, and Jarrell 1997). Board independence, however, is negatively and significantly related to contemporaneous, next year's, and next two years' operating performance. This result is surprising, especially considering the recent emphasis placed on board independence by the stock exchanges' amended listing requirements post-Enron. Still, the result is consistent with prior literature on boards.

Exhibit 6.1 also contains some probative evidence on commercial indexes. The TCL compliance rating is unrelated to the next year's and the next two years' operating performance and its relation to contemporaneous operating performance is negative but only marginally significant. Furthermore, Brown and Caylor's (2006) Gov-Score, which uses the components of ISS's assessment of acceptable governance practices, is unrelated to contemporaneous and next year's operating performance. These findings highlight the problems of constructing a governance index using multiple indicators of board structure and processes, charter provisions, and management compensation structure.

As noted earlier, while these features characterize a company's governance, construction of a governance index requires the daunting task of properly weighting the various components. The failure to find a relationship between these multiple-dimension indexes and performance may well be a function of inapposite weights on the components, rather than the true absence of a relation between performance and governance. Even when using a smaller set of ISS variables—as is the case with Brown and Caylor's (2006) Gov-7 index—there is no consistent, significant relationship between better governance and better performance. By contrast, when the same analysis is performed using Glass Lewis's Board Accountability Index, which is related to Bebchuk et al.'s (2009) E-Index (the correlation between these two indexes is 0.99), not surprisingly the results were qualitatively very similar to those for the G- and E-Indexes. Better-governed firms (lower index values) have higher contemporaneous and subsequent operating performance, but no significant relation exists between the Board Accountability Index and stock returns.

Additionally, Bhagat and Bolton (2008) find that the G-Index and median director ownership are uncorrelated. This finding suggests that a composite measure of governance that combines the information contained in the G-Index and median director ownership might be a more powerful predictor of operating performance than either measure by itself. For each year, all firms are ranked from best governed to worst governed with respect to each of the two governance variables. The sum of these two ranks provides a composite governance score (Composite G-Ownership index) for each year for each sample firm. Consistent with Bhagat and Bolton's hypothesis, the combined measure of governance outperforms either of the two measures taken separately. They find that a 1 percent improvement in governance as measured by the composite index leads to a 1.874 percent change in operating performance in the current period, a 1.567 percent change in next year's operating performance, and a 1.520 percent change in the next two years' operating performance. The respective changes per 1 percent governance improvement for the G-Index alone are 0.854 percent, 0.763 percent, and 0.287 percent, respectively.

The analysis by Bhagat and Bolton (2008) summarized in Exhibits 6.1 and 6.2 does not compare the performance of the most prominent commercial index (the one devised by ISS) and other commercial indexes, as providers do not publicly disclose the details of their index's construction. It does include the following: (1) TCL's compliance benchmark rating (the index that TCL deemphasized of its two rankings); (2) Glass Lewis's index (which is a minor tweaking of the E-Index); (3) Brown and Caylor's Gov-Score (as the closest approximate to ISS's index, by a straightforward tallying of 51 governance components out of the more than 60 factors employed by ISS in a more complicated, proprietary weighting system); and (4) Brown and Caylor's Gov-7, which uses only seven of the Gov-Score components.

There is no plausible reason to expect that commercial indexes that are not analyzed would perform any better than the indexes with a family resemblance that are investigated. To any reasonable observer, the burden of proof concerning whether ISS's index would perform better than its simplified version, the Gov-Score, ought to be placed on ISS because it is in possession of the relevant data. In support of this contention, ISS describes a process in which it constantly updates the weighting algorithm, suggesting that the index might not predict performance because the firm feels a continual need to tinker with it. Furthermore, the Bhagat and Bolton (2008) results suggest that the more components in an index, the less likely it is to be positively associated with performance. In Exhibits 6.1 through 6.3 of their study, Gov-Score, the index with the highest number of components, fared worse than those with fewer components, including the single board characteristics. This finding is consistent with the fact that governance components may interact as substitutes and not complements. With regard to the other commercial indexes that are not analyzed, they could possibly do better than those investigated. TCL's preferred ranking system and GovernanceMetric's index have very few gradations across firms. Therefore, they would intuitively appear to be even less capable of predicting small differences in performance than the analyzed indexes, which have greater variation.

Finally, recent work by Daines, Gow, and Larcker (2008) investigates whether three commercial indexes (ISS, TCL, and GovernanceMetrics) can predict future performance. Their study provides additional support for the extrapolation of the limitations of academic indexes to commercial products: The authors find no systematic relationship between the indexes and performance. Although they do not employ a simultaneous equation methodology, Daines et al.'s results suggest that the commercial indexes perform even more poorly than the academic indexes.

In summary, the findings in Exhibits 6.1 and 6.2 suggest that certain complex measures of corporate governance—the G- and E-Indexes—and certain simple measures—director ownership and CEO-chair separation—are positively associated with current and future operating performance. This further implies that there is no obvious benefit to using those more complex measures. Indeed, governance indexes that comprise more dimensions than the G- and E-Indexes and are closer in form to indexes marketed by commercial vendors such as TCL and ISS are not even related to future performance. The combination of only one of those dimensions, median outside director ownership, with the G-Index appears to have a greater impact on future operating performance than any of the governance indexes alone.

CORPORATE GOVERNANCE AND DISCIPLINARY MANAGEMENT TURNOVER AFTER POOR PERFORMANCE

Although the analysis up to now has focused on the relationship between governance and overall performance, governance matters may possibly matter most for a firm experiencing a crisis or needing to make a critical decision such as one regarding a change in senior management. In this regard, governance may be more important for imposing discipline and providing fresh leadership when the corporation is performing poorly than in the ordinary course of events.

To investigate this possibility, Bhagat and Bolton (2008) examine the impact on management turnover following poor performance of the academic governance indexes and single board governance attributes. They estimate a multinomial logit regression in which the dependent variable is equal to zero if no turnover occurs in a firm-year, one if the turnover is disciplinary (i.e., the manager appeared to have been dismissed because of poor performance), and two if the turnover is nondisciplinary (i.e., the dismissal is not based on performance). They classify CEO turnover as *nondisciplinary* if the CEO died, if the CEO is older than 63, if the change is the result of an announced transition plan, or if the CEO stays on as chairman of the board for more than a year. Bhagat and Bolton classify CEO turnover as *disciplinary* if the CEO resigns to pursue other interests, if the CEO is terminated, or if no specific reason is given. Using the past two years' stock return as the performance measure, they estimate the following baseline equation:

$$\text{Type of CEO Turnover} = g_1\left(\text{Past two years' stock return}, Z_1, \varepsilon_1\right) \qquad (6.5)$$

The Z_1 vector of controls includes CEO ownership, CEO age, CEO tenure, firm size, industry return, and year dummy variables; these controls are suggested by Engel, Hayes, and Wang (2003) and Farell and Whidbee (2003). The baseline results indicate that a firm's stock market returns during the previous two years, CEO stock ownership, and CEO tenure are significantly and negatively related to disciplinary CEO turnover. These findings are consistent with the prior literature. Bhagat and Bolton (2008) further find that the prior two years' returns of firms in the industry are significantly and positively related to disciplinary CEO turnover. In other words, if prior industry performance has been good, the probability of disciplinary CEO turnover increases, regardless of the particular company's performance. Similarly, if prior industry performance has been poor, the probability of disciplinary CEO turnover decreases, regardless of the particular company's performance.

To determine the role that governance plays in CEO turnover, Bhagat and Bolton (2008) create an interactive variable that is the product of the past two years' stock returns and the governance variable. The reasoning behind this construct is that if the firm is performing adequately, good governance should not lead to CEO turnover. Only when performance is poor would the expectation be that better-governed firms are more likely to replace the CEO. To measure this effect, Bhagat and Bolton estimate the following modified version of equation (6.5):

$$\text{Type of CEO Turnover} = g_2(\text{Past two years' stock return, Governance, Past two years' stock return} \times \text{Governance}, Z_1, \varepsilon_2) \qquad (6.6)$$

As summarized in Exhibits 6.3 and 6.4, Bhagat and Bolton (2008) find that when including the governance variables, the prior return variable is insignificant in seven of the nine cases, suggesting that poor performance alone is not enough to lead to a change in senior management. In addition, the governance variable by itself is statistically insignificant in most cases. This finding suggests no relationship between good governance per se and disciplinary turnover (or that the literature's definition of good governance is misplaced, at least with respect to disciplinary turnover). The analyses of Exhibits 6.3 and 6.4 do not control for the endogeneity of the relation between performance and governance. The results taking turnover endogeneity into account are entirely consistent with the results reported in the tables.

The key variable for determining whether governance is related to disciplinary turnover for poorly performing firms, however, is the interactive term. When governance is measured by either the percentage of independent directors or the dollar value of the median outside director's stock ownership, the interactive term is negative and statistically significant. These findings suggest that good governance, as measured by those single board attributes, increases the probability of disciplinary turnover for poorly performing firms. The interactive term is significantly negative for CEO-chair duality, which means that when the CEO is also the chair, he is more likely to experience disciplinary turnover given poor firm performance.

The governance indexes do not fare as well as the single governance measures in predicting good performance when performance is measured by forced CEO turnover following poor financial performance. The interaction terms with Gompers et al.'s (2010), Bebchuk et al.'s (2009), and Glass Lewis's measures of good governance are negatively related to the probability of disciplinary turnover for poorly performing firms. These findings indicate that better-governed firms, as measured by those three indexes, are less likely to experience disciplinary management turnover in spite of their poor performance. In addition, the interaction

Exhibit 6.3 Multinomial Logit Model for Disciplinary CEO Turnover

This table presents the results from multinomial logistic regressions estimating the probability of CEO turnover. The dependent variables are type of CEO turnover: 1 = disciplinary turnover, 2 = nondisciplinary turnover, 0 = no turnover. No turnover is the baseline category. The following control variables are included but not shown in the table: Firm's stock market returns during the previous two years, CEO stock ownership, CEO tenure, firm size, industry returns during the previous two years, and year dummy variables. The *p*-values are in parentheses.

Dependent Variable: Disciplinary Turnover							
	Governance Variable						
	GIM G-Index	**BCF E-Index**	**TCL Benchmark Score**	**BC Gov-Score**	**$ Value of Median Director's Holdings**	**CEO-Chair Duality (= 1 if Dual)**	**% of Directors Independent**
Governance	−0.040	−0.009	0.018	−0.064	−0.062	−0.790	−0.911
	(0.38)	*(0.92)*	*(0.24)*	*(0.21)*	*(0.26)*	*(0.00)*	*(0.09)*
(Return, Last two years ×	−0.480	−0.877	0.033	0.038	−0.284	−1.381	−4.416
Governance)	*(0.00)*	*(0.00)*	*(0.49)*	*(0.84)*	*(0.00)*	*(0.04)*	*(0.00)*
Control variables	Included	Included	Included	Included	Included	Included	Included
Years included	2000–2002	2000–2002	2001–2002	2002	2000–2002	2000–2002	2000–2002
Sample size	2,036	2,036	2,195	788	3,166	3,228	3,228

Exhibit 6.4 Multinomial Logit Model for Nondisciplinary CEO Turnover

This table presents the results from multinomial logistic regressions estimating the probability of CEO turnover. The dependent variables are type of CEO turnover: 1 = disciplinary turnover, 2 = nondisciplinary turnover, 0 = no turnover. No turnover is the baseline category. The following control variables are included but not shown in the table: Firm's stock market returns during the previous two years, CEO stock ownership, CEO tenure, firm size, industry returns during the previous two years, and year dummy variables. The *p*-values are in parentheses.

Dependent Variable: Nondisciplinary Turnover								
	Governance Variable							
	Baseline Performance	**GIM G-Index**	**BCF E-Index**	**TCL Benchmark Score**	**BC Gov-Score**	**$ Value of Median Director's Holdings**	**CEO-Chair Duality (= 1 if Dual)**	**% of Directors Independent**
Governance	—	0.014	0.078	0.002	−0.067	−0.028	−1.133	0.236
	—	*(0.70)*	*(0.26)*	*(0.87)*	*(0.13)*	*(0.55)*	*(0.00)*	*(0.57)*
(Return, Last two years × Governance)	—	0.017	0.034	0.006	0.045	0.084	−0.152	−0.875
	—	*(0.88)*	*(0.88)*	*(0.82)*	*(0.79)*	*(0.27)*	*(0.68)*	*(0.37)*
Control variables	Included	Included	Included	Included	Included	Included	Included	
Years included	2000–2002	2000, 2002	2000, 2002	2001–2002	2002	2000–2002	2000–2002	2000–2002
Sample size	3,364	2,036	2,036	2,195	788	3,166	3,228	3,228

terms with the TCL compliance rating, Gov-Score, and Gov-7 measures of good governance are unrelated to the probability of disciplinary turnover for poorly performing firms. These findings again appear to underscore the hazard of constructing a governance index using multiple indicators of board structure and processes, charter provisions, and management compensation structure.

In sum, of all the measures of governance quality evaluated by Bhagat and Bolton (2008), only the outside directors' stock ownership measure is related to multiple measures of performance: firms' future accounting profitability and disciplinary management turnover upon poor performance. This finding indicates more convincingly than the findings regarding accounting performance that the more complex measures of firms' governance quality generated by index construction need not be superior to a single governance variable. It also provides support for proposals to compensate directors with stock.

SUMMARY AND CONCLUSIONS

Corporate governance is the set of processes that provides an assurance to outside investors of a fair return on their investment. This chapter has focused on the empirical evidence of the relationship between corporate governance and performance. While the findings in the earlier literature are mixed, the recent literature documents that better governance is sometimes related to some measures of performance. In particular, governance as measured by the Gompers et al. (2010) and Bebchuk et al. (2009) indexes, stock ownership of board members, and CEO-chair separation is significantly positively correlated with better contemporaneous and subsequent accounting measures of operating performance. Commercial indexes such as those provided by TCL and ISS are not related to future operating performance. In addition, none of the widely used academic governance indexes or individual governance mechanisms associated with characteristics of the board of directors is correlated with future stock market performance. In several instances, inferences about the stock market performance and governance relationship depend on whether one takes into account the endogenous nature of the relationship between governance and stock market performance.

Finally, another measure of performance by which to evaluate the effectiveness of a governance mechanism is whether management is replaced after poor firm performance. The probability of disciplinary management turnover given poor performance is positively correlated with stock ownership of board members and with board independence. However, better-governed firms as measured by the Gompers et al. (2010) and Bebchuk et al. (2009) indexes and various commercial indexes are less likely to experience disciplinary management turnover in spite of their poor performance.

The preceding evidence provides a strong empirical argument for considering dollar ownership of the board members as a good measure of the quality of corporate governance of U.S. firms, and as preferable to more complex measures of corporate governance, including widely used governance indexes. These findings have important implications for researchers, senior policy makers, and corporate boards. In general, no one measure of corporate governance is appropriate for evaluating a firm's governance quality. The best measure of governance varies with the context for which it is to be used, as different measures of good governance are correlated with different performance measures. The measure also may vary with firm characteristics. But if one measure were to be chosen on which to expend efforts to improve corporate governance, the focus should be on stock ownership of board members. In contrast to other measures, board members' stock ownership is positively related both to future operating performance and to the probability of disciplinary management turnover in poorly performing firms.

DISCUSSION QUESTIONS

1. What methodological reasons might lead researchers investigating the relation between governance and performance to disregard the endogeneity issue and not use a simultaneous equations approach?
2. What are the implications of the research discussed in the chapter for regulations adopted by Congress and the stock exchanges following the Enron and other accounting scandals that mandated a variety of board-related corporate governance mechanisms for publicly traded firms? Note that stock ownership is not one of the new regulations.
3. Many nations, led by the United Kingdom but now extending to all of the members of the European Union and Canada, have adopted a "comply or explain" approach to corporate governance, setting up a list of best practices with which listed firms are to comply, or providing an explanation for their noncompliance. Some have advocated that the United States should follow such an approach. Discuss how to evaluate such a regulatory result given the research on governance indexes described in this chapter.
4. Say-on-pay initiatives allowing shareholders to vote on management compensation packages have been used in Europe for years but are still rare in the United States. What are the advantages and disadvantages of practices that allow shareholders to take more active roles in direct firm governance?

REFERENCES

Bebchuk, Lucian, Alma Cohen, and Allen Ferrell. 2009. What matters in corporate governance? *Review of Financial Studies* 22 (2): 783–827.

Berle, Adolph A., and Gardiner Means. 1932. *The modern corporation and private property*. New York: Macmillan.

Bhagat, Sanjai, and Bernard Black. 1999. The uncertain relationship between board composition and firm performance. *Business Lawyer* 54 (3): 921–963.

Bhagat, Sanjai, Bernard Black, and Margaret Blair. 2004. Relational investing and firm performance. *Journal of Financial Research* 27 (1): 1–30.

Bhagat, Sanjai, and Brian Bolton. 2008. Corporate governance and firm performance. *Journal of Corporate Finance* 14 (3): 257–273.

Bhagat, Sanjai, Brian Bolton, and Roberta Romano. 2008. The promise and peril of corporate governance indices. *Columbia Law Review* 108 (8): 1803–1882.

Bhagat, Sanjai, Brian Bolton, and Ajay Subramanian. 2010. Manager characteristics and capital structure: theory and evidence. *Journal of Financial and Quantitative Analysis*, forthcoming.

Bhagat, Sanjai, Dennis C. Carey, and Charles M. Elson. 1999. Director ownership, corporate performance, and management turnover. *Business Lawyer* 54 (3): 885–919.

Bhagat, Sanjai, and Richard Jefferis. 2002. *The econometrics of corporate governance studies*. Cambridge, MA: MIT Press.

Brickley, James A., Jeffrey L. Coles, and Gregg Jarrell. 1997. Leadership structure: Separating the CEO and chairman of the board. *Journal of Corporate Finance* 3 (3): 189–220.

Brown, Lawrence D., and Marcus L. Caylor. 2006. Corporate governance and firm valuation. *Journal of Accounting and Public Policy* 25 (4): 409–434.

California Public Employees' Retirement System (CalPERS). 2008. *Global Principles of Accountable Corporate Governance*. http://www.calpers-governance.org/principles/docs/2008-8-18-global-principles-accountable-corp-gov-final.pdf.

Core, John E., Wayne R. Guay, and Tjomme O. Rusticus. 2006. Does weak governance cause weak stock returns? An examination of firm operating performance and investors' expectations. *Journal of Finance* 61 (2): 655–687.

Council of Institutional Investors (CII). 2008. The Council of Institutional Investors Corporate Governance Policies § 5. http://www.cii.org.

Cremers, K. J. Martijn, and Vinay B. Nair. 2005. Governance mechanisms and equity prices. *Journal of Finance* 60 (6): 2859–2894.

Daines, Robert, Ian Gow, and David Larcker. 2008. Rating the ratings: How good are commercial governance ratings? John M. Olin Program in Law and Economics. Working paper 360, Stanford Law School.

Demsetz, Harold. 1983. The structure of ownership and the theory of the firm. *Journal of Law and Economics* 26 (2): 375–390.

Eisenberg, Melvin A. 1976. *The structure of the corporation: A legal analysis*. Boston: Little, Brown.

Engel, Ellen, Rachel M. Hayes, and Xue Wang. 2003. CEO turnover and properties of accounting information. *Journal of Accounting and Economics* 36 (1–3): 197–226.

Fama, Eugene F. 1980. Agency problems and the theory of the firm. *Journal of Political Economy* 88 (2): 288–307.

Fama, Eugene F., and Michael C. Jensen. 1983. Separation of ownership and control. *Journal of Law and Economics* 26 (2): 301–325.

Farell, Kathleen A., and David A. Whidbee. 2003. The impact of firm performance expectations on CEO turnover and replacement decisions. *Journal of Accounting and Economics* 36 (1–3): 165–196.

Gillan, Stuart L., Jay C. Hartzell, and Laura T. Starks. 2007. Tradeoffs in corporate governance: Evidence from board structures and charter provisions. Working paper, University of Texas at Austin.

Gompers, Paul A., Joy L. Ishii, and Andrew Metrick. 2010. Corporate governance and equity prices. *Quarterly Journal of Economics* 118 (1): 107–155.

———. 2010. Extreme governance: An analysis of dual-class firms in the United States. *Review of Financial Studies* 23 (3): 1051–1088.

Grossman, Sanford J., and Oliver D. Hart. 1983. An analysis of the principal-agent problem. *Econometrica* 51 (1): 7–45.

———. 1986. The costs and benefits of ownership: A theory of vertical and lateral integration. *Journal of Political Economy* 94 (4): 691–719.

Hart, Oliver, and John Moore. 1990. Property rights and the theory of the firm. *Journal of Political Economy* 98 (6): 1119–1158.

Hermalin, Benjamin, and Michael Weisbach. 2003. Boards of directors as an endogenously determined institution: A survey of the economic evidence. *Economic Policy Review* 9 (1): 7–26.

Himmelberg, Charles P., R. Glenn Hubbard, and Darius Palia. 1999. Understanding the determinants of managerial ownership and the link between ownership and performance. *Journal of Financial Economics* 53 (3): 353–384.

Holmström, Bengt. 1979. Moral hazard and observability. *Bell Journal of Economics* 10 (1): 74–91.
Jensen, Michael C. 1986. Agency costs of free cash flow, corporate finance, and takeovers. *American Economic Review* 76 (2): 323–329.
Lehn, Kenneth, Sukesh Patro, and Mengxin Zhao. 2006. Governance indices and valuation: Which causes which? Working paper. http://papers.ssrn.com/sol3/papers.cfm?abstract_id=810944.
McConnell, John J., and Henri Servaes. 1990. Additional evidence on equity ownership and corporate value. *Journal of Financial Economics* 27 (2): 595–612.
Mehran, Hamid. 1995. Executive compensation structure, ownership, and firm performance. *Journal of Financial Economics* 38 (2): 163–184.
Morck, Randall, Andrei Shleifer, and Robert W. Vishny. 1988. Management ownership and market valuation. *Journal of Financial Economics* 20 (1/2): 293–315.
Myerson, Roger. 1979. Incentive compatibility and the bargaining problem. *Econometrica* 47 (1): 61–73.
Romano, Roberta. 1996. Corporate law and corporate governance. *Industrial and Corporate Change* 5 (2): 277–339.
———. 2001. Less is more: Making institutional investor activism a valuable mechanism of corporate governance. *Yale Journal on Regulation* 18 (2): 174–251.
Shleifer, Andrei, and Robert W. Vishny. 1997. A survey of corporate governance. *Journal of Finance* 52 (2): 737–783.
Stulz, René M. 1988. Managerial control of voting rights: Financing policies and the market for corporate control. *Journal of Financial Economics* 20 (1/2): 25–54.

ACKNOWLEDGMENTS

This chapter draws heavily from Bhagat and Bolton (2008) and Bhagat, Bolton, and Romano (2008).

ABOUT THE AUTHORS

Sanjai Bhagat is professor of finance at the University of Colorado at Boulder. He has published extensively in the leading finance and law academic journals such as the *Journal of Finance, Journal of Financial Economics, American Law and Economics Review, Columbia Law Review,* and *Journal of Corporation Law*. He is a board member of Integra Ventures, a venture-capital company, and of the National Association of Corporate Directors, Colorado Chapter. He is also a founding director of the TiE-Rockies (The Indus Entrepreneurs), a professional group serving technology entrepreneurs. He has served as the associate editor for the *Journal of Financial and Quantitative Analysis, Journal of Financial Research,* and *Journal of Corporate Finance.*

Brian Bolton is an assistant professor of finance at the University of New Hampshire's Whittemore School of Business and Economics. His research focuses on recent developments in corporate governance, capital structure, and financial institutions. His work has been published in the *Columbia Law Review, Journal of Financial and Quantitative Analysis, Journal of Corporate Finance,* and other business journals and has been presented at leading finance and economics conferences around the world. Professor Bolton has received numerous research awards, teaching awards, and research grants. Before academia, he had a career working with a private equity fund and a financial consultancy.

Roberta Romano is the Oscar M. Ruebhausen Professor of Law at Yale Law School and director of the Yale Law School Center for the Study of Corporate Law. She is a fellow of the American Academy of Arts and Sciences, a research associate of the National Bureau for Economic Research, a fellow of the European Corporate Governance Institute, and a past president of the American Law and Economics Association. She is the author of *The Genius of American Corporate Law* (AEI Press, 1993) and *The Advantage of Competitive Federalism for Securities Regulation* (AEI Press, 2002). Professor Romano is also series editor of the *Foundations of Law* reader series of Foundation Press and editor of the volume in the series entitled *Foundations of Corporate Law, 2d ed.* (Foundation Press, 2010). Her research has focused on state competition for corporate charters, the political economy of takeover regulation, shareholder litigation, institutional investor activism in corporate governance, and the regulation of financial instruments and securities markets.

CHAPTER 7

International Corporate Governance Research

DIANE K. DENIS
Professor and Duke Realty Chair in Finance, Purdue University

INTRODUCTION

Denis and McConnell (2003) published a survey of research on international corporate governance that divided the body of international corporate governance research into two generations. The first generation included studies of various aspects of governance in individual countries other than the United States. When that survey was published such studies dominated the body of international corporate governance research. Collectively, these studies provided much information about governance in individual countries and revealed differences across these countries. The second-generation studies were more comparative in nature, examining multiple countries in a given study. These geographically diverse samples allowed their authors to more systematically document differences in corporate governance around the world. More importantly, the opportunity to simultaneously examine data from multiple countries allowed the authors to develop and test broader hypotheses about the factors underlying the observed governance differences.

Both the first and second generations of international corporate governance research have continued to expand since 2003. Along the way, non-U.S. research has increasingly become part of the mainstream of corporate governance research. Thus, the chapters in this book that are dedicated to the various individual governance mechanisms are likely to include findings from the first generation of international corporate governance research. This chapter focuses instead on the second generation of international corporate governance research. In particular, the chapter emphasizes those studies that increase understanding of the factors that underlie differences across countries, the implications of these differences for national economies and the individual firms operating within them, and the ongoing evolution of corporate governance around the world.

This chapter is not meant to be a comprehensive survey of second-generation international corporate governance research. Instead, it seeks to reference a representative set of relevant papers with the goal of providing a clear and uncluttered summary of the major issues and viewpoints regarding corporate governance across countries. The papers referenced here make important contributions to the literature but they are not the only papers that do so. The reader interested in delving into these topics in greater depth will find a wealth of interesting and relevant research available elsewhere.

Defining Corporate Governance

The realization of a potentially profitable business opportunity requires a variety of inputs, including entrepreneurial ideas, managerial skill, labor skill, and financial capital. Individual participants in an economy are endowed with some but not all of these attributes. Thus, economic development requires that numerous disparate parties be brought together, each of them contributing necessary inputs with the expectation of earning a return on the assets they provide. The corporate form provides for the existence of a separate legal entity to which such inputs can be contributed and in which their providers can hold a return-generating stake. The long-term and continued existence of the corporate form around the world attests to its efficiency as a means of allocating disparate economic resources to their combined highest-valued uses.

The corporate form is not without its problems. Disparate economic agents bring with them disparate and potentially conflicting interests. The set of conflicts that have generated the most interest and attention are those that prevent suppliers of financial capital from fully realizing appropriate returns. The most generally accepted definition of corporate governance is that it is the set of mechanisms that ensures that the suppliers of financial capital to corporations receive an appropriate return on their investment. (Shleifer and Vishny 1997).

Not everyone shares this view of corporate governance, in which the returns to suppliers of capital appear to be of primary concern. Proponents of a stakeholder theory of the firm suggest that governance should concern itself with providing appropriate returns to all stakeholders. This chapter adopts the traditional definition of corporate governance, which focuses on providers of capital, particularly the shareholders as the residual claimants. However, the priority afforded to different categories of stakeholders varies internationally. In addition, the particular priorities within a country can influence the system of governance in that country no matter what definition of governance is considered. For example, Atanassov and Kim (2009) find that the priority afforded to the labor force varies across countries. Given the obvious potential for conflicts of interest between labor and investors, the authors hypothesize that the relative influence of these two parties will influence the governance system within firms and countries and document evidence consistent with this hypothesis.

Corporate Governance Mechanisms

What, then, are the mechanisms that can protect the appropriate returns to shareholders from expropriation by those who control the assets of the corporation? The first generation of corporate governance research focused almost exclusively on firm-specific mechanisms. These include internal mechanisms such as the board of directors, executive compensation plans, and the ownership structure of individual firms, as well as such external mechanisms as the market for control of individual firms. In addition to documenting considerable variation across individual firms, this cumulative body of research pointed to systematic differences across countries in the mix of governance forms employed by the individual firms within countries. The second generation of international governance research explores the factors that influence these systematic differences, which include countries' legal systems—in particular the degree of investor protection afforded by their laws—and various other cultural and social factors. In addition, this research suggests that countries' governance systems both affect and are affected by levels of economic and financial development within countries and the degree of financial globalization across countries.

The remainder of the chapter consists of the following sections. The next section explores factors that influence country-level governance and the role that governance plays in economic and financial development within economies. Following that is a section on firm-level governance and the ways in which it interacts with country-level governance. The evolution of international corporate governance to date and its potential future are discussed in two additional sections. The final section summarizes and concludes.

INFLUENCE OF LEGAL, POLITICAL, AND CULTURAL FACTORS ON COUNTRY-LEVEL GOVERNANCE

The most noticeable difference in governance systems across countries is in the ownership structure of individual firms. While there is variation in ownership structure across firms within a country, certain broad patterns are observed. In countries such as the United States and the United Kingdom, many firms are widely held by a large number of small shareholders. Elsewhere in Europe and in the world, shareholding tends to be more concentrated, with large holdings by family members or by other individuals, corporations, financial institutions, or the government. Such differences affect the fundamental nature of the agency problem that must be solved. In widely held firms, the primary conflict of interest is between the atomistic shareholders who own the firm and the managers who control the firm. That is, shareholders' wealth is most likely to be expropriated by managers whose ownership stake in the firm may also be quite small. When shareholdings are more concentrated, the larger shareholders in the firm have greater influence, which better enables them to avoid expropriation of their own resources. However, concentrated ownership also better enables large shareholders to expropriate resources from the smaller shareholders who lack such influence. Thus, in such firms, the most important conflict of interest is between majority and minority shareholders.

Several stylized differences in other corporate governance mechanisms follow from the observed differences in ownership structure. In countries characterized by more concentrated ownership of firms, boards of directors are typically less independent, firms offer lower and less equity-based compensation to top executives, and takeover markets are smaller and less hostile.

What Drives Country Differences in Ownership Structure?

The origins of country differences in ownership structure have been the subject of much attention and some debate among financial economists.

The Role of Investor Protection

La Porta, Lopez-de-Silanes, Shleifer, and Vishny (1998) published a seminal paper proposing that the differences in ownership structure observed in individual countries around the world are due to differences in the legal systems within those countries, specifically the degree to which the law protects investors of financial capital from expropriation. They hypothesize that diffuse ownership by many small investors will exist only if such laws exist and are strongly enforced. Where legal protection of investors is weak, shareholders will only feel assured of earning an appropriate return on their investment if they hold large enough stakes to have a meaningful degree of control over the firm. La Porta et al. find evidence consistent with their hypothesis: They document a strong negative correlation between ownership concentration and the strength of investor protection at the country level.

In seeking to explain these differences in investor protection, La Porta et al. (1998) hypothesize that countries' laws and therefore the degree of investor protection they provide are influenced by the origins of their legal systems. They identify four major legal families—common law, German civil law, Scandinavian civil law, and French civil law—and measure the strength of investor protection provided by the legal systems of individual firms within each family. Consistent with their hypothesis, they find that the degree of investor protection varies systematically across these families: Common law countries provide the strongest degree of investor protection and French civil law countries provide the weakest. The authors conclude that legal origin is an important determinant of the degree of investor protection and, therefore, of corporate ownership structure.

La Porta, Lopez-de-Silanes, and Shleifer (2008) further develop legal origins theory and characterize legal origin as a style of social control of economic life. They suggest that civil law is designed to support government-desired outcomes and is therefore characterized by greater government ownership and regulation. By contrast, common law is designed to support private market outcomes and therefore involves lower formalism of judicial procedures and greater judicial independence.

Citing a long tradition in economics of viewing culture as a determinant of economic growth, Stulz and Williamson (2003) consider the effect of culture on the degree of investor protection. Using religion and language as simple proxies for culture, they find evidence of a relationship between culture and the degree of investor protection. Specifically, they discover that protestant civil law countries protect creditor rights better than Catholic civil law countries and conclude that with respect to creditor rights in particular, a country's creditor rights are better explained by the country's prominent religion than by its legal origin.

Other Influences on Corporate Ownership Structure

In characterizing legal origin as the primary determinant of corporate ownership structure, La Porta et al. (1998) treat countries' legal origins as exogenous, having been imposed through conquest and colonization. These fundamental characteristics of legal systems are then assumed to have remained in place over time. However, numerous other economic and legal scholars question the exogeneity of legal systems and/or their impact on corporate structure.

Roe (1997 and 2006) considers investor protection and legal institutions to be important determinants of corporate ownership structure but rejects the notion that legal origin is their foundation. He believes that twentieth century politics and history are responsible for the evolution of corporate structure and advocates a political economy approach that considers how political institutions interact with preferences to create policy outcomes. For example, legal origins theory posits that U.S. firms are more diffusely owned because stronger investor protection increases the willingness of investors to take small, noncontrolling positions in firms. Implicit in this view of the world is an assumption that diffuse ownership is a superior outcome. Roe suggests instead that U.S. firms may be more widely held due to restrictions on the size and scope of U.S. financial institutions, restrictions stemming from American populism and interest group politics. These restrictions essentially mean that concentrated ownership by financial institutions is unavailable to U.S. firms, forcing them to evolve to make the best use of other governance tools. Roe allows for the possibility that some U.S. firms would be better off with the concentrated ownership structure currently unavailable to them.

Legal origins theory characterizes civil law as being more regulatory in nature, whereas common law allows for greater judicial independence. Roe (2006) suggests that this presumed difference between common law and civil law has narrowed over time. Judges have become less important in common law countries and regulation has increased. Roe indicates that financial markets in the United States are in fact more regulated than in some civil law countries.

Roe (2006) accepts the importance of legal systems but differs in his view of how they develop. In contrast, Easterbrook (1997) raises the more basic question of whether legal differences really matter for corporate structure. He points out that any individual country is made up of many corporations with different and often competing agendas. Under such conditions, firms will take the law as given and adapt to any constraints they impose. Thus, for example, U.S. financial intermediaries may avoid holding large positions in individual firms for economic reasons. In an efficient market, the costs of holding undiversified blocks in public corporations may exceed the benefits of doing so. Easterbrook believes that markets beat political process every time and suggests that corporate law is more enabling in the United States because jurisdictions must compete against each other in the market for incorporations.

Pagano and Volpin (2005) develop and test a political theory in which the degree of investor and employment protection are influenced by the nature of countries' electoral systems: A proportional system results in weaker investor protection and stronger employment protection than does a majoritarian system. Perotti and von Thadden (2006) develop a model in which the concentration of financial wealth in democratic countries affects the level of investor protection: The less concentrated financial wealth is—and therefore the more people in the economy holding financial wealth—the greater the political support for investor protection.

La Porta et al. (2008) bring all of these ideas together and test them in a unified framework. They conclude that their evidence continues to support legal origin as the strongest determinant of legal rules and regulations and, therefore, of corporate structure. They acknowledge that the empirical issues have not all been settled. Understanding the factors that influence the development of corporate structure around the world is not simply an academic exercise. To the extent that countries will continue to evolve—particularly current and future emerging economies that are in the early stages of development—decision makers must understand the most beneficial ways of bringing about this evolution. This requires understanding how corporate governance systems develop and how they evaluate the quality of alternative systems.

Country Governance and Economic and Financial Development

The evidence cited thus far suggests that investor protection and ownership structure vary systematically and in related ways across countries. It does not, however, establish whether such governance differences matter. Numerous researchers address the question of whether there are systematic differences in the quality of country governance systems around the world.

By starting from the assumption that economic and financial development are good for a country, then the quality of a governance system can be measured in part by the extent to which it is associated with such development at the country level. This is not to say that all parties within all countries are interested in development. Rajan and Zingales (2003), for example, develop a model in which those in power in an underdeveloped economy may oppose development due to the competition that it would create. Their ability to hinder such development would be evidence that country governance is ineffective.

There is evidence that the variation in governance systems around the world is associated with varying levels of financial development. La Porta, Lopez-de-Silanes, Shleifer, and Vishny (1997) hypothesize that countries whose laws and law enforcement offer strong investor protection will have more extensive capital markets. They measure the ability of firms in 49 countries to raise external finance through debt or equity and find evidence strongly consistent with their hypothesis. Firms in common law countries have access to the largest and broadest capital markets, while those in French civil law countries have the least developed capital markets. Stulz and Williamson (2003) present evidence that stock market development is correlated with a country's legal origin, showing greater development in common law countries. Rossi and Volpin (2004) provide evidence that investor protection also affects the development of markets for corporate control. They examine merger and acquisition activity in 49 countries and find that the volume of such activity is higher in countries with better accounting standards and stronger shareholder protection.

A related body of literature provides evidence that better financial development translates into greater economic development. Rajan and Zingales (1998) hypothesize that financial development leads to economic development by reducing the cost of external finance. They find evidence consistent with this hypothesis. Specifically, they find that industries that are more dependent on external finance develop more quickly if they are located in more financially developed countries. Demirguc-Kunt and Maksimovic (1998) compare the actual growth rates of firms in 30 countries to estimates of the growth rate they could achieve with access to long-term financial capital. They find that an active stock market and high respect for legal norms are associated with firm growth financed by long-term external financing.

While this literature implies that higher-quality country-level governance leads to greater financial and economic development, there is also evidence that better financial and economic development lead to better governance at the firm level.

Doidge, Karolyi, and Stulz (2007) hypothesize that decision makers within firms trade off the costs and benefits of adopting firm-level governance. The primary benefit of better corporate governance is a lower cost of external finance. Firms in countries with low levels of economic development have less need for external capital and therefore less potential benefit to be gained in return for the cost of giving up private benefits of control by voluntarily improving governance. The authors examine the determinants of firm-level governance quality in 22 countries and find that country characteristics explain far more of the variance in governance ratings than do firm-level characteristics.

CORPORATE GOVERNANCE AT THE FIRM LEVEL

As discussed, differences in the strength of investor protection across countries lead to important differences in the development of their financial markets. Such differences have potentially important implications for the individual firms within these countries. A firm needs capital to grow. Unless it can credibly commit to providing an appropriate return to investors, the firm will suffer in terms of access to and cost of external finance. Firms in countries whose laws provide weak investor protection are at a disadvantage in terms of their ability to provide such commitment.

The Effects of Ownership Structure

Evidence shows that firms in weak investor protection countries have more concentrated ownership structures. Does the presence of large investors overcome the negative effects of weak country laws? The evidence suggests that the answer depends on the nature of large investors' holdings. Large shareholdings by investors give them more influence over the firm, reducing the likelihood that the firm's management will expropriate their returns. However, large shareholders can and do expropriate resources from minority shareholders through such activities as the consumption of perquisites or the transfer of assets from the firm to other entities that benefit the controlling shareholders. These are private benefits of control, and the literature suggests that their incidence and scope are magnified when large shareholders' control rights in a firm exceed their cash flow rights. This disparity is common in many countries and can be achieved through pyramid structures, cross shareholding, and classes of shares with super voting rights.

Dyck and Zingales (2004) examine the differences between the premiums paid for block share purchases of voting and nonvoting securities in 39 countries as a measure of the private benefits of control. Their results indicate that this premium varies greatly across countries and firms and is significantly negatively related to countries' degree of investor protection. Nenova (2003) isolates control and vote values from the stock prices of dual-class firms in 18 countries and estimates that controlling shareholders extract average private benefits of control ranging from zero to 50 percent of firm value. Variables related to the legal environment explain 75 percent of the variation across countries.

The existence of private benefits of control does not necessarily indicate that the concentrated ownership structures adopted by firms in weak investor protection countries are suboptimal. These benefits could be an efficient way to compensate large shareholders for the costs of holding a less diversified portfolio. Consistent with this, La Porta, Lopez-de-Silanes, Shleifer, and Vishny (2002) find that firm valuations are higher in firms whose controlling shareholders own significant cash flow rights. This relationship does not hold in the many cases in which controlling shareholders hold control rights that are much more significant than the cash flow rights associated with them.

Morck, Wolfenzon, and Yeung (2005) consider the concentration of corporate control in the hands of an elite group of investors whose capital investments are not commensurate with their control rights, which they term *economic entrenchment*, to be a problematic corporate governance structure. They suggest that if a few such investors have wide control of an individual economy, this can have negative effects on rates of innovation, economy-wide resource allocation, and economic growth. Consistent with this notion, John, Litov, and Yeung (2008) find evidence that corporate risk taking is positively related to the degree of investor protection.

Interactions between Country-Level and Firm-Level Governance

Easterbrook (1997) suggests that organizations adapt to their surroundings. Individual firms do have some control over their own governance systems. Those firms that have a demand for external finance will seek to improve their own governance as long as the costs of doing so do not exceed the benefits that come from access to lower-cost capital. Firms may be able to partially offset weak country-level governance by adopting stronger firm-level corporate governance. In addition, as financial markets become more global in nature, firms' access to capital and the market for control of their assets can extend past country borders, expanding the set of governance mechanisms in additional ways.

Numerous studies provide evidence that firms and control markets adapt to country governance systems. Durnev and Kim (2005) examine governance quality measures in 859 firms in 27 countries, focusing specifically on the variation in total quality across firms within a given country. They find that the variation within individual countries is wide and that it is greatest in the countries with the weakest legal protection. This is consistent with firms needing to adopt alternative firm-level governance characteristics when country-level governance is not sufficient to reassure potential investors. The wide variation within such countries also indicates, however, that not all firms that face weak country governance regimes choose to improve governance at the firm level. Durnev and Kim find that firms are more likely to increase their total governance quality when they have more profitable investment opportunities, greater need for external financing, and a higher concentration of share ownership. These results provide further evidence that firms trade off costs and benefits when determining whether to adopt specific governance mechanisms.

Dahya, Dimitrov, and McConnell (2008) provide evidence that firms can offset the negative effects of weak country-level protection by appointing a more independent board of directors. In a sample consisting of firms from 22 countries, they find that corporate value is positively related to the proportion of the directors on the board who are independent of the dominant shareholder, and that this relationship is stronger in weak investor protection countries.

The increasing globalization of financial markets provides other means by which individual firms can circumvent poor country-level governance systems.

One way to do so is to list their shares on the exchanges of stronger governance countries, thereby subjecting themselves to more stringent country laws and listing requirements and increasing the pool of financial capital to which they have access. Doidge, Karolyi, and Stulz (2004) provide evidence that foreign firms that list in the United States perform better than those that do not. They attribute this superior performance to the increased ability of these firms to undertake valuable growth opportunities. The increased firm value associated with undertaking such opportunities provides controlling shareholders with the incentive to give up private benefits of control by submitting to increased regulation. Reese and Weisbach (2002) show that cross-listings in the United States are more likely to be made by firms in weaker-protection French civil law countries. They suggest that the protection of minority shareholders is an important reason for listing. Reese and Weisbach also find that firms cross-listing in the United States are more likely to issue equity following their listings and that such equity issues are larger for French civil law countries.

The globalization of the financial market also provides opportunities for foreign investors to initiate firm-value-increasing transactions. Aggarwal, Erel, Ferreira, and Matos (2009) find that institutional investors from strong investor protection countries play an important role in pushing for governance improvements in weak investor protection countries. Rossi and Volpin (2004) examine cross-border mergers and acquisitions and find that the targets of such transactions are more likely to be from weak investor protection countries and the acquirers are more likely to be from strong investor protection countries. Anecdotal evidence suggests that targets almost always adopt the governance standards of the acquirer rather than the reverse.

THE EVOLUTION OF COUNTRY GOVERNANCE SYSTEMS

Clearly there is significant variation in the quality of governance systems around the world, implying that improvements in governance could potentially increase levels of financial and economic development in some countries as well as the value of some individual firms. High levels of interest in corporate governance on the part of governments, the media, institutions, and institutional watchdogs have led to increasing awareness of and attention to governance worldwide. Has this attention and potential translated into changes and, in particular, improvements in corporate governance? If changes are occurring, is convergence in worldwide governance systems occurring?

Country-level corporate governance mechanisms are one aspect of a complex interaction involving legal systems, politics and history, culture, and financial and economic development. The debate regarding the fundamental influences on country-level governance has implications for the likelihood that change will be observed. If legal origin is the primary determinant of country-level governance, one should not expect to see fundamental governance changes. However, to the extent that politics and development are important determinants, change is more likely.

Enriques and Volpin (2007) identify four legal tools that governments can use to protect investors from dominant shareholders and insiders more generally. These legal tools include enhancing disclosure requirements, strengthening requirements concerning the composition and role of the board of directors, empowering shareholders, and strengthening public enforcement. The authors evaluate governance reforms in France, Germany, and Italy from 1991 to 2005 and find that all three countries have enacted significant corporate law reforms aimed at accomplishing these four goals. These reforms have most often been patterned after U.S. corporate law. Enriques and Volpin question whether this is appropriate, given the fundamental differences in ownership structure between Europe and the United States. They believe that much more needs to be done to resolve problems in Europe related to the private benefits of control, particularly with respect to self-dealing in related-party transactions.

Focusing on these same four categories of reform, Lu (2009) examines corporate governance reforms (CGR) in 40 countries. She defines a CGR as a deliberate intervention in corporate governance traditions by the state, security regulators, the stock exchange, or others. In order to qualify as a CGR, the reform must involve legal rules or require that firms that do not comply explain why they do not. Recommendations to which compliance is purely voluntary do not qualify. Using this definition Lu finds that 31 of the 40 countries undertook at least one major corporate governance reform between 1999 and 2007.

Lu (2009) points to three primary motivations for country-level governance reforms: international pressure, financial crises, and corporate scandals. International pressure comes from the increasing need to be competitive in an international market and also from the Organisation for Economic Co-operation and Development (OECD), which issued influential corporate governance principles in 1999 and 2004.

Stulz and Williamson (2003) provide evidence consistent with an important role for competitive pressures brought on by increased financial globalization. They hypothesize that the importance of cultural influences on countries should decline with countries' openness to international trade. Countries that want to participate in international markets must be able to attract trading partners who will expect that their rights will be enforced. More exposure to other countries dilutes cultural influences and exposes firms to competition that requires them to operate more efficiently. Thus, firms will lobby for institutions that help them be more competitive. Evidence provided by Stulz and Williamson is consistent with their hypothesis: Culture has less impact on investor protection in countries with greater amounts of international trade.

Clarke (2009) assesses the effectiveness of one particular corporate governance reform: the 2004 European Union Takeover Directive. This directive stemmed from a desire on the part of the European Union (EU) to increase international competitiveness, combined with a belief that regulation of the takeover market is important to integrating the EU market. This view originated during the 1970s and was explicitly called for in a 1985 white paper but only came about with the 2004 directive that took effect in 2006. The directive seeks to provide harmonization across EU countries while also providing for flexibility and differences across member states. One of the more significant differences among EU countries concerns their attitudes towards corporate social responsibility, particularly with respect to employees. Clarke suggests that the general consensus is that the directive has not been particularly effective in liberalizing the EU takeover market. Some EU states have implemented the directive in a protectionist way, which was not its intended purpose.

Overall, the evidence suggests that country-level corporate governance is evolving around the world and that movement is most often in the direction of more disclosure, more prescribed boards of directors, more involved shareholders, and more effective law enforcement. What little evidence there is on the effectiveness of these reforms is mixed. Many of the major country governance reforms are relatively recent. Thus, drawing broad conclusions about their overall effectiveness is premature.

THE FUTURE OF CORPORATE GOVERNANCE

International corporate governance research to date provides much information about how and why companies employ various governance mechanisms around the world, about the ways in which they interact and evolve, and about the nature and effectiveness of the various systems that have been in place. Two broad questions arise when contemplating the future of corporate governance around the world: Where is corporate governance headed, and where should it be headed? The uniformity of corporate governance reforms in both developed and developing countries leaves the impression that governance around the world is converging towards a common set of country-level governance regulations.

However, there has been no systematic evidence of convergence or even movement in the systematically varying ownership structures that arguably represent the most fundamental difference in governance systems across countries. Bebchuk and Roe (1999) develop a model of path dependence of corporate structure in which corporate structure at any point in time depends on corporate structure in the past. They consider path dependence to be a powerful force. In addition, they suggest that it explains the persistence in country ownership structures to date and supports a prediction that they may continue to persist, even in the face of globalization and the resulting increase in competitive pressure. La Porta et al. (2000) advocate a move away from concentrated ownership structures but acknowledge the difficulty of accomplishing such a move in the face of significant interest-group politics.

If ownership structure differences persist across countries, then whether convergence in regulation should be expected or efficient is unclear. Zumbansen (2009) discusses tensions in the European Union between the desire to enhance international competitiveness and long-standing differences among member states. He warns that one size does not fit all and that nations cannot transplant legal institutions uncritically. He advocates for regulatory governance by benchmarking and disseminating nonbinding objectives and standards, resulting in regulation that is flexible and indirect.

Other authors also warn against excessive regulation of governance systems and the temptation to prescribe uniform solutions. Hart (2009) lays out the conditions under which regulation is necessary and efficient but suggests that governance regulation is more often an inefficient response to the public's call for action after a crisis. He considers the Sarbanes-Oxley Act, enacted in the United States in response to a series of corporate scandals, to have been one such inefficient response. Roe (1997, 21) states "... we should also resist the temptation to add up the costs and benefits of each national governance system, pronounce one the winner, and then use law to move a system to the preferred governance model." Roe instead encourages competition between governance systems with nations adopting the system that is most individually efficient.

The Economic Crisis

The evolution of governance systems to date has come about at least partly in response to major events in financial markets, particularly financial crises in various countries. Thus, the systems observed around the world reflect the ways in which these countries responded to crisis. La Porta et al. (2008) suggest that country responses to financial crises are affected by their legal origin: When the market system gets into trouble, civil law seeks to repress markets and replace them with state mandates while common law seeks to shore up markets. However, La Porta et al. (p. 327) state that:

> *As long as the world economy remains free of war, major financial crises, or other extraordinary disturbances, the competitive pressures for market-supporting regulation will remain strong and we are likely to see continued liberalization. Of course, underlying this prediction is a hopeful assumption that nothing like World War II or the Great Depression will repeat itself. If it does, countries are likely to embrace civil law solutions, just as they did back then.*

Whether the financial problems that began in 2007 and reached crisis stage in 2008 are on par with the Great Depression, these problems are likely of sufficient scope and magnitude to threaten a continued focus on market-supporting regulation. With the crisis still ongoing, there is already considerable evidence that significant changes in economic structure are likely. The rout in markets worldwide has led many to question the viability of capitalism and its fundamental dependence upon markets and market solutions. Government participation in economies is at unprecedentedly high levels in even the most market-based economies, including the United States, and calls for increased regulation are coming from many corners. There is reason to be concerned that policy makers' responses to short-term economic problems could inhibit the long-term viability of market economies.

Among the general calls for increases in regulation are calls for more direct participation by governments in establishing corporate governance systems. The role that corporate governance played in the current situation is subject to debate. The credit-based transactions that were ultimately the undoing of markets had, mistakenly or not, been shareholder value increasing for some time. Whatever the reality, there is widespread perception that poor corporate governance is a major culprit. Zingales (2009) suggests that increasing use of the financial markets for retirement investment has made these markets more important to ordinary people. The public's perception is that they have been defrauded by managers who have not been accountable to anyone. Markets cannot survive without trust, and trust cannot be restored until such perceptions are confronted.

Future Direction

Regulatory changes are inevitable following an economic crisis, but avoiding the pitfalls associated with regulating in response to crisis is important. Zingales (2009) points out that regulation arising during recessions tends to overweight recent experiences, rather than looking ahead to the future, and that the political need for quick response does not allow for the careful study needed to determine the optimal response.

Governance changes stemming from the 2008–2009 economic crisis are already observed. Ownership concentration is increasing even in common law countries such as the United States, as the government takes significant, albeit purportedly short-term, stakes in major firms. The worldwide supply of financial capital for investment purposes is greatly reduced at present, rendering ineffective the competitive pressure associated with the globalization of financial markets. Thus, in the short run, changes in governance systems will come largely as a result of increased regulation. These regulatory changes should be designed not to impede a longer-term return to free-flowing markets for financial and economic development.

The need for transparency features prominently in many calls for reform, and it is in the area of enhanced disclosure that regulation has the most potential to restore trust in markets without displacing a priority role for markets in corporate structure and governance. Zingales (2009) advocates increased disclosure across the economy including in such private markets as hedge funds and private equity. He cautions that the cost of such regulation, particularly in terms of its competitive effects, must not exceed its benefits. Stulz (2009) points out that enhanced disclosure must go hand in hand with effective public enforcement. Investors must be confident that if disclosure reveals that firm controllers are pursuing value-decreasing actions there will be mechanisms to ensure such behavior can be altered.

Also popular are calls for increased participation by shareholders in the corporations in which they hold stakes. The potential effectiveness of regulation in this area is much less clear. Holding a stake in a firm does not in and of itself confer upon shareholders the knowledge or expertise needed to make sound decisions. Zingales (2009), however, advocates for an increased role for independent institutional investors in appointing directors, suggesting that such a change will improve governance by giving directors an incentive to develop a reputation for acting in shareholders' interests, rather than in the interests of the managers who currently play important roles in appointing them.

The greatest risk with respect to regulation is the loss of flexibility that it necessarily entails. Policy makers and lawmakers alike need to carefully evaluate both the costs and benefits of any potential regulation. One size does not fit all. In the longer run, the very diverse firms and countries that make up the world economy must be able to evaluate and choose among competing systems of corporate governance. Advocating a world in which governments regulate ownership structures or board structures is dangerous precisely because there is not one best ownership structure or one best board structure. A multitude of factors at both the country and individual firm levels influences the particular mix of corporate governance mechanisms that will be most effective for a given firm. The goal, then, should be a world in which governance systems are determined primarily by informed economic agents making choices in relatively free markets for financial capital and investment opportunities.

Research in international corporate governance plays an important role in informing economic agents about their choices and the potential consequences. Such information is more important than ever as people navigate through difficult times and the ongoing expansion of data from around the world greatly facilitates the examination of important questions. In addition, times of significant and relatively discrete change provide for new and interesting data points and new opportunities to evaluate consequences and draw conclusions from them.

SUMMARY AND CONCLUSIONS

Corporate governance systems vary considerably around the world in terms of their particular mix of mechanisms and of the resulting effectiveness with which they assure suppliers of an appropriate return on the capital they invest. These differences matter. Corporate governance is an important facet of a complex interaction that also involves legal systems, financial and economic development, politics, history, and culture.

The most fundamental difference among governance systems across countries is in the typical ownership structures of firms within them, which ranges from widely held to concentrated among large shareholders. Researchers and others pose many explanations for these differences including legal origin, politics, history, and culture. These factors are interrelated and each most likely influences corporate ownership structure to varying degrees.

The basic agency problem in widely held firms is the potential for conflicts of interest between managers and shareholders. Concentrated ownership reduces this agency problem because large shareholders have more incentive and ability to influence managers and evidence suggests that, ceteris paribus, the concentration of cash flow rights is value-increasing. There are private benefits of control and some of these enable large shareholders to divert resources from the firm—and therefore from minority shareholders—to themselves. This is the basic agency problem in such firms, and evidence suggests that it is value-decreasing and most prevalent when large shareholders' control rights greatly exceed their cash flow rights.

There are considerable differences in the quality of country governance systems and of firms' total governance systems. These differences affect financial and economic development within countries. Suppliers of capital are more willing to invest when governance systems provide them with greater assurance of being able to earn an appropriate return on their investment. The relationship works in the other direction as well. Greater levels of financial and economic development provide more investment opportunities, providing firm controllers with greater incentive to incur the cost of improved governance in order to realize the increased access to and reduced cost of financial capital that it provides.

Firms that have good investment opportunities while facing poor country-level governance commit to potential investors by adopting appropriate firm-level governance mechanisms or by listing their securities in stronger governance countries and thereby subjecting themselves to those stronger laws. Where such efforts are unsuccessful, an increasingly global market for corporate control allows institutional investors and acquirers from countries with strong country governance to take value-increasing positions in firms from weak governance countries.

Country governance regulations have evolved considerably over the past 10 years, generally in similar directions. Judging the effectiveness of some of these reforms is premature. In the meantime, the economic crisis and economic agents' short-term responses to the crisis have temporarily altered many aspects of corporate governance systems worldwide. As significant events often do, the crisis provides both the impetus and the data needed to evaluate governance systems in new ways. The goal should be systems of laws worldwide that provide for vibrant financial and economic markets in which countries and firms have the ability and the incentive to choose governance systems that maximize their economic value.

DISCUSSION QUESTIONS

1. Allen, Qian, and Qian (2005) present China as a notable counterexample to the law, finance, and growth literature. China's legal and financial systems are not well-developed and yet China has been one of the fastest growing economies in the world. What factors might explain China's ability to grow despite relatively weak institutions?
2. How has the globalization of financial markets expanded the ways in which the quality of governance can be increased for individual firms?
3. From the perspective of a large shareholder, what are the potential costs and benefits of adopting more stringent governance mechanisms?
4. Propose and discuss the potential governance-related impact of one actual or proposed government response to the financial crisis of 2008–2009.

REFERENCES

Aggarwal, Reena, Isil Erel, Miguel A. Ferreira, and Pedro P. Matos. 2009. Does governance travel around the world? Evidence from institutional investors. Working paper, Charles A. Dice Center for Research in Financial Economics and Fisher College of Business Working Paper Series.

Allen, Franklin, Jun Qian, and Meijun Qian. 2005. Law, finance, and economic growth in China. *Journal of Financial Economics* 77 (1): 57–116.

Atanassov, Julian, and E. Han Kim. 2009. Labor and corporate governance: International evidence from restructuring decisions. *Journal of Finance* 64 (1): 341–374.

Bebchuk, Lucien, and Mark Roe. 1999. A theory of path dependence in corporate governance and ownership. *Stanford Law Review* 52 (1): 127–170.

Clarke, Blanaid. 2009. The takeover directive: Is a little regulation better than no regulation? *European Law Journal* 15 (2): 174–197.

Dahya, Jay, Orlin Dimitrov, and John J. McConnell. 2008. Dominant shareholders, corporate boards, and corporate value: A cross-country analysis. *Journal of Financial Economics* 87 (1): 73–100.

Demirguc-Kunt, Asli, and Vojislav Maksimovic. 1998. Law, finance, and firm growth. *Journal of Finance* 53 (6): 2107–2137.

Denis, Diane K., and John J. McConnell. 2003. International corporate governance. *Journal of Financial and Quantitative Analysis* 38 (1): 1–36.

Doidge, Craig G., G. Andrew Karolyi, and René M. Stulz. 2004. Why are foreign firms listed in the U.S. worth more? *Journal of Financial Economics* 71 (2): 205–238.

———. 2007. Why do countries matter so much for corporate governance? *Journal of Financial Economics* 86 (1): 1–39.

Durnev, Art, and E. Han Kim. 2005. To steal or not to steal: Firm attributes, legal environment, and valuation. *Journal of Finance* 60 (3): 2741–2771.

Dyck, Alexander, and Luigi Zingales. 2004. Private benefits of control: An international comparison. *Journal of Finance* 59 (2): 537–600.

Easterbrook, Frank. 1997. International corporate differences: Markets or law? *Journal of Applied Corporate Finance* 9 (4): 23–30.

Enriques, Luca, and Paolo Volpin. 2007. Corporate governance reforms in Continental Europe. *Journal of Economic Perspectives* 21 (1): 117–140.

Hart, Oliver. 2009. Regulation and Sarbanes-Oxley. *Journal of Accounting Research* 47 (2): 437–445.

John, Kose, Lubomir Litov, and Bernard Yeung. 2008. Corporate governance and risk taking. *Journal of Finance* 63 (4): 1679–1728.

La Porta, Rafael, Florencio Lopez-de-Silanes, and Andrei Shleifer. 2008. The economic consequences of legal origins. *Journal of Economic Literature* 46 (2): 285–332.

La Porta, Rafael, Florencio Lopez-de-Silanes, Andrei Shleifer, and Robert W. Vishny. 1997. Legal determinants of external finance. *Journal of Finance* 52 (3): 1131–1150.

———. 1998. Law and finance. *Journal of Political Economy* 106 (6): 1113–1155.

———. 2000. Investor protection and corporate governance. *Journal of Financial Economics* 58 (1): 3–27.

———. 2002. Investor protection and corporate valuation. *Journal of Finance* 57 (3): 1147–1170.

Lu, Yao. 2009. Cross-border target selection and investor protection disparity. Working paper, International Policy Center, Gerald R. Ford School of Public Policy, University of Michigan.

Morck, Randall, Daniel Wolfenzon, and Bernard Yeung. 2005. Corporate governance, economic entrenchment, and growth. *Journal of Economic Literature* 43 (3): 655–720.

Nenova, Tatiana. 2003. The value of corporate voting rights and control: A cross-country analysis. *Journal of Financial Economics* 68 (3): 325–352.

Pagano, Marco, and Paolo F. Volpin. 2005. The political economy of corporate governance. *American Economic Review* 95 (4): 1005–1030.

Perotti, Enrico C., and Ernst-Ludwig von Thadden. 2006. The political economy of corporate control and labor rents. *Journal of Political Economy* 114 (1): 145–174.

Rajan, Raghuram G., and Luigi Zingales. 1998. Financial dependence and growth. *American Economic Review* 88 (3): 559–586.

———. 2003. The great reversals: The politics of financial development in the twentieth century. *Journal of Financial Economics* 69: 1, 5–50.

Reese, William. A., Jr., and Michael S. Weisbach. 2002. Protection of minority shareholder interests, cross-listings in the United States, and subsequent equity offerings. *Journal of Financial Economics* 66 (1): 65–104.

Roe, Mark J. 1997. The political roots of American corporate finance. *Journal of Applied Corporate Finance* 9 (4): 8–22.

———. 2006. Legal origins, politics, and modern stock markets. *Harvard Law Review* 120 (2): 460–527.

Rossi, Stefano, and Paolo F. Volpin. 2004. Cross-country determinants of mergers and acquisitions. *Journal of Financial Economics* 74 (2): 277–304.

Shleifer, Andrei, and Robert W. Vishny. 1997. A survey of corporate governance. *Journal of Finance* 52 (2): 737–783.

Stulz, René. 2009. Securities laws, disclosure, and national capital markets in the age of financial globalization. *Journal of Accounting Research* 47 (2): 349–390.

Stulz, René M., and Rohan Williamson. 2003. Culture, openness, and finance. *Journal of Financial Economics* 70 (3): 313–350.

Zingales, Luigi. 2009. The future of securities regulation. *Journal of Accounting Research* 47 (2): 391–425.

Zumbansen, Peer. 2009. "New governance" in European corporate law regulation as transnational legal pluralism. *European Law Journal* 15 (2): 246–276.

ABOUT THE AUTHOR

Diane K. Denis joined the Krannert School of Management at Purdue University in 1995, following six years on the faculty at Virginia Polytechnic Institute and State University. Professor Denis has published widely in the fields of corporate governance and corporate finance in such journals as the *Journal of Financial Economics*, *Journal of Finance*, and others. She is the co-editor of a two-volume book of readings on international corporate governance and is associate editor for a number of finance journals. Professor Denis's teaching interests are in corporate finance, mergers and acquisitions, and international finance. She has won several teaching awards and is a fellow of Purdue University's Teaching Academy. Professor Denis received a BS in finance from Oakland University in 1980, an MBA from the Cranfield Institute of Technology in the United Kingdom in 1981, and a PhD in finance from the University of Michigan in 1990.

CHAPTER 8

Agency Theory: Incomplete Contracting and Ownership Structure

IAIN CLACHER
Lecturer, Leeds University Business School

DAVID HILLIER
Professor of finance, University of Strathclyde

PATRICK McCOLGAN
Senior Lecturer, University of Strathclyde

INTRODUCTION

Since the seminal work of Jensen and Meckling (1976), proposing a theory of the firm based upon conflicts of interest between various contracting parties—namely shareholders, corporate managers, and debt holders—a vast literature has developed to explain both the nature of these conflicts and the means by which they may be resolved. To fully summarize the research that has been conducted in the field of agency relationships would be almost impossible. This chapter thus provides an overview of the major research themes that have emerged and their implications with respect to current thinking in the area.

To this end, the chapter addresses two major strands of the literature. The first strand deals with Type I agency costs that occur as a result of incomplete contracting between managers and shareholders (Jensen and Meckling 1976). The second strand discusses Type II agency costs where conflicts occur between majority and minority shareholders. Framing these issues is the nature of a corporation's regulatory environment, strength of investor protection, and financial market development (La Porta, Lopez-de-Silanes, Shleifer, and Vishny 2000 and 2002).

The remainder of the chapter proceeds as follows. The first half of the chapter discusses agency costs in widely held corporations. This is the classic view of agency costs where conflicts exist between managers and shareholders. This section focuses on Type I agency costs including monitoring costs, bonding costs, and residual loss. Next, the chapter considers the source of agency conflicts in widely held firms, including moral hazard, earnings retention, time horizon conflicts, and managerial risk aversion.

The second half of the chapter discusses Type II agency costs, where agency conflicts are between large/controlling shareholders and small/noncontrolling shareholders. Specifically considered is how relevant Type II agency costs are to both U.S. corporations and foreign firms. The final sections of the chapter consider family firms and controlling minority shareholders, followed by a summary and conclusions.

AGENCY COSTS IN WIDELY HELD CORPORATIONS

Jensen and Meckling (1976) define the agency relationship as a contract in which one party (the principal) gives another party (the agent) decision-making authority to perform some service on its behalf. In the classical principal-agent problem, professional managers assume the role of the agent who acts on behalf of the company's shareholders—the principal. The basic agency problem arises because of a separation between decision making, which is carried out by professional managers, and the bearing of residual risk by shareholders. Shleifer and Vishny (1997) describe the agency problem as referring to the difficulties faced by financiers in ensuring that their funds are not expropriated or wasted on unattractive projects. Within this framework shareholders are assumed to derive purely financial benefits from ownership of their equity investments.

Agency problems cannot be costlessly controlled because of the impossibility of perfectly contracting for the actions of an agent whose decisions affect both his own welfare and the welfare of the principal (Brennan 1995). Shleifer and Vishny (1997) argue that because complete contracts between managers and shareholders are unfeasible, shareholders must allocate residual control rights for given circumstances. These residual control rights are typically retained by those who are best qualified to use them—the company's managers.

Because management controls the firm, managers have the ability to realize private benefits of control that are unavailable to the company's shareholders. Jensen and Meckling (1976) argue that this inefficiency is reduced with the increase of managerial incentives to make value-maximizing decisions. The authors suggest that agency costs arise because providing managers with the appropriate incentives to act in the best interest of company shareholders imposes costs on the principals.

As with any other costs, financial markets recognize agency relationship issues and reflect these in a company's share price. Type I agency costs can be seen as the value loss to shareholders arising from the cost of minimizing divergences of interest between company shareholders and corporate managers. Jensen and Meckling (1976) define agency costs as the sum of monitoring costs, bonding costs, and residual loss.

Monitoring Costs

The actions of company management are monitored with the understanding that they are judged on the extent to which they have maximized some observable measure(s) of shareholder wealth. Monitoring costs are expenditures paid by the principal to measure, observe, and control an agent's behavior. These costs may include audits, writing executive compensation contracts, and ultimately the cost of hiring and firing top managers. Initially the principal pays these costs, but

Fama and Jensen (1983) argue that the agent will ultimately bear monitoring costs because the agent's compensation will be adjusted to cover these costs.

Legislation and codes of best practice may also affect certain aspects of monitoring. For example, UK companies are required to provide statements of compliance with the Combined Code on Corporate Governance (2008), resulting from the reports of the Cadbury (1992), Greenbury (1995), Hampel (1998), and Higgs (2003) committees. The Code emphasizes the monitoring role of control systems that are believed to reduce agency conflicts between shareholders and managers. Noncompliance must be disclosed and explained, and the attention brought by these disclosures represents an additional source of monitoring to company management.

Denis, Denis, and Sarin (1997) contend that effective monitoring will be restricted to certain groups or individuals. Such monitors must have both the necessary expertise and the financial incentive to monitor company management. Additionally, these monitoring parties must provide a credible threat to management's control over the firm.

Burkart, Gromb, and Panunzi (1997) provide a more cautious view of monitoring. Excessive monitoring will constrain managerial initiative and entrepreneurship. They argue that monitoring will be costly because a reduction in managerial discretion will harm outside shareholders who do not have the human capital to exploit arising opportunities facing the firm. Short, Keasey, Wright, and Hull (1999) provide a discussion of how published codes of best practice in the United Kingdom have increased the level of monitoring of managers but also provided a deterrent to managerial entrepreneurship. The optimal level of monitoring will therefore be specific to an individual company's contracting environment (Himmelberg, Hubbard, and Palia 1999).

Bonding Costs

If agents ultimately bear monitoring costs, they are likely to set up structures that will see them acting in shareholders' best interests, or compensating them accordingly if not. The costs of establishing and adhering to these systems are known as *bonding costs* (Jensen and Meckling 1976). Bonding costs, which are not always financial, are borne by agents. For example, bonding costs may include the effort of providing timely and accurate information to external shareholders. The ability to impose such costs on managers is finite, however, and agents will stop incurring bonding costs when the marginal reduction in monitoring costs equals the marginal increase in bonding costs.

Denis (2001) argues that the best solution to a Type I agency problem is to provide managers with a contract to bond them to do exactly as shareholders want in any given state of nature. As she notes, this is unfeasible due to the impossibility of contracting for all possible future states. Further, even if such contracting were practicable, the excessive costs of attempting to do so would prevent such actions from being taken. Such a contract would also assume that shareholders are actually aware of the optimum decision in any given state. If this were so, shareholders would be less inclined to hire professional managers in the first instance as they would have better decision-making skills than the managers in their employ. In this situation, the employment of professional managers would simply be an unnecessary cost. In practice, bonding provides a means for ensuring that managers do some of what shareholders would prefer by writing less than perfect contracts.

Residual Loss

Despite the effects of both monitoring and bonding, the interests of managers and shareholders are still unlikely to be fully aligned. Therefore, agency losses arise from conflicts of interest. Jensen and Meckling (1976) define this loss as a *residual loss*, which represents the net loss (in excess of any accrued benefits) from enforcing suboptimal incentive contracts.

Because managerial actions are unobservable ex ante, fully contracting for every state of nature is impractical (Denis 2001). The result is an optimal level of contracting with a given level of residual loss. This may be viewed as representing a trade-off between overly constraining management and providing them with the discretion to pursue their own self-serving corporate policies.

SOURCES OF AGENCY CONFLICTS

Agency problems arise from conflicts of interest between two parties to a contract and as such are almost limitless in nature. However, theoretical and empirical research has developed in four key areas: moral hazard, earnings retention, time horizon, and risk aversion. This section provides a discussion of these major themes and the empirical research that has been conducted in these areas. Much of the discussion provided in this section focuses exclusively on theoretical and empirical research in market-based economies where legal protection of investors is strong. Shleifer and Vishny (1997) argue that expropriation of shareholders in such systems is generally more subtle. Yet in less developed economies, expropriation tends to be blatant and obvious, resulting in large premiums for controlling ownership stakes which can minimize the likelihood of expropriation. These issues are discussed in more detail in the latter part of the chapter.

Moral Hazard Agency Conflicts

Jensen and Meckling (1976) first proposed a moral hazard explanation for agency conflicts. Assuming a situation where a single manager owns the firm, they developed a model whereby the incentive of the manager to undertake private perquisite consumption (defined as an incidental payment, benefit, privilege, or advantage over and above regular income), rather than invest in positive net present value (NPV) projects, increases as the manager's ownership stake in the company declines. This framework is easily applied to companies where ownership structure is diverse and corporate managers do not own a substantial proportion of their company's shares, such as in the United States and United Kingdom.

Shleifer and Vishny (1989) argue that rather than not investing, managers may choose to invest in assets best suited to their personal skills. The value of these investments will therefore be higher to the firm's shareholders under the incumbent manager than under the next best replacement candidate, even when the investments are not value maximizing to shareholders. Such investments increase the individual manager's value to the firm and the costs of replacing him, thereby allowing managers to extract higher levels of compensation from the company and providing them with greater discretion over future policies.

Moral hazard problems are likely to be more extensive in larger companies (Jensen 1993). While large firms attract more external monitoring from regulators, analysts, and institutions, their large size expands the complexity of the firm's contracting nexus almost exponentially. This will increase the difficulty of effective monitoring and also increase its cost. Further, Jensen (1986) argues that in larger, more mature companies, free cash flow problems will heighten the difficulties created by moral hazard. Where managers have such funds at their disposal without any strong incentives to invest, the scope for private perquisite consumption is vastly increased as monitoring how managers use corporate funds becomes more difficult.

Moral hazard problems are also related to a lack of managerial effort. Although directly measuring such shirking of responsibilities by directors is not easy, Rosenstein and Wyatt (2006) find that company stock prices decline upon the announcement of the appointment of an executive director to the board of another company. This is consistent with diminishing managerial effort damaging corporate value.

Earnings Retention Agency Conflicts

Denis (2001) argues that moral hazard–based agency theories are of relatively lesser importance than other theories of conflicts of interest between managers and shareholders. Brennan (1995) also contends that moral hazard–based theories oversimplify the agency problem as one of effort aversion. Grandiose managerial visions and cash distribution to shareholders may be of greater concern to company shareholders. Here, the problem of overinvesting may be considerably more important than that of perquisite consumption and the resulting underinvestment.

Studies of compensation structures generally find that executive remuneration is an increasing function of company size. For example, Jensen and Murphy (1990) and Conyon and Murphy (2000) discuss providing management with a direct incentive to focus on size growth, rather than growth in shareholder returns. Jensen (1986) contends that managers prefer to retain earnings, whereas shareholders prefer higher levels of cash distributions, especially where the company has few positive NPV investment opportunities. Jensen defines *free cash flow* as those funds generated by the company's existing assets in excess of those required to finance all available positive NPV investment opportunities. By definition, managers should not use this cash for further investment opportunities but should retain such funds in securities that generate a reasonable return to investors or distribute the cash to shareholders through dividends or share repurchases.

Chief executive officers (CEOs) and top management in general benefit from retained earnings because size growth grants them a larger power base, greater prestige, and an ability to dominate the board of directors and award themselves higher levels of remuneration (Jensen 1986 and 1993). This reduces the amount of firm-specific risk within the company and therefore strengthens executive job security. Shleifer and Vishny (1989) also suggest that committing free cash flow to manager-specific investments raises the cost of replacing the incumbent manager and allows the manager to extract higher levels of remuneration and power from the company.

Demsetz and Lehn (1985) also contend that a given level of control over the company requires a lower equity stake as the relative size of a firm increases.

Finance theory dictates that investors will already hold well-diversified portfolios. As a result, earnings retention and further corporate diversification may be incompatible with their interests. Empirical evidence suggests that such strategies are ultimately damaging to shareholder wealth. Lang and Stulz (1994) and Berger and Ofek (1995) find that the value of companies operating in multiple areas of business is lower than the theoretical aggregate value of the component parts of the individual business units. Lang, Poulsen, and Stulz (1995) develop a financing hypothesis of asset sales in which they argue that managers value both size and control over firms and sell assets only when alternative financing sources are too expensive. In examining the stock price reaction to the announcement of such sales, the authors find that when the company retains and reinvests the proceeds, a significantly negative reaction occurs. However, when the company returns the proceeds to financial claimants, announcements elicit a significantly positive abnormal stock price reaction. Denis et al. (1997) also find that companies subsequently reversing diversification strategies are more likely to have negative excess values, based upon comparing the market value of the combined firm to the disaggregated sum of its parts. Overall, these findings suggest that managerial discretion over free cash flow is value-destroying for company shareholders.

Morck, Shleifer, and Vishny (1990) find evidence that company managers overpay when making acquisitions because they pursue private objectives of size, growth, and unrelated diversification over the goal of shareholder wealth maximization. Such acquisitions reduce shareholder wealth, as is reflected in the negative stock price reaction for bidding companies on the date of the bid announcement. Specifically, purchases of companies for the purposes of unrelated diversification, acquiring growth opportunities, and acquisitions made by poorly performing firms elicit the worst stock price reaction. Each of these forms of acquisition provides private benefits to bidding company management, which do not necessarily accrue to their shareholders.

Earnings retentions reduce the need for outside financing when managers require new funds for investment projects. Yet despite the potential costs of raising new capital (Myers 1984), external markets provide a potentially important monitoring function in constraining grandiose managerial investment policies (Easterbrook 1984). Earnings retention reduces the likelihood of external monitoring that encourages management to undertake value-maximizing decisions.

Time Horizon Agency Conflicts

Conflicts of interest may also arise between shareholders and managers regarding the timing of cash flows. Shareholders are assumed to be concerned with all future cash flows of the company into the indefinite future, as these are reflected in the current share price. However, management may only be concerned with company cash flows for their term of employment, leading to a bias in favor of short-term projects with high accounting rates of return at the expense of long-term positive-NPV investments.

The extent of this problem is heightened as top executives approach their retirement or make plans to leave the company. Dechow and Sloan (1991) examine research and development (R&D) expenditures as top executives approach retirement and find a declining trend. R&D expenditures represent an accounting expense that reduces performance-related executive compensation in the short term. These findings may be explained by the fact that retiring executives will not be around to reap the benefits of such investments.

Impending retirement may also lead to management using subjective accounting practices to manipulate earnings before leaving office in an attempt to maximize performance-based bonuses (Healy 1985). Any attempt to uncover evidence of such manipulations is problematic because management has incentives to both increase and reduce reported income due to earnings management and weak incentives related to performance

Pourciau (1993) examines accounting accruals and write-offs surrounding *non-routine* CEO turnover—that is, where managers have been forced from their position. She finds evidence that managers use accruals and write-offs to actually reduce reported income rather than to increase reported profits. Murphy and Zimmerman (1993) also examine a series of discretionary accounting practices and expenditures surrounding CEO turnover. They conclude that changes in these policies arise due to poor performance rather than attempts to manage earnings. In contrast to Dechow and Sloan (1991), Murphy and Zimmerman find little evidence that managers seek to manage reported earnings when they approach their retirement age.

Managerial Risk Aversion Agency Conflicts

Conflicts relating to managerial risk aversion arise because of portfolio diversification constraints. Fama (1980) argues that company managers rent a substantial fraction of their wealth—namely their human capital stock—to the company that employs them. The rental rates for their human capital depend upon the success or failure of the company during their tenure.

Should private investors want to diversify their holdings they can do so at little cost. However, company managers are more akin to individuals holding a single stock in the company that employs them. As such, shareholders are considered to be concerned only with systematic risk, whereas company managers are concerned with both systematic and unsystematic (firm-specific) risk. Denis (2001) comments that the majority of a company manager's human capital is tied to the firm for which they work. Therefore, their income is largely dependent upon the performance of their company. As a consequence, managers may pursue investment and financing policies that minimize the risk of their company's equity (Jensen 1986).

Himmelberg et al. (1999) find evidence consistent with this idea and report that increases in idiosyncratic stock price risk correlate with reductions in managerial ownership. By contrast, Demsetz and Lehn (1985) find that ownership by large shareholders is a quadratic function of various measures of company risk. Ownership initially increases with risk and then declines at higher levels. The authors attribute the initial increase to the greater control potential from higher ownership concentration in companies operating in noisier environments.

The risk aversion problem is heightened when executive pay is composed largely of a fixed salary or where managers' specific skills are difficult to transfer from one company to another. Risk-increasing investment decisions may also increase the likelihood of bankruptcy. Such a corporate event will severely damage a manager's reputation and will increase his difficulty in finding alternative employment opportunities. For example, Gilson (1989) finds that managers who lost their jobs as a result of poor long-run performance and financial distress in their companies are subsequently unable to find employment as the CEO of another exchange-listed company.

Managerial risk aversion will also affect the financial policy of the firm. Higher debt is expected to reduce agency conflicts (Jensen 1986) and also carries potentially valuable tax shields (Myers 1984). Yet Brennan (1995) argues that risk-averse managers prefer equity financing because debt increases the risk of default and bankruptcy.

OWNERSHIP STRUCTURES AND TYPE II AGENCY COSTS

So far, the chapter has focused on firms with a distinct separation of ownership and control. In the Jensen and Meckling (1976) scenario, managers expropriate wealth from shareholders due to incomplete contracting between the principals and their agents. One question that must be addressed is whether the Jensen and Meckling agency cost theory holds true across all firms. Clearly, the theory has intuitive appeal and many of the implications of the theory are testable. However, the base case of zero agency cost, where there is one managerial owner, is problematic to observe in reality. Thus, estimating agency costs in owner-managed firms was, until relatively recently, an issue that finance theory had not sufficiently addressed. Using a sample of small U.S. corporations, Ang, Cole, and Lin (2000) empirically analyze this issue. They show that agency costs are higher both where outside managers are being employed and where there are more nonmanager shareholders, and increase as managerial share ownership decreases. As a result, the predictions of Jensen and Meckling's principal agent model clearly affect firms in reality, at least in the United States.

The concept of a widely held firm with atomistic shareholder base in the Jensen and Meckling (1976) framework is an atomistic kind of firm that Berle and Means (1932) also envisaged. Berle and Means argue that managers control corporations because individual shareholders do not own enough equity to exert substantial influence over incumbent managers. A widely held ownership structure, however, is not the norm for most countries across the world, where small family groups and governments own and control many firms.

Ownership around the World

La Porta, Lopez-de-Silanes, and Shleifer (1999) analyze the ownership of the 20 largest corporations in 27 countries around the world and find that most companies are closely held by a small number of controlling shareholders. As La Porta et al. (p. 2) note, ". . . the principal agency problem in large corporations around the world is that of restricting expropriation of minority shareholders by the controlling shareholders, rather than that of restricting empire building by professional managers unaccountable to shareholders." This is known as a Type II agency cost.

To date, much of the research into agency relationships and agency costs has concerned typically large U.S. corporations. As Holderness (2009, 1377) states, "Two stylized facts dominate the thinking about ownership concentration of public corporations—U.S. firms are generally diffusely owned, and U.S. firms are more diffusely owned than comparable firms elsewhere." However, Holderness finds that the vast majority of U.S. firms (nearly 90 percent) actually have average aggregate block holdings comprising 39 percent of outstanding equity. This evidence suggests that the United States may not have a markedly different ownership structure from that of other countries. As such, understanding Type II agency costs is likely to be just as relevant for the United States as other countries where Type II agency issues dominate.

Anderson and Reeb (2003a) show that one-third of S&P 500 firms are controlled or run by a founding family member. This is further evidence that typical U.S. corporations cannot be characterized as being widely held with nonshareholder professional managers at the helm. In family firms, Type I agency issues are not as relevant as Type II agency issues because managers are very much synonymous with their controlling shareholder base (Demsetz and Lehn 1985). As Anderson and Reeb note, family owners have in-depth knowledge of their business. Chen (2006) argues that managers are less likely to manipulate financial accounts because family owners not only monitor the management more closely but also have a detailed knowledge of the business, thereby increasing the difficulty for managers to undertake typical Type I agency behavior. For example, Bergstresser, Desai, and Rauh (2006) show that managers manipulate corporate pension accounts to maximize the value of executive stock options and to meet earnings targets.

The Importance of Minority Shareholder Rights

Ownership and control are two important factors in examining corporate structures but they have very different implications for the firm. In a corporate environment with weak investor protection, the benefits that can accrue for controlling shareholders are substantial. As La Porta et al. (2000, 13) state, "When the insiders actually do expropriate, the so-called private benefits of control become a substantial share of the firm's value."

The trade-offs here are complex and raise the question of what the optimal ownership structure in a firm is vis-à-vis control rights and cash flow rights (Grossman and Hart 1980). As the shares of the firm become more widely held, the likelihood of expropriation by management increases, and so the risk of Type I agency costs increases (La Porta, Lopez-de-Silanes, Shleifer, and Vishny 1998). Yet, where there are strong legal systems, shareholders have legal recourse with managers of the firm through the courts. A class action law suit is an example of this (Ali, Chen, and Radhakrishnan 2007). As a result, managers are less likely to undertake excessive expropriation in environments with strong investor protection because shareholders can more ably hold managers accountable.

Alternatively, where legal enforcement is weak and investor protection is low, large controlling stakes may help to mitigate Type I agency costs. If shareholders have a large or controlling stake, they have much of their personal wealth tied to the success of the firm. This provides an incentive for blockholders to actively monitor managers and hold management accountable, thereby reducing the likelihood of

Type I agency costs (Volpin 2002). The downside of having large controlling stakes is offset by the higher probability of wealth expropriation by the same shareholders.

Bennedsen and Wolfenzon (2000) argue that the preceding scenario may not necessarily hold. They posit that splitting ownership among a number of large blockholders is possible in order to reduce expropriation. In this situation, there is no controlling shareholder and so any decisions made must be by majority agreement. As a result of their individual cash flow rights, the controlling shareholders' best strategy may be to distribute cash in the form of dividends as there is insufficient individual wealth to effectively expropriate from the minority shareholders.

Advantages of Family Firms Ownership Structures

Type I agency problems can be succinctly summed up as a situation whereby managers do not always act in the best interests of shareholders. There are many reasons such problems do not exist (or are not as prevalent) in family-owned firms. First, family owners do not hold a diversified portfolio and their personal wealth is highly correlated to the success or failure of the firm. For example, for the Forbes 400 Wealthiest Americans, Anderson and Reeb (2003a) find that, on average, more than 69 percent of individuals' wealth is dependent on their controlling stakes in corporations.

Consequently, this exposure to the firm motivates family owners to actively monitor management, which reduces the free-rider problem that occurs under diffuse ownership (Demsetz and Lehn 1985). The free-rider problem with Type I agency relationships occurs because the cost of monitoring management for a small shareholder is considerably in excess of any gains that would be directly attributable to the shareholder undertaking such actions. Further, the monitoring of management will benefit all other shareholders without having to bear the cost of monitoring themselves. Because small shareholders are not incentivized to actively monitor managers, they free-ride on the efforts of others.

Family owners have different investment objectives from normal shareholders because family owners are likely to have a much longer investment horizon than nonfamily shareholders. This occurs because one of the investment goals of the family owners is intergenerational ownership transfer where the control of the family's wealth is passed from one generation to the next (Basu, Dimitrova, and Paeglis 2009).

As a result of longer investment horizons, family-run firms are less likely to suffer myopic investment problems (Stein 1988 and 1989). Myopic investments typically occur where Type I agency problems exist and managers invest to increase their labor market value, which is not necessarily in the best interest of shareholders (Campbell and Marino 1994).

Type II Agency Problems

Controlling Minority Shareholders

Type II agency problems occur as a consequence of conflicts between controlling and noncontrolling shareholders. One scenario where this occurs is through the ownership of dual-class shares. Founding family owners may have substantial control over the firm despite owning only a small fraction of the total shares in issue. For example, Google has both A-Class shares held by the founders and B-Class shares held by public investors. Given that A-Class shares have 10 votes and B-Class shares have only 1 vote per share, founder members have a level of voting power that exceeds their cash flow rights.

Dual-class stock also allows controlling minority shareholders to protect themselves from other governance mechanisms such as the market for corporate control (Cronqvist and Nilsson 2003). Controlling minority shareholders engage in trading off the costs and benefits of expropriation of noncontrolling shareholders (La Porta et al. 2002).

In analyzing the Swedish case, Cronqvist and Nilsson (2003) show that controlling minority shareholders use dual-class shares and other control mechanisms more frequently to retain control significantly above their cash flow rights. The agency cost of using such mechanisms is considerable, between 6 percent and 25 percent of corporate value.

By controlling the firm through majority voting rights, family owners can undertake actions that expropriate wealth from noncontrolling shareholders. As Gilson and Gordon (2003) suggest, this occurs because the controlling stake allows family owners to marginalize noncontrolling owners. One way in which private benefits can be extracted is through related-party transactions (Anderson and Reeb 2003a). Related-party transactions take place when the groups in the deal have a prior relationship. Such actions can include targeted share issues and repurchases of shares, asset transfers, entrenchment, and tunneling (Volpin 2002). When managers undertake related-party transactions, they are essentially asset-stripping one firm by selling its assets and securities at below market value to another firm under their control (La Porta et al. 2000).

Investment Motives in Family Firms

Controlling family ownership may also lead to suboptimal investment decisions. As noted earlier, one of the investment goals of family firms is likely to be intergenerational ownership transfers. This can also be viewed as a nonpecuniary benefit of control because utility may be derived by passing the firm from one generation to the next (Andres 2008). Consequently, controlling family members may tend to be more risk averse to ensure that this event transpires.

In such a situation, family-controlled firms may undertake strategies that are not necessarily in the interest of noncontrolling or minority shareholders. One strategy may be to undertake unrelated diversification to lessen the cash flow risks of the main business of the firm. Further, family controlled firms may employ a suboptimal capital structure by not using an optimal amount of debt in the financing mix due to a fear of bankruptcy (Anderson and Reeb 2003b). Clearly both of these situations could impose costs on minority shareholders. First, if small shareholders already hold well-diversified portfolios, they do not benefit from unrelated corporate diversification. Second, not exploiting the optimal financing mix available to the firm may result in a loss of value to minority shareholders because the firm does not use the maximum debt interest tax shield available. Interestingly, in their analysis of U.S. family firms, Anderson and Reeb find that family firms have a lower degree of diversification and comparable leverage ratios relative to nonfamily firms.

Hagelin, Holmen, and Pramborg (2006) analyze risk management in Swedish firms with dual-class shares. Their analysis separates out family-owned firms where the family wealth is diversified from those where family wealth is tied up in the firm. Consistent with Anderson and Reeb (2003b), the results of Hegelin et al. show that where the owner's wealth is diversified, no difference exists in corporate risk relative to non-family-run firms. However, when the owner's wealth is undiversified, the firms have less debt and use their controlling stake to reduce the risk for their wealth.

Costs of Succession

One consequence of the succession motive of family firms is that as the firm passes from one generation to the next, a loss of talent and expertise occurs. Morck et al. (2000) argue that much of the talent and skill that led to success is only partially transferred from one generation to the next. Consequently, skill and talent revert towards the mean over time. As a result of successive intergenerational transfers of the firm, firm performance will decrease and adversely affect small shareholders.

This process of succession can also result in the managerial entrenchment of family members on the board. For example, when Rupert Murdoch placed his 30-year old son, James Murdoch, as CEO of BSkyB Plc, a considerable outcry occurred from shareholders concerned about the independence of the firm. Such a reaction by the market is consistent with the work of Pérez-González (2006), who finds that when family heirs are appointed to the board, a significantly negative stock market reaction occurs following the announcement.

Again consistent with the view that descendent CEOs destroy value, Villalonga and Amit (2006) find that value is created when there is significant family ownership and the founder is the CEO or chairman. The founder premium is lower, however, in firms with dual-class shares and pyramid ownership structures. Further, relative to standard Type I agency costs between managers and shareholders, the cost of Type II agency relationships in firms where the CEO is a descendent of the founder is considerably higher.

As Shleifer and Vishny (1997) posit, by allowing for the entrenchment of family members, founders may continue to be involved in running the family business even when it is not in the best interests of the firm and its shareholders. The authors argue that this is one of the largest agency costs that family owners can impose on noncontrolling shareholders because of the loss of value.

Other theories may explain the actions of family firms in this respect. The most notable of these is stewardship theory, where managers do not act to maximize their personal utility through perquisite consumption (Chrisman, Chua, Kellermanns, and Chang 2007). Stewardship theory contends that managers will, on average, undertake actions for the good of the firm (Davis, Schoorman, and Donaldson 1997). In this situation managers place less emphasis on their own personal goals relative to the goals of the firm. Further, when family managers run the firm, there may be other nonfinancial goals that are in the interest of both family managers and family owners (Corbetta and Salvatto 2004). Arguably, succession and intergenerational ownership transfers may be one such motive.

Chrisman et al. (2007) empirically examine whether family businesses exhibit signs of agency theory relationships or whether stewardship theory relationships dominate. Their results show greater evidence of agency-based relationships, and demonstrate that family managers are subject to the type of controls that would be placed on non–family members to limit expropriation.

SUMMARY AND CONCLUSIONS

Agency costs within firms are complex. They are dependent upon a wide range of motives, incentives, and structures. In the classic view of the corporation as posited by Berle and Means (1932) and formalized by Jensen and Meckling (1976), agency costs occur between managers and shareholders as a result of incomplete contracting. These Type I agency costs result when manager and shareholder goals are not aligned, resulting in managers undertaking perquisite consumption and expropriating wealth from shareholders.

The view of an atomistic shareholder base is not an ownership structure that is common across the world. Having ownership structures where a large blockholder is in control or where a controlling minority stake exists is more common. Controlling minority stakes allows an individual to exercise control over the firm in excess of the cash flow rights for which his stake permits. In this situation, Type II agency costs are much more relevant because there is a risk of the controlling shareholder undertaking actions that expropriate the noncontrolling shareholders.

DISCUSSION QUESTIONS

1. Agency problems are a result of incomplete contracting and the separation of ownership and control. Assuming the firm has a diffuse shareholder base, what type of agency problems can occur in a firm?
2. Corporate ownership around the world differs markedly from the diffuse ownership structures that are assumed to dominate capital markets. Describe the type of agency issues that occur where minority shareholders have corporate control.
3. If firms have controlling minority shareholders, Type I agency relationships are not as predominant as Type II agency relationships. Why does this occur?
4. Family firms have a wide range of incentives that may not be in the interest of diversified shareholders. Discuss the main issues surrounding succession and family entrenchment.

REFERENCES

Ali, Ashiq, Tai-Yaun Chen, and Suresh Radhakrishnan. 2007. Corporate disclosures by family firms. *Journal of Accounting and Economics* 44 (2): 238–286.

Anderson, Ronald C., and David M. Reeb. 2003a. Founding-family ownership and firm performance: Evidence from the S&P 500. *Journal of Finance* 58 (3): 1301–1328.

———. 2003b. Founding-family ownership corporate diversification and leverage. *Journal of Law and Economics* 46 (2): 653–684.

Andres, Christian. 2008. Large shareholders and firm performance—an empirical examination of founding family ownership. *Journal of Corporate Finance* 14 (4): 431–445.

Ang, James S., Rebel A. Cole, and James W. Lin. 2000. Agency costs and ownership structure. *Journal of Finance* 55 (1): 81–106.

Basu, Nilanjan, Lora Dimitrova, and Imants Paeglis. 2009. Family control and dilution in mergers. *Journal of Banking & Finance* 33 (5): 829–841.

Bennedsen, Morton, and Daniel Wolfenzon. 2000. The balance of power in closely held corporations. *Journal of Financial Economics* 58 (2): 113–39.

Berger, Philip G., and Eli Ofek. 1995. Diversification's effect on firm value. *Journal of Financial Economics* 37 (1): 39–65.

Bergstresser Daniel, Mihir Desai, and Joshua Rauh. 2006. Earnings manipulation, pension assumptions and managerial investment decisions. *Quarterly Journal of Economics* 121 (1): 157–195.

Berle, Adolf, and Gardiner Means. 1932. *The modern corporation and private property*. New York: Harcourt, Brace and World.

Brennan, Michael J. 1995. Corporate finance over the past 25 years. *Financial Management* 24 (2): 9–22.

Burkart, Mike, Denis Gromb, and Fausto Panunzi. 1997. Large shareholders, monitoring, and the value of the firm. *Quarterly Journal of Economics* 112 (3): 693–728.

Cadbury, Adrian. 1992. *Codes of best practice. Report from the Committee on Financial Aspects of Corporate Governance*. London: Gee Publishing.

Campbell, Tim S., and Anthony M. Marino. 1994. Myopic investment decisions and competitive labour markets. *International Economic Review* 35 (4): 855–875.

Chen, Tai-Yaun. 2006. CEO compensation contracts of family firms. Working paper, University of Ontario.

Chrisman, James. J., Jess H. Chua, Franz W. Kellermanns, and Erick P. C. Chang. 2007. Are family managers agents or stewards? An exploratory study in privately held firms. *Journal of Business Research* 60 (1): 1030–1038.

The Combined Code on Corporate Governance. 2008. London: Financial Reporting Council.

Conyon, Martin J., and Kevin J. Murphy. 2000. The prince and the pauper? CEO pay in the US and UK. *Economic Journal* 110 (467): 640–671.

Corbetta, Guido, and Carlo Salvatto. 2004. Self-serving or self actualizing? Models of man and agency costs in different types of family firms: A commentary on "Comparing agency costs of family and non-family firms: Conceptual issues and exploratory evidence." *Entrepreneurship, Theory and Practice* 28 (2): 355–362.

Cronqvist, Henrik, and Mattias Nilsson. 2003. Agency costs of controlling minority shareholders. *Journal of Financial and Quantitative Analysis* 38 (4): 695–719.

Davis, James H., F. David Schoorman, and Lex Donaldson. 1997. Toward a stewardship theory of management. *Academy of Management Review* 22 (1): 20–47.

Demsetz, Harold, and Kenneth Lehn. 1985. The structure of corporate ownership: Causes and consequences. *Journal of Political Economy* 93 (6): 1155–1177.

Dechow, Patricia M., and Richard G. Sloan. 1991. Executive incentives and the horizon problem: An empirical investigation. *Journal of Accounting and Economics* 14 (1): 51–89.

Denis, David J., Diane K. Denis, and Atulya Sarin. 1997. Agency problems, equity ownership, and corporate diversification. *Journal of Finance* 52 (1): 135–160.

Denis, Diane K. 2001. Twenty-five years of corporate governance research ... and counting. *Review of Financial Economics* 10 (3): 191–212.

Easterbrook, Frank H. 1984. Two agency cost explanations of dividends. *American Economic Review* 74 (4): 650–659.

Fama, Eugene F. 1980. Agency problems and the theory of the firm. *Journal of Political Economy* 88 (2): 288–307.

Fama, Eugene F., and Michael C. Jensen. 1983. Separation of ownership and control. *Journal of Law and Economics* 26 (2): 301–325.

Gilson, Ronald J., and Jeffrey N. Gordon. 2003. Controlling shareholders. *University of Pennsylvania Law Review* 152 (2): 785–843.

Gilson, Stuart C. 1989. Management turnover and financial distress. *Journal of Financial Economics* 25 (2): 241–262.

Greenbury, Richard. 1995. Directors' remuneration: Report of a study group chaired by Sir Richard Greenbury. London: Gee Publishing.

Grossman, Sanford J., and Oliver D. Hart. 1980. Takeover bids, the free rider problem and the theory of the corporation. *Bell Journal of Economics* 11 (1): 42–64.

Hagelin, Niclas, Martin Holmen, and Bengt Pramborg. 2006. Family ownership, dual-class shares, and risk management. *Global Finance Journal* 16 (3): 283–301.

Hampel, Ronnie. 1998. Committee on corporate governance: Final report. London: Gee Publishing.

Healy, Paul M. 1985. The effect of bonus schemes on accounting decisions. *Journal of Accounting and Economics* 7 (1–3): 85–108.

Higgs, Derek. 2003. Review of the role and effectiveness of non-executive directors. London: Gee Publishing.

Himmelberg, Charles P., Glenn R. Hubbard, and Darius Palia. 1999. Understanding the determinants of managerial ownership and the link between ownership and performance. *Journal of Financial Economics* 53 (3): 353–384.

Holderness, Clifford G. 2009. The myth of diffuse ownership in the United States. *Review of Financial Studies* 22 (4): 1377–1408.

Jensen, Michael C. 1986. The agency costs of free cash flow: Corporate finance and takeovers. *American Economic Review* 76 (2): 323–329.

———. 1993. The modern industrial revolution, exit and the failure of internal control systems. *Journal of Finance* 48 (3): 831–880.

Jensen, Michael C., and William H. Meckling. 1976. Theory of the firm: Managerial behavior, agency costs and ownership structure. *Journal of Financial Economics* 3 (4): 305–360.

Jensen, Michael C., and Kevin J. Murphy. 1990. Performance pay and top management incentives. *Journal of Political Economy* 98 (2): 225–264.

La Porta, Raphael, Florencio Lopez-de-Silanes, and Andrei Shleifer. 1999. Corporate ownership around the world. NBER Working paper 6625.

La Porta, Raphael, Florencio Lopez-de-Silanes, Andrei Shleifer, and Robert W. Vishny. 1998. Law and finance. *Journal of Political Economy* 106 (6): 1113–1155.

———. 1999. The quality of government. *Journal of Law, Economics and Organisation* 15 (1): 222–279.

———. 2000. Investor protection and corporate governance. *Journal of Financial Economics* 58 (1–2): 3–27.

———. 2002. Investor protection and corporate valuation. *Journal of Finance* 57 (3): 1147–1170.

Lang, Larry, Annette Poulsen, and René Stulz. 1995. Asset sales, firm performance, and the agency costs of managerial discretion. *Journal of Financial Economics* 37 (1): 3–37.

Lang, Larry, and René Stulz. 1994. Tobin's Q, corporate diversification, and firm performance. *Journal of Political Economy* 102 (6): 1248–1280.

Morck, Randall, Andrei Shleifer, and Robert W. Vishny. 1990. Do managerial objectives drive bad acquisitions? *Journal of Finance* 45 (1): 31–48.

Morck, Randall, David A. Strangeland, and Bernard Yeung. 2000. Inherited wealth, corporate control and economic growth: The Canadian disease? NBER Working paper 6814.

Murphy, Kevin, and Jerry Zimmerman. 1993. Financial performance surrounding CEO turnover. *Journal of Accounting and Economics* 16 (1–3): 273–315.

Myers, Stewart C. 1984. The capital structure puzzle. *Journal of Finance* 39 (3): 575–592.

Pérez-González, Francesco. 2006. Inherited control and firm performance. *American Economic Review* 96 (5): 1559–1588.

Pourciau, Susan. 1993. Earnings management and non-routine executive changes. *Journal of Accounting and Economics* 16 (1-3): 317–336.

Rosenstein, Stuart, and John G. Wyatt. 2006. Shareholder wealth effects when an officer of one corporation joins the board of directors of another corporation. *Managerial Decision Economics* 15 (4): 317–327.

Shleifer, Andrei, and Robert W. Vishny. 1989. Management entrenchment: The case of manager-specific investments. *Journal of Financial Economics* 25 (1): 123–139.
———. 1997. A survey of corporate governance. *Journal of Finance* 52 (2): 737–783.
Short, Helen, Kevin Keasey, Mike Wright, and Alison Hull. 1999. Corporate governance: From accountability to enterprise. *Accounting and Business Research* 29 (4): 337–352.
Stein, Jeremy. 1988. Takeover threats and managerial myopia. *Journal of Political Economy* 96 (1): 61–80.
———. 1989. Efficient capital markets, inefficient firms: A model of myopic corporate behavior. *Quarterly Journal of Economics* 106 (4): 655–669.
Villalonga, Belen, and Raphael Amit. 2006. How do family ownership, control and management affect firm value? *Journal of Financial Economics* 80 (2): 385–417.
Volpin, Paolo F. 2002. Governance with poor investor protection: Evidence from top executive turnover in Italy. *Journal of Financial Economics* 64 (1): 61–90.

ABOUT THE AUTHORS

Iain Clacher is a lecturer in accounting and finance at Leeds University Business School. His current research focuses on final salary pension schemes of UK corporations. His PhD thesis research analyzed fair value pension accounting, pension risk, and pension plan funding. His other research interests include corporate governance, corporate social responsibility, socially responsible investment, international accounting standards, and sovereign wealth funds. He is co-author of *Fundamentals of Corporate Finance: European Edition* (McGraw-Hill, 2011) with David Hillier, Stephen Ross, Randolph Westerfield, and Bradford Jordan. He has also been involved in work for the City of London Corporation and The Work Foundation, United Kingdom.

David Hillier is a professor of finance at the University of Strathclyde. Professor Hillier has published a wide range of peer-reviewed academic articles on corporate governance, corporate finance, insider trading, asset pricing, precious metals, auditing, and market microstructure. His research has attracted an ANBAR citation and a best paper prize from one of the top finance and management journals in Southeast Asia. He is on the editorial board and reviews for many of the world's top finance journals. Professor Hillier is a co-author of the European editions of *Financial Markets and Corporate Strategy* (McGraw-Hill, 2008), *Corporate Finance* (McGraw-Hill, 2010), and *Fundamentals of Corporate Finance* (McGraw-Hill, 2011).

Patrick McColgan has been a senior lecturer in finance at the University of Strathclyde since 2007. He studied accounting and finance at undergraduate and postgraduate level at the University of Strathclyde between 1996 and 2003 and was employed as a lecturer in finance at the University of Aberdeen between 2003 and 2007. His teaching interests include corporate finance, corporate governance, personal finance, and investment management. His research focuses in the general area of corporate finance and specifically corporate governance and corporate restructuring, relative to which he has published numerous international peer-reviewed articles. More recently he has been researching security issuance.

CHAPTER 9

Theories and Models of Corporate Governance

THOMAS W. JOO
Professor of Law, University of California, Davis

INTRODUCTION

Corporate governance is often said to chiefly concern the "internal" governance of corporations: that is, the relationship among the participants in the corporate enterprise. Internal governance is sometimes distinguished from "external" regulation of the nominally private business corporation by the state. But the internal and external aspects of governance are intertwined and not mutually exclusive. Any state regulation that affects an enterprise at the corporate level will also affect the private claimants that compose it, possibly altering their relationships. Moreover, any internal relationship within a corporation exists, for better or for worse, within legal frameworks created by governments. Thus, even as the contemporary legal discourse on corporate governance purports to focus on internal matters, it advances arguments regarding the extent to which internal relationships are, and should be, structured by private claimants, and the extent to which they are, or should be, structured externally by the state.

These issues are often framed in terms of a debate over the nature or essence of the corporation. This chapter presents a brief historical survey of essentialist models of the corporation, with special emphasis on the contemporary theory known as "contractarianism." Recurring questions include who owns the corporation, whether a corporation is an artificial phenomenon created by state fiat or a natural by-product of human interaction, whether the corporation is an entity separate from its constituent individuals, and why decision-making authority is concentrated in professional managers. The shifting answers to these questions are presented as justifications for, or critiques of, the existing corporate governance regime, but can also be seen as shorthand for unspoken normative assumptions about the respective roles of the group, the state, and the individual.

This chapter consists of seven sections. The first section addresses "artificial entity" theory, which focuses on the relationship between the corporation and the state. The second discusses "aggregation" theory, which portrays the corporation as indistinguishable from natural individual interaction and deemphasizes the role of the state. The third section discusses the "fiduciary" model as a response to concentrated management power. The model posits that shareholders are the owners of the corporation, to whom managers are accountable as agents. The fourth section introduces "managerialism," which defends concentrated, hierarchical decision making. The fifth describes the contemporary contractarian model, which has dominated the field for the past two decades but has drawn increasing criticism. The sixth section examines post-contractarian directions. The final section describes nascent new developments in corporate governance theory.

ARTIFICIAL ENTITY THEORY

Until about the mid-1800s, American corporations, like British corporations before them, were created exclusively by special enabling legislation and were rarely business corporations in the contemporary sense. A state's legislature would pass legislation that recognized a corporation and prescribed its powers and its purpose, which was normally for public benefit, such as a church or school, or a toll road or bridge. Because the state was at least formally responsible for the corporation's existence, British and early American law routinely referred to corporations as "artificial entities."

In *Trustees of Dartmouth College v. Woodward* (1819), the leading corporate law case from this period, the United States Supreme Court stated that corporations are "artificial entities." However, the Court specifically rejected the argument that corporations are created by a *unilateral* act of the state. Rather, the corporate charter of Dartmouth College was a *bilateral* "contract" between the state and Dartmouth's incorporators, under which the state awarded corporate status in exchange for the incorporators' promise to engage in educational pursuits for the benefit of the public. The Contracts Clause of the U.S. Constitution forbids the states of the Union from "impairing" existing contract obligations, and thus the Court held that New Hampshire could not unilaterally revoke or amend Dartmouth's charter. Following the contract argument to its conclusion, however, the Court also held that a state could amend the corporate charter *if* the contract so provided: that is, if power were reserved at the time of chartering. (All states' corporation codes now have provisions to this effect.)

According to *Dartmouth College*, corporate status makes an enterprise subject to no more (and no less) regulation than a natural person. The states' authority to impose economic regulations on natural and artificial subjects alike is derived from the states' inherent power to regulate public welfare. Under this so-called "police power" doctrine, the Supreme Court held, for example, that even though a corporation's charter authorized it to hold a lottery for 25 years, a subsequent state constitutional revision outlawing lotteries did not violate the Contracts Clause. Although the charter was a contract, "no legislature can bargain away the public health or the public morals" (*Stone v. Mississippi*, 1880). Although *Dartmouth College* was ambivalent about the regulatory implications of the artificial entity theory, it also made clear that a corporation's charter and enabling legislation determined its powers. Thus, the artificial entity theory is often invoked to justify regulation. Until well into the twentieth century, the Supreme Court used this argument to justify two kinds of state action against corporations. First, the Court often invalidated corporate actions on the grounds that they had exceeded their chartered powers, a doctrine known as *ultra vires*. Second, the Court allowed states to place special requirements on out-of-state corporations. Because a corporation's home state gave it the privilege to do business in the corporate form, the power to grant those privileges did not extend beyond the borders of the home state (Horwitz 1992).

Bratton (1989) argues that while theory has vacillated between individual and entity conceptions, corporate doctrine has been "nonevolutionary" and has generally refused to adopt any one essentialist characterization of the corporation. Indeed, while artificial entity theory has continued to appear sporadically in U.S. Supreme Court jurisprudence to justify government regulation, the Court never seems to have committed to any one model. For example, Chief Justice Marshall, the author of *Dartmouth,* wrote in another opinion for the Court that although a corporation may be an artificial entity for *some* purposes, courts could, "for legitimate purposes," consider it as nothing but a group of individuals (*Bank of the United States v. Devaux*, 1809).

AGGREGATION THEORY

When American states in the Jacksonian era began granting special incorporations to businesses that lacked significant public purposes, some criticized such incorporations as examples of favoritism. Special incorporation was therefore eventually replaced by general incorporation statutes that granted incorporation as a matter of course (Dodd 1954). As special incorporation was replaced by general incorporation, the role of the state in any given incorporation became less apparent than the role of entrepreneurs and investors in creating the underlying enterprise.

Not coincidentally, this antistatist model came to prominence in America during the late nineteenth century, at the confluence of laissez-faire ideology, a period of fear of European socialism, and the rise of large, politically powerful business corporations such as railroads and large banks. Around the same time, the U.S. Supreme Court's broad police-power justification of state regulation stood in tension with a line of state court cases holding that the "due process" clauses in state constitutions limited states' ability to regulate private property. Around the turn of the twentieth century, federal courts' deference to police power began to give way to the doctrine of "substantive due process," which held that the U.S. Constitution protected economic and property rights against state regulation.

In the late nineteenth century, Taylor (1884) and other theorists articulated a view of the corporation that rejected both the artificial and the entity characterizations. They deemphasized the state and the group in favor of the individual. According to Taylor, corporate law governs corporations because individuals voluntarily subject themselves to the rules of law. Taylor expanded the *Dartmouth College* view of a charter as a contract with the state, characterizing the charter as also embodying an agreement among the incorporators to be bound by the terms of the charter and of the law. Furthermore, according to Taylor (pp. 504–505), shareholders agree to majority voting and management control by directors and officers; this contract prescribes and limits the powers of directors. Taylor (p. iv) also argued that the view of a corporation as an entity had "outlived its usefulness"; instead, a corporation should be viewed in terms of the real persons who composed it and the relationships among them.

While doctrine did not generally incorporate this theory, some federal cases held that corporations were nothing more than "aggregations of individuals" (*San Mateo v. Southern Pacific Railroad* 1882, 734). These cases held that state regulation of corporate activity amounted to a deprivation of those individuals' property and eventually led to the constitutional protection of economic rights under the aforementioned rubric of substantive due process. Thus, the equation of corporations with their component individuals was part of an effort to rein in economic regulation generally. When the Supreme Court eventually addressed the constitutionality of corporate regulations, however, it simply asserted corporate constitutional rights without explanation (*Santa Clara v. Southern Pacific Railroad* 1886). Bearing out Bratton's "nonevolutionary" description of doctrine, the Court did not explicitly invoke aggregation or any other essentialist theory.

MANAGERIAL POWER IN CORPORATE THEORY I: THE FIDUCIARY MODEL

The aggregation theory was short-lived probably because it conflicted descriptively with the rise of large corporations, such as railroads, whose shareholders were increasingly passive investors in enterprises founded and managed by others. The power of professional managers raised a long-running concern of corporation theory. Smith (1776, 700) famously argued that the directors of joint-stock companies, being "the managers rather of other people's money than of their own," will tend to indulge in "negligence and profusion" in the operation of such companies.

This "other people's money" problem is hardly unique to the corporate context. In trust law and agency law, a principal party gives a "fiduciary" (trusted person) the power to control the principal's property. The fiduciary lacks ownership interest in the property and is obligated to use his control for the benefit of the principal (or a third party).

Corporate law has long referred to corporate directors and officers variously as fiduciaries, agents, or trustees of shareholders. This shareholder-centered model emphasizes that directors and officers owe "fiduciary duties" to shareholders, who are the rightful owners of the firm. But this only centers the analysis on the relationship between shareholders and management. It says very little, descriptively or normatively, about the content of that relationship, or whether it should be governed by the law or left to the parties. Fiduciary duties vary by context: The legal rights and duties of trustees differ from those of agents, and the rights of any given fiduciary may vary based on the nature of the task and agreements with the principal. The rights of principals are similarly mutable: They can trade away some or all of their ownership rights to third parties or even to their fiduciaries.

Moreover, the fiduciary model does not explain *why* shareholders are the focus of corporate governance. Most contemporary adherents of the fiduciary model simply take this focus for granted. But before shareholder limited liability became the general rule in the 1890s, some courts referred to corporate capital as a trust for the benefit of a corporation's *creditors* (Dodd 1954, 91–93). Furthermore, before stock-issuing business corporations were widespread, *Dartmouth College* focused on the relationship between the *incorporators* and the state.

Despite pervasive rhetoric of fiduciary duty, corporate law has long limited shareholders' power to control the directors or officers who are purportedly shareholders' agents. State laws vest management authority in directors, and by the early twentieth century, according to Horwitz (1992, 99), director authority was considered *original*, not delegated by shareholders. Even majority resolutions of shareholders cannot override directors' authority to manage the corporation. Shareholders may sue corporate fiduciaries for acts of disloyalty and self-dealing, but not for negligence or poor performance. Instead, courts give great deference to management's business decisions, even those that turn out to have been hasty or ill-considered. Gevurtz (1994) traces this doctrine, known today as the "business judgment rule," at least as far back as an 1829 case, *Percy v. Millaudon*. That case articulated the enduring argument that relaxing legal duties for managers actually *improves* corporate governance because strict duties only deter qualified individuals from becoming corporate directors. Although cases and commentators often state that directors have a fiduciary duty to maximize shareholder wealth, the deference of the business judgment rule renders such a duty unenforceable. The supposed duty might be impossibly vague in any event, as shareholder wealth is difficult to define: Business decisions that increase share price in the short term might harm long-term firm value, and vice versa.

MANAGERIAL POWER IN CORPORATE THEORY II: MANAGERIALISM

Because the aggregation theory did not satisfactorily account for the hierarchical nature of corporate governance, legal theorists advanced a "natural entity" theory that derived from Continental theory. The concept of the corporation as an entity separate from the human beings who compose it explained why power need not be dispersed among the entire membership. The characterization of this entity as "natural" legitimated this concentration of power. Like aggregation theory, it also appealed to the theory of economic rights reflected in substantive due process jurisprudence. The natural entity theory was a major departure from aggregation theory, however, in that the "natural" phenomenon and the holder of economic rights was the corporation itself rather than its constituent individuals.

Dodd (1932) argued that the centralization of corporate control offered an opportunity to direct corporate wealth and power to serve broader social interests. Strict accountability to shareholders, Dodd argued, would require corporate management to serve shareholders' narrow, selfish desire for short-term investment returns. If liberated from enforceable obligations to shareholders, directors could manage corporate wealth and influence as "trustees" for society generally. While this argument had no explicit essentialist content, it was a refutation of the aggregate and fiduciary models. This argument was generally consistent with the natural entity theory's distinction between the corporation and its constituent individuals.

Although Berle (1931) made a famous defense of the fiduciary model, his best-known work upended that view. Berle and Means (1932) argued that the concentration of power in management rendered the large, publicly traded corporation fundamentally different from our traditional notion of private property. Shareholders, as passive owners of corporations, had abdicated the property owner's traditional control and responsibility to professional managers, and managers had far-reaching powers that did not require them to manage the corporation in the interest of its owners. Thus, Berle and Means (p. 356) state, "they have placed the community in a position to demand that the modern corporation serve not alone the owners or the control but all society." While Dodd had put his faith in the wisdom and conscience of the business elite in identifying the public interest, Berle and Means entrusted this task to "the community." Their conclusion left critical ambiguities, however, in that it failed to define the community or to specify whether "demand" referred to mere exhortation or coercive regulation.

Bratton and Wachter (2008) trace Berle's revised view of corporate social responsibility to the Continental philosophy of "corporatism." Like natural entity theory, corporatism recognizes the role of groups such as unions and corporations. According to Bratton and Wachter (p. 113), corporatism also "emphasizes cooperative relationships among groups and between the state and the different groups" in the identification and realization of the public interest. Bratton and Wachter also attribute Dodd's similar characterization to the influence of corporatism. Perhaps because corporatism is so alien to the American tradition of individualism, Berle and Means' plea for social responsibility has been all but forgotten. However, their description of the "separation of ownership and control" has, ironically, had enduring influence in shareholder-centered corporate governance theory.

Dewey (1926) called for an end to the long tradition of essentialist corporate theorization. In classic Legal Realist fashion, he argued that essentialist models were indeterminate and thus unhelpful. The various essentialist models could be employed to support varying conclusions about corporations' legitimacy and their relationship to the state. Under the influence of pragmatic ideologies like Realism, not to mention the exigencies of the Depression, American legal thought lost interest in formal essentialist models of the corporation. The New Deal challenged and temporarily reversed the turn-of-the-century move toward economic conservatism. In the late 1930s, the Supreme Court began to reject substantive due process and uphold both state and federal economic regulation. But once again, it avoided corporate essentialism. Instead, the Supreme Court justified government economic regulation on broad assertions of government authority. Thus, as in its earlier substantive due process and corporate rights jurisprudence, the Supreme Court required no theory of the corporation.

Many mid-century theorists accepted and sought to address the descriptive reality of "managerialism"—that large corporations were run by professional management and exerted significant economic and social influence. They tended to avoid express essentialization, but their focus on the corporate institution shows the influence of natural entity and corporatist theories. Alfred Chandler (1977) characterized the rise of centralized management control in the twentieth century as an efficient means of coordinating large-scale production. Galbraith (1967) argued that because corporate managements were beyond shareholder control, they were answerable only to the state. Thus the economy was no longer controlled by small investors and entrepreneurs, but had become a partnership between government and large corporations.

In the 1970s, corporate bankruptcies, the decline of American industry, and destructive corporate behavior contributed to growing resentment toward large corporations. Social advocates called for greater corporate accountability to society, while shareholder advocates called for greater management accountability to shareholders. This was reminiscent of the Berle-Dodd debate and consistent with the general post-Watergate demand for greater accountability. In this context, Eisenberg (1976) developed the model of the "monitoring board." He observed that directors of large corporations delegate most managerial power to professional executives who are beyond shareholder control. Normatively, he argued that boards should not be viewed as part of management; rather, they should focus on the distinct task of monitoring the corporation's managers. By distinguishing between directors and executives and enlisting directors as shareholders' agents to control executives, Eisenberg adapted the fiduciary model to contemporary conditions and offered a specific solution to the venerable "other people's money" problem. This highly influential view has led to the common contemporary practice of majority-independent corporate boards, rather than boards dominated by the corporation's own executives.

CONTRACTARIANISM

Familiar historical themes and fundamental normative conflicts recur in contemporary corporate governance theory. Fiduciary rhetoric continues to dominate mainstream doctrine. But a revised version of contract-based theory has come to dominate theory and to exert influence on doctrine. The latter half of the twentieth century saw a decline in the influence of Legal Realism and revivals of both conservative economic theory and essentialist corporate theory. It also saw developments in contract theory that rehabilitated the nineteenth-century aggregation theory. As noted earlier, the aggregation theory had failed in part because it could not explain the hierarchical governance of the large, publicly traded corporation in terms of individuals' voluntary contracts. Developments in economic and legal theories of contract now made such an explanation possible. While there is considerable diversity of approach among contract-based corporate theories in economics and law, the theories can be loosely grouped under the rubric of "contractarianism."

As in its earlier incarnation, the renewed focus on contract resonated with two fundamental and related traditions in American political, economic, and legal thought: first, the libertarian notion that consent confers moral legitimacy; and second, the economic notion (famously expressed in Smith's metaphor of the invisible hand) that individual, decentralized consensual exchanges allocate economic goods so as to maximize overall social utility. More generally, contractarianism (like aggregation theory and natural entity theory) invoked the notion of a corporation as the *natural* outcome of *private* interaction, as distinct from an *artificial* state creation. The renewed dominance of these concepts in late-twentieth-century corporate theory can be seen as part of the broader neoconservative revolution.

Developments in Contract Theory

The formal and doctrinally rigid concept of contract in nineteenth-century law probably contributed to the short life of contract-based corporate theory in that era. The traditional legal concept of "contract" refers to certain kinds of legally enforceable obligations. In nineteenth-century doctrine, the enforceability of contract was typically attributed to bargaining and the voluntary exchange of discrete promises, along with a number of technical legal requirements. The United States Supreme Court in *Dartmouth College* relied on a literal and technical notion of contract as an explicit and discrete bargain. Dartmouth's corporate charter had legal status because the incorporators had promised to engage in educational activities in exchange for the state's promise to grant them the legal powers of a corporation. Contract-based models such as Taylor's (1884), however, were conclusory, vaguely sketched, and did not even attempt to satisfy the doctrinal requirements of contract law.

The retheorization of contract as a broader concept in twentieth-century economics and law allowed contract-based corporate theory to return with much greater success. Contemporary contractarianism is remarkably similar to Taylor's (1884) contractual conception, but is far more detailed and finely theorized. In the twentieth century, legal theory and doctrine developed a more expansive concept of contract. Economists used the term to include all voluntary relationships between market participants regardless of exchange or legal enforceability. This broadened definition both coincided with and strongly influenced the roughly contemporaneous expansion of the legal theory of contract. The traditional concept of contract as the exchange of discrete, negotiated terms gave way in the twentieth century as contracts, in practice, were often forms whose terms were offered in preprinted documents with little or no opportunity for negotiation. While some have argued (and continue to argue) that these so-called "adhesion contracts" are less than consensual, others argue that signing a form indicates consent regardless of whether the signer has read or understood the terms. Furthermore, market competition theory suggests that even in the absence of negotiation, form contract providers cannot force unfair terms onto consumers, who can simply take their business elsewhere.

"Relational" contract theory further expanded the notion of contract. Largely credited to MacNeil (1978), it argued both normatively and descriptively that parties entering into contracts did not simply exchange discrete promises to perform narrowly specified obligations. Rather, they transacted within a complex context of social relationships such that the discrete terms of a contract were only part of a deeper, ongoing relationship whose precise content was open-ended and flexible.

Under the theory of "incomplete contracts," as discussed in Hart and Moore (1988), practical limitations such as transaction costs and information costs prevent parties from making agreements that completely and explicitly account for all possible contingencies. Form and relational contracts can be seen as addressing these limitations by reducing transaction costs. Form contracts provide detailed sets of terms without bargaining or drafting. The theory of relational contract suggests that contracts need not expressly provide for all contingencies, as they establish a general relational context in which to address such contingencies.

Contract Theory and Corporate Theory

Coase (1937) is credited with introducing transaction-cost analysis to the theory of the business firm. While accepting the neoclassical economic premise that market exchange is in theory the most efficient method of allocating resources, Coase noted that completing market exchanges can in practice be obstructed by transaction costs, such as shopping for and negotiating deals. He maintained that business enterprises are commonly organized as firms because conducting large-scale production by multiple discrete market transactions would entail excessively high transaction costs. Thus, he argued, entrepreneurs bring production under the single roof of a firm, where production tasks are governed not by contract but by the fiat of the entrepreneur.

Contractarian corporate governance theory owes much to Coase (1937), but crucially rejects his characterization of the firm as an exception to market contracting. Alchian and Demsetz (1972) argued that an entrepreneur does not exercise fiat over the workers he employs. Rather, they reasoned, an employer is a purchaser of the worker's labor and as such has no more despotic power over a worker than a shopper has over the grocer he patronizes. The relationship is a bargained-for economic exchange: that is, a contract.

Following Alchian and Demsetz (1972), who focus on the firm as a way of organizing production, orthodox economic and legal theory applied the contractual model to the corporate form of organizing capital and governance. Jensen and Meckling (1976) famously gave Adam Smith's "other people's money" problem formal theoretical structure and renamed it the phenomenon of "agency cost." Alchian and Demsetz (pp. 5–6) view stocks and bonds as contractual solutions to the question of how to structure principal-agent relationships to minimize agency cost; that is, to "maximize the principal's welfare, and given that uncertainty and imperfect monitoring exist." Stocks, bonds, and other contracts made up a corporation, which was nothing more than a "nexus of contracts."

The efficient capital markets hypothesis (EMH or ECMH), pioneered by Fama (1970), further buttressed the new contractarian theory of the firm and particularly its extension to the corporation. Efficient capital markets protect the purchasers of securities just as competitive product markets protect consumers who sign form contracts. According to EMH, the price of a corporation's publicly traded securities reflects all available information about that security. This theory provides legal scholars with a response to the argument that management had undue power in relation to shareholders. EMH suggests that the market value of the terms of the relationship between management and shareholders in any given firm, as determined by state corporations law, federal securities law, charter, bylaws, management skill, and so on, is reflected in the market price the shareholder paid for his stock, regardless of whether he was aware of any of that information. The capital market has, in effect, bargained for a fair price for those terms, which investors then consent to pay. Efficient capital markets further assure the consensual nature of corporate governance by facilitating a "market for corporate control" that disciplines management: Capital markets translate poor management or exploitative governance terms into reduced stock prices, and extreme declines in stock price leave management vulnerable to hostile takeovers.

Although contractarianism suggests that law is unnecessary, corporate law does exist, suggesting that government plays at least some role in shaping the corporation. Contractarian theorists have accounted for the role of the state by subsuming politics and law into a market model. In doing so, the theory reflects the influences of form, relational and incomplete contract theory, and EMH. Black (1990), for example, argued that the role of corporate governance law is to provide a kind of form contract that mimics the efficient governance terms that most corporations would reach through market contracting anyway, while relieving parties of the transaction costs of actually conducting bargaining. This form contract is only a default governance regime, however. State law allows most governance rules to be altered in the corporate charter. Thus, parties can vary aspects of the form contract if they wish and economize on transaction costs by limiting negotiations to only those terms they wish to change. Relational contract theory helps explain broad principles of corporate law, such as fiduciary duties, as elements of the corporate form contract. The lack of specificity in these principles does not render them noncontractual: Contracts are not limited to imposing discrete rights and duties, but may also establish general relational frameworks.

The "regulatory competition" theory offers an explanation of how U.S. law can produce efficient default rules for corporate governance (Romano 1993). While federal law governs publicly traded securities, the law of the state of incorporation traditionally governs much of the relationship between corporate shareholders and management. The regulatory competition theory posits that states themselves are market actors competing with other states to attract incorporations. Earlier observers claimed (and many continue to claim) that this competition results in a race to the bottom, in which states compete to offer governance rules that favor incorporators and management at the expense of shareholders. Regulatory competition theory, however, holds that states race to the top, not the bottom. Incorporators and managers must migrate to the most efficient governance regimes or efficient capital markets will punish their stock prices. Thus, the theory holds, states compete to provide the most efficient regulatory regimes. States do not coerce shareholders to follow corporate law; rather, shareholders choose the state law they wish to follow. In contrast to the competitive market for charters, the federal government holds a regulatory monopoly on securities law. Regulatory competition theorists have therefore called for the devolution of securities regulation to state governments or liberalized treatment of securities registered in foreign jurisdictions.

In addition to downplaying the role of the state, the contractarian model also deemphasized the role of the shareholder. The fiduciary model had described the relationship between shareholders and management as hierarchical, with managers subservient to their shareholder principals. The decomposition of the corporation into a set of contracts, however, questioned the traditional concept of the shareholder-owned corporation. Fama (1980) explained the supposedly problematic separation of ownership from control as merely the result of distinct markets (and therefore distinct contracts) for two factors of production: risk bearing and management. If governance power is allocated by bargaining, the resultant contract should be expected to protect management interests as well as shareholder interests. Moreover, taken to its logical extreme, the contractarian model questions not only the privileging of shareholders over management, but also the very focus on shareholder-management relations. As Klein (1982) pointed out, contractarianism holds that shareholders are only one among many classes of potential claimants and contracts governing shareholder rights constitute just one among the many types of contracts that make up the corporation.

Challenges and Refinements

Some theorists rejected contractarianism because it tended to privilege shareholders at the expense of parties with whom the corporation had no contracts, such as communities affected by corporate activity, or parties with ostensibly narrow explicit contracts such as workers or bondholders. This perspective, sometimes referred to as the "stakeholderist" or "other constituencies" view, is well represented in Mitchell (1995). It was particularly salient during the hostile takeover wave of the 1980s. Hostile takeovers were justified as making profits for shareholders, but the stakeholderists argued that those profits were often gained at the expense of employees and local economies.

Some stakeholder advocates' arguments are reminiscent of Dodd's (1954) reliance on corporate directors' discretion to define and serve the public interest. Others, such as Greenfield (2006, 123), argue for regulation on the grounds that "corporate law is public rather than private law," due to the impact of corporate activity on multiple constituents across society. Still others assign a more active role to nonshareholder constituencies, in the manner of Berle and Means (1932). For example, the "power model," a noncontractual approach advanced by Dallas (1988), holds that the goals a corporation pursues are determined by the outcomes of an ongoing power struggle among various constituencies competing to influence corporate goals. While this is largely consistent with contractarianism's rejection of shareholder-centrism, it expands the scope of inquiry by emphasizing that constituencies that engage in no formal economic transactions with the corporation (such as neighboring communities or environmental advocates) can at least theoretically participate in the struggle to determine the goals of the corporation. Furthermore, the power model recognizes that political processes shape law and thus shape corporations. It also emphasizes that the existing allocation of governance power is only the temporary result of current conditions, a point that is consistent with contractarianism but rarely emphasized.

As noted earlier, contractarianism questioned the received wisdom of the fiduciary model. Some theorists have sought to restate shareholder-centric corporate governance in contractarian terms. According to this approach, shareholder rights are the most efficient way of compensating shareholders for risking their capital in the corporate enterprise. According to Easterbrook and Fischel (1983, 403), management should be (and is) responsive to shareholder wealth concerns because shareholders "receive most of the marginal gains and incur most of the marginal costs" of corporate activity and thus have incentive to make efficient business decisions. While governance structures are open-ended and resist definition in discrete terms, the relational contract perspective suggests that they may nonetheless constitute contracts and that their open-endedness is in fact a common feature of contracts.

As a descriptive matter, however, the apology for shareholder-centrism tends to overstate the actual rights of shareholders. The hierarchical corporate governance structure that arose a century ago remains the rule today. While shareholders vote for directors, directors typically run unopposed, and while incumbent boards may use corporate resources and mailings to make nominations, shareholders may not. Directors delegate most managerial power to appointed executives whom shareholders have no power to remove. The deferential business judgment rule also remains a centerpiece of corporate law. A recent leading case, *In re Walt Disney Company Derivative Litigation* (2006, 55), confirmed the deferential approach by holding that directors whose conduct "fell significantly short of the best practices of ideal corporate governance" were not liable because the standard of legal liability is considerably lower than "best practices."

Contractarian theorists have more recently formulated models that account for hierarchical corporate governance. The two leading legal models in this vein are the "team production" and "director primacy" models. Both focus on the board, reflecting Eisenberg's (1976) influential distinction between boards and executives.

The theories posit that the board's function is much broader than monitoring, however. Taking advantage of the broad contemporary notions of contract, they suggest that corporate constituents have contracted to give directors broad discretion over corporate affairs for the ultimate benefit of corporate constituents. As Bainbridge (2008, 45), the author of the director primacy model, argues: "The firm's constituents voluntarily enter into a relationship in which they accept the power of fiat, while reserving the right to dissociate from the firm." The idea of voluntary submission to fiat may seem oxymoronic in a narrowly literal sense. As transaction cost theory and the related incomplete and relational contracting perspectives suggest, however, consenting to fiat may be an efficient way to assign corporate governance powers. Explicitly defining all rights and duties would entail prohibitive transaction costs. Further, diversified investors lack the time and expertise to participate actively in governance.

While the team production and director primacy models agree that hierarchical governance results from a contract between directors and corporate constituents, they differ sharply on the identity of the relevant constituents. Under the team production theory espoused by Blair and Stout (1999), the board of directors contracts with *all* constituents, who authorize the board to run the enterprise with broad discretion to balance all constituents' interests. The weight given to each constituent's interests will be influenced by that constituent's bargaining power relative to the board and the other constituents. Like Dodd's (1954) model of broad director trusteeship and Dallas's (1988) power model, the team production model could thus turn corporate priorities in almost any conceivable direction. But Dodd's model rests on a faith in directors' assessment of the public interest, and Dallas argues that any political interest group could attempt to influence corporate goals. Compared to those models, team production narrows the scope of director discretion and the relevant constituencies. It contends that directors balance the self-interest of multiple contracting parties in accordance with each constituent's relative economic value to the enterprise. This eliminates parties affected by the corporation who do not have contracts with the corporation and limits directors' role to balancing contract claims, rather than serving the public interest.

The director primacy model further narrows the scope of director duty. Unlike the team production theory, under which the ultimate purpose of the corporate enterprise is negotiated among all its constituents, the director primacy model maintains that shareholders hire directors to maximize shareholder wealth and are thus the only constituents of directors. Bainbridge (2008) argues that making directors answerable to multiple constituents, as the team production model purports to do, renders their duties indeterminate and makes governance decisions difficult, freeing directors from accountability. Bainbridge (p. 66) notes that this indeterminacy would raise the cost of capital: "Shareholders will view a director preference for other constituencies as a risk demanding compensatory returns." While the team production model holds that directors will focus on shareholder wealth only as long as the competition for capital requires it, the director primacy model sees the rule as inflexible because shareholders, relative to other contractual constituents such as bondholders or employees, are less able to negotiate for specific contractual protections.

Under the director primacy model, shareholders voluntarily assume the risk of bad corporate leadership with their only immediate recourse being to sell their shares. Directors are disciplined not by legal duties to shareholders but by the capital market and the market for corporate control. This approach answers the criticism, noted earlier, that a duty to maximize shareholder wealth is a meaningless constraint because it is vaguely defined and cannot be enforced in court: Shareholders define wealth maximization as they wish and enforce their definitions through investment decisions rather than lawsuits. The use of the term "contract" in this context, however, brings up a deep irony of the contractarian model's success in the legal academy. Until the relatively recent entry of economic contractarian discourse into legal theory, "contract" was typically used in law to distinguish legally enforceable obligations from unenforceable ones. (Precisely what obligations are enforceable, and which of these are properly called contracts, were, and remain, highly contested.) While some early legal contractarians insisted that corporate governance consisted of legally enforceable contracts, contractarian legal theorists now much more commonly use the term "contract" in the nonlegal sense of a voluntary interaction. Bainbridge (2008, 45), for example, specifies that many of the contracts that make up corporations in his model are "unenforceable." Thus the concept of "contract" so central to the legal theory of corporate governance is no longer a legal concept.

The main normative challengers to director-led hierarchy are advocates of increased shareholder governance power, such as Bebchuk (2005). The challengers maintain that director discretion does not maximize either shareholder wealth or the joint corporate product. They argue that capital markets are insufficient to prevent directors' inattention, self-dealing, or capture by executives. The conflict has played out in practical issues, such as whether shareholders should have increased ability to nominate directors and approve executive compensation. As with many post-Realist approaches to the subject, shareholder advocates do not rely on a uniform comprehensive essentialist model. Their position is consistent with the tradition of the fiduciary model and the accountability debate between Berle (1931) and Dodd (1954), but is sometimes presented as an attempt to reform governance "contracts" that have been distorted by market failures.

As a descriptive matter, many corporate governance scholars argue that the analytical focus on directors is misplaced. They argue that real power belongs to CEOs and other senior executives. They maintain that the role of the board is merely nominal and boards do not engage in active monitoring or managing. Anecdotally, many high-profile incidents have shown passive boards failing to oversee executive management. Board passivity has been blamed in part for the failure of Enron Corporation and many of its contemporaries. Leading cases on directors' duties such as *In re Caremark Int'l, Inc., Derivative Litigation* (1996) and the aforementioned *Walt Disney* (2006) hold that directors need to engage in only minimal oversight. While the high salaries of American CEOs are sometimes defended as economically justified, they are popularly understood as proof that CEO power trumps shareholder interests and board oversight. Bebchuk and Fried (2004) have advanced empirical research in support of this managerialist intuition. Bainbridge (2008), however, cites other evidence suggesting boards have become more active in recent years in response to such criticism.

The coming years may yield new insight into the role of corporate boards as board behavior leading up to the 2008 financial crash comes under legal scrutiny. Unfortunately, directly observing boards in action is difficult and practices vary by corporation, so scholars on both sides of the descriptive debate must rely on anecdotal and circumstantial evidence. Indeed, it may be an overgeneralization to posit that corporate control lies with either directors or executives. As a descriptive matter, different corporations allocate power differently between their boards and executives (not to mention other constituents, such as shareholders, creditors, and labor). As a normative matter, different allocations of power may be preferable in different situations. In contractarian terms, shareholders (and perhaps other constituents) could be said to contract in some instances for directorial control of the enterprise and in some instances for executive control. Indeed, portfolio theory would seem to suggest investors would prefer a marketplace with a variety of different governance arrangements.

POST-CONTRACTARIAN DIRECTIONS

Although contractarianism remains the dominant theory approach in legal academia, many of its underlying assumptions are being questioned. "Behavioral finance," pioneered by De Bondt and Thaler (1985), predicts and describes certain types of irrational investment behavior. The theory has made significant inroads into the legal academy through the work of Langevoort (2002) and others. The regulatory competition thesis has also been challenged. Kahan and Kamar (2002), for example, argue that the states do not engage in anything resembling market competition.

After decades of model-building based on efficient-market and contractarian theories, the current state of corporate governance theory might be characterized as a model-destroying phase. Confidence in the efficiency of capital markets and in rational economic behavior more generally has been battered by the evidence of market irrationality in the financial crash of 2008 and the dot-com bubble. Some of the most famous advocates of EMH, from Eugene Fama in academia to Alan Greenspan in government, have recently expressed doubts about market rationality. Some defenders of the old models complain that the new theorists offer no comprehensive alternative models, citing the aphorism, "It takes a model to beat a model." Behavioral finance so far does not seem to offer an elegant, parsimonious theory comparable to the rational behavior model. That apparent weakness, however, may in fact be its most significant contribution. As the best theorists appreciate, rational behavior theory, and grand constructs generally, offer ease of comprehension at the cost of oversimplification. The spectacular recent failures in the financial markets illustrate how the costs of oversimplification can outweigh the benefits.

SUMMARY AND CONCLUSIONS

While contractarianism relies heavily on assumptions about the efficiency of capital or regulatory markets, a different kind of contract-based justification of corporate governance could proceed without them. By incorporating efficient-market assumptions, contractarianism makes two claims: that governance is consensual and that it is efficient. The two claims, though related, appeal to two independent normative commitments. Assume for the sake of argument that markets and the governance contracts they produce are inefficient. On the one hand, technocrats, such as government agencies or stock-exchange officials, might produce more efficient terms in at least some circumstances. The question would arise whether the economic gain in efficiency would justify the political loss of self-determination. On the other hand, governance that is contractual (in the economic sense of the term) would be by definition consensual even if it were inefficient. This fact raises the reverse of the previous question: whether the political value of liberty would justify an economically inefficient system. By assuming that unregulated markets are efficient, contractarianism conflates the two values of liberty and efficiency, obscuring their independent normative importance and the tension between them. As economic thinking came to pervade political and moral reasoning in recent decades, efficiency (in the sense of greater aggregate social wealth) became increasingly important relative to other values such as promise, consent, and equity. Whether the current financial crisis marks another cyclical shift in values remains to be seen.

The point here is not to argue that evidence of market inefficiency now requires theorists to choose between central economic planning and liberty. There are, of course, compromises that would reconcile markets and efficiency, such as the argument that markets, however inefficient, are more efficient than regulation. The purpose here is a broader focus on models (including contractarianism) and their usefulness in concentrating normative discussion.

Essentialist models, even those that primarily describe corporate governance, serve to justify the status quo or argue for reform. For example, by describing corporate governance as contractual, contractarianism justifies the permissive nature of most of existing corporate law, while implying that mandatory legal rules are improper. Dewey (1926) complained that the normative conclusions of essentialist models were logically indeterminate. As Hager (1989) has argued, however, legal concepts draw their strength not only (or even primarily) from logic but also from their appeals to preexisting normative visions. Those visions tend to change with time.

Furthermore, as Horwitz (1992, 68) has argued, a given model's normative applications may become limited as it develops particular normative associations through "history and usage." For example, when ideas such as natural entity and corporatism first appeared, they provided potential justifications for either managerialist control, as Dodd (1932) argued, or regulation in the public interest, as Berle and Means (1932) seemed to suggest. They lost that potential ability to justify normative arguments because they acquired undesirable normative associations unrelated to their actual content: The general emphasis on groups as entities may have been too reminiscent of socialism and communism and too alien to American individualism. Further, as Bratton and Wachter (2008) argue, fascist regimes of the 1930s expressly adopted corporatist theory. Similarly, contractarianism has the potential to broaden the definition of corporate constituents, but has also been associated with favoring the shareholder contract over all others. Thus, attempts to define corporate *contracts* to include informal guarantees to workers and communities affected by plant closings, while consistent with relational contract theory, have not been successful.

As Dewey (1926) argued, models often masquerade as proofs of normative positions that are external to the models. But as the foregoing analysis has attempted to show, models can be useful in identifying and isolating the normative commitments they assume and appeal to. This kind of analysis need not be reserved for retrospective historical commentary. Careful construction of models should include contemporaneous acknowledgment and examination of these commitments. Among corporate theorists, Bainbridge (2008) is particularly and unusually candid in this regard. Legal doctrine necessarily strikes compromises among competing normative visions or chooses among them. Theorists should use abstract models not to disguise these unspoken normative visions but to flush them out and clearly define them. Theorists and lawmakers can then apply themselves to debating the wisdom of the law's choice of normative goals and its success at realizing those goals.

DISCUSSION QUESTIONS

1. Who are the owners of a corporation: shareholders, bondholders, workers, society, or someone else? What is the meaning of the statement that some constituency *owns* a corporation? What is the difference between an *ownership* relationship and a *contract* relationship to the corporation? Are these two kinds of relationships superior to other kinds of relationships?
2. Should the goals of a corporation be determined by a judicially enforceable duty to maximize shareholder wealth, the outcome of a political struggle to set priorities in the public interest, management discretion, or in some other way? Why? Can models or theories of the corporation help answer this question, or question 1?
3. One model of the corporation common in popular discourse but not discussed here is *corporate democracy*. Analyze this model with an eye to what the chapter calls "identifying and isolating" the normative commitments embedded in it.
4. As Bratton (1989) points out, corporate law doctrine has avoided committing itself to any one essentialist model of the corporation. What are the advantages and drawbacks of this approach as compared to the theoretical search for a single unifying model?

REFERENCES

Alchian, Armen A., and Harold Demsetz. 1972. Production, information costs, and economic organization. *American Economic Review* 62 (5): 777–795.

Bainbridge, Stephen M. 2008. *The new corporate governance in theory and practice.* New York: Oxford University Press.

Bebchuk, Lucian Arye. 2005. The case for increasing shareholder power. *Harvard Law Review* 118 (3): 833–914.

Bebchuk, Lucian, and Jesse Fried. 2004. *Pay without performance: The unfulfilled promise of executive compensation.* Cambridge: Harvard University Press.

Berle, Adolf. A., Jr. 1931. Corporate powers as powers in trust. *Harvard Law Review* 44 (7): 1049–1074.

Berle, Adolf. A., Jr., and Gardner C. Means. 1932. *The modern corporation and private property.* New York: The Macmillan Company.

Black, Bernard S. 1990. Is corporate law trivial? A political and economic analysis. *Northwestern University Law Review* 84 (2): 542–597.

Blair, Margaret M., and Lynn A. Stout. 1999. A team production theory of corporate law. *Virginia Law Review* 85 (2): 247–328.

Bratton, William W., Jr. 1989. The new economic theory of the firm: Critical perspectives from history. *Stanford Law Review* 41 (6): 1471–1528.
Bratton, William W., Jr., and Michael L. Wachter. 2008. Shareholder primacy's corporatist origins: Adolf Berle and the modern corporation. *Journal of Corporation Law* 34 (1): 99–152.
Chandler, Alfred D., Jr. 1977. *The visible hand: The managerial revolution in American business.* Cambridge: Belknap Press of Harvard University Press.
Coase, R. H. 1937. The nature of the firm. *Economica* 4 (16): 386–405.
Dallas, Lynne L. 1988. Two models of corporate governance: Beyond Berle and Means. *University of Michigan Journal of Law Reform* 22 (1): 19–116.
De Bondt, Werner F. M., and Richard Thaler. 1985. Does the stock market overreact? *Journal of Finance*, 40 (3): 793–808.
Dodd, E. Merrick, Jr. 1932. For whom are corporate managers trustees? *Harvard Law Review* 45 (7): 1145–1163.
———. 1954. *American business corporations until 1860 with special reference to Massachusetts.* Cambridge: Harvard University Press.
Dewey, John. 1926. The historic background of corporate legal personality. *Yale Law Journal* 35 (6): 655–673.
Easterbrook, Frank H., and Daniel R. Fischel. 1983. Voting in corporate law. *Journal of Law and Economics* 26 (2): 395–427.
Eisenberg, Melvin Aron. 1976. *The structure of the corporation: A legal analysis.* Boston: Little, Brown.
Fama, Eugene F. 1970. Efficient capital markets: A review of theory and empirical work. *Journal of Finance* 25 (2): 383–423.
Fama, Eugene F. 1980. Agency problems and the theory of the firm. *Journal of Political Economy* 88 (2): 288–307.
Galbraith, John Kenneth. 1967. *The new industrial state.* Boston: Houghton Mifflin.
Gevurtz, Franklin A. 1994. The business judgment rule: Meaningless verbiage or misguided notion? *Southern California Law Review* 67 (2): 287–337.
Greenfield, Kent. 2006. *The failure of corporate law.* Chicago: University of Chicago Press.
Hager, Mark. 1989. Bodies politic: The progressive history of organizational "real entity" theory. *University of Pittsburgh Law Review* 50 (2): 575–654.
Hart, Oliver, and John Moore. 1988. Incomplete contracts and renegotiation. *Econometrica*, 56 (4): 755–785.
Horwitz, Morton J. 1992. *The transformation of American law, 1870–1960: The crisis of legal orthodoxy.* New York: Oxford University Press.
Jensen, Michael C., and William H. Meckling. 1976. Theory of the firm: Managerial behavior, agency costs and ownership structure. *Journal of Financial Economics* 3 (4): 305–360.
Kahan, Marcel, and Ehud Kamar. 2002. The myth of state competition in corporate law. *Stanford Law Review* 55 (3): 679–749.
Klein, William A. 1982. The modern business organization: Bargaining under constraints. *Yale Law Journal* 91 (8): 1521–1564.
Langevoort, Donald C. 2002. Taming the animal spirits of the stock markets: A behavioral approach to securities regulation. *Northwestern University Law Review* 97 (1): 135–188.
MacNeil, Ian R. 1978. Contracts: Adjustment of long-term economic relations under classical, neoclassical, and relational contract law. *Northwestern University Law Review* 72 (6): 854–905.
Mitchell, Lawrence E., ed. 1995. *Progressive corporate law.* Boulder, CO: Westview Press.
Romano, Roberta. 1993. *The genius of American corporate law.* Washington, DC: AEI Press.
Smith, Adam. 1776. *An inquiry into the nature and causes of the wealth of nations.* New York: Modern Library. (Cited from Cannan edition, 1937.)
Taylor, Henry O. 1884. *A treatise on the law of private corporations having capital stock.* Philadelphia: Kay & Brother.

CASE LAW

Bank of the United States v. Devaux, 9 U.S. 61 (1809).
In re Caremark Int'l., Inc., Derivative Litigation, 698 A.2d 959 (Del.Ch. 1996).
In re Walt Disney Co. Derivative Litigation, 906 A.2d 27(Del. 2006).
Percy v. Millaudon, 8 Mart. (n.s.) 68 (La. 1829).
San Mateo v. Southern Pacific Railroad, 13 F. 722 (C.C.Cal. 1882).
Santa Clara v. Southern Pacific Railroad, 118 U.S. 394 (1886).
Stone v. State of Mississippi, 101 U.S. 814 (1880).
Trustees of Dartmouth College v. Woodward, 17 U.S. 518 (1819).

ABOUT THE AUTHOR

Thomas W. Joo is a professor of law at the University of California, Davis, School of Law. He is the editor of *Corporate Governance: Law, Theory and Policy* (Carolina Academic Press, 2nd ed., 2010) and the author of numerous law journal articles on corporate governance, contracts, and critical race theory. Prior to joining the UC Davis faculty, he served as clerk to the Honorable Judge Wilfred Feinberg of the United States Court of Appeals for the Second Circuit and as an associate at the law firm of Cleary Gottlieb Steen and Hamilton. Professor Joo received his JD from Harvard Law School. The author would like to thank the UC Davis School of Law for financial support and Adam Lunceford for research assistance.

CHAPTER 10

Unfettered Agents? The Role of Ethics in Corporate Governance

DONALD NORDBERG
Senior Lecturer, Westminster Business School

INTRODUCTION

> *The directors . . . being the managers rather of other people's money than of their own, it cannot well be expected that they should watch over it with the same anxious vigilance with which the partners in a private copartnery frequently watch over their own. Like the stewards of a rich man, they are apt to consider attention to small matters as not for their master's honour, and very easily give themselves a dispensation from having it. Negligence and profusion, therefore, must always prevail, more or less, in the management of the affairs of such a company.*
>
> (Smith 1776/1904, V.1.107)

Headlines do not tell the whole story, but they highlight the issues. Sometimes a phrase speaks volumes: fat cat, poison pill, say on pay, whistle-blower, and watchdog. Sometimes just the names can tell a tale: Maxwell, Polly Peck, Enron, WorldCom, Ahold, Parmalat, Bear Stearns, and Lehman Brothers.

From the earliest days of the corporation, scholars, practitioners, and business executives have worried about how to control the unfettered agent. Once owners no longer want to manage their businesses and hire others to take their place, they face a problem. Specifically, the owners' agent might not watch over the business with the same anxious vigilance as the owner. Adam Smith was mindful of this, though perhaps too polite to say that the agent might prove self-serving and not just act as the "stewards of a rich man." He may not have imagined these agents would go on to aspire to become truly rich men themselves.

More than half a century later, Mill (1848/1909, I.9.15) drew a fresh distinction between managers (what he called the "administration by hired servants") and the oversight of directors. These directors held only a small proportion of the capital and divided their time between other occupations. According to Mill (I.9.17), they could not be expected to take great care with "small gains and small savings." What today are called *outside directors* in the United States and *nonexecutives* in Great Britain are agents monitoring the work of another set of agents, the managers. Directors often lack the time and, in some cases, the commitment to attend to the business and managers they are meant to oversee.

By the time of the Wall Street Crash in 1929 and the subsequent Great Depression, an added complication existed. The *joint stock companies* of the Victorian era had evolved into the *modern corporation* of Adolf Berle and Gardiner Means. Although these companies would be dwarfed by those of today, they seemed giants at the time. Their stock was held in small amounts by distant owners who lacked the economic clout to assert their moral rights over the corporation and its wealth. Berle and Means (1932/1991, 8) worried that the separation of ownership and control was inevitable and "destroys the very foundation on which the economic order of the past three centuries has rested."

That foundation was the careful investment of capital to create products that could be sold at a profit. This created more capital to be invested, resulting in a virtuous cycle. The owner might leave day-to-day management to pursue another business or take leisure time. At the owner's death, the heirs may be unable or unwilling to manage. Entrepreneurial owners might not be equipped mentally to run a large-scale business so they turn to professional managers to pick up the reins. Viewed in economic terms, these actions yield benefits but entail costs. What arises is at least superficially a simple calculus: Measure the benefits, including the opportunities gained from not having to manage the business, and subtract the costs. The extra benefits of a diligent and competent manager might well justify a large cash payment, perhaps even a share of the business. The "net benefits" of a slothful or deceitful one, however, could be ruination. Gathering the information needed to recruit the diligent rather than the slothful manager has a cost that must be added to the equation. Paying someone else to interpret that information adds another cost.

Monitoring and controlling the agent is still possible for the owner with a large stake in the business and perhaps worth the cost of doing so. But what of all the distant shareholders who have only a small stake? What of the specialized investment firms that have a small stake in many businesses? In the modern corporation, Berle and Means (1932/1991) saw situations in which none of the owners thought they could justify the cost of monitoring and control. In the Crash of 1929 and the Great Depression that followed, Berle and Means saw the consequences of owners' collective nonaction: the macroeconomic cost of the unfettered agent.

Even without a stock market crash, the agent can do damage. What happens when the agents are self-serving, extracting more than their fair share of the proceeds of the business? Without controls, the unfettered agent might drain away the profits, essentially stealing the owners' property. Some of these actions will be governed under law and contract. Between the scope of law and the many individual decisions that managers and directors make, however, lies a large pool of actions where agents exercise discretion and decide upon what is fair. If Berle and Means (1932/1991) were right and the "very foundation" of economic order had been "destroyed," then perhaps a phenomenon exists with moral rather than just economic implications. What role then does ethics play in the governance of the modern corporation?

Nordberg (2009) notes that ownership of the modern corporation that Berle and Means (1932/1991) described has changed somewhat in the intervening decades. Through collective investment vehicles such as mutual funds, pension funds, hedge funds, equity derivatives, stock lending, and other new instruments, ownership of companies has taken on a more complex meaning. The separation of ownership from control is more pronounced and less complete than in the corporation described by Berle and Means. Short-selling opens the possibility that the economic interests of some shareholders could be opposite those of others, and even perverse to the interests of the business. Directors are charged in law with looking after the interests of the business—the company and its shareholders—duties that open new sorts of obligations. The requirements differ from jurisdiction to jurisdiction, making directors (and indeed the law) less certain that the interests of the company and of its shareholders are one and the same thing. In the face of many claims on the company's resources, how does a director decide which course of action is right and which apportionment of the company's resources fair?

This chapter provides an examination of the various theoretical approaches that scholars have used to describe directors' duties. It also sets these against the major currents of thought about ethics to help provide an understanding of what philosophical assumptions underpin the many prescriptions of good governance. Finally, the chapter considers to what extent those concepts provide the locus of how directors decide.

CORPORATE GOVERNANCE IN THEORY

The development of corporate governance theory mirrors closely what MacAvoy and Millstein (2003) called the "recurrent crisis" facing corporations and the system of capitalism on which they are based. The 1929 Crash sparked not only the Berle and Means (1932/1991) reflections on the problems presented by the evolution of corporations but also led to new ways of thinking about the economic purpose of corporations. Coase (1937) argued that by reducing the cost of producing goods and services, corporations enhance what economists call *utility*, the usefulness of the outcome. Corporations, however, did not necessarily need to get larger, more remote, and more powerful at the expense of efficiency in creating goods and services.

During World War II, the corporation became subordinated to the needs of the state. This led to a hiatus in the debate over corporate purpose and direction. In the benign decades of economic recovery that followed, corporations basked in growth and shareholders grew complacent with regular dividends and capital gains. With a change in the macroeconomy in the 1970s characterized by stagflation, a shift occurred in the nature of shareholding and a related concern that corporations were no longer serving the needs of owners. The new owners were increasingly institutional investors with a louder voice than the distant, small shareholders whose interests Berle and Means (1932/1991) had at heart. Some began to question current arrangements with the intent of making owners less distant from managers and boards.

Corporate governance thinking developed slowly in subsequent years until a crisis of confidence emerged in the early 1990s. In the United Kingdom, a series of corporate frauds led to questions about how boards neglected the interests of owners and, at times, worked directly against owners' interests. Reforms in law and custom-and-practice followed, but so, too, did another crisis. Enron collapsed in 2001 and WorldCom in 2002. In the following years, a host of other U.S. companies collapsed that were promptly followed by the fall of Parmalat and Ahold in Europe and HIH in Australia. More changes in law and custom-and-practice ensued. In 2007–2008 came the collapse of Bear Stearns, Lehman Brothers, and much of the global banking industry. These failures again ignited concerns that corporate managers were out of control and that boards of directors had not carried out their responsibilities or were complicit.

Agency Theory

The issue raised by Smith (1776/1904), Mill (1848/1909), and later by Berle and Means (1932/1991) is often called the *agency problem*. Agency theory holds that managers, without a stake in the business, can only be expected to work in their own interests. The theory further assumes that shareholders hold a singular perspective of maximizing their wealth through share price increases or through dividend payments. In this view, managers and shareholders hold the same economic goal—to maximize their personal well-being. However, in pursuing their individual well-being, the interests of managers and shareholders may diverge. Jensen and Meckling (1976) first articulated this view at the same time that emerging theories of corporate finance—the efficient market hypothesis (EMH) and modern portfolio theory (MPT)—raised questions about the value of conglomerate corporations, presumably built up by self-serving and increasingly powerful agents. No longer was the manager the timid, risk-averse, inattentive agent imagined by Smith and Mill. Modern corporations with their chief executive officers (CEOs) had become empires built on someone else's money.

The increased scope for malfeasance and misdemeanors, as well as empire-building, led to calls for greater control. Following the lead of Jensen and Meckling (1976), agency theorists developed a variety of prescriptions about how to monitor managers and provide incentives to align managers' interests with the interests of shareholders. Scholars, including Fama (1980) and Eisenhardt (1989), developed a basis of thinking that would come to dominate the discussion of corporate governance. Others contributing to this discussion include D'Aveni and Kesner (1993), Bebchuk (2005), Gomez-Mejia and Wiseman (2007), Zahra (2007), Kumar and Sivaramakrishnan (2008), and McKnight and Weir (2009).

Prescriptive uses of agency theory build upon the notion that agents and principals share a self-serving motivation for wealth creation. By giving top managers a stake in the business and its outcomes, the interests of the agents will be more in line with those of the principals. This theoretical perspective laid the foundation for a growing reliance on incentive pay based on financial targets and stock options that focused managers on the task of creating shareholder value. The recipe involved a combination of profits to fund dividends, share buybacks, and organic growth; and leverage to fund acquisitions and increase earnings per share, leading to share price appreciation and eventual capital gains. The agency perspective insists that the purpose of the corporation is to create wealth for its owners. Sharing wealth with managers—an agency cost—is justified provided that managers create substantially more wealth than they receive. But the portion shared with managers might not be enough to solve the agency problem.

To prevent fraud and misdemeanor, corporations also needed stronger boards. Such boards should consist of more than just cronies of the CEO or big-name trophy directors who paid little attention to the business. Boards needed to act as controllers of managers. Hence, the emphasis shifted to independent outside directors strong enough to stand up to the CEO and override decisions when necessary. Boards represent another direct agency cost. When boards do not work, further layers are needed, including independent audit committees, direct nomination of directors by shareholders, annual election of directors, and named senior independent directors to give institutional investors direct access to a potentially countervailing voice in the boardroom. Tying managers down from a sufficient number of directions will fetter the agent to the interests of the principal. Each of these controlling actions, however, involves a cost.

Stewardship Theory

To some scholars and many businesspeople, the agency portrait of the manager seems unduly pessimistic. Are managers really so self-serving? Is money their only motivation? Is a business nothing more than a nexus of contracts, as Coase (1937), Williamson (1985 and 1988), and Eisenhardt (1989) argue, with the purpose of efficiency?

Donaldson and Davis (1991) thought such questions were at odds with the realities they saw. That is, the economic model of man in agency theory captured only one aspect of how executives and directors view their work. They advanced a competing notion: Managers generally seek to do a good job of looking after the assets they control for the good of the company. The approach of Donaldson and Davis (p. 51), which arises from psychology rather than economics, views people in organizations as "motivated by a need to achieve, to gain intrinsic satisfaction through successfully performing inherently challenging work, to exercise responsibility and authority, and thereby to gain recognition from peers and bosses." If correct, then exactly the opposite response might occur from managers and boards of directors from that predicted by agency theory.

Perhaps the most central provision of good corporate governance is the separation of the chairman and CEO positions. Agency theory suggests that having a strong chairman, one able to challenge the CEO, would curb executive power. Though initially an added cost, this separation would pay for itself by reducing the cost of the unfettered agent. But if stewardship theory is right and executives are not merely self-interested actors, then a dual chair-CEO would provide clearer focus and lead to stronger value creation and not mere cost control.

Using data from U.S. companies, Donaldson and Davis (1991) show that companies with joint chair-CEOs produced better financial performance, irrespective of specific incentives to align executive pay with shareholder interests. The authors question the premise implicit in normative uses of agency theory that the primary role of the board is to monitor managers. Donaldson and Davis argue that agency theory, with its roots in organizational economics and transaction-cost approaches, takes a reductionist view of behavior. Stewardship theory, by contrast, with roots in psychology and organizational behavior, involves an optimistic view of managerial motivation, one that values the notions of higher motivations in the hierarchy of an executive's needs (Maslow 1943 and 1954).

This view is not blind to the possibility that executives might work mainly for money. Davis, Schoorman, and Donaldson (1997) suggest a contingency approach that balances the economic forces of agency theory and the psychological forces of stewardship theory, with the outcome dependent upon the company's circumstances. Managers who identify more with the company, who are more committed to its values, and who are more intrinsically motivated, are more likely to take a stewardship approach. Stewards are more likely than agents to value higher-order needs.

Davis et al. (1997) provide clues to help identify when senior managers are more likely to see themselves as stewards rather than agents. Stewards are more likely to rely on personal sources of power—*expert* and *referent* in the sense of French and Raven (1959)—while agents use institutional sources of power (French and Raven's *legitimate*, *coercive*, and *reward* power). Stewards are also more likely to adopt collectivist goals rather than individual goals and thrive in cultures with "low power distance" (Hofstede 1980). Stewards should thrive, therefore, in situations of trust, where agents might prove exploitative. The prescriptions of agency theory, with their reliance on control over managerial action, would be the wrong approach to take with managers who see themselves as stewards.

Davis et al. (1997) suggest that agency and stewardship theory taken together represented something of a prisoner's dilemma, the problem often seen as the center of game theory. If managers acted as agents and shareholders expected them to do so, then a high degree of control through a strong and independent board focused on monitoring management's actions would minimize risk. If executives acted as stewards and shareholders expected them to do so, then the ensuing trust would be rightly placed. That is, managers would concentrate on value creation, resulting in greater gains. The dilemma heightens when shareholders and executives differ in their view of their roles. If shareholders expect stewardship but executives act as agents, the executives could siphon off value from the company for private use. If executives are inclined towards stewardship and shareholders respond with the strong monitoring appropriate for agents, executives would become frustrated and leave, or work in suboptimal ways.

Why, then, is there so much emphasis on agency? Davis et al. (1997) propose that concerns in the literature of corporate governance arise from shareholders being risk averse. Mainstream institutional investors are, after all, a rather conservative group. They seek predictable returns, so the checks and balances implied in stronger board monitoring is a means of minimizing risk. The imprint of shareholder risk aversion appears in the debate over the original Cadbury Code (Cadbury 1992) and its subsequent development (Greenbury 1995; Hampel 1998; Higgs 2003; Financial Reporting Council 2006 and 2008) in the United Kingdom, in the formation of governance codes in other countries (Veniot 1995; Cromme Commission 2002/2007; Lippens 2004; OECD 2004, among others), and in the efforts of activist pension funds lobbying for similar positions in the United States. Marxist scholars such as Lysandrou and Stoyanova (2007) see in investors' demands for good governance an attempt to turn corporate earnings into a commodity in which a steady flow of dividends is more important than value creation.

Risk aversion can, however, lead companies to forgo opportunities. This sentiment might, even more than personal greed, explain the discomfort many executives expressed after the adoption of both the Sarbanes-Oxley Act of 2002 in the United States and the board governance guidelines by NASDAQ (2002) and the New York Stock Exchange (2003) as well as the codes of conduct proliferating around the world (Aguilera and Cuervo-Cazurra 2009). This focus in codes on formal elements of corporate governance practice has led to complaints from boards that governance has gone over the top (Brabeck-Letmathe 2005;

Nordberg 2007b). As discussed by Maharahj (2008, 77), consider the unidentified executive who complained that "a few bad actors have caused huge changes, where we are proscribing solutions . . . it is almost like the innocent being punished while the guilty go free."

Treating stewards as if they were agents introduces a new agency cost: the opportunity cost of misplaced fears. If the unfettered agent represents a potentially dangerous cost to the business, so too does the fettered steward.

Stakeholder Theory

Corporate governance theory has long contrasted two roles for the board—control and value creation—but now includes a further strand: stakeholder theory. This theory traces its roots to the radical thinking of Freeman (1984). In what might be called its weak form, the once revolutionary ideas of stakeholder theory now seem self-evident: Suppliers, customers, and employees all contribute to the business. Insofar as treating stakeholders well is instrumental to corporate financial performance, it makes economic sense to shareholders to also look after stakeholder interests. This view sat comfortably alongside a parallel shift in emphasis in strategy toward a resources-based approach (Wernerfelt 1984; Barney 1995) and in accounting and marketing toward the importance of nonfinancial metrics (Kaplan and Norton 1992; Rust, Lemon, and Zeithaml 2004).

The corporate governance literature now abounds with references to stakeholder theory. Germany, with its two-tier system of boards, is perhaps the extreme example of stakeholder theory. German law grants seats on the senior or *supervisory* board to members of the workforce. For a long period, banks and insurance companies also had privileged board positions as holders of large blocks of equity. In addition, Japan has a stakeholder orientation owing to the favored treatment of suppliers and customers in the families of companies known as *keiretsu*, as well as in the common practice of assuring jobs for life.

These approaches developed many admirers, especially in the 1980s when German economic performance was the envy of all and Japanese industry began to dominate large swathes of global manufacturing. But these countries have come under increasing strain in the past decade. Globalization of portfolio investment and the decisions by German banks to sell off their strategic stakes led German companies to place more emphasis on financial performance. Japan's lost decade of economic growth in the 1990s and early 2000s put strains on the *keiretsu* as the banking system went through consolidation and many companies ended paternalistic employment practices.

In formulating the theory, Freeman (1984) exploits a rhetorical device embedded in his neologism to make people think that *stakeholders*—employees, customers, suppliers and others—are owed a duty of care akin to that of *stockholders*. According to Freeman (p. 45), words "make a difference in how we see the world. By using the term 'stakeholder' managers and theorists alike will come to see these groups as having a 'stake.'" Freeman lays the groundwork for a strong version of stakeholder theory. In particular, he challenges the assumption that directors and managers have their sole or even primary duty to shareholders. This approach to stakeholder theory has shaped the thinking behind corporate social responsibility. Calls for "sustainability" and concern for a "triple bottom line" (Elkington 1999) evoke a similar theoretical basis. Sustainability has become for some writers the alter-ego of corporate social responsibility (Grayson, Lemon, Slaughter, Rodriguez, Jin, and Tay 2008).

This approach competes with agency and stewardship theory for the attention of directors as they decide what actions to take. Fettering the agent in this way can entail costs, especially when stakeholders must be considered as more than an instrument of profit generation.

Narrow Stewardship

Directors may, however, take yet another view of their responsibilities. They may see themselves as stewards of some aspect of the organization, an aspect they regard as particularly important. In this narrow sense, directors act as stewards of special interests. A family retains seats on the board of a company that its members founded but no longer control. Hence, its directors see themselves as protecting the interests of the family and not other shareholders, stakeholders, or even the company as a whole. Another example is a director appointed by banks as a condition of a loan. This director will probably have the bank's interests at heart, whatever the law might say, and advocate policies to improve cash flow rather than to invest in new facilities, irrespective of the promised long-term gains. In such cases, the director's stance may lead to actions that put neither shareholder value nor other stakeholder interests at the fore.

In other cases, directors may act as stewards of the principles or traditions of the business. This form of stewardship often occurs in companies with a strong ethos. For example, when Anita Roddick created The Body Shop, her cosmetics manufacturing and retailing business, the company won a loyal following of customers who shared her views that companies should not test cosmetics on animals. After the firm went public, directors were expected to uphold that view even if did not always seem to maximize net present value. They were asked, in effect, to become stewards of an ethical principle.

Many important news organizations operate on narrow stewardship, sacrificing profitability for the integrity of their reporting. Integrity contributes to the brand, attracting customers and arguably generating profits in the long term. The financial results of news companies cast doubt upon that view. Like many newspapers, the *New York Times* has operated for a century, in effect, as a family trust. The company makes less money than it might because it spends more than necessary on reporting and editing the news. Unlike some other great newspapers, including *Le Monde* in France or the *Süddeutsche Zeitung* in Germany, the *New York Times* is a listed corporation with attendant demands from shareholders for a return on their investment. Reuters embedded in its corporate governance structures a separate board to overrule decisions by the main board that would endanger the objectivity of reporting. At its rival Dow Jones, which owns the *Wall Street Journal*, family shareholders controlled the company through disproportionate voting rights and were able to elect directors who invested in news gathering even when it came into conflict with profitability. The situation continued for many years until the family fell out over the relative value of editorial integrity and the value of a hostile takeover bid from Rupert Murdoch's News Corporation (Nordberg 2007a).

Narrow stewardship also has costs. So how does a director decide which approach to take?

ETHICS IN CORPORATE GOVERNANCE

So far, this chapter has examined the work of directors through lenses of theories that vie to explain how directors reach their decisions, as well as how they ought to reach their decisions. But these theories do more than describe how directors think and act. Because concern for corporate governance arose from the misdeeds of corporate executives and the apparent blindness of boards, corporate governance and the literature about it has a strong normative flavor. What should boards do? Moreover, corporate governance concerns policy making. Underpinning each perspective is an oft-hidden ethical understanding that requires exploration to avoid blindly moving from *is* to *ought*.

Two broad approaches to the topic of ethics have competed for supremacy in helping people decide how they ought to act: the teleological and the deontological. The first approach is based on an assessment of the consequences of an action, while the other is based on a determination of an *a priori* sense of what is good, right, and just.

Teleology in Corporate Governance

Much of the development of both capitalism and neoclassical economics is based on the notion developed from Smith (1776/1904) that people select a course of action based on the value it creates. Individuals' wishes may well be moderated and even blocked by the invisible hand of market competition, and that dynamic calculus provides the basis for deciding which actions are best. Consequences determine the rightness of the action. Called *teleology* from the Greek word for purpose, this approach looked to the individual businessman in the late eighteenth century rather like the ethical stance Bentham (1789/1904) called *utilitarian*. He saw individuals acting in their own interests, balancing pain and pleasure to achieve an outcome with the greatest utility. *Utility*, the satisfaction or happiness that an individual derives from a course of action, underlies the equations in many economic models. As Frankena (1963) discusses, this philosophy is also known as *ethical egoism*.

With the Industrial Revolution and proliferation of the joint stock company, that calculus became more complex. Mill's (1863/1991) version of utilitarianism tried to take that into account with his "greatest happiness principle," often elaborated as the "greatest good for the greatest number." Utility functions pervade discussions of micro- and even macroeconomics. In many ways, this concept forms the foundation of shareholder value. If the role of corporate governance is to maximize utility, this role demands a dual focus from the board to enforce it: (1) increasing the value of the business and (2) monitoring performance of the executive to prevent catastrophic or just undue loss. Empirical studies of boards (Forbes and Milliken 1999; McNulty and Pettigrew 1999; Stiles and Taylor 2001; Useem 2003) suggest directors have limited impact on strategy formation (for an overview, see

Pugliese, Bezemer, Zattoni, Huse, Van den Bosch, and Volberda [2009]). Thus, the fact that more attention has been paid to monitoring and control is not surprising.

Philosophers have criticized Mill's approach on many grounds, not least of which is that *happiness* is amorphous and subjective. The contemporary English philosopher Scruton (1994, 283) calls this consequences-based approach "part of the moral idiocy of the English," a reference to Bentham, Mill, and their followers. Both happiness and money lack a firm basis of comparison: $100 means something very different to a pauper and a billionaire. As a result, the calculus of the greatest happiness is at best complex and at worst meaningless. In corporate governance, seeing shareholder value as the ultimate utility has many problems, as explored in Chapter 21, "The Politics of Shareholder Activism." But the strength of Mill's reasoning has won many supporters, especially in the ranks of economists who educate businesspeople and financial market specialists who promote shareholder value as the right aim for a business. The main alternative to utilitarianism is one that many businesspeople find unpalatable.

Deontological Views of the Board

Competing against the utilitarian view of right and wrong is the other main strand of modernist ethics: the notion that some things and actions have intrinsic value. These final goods should be sought for themselves, not because they lead to something else. Some might even lead to what Bentham and Mill saw as the opposite of happiness—pain. Immanuel Kant's categorical imperative laid the cornerstone in the eighteenth century, a notion of a priori goods that could be derived from reason alone. An action was right if and only if the actor would think it right for all other people. A version of the Golden Rule in Christian faiths but derived, as Kant (1785/1964, 17) maintained, solely by reason, it holds there is a greater good "not derived from the goodness of the results which it produces."

Just as much of the literature of neoclassical economics has an orientation around utility, much mainstream discussion of corporate ethics takes its cue from Kant's deontology, with its roots in the Greek word for duty. The literature examines the concept of duty both explicitly (Evan and Freeman 1993; Bowie 1999; Morrell 2006) and implicitly (Freeman and Evan 1990; Freeman 1994; Donaldson and Preston 1995; Mitchell, Agle, and Wood 1997; Hasnas 1998; Crowther and Rayman-Bacchus 2004).

In its narrow form, stewardship theory can be viewed as having deontological roots, looking after specific aspects of the business. What businesses and lobbying organizations call *ethical* sourcing of raw materials or *ethical* supply chain management, for example, has as its ethical basis the presumption of a duty to suppliers transcending the mere contract, even if that contract is freely negotiated. Ethical investors seem willing to forgo short-term superior profits and capital gains on the principle that the practices they see as ethical are good in themselves. There is an alternative interpretation, one invoking the use of *enlightened self-interest*. In this view businesspeople are, in fact, judging the rights by its outcomes, by viewing such ethical practices as leading to better financial performance in the future.

Much of stakeholder theory, especially what is called the strong form, assumes a deontological view. As Kant argued that people may not, under the categorical imperative, be used merely as an instrument—the means to something else—so too employees, suppliers, and customers may not be treated merely as instruments of corporate profitability. Corporations have a duty to these other groups, something that qualifies the extent of the company's sole or primary duty to shareholders, and that moderates these shareholder obligations through some balancing of interests. When the economist Friedman (1970) famously declared that the firm's only social responsibility was to increase its profits, he was not declaring a preference for unethical behavior by businesses. Quite the contrary, he was indicating a preference for a teleological view of ethics against the deontological one that lies beneath the lobbying for corporate social responsibility.

Deontology has not solved the problem of ethics, either. Kant attempted to reason his way to the categorical imperative without reference to God, through using reason alone. The difficulties in his logic aside, many philosophers see Kant's view as still resting on faith—perhaps even individual faith—and becoming in effect, as MacIntyre (1998, 190) notes, "parasitic upon some already existing morality."

The Virtuous Director

These competing views of ethics have led to a long debate, with origins in modernist thinking and assumptions that reason alone would provide the answer. Rawls (1999) sought an answer in his notion of "justice as fairness." Justifying some redistribution of wealth while seeking not to impede enterprise, Rawls takes an approach he is said to have thought of as "operationalizing Kant" (see the preface of Binmore 2005). But the frustration in evidence among philosophers over the central problem of ethics does not often reach the textbooks on corporate ethics and less so the literature on corporate governance or social responsibility. Some scholars and, in practice, businesspeople have turned away from the argument between deontology and utilitarianism and toward the pragmatism of American thinkers such as John Dewey and William James, and more recently Richard Rorty. Their views are sometimes summarized, perhaps flippantly, as "if it works, it is right." Another view can be seen in the later work of the economist and game theorist Binmore (2005), who argues that a *natural* view of justice sees ethics on an evolutionary path, adapting to our greater knowledge and changing circumstances. Such notions, whether overtly postmodern or drawn from notions of bounded rationality, can be intellectually very satisfying to contemplate. But they may leave a director seeking the "right" basis for a decision rather less than satisfied.

The malaise of ethics has sent some philosophers back to the Greeks. What scholars including MacIntyre (1985), Charles Taylor (1991), and Richard Taylor (2002) found includes a different notion of ethics, one based not on good and bad, right and wrong, but nonetheless relevant to corporate directors: virtue. Employing Aristotle's view of personal happiness, Richard Taylor points toward creative intelligence as the rightful aspiration of mankind, while Charles Taylor draws a portrait of the authenticity of the artist in a system that sees reason to constrain the individual in the interests of the community. These more individual notions of virtue contrast with MacIntyre's view of virtue as striving for the internal goods within a community.

The link to the ethics of corporate governance comes in what directors aspire to achieve. It points toward another view of the corporation, something more than maximizing the net present value of future cash flows or serving as a nexus of contracts to minimize transaction costs. But this view is also different from the so-called *responsible* corporation that makes many businesspeople seethe about do-gooders who stop the corporation doing some really good work and creating some really good products. What virtue consists of may change with the business and environmental climate. Virtue may change as people come to better understand the business, customers, or the potential of a technology to do something customers never thought they wanted. The constant in this is that virtue is the striving.

SUMMARY AND CONCLUSIONS

For the director seeking an ethical basis for decisions, the unsettled debate over ethics may also be unsettling. But a director can at least compare theories of corporate governance, especially as they move from *is* to *ought*, to see which ethical assumptions are embedded in the theories and so which elements of the unresolved ethical debate they contain (Nordberg 2008). Exhibit 10.1 provides a summary of these issues.

Agency theory provides a solution to the problem of the unfettered agent. It assumes that the manager left alone will act in a purely self-interested way. It leads people, as *is* becomes *ought*, to build incentives designed to keep the agent aligned with the interests of owners. People build layers of governance mechanisms—boards and their committees, gatekeepers such as credit rating agencies and external auditors, accounting standards, and disclosure requirements—in

Exhibit 10.1 Ethical Perspectives on Corporate Governance

This table indicates three theoretical perspectives on corporate governance. Because each has different embedded ethical assumptions, each perspective points toward differing outcomes. These suggest a more complex range of considerations than that portrayed in governance literature focused on agency theory with its emphasis on the board's role as monitoring and controlling management.

Ethical Basis	Individual Focus	Corporate Focus
Teleological ethics	Governance approach: agent-principal Ethical assumption: ethical egoism Outcome: greed is good; unfettered agent	Governance approach: shareholder value Ethical assumption: utilitarian Outcome: directed greed; channeled agent
Deontological ethics	Governance approach: narrow stewardship Ethical assumption: personal duty Outcome: potential for interpersonal conflicts	Governance approach: strong stakeholder Ethical assumption: social responsibility Outcome: potential for suboptimal performance through goal confusion
Virtue ethics	Governance approach: personal stewardship Ethical assumption: higher-order personal achievement Outcome: esteem, self-actualization	Governance approach: collective stewardship Ethical assumption: higher-order collective achievement Outcome: long-term value creation

the hope of channeling the agent to work in a certain way. They do so because they believe the agent is an ethical egoist, a Benthamite, seeking to maximize personal happiness, unwilling and perhaps even incapable of seeking a larger good—in short, the unfettered agent. Firms create incentives such as stock options to turn the agent into a utilitarian manager in the mold of John Stuart Mill, an ethical collectivist, creating shareholder value along the way. This approach seeks to replace the vagueness of the greatest happiness principle that Mill proposed with a more concrete measure: the sum of dividends and capital gains that together will make the greatest number of institutional shareholders happy. This principle can break down nonetheless when differing shareholder interests collide (Nordberg 2009), as they do, when some shareholders seek a good that they see as greater than shareholder value.

That conflict may come through a director's duty to one set of shareholder aims or to other a priori obligations. These claims, whether on behalf of a narrow interest or the broader faith that such good actions lead to better financial performance, are deontological in origin and a good that is independent of its outcomes. When such a duty arises through narrowly defined, personal views of stewardship, the potential for interpersonal conflict arises as goals compete and directors push their own causes. A strong stakeholder approach, placing multiple, conflicting demands on the resources of the corporation, creates the potential for confusion over aims and direction. Businesspeople, as given voice by Friedman (1970), often cite the resulting lack of clarity about purpose as the reason that the more strident demands for corporate social responsibility are impractical.

Many businesspeople aspire to the notion that they are indeed stewards. They personally seek to do the best they can, which results in doing the best they can for the company. Stewardship is in evidence among those who bemoan how the corporate governance "industry" has forced them to focus more on monitoring and control than on value creation (Brabeck-Letmathe 2005). As a result, the board's agenda has become increasing imbalanced (Nordberg 2007b). Stewardship is present in those directors of companies who see the reputation of their profession sullied by the excesses of those unfettered agents among their ranks (Maharaj 2008). Stewardship also exists in the crop of new outside directors who risk shareholder lawsuits for an often modest director's fee because they believe with Weinberg (2006) that "[s]erving on a board is like taking on a position in public service."

Here virtue ethics in operation is present. This statement shows an aim embracing something other than a focus on delivering earnings per share this quarter that exceed analyst estimates, timed to be published just as the stock options of senior management vest. The individual and corporate goals of utilitarian approaches to business seem to require mechanisms to keep them in line, while the individual and corporate goals of a duty-based system of ethics entail internal conflicts. In a virtue-based system, individual and collective aims seem to be self-reinforcing.

However, hoping that managers and the directors that shareholders hire to oversee them will act as stewards may not be enough. But mechanisms of corporate governance aimed at fettering the agent may, as Davis et al. (1997) suggest, leave the would-be steward frustrated or turn the steward into an agent seeking to cast off his chains. What perhaps most needs to be found in corporate governance is a mechanism to identify who is likely to be a steward and who the unfettered agent.

DISCUSSION QUESTIONS

1. In what ways might an unfettered agent cause catastrophic damage to the company? How could one extract personal gain and at the expense of whom?
2. In what ways can restricting the agent limit the potential of the company? Think in particular about the ways in which senior managers and then boards of directors contribute to strategy development and implementation.
3. Consider the following two statements: (1) "Every decision the board makes, even the choice of wine with dinner, involves an ethical choice"; and (2) "The corporation is a means of organizing economic activity. Economics and ethics have nothing to do with each other." What economic and ethical assumptions does each make?
4. How can people monitor and control the actions of an agent without unwittingly failing to nurture sentiments of stewardship among directors and senior managers?

REFERENCES

Aguilera, Ruth V., and Alvaro Cuervo-Cazurra. 2009. Codes of good governance. *Corporate Governance: An International Review* 17 (3): 376–87.

Barney, Jay B. 1995. Looking inside for competitive advantage. *Academy of Management Executive* 9 (4): 49–61.

Bebchuk, Lucian Arye. 2005. The case for increasing shareholder power. *Harvard Law Review* 118 (3): 833–914.

Bentham, Jeremy. 1789/1904. An introduction to the principles of morals and legislation. Oxford: Clarendon Press. http://www.econlib.org/library/Bentham/bnthPML.html.

Berle, Adolf A., and Gardiner C. Means. 1932/1991. *The modern corporation and private property*. New Brunswick, NJ: Transaction Publishers.

Binmore, Ken. 2005. *Natural justice*. New York: Oxford University Press.

Bowie, Norman E. 1999. *Business ethics: A Kantian perspective*. Oxford: Blackwell.

Brabeck-Letmathe, Peter. 2005. Corporate governance—A European vantage point. Speech given at Boston College, March 8 (Nestlé SA). http://www.nestle.com/MediaCenter/SpeechesAndStatements/AllSpeechesAndStatements/03_08_2005.htm.

Cadbury, Adrian. 1992. The financial aspects of corporate governance, known as the Cadbury Code. http://www.ecgi.org/codes/documents/cadbury.pdf.

Coase, Ronald H. 1937. The theory of the firm. *Economica* 4 (16): 386–405.

Cromme Commission. 2002/2007. German corporate governance code. Government Commission of the German Corporate Governance Code. http://www.corporate-governance-code.de.

Crowther, David, and Lez Rayman-Bacchus (eds.). 2004. *Perspectives on corporate social responsibility*. Aldershot: Ashgate.

D'Aveni, Richard A., and Idalene F. Kesner. 1993. Top managerial prestige, power and tender offer response: A study of elite social networks and target firm cooperation during takeovers. *Organization Science* 4 (2): 123–151.

Davis, James H., F. David Schoorman, and Lex Donaldson. 1997. Toward a stewardship theory of management. *Academy of Management Review* 22 (1): 20–47.

Donaldson, Lex, and James H. Davis. 1991. Stewardship theory or agency theory: CEO governance and shareholder returns. *Australian Journal of Management* 16 (1): 49.

Donaldson, Thomas, and Lee E. Preston. 1995. The stakeholder theory of the corporation: Concepts, evidence, and implications. *Academy of Management Review* 20 (1): 65–91.

Eisenhardt, Kathleen M. 1989. Agency theory: An assessment and review. *Academy of Management Review* 14 (1): 57–74.

Elkington, John. 1999. *Cannibals with forks: The triple bottom line of 21st century business.* Oxford: Capstone.

Evan, William M., and R. Edward Freeman. 1993. A stakeholder theory of the modem corporation: Kantian capitalism. In *Ethical Theory and Business*, ed. Tom L. Beauchamp and Norman E. Bowie. Upper Saddle River, NJ: Prentice Hall.

Fama, Eugene F. 1980. Agency problems and the theory of the firm. *Journal of Political Economy* 88 (2): 288–307.

Fama, Eugene F., and Michael C. Jensen. 1983. Separation of ownership and control. *Journal of Law and Economics* 23 (2): 301–325.

Financial Reporting Council. 2006. Review of the 2003 Combined Code: The findings of the review. London. http://www.frc.org.uk/documents/pagemanager/frc/Combined%20Code%20review%20main%20findings%2018%20January%202006.pdf.

———. 2008. Combined Code on Corporate Governance. http://www.frc.org.uk/documents/pagemanager/frc/Combined_Code_June_2008/Combined%20Code%20Web%20Optimized%20June%202008(2).pdf.

Forbes, Daniel P., and Frances J. Milliken. 1999. Cognition and corporate governance: Understanding boards of directors as strategic decision-making groups. *Academy of Management Review* 24 (3): 489–505.

Frankena, William K. 1963. *Ethics*. Englewood Cliffs, NJ: Prentice-Hall.

Freeman, R. Edward. 1984. *Strategic management: A stakeholder approach*. Boston: Pitman Publishing.

———. 1994. The politics of stakeholder theory: Some future directions. *Business Ethics Quarterly* 4 (4): 409–422.

Freeman, R. Edward, and William M. Evan. 1990. Corporate governance: A stakeholder interpretation. *Journal of Behavioral Economics* 19 (4): 337–359.

French, J. R. B., Jr., and B. Raven. 1959. The bases of social power. In *Studies in Social Power*, ed. Dorwin Cartwright. Ann Arbor: University of Michigan.

Friedman, Milton. 1970. The social responsibility of business is to increase its profits. *New York Times Magazine*, September 13, 122–26.

Gomez-Mejia, Luis R., and Robert M. Wiseman. 2007. Does agency theory have universal relevance? A reply to Lubatkin, Lane, Collin, and Very. *Journal of Organizational Behavior* 28 (1): 81–88.

Grayson, David, Mark Lemon, Sarah Slaughter, Miguel Angel Rodriguez, Zhouying Jin, and Simon Tay. 2008. A new mindset for corporate sustainability. British Telecommunications plc and Cisco Systems Inc. http://www.biggerthinking.com/docs/en/a_new_mindset_white_paper.pdf.

Greenbury, Richard. 1995. Directors' remuneration: Report of the study group. *European Corporate Governance Institute*, Brussels. http://www.ecgi.org/codes/documents/greenbury.pdf.

Hampel, Ronnie. 1998. Committee of Corporate Governance—final report. London: Gee Publishing. http://www.ecgi.org/codes/documents/hampel.pdf.

Hasnas, John. 1998. The normative theories of business ethics: A guide for the perplexed. *Business Ethics Quarterly* 8 (1): 19–42.

Higgs, Derek. 2003. Review of the role and effectiveness of non-executive directors. London: U.K. Department of Trade and Industry. http://www.ecgi.org/codes/documents/higgsreport.pdf.

Hofstede, Geert. 1980. *Culture's consequences: International differences in work-related values.* Beverly Hills, CA: Sage.

Jensen, Michael C., and William H. Meckling. 1976. Theory of the firm: Managerial behavior, agency costs and ownership structure. *Journal of Financial Economics* 3 (4): 305–360.

Kant, Immanuel. 1785/1964. *Groundwork of the metaphysic of morals*. Trans. H. J. Paton. New York: Harper Torchbooks.

Kaplan, Robert S., and David P. Norton. 1992. The balanced scorecard—measures that drive performance. *Harvard Business Review* 70 (1): 71–79.
Kumar, Praveen, and K. Sivaramakrishnan. 2008. Who monitors the monitor? The effect of board independence on executive compensation and firm value. *Review of Financial Studies* 21 (3): 1371–1401.
Lippens, Maurice. 2004. The Belgian code on corporate governance. Brussels. http://www.ecgi.org/codes/documents/bel_code_dec2004_en.pdf.
Lysandrou, Photis, and Denitsa Stoyanova. 2007. The anachronism of the voice-exit paradigm: Institutional investors and corporate governance in the UK. *Corporate Governance: An International Review* 15 (6): 1070–1078.
MacAvoy, Paul, and Ira Millstein. 2003. *The recurrent crisis in corporate governance*. Basingstoke: Palgrave Macmillan.
MacIntyre, Alasdair. 1985. *After virtue: A study in moral theory*. London: Duckworth.
———. 1998. *A short history of ethics*. London: Routledge.
Maharaj, Rookmin. 2008. Corporate governance, groupthink and bullies in the boardroom. *International Journal of Disclosure and Governance* 5 (1): 69–92.
Maslow, Abraham H. 1943. A theory of human motivation. *Psychological Review* 50 (4): 370–396.
———. 1954. *Motivation and personality*. New York: Harper & Row.
McKnight, Phillip J., and Charlie Weir. 2009. Agency costs, corporate governance mechanisms and ownership structure in large UK publicly quoted companies: A panel data analysis. *Quarterly Review of Economics and Finance* 49 (2): 139–158.
McNulty, Terry, and Andrew Pettigrew. 1999. Strategists on the board. *Organization Studies* 20: 47–74.
Mill, John Stuart. 1848/1909. Principles of political economy with some of their applications to social philosophy. William J. Ashley (ed.). *Library of Economics and Liberty* ed. London: Longmans, Green and Co. http://www.econlib.org/library/Mill/mlP.html.
———. 1863/1991. Utilitarianism. In *John Stuart Mill: On Liberty and Other Essays*, ed. John Gray. Oxford: Oxford University Press.
Mitchell, Ronald K., Bradley R. Agle, and Donna J. Wood. 1997. Toward a theory of stakeholder identification and salience: Defining the principle of who and what really counts. *Academy of Management Review* 22 (4): 853–886.
Morrell, Kevin. 2006. Governance, ethics and the national health service. *Public Money & Management* 26 (1): 55–62.
NASDAQ. (2002). Summary of NASDAQ corporate governance proposals. http://www.nasdaq.com/about/Corp_Gov_Summary101002.pdf.
New York Stock Exchange. 2003. Final NYSE corporate governance rules. http://www.ecgi.org/codes/documents/finalcorpgovrules.pdf.
Nordberg, Donald. 2007a. News and corporate governance: What Dow Jones and Reuters teach us about stewardship. *Journalism: Theory, Practice and Criticism* 8 (6): 718–735.
———. 2007b. Rebalancing the board's agenda. *Journal of General Management* 33 (2): 13–23.
———. 2008. The ethics of corporate governance. *Journal of General Management* 33 (6): 35–52.
———. 2009. Politics in corporate governance: How power shapes the board's agenda. Centre for International Business and Sustainability. http://ssrn.com/abstract=1332310.
OECD. 2004. *OECD Principles of Corporate Governance, Revised*. Paris: Organization for Economic Co-operation and Development. http://www.oecd.org/dataoecd/32/18/31557724.pdf.
Pugliese, Amedeo, Pieter-Jan Bezemer, Alessandro Zattoni, Morten Huse, Frans A. J. Van den Bosch, and Henk W. Volberda. 2009. Boards of directors' contribution to strategy: A literature review and research agenda. *Corporate Governance: An International Review* 17 (3): 292–306.

Rawls, John. 1999. *A theory of justice*. Cambridge, MA: Belknap Press.
Rust, Roland T., Katherine N. Lemon, and Valarie A. Zeithaml. 2004. Return on marketing: Using customer equity to focus marketing strategy. *Journal of Marketing* 68 (1): 109–127.
Scruton, Roger. 1994. *Modern philosophy*. New York: Allen Lane.
Smith, Adam. 1776/1904. *The wealth of nations*. London: Methuen & Co. http://www.econlib.org/library/Smith/smWNCover.html.
Stiles, Philip, and Bernard Taylor (2001). *Boards at work—How directors view their roles and responsibilities*. Oxford: Oxford University Press.
Taylor, Charles. 1991. *The ethics of authenticity*. Cambridge, MA: Harvard University Press.
Taylor, Richard. 2002. *Virtue ethics: An introduction*. Amherst, NY: Prometheus Books.
Useem, Michael. 2003. Corporate governance is directors making decisions: Reforming the outward foundations for inside decision-making. *Journal of Management and Governance* 7 (3): 241–253.
Veniot. 1995. The boards of directors of listed companies in France. Paris: CNPF and AFEP. http://www.ecgi.org/codes/documents/vienot1_en.pdf.
Weinberg, Peter. 2006. Boardroom culture must embrace directors. *Financial Times* London. http://search.ft.com/ftArticle?id=061117001294.
Wernerfelt, Birger. 1984. A resource-based view of the firm. *Strategic Management Journal* 5 (2): 171–180.
Williamson, Oliver E. 1985. *The economic institutions of capitalism*. New York: Free Press.
———. 1988. Corporate finance and corporate governance. *Journal of Finance* 43 (3): 567–591.
Zahra, Shaker A. 2007. An embeddedness framing of governance and opportunism: Towards a cross-nationally accommodating theory of agency—critique and extension. *Journal of Organizational Behavior* 28 (1): 69–73.

ABOUT THE AUTHOR

Donald Nordberg is senior lecturer in strategy and corporate governance at Westminster Business School and honorary visiting professor of journalism at City University, London. In a career in financial journalism and investor relations, he has been a correspondent and senior editorial executive for Reuters in Germany, Switzerland, the United Kingdom, and the United States and served as senior adviser to The Conference Board in Europe. He has degrees from the University of Illinois and Warwick Business School in England. His articles have appeared in the *Journal of General Management*; the *Journal of Financial Regulation and Compliance*; *Journalism: Theory, Practice and Criticism*; and others.

PART TWO

Internal Governance

Boards of Directors

Compensation, Ownership, and Turnover

CHAPTER 11

Board Composition and Organization Issues

MATTEO TONELLO
Director, Corporate Governance Research, The Conference Board

INTRODUCTION

In the past decade, U.S. public companies have responded to pressures from regulators and shareholders by strengthening the independence and expanding the expertise of their boards of directors. In particular, the Sarbanes-Oxley Act of 2002, subsequent rules by the Securities and Exchange Commission (SEC), and securities exchange listing provisions have brought changes in corporate board composition and imposed new standards of integrity for the performance of its functions (Tonello and Brancato 2007; Monks and Minow 2008). Some organized investors, including large public and private pension funds as well as activist hedge funds, have been taking unprecedented steps to monitor the governance structure of their portfolio companies. Today, they urge boards to repeal bylaws on classification and depart from the default rule of plurality voting in directors' elections (Davis, Lukomnik, and Pitt-Watson 2006; Park and Tonello 2009).

According to New York Stock Exchange (NYSE) rules, the nominating committee, as part of the director selection process, should "identify individuals qualified to become board members, consistent with the criteria approved by the board" and disclosed in its governance guidelines (NYSE 2009, Section 303A[4][a]). The composition and skill set of a board should depend on the company's strategic vision and particular challenges. As companies experience evolving business circumstances, the desired composition of the board may also change, requiring firms to regularly revisit director qualifications (Heslin and Donaldson 1999). An ideal board comprises a mix of knowledge and expertise in accounting and finance, risk management, strategic and business planning, legal and compliance, human resources, marketing, international trade, and industry-specific research and development (R&D).

In the post-Enron business environment, a growing number of companies have found attracting and retaining qualified directors increasingly more difficult. This is partially due to strict director independence rules and the requirement that companies appoint a financial expert to their audit committee (per SEC Regulation S-K, Item 401[h]). Qualified directors may also be more reluctant to join new boards because of increased scrutiny by enforcement agencies and institutional investors.

This figure shows the background of members on the board of directors in 1998. Over the years, active and retired CEOs and COOs have consistently been at the top of boards' wish lists.

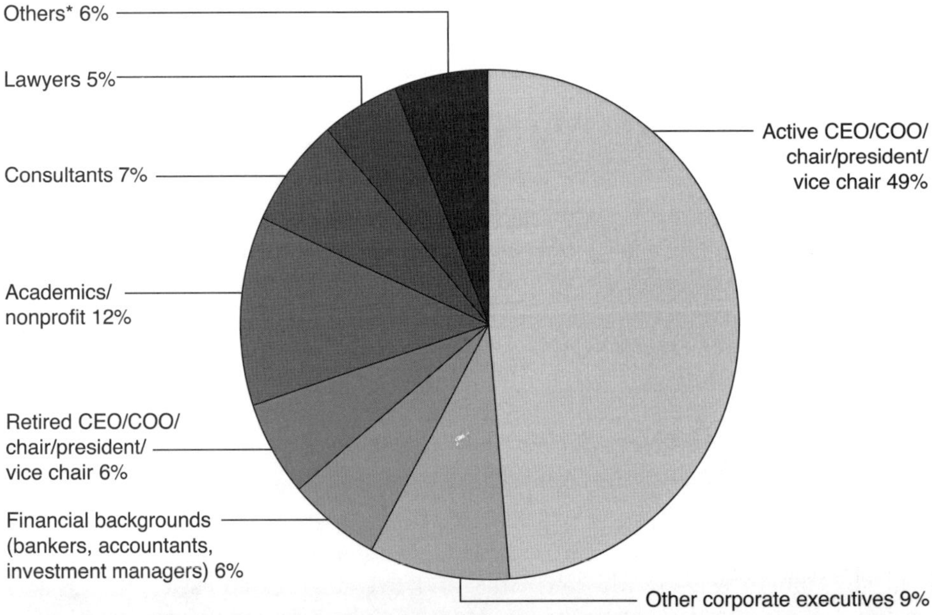

*Mostly retired government and military officials, plus a few other retired professionals

Exhibit 11.1 Director Background, 1998
Source: 2008 Spencer Stuart Board Index (Spencer Stuart 2008, 12). Based on an analysis of proxy filings by S&P 500 companies.

Other factors include a potential for greater liability and the time commitment that is now required by the job. Studies show a decreased propensity of active chief executive officers (CEOs) to join the boards of other companies. However, the prestige of the position as well as the opportunity to gain knowledge, add value, and network will continue to serve as important motivators for attracting new talent to the boardroom (Daum 2008). As a practical matter, companies continue to successfully nominate individuals from the ranks of retired CEOs, chief financial officers (CFOs), heads of large corporate operating divisions, academics, and leaders of prominent scientific, nonprofit, or governmental organizations. Exhibits 11.1 and 11.2 show the changes in directors' backgrounds from 1998 to 2008.

ANATOMY OF A CORPORATE BOARD

The Conference Board, the New York-based independent research organization, annually analyzes board composition and director qualifications for business corporations listed on U.S. securities exchanges. The information is organized according to 22 industry categories and 10 revenue groups (ranging from a few million dollars to over $10 billion of revenues) and is based on the review of SEC filings as

This figure shows the background of members on the board of directors in 2008. As a result of regulatory requirements and stricter governance standards, the number of directors with financial backgrounds has increased substantially in the past decade.

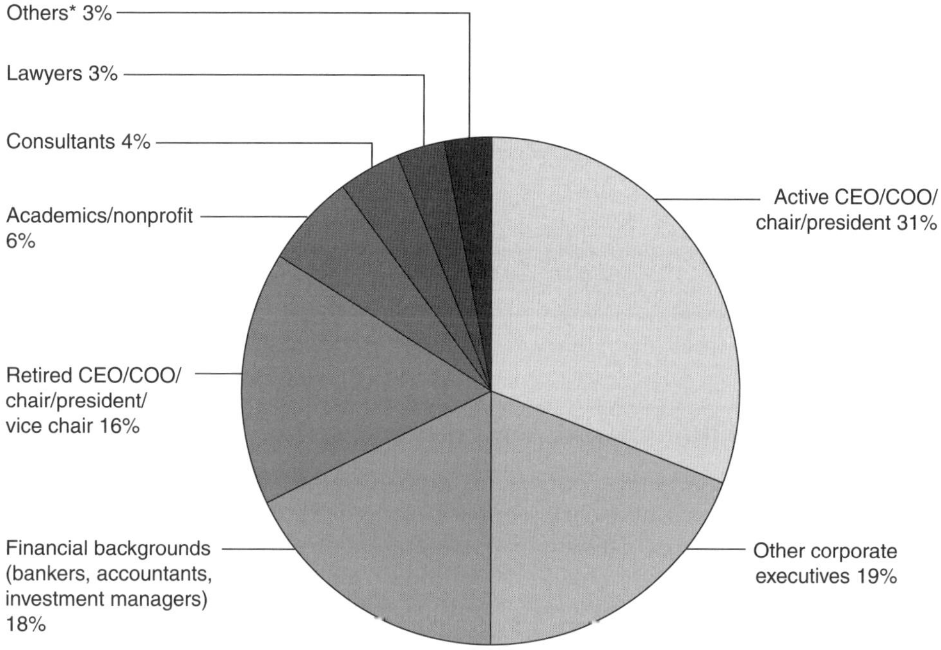

*Mostly retired government and military officials, plus a few other retired professionals

Exhibit 11.2 Director Background, 2008
Source: 2008 Spencer Stuart Board Index (Spencer Stuart 2008, 12). Based on an analysis of proxy filings by S&P 500 companies.

well as a survey of corporate secretaries (Hallock, Tonello, and Torok 2008). What follows are the major takeaways.

Board Size and Diversity

Most companies have between 9 and 12 board members. There is little variation in the number of directors from industry to industry but boards tend to be larger as corporate revenue increases. Similarly, the largest companies are more likely to have at least one woman (100 percent), one academic (55.6 percent), and one person of color (88.9 percent) on their board. Among companies in the bottom decile in terms of revenues, those numbers are much smaller: 62.5 percent, 34.4 percent, and 28.1 percent, respectively. The optimal board size is determined by the trade-off between two opposing needs. Boards need to be large enough to accommodate the necessary skill sets and competencies, but still be small enough to promote cohesion, flexibility, and effective participation (Raheja 2005). Exhibits 11.3 and 11.4 illustrate minority representation in corporate boards across industries and revenue groups.

Exhibit 11.3 Diversity and Minority Representation by Industry

This table shows the percentage of diversity and minority representation, partitioned by industry. Nonfinancial services have the highest percentage of at least one member in each minority category.

	Manufacturing	Financial Services	Nonfinancial Services
Women	83.5%	78.0%	86.0%
Academics	37.7	39.8	56.5
Non-U.S. professionals	24.7	16.1	28.3
African-American	40.0	43.2	54.4
Hispanic	16.5	19.5	26.1
Other minority	4.7	4.2	8.7

Source: The Conference Board.

Director Independence and Affiliations

Although numerous scholars continue to express skepticism about a correlation between board independence and firm performance (Bhagat and Black 2002; Romano 2006), trends in nominating more independent directors have been observed since the corporate scandals of 2001–2002. Today, more than two-thirds of board members across industries are considered independent directors as defined by major securities exchange listing standards (see the following section on board independence), and the percentage of independent directors increases with company size. Most boards only count one to two members who are employees or otherwise affiliated with the company (e.g., due to former employment or providing professional services, such as legal or management consulting assistance). As

Exhibit 11.4 Diversity and Minority Representation by Revenue

This table shows the percentage of diversity and minority representation, partitioned by revenue. In general, the larger the company size, the more diverse is the composition of the corporate board, with at least one member of the following categories.

Revenues in Millions	Women	Academics	Non-U.S. Professionals	African-American	Hispanic	Other Minority
$0 to < $121.6	62.5%	34.4%	6.3%	28.1%	6.3%	9.4%
121.6 to < 224.1	63.6	45.5	9.1	18.2	0.0	0.0
224.1 to < 365.1	76.5	35.3	5.9	5.9	5.9	0.0
365.1 to < 581.9	80.0	33.3	20.0	26.7	13.3	13.3
581.9 to < 887.0	62.5	31.3	18.8	6.3	0.0	0.0
887.0 to < 1,278.9	70.0	35.0	20.0	25.0	20.0	10.0
1,278.9 to < 2,126.7	79.0	31.6	26.3	31.6	15.8	0.0
2,126.7 to < 3,848.5	87.5	50.0	12.5	41.7	20.8	0.0
3,848.5 to < 9,153	90.2	43.9	24.4	58.5	19.5	12.2
≥ 9,153	100.0	55.6	38.9	88.9	44.4	1.9

Source: The Conference Board.

Exhibit 11.5 Board Size and Director Affiliations by Industry

This table shows board size and director affiliations, partitioned by industry. Little variation exists in the number of corporate directors. Among industries, the number of directors who are employees of or otherwise affiliated with the company varies from two to three.

	Manufacturing	Financial Services	Nonfinancial Services
Board size	10	10	12
Independent directors	8	7	9
Directors who are current employees	1	2	1
Directors affiliated with the company	1	1	1

Source: The Conference Board.

many as 4 out of 10 board members have retired from a previous career and become professional directors. Exhibits 11.5 and 11.6 describe director independence and affiliations across industries and company size groups. Exhibits 11.7 and 11.8 illustrate the adoption of director policies restricting contemporaneous service on multiple corporate boards.

Board Classification

In recent years, growing support for shareholder resolutions requesting to declassify boards has resulted in a steady decline in staggered structures—that is, where directors are subject to staggered terms, typically running three years so that only one-third of the board stands for election each year (Ganor 2008). Today, many

Exhibit 11.6 Board Size and Director Affiliations by Revenue

This table shows board size and director affiliations, partitioned by revenue. Board size varies more among revenue groups. Most companies have only one affiliated director (e.g., a provider of professional services to the organization).

Revenues in Millions	Board Size	Independent Directors	Directors Who Are Current Employees	Directors Affiliated with the Company
$0 to 121.6	10	6	3	1
121.6 to 224.1	11	6	1	1
224.1 to 365.1	9	6	2	0
365.1 to 581.9	9	6	1	1
581.9 to 887.0	8	7	0	1
887.0 to 1,278.9	10	7	1	1
1,278.9 to 2,126.7	10	8	2	1
2,126.7 to 3,848.5	10	7	1	1
3,848.5 to 9,153	10	8	2	1
≥ 9,153	12	10	2	1

Source: The Conference Board.

Exhibit 11.7 Service on Multiple Boards by Industry

This table shows company policies regarding service on multiple boards, partitioned by three industry groups—manufacturing, financial services, and nonfinancial services. A great majority of companies permit their board members to also serve on three or more other for-profit boards.

	Manufacturing	Financial Services	Nonfinancial Services
Companies limiting multiple board services	44.7%	40.7%	50.0%
Policy for board members:			
No other board service permitted	0.0	0.0	5.0
One other board service permitted	0.0	2.4	0.0
Two other boards service permitted	12.5	19.1	10.0
Three or more other boards service permitted	87.5	78.6	85.0
Policy for senior executives:			
No other board service permitted	12.5	0.0	22.2
One other board service permitted	37.5	28.6	55.6
Two other boards service permitted	37.5	42.9	22.2
Three or more other boards service permitted	12.5	28.6	0.0

Source: The Conference Board.

companies have abandoned classifications. Findings for 2008 indicate considerable variation in this area across revenue, with the lowest percentage of classified boards among companies in the highest revenue categories.

Classified boards appear to be conducive to complacency as well as to excessive stability and continuity. Specifically, staggered structures may make hostile takeover attempts more difficult (Bebchuk, Coates, and Subramanian 2002). When a board is staggered, hostile bidders must win more than one proxy fight at successive shareholder meetings to exercise control of the target firm. Particularly in combination with a poison pill, a staggered board that cannot be dismantled or evaded is one of the most potent takeover defenses available to U.S. companies. By contrast, due to the rapid decline in valuation of public companies registered since late 2007, some corporations with declassified boards have found themselves dangerously exposed to attack by strategic acquirers and activist investors (Alexander 2009). Exhibits 11.9 and 11.10 illustrate the percentage of corporate boards that are declassified, respectively by industry and revenue groups.

Board Leadership

Governance activists have also been campaigning for the separation of the board chairman and CEO positions and the establishment of independent board leadership (Alogna, Pargendler, and Thompson-Mann 2009). Recent data shows that the percentage of companies with a lead or presiding independent director increases with revenue, whereas the percentage of companies with a non-CEO chair declines. This may also be explained by the fact that NYSE rules now require that

Exhibit 11.8 Service on Multiple Boards by Revenue

This table shows the policy for board members and senior executives for service on multiple boards, partitioned by revenue. No correlation exists between company size and limits on the number of boards on which a director may serve.

		Policy for Board Members				Policy for Senior Executives			
Revenues in Millions	**Companies Limiting Multiple Board Services**	**No Other Board Service Permitted**	**One Other Board Service Permitted**	**Two Other Boards Services Permitted**	**Three or More Other Boards Service Permitted**	**No Other Board Service Permitted**	**One Other Board Service Permitted**	**Two Other Boards Service Permitted**	**Three or More Other Boards Service Permitted**
$0 to < $121.6	12.5%	33.3%	0.0%	33.3%	33.3%	0.0%	0.0%	100.0%	0.0%
121.6 to < 224.1	27.3	0.0	0.0	0.0	100.0	50.0	0.0	50.0	0.0
224.1 to < 365.1	47.1	0.0	0.0	14.3	85.7	50.0	0.0	50.0	0.0
365.1 to < 581.9	53.3	0.0	0.0	37.5	62.5	0.0	100.0	0.0	0.0
581.9 to < 887.0	31.3	0.0	0.0	0.0	100.0	0.0	33.3	33.3	33.3
887.0 to < 1,278.9	25.0	0.0	0.0	20.0	80.0	0.0	50.0	0.0	50.0
1,278.9 to < 2,126.7	31.6	0.0	0.0	20.0	80.0	0.0	66.7	33.3	0.0
2,126.7 to < 3,848.5	58.3	0.0	0.0	0.0	100.0	20.0	0.0	60.0	20.0
3,848.5 to < 9,153	56.1	0.0	4.8	28.6	66.7	0.0	50.0	37.5	12.5
≥ 9,153	61.1	0.0	0.0	4.0	96.0	5.6	38.9	33.3	22.2

Source: The Conference Board.

This figure shows the percentage of companies with a classified board, partitioned by manufacturing, financial services, and nonfinancial services. The majority of manufacturing companies have a classified board.

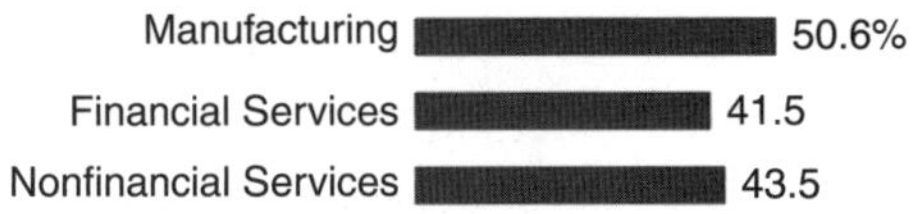

Exhibit 11.9 Board Classification by Industry
Source: The Conference Board.

member-listed companies have an outside director preside over executive sessions of board meetings (see the later section on board leadership).

Age, Director Tenure, and Retirement Policies

Firms are adopting retirement policies, based on tenure or director age, as a means to encourage dynamism and innovation in board composition. Tenure limits are also a way to avoid the tough decision of asking a nonperforming director to retire. Although mandatory retirement can provide boards with fresh perspectives, it can also deprive them of seasoned and experienced individuals who are familiar with the business strategy and the current challenges facing the company. The percentage of boards following such policies is lowest among companies in the lowest revenue groups (21.9 percent) and highest among the largest organizations (up to 92.6 percent). The median age of directors ranges from the mid-50s to the mid-60s, while the median mandatory retirement age is 72. For the most part,

This figure shows the percentage of companies with a classified board, partitioned by revenues. Only a quarter of the largest companies have a classified board.

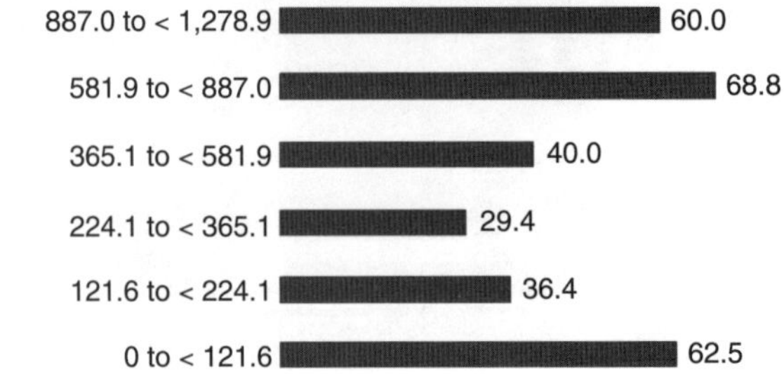

Exhibit 11.10 Board Classification by Revenue
Source: The Conference Board.

This figure shows the percentage of companies in manufacturing, financial services, and nonfinancial services with a mandatory retirement age. Of the three groups, manufacturing has the highest percentage of firms having a mandatory retirement age.

Exhibit 11.11 Retirement Policies (Based on Age) by Industry
Source: The Conference Board.

smaller companies have younger directors than do larger companies. Exhibit 11.11 shows companies across major business industries that are currently adopting retirement policies. Exhibit 11.12 illustrates such data based on a corporate revenue breakdown.

BOARD INDEPENDENCE

While boards traditionally performed almost exclusively an advisory role, today's boards have evolved to become active fiduciaries in the exercise of their oversight responsibilities. From this standpoint, the company must be able to rely on the independent judgment of its directors. Although defined by regulatory standards, independence (in thought and action) from management's influence should always be evaluated qualitatively and on a case-by-case basis, before each election and as part of the annual board assessment process.

In considering independence, the firm should focus not only on the formal review of the nominee's background, current professional activities, and economic and family relationships, but also on whether the prospective director can, in fact,

Exhibit 11.12 Retirement Policies (Based on Age) by Revenue

This table shows the distribution of companies having a mandatory retirement age, partitioned by the firm's revenues in millions of dollars. The median mandatory retirement age is 72.

Revenues in Millions	Companies with Mandatory Retirement Age	Median Mandatory Retirement Age
$0 to < $121.6	21.9%	72
$121.6 to < 224.1	63.6	72
224.1 to < 365.1	52.9	72
365.1 to < 581.9	46.7	72
581.9 to < 887.0	37.5	74
887.0 to < 1,278.9	75.0	72
1,278.9 to < 2,126.7	52.6	70
2,126.7 to < 3,848.5	62.5	72
3,848.5 to < 9,153	75.6	72
≥ 9,153	92.6	72

Source: The Conference Board.

perform her duties without being subject to the influence of management. As some of the recent corporate scandals suggest, even boards meeting formal qualification criteria may not act as a strong independent check on management. Qualitative aspects of director independence should comprise the will to interact with senior executives as well as the confidence and expertise to ask the hard questions required to provide effective oversight.

Formal Assessment: Regulatory Standards

The Sarbanes-Oxley Act and the SEC rules adopted after its enactment do not prescribe independence standards relating to members of corporate boards other than audit committee members (Section 301 of the Sarbanes-Oxley Act of 2002 and Section 10A of the Securities Exchange Act of 1934). Instead, this requirement stems from the NYSE and NASDAQ listing rules which mandate establishing a board composed of a majority of independent directors and the disclosure of their names in the annual proxy statement. While anticipating all situations in which a director may be involved is not possible, the NYSE and NASDAQ recognize that certain personal and professional relationships can compromise a director's independence. Therefore, each of the two self-regulatory organizations has created lists of relationships that are incompatible with a finding of independence. To this day, empirical evidence regarding the value of these independence criteria remains mixed (Gupta and Fields 2009).

The NYSE and NASDAQ have also adopted practices and procedural requirements to empower outside directors to act free from management's influence. For example, to facilitate an open and objective discussion about management performance and business conduct, both organizations require nonexecutive members of boards to meet at regularly convened executive sessions without management or employee directors. A listed company must disclose in its annual proxy statement the name of the director who will preside at these sessions or the procedure by which the presiding director is chosen for each session. Also, the company must disclose a method for interested parties to communicate directly with the presiding or lead director or with the group of nonexecutive directors in its entirety.

NYSE

Under NYSE standards, the board of directors must affirmatively determine—taking into account all of the "relevant facts and circumstances"—that a director has no material relationship with the company (either directly or indirectly) for that director to be considered independent (Section 303A of the *NYSE Listed Company Manual*, as last amended on August 15, 2008; SEC Release No. 34-58367). The basis for a board's determination that a relationship is not material is required to be disclosed in the company's annual proxy statement. Under the rules, a director cannot be considered independent until three years after the end of any of the following relationships:

- The director (or an immediate family member of the director) is an executive officer of the issuer.
- The director (or an immediate family member of the director) receives more than $120,000 per year in direct compensation from the company, other than

director and committee fees and pension or other forms of deferred compensation for prior service (provided such compensation is not contingent in any way on continued service).

- The director (or an immediate family member of the director) is employed as an executive officer of another company that makes payments to or receives payments from the listed company for property or services in an amount that exceeds the greater of $1 million or 2 percent of such company's annual consolidated gross revenues.
- The director (or an immediate family member) is employed as an executive officer of a company where any of the issuer's present executive officers at the same times serves or served on that company's compensation committee.
- The director is a partner or an employee of the internal or external auditor of the issuer or has an immediate family member who is a partner or an employee of the firm and personally worked on the issuer's audit.

NASDAQ

Similar director independence criteria are promulgated by NASDAQ rules (Rule 5605[a][2]). More specifically, a director of a NASDAQ-listed company cannot be considered independent until three years after the end of any of the following relationships:

- The director is employed by the issuer or any of its parents or subsidiaries.
- A family member of the director is an executive officer of the issuer or any of its parents or subsidiaries.
- The director (or an immediate family member of the director) accepted any payments from the issuer or any parent or subsidiary in excess of $120,000 per year (except for compensation for board or board committee service, payments arising solely from investments in the issuer's securities, and benefits under a tax-qualified retirement plan).
- The director (or an immediate family member of the director) is an executive officer or an equivalent officer of any entity that makes payments to or receives payments from the listed company for property or services that exceed 5 percent of the recipient's consolidated gross revenues for that year, or $200,000, whichever is more (except for payments arising solely from investments in the company's securities or payments under nondiscretionary charitable contribution matching programs).
- A director (or an immediate family member of the director) is employed as an executive officer of a company where any of the present executive officers of the issuer at the same time serves on that company's compensation committee.
- A director (or an immediate family member of the director) is or was a partner of the issuer's external auditor or an employee of the external auditor that worked on the issuer's audit.

Various formal criteria to evaluate independence have also been advocated by The Conference Board Commission on Public Trust and Private Enterprise as well as by The Business Roundtable, the California Public Employees' Retirement

System (CalPERS), the National Association of Corporate Directors (NACD), and the Teachers Insurance and Annuity Association-College Retirement Equities Fund (TIAA-CREF).

Contextual Assessment: Delaware Law

Most Delaware court decisions concerning director independence have focused on economic ties and whether directors were under the "dominion and control" of a fellow director or senior executive. However, with the 2003 ruling in the *Oracle* case—regarding the impartiality of two outside directors appointed to a special litigation committee—the Court of Chancery expanded its review to a wider array of personal and professional relationships (including economic, social, philanthropic and personal relationships) to conclude that, despite the lack of economic ties, the special litigation committee was "fraught with conflicts" (*In re Oracle Corp. Derivative Litigation*, 824 A.2d 917 [Del. Ch. 2003]). In the decision, Vice Chancellor Strine explained that (p. 919)

> *[t]his contextual approach is a strength of our law, as even the best minds have yet to devise across-the-board definitions that capture all of the circumstances in which the independence of directors might reasonably be questioned. By taking into account all circumstances, the Delaware approach undoubtedly results in some level of indeterminacy, but with the compensating benefit that independence determinations are tailored to the precise situation at issue.*

The Oracle decision generally indicates that, despite definitions by regulatory agencies or other attempts to codify independence standards, Delaware courts expect boards of directors to assess the particular circumstances and establish a degree of independence that goes beyond the baseline requirements (and include, for example, matters such as the length of service on a board or committee and the robustness of the nomination process adopted to select a certain board member). According to *In re Oracle Corp.* (2003, 917), "It will no longer be sufficient (if it ever was) for boards of directors to focus on . . . the existence of personal material economic interests when evaluating possible sources of impermissible bias. Instead, the independence inquiry will depend on whether a director is unable to make a decision with only the best interests of the corporation in mind for *any* substantial reason." This approach is consistent with a commentary published by Vice Chancellor Strine in 2002, in the aftermath of the Enron case, where he wrote that "[t]he question of whether a director can act independently is inherently situational" (Strine 2002, 1378).

Over the past few years, The Conference Board has been documenting a strong trend toward board independence which exceeds the minimum standards set by major self-regulatory organizations. In 2008, across industries, companies consistently reported that independent directors constitute more than 70 percent of their board membership. In general, the number of directors who are independent under major securities exchange standards increases with company size. Although 77.8 percent of the directors in the smallest revenue group surveyed

This figure shows the percentage of independent directors partitioned by industry. The median percentage of independent directors ranges from 71.4 to 86.6.

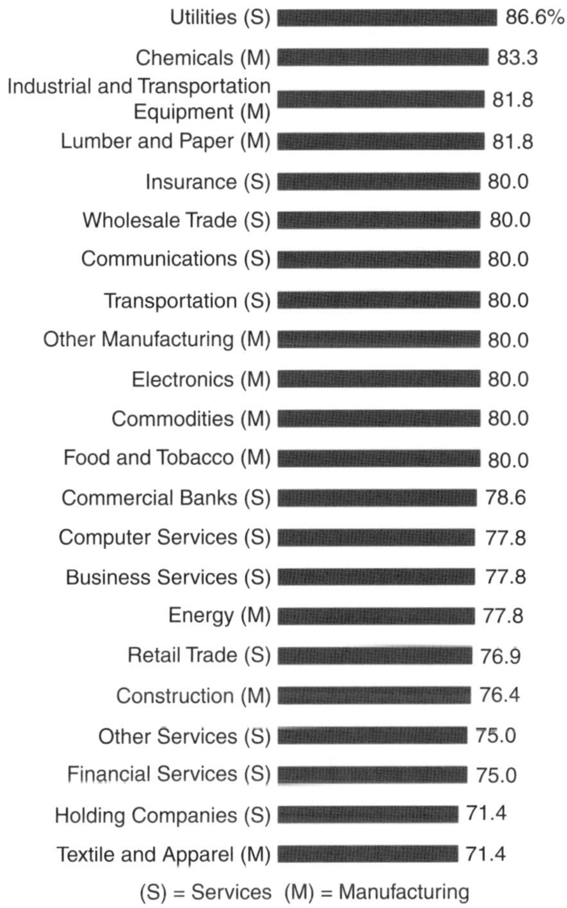

Exhibit 11.13 Independent Directors by Industry
Source: The Conference Board.

by The Conference Board meet baseline independence requirements, this median increases to 84.6 percent among the largest companies (Hallock et al. 2008). Exhibits 11.13 and 11.14 discuss survey findings on director independence, based on industry and revenue groups.

Disclosure Requirements

For the past few years, issuers have been required to disclose information in SEC filings regarding director independence and other corporate governance matters. The SEC has consolidated these requirements under new Item 407 of Regulation S-K (SEC Release No. 33-8732; 34-54302, August 11, 2006). Registrants must disclose

This figure shows the percentage of companies with independent directors, partitioned by revenues. As company revenue increases, so does the percentage of independent directors.

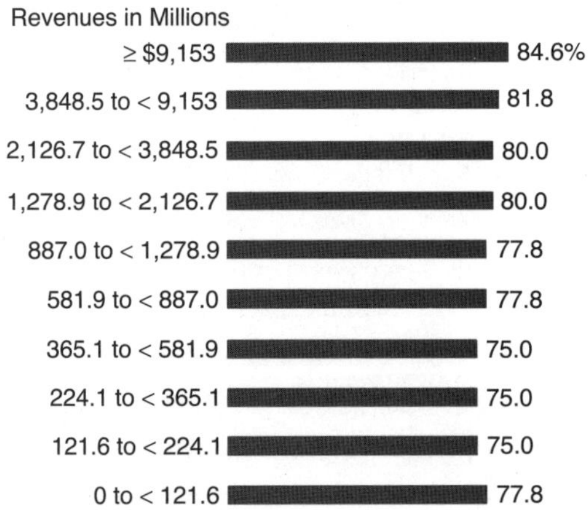

Exhibit 11.14 Independent Directors by Revenue
Source: The Conference Board.

information about director independence; nominating, audit, and compensation committees; and shareholder communications by:

- Identifying each independent director of the company (and the nominees for director when the information is being presented in a proxy or information statement) as measured by the company's definition of independence.
- Identifying any members of the compensation, nominating, and audit committees whom the company has *not* identified as independent under such definition.
- Describing, by specific category or type, any related-party transactions, relationships, or arrangements *not* otherwise disclosed and that were part of the board of directors' consideration in determining that the independence standard has been met as to each independent director or director nominee.
- Providing the number of board meetings during the fiscal year and certain attendance information, including the board's policy on attendance at annual shareholder meetings and attendance information with respect to the last annual meeting.
- Identifying any standing audit, nominating, and compensation committees; their membership composition; and the number of meetings, together with certain descriptive information regarding such committees and their membership. If the registrant does not have a standing nominating or compensation committee, or committees performing similar functions, the registrant must provide the basis for the view of the board of directors that it is appropriate not to have such a committee and identify each director who participates in the consideration of director nominees and/or executive officer and director compensation, as applicable.
- Disclosing information about the audit committee's independence and expertise, and about the process for shareholders to send communications to

the registrant's board of directors. If there is no process, the basis for the board's view that it is appropriate not to have such a process and, if not all shareholder communications are sent directly to board members, a description of the process for determining which communications will be provided to board members.

BOARD LEADERSHIP

Traditionally, in U.S. public companies, the CEO heads the management team that the board oversees and also serves as a member of the board. Those who support the preservation of this traditional structure of *duality* argue that single leadership fosters greater operational efficiency, facilitates internal communication from and to the board, and ultimately enables better business performance (Berg and Smith 1978; Chaganti, Mahajan, and Sharma 1985; Baliga, Moyer, and Rao 1996; Brickley, Coles, and Jarrell 1997). The Business Roundtable, for example, believes that most American corporations have been "well served" by a structure where the CEO also operates as chairman of the board, because it bridges management and directorship levels while ensuring that both act with commonality of purpose (Business Roundtable 2005). By contrast, detractors of this practice observe that separating the roles gives boards an organizational basis for acting independent of management and avoiding dangerous instances of CEO imperialism (Park and Goyal 2002; Coombes and Wong 2004).

However companies decide this structural issue, today's boards are unquestionably expected to establish procedural safeguards necessary to avoid conflicts of interests and to ensure appropriate balances of power. The role of outside directors has been transformed over the years as boards were expanding their expertise and intensifying their monitoring activities. The new regulatory and enforcement environment emphasized the board's ability to analyze strategic and governance issues objectively; as a result, outside directors should be able to rely on their leader as an example of independence and autonomy from senior management. In 2003, the Commission on Public Trust and Private Enterprise, an entity convened under the auspices of The Conference Board to address the confidence decline that followed the Enron scandal, concluded that such balance of power can be achieved by adopting one of the following approaches (The Conference Board 2003).

- *Separating the roles of board chairman and CEO and appointing an independent lead director.* This approach clearly delineates the roles and responsibilities of the chairman and CEO and provides the greatest potential for creating appropriate checks and balances between the board and management. In this scenario, the chairman would have such responsibilities as presiding at board meetings; having ultimate approval over board agendas, length of discussion time for agenda items, and information flow to the board; and working with the corporate governance committee to coordinate CEO and board assessments.
- *Appointing a lead, presiding, or senior independent director.* This approach could be employed when boards do not choose to separate the chairman and CEO positions, or when the roles are separated but the appointed chairman is not an independent director. In this scenario, the lead, presiding, or senior

director should not be a member of management or have any conflicting ties to the CEO. Preferably, he should meet the independence requirements under applicable listing standards. The presiding director (or other equivalent designation) would have such responsibilities as chairing executive sessions, serving as the principal liaison between management and independent directors, and working closely with the chairman to finalize board meeting agendas. The lead or presiding director would also be in charge of meetings of independent directors and have approval over information flow to the board and other operational aspects.

Although the combined function remains the prevalent practice among U.S. public companies, splitting the role of chairman and CEO has been gaining momentum in recent years. In particular, in 2008, support for proposals calling for an independent board chair climbed by more than five percentage points to nearly 30 percent of affirmative votes cast. Activists supporting these propositions argue that oversight of the chief executive by an independent chair might have helped mitigate the risk-taking that contributed to the recent financial meltdown (RiskMetrics 2008). Proxy filings analyzed by The Conference Board indicate that the percentage of companies with a lead or presiding independent director increases with revenue, whereas the percentage of those with a non-CEO chair declines, suggesting that companies view the roles as overlapping rather than complementary. For example, only 29.3 percent of large companies with revenues of $9 billion or more report separating the CEO and board chairman positions; however, 68.1 percent of the same sample report having appointed a lead director. Variations can also be observed from industry to industry, with only 31.6 percent of companies in the energy industry with a non-CEO chair compared to over 50 percent in other sectors, including insurance and financial services (Hallock et al., 2008). Board leadership types adopted by companies are illustrated in Exhibits 11.15 and 11.16.

These trends may also be explained by the fact that current NYSE rules require that an outside director preside over executive sessions of the boards of listed companies (NYSE 2009, Section 303A.3). Thus, companies with CEOs functioning as board chairmen—almost 70 percent of companies in the energy industry—would automatically comply with the requirement by appointing an independent director to perform in such leadership capacity during executive sessions. Some NYSE members have even chosen to rotate the position and disclose multiple lead directors on the theory that the rotation system avoids exposing a single director—by virtue of his leadership role—to a greater degree of liability than fellow members. This is consistent with the commentary to the previously mentioned NYSE rule, according to which:

> *[t]here need not be a single presiding director at all executive sessions of the non-management directors. If one director is chosen to preside at these meetings, his or her name must be disclosed in the company's annual proxy statement or, if the company does not file an annual proxy statement, in the company's annual report on Form 10-K filed with the SEC. Alternatively, a company may disclose the procedure by which a presiding director is selected for each executive session. For example, a company may wish to rotate the presiding position among the chairs of board committees.*
>
> (Commentary to *NYSE Listed Company Manual*, Section 303A.3)

This figure shows the percentage of companies who have lead directors and those who have non-CEO chairs, partitioned by industry. The presence of a lead independent director ranges from a low 30.6 percent in financial services to a high 62.2 percent in the energy industry.

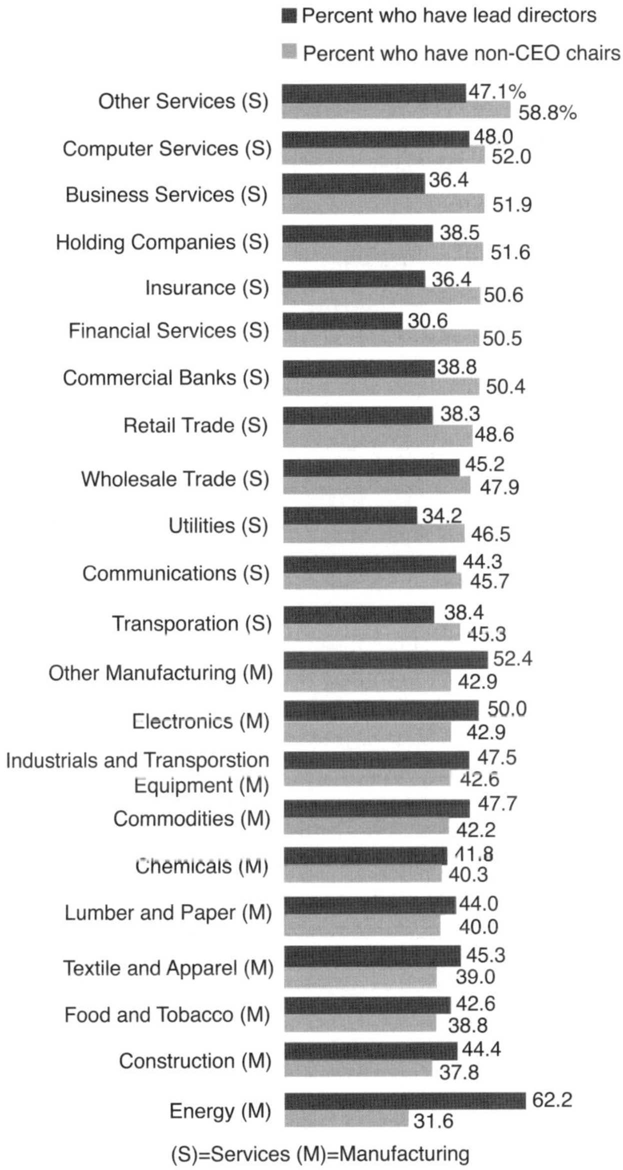

Exhibit 11.15 Board Leadership Type by Industry
Source: The Conference Board.

This figure shows the percentage of companies who have lead directors and those who have non-CEO chairs, partitioned by revenue. The percentage of companies with a lead director increases with revenue, while the percentage of companies with a non-CEO chair declines.

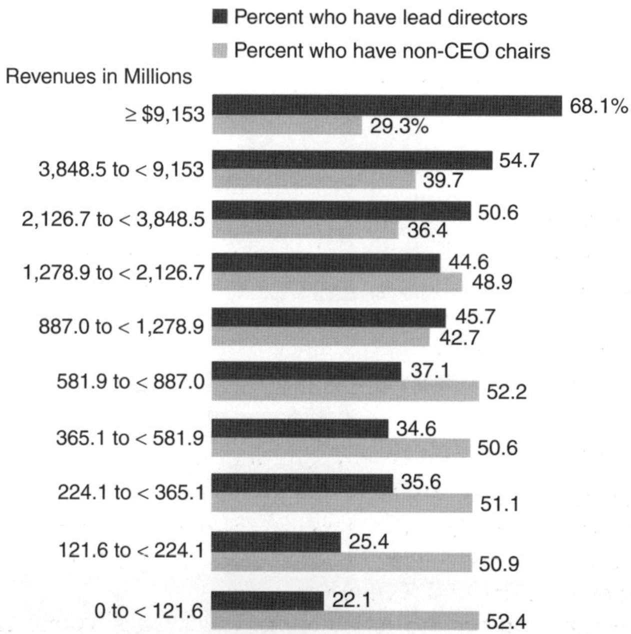

Exhibit 11.16 Board Leadership Type by Revenue
Source: The Conference Board.

BOARD COMMITTEES

The typical board of directors avails itself of committees to enhance the overall effectiveness of its oversight and ensure focus on matters of particular concern. A committee structure permits a better allocation of skills and responsibilities among subgroups of directors and addresses the increasing need to dedicate more time and in-depth analysis to key areas of the business (Klein 1998; Spira and Bender 2004).

As a result of the expansion of board responsibilities documented in the past decade, the establishment of certain standing committees is now prescribed either by law or regulatory standards. Specifically, the Sarbanes-Oxley Act of 2002 and subsequent SEC rules require that audit committees be composed entirely of independent directors (Section 301 of the Sarbanes-Oxley Act of 2002 and Rule 10A-3 under the Securities Exchange Act of 1934). The NYSE prescribes to all listed companies the formation of nominating, audit, and compensation committees composed of directors meeting stock exchange independence standards (NYSE 2009, Section 303A.04). NASDAQ rules strengthen independent oversight of nomination and compensation decisions but do not require the formation of dedicated committees.

Boards may choose to establish other standing committees with a specific focus on strategy and risk, succession planning, technology, public affairs, and other substantive issues of particular concern to the business (Tonello 2007). In some regulated industries, special legislation may require or encourage the delegation of certain oversight functions to similar ad hoc committees. Finally, from time to time, the board may create a special committee to undertake urgent tasks (e.g., oversee an internal investigation on potential wrongdoing or provide recommendations regarding a situation of crisis (Bergen 2009).

Facts and Statistics

Research conducted by The Conference Board shows that virtually all public companies rely on audit, compensation, and nominating/governance committees of the board. Other board functions increasingly delegated to standing committees include finance and corporate social responsibility. The median size of a standing committee varies from three to five members (Hallock et al. 2008). Exhibits 11.17 and 11.18 display statistical information on existing board committees.

Nominating/Corporate Governance Committees

- In 2008, virtually all S&P 500 companies had a nominating/corporate governance committee. Virtually all members are independent.
- Nominating committees vary in size between three and six members, depending on industry and revenue groups.
- The average number of nominating/governance committee meetings dipped from 5 in 2007 to 4.5 in 2008.

Exhibit 11.17 Types of Board Committees, by Industry

This table shows the percentage of companies in manufacturing, financial services, and nonfinancial services having various types of committees. Most companies' boards have audit, compensation, and nominating/governance committees.

Company Has Committee	Manufacturing	Financial Services	Nonfinancial Services
Audit	100.0%	96.6%	100.0%
Compensation	97.7	95.8	89.1
Nominating/Governance	95.3	83.1	87.0
Executive	36.5	44.9	58.7
Succession Planning	0.0	2.5	0.0
Finance	25.9	34.8	26.1
Ethics	1.2	0.9	2.2
Human Resources	3.5	5.1	6.5
Pension and Benefits	4.7	1.7	4.4
Stock Option	3.5	1.7	4.4
Environmental and Corporate Responsibility	15.3	6.8	2.2
R&D/Innovation	5.9	0.0	0.0
Political Contributions	1.2	0.9	2.2

Source: The Conference Board.

Exhibit 11.18 Types of Board Committees, by Revenue

This table shows the percentage of companies with different committees, partitioned by company revenues. Environmental and social responsibility committees are increasingly present in boards of larger companies.

	Revenues in Millions						
Company Has Committee	**\$0 to < \$121.6**	**\$121.6 to < \$224.1**	**\$224.1 to < \$365.1**	**\$365.1 to < \$581.9**	**\$2,126.7 to < \$3,848.5**	**\$3,848.5 to < \$9,153**	**≥ \$9,153**
Audit	93.8%	100.0%	100.0%	100.0%	100.0%	97.6%	100.0%
Compensation	90.6	100.0	94.1	100.0	91.7	92.7	98.2
Nominating/Governance	78.1	81.8	88.2	86.7	87.5	90.2	96.3
Executive	31.3	45.5	35.3	33.3	41.7	46.3	59.3
Succession Planning	6.3	0.0	0.0	0.0	4.2	0.0	1.9
Finance	25.0	9.1	5.9	6.7	33.3	34.2	55.6
Ethics	0.0	0.0	0.0	0.0	4.2	2.4	3.7
Human Resources	9.4	9.1	0.0	0.0	16.7	2.4	3.7
Pension and Benefits	3.1	9.1	11.8	6.7	4.2	0.0	0.0
Stock Option	3.1	0.0	0.0	6.7	12.5	0.0	3.7
Environmental and Corporate Responsibility	0.0	0.0	5.9	0.0	20.8	4.9	22.2
R&D/Innovation	3.1	0.0	5.9	0.0	4.2	0.0	1.9
Political Contributions	3.1	9.1	0.0	0.0	4.2	0.0	0.0

Source: The Conference Board.

- Retired and active chairmen, presidents, and CEOs are most in demand as chairmen of nominating/governance committees. Together, these groups make up 60 percent of nominating committee chairmen. The next most sought-after candidates are academics and nonprofit executives.

Compensation Committees

- In 2008, all S&P 500 companies had a dedicated compensation committee composed of independent members.
- Compensation committees vary in size between three and six members, depending on industry and revenue groups.
- Compensation committees met for an average of 6.6 times in 2008 (an increase from 5.8 in 2003). Approximately 30 percent of compensation committees met 8 or more times, up from 19 percent in 2007, and one met 21 times.
- Retired and active chairmen, presidents, and CEOs are most in demand as chairmen of compensation committees. Together, these groups make up 60 percent of compensation chairmen. The next most sought-after chairman candidates are other corporate executives (both active and retired).

Audit Committees

- In 2008, all S&P 500 companies had an audit committee composed of independent members.
- Audit committees vary in size between three and seven members, depending on industry and revenue groups.
- On average, audit committees met 9.1 times in 2008 (down slightly from a peak of 9.5 percent in 2006 and 2007). However, 29 percent of audit committees convened 11 or more times, and 1 percent met 28 times.
- Retired and active company chairmen, presidents, and CEOs are most in demand as chairmen of audit committees. Together, these groups comprise 43 percent of audit committee chairmen. The next most sought-after chairman candidates are active or retired CFOs, treasurers, and financial managers (15 percent), followed by accountants and investors (at 9 percent and 8 percent, respectively).

Formation and Operational Issues

Often the responsibility of the nominating/corporate governance committee is to make recommendations on and oversee the internal organization of the board, including the need to form standing or special committees, their assignments, and member qualifications. Similarly, the governance committee is responsible for establishing procedures to periodically assess the performance of the board and its committees (NYSE 2009, Sections 303A.04[a], 303A.05[a], and 303A.07[c]). An effective organizational structure should require that:

- Each committee has a written charter delineating the committee's composition, duties, and reporting lines.
- The full board reviews and approves the committee charter at least annually.
- The committee charter is publicly available, as the performance of the committee and its members should be assessed vis-à-vis the responsibilities described in the document.

The full board of directors should periodically expect recommendations by the corporate governance committee and reevaluate the internal delegation of functions based on actual circumstances facing the company. Similarly, committees should update the full board regarding their activities on a regular basis via oral or written reports. In certain circumstances, the board should consider requesting minutes of committee meetings.

While the board should ensure that committees retain experienced individuals, it may also adopt a policy of rotating members and chairmen to provide a fresh perspective to their operations and expose directors to different business aspects (Tonello and Brancato 2007).

BOARD OPERATIONS

Directors should remain apprised of best practices regarding board operations, including the conduct of meetings and executive sessions, the compilation of the agenda, the circulation of preparatory materials, the use of external advisers, and the adoption of policies on record keeping and voting.

In the past decade, serving on a board has become a significant commitment, both in terms of time and attention required. Not only must directors participate in board meetings and be willing to serve on committees, but they also should expect to dedicate time to reviewing relevant materials and preparing a thoughtful contribution to the discussion and deliberation process. More frequently now than in the past, due to the direct oversight exercised by the board on key aspects of the business (including internal controls, compliance programs, and risk management procedures), directors are asked or feel the need to visit corporate facilities and meet with senior management or other employees. Ultimately, the dedication expected from a director varies considerably based on the size and complexity of the organization, as well as the issues it faces in the given circumstances. Needless to say, a member of the board would need to be more closely involved in times of financial distress and during management succession or change-of-control situations (Alexander 2009; Bergman 2009).

Frequency of Meetings

Boards of directors hold scheduled meetings on a regular basis throughout the year and at least before the quarterly release of financial information to the market. In addition to scheduled meetings, special meetings may be prompted by emergencies or other particular circumstances.

Public data analyzed by The Conference Board show that the frequency of board meetings varies minimally based on the size of the company as well as across industries, with the average number of scheduled meetings being 7 or 8 per year. However, for each of the industry and revenue groups in the sample, a consistent number of companies (approximately 10 percent) meet as often as 12 to 15 times per year, indicating that—irrespective of the business size and economic sector—extraordinary events may occur and require special dedication by directors on a continuous and planned basis. In addition to full board meetings, directors serving on standing committees reconvene 6 to 9 times per year, with audit committees meeting more frequently (9.1 times per year, on average) than compensation committees (6.6 times) and nominating/corporate governance committees (4.6 times) (Hallock et al. 2008). Exhibits 11.19 and 11.20 describe the frequency of board meetings in different business industries and company size groups.

Attendance Policies

Engagement in the workings of the board is a crucial metric in any director assessment process. To encourage participation, companies tend to adopt formal meeting attendance policies for board members.

The majority of public corporations surveyed by The Conference Board pay directors a fee for each of the board or committee meetings they attend, whereas only a small group of respondents report that they penalize low attendance (for example, by means of a policy requiring directors to forfeit a portion of their compensation if they miss more than a certain number of meetings). The inability to attend over 75 percent of the board meetings is required to be publicly disclosed in the company's proxy statements (Item 7[f] of the Schedule 14A to be filed under the Securities Exchange Act of 1934). Exhibits 11.21 and 11.22 illustrate the adoption of attendance policies.

Executive Sessions

To empower the corporate board to serve as a more effective check on management, the major securities markets require companies to schedule regular executive sessions in which outside directors can openly discuss business issues without being subject to the influence of senior executives. (See, for example, NYSE [2009], Section 303A.03; and NASDAQ Rule 5605[b][2].) Executive sessions merely constitute a discussion forum and are not the venue for directors to take formal actions on behalf of the full board. Detailed minutes are not customary and, in fact, may discourage a candid participation (Krus 2006).

Under NYSE listing standards, in particular, the board must adopt a policy for regular scheduling of executive sessions. This avoids the situation in which directors hesitate to call a session due to the negative inference of such a request and the risk of compromising relations with the CEO or other executives. If nonindependent directors are normally admitted to executive sessions, then at least once a year the board should schedule an executive session of independent directors only.

An outside director must preside over each executive session, but there is no requirement that the same individual assumes the leading role at all of these meetings. If the board appoints only one lead director, his name must be disclosed in the company's annual proxy statement or annual report filed with the SEC. Alternatively, the company must disclose the procedure by which a presiding director is chosen for each session. For example, a company may want to rotate the presiding position among the chairs of standing board committees.

For interested parties to make their concerns known to outside directors, the company must disclose—also on proxy statements or the annual report—a method for such parties to communicate directly with the presiding director or with outside directors as a group. For this purpose, companies may, if they wish, utilize the same procedures they have established for the receipt and treatment of complaints or

Exhibit 11.19 Frequency of Board Meetings, by Industry

This table shows the number of annual board meetings, partitioned by industry. The median corporate board meets between seven and nine times annually.

		Number of Meetings Annually					
Industry	**Number of Companies**	**10th Percentile**	**25th Percentile**	**Mean**	**Median**	**75th Percentile**	**90th Percentile**
Business Services (S)	101	4	5	8	7	10	12
Chemicals (M)	203	5	6	8	8	10	13
Commercial Banks (S)	187	5	6	9	9	12	14
Commodities (M)	90	4	5	7	6	9	11
Communications (S)	91	4	6	9	8	10	15
Computer Services (S)	154	4	6	9	8	11	17
Construction (M)	28	4	6	8	8	10	13
Electronics (M)	154	5	6	9	8	11	14
Energy (M)	109	4	5	9	7	12	14
Financial Services (Nonbanking) (S)	70	5	5	10	8	12	17
Food and Tobacco (M)	50	4	5	7	6	9	12
Holding Companies (S)	127	4	5	9	7	11	14
Industrial and Transportation Equipment (M)	172	4	5	7	6	9	12
Insurance (S)	111	4	4	7	7	9	12
Lumber and Paper (M)	42	4	5	7	7	9	10
Other Manufacturing (M)	139	4	5	8	7	9	15
Other Services (S)	107	4	5	8	7	10	15
Retail Trade (S)	129	4	5	8	7	10	13
Textile and Apparel (M)	17	4	6	8	7	8	11
Transportation (S)	67	4	5	7	6	8	13
Utilities (S)	98	5	6	8	8	10	13
Wholesale Trade (S)	73	4	5	8	7	9	13

(S) = Services (M) = Manufacturing
Source: The Conference Board.

Exhibit 11.20 Frequency of Board Meetings, by Revenue

This table shows the number of annual board meetings, partitioned by company revenues. The smallest companies meet just as often as the largest companies.

Revenues in Millions	Number of Companies	Number of Meetings Annually: 10th Percentile	25th Percentile	Mean	Median	75th Percentile	90th Percentile
$0 to < $121.6	231	4	5	8	7	10	14
121.6 to < 224.1	232	4	5	9	8	12	15
224.1 to < 365.1	233	4	5	8	7	11	13
365.1 to < 581.9	231	4	5	8	7	10	14
581.9 to < 887.0	232	4	5	8	7	10	14
887.0 to < 1,278.9	232	4	5	8	7	10	14
1,278.9 to < 2,126.7	233	4	5	8	7	10	12
2,126.7 to < 3,848.5	231	4	6	8	7	10	13
3,848.5 to < 9,153	232	5	6	8	7	9	13
≥9,153	232	6	6	9	8	10	12

Source: The Conference Board.

Exhibit 11.21 Board Attendance Policies by Industry

This company shows board attendance policies of firms, partitioned by manufacturing, financial services, and nonfinancial services. The majority of companies pay meeting attendance fees. A smaller number penalize low attendance.

	Manufacturing	Financial Services	Nonfinancial Services
Companies that penalize low attendance	2.4%	4.2%	15.2%
Companies that pay meeting attendance fees	52.9	64.4	65.2

Source: The Conference Board.

concerns on accounting or auditing practices, in compliance with the Exchange Act (Section 10A[m][4] and Rule 10A-3[b][3]).

Use of External Advisers

The board or its committees should hire external experts such as counsel, consultants, and other professionals to the extent that additional expertise is deemed necessary to fulfill the board's fiduciary duties. In order to avoid conflicts of interest, external experts and consultants should have a direct line of communication and reporting responsibility to the board, not to management (Brancato and Rudnick 2006). Boards do not require management approval to hire their own advisers. The Sarbanes-Oxley Act of 2002 authorizes independent audit committees to hire their own advisers at company expense (Section 10A[m][5] of the Securities Exchange Act of 1934, amended by Section 301 of the Sarbanes-Oxley Act).

Exhibit 11.22 Board Attendance Policies by Revenue

This table shows attendance policies of companies, partitioned by revenues. The percentage of companies paying meeting attendance fees varies greatly by revenue size.

Revenues in Millions	Companies That Penalize Low Attendance	Companies That Pay Meeting Attendance Fees
$0 to < 121.6	21.9%	65.6%
121.6 to < 224.1	0.0	72.7
224.1 to < 365.1	5.9	64.7
365.1 to < 581.9	0.0	86.7
581.9 to < 887.0	0.0	62.5
887.0 to < 1,278.9	5.0	70.0
1,278.9 to < 2,126.7	0.0	84.2
2,126.7 to < 3,848.5	8.3	70.8
3,848.5 to < 9,153	2.4	53.7
≥9,153	3.7	35.2

Source: The Conference Board.

SUMMARY AND CONCLUSIONS

This chapter examines the composition of boards of directors of U.S. public companies and is based on empirical research conducted by The Conference Board, the New York–based business membership organization. In the past decade, public corporations in the United States have responded to pressures from market regulators and gatekeepers by strengthening their management oversight process and adopting a wide range of best governance practices. Proxy statement analyses and survey findings reveal that today's corporate boards are increasingly independent from senior executives. Directors' independence results from several factors, including the limited number of directors who are employees or otherwise affiliated with the company; a more diverse array of backgrounds, both personal and professional; the steady decline in the use of classified structures; the widespread institution of lead directors to counterbalance CEO influence; and the adoption of stricter retirement and tenure policies.

Board practices appear to have improved dramatically even at an operational level. Major responsibilities such as audit and compensation oversight are handled more efficiently through standing committees composed of smaller subgroups of independent directors. Meetings can be as frequent as 12 times per year, and companies often encourage engagement through attendance policies and other incentives. Boards conduct executive sessions to favor candid discussions among outside directors and to provide additional opportunities to coordinate their initiatives within the full board.

DISCUSSION QUESTIONS

1. What are the driving factors of the process undergone in the past decade by U.S. corporate boards of directors to strengthen their independence and professional expertise?
2. Discuss the reasons today's corporate boards may find attracting and retaining qualified directors difficult.
3. What aspects should a thorough evaluation of director independence encompass?
4. What considerations should a company make in choosing the most appropriate board leadership structure?
5. What policies do companies use to encourage board meeting attendance?

REFERENCES

Alexander, Frederick H. 2009. *The role of the board in turbulent times: Responding to unsolicited takeover offers*. New York: The Conference Board, Inc.

Alogna, Stephen, Mariana Pargendler, and Meagan Thompson-Mann. 2009. Chairing the board: The case for independent leadership in corporate America. Yale School of Management—Millstein Center for Corporate Governance and Performance Policy Briefing 4, 1–24.

Baliga, B. Ram, Charles R. Moyer, and Ramesh S. Rao. 1996. CEO duality and firm performance: What's the fuss? *Strategic Management Journal* 17 (1): 41–53.

Bebchuk, Lucian A., John C. Coates, and Guhan Subramanian. 2002. The powerful anti-takeover force of staggered boards: Theory, evidence, and policy. *Stanford Law Review* 54 (5): 887–951.

Berg S. V. and S. K. Smith. 1978. CEO and board chairman: A quantitative study of dual vs. unitary board leadership. *Directors & Boards* 3 (1): 34–39.

Bergen, Robin. 2009. *The role of the board in turbulent times: Overseeing internal investigations*. New York: The Conference Board, Inc.

Bergman, Mark S. 2009. *The role of the board in turbulent times: Assessing corporate strategy, liquidity needs, strategic transactions, internal controls and disclosure*. New York: The Conference Board, Inc.

Bhagat, Sanjai, and Bernard S. Black. 2002. The non-correlation between board independence and long-term firm performance. *Journal of Corporation Law* 27: 2, 231–273.

Brancato, Carolyn K., and Alan Rudnick. 2006. *The evolving relationship between compensation committees and consultants*. New York: The Conference Board, Inc.

Brickley, James A., Jeffery L. Coles, and Gregg Jarrell. 1997. Leadership structure: Separating the CEO and chairman of the board. *Journal of Corporate Finance* 3 (3): 189–220.

Business Roundtable. 2005. *Principles of corporate governance*. Washington, D.C.: Business Roundtable.

Chaganti, Rajeswararao S., Vijay Mahajan, and Subhash Sharma. 1985. Corporate board size, composition and corporate failures in retailing industry. *Journal of Management Studies* 22 (4): 400–417.

Coombes, Paul, and Simon C. Y. Wong. 2004. Chairman and CEO—One Job or Two? *McKinsey Quarterly* 2: 42–47.

Davis, Stephen, Jon Lukomnik, and David Pitt-Watson. 2006. *The new capitalists: How citizen investors are reshaping the corporate agenda*. Boston: Harvard Business School Press.

Daum, Julie. 2008. *Trends in board membership: The rise of the first-time director*. New York: Spencer Stuart.

Ganor, Mira. 2008. Why do managers dismantle staggered boards? *Delaware Journal of Corporate Law* 33 (1): 149–198.

Gupta, Manu, and Paige L. Fields. 2009. Board independence and corporate governance: Evidence from director resignations. *Journal of Business Finance and Accounting* 36 (1–2): 161–184.

Hallock, Kevin F., Matteo Tonello, and Judit Torok. 2008. *Directors' compensation and board practices in 2008*. New York: The Conference Board Inc.

Heslin, Peter A., and Lex Donaldson. 1999. An organizational portfolio theory of board composition. *Corporate Governance: An International Review* 7 (1): 81–88.

In re Oracle Corp. Derivative Litigation, 824 A.2d 917 (Del. Ch. 2003).

Klein, April. 1998. Firm performance and board committee structure. *Journal of Law and Economics* 41 (1): 275–303.

Krus, Cynthia M. 2006. *Corporate secretary's answer book*. New York: Aspen Publishers, Inc.

Monks, Robert A. G., and Nell Minow. 2008. *Corporate governance*. Hoboken, NJ: John Wiley & Sons.

National Association of Securities Dealers Quotation System (NASDAQ). NASDAQ Rule 5605(b)(2).

New York Stock Exchange (NYSE). 2009. *NYSE Listed Company Manual*.

Park, Chul W., and Vidhan K. Goyal. 2002. Board leadership structure and CEO turnover. *Journal of Corporate Finance* 8 (1): 49–66.

Park, Damien J., and Matteo Tonello. 2009. *The role of the board in turbulent times: Avoiding shareholder activism*. New York: The Conference Board, Inc.

Raheja, Charu G. 2005. Determinants of board size and composition: A theory of corporate boards. *Journal of Financial and Quantitative Analysis* 40 (2): 283–306.

RiskMetrics Group. 2008. *2008 Postseason report summary*. New York: RiskMetrics Group.

Romano, Roberta. 2006. The Sarbanes-Oxley Act and the making of quack corporate governance. *Securities Law Review* 38 (3): 462–483.
Securities and Exchange Commission (SEC). 2006. SEC Release No. 33-8732; 34-54302, August 11. www.sec.gov.
———. 2008. Release No. 34-58367, August 15. www.sec.gov.
Spira, Laura F., and Ruth Bender. 2004. Compare and contrast: Perspectives on board committees. *Corporate Governance: An International Review* 12 (4): 489–499.
Strine, Leo E. 2002. Derivative impact? Some early reflections on the corporation law implications of the Enron debacle. *Business Lawyer* 57 (4): 1371–1402.
The Conference Board. 2003. *Commission on public trust and private enterprise: Findings and recommendations*. New York: The Conference Board, Inc.
Tonello, Matteo. 2007. *Emerging governance practices in enterprise risk management*. New York: The Conference Board, Inc.
Tonello, Matteo, and Carolyn Brancato. 2007. *Corporate governance handbook 2007: Legal standards and board practices*. New York: The Conference Board, Inc.

ABOUT THE AUTHOR

Matteo Tonello is director of corporate governance at The Conference Board in New York. For The Conference Board, he has conducted corporate governance, regulatory compliance, and risk management analyses and research in collaboration with leading corporations, institutional investors, and professional firms. Also, he has participated as a speaker and moderator in educational programs on governance best practices. Matteo Tonello is co-chair of The Conference Board Expert Committee on Shareholder Activism and has recently served on the Technical Advisory Group to The Conference Board Task Force on Executive Compensation. Before joining The Conference Board, he practiced corporate law at Davis Polk & Wardwell. He is a graduate of Harvard Law School and the University of Bologna.

CHAPTER 12

Board Diversity

DANIEL FERREIRA
Associate Professor (Reader), London School of Economics

INTRODUCTION

The board of directors is the most important decision-making body in a corporation. Boards are responsible for approving major strategic and financial decisions, such as mergers and acquisitions (M&As) and changes in capital structure, and also for the most important task of all, which is to hire and fire top executives. Not surprisingly, substantial research focuses on the workings of corporate boards. But researchers focus on varying aspects of boards. Some view boards as groups of diverse individuals who have different biases and prejudices and whose behavior is affected by social constraints and power relations. This perspective suggests that director heterogeneity plays a key role in how boards function. In contrast, most researchers in economics consider the board as a single entity. The only heterogeneity considered is whether directors are independent from managers. All other director characteristics are usually deemed unimportant unless they are somehow related to (formal or real) independence. More recently, an increasing amount of economic research on board diversity can be found in the academic pipelines

This chapter discusses current board diversity literature. The chapter mainly focuses on the recent contribution of economists to this topic but also provides some discussion of the noneconomic literature. Specifically, the chapter attempts to provide partial answers to three questions: What can be learned about diversity by studying boards? What can be learned about corporate governance from studies of board diversity? Is research on board diversity useful for policy discussions?

Directors may differ in many important characteristics, such as educational and functional background, industry experience, social connectedness, insider status, gender, and race. The goal of this chapter is not to discuss each of these characteristics in isolation but to use some examples to illustrate what can be learned from this research area. These examples are predominantly taken from the literature on demographic characteristics of directors. In particular, this chapter focuses mainly on gender and only briefly discusses other characteristics.

The chapter starts by discussing how economics and management scholars differ in their theoretical analyses of boards and board diversity more specifically. It then discusses a more practical issue: the costs and benefits of board diversity. After a brief overview of the literature on board diversity, the chapter examines gender diversity in the boardroom in more detail. The end of the chapter provides a summary of its main points in the form of some tentative answers to the three questions previously stated.

BOARD DIVERSITY, ECONOMIC THEORY, AND MANAGEMENT THEORIES

In economics, theoretical analyses of corporate boards usually abstract from the process of how board members reach an agreement (Hermalin and Weisbach 1998; Adams and Ferreira 2007). Whenever directors are treated as heterogeneous, this typically occurs because of their status as corporate insiders or outsiders (e.g., Raheja 2005). Accordingly, most of the existing empirical research in economics disproportionately focuses on the distinction between independent and nonindependent directors as the main source of director heterogeneity (see, for example, the survey by Adams, Hermalin, and Weisbach [2010]).

Unlike economists, management scholars normally create taxonomies to describe different views of boards. For example, the view that boards perform an important monitoring role is usually called the *agency* perspective. As an alternative or a complement to the agency view, some management scholars propose a *resource dependence* perspective (Pfeffer and Salancik 1978). Directors are viewed as providing important resources to the firm such as connections to key outsiders (regulators, suppliers, financiers, and others) and advice and counsel. When considering directors as resource providers, various dimensions of director diversity clearly become important. Thus, most of the original research on board composition beyond independence has been done by management scholars, especially those in the resource dependence tradition.

A sense arises that the approach adopted by management scholars is richer than the one adopted by most economists. Management scholars have no difficulties working with many theories at the same time. For example, Hillman and Dalziel (2003) discuss the possible relations between firm performance and board composition accounting for both agency and resource dependence perspectives. In contrast, economists normally only consider the monitoring role of boards (the agency perspective in the management jargon).

Despite some remaining skepticism, the dual role of boards is now becoming a mainstream idea in the economics literature. For example, Adams and Ferreira (2007) develop a formal model of boards, taking into account the dual role of boards as monitors and advisers of management. Skeptics of the economic approach will point out that a mathematical model of the dual role of boards is unnecessary. After all, management scholars have always considered boards to have this dual role. But economists think differently. They would ask: Why can't firms separate the two roles? Why not hire a group of people to monitor the chief executive officer (CEO) and another one to provide advice and other resources?

The analysis in Adams and Ferreira (2007) explains why separating the two functions of boards is not always desirable. First, directors should perform these two tasks because the same information that is used for monitoring purposes is also relevant for advising managers. But a second and subtler reason exists for combining the two functions in one board: A CEO is more likely to reveal firm-specific information to outside directors if he expects this information to improve the quality of advice provided by directors. Thus, a board with a superior advisory capability is likely to become better informed.

Today, both economists and management scholars tend to assign to boards the dual role of monitors and advisers of management. Whether boards perform such functions effectively is still a controversial issue. Powerful executives are likely to influence the nomination process in favor of those directors who are more likely to help managers achieve their self-serving goals (Hermalin and Weisbach 1998). Consequently, some view board composition as the outcome of choices made by executives in their attempt to reduce the effectiveness of monitoring by boards. This is also known as the *managerial power* view of boards.

What both the economic approach and the managerial approach have in common is the idea that firms choose directors for their characteristics. Different board compositions provide diverse connections with the outside environment (competitors, suppliers, investors, politicians, the media, and others). Director characteristics could affect directors' competence and incentives to monitor and advise managers, and thus could be chosen either to maximize shareholder value or to protect the interests of executives.

BENEFITS AND COSTS OF DIVERSITY

From a practical perspective, if firms want to choose the composition of their boards in order to maximize firm value, they should have at least a qualitative idea about the trade-offs of demographic diversity. This section discusses various potential benefits and costs of board diversity featured in the academic literature.

Potential Benefits of Board Diversity

- *Creativity and different perspectives.* People from different backgrounds and with different life experiences are likely to approach similar problems in different ways. Some evidence indicates that more diverse groups foster creativity and produce a greater range of perspectives and solutions to problems (e.g., Wiersema and Bantel 1992; Watson, Kumar, and Michaelsen 1993). That is, diverse groups are less likely to suffer from *groupthink*. Dissimilar group members may also contribute to group creativity by acquiring information through a more diverse set of sources. For example, minority members' networks may give them access to unique information sources (Granovetter 1973).
- *Access to resources and connections.* By selecting directors with different characteristics, firms may gain access to different resources. For example, directors with financial industry experience can help firms gain access to specific investors. Directors with political connections may help firms deal with regulators or win government procurement contracts. These reasons probably cannot explain a demand for some other demographic characteristics such as gender, age, or ethnicity.
- *Career incentives through signaling and mentoring.* Diversity in the boardroom may signal to lower-level employees that the company is committed to the promotion of minority workers or at least that their minority status

is not a hindrance to their careers in the company. Because mentoring is likely to be important for career advancement, boardroom diversity may also be beneficial for the careers of minority top executives, although whether outside directors engage in mentoring relationships with executives is not obvious. Because promotions at the highest levels are likely to be discussed in the boardroom, boardroom diversity is also a means of committing to a policy of nondiscrimination against minority managers.

- *Public relations, investor relations, and legitimacy.* Some firms may benefit more from conforming to societal expectations than others. For example, consumer goods firms may want to cultivate an image of social responsibility. Firms in which institutional investors comprise a larger fraction of their shareholder bases may surrender to investors' demands for board diversity. Those types of firms are more likely to pay attention to director demographics, especially gender and ethnicity. For those firms, having a more diverse board can be a means of acquiring legitimacy in the view of the public, the media, and the government.

Potential Costs of Board Diversity

- *Conflict, lack of cooperation, and insufficient communication.* The social psychology literature provides evidence on the relationship between demographic similarity and attraction (Zander 1979). In the management literature, Lau and Murnighan (1998, 328) develop the concept of group *faultlines* as "hypothetical dividing lines that may split a group into subgroups based on one or more attributes." Salient demographic characteristics may split groups into implicit subgroups. Demographic dissimilarity may limit communication among subgroups, create conflict, and reduce interpersonal attraction and group cohesiveness.

  In the case of corporate boards, perhaps a key problem associated with diversity is the possibility of communication breakdowns between top executives and minority outside directors. As Adams and Ferreira (2007) point out, outside directors rely on executives to gain access to firm-specific information. Executives may perceive demographically dissimilar directors as sharing different values and espousing dissimilar views. The reluctance of executives to share information with minority outside directors could compromise board effectiveness.
- *Choosing directors with little experience, inadequate qualifications, or who are overused.* An indirect cost of choosing directors mainly for their demographic characteristics is the possibility of neglecting other important characteristics. Take, for example, the case of gender diversity. Because the proportion of women in top executive positions is small but growing, a preference for female directors may lead to a board that is disproportionately young and little-experienced. Furthermore, because qualified minority candidates may be in short supply, minority directors are likely to accumulate more board seats than the average director. Busy directors are possibly less effective than non-busy ones.
- *Conflicts of interests and agenda pushing.* Some directors may be more interested in pushing their own personal agenda even at the expense of the

company's profits. Perhaps more problematic is the case in which directors also represent the interests of outsiders (for example, directors with financial industry connections). A more diverse board may be in greater risk of being influenced by directors with distinct personal and professional agendas. The cause of this risk is not diversity per se, but an insufficient alignment with shareholders' interests. An excessive focus on some characteristics (e.g., functional background) as a criterion for selecting directors may have the unintended consequence of appointing directors whose loyalties lie elsewhere.

A SELECTIVE OVERVIEW OF THE EMPIRICAL LITERATURE ON BOARD DIVERSITY

Management scholars with backgrounds in sociology and social psychology were among the first to conduct statistical studies of board composition. Pfeffer (1972) should perhaps be credited as the pioneer of this field. Pfeffer views boards mainly as a mechanism for co-opting other external organizations and individuals, which is consistent with his view of firms as dependent on external resources. He hypothesizes that board composition in terms of insiders and outsiders, the number of directors with financial expertise, and the number of lawyers on boards depends on the firm's need for creating links with the external environment (for example, the need to deal with regulators and banks).

Pfeffer's (1972) idea that the board is an instrument for dealing with the firm's external environment underlies much of the research in board diversity. For example, Agrawal and Knoeber's (2001) investigation of the appointment of directors with political connections is motivated by this idea. They find that firms in industries that are more dependent on the government have more directors with political connections.

Goldman, Rocholl, and So (2009) find evidence consistent with the hypothesis that the appointment of politically connected directors affects shareholder value. In particular, they find that a portfolio of firms with Republican directors outperforms a similar portfolio of Democratic firms after the 2000 presidential election. In a companion paper, Goldman, Rocholl, and So (2008) show evidence of at least one mechanism by which political connections can affect firm value: by affecting the probability of winning government procurement contracts.

While the case of politically connected directors fits well with the resource dependence view of boards, the case of directors with financial expertise is more complicated. Kroszner and Strahan (2001) discuss the potential conflicts of interests associated with the presence of bankers on boards. Güner, Malmendier, and Tate (2008) present evidence suggesting that firms with directors with financial industry experience tend to borrow too much with respect to their investment opportunities and to engage too frequently in value-destroying M&As. The authors claim that directors with financial expertise may distort their advice towards excessive borrowing and M&A activities in order to benefit commercial and investment banks.

As the case of bankers on boards suggests, the conflict-of-interest problem is the flip side of the resource dependence story. Bankers may be providers of resources to banks and not to the firms in which they serve as directors.

Knyazeva, Knyazeva, and Raheja (2009) study heterogeneity in directors' characteristics such as the number of board appointments, their experience in other firms and industries, and their equity ownership in the firm. They find substantial variation in board heterogeneity that is explained by industry- and firm-level variables. Once more, this evidence provides support for the resource dependence view. The authors also document correlations between some dimensions of board heterogeneity and firm performance.

The resource dependence view seems particularly useful when applied to characteristics such as functional background, experience, and social and political connections. But it is of limited appeal as a means to understanding the role of other demographic characteristics of directors. Understanding the role of characteristics such as gender or age requires paying attention to the impact of demographic diversity on director behavior and board dynamics.

James Westphal and his co-authors have produced some of the most original research on board diversity to date, using data from surveys of directors in large U.S. companies. Westphal and Zajac (1995) argue that CEOs prefer to work with demographically similar directors. Thus, CEOs who can influence the director nomination process will try to hire directors who are demographically similar to themselves. They also find evidence that CEO compensation is higher when CEOs and directors are demographically similar.

Westphal and Milton (2000) find that minority directors have more influence on board decisions if they have prior experience in a minority position on other boards and if they have social network ties to majority directors through common memberships on other boards. Westphal and Bednar (2005) argue that demographic homogeneity among directors (with respect to gender, functional background, education, and industry experience) increases the likelihood that directors will express their concerns in board meetings. Westphal and Stern (2006) show results suggesting that managers from a demographic minority group or without elite credentials are more likely to use interpersonal influence to obtain board appointments.

In summary, there are some important practical lessons from the academic literature on board diversity:

- Firms appear to choose directors for their characteristics; different types of firms choose different levels of director heterogeneity.
- Firms choose directors as a means to deal with the external environment.
- CEOs and top executives appear to prefer directors who are similar to themselves.
- Social networks and commonality of backgrounds appear to affect director appointments and the dynamics of the board.
- Directors from minority groups perceive their minority status as a hindrance to their work as a director.
- Minority directors may serve interests other than those of shareholders.

GENDER DIVERSITY IN THE BOARDROOM

This section discusses gender diversity in boards. The following relies extensively on research conducted by Adams and Ferreira (2009).

Women hold few corporate board seats. In the United States, women held 15.2 percent of Fortune 500 board seats in 2008 (Catalyst 2009). The percentage of female directors in Japan, Europe, Australia, and Canada is estimated to be 0.4 percent, 8.0 percent, 8.7 percent, and 10.6 percent, respectively (Equal Opportunity for Women in the Workplace Agency [EOWA] 2006; European Professional Women's Network [EPWN] 2004).

This relative underrepresentation of women in the boardroom has not gone unnoticed. Catalyst, a nonprofit organization committed to promote women in business, has been publishing a census of women in Fortune 1000 boards since 1993. The Higgs report (Higgs 2003) and the Tyson report (Tyson 2003) call for increased representation of women on British boards. In some countries, legislative initiatives to promote women on boards are gaining momentum. In Norway, since January 2008 all listed companies must abide by a 40 percent gender quota for female directors or face dissolution. Spain has enacted a law requiring companies to increase the share of female directors to 40 percent by 2015.

The remainder of this section provides an overview of the empirical evidence on female directors in publicly listed U.S. firms. The analysis is based on an unbalanced panel of director-level data for Standard & Poor's (S&P) 500, S&P MidCaps, and S&P SmallCap for the period 1996–2003, which is the same sample used in Adams and Ferreira (2009).

Women on Boards: Who Are They?

A first question is whether female directors are different from their male counterparts in terms of observable characteristics. Exhibit 12.1 provides some answers. As Exhibit 12.1 shows for a sample of U.S. firms from 1996 through 2003, female directors have more directorships and shorter tenure than male directors. They are also younger and less likely to be retired from their main occupation than male directors. These differences are all statistically significant.

These simple statistics are highly revealing. The evidence on tenure and age confirms the impression that female directors are, on average, less experienced, but also that there is a trend towards having more women on boards. Female directors are slightly busier than male directors, providing evidence consistent with the view that firms actively seek female directors but female directors are in short

Exhibit 12.1 Difference in Characteristics between Female and Male Directors

This table provides a contrast between women and men on four director characteristics. The sample consists of an unbalanced panel of 86,714 director-level observations from 1,939 U.S. firms (S&P 500, S&P MidCap, and S&P SmallCap firms) for the period 1996–2003.

Director Characteristic	Women	Men
Number of directorships	2.1	1.9
Tenure as director	7.2 years	10.0 years
Age	55.0 years	59.0 years
Percentage of retired directors	10%	19%

supply. The magnitude of the difference in the number of directorships appears small, perhaps suggesting that women might not be much busier than men. But the evidence on the proportion of retired directors again suggests that women might be busier; men are twice as likely to be retired as women.

Another characteristic in which male and female directors clearly differ is their status as independent. In the full sample of Adams and Ferreira (2009), the average proportion of independent directors is 63 percent; female directors are classified as independent in 80 percent of the cases.

The similarities must also not be overlooked. The average male or female director is above 55 years old, has two directorships, has been on the same board for at least seven years, and has another main occupation.

Characteristics of Firms with Women on Their Boards

An interesting issue is whether firms with and without female directors differ. There are several reasons this might be the case. For example, women may be more likely to be on the board of firms in particular industries, perhaps due to some industries having more diverse workforces.

Exhibit 12.2 provides summary statistics for the fraction of women on boards in selected two-digit standard industrial classification (SIC) codes. Female directors are less prevalent in firms that deal with infrastructure, energy, or electronics as compared to firms in consumer goods. Casual observation suggests that the consumers of the products from the latter five industries in Exhibit 12.2 are more likely to be diverse. Having a woman's perspective may be particularly valuable in such industries.

According to Hillman, Shropshire, and Cannella (2007), firms with female directors are larger and older, have more directors who sit on other boards with

Exhibit 12.2 Percentage of Female Directors in Selected Industries

This table presents the percentage of female directors, partitioned by industry. The sample consists of an unbalanced panel of 86,714 director-level observations from 1,939 U.S. firms (S&P 500, MidCap, and SmallCap firms) for the period 1996–2003.

Industry	N	Female Directors %
Special trade contractors	11	2
Oil and gas extraction	292	4
Transportation services	36	4
Water transportation	46	4
Electronic and other equipment	794	5
Paper and allied products	203	8
Eating and drinking places	169	9
Transportation by air	93	9
Furniture and home furnishings stores	58	10
Leather and leather products	40	14
Tobacco products	9	15
Apparel and accessory stores	164	15
Food stores	76	15
Real estate	6	16

female directors, and are in industries with a higher proportion of women in the workforce. Adams and Ferreira (2009) report that firms with female directors are larger, have more business segments, have larger boards, have worse performance in terms of Tobin's q (market value of assets over book value of assets) but better performance in terms of return on assets (ROA), and have lower stock return volatility than firms without female directors.

Do Women Change Boards?

Attendance at Board Meetings

Knowing much about what goes on in the boardroom is difficult. Minutes of meetings and voting outcomes are understandably treated as secret documents, when they exist at all. Thus, measuring the individual contribution of each director to the decision-making process is usually impossible. An exception exists with respect to attendance at board meetings. A Securities and Exchange Commission's (SEC) rule requires firms listed in the United States to disclose the names of those directors who missed more than 25 percent of the meetings in a year. Thus, identifying which directors had severe attendance problems in any given year is possible (Adams and Ferreira 2008).

The analysis in Adams and Ferreira (2009) suggests that female directors are significantly less likely to experience severe attendance problems. Furthermore, male attendance also appears to improve in boards with relatively more female directors. These results suggest that the addition of women to boards changes the behavior of all board members.

Of course, knowing whether attendance is important in practice is not obvious. But attendance behavior has improved dramatically after the Sarbanes-Oxley Act of 2002. The most recent data suggest that the proportion of directors with severe attendance problems is now almost zero. Thus, one of the consequences of the new emphasis on outside directors' responsibilities apparently was to eliminate absenteeism. The key lesson from the attendance data, however, is that more women on boards is associated with a more active board.

Board Committee Composition

Another way of trying to understand how women change boards is to see how they are deployed. Committees do most of the real work in boards. Unlike the board as a whole, board committees such as audit, nominating, corporate governance, compensation, and executive committees specialize in narrowly defined tasks. The first four committees are usually considered the most important monitoring committees (Kesner 1988; Adams and Ferreira 2009). The executive committee is mostly responsible for serving as a stand-in to act in lieu of a full board when immediate actions are needed, counseling the CEO, and overseeing the activities of other board committees (Kesner 1988).

Kesner (1988) has the pioneering work on the composition of board committees. She analyzes a cross-sectional sample of 250 Fortune 500 companies in 1983. In that sample, the proportion of female directors is a mere 3.6 percent. She finds only weak evidence that gender matters for committee appointments: Female directors are underrepresented in executive and nominating committees, but not in compensation and audit committees. She interprets the results with caution, admitting that due to the small cross-sectional sample, she cannot conclude whether gender or other characteristics drive committee assignments.

Bilimoria and Piderit (1994) reinvestigate these issues in a cross-sectional sample of 270 Fortune 500 firms in 1984. They find that women are significantly less likely to be appointed to compensation committees, as well as finance and executive committees, but are more likely to be part of public affairs committees. Despite using a similarly small cross-sectional sample, they interpret their findings much more provocatively and claim to find evidence for sex-based discrimination in committee appointments.

Adams and Ferreira (2009) analyze the issue of committee membership using data during 1996–2003. Due to the size (more than 1,900 firms) and the panel nature of the data, they can provide results that are more reliable than the ones from the previous studies. In particular, their study controls for various firm and director characteristics as well as for time-invariant firm characteristics through firm fixed effects regression methods. Analyzing only monitoring committees, Adams and Ferreira find that female directors are more likely to be appointed to audit, corporate governance, and nominating committees than male directors. Yet female directors are less likely to be appointed to compensation committees than male directors.

These most recent data paint a more complicated picture of women in the boardroom. There is no clear sign of discrimination against women in monitoring committee appointments. If anything female directors appear to have a greater chance of being deployed to audit, nominating, and corporate governance committees than men. Still, women are underrepresented in compensation committees and they also do not appear to affect CEO compensation (Adams and Ferreira 2009). Westphal and Zajac (1995) argue that demographic similarity between CEOs and directors is associated with higher CEO compensation. Thus, CEO influence on the composition of board committees is one possible explanation for the relative underrepresentation of women on compensation committees. An open question for future research is whether the increasing number of women on boards will eventually lead to more women on compensation committees and whether that will affect CEO compensation.

Director Compensation Structure

Despite not having a discernible impact on CEO compensation, female directors appear to affect director compensation. Adams and Ferreira (2009) show that the proportion of overall director compensation that is paid in stock options and deferred shares is higher in firms with relatively more women on boards. However, there is no clear impact on the overall level of director pay. Whether equity-based compensation for directors is good or bad depends on one's view of how stock markets work. Stock ownership aligns directors' and shareholders' interests in relatively efficient markets, when no significant distinction between long-term and short-term shareholders exists.

Does Gender Diversity Affect Firm Outcomes?

CEO Turnover

One of the most interesting results in the board diversity literature is the impact of board gender diversity on CEO turnover. From a theoretical viewpoint, whether and how diversity should matter for CEO turnover is unclear. Westphal and Bednar's (2005) *pluralistic ignorance* theory of boards suggests that demographic homogeneity among directors would make them more willing to take action after problems are encountered. Thus, according to this view, a more homogeneous board would take action more frequently after poor financial performance, perhaps replacing the CEO more often in such cases. The evidence in Adams and Ferreira (2009) suggests that the opposite is true: CEO turnover is more sensitive to stock return performance in firms with relatively more women on boards. This result suggests that boards with relatively more female directors are more likely to hold CEOs accountable for poor stock price performance.

Stock Return Volatility

Ferreira (2002) is the first to investigate the relation between gender diversity in the boardroom and stock return volatility. A positive relation between volatility and gender diversity is perhaps the most robust finding in this literature. Farrell and Hersch (2005), Hillman et al. (2007), and Adams and Ferreira (2009) also report a similar finding. Although this is a very robust finding, the literature has not yet fully addressed it. Further work is still needed to make sense out of this evidence.

Market Value and Operating Performance

No question has attracted more attention in this literature than the link between women on boards and the bottom line. Catalyst, a nonprofit organization seeking to promote women in business, regularly produces reports showing correlations between accounting performance and the presence of female directors on the boards of Fortune 500 firms. Those reports receive substantial media attention. The evidence is usually that the presence of women on boards correlates positively with measures of accounting performance such as return on equity (ROE). Despite the usual disclaimer that "correlation does not imply causation" that accompanies those reports, the language and the use of those reports implicitly suggest that having more women on boards is a way of improving financial performance. For example, Catalyst (2007, 1) states that "companies with more women board directors outperform those with the least by 53 percent." Most of the media coverage also interprets these results in a similar fashion.

Such evidence does not present an obvious case for the promotion of women in the boardroom. This point is further discussed in the conclusions. The following discussion presents the existing evidence in more detail.

Keeping in mind that Catalyst's reports are not scholarly research is important. Although academics help Catalyst researchers, the final reports from Catalyst do not undergo peer review and are not published in academic journals. The empirical findings in such reports are usually simple raw correlations without taking into account other possible determinants of firm performance. Furthermore, they are mostly cross-sectional and do not consider how performance changes after adding women to the board.

Academic literature exists that appears to give credence to Catalyst's results. For example, Carter, Simkins, and Simpson (2003) document a positive relationship between gender and ethnic diversity of the board and corporate performance, as proxied by Tobin's q. Carter, D'Souza, Simkins, and Simpson (2008) follow up that study and document additional evidence consistent with a positive impact of gender diversity on the market value of firms. Erhardt, Werbel, and Shrader (2003) provide evidence that board diversity is positively correlated with accounting measures of performance. Some other papers fail to find any statistically significant results (Farrell and Hersch 2005; Rose 2007, using data from Denmark).

Adams and Ferreira (2009) show the results of regressions of Tobin's q and ROA on the fraction of women on boards. After controlling for a long list of possible covariates, a positive relation between performance and board gender diversity is revealed. Although the statistical significance of the estimates is not particularly impressive, the positive correlation between performance and board diversity is compatible with some previous results such as those of Catalyst and Carter et al. (2003).

To address the causation versus correlation issue, Adams and Ferreira (2009) consider the problem of omitted variables. Gender diversity could correlate with omitted firm-specific variables such as corporate culture. Firms that are more progressive may have better performances and also more female directors. One way of taking into account time-invariant firm characteristics is to run firm fixed effects regressions. This basically amounts to considering only how within-firm changes in board diversity correlate with changes in firm performance.

Adams and Ferreira (2009) show a surprising result: The inclusion of firm fixed effects flips the sign of the estimated coefficients on the fraction of female directors. That is, now the (conditional) correlation between performance (ROA and Tobin's q) and board gender diversity is negative and statistically significant (at the 10 percent level). Clearly, the fixed effects results suggest that firm-specific omitted variables are an important enough concern to cast doubt on a causal interpretation of the widely publicized positive relation between profits and women on boards.

Of course, the fixed effects results also do not establish the direction of causality. Past and expected future performance may influence firms' decisions to select female directors. Baysinger and Butler (1985, 114) argue that "top-performing firms may be willing to invite independent directors onto their boards in order to appear progressive." A similar argument could be made for the selection of women to boards. If female directors are appointed because of tokenism, boards may choose female directors when they believe they can afford to have tokens. By contrast, Ryan and Haslam (2007) argue that women face a "glass cliff" in that they are more likely to be appointed to leadership positions where change is required, for example, following poor performance. Finally, women may also use firm performance as a criterion for accepting a directorship. All of these arguments suggest that corporate performance could influence the proportion of women on the board and highlight the importance of disentangling causality.

A typical way of addressing the causality issue is by means of instrumental variables (IV) methods. These methods identify causality only under very strong and usually unrealistic assumptions. Thus, any claims of detecting causality by means of IV methods should be taken cautiously. Adams and Ferreira (2009) find that, if the number of male director connections to female directors on other boards is used as an instrument for the fraction of women on boards, the impact of an increase in the fraction of female directors on both Tobin's q and ROA is negative in their sample.

The key message from Adams and Ferreira (2009) is that the impact of board diversity on performance is likely to be heterogeneous: Some firms benefit from more diversity while others do not. They hypothesize that female directors are more likely to be truly independent from managers (the evidence supports this view) and as such more likely to be tough monitors. But because an excessive emphasis on monitoring can be counterproductive at times, additional monitoring can harm performance in firms that are otherwise well governed. Adams and Ferreira provide some suggestive evidence in this direction.

An alternative method for ascertaining causality is to look for exogenous changes in the environment forcing firms to change the composition of their boards. Ahern and Dittmar (2009) exploit the introduction of a mandatory 40 percent female quota on boards of Norwegian firms. They find that firms that adjust to this new level suffer a significant negative reduction in market value.

Some Methodological Issues

Unfortunately, some of the authors in this literature do not acknowledge the limitations of IV methods. Some appear to believe that using two- or three-stage least squares, generalized method of moments (GMM), and dynamic panel methods somehow solve the causality problems. These are all variants of IV methods and as such are only useful if the chosen instruments are valid. Contrary to what some believe, the validity of all assumptions necessary for identification cannot be tested by statistical methods.

Choosing instruments in an arbitrary fashion can lead to almost any result. For example, Carter et al. (2003) estimate a system of equations in which Tobin's q depends on gender diversity and gender diversity depends on Tobin's q. The excluded variables from the diversity equation are board meetings, a dummy indicating that directors receive stock compensation, insider ownership, and ROA. They provide no rationale for these identification assumptions. To put it simply, why should ROA be assumed not to affect board diversity?

Although so-called natural experiments such as the one provided by the introduction of gender quotas in Norway are a promising way of sorting out causality, they also have limitations. The main problem is the lack of a randomly chosen control group—that is, a group of firms that are not affected (or are expected to be less affected) by the proposed legislation. Ahern and Dittmar (2009) avoid this problem by considering changes in performance following large changes in board composition, exploiting the fact that not all firms adjust to the quota level at the same time. The problem with this approach is that the timing of the adjustment is endogenously chosen by firms. If the timing of the adjustment is driven by past or expected performance, this identification strategy may not be valid.

Board Diversity and Firm Performance: The Way Forward

The evidence in Adams and Ferreira (2009) is compatible with the view that board diversity has costs and benefits. Their evidence also suggests that the balance between these benefits and costs varies across firms. Further research on the impact of board composition on firm performance is likely to generate new insights about the potential costs and benefits of heterogeneity in director characteristics.

An example is the recent work by Anderson, Reeb, Upadhyay, and Zhao (2009). They analyze the impact of board heterogeneity on firm performance taking into account six director characteristics: education, experience, profession, gender, ethnicity, and race. To address endogeneity problems, they use the heterogeneity of the county of the firm's corporate headquarters as an instrument for board diversity and they also run first-difference regressions. They find an overall positive effect of their diversity index on Tobin's q in a sample of Russell 1000 firms in 2003 and 2005. Consistent with diversity having costs and benefits, they find that the impact of board diversity on performance varies with firm characteristics. In particular, the authors report that board diversity has a beneficial effect in more complex firms, but a detrimental one in less complex firms. Similarly, board diversity is particularly beneficial in firms with high levels of a proxy variable for CEO power.

SUMMARY AND CONCLUSIONS

We return now to the three questions asked at the beginning of this chapter.

What Do We Learn about Diversity by Studying Boards?

Diversity affects the way groups behave. The composition of boards seems to affect directors' attendance behavior and the number of scheduled board meetings. Demographic dissimilarity in the boardroom seems to affect incentives for replacing CEOs, the director nomination process, and the design of compensation systems.

The study of diversity also helps to understand discrimination in business situations. Some use research findings that women are underrepresented in some key board committees as evidence of discrimination. Because evidence from more recent data also suggests that women are overrepresented in some important committees, the overall findings of discrimination on the basis of committee assignments are weak.

Others view a positive relation between profits and board diversity as evidence of discrimination. *Taste-based* discrimination implies that firms forgo profits to avoid hiring minority workers. This is particularly plausible in the case of corporate boards because some firms may not be governed in the interests of shareholders due to agency problems. Research findings suggest that some firms would benefit from more diversity, but positive discrimination also exists, suggesting that some firms forgo profits in favor of a more diverse board.

What Do We Learn about Corporate Governance from Studies of Board Diversity?

Studies of board diversity indicate that boards matter. In particular, board composition is correlated with various firm characteristics and outcomes. Firms in various industries choose different board compositions. Board diversity seems to affect corporate performance, but in diverse ways depending on the characteristics of the firm.

The evidence supports the view that directors perform multiple functions. They monitor managers, give advice on strategic issues, and provide access to crucial external resources. The need to balance these multiple roles requires close attention to board composition in terms of directors' personal characteristics.

Board diversity research also reveals some potential flaws in existing governance practices. Research suggests that CEO pay is higher in firms in which directors are demographically similar to the CEO. Evidence also indicates that female directors are underrepresented in compensation committees that set CEO compensation, despite being overrepresented in other monitoring committees (Adams and Ferreira 2009). Knowing whether CEO pay levels would change if there were more diversity in compensation committees is an empirical issue that deserves further scrutiny.

Board Diversity: Policy Concerns

Some in academia and the media have used the positive association between certain measures of financial performance and the presence of women on boards to make a business case for women in the boardroom. For example, Nowicki (2009, 2) cites Catalyst's reports and asks "what can be done to increase the number of women directors, serving in the Fortune 500 in these challenging economic conditions, given the correlation between women directors and firm performance?" Tuhus-Dubrow (2009, 1) cites research on women on boards and top management teams to conclude that there is "a new reason for businesses to promote women: it's more profitable."

Whether such arguments are helpful in advancing women in the boardroom is doubtful. Making a business case for women in the boardroom on the basis of statistical evidence linking women to profits obviously creates the possibility of a business case against women if the evidence turns out to suggest that women reduce profits. Conservative newspapers have used the evidence in Adams and Ferreira (2009) in exactly this way. The evidence on Norwegian quotas is also likely to be used by antidiversity constituencies.

The research on board diversity is best used as a means to understand the costs and benefits of diversity in the workplace and to study corporate governance issues. There are fruitful lessons for the practice of business. But correlations between profits and diversity in either direction are unlikely to be of much guidance for policy debates.

DISCUSSION QUESTIONS

1. From the point of view of shareholders, what are the main costs and benefits of board diversity?
2. What are the key findings from the board diversity literature?
3. Why does the proportion of female directors vary across industries?
4. What could explain the statistical evidence on the relation between profits and gender diversity in the boardroom?

REFERENCES

Adams, Renée, and Daniel Ferreira. 2007. A theory of friendly boards. *Journal of Finance* 62 (1): 217–250.

———. 2008. Do directors perform for pay? *Journal of Accounting and Economics* 46 (1): 154–171.

———. 2009. Women in the boardroom and their impact on governance and performance. *Journal of Financial Economics* 94 (2): 291–309.

Adams, Renée B., Benjamin E. Hermalin, and Michael S. Weisbach. 2010. The role of boards of directors in corporate governance: A conceptual framework and survey. *Journal of Economic Literature* 48 (1): 58–107.

Agrawal, Anup, and Charles Knoeber. 2001. Do some outside directors play a political role? *Journal of Law and Economics* 44 (1): 179–198.

Ahern, Kenneth R., and Amy K. Dittmar. 2009. The changing of the boards: The value effect of a massive exogenous shock. Working paper, University of Michigan.

Anderson, Ronald C., David M. Reeb, Arun Upadhyay, and Wanli Zhao. 2009. The economics of director heterogeneity. Working paper, Temple University.

Baysinger, Barry D., and Henry N. Butler. 1985. Corporate governance and the board of directors: Performance effects of changes in board composition. *Journal of Law, Economics, and Organization* 1 (1): 101–124.

Bilimoria, Diana, and Sandy K. Piderit. 1994. Board committee memberships: Effects of sex-based bias. *Academy of Management Journal* 37: 6, 1453–1477.

Carter, David A., Betty J. Simkins, and W. Gary Simpson. 2003. Corporate governance, board diversity, and firm value. *Financial Review* 38 (3): 33–53.

Carter, David A., Frank D'Souza, Betty J. Simkins, and W. Gary Simpson. 2008. The diversity of corporate board committees and financial performance. Working paper, Oklahoma State University.

Catalyst. 2007. *The bottom line: Corporate performance and women's representation on boards.* New York: Catalyst.

———. 2009. *2008 Catalyst census of women board directors of the Fortune 1000*. New York: Catalyst.

Equal Opportunity for Women in the Workplace Agency (EOWA). 2006. 2006 EOWA Australian Census of Women in Leadership. www.eowa.gov.au.

Erhardt, Niclas L., James D. Werbel, and Charles B. Shrader. 2003. Board of director diversity and firm financial performance. *Corporate Governance: An International Review* 11 (2): 102–111.

European Professional Women's Network (EPWN). 2004. The European PWN board women monitor. www.europeanpwn.net/index.php?article_id=8.

Farrell, Kathleen A., and Philip L. Hersch. 2005. Additions to corporate boards: The effect of gender. *Journal of Corporate Finance* 11 (1): 85–106.

Ferreira, Daniel. 2002. *Essays on the economics of organizations*. PhD Dissertation. Chicago: The University of Chicago, Department of Economics.

Goldman, Eitan, Jörg Rocholl, and Jongil So. 2008. Political connections and the allocation of procurement contracts. Working paper, Indiana University.

———. 2009. Do politically connected boards affect firm value? *Review of Financial Studies* 22 (6): 2331–2360.

Granovetter, Mark. 1973. The strength of weak ties. *American Journal of Sociology* 78 (6): 1360–1380.

Güner, A. Burak, Ulrike Malmendier, and Geoffrey Tate. 2008. Financial expertise of directors. *Journal of Financial Economics* 88 (2): 323–354.

Hermalin, Benjamin E., and Michael S. Weisbach. 1998. Endogenously chosen boards of directors and their monitoring of the CEO. *American Economic Review* 88 (1): 96–118.

Higgs, Derek. 2003. Review of the role and effectiveness of nonexecutive directors. www.dti.gov.uk/cld/non_execs_review.
Hillman, Amy I., and Thomas Dalziel. 2003. Boards of directors and firm performance: Integrating agency and resource dependence perspectives. *Academy of Management Review* 28 (3): 383–396.
Hillman, Amy J., Christine Shropshire, and Albert A. Cannella, Jr. 2007. Organizational predictors of women of corporate boards. *Academy of Management Journal* 50 (4): 941–952.
Kesner, Idalene F. 1988. Directors' characteristics and committee membership: An investigation of type, occupation, tenure, and gender. *Academy of Management Journal* 31: 1, 66–84.
Knyazeva, Anzhela, Diana Knyazeva, and Charu Raheja. 2009. The benefits of focus vs. heterogeneity: An analysis of corporate boards. Working paper, University of Rochester and Wake Forest University.
Kroszner, Randall S., and Philip E. Strahan. 2001. Bankers on boards: Monitoring, conflicts of interest, and lender liability. *Journal of Financial Economics* 62 (3): 415–452.
Lau, Dora C., and I. Keith Murnighan. 1998. Demographic diversity and faultlines: The compositional dynamics of organizational groups. *Academy of Management Review* 23 (2): 325–040.
Nowicki, Elizabeth A. 2009. Economic concerns, beleaguered corporations, and women in corporate boardrooms. Working paper, Tulane Law School.
Pfeffer, Jeffrey. 1972. Size and composition of corporate boards of directors: The organization and its environment. *Administrative Science Quarterly* 17 (2): 218–228.
Pfeffer, Jeffrey, and Gerald R. Salancik. 1978. *The external control of organizations: A resource dependence perspective*. New York: Harper & Row.
Raheja, Charu. 2005. Determinants of board size and composition: A theory of corporate boards. *Journal of Financial and Quantitative Analysis* 40 (2): 283–306.
Rose, Casper. 2007. Does female board representation influence firm performance? The Danish evidence. *Corporate Governance: An International Review* 15 (2): 404–413.
Ryan, Michelle K., and S. Alexander Haslam. 2007. The Glass Cliff: Exploring the dynamics surrounding women's appointment to precarious leadership positions. *Academy of Management Review* 32 (2): 549–572.
Tuhus-Dubrow, Rebecca. 2009. The female advantage. *Boston Globe*, May 3. Ideas Section, 1.
Tyson, Laura. 2003. The Tyson report on the recruitment and development of nonexecutive directors. www.london.edu/tysonreport.
Watson, Warren E., Kamalesh Kumar, and Larry K. Michaelsen. 1993. Cultural diversity's impact on interaction process and performance: Comparing homogeneous and diverse task groups. *Academy of Management Journal* 36 (3): 590–602.
Westphal, James D., and Michael K. Bednar. 2005. Pluralistic ignorance in corporate boards and firms' strategic persistence in response to low firm performance. *Administrative Science Quarterly* 50 (2): 262–298.
Westphal, James D., and Laurie P. Milton. 2000. How experience and network ties affect the influence of demographic minorities on corporate boards. *Administrative Science Quarterly* 45 (2): 366–398.
Westphal, James D., and Ithai Stern. 2006. The other pathway to the boardroom: Interpersonal influence behavior as a substitute for elite credentials and majority status in obtaining board appointments. *Administrative Science Quarterly* 51 (1): 169–204.
Westphal, James D., and Edward J. Zajac. 1995. Who shall govern? CEO/board power, demographic similarity, and new director selection. *Administrative Science Quarterly* 40 (1): 60–83.
Wiersema, Margarethe F., and Karen Bantel. 1992. Top management demography and corporate strategic change. *Academy of Management Journal* 35 (1): 91–121.
Zander, Alvin. 1979. The psychology of group processes. *Annual Review of Psychology* 30: 417–451.

ABOUT THE AUTHOR

Daniel Ferreira joined the London School of Economics and Political Science in 2006 after previous appointments as assistant professor in Portugal, Sweden, and Brazil. He became reader in finance (i.e., associate professor with tenure) in 2008. Dr. Ferreira has published widely on corporate governance and corporate finance in such journals as the *Journal of Finance, Journal of Financial Economics, Review of Financial Studies, Journal of Accounting and Economics*, and *Review of Economic Studies*, among others. He is also the director of the Corporate Finance and Governance program at the Financial Markets Group (FMG) and a research associate at the Center for Economic Policy Research (CEPR) and the European Corporate Governance Institute (ECGI). Dr. Ferreira received a PhD in economics from the University of Chicago in 2002.

CHAPTER 13

Board Subcommittees for Corporate Governance

ZABIHOLLAH REZAEE
Thompson-Hill Chair of Excellence, Professor of Accountancy,
University of Memphis

INTRODUCTION

Boards of directors are responsible for overseeing firms' strategic decisions, financial reporting procedures, internal control systems, risk assessment activities, audit practices, and corporate governance systems to protect and promote shareholders' interests. The board generally delegates these oversight functions to various board subcommittees, with the full board maintaining responsibility and accountability for the delegated functions. In the United States, stock exchange listing standards require that companies establish at least three board subcommittees: the audit committee, the compensation committee, and the nominating/governance committee (NYSE 2003). These three subcommittees must be composed solely of independent directors as defined by the exchange. Companies may also form other special committees (e.g., executive, finance, budget, risk management, litigation, and mergers and acquisitions) to address special board projects. This chapter discusses the three mandatory board subcommittees for listed companies and various other subcommittees the board may create.

IMPORTANCE OF BOARD SUBCOMMITTEES

Boards of directors typically fulfill their fiduciary duties through subcommittees to make efficient use of the time and expertise of individual directors. Board subcommittee formations and assignments depend on the type and size of the company, board characteristics, and delegated fiduciary duties. Because subcommittees of the board of directors are a subset of the board, they perform tasks and make recommendations for final approval by the entire board. Board subcommittees generally function independently from one another with sufficient authority, resources, and assigned responsibilities to effectively assist the entire board in fulfilling its fiduciary duties. Subcommittees should possess attributes that assist the full board in balancing its role as a watchdog or monitor and its role as managerial adviser.

- The 2008 survey of the Spencer Stuart Board Index (2008) reveals that S&P 500 companies, on average, maintain 4.2 board subcommittees.
- Many companies (more than 33 percent) have just the three mandatory subcommittees (audit, compensation, and nominating/governance); 25 percent of firms report five subcommittees (the three mandatory committees plus, most frequently used, an executive and finance subcommittee).
- Post Sarbanes-Oxley (SOX), the number of S&P 500 firms with six or more subcommittees is substantially down.
- For all S&P 500 firms in 2008, the three mandatory subcommittees (audit, compensation, and nominating/governance) are composed entirely of independent directors.
- A small but growing number of S&P 500 firms have added subcommittees focused on public policy, corporate and social responsibility (11 percent); science and technology (6 percent); environment, health, and safety (4 percent); and legal/compliance issues (4 percent).

AUDIT COMMITTEE

Recent financial crises and analysis of troubled banks and companies point to lapses in audit committees' oversight function. This raises the question: What role did audit committees play in overseeing risk assessment of subprime loans? Audit committees should function to protect investor interests by taking the lead on oversight responsibilities in the areas of internal controls, financial reporting, risk assessment, audit activities, and compliance with applicable laws and regulations. In the post-Sarbanes-Oxley (SOX) period, the audit committee selects the firm's external auditor, reviews the company's annual audited financial statements, and interacts with internal auditors to examine matters pertaining to internal control structure.

Securities and Exchange Commission (SEC 2003a) rules prohibit the listing of any security of an issuer (public company) that is not in compliance with the audit committee requirements established by SOX. These requirements (SEC 2003a) pertain to:

- The independence of audit committee members.
- The audit committee's responsibility to appoint and oversee the company's independent accountant.
- Procedures for handling complaints regarding the company's accounting practices.
- The authority of the audit committee to engage advisers.
- Funding for the independent auditor and any outside advisers engaged by the audit committee.

SOX stipulates that the audit committee maintain responsibility for hiring, overseeing, compensating, and firing external auditors. Effective, open, and candid communication between the audit committee and external auditors shields auditors from the undue influence of management. The audit committee must approve all audits and any permissible non-audit consulting services provided by the external auditors to the company. The audit committee should have access to and, when warranted, review all engagement letters signed between the independent auditors and their clients for audit and non-audit consulting services. The audit committee should receive from the independent auditors a detailed summary of each engagement describing the service involved, related fees, and assurance that the provided services are compatible with the auditor independence rules. In the post-SOX era, independent external auditors work with management at the direction of the audit committee.

Evolution of the Audit Committee

The evolution of audit committees reveals that many companies voluntarily established audit committees in the mid-twentieth century to provide more effective communication between the board of directors and external auditors. Traditionally, audit committees have acted as a liaison between management and external auditors in selecting auditors to preserve auditors' independence, reviewing a company's annual audited financial statements, and interacting with internal auditors in reviewing matters pertaining to internal control structure. Several pre-SOX reports (Treadway Commission 1987; Section 363.5 of FDIC Improvement Act 1993; Blue Ribbon Committee 1999; Public Oversight Board Panel on Audit Effectiveness 2000) address the role of the board of directors and its representative audit committee in overseeing corporate governance, the financial reporting process, the internal control structure, and audit functions. These reports discuss audit committees' structure and organization and suggest guidelines regarding functions, responsibilities, and activities of audit committees without mandating any specific requirements.

National Commission on Fraudulent Financial Reporting (Treadway Commission 1987)

The report of the Treadway Comission (1987) made 11 recommendations about the structure and role of the audit committee. These recommendations represent the first guidelines covering audit committee responsibilities and set standards based on best practices rather than on common practices. Three of the 11 recommendations of the Treadway Report pertain to audit committee structure. The first recommendation states that the SEC should require all publicly traded companies to establish audit committees composed solely of independent directors. The second recommendation proposes that all public companies establish a written charter for the audit committee, specifying its mission, objectives, role, and responsibilities. The third recommendation suggests that audit committees have adequate resources and authority to discharge their responsibilities.

The Treadway Report further provides eight recommendations about the role, responsibilities, and function of audit committees. These recommendations expand the audit committees' responsibilities to:

1. Oversee the quarterly reporting process and approve quarterly financial statements.
2. Sign a letter for inclusion in the annual reports describing the committee's responsibilities, activities, and accomplishments during the year.
3. Review annually management programs to monitor compliance with the code of business conduct in resolving conflicts of interest and, accordingly, assist management in preventing and detecting fraud.
4. Assume informal, vigilant, and effective oversight of the financial reporting process and the company's internal controls.
5. Ensure that the internal auditor's involvement in the audit of the entire financial reporting process is appropriate and properly coordinated with the independent public accountant.
6. Review management's evaluation of the factors assisting public accountants in preserving their independence.
7. Advise management when it seeks a second opinion on a significant accounting issue, such as important accounting policies or determination of accounting estimates.
8. Review management's plans for engaging the company's independent public accountant to perform any attestation function, such as management advisory services and review services.

FDICIA

The U.S. Congress passed the Federal Deposit Insurance Corporation Improvement Act of 1991 (FDICIA) in response to the savings and loan debacle. The FDICIA (FDIC 1991) requires that managers and independent auditors of depository institutions report on the effectiveness of internal controls over financial reporting. Regulations on FDIC Improvement Act of 1991 requires large financial institutions (more than $3 billion in assets) to establish an independent audit committee of outside, nonexecutive board members. The financial institution's full board is responsible for determining whether its audit committee complies with the FDIC independence rules and whether audit committee members have the necessary experience, financial literacy, and banking qualifications to fulfill their assigned responsibilities.

POB Report

The report of the Public Oversight Board (POB), entitled "The Panel on Audit Effectiveness Report and Recommendations," was issued in August 2000 (POB 2000). The 2000 panel was established in 1998 at the request of Arthur Levitt, the former chair of the SEC, to investigate the way independent audits are performed in light of recent changes in the business environment, such as globalization and technological advances. The 2000 report was addressed to several constituents of audited financial statements including audit committees, public accounting firms, the SEC, the standard setters, and the public. The report recommended that audit committees preapprove non-audit services (beyond a minimum threshold) that may affect auditors' independence when performing financial statement audits.

The 2000 panel, recognizing the importance of audit committees in the governance process, recommended that the SEC Public Sector require CPA firms to report annually to audit committees the total fees received by the audit firm for non-audit services such as management advisory and other non-alternative services. Further, external auditors should disclose all factors and relationships between the auditor and the client that may affect auditors' independence.

The Blue Ribbon Committee (BRC) Report

The Blue Ribbon Committee (BRC 1999) issued its report in February 1999 consisting of 10 recommendations to improve the effectiveness of audit committees and 5 guiding principles for audit committee best practices. The recommendations set forth by the BRC (1999), the rules adopted by the New York Stock Exchange (NYSE) and National Association of Securities Dealers (NASD), and the regulations established by the SEC have fundamentally defined the nature, functions, and duties of public audit committees. The BRC (1999) recommended five guiding principles to improve audit committee effectiveness in overseeing the accountability of corporate governance, the reliability of internal control structures, and the appropriateness of audit functions (BRC 1999). These principles are as follows:

1. The audit committee should play a key role in monitoring the component parts of the audit process.
2. Independent communication and information should flow between the audit committee and internal auditors.
3. Independent communication and information should flow between the audit committee and outside auditors.
4. Candid discussions should be held with management, the internal auditor, and the outside auditors regarding issues requiring judgment and impacting quality.
5. Audit committee members must be diligent and knowledgeable.

Audit Committees in the Post-SOX Era

The rash of financial statement fraud cases at the turn of the twenty-first century and their persistence in recent years raises this question of "Where was the audit committee?" This concern encouraged policy makers and regulators to take action to ensure the integrity and quality of the financial reporting process. The passage of SOX in July 2002 set new requirements for public-company audit committees to oversee companies' financial reports. SEC rules and stock exchange listing standards also provide guidance for the formation, structure, and responsibilities of audit committees. These standards suggest that audit committees meet at least three times per year (SOX 2002).

SOX Provisions Pertaining to Audit Committees

SOX (2002) expands audit committee responsibilities and requires committees to include more independent directors. The Act mandates that publicly traded companies maintain a standing audit committee that ensures full compliance with

SOX provisions. Audit committees have a primary responsibility of appointing external auditors, as well as overseeing their work and managing their compensation. Concisely, audit committees are directly responsible for establishing oversight mechanisms for financial disclosures of U.S. corporations and therefore should be independent from management. The audit committee's role has also broadened to include active participation in the firm's corporate governance practices, internal controls, and financial reports. At least one member of the audit committee has to be classified as a *financial expert* with other members maintaining an adequate knowledge of finance.

SEC Rules on Audit Committees

The SEC has been a longtime advocate of audit committees. Until recently, however, the SEC has stopped short of making audit committees a requirement for publicly traded companies. In December 1999, the SEC adopted audit committee rules in response to the Blue Ribbon Committee Report and Recommendations. The rules require disclosure on the existence, composition, charter, and function of audit committees. Among other things, the SEC rules (SEC 2000) require that (1) proxy statements include a report from the audit committee; (2) publicly traded companies disclose in their proxy statements whether their audit committee has a written charter, and file a copy of their charter every three years; and (3) public companies disclose in their proxy statements certain information pertaining to the independence of audit committee members.

In 2003, the SEC issued rules regarding Sections 406 and 407 of SOX (SEC 2003b) that require audit committees to prepare, present, and report audit and audit committee information in annual proxy statements. The following information became mandatory for the audit committee: to discuss the annual financial statements with management, to discuss audit-related matters with external auditors, and to confirm that the committee received external auditor's disclosure in compliance with auditor independence rules. After meeting those three requirements, the audit committee must make a decision whether to include audited financial statements in the company's annual report. Establishing a charter for the audit committee is highly recommended and, if established, a copy of the charter must be released in the proxy statement at least once every three years.

National Stock Exchanges Requirements

National stock exchanges in the United States, including the NYSE, AMEX, and NASDAQ (NYSE 2003) require that listed companies have audit committees with membership limited primarily to independent directors. In the post-SOX era, the exchanges have also revised their audit committee standards to comply with SOX and SEC provisions. To meet financial literacy requirements, the exchanges stipulate that an audit committee member should have a basic understanding of fundamental financial statements and an understanding of the specific company's operations. This requirement suggests that a sufficient, rather than a thorough understanding of generally accepted accounting principles (GAAP) satisfies the financial literacy requirement of the rules. The audit committee should not only understand the appropriateness and applications of accounting principles, methods, and procedures, but should also be able to challenge management on its application. In addition, NYSE rules require that audit committees closely monitor information given to analysts, carefully examine underlying managerial judgments affecting financial reports, and undergo annual evaluations.

Audit Committee Structure

The structure of the audit committee can have a major impact on its effectiveness. Structure encompasses the committee's size and composition, independence, qualifications, attributes, and resources.

Committee Size and Composition

Corporate governance reforms (SOX, SEC rules, and listing standards) require that the audit committee should be composed solely of at least three independent directors. The size of the audit committee usually ranges from three to five members. The 2006 Ernst and Young Committee Survey and Industry Insights (E&Y 2006) show that:

- About 26 percent of audit committee members are active chairs, presidents, or CEOs of other firms or organizations.
- Ninety-one percent of audit committee members are above 50 years old, but only 42 percent are full-time outside employees.
- Audit committees prefer to hire individuals with strong financial backgrounds (34 percent) or CEO/executive experience (24 percent).
- Average compensation for a committee member grew from $100,000 in 2005 to $120,000 in 2006.
- About 12 percent of audit committee members are active and retired human resources, strategy, and operations professionals.

Independence

Audit committees should be composed of nonexecutive and independent directors. According to SEC rules and listing standards, audit committee members are considered to be independent if they have not been employed by the company or its affiliates within the past five years, not received any compensation other than their board pay, not provided any advisory or consulting services to the company or its affiliates, and not been a member of the immediate family of any of the company's executives or its affiliates within the past five years (SEC 2003c).

Member Qualifications and Attributes

As a general rule, audit committee members should be independent, financially literate, able and willing to assume the assigned responsibilities, use proper judgment, maintain objectivity and confidentiality, and exercise due care. Recent corporate governance reforms (SOX, SEC rules, and listing standards) and best practices require that at least one of the members of the audit committee should be designated as a financial expert whereas the other members should be financially literate. The SEC (SEC 2003b) defines an audit committee financial expert as a person who has (1) an understanding of GAAP and financial statements; (2) the ability to assess the general application of GAAP in connection with the accounting for estimates, accruals, and reserves; (3) adequate experience in preparing, auditing, analyzing, or evaluating financial statements; and (4) an understanding of audit committee responsibilities pertaining to corporate governance, financial reporting, internal controls, risk assessment, and audit functions. Public companies must disclose a designated financial expert. If a company discloses that the financial expert serves on the audit committee, the name of the expert must also be disclosed. Companies may disclose more than one audit committee financial expert (SEC 2003b).

Audit Committee Meetings

Audit committees meet regularly to discuss their tasks and assist the entire board with its advisory and oversight function. Audit committees should meet at least four times a year to review quarterly financial and internal control reports. The frequency of audit committee meetings depends on the extent of the audit committee's assigned responsibilities by the entire board. The 2008 survey of the Spencer Stuart Board Index (SSBI 2008) survey indicates that:

- S&P 500 company audit committees met 9.1 times in 2007; in comparison, audit committees met 9.5 times in 2006 and 8.7 times in 2004. Only 1 percent of S&P 500 companies had three or fewer audit committee meetings in 2006, compared to 91 percent in 2002.
- A total of 41 percent of audit committees met 8 to 10 times in 2007, compared to none in 2002.
- Only 14 percent of audit committees met more than 14 times in 2007.

Audit Committee Responsibilities

In the post-SOX era, review of the effectiveness of internal control over financial reporting (ICFR) and reliability of financial statements is an essential part of audit committees' roles and responsibilities. Audit committees hold three key responsibilities: overseeing internal controls, ensuring the integrity of financial reports, and coordinating audit activities.

Internal Controls

The audit committee oversees the adequacy and effectiveness of the company's internal control structure to assure the efficiency and effectiveness of operations, the reliability of financial reporting, and compliance with applicable laws and regulations. The committee's oversight of Section 404 on internal control is becoming increasingly important as public companies are required to certify their ICFR. The audit committee (1) knows the senior executive who is directly responsible and ultimately accountable for Section 404 compliance; (2) understands the process of establishing and maintaining adequate and effective internal controls; (3) understands procedures for assessing the effectiveness of both the design and operation of ICFR; (4) understands the proper documentation of compliance with Section 404; (5) reviews management's report on the effectiveness of ICFR; (6) reviews auditor reports expressing an opinion on management's assessment of the effectiveness of ICFR; (7) evaluates the identified significant deficiencies and material weaknesses in internal control; (8) assesses satisfaction with management and auditor efforts and reports on ICFR; and (9) ensures that management has properly addressed the identified material weaknesses.

In February 2005, the American Institute of Certified Public Accountants (AICPA 2005) issued a report entitled *Management Override of Internal Controls: The Achilles' Heel of Fraud Prevention*. This report offers several recommendations and actions that audit committees can take to address the risk of management override of ICFR. These recommendations are: (1) exercise an appropriate level of skepticism; (2) strengthen the audit committee's understanding and knowledge of the company's business and industry to identify and assess business and financial risks that increase the likelihood of financial statement fraud; (3) brainstorm and openly discuss among its members the potential for fraud, including identification of events and transactions that are most likely to be susceptible to fraud; (4) establish and use business codes of conduct to assess financial culture by ensuring that management practices and promotes an "appropriate tone at the top" of promoting ethical behavior and legal conduct throughout the company; (5) cultivate a vigorous whistle-blower program to receive tips regarding fraud and concerns from employees, suppliers, customers, and others; and (6) establish a broad information and feedback network that extends beyond senior management and requires the audit committee to communicate with the internal auditor, independent auditors, compensation committee, and key employees about the likelihood of occurrence of fraud, and how to prevent and detect fraud (AICPA 2005).

The audit committee is responsible for addressing internal control activities and asking the following questions.

- What are the internal control priorities?
- Are there adequate internal control investments?
- Are internal control resources properly allocated?
- Is the company getting the correct return for its investment in internal control?
- Are entity-level controls adequate and effective?
- Are process-level controls adequate and effective?
- Have management and the independent auditor coordinated their plans to implement the requirements of the SEC's Interpretive Guidance and the Public Company Accounting Oversight Board's (PCAOB) Auditing Standard No. 5?
- Are the design and operation of ICFR effective?
- Are the design and operation of internal control over operational performance (ICOP) effective?
- Are the design and operation of internal control over compliance functions (ICCF) effective?
- Is the management report on ICFR appropriate?
- Is the independent auditor's report on ICFR appropriate?
- What are the causes and effects of reported material weaknesses in ICFR?
- What, if any, remediating actions have been taken or are planned by management to correct reported material weaknesses?

- Has the independent auditor issued a report on management corrections of the reported material weaknesses?
- What are the effects of internal control significant deficiencies and material weaknesses on potential misstatements in financial statements?

Financial Reporting

The audit committee oversees the financial reporting process by reviewing annual and quarterly financial statements including (1) management discussion and analysis (MD&A); (2) accounting principles, practices, estimates, and reserves; and (3) independent auditors' suggestions, comments, and adjusting and classification entries. The committee is responsible for overseeing the integrity, reliability, quality, and transparency of the company's financial disclosures. In the post-SOX period, the audit committee prepares and submits a formal annual report to the shareholders stating that (1) financial statements prepared in accordance with GAAP are included in the annual report on Form 10-K or Form 10-KSB; (2) the committee adopted a charter and has satisfied its oversight responsibilities as specified in the proxy statement; (3) the committee reviewed the audited financial statements with management; (4) the committee discussed with the independent auditor those matters required to be communicated to the committee in accordance with generally accepted auditing standards (GAAS); (5) the committee received the independent disclosures from the independent auditor and discussed the matters relevant to auditor independence; and (6) the committee discussed with management and the independent auditor their reports on ICFR.

Audit Activities

The audit committee has the responsibility for overseeing both internal and external audit activities. The committee has the direct responsibility for hiring, compensating, and firing the company's independent auditor and chief audit executive (CAE, the head of the internal audit department). Sections 201 and 202 of the Sarbanes-Oxley Act of 2002 (SOX 2002) require the company's audit committee to preapprove all audit and permissible non-audit services. The audit committee must establish preapproval policies and procedures to (1) increase the committee's knowledge and understanding of all permissible non-audit services; (2) evaluate the qualifications of providers of preapproved non-audit services; and (3) select the best provider, considering reinforcement of auditor independence from management. Although SOX and SEC-related implementation rules permit certain tax services to be performed by the company's independent auditor contemporaneously with audit services, the PCAOB in its Ethics and Independence Rule 3523 (PCAOB 2007) limits the performance of various tax services such as tax shelters.

In addition to the aforementioned responsibilities, audit committees typically perform other tasks including (1) participating with other board committees (compensation and nominating) in overseeing the effectiveness of corporate governance without assuming a managerial responsibility; (2) overseeing the establishment and enforcement of the company's code of ethical conduct to ensure an appropriate tone-at-the-top policy carries throughout the company; (3) overseeing the establishment and enforcement of whistle-blower programs in compliance with the requirements of SOX (2002) and SEC-related rules; and (4) overseeing the company's enterprise risk management and ensuring its suitability to identifying business events and their related risks (Rezaee 2006).

Audit Committee Compensation

In the post-SOX era, audit committee compensation has substantially increased because of the increased audit committee activities in terms of the frequency and length of meetings. The 2008 Spencer Stuart Board Index (SSBI 2008) survey shows that:

- There is a trend toward increasing retainer compensation instead of meeting fees. The average retainer amount paid to audit committee members by S&P 500 companies in 2007 was $74,872, which represents a 71 percent increase from 2003.
- The maximum retainer fee for an audit committee member was $280,000 with a majority paid in equity-based forms. Audit committee members and compensation committee members receive the most compensation, and audit committee chairs earn more, on average, than compensation committee members.
- The most common amount paid to members of an audit committee for a phone meeting is $750, while face-to-face meetings are $2,000 for audit committee members and $1,500 for compensation committees.
- Stock grants are a popular means of compensation and have become much more common than options.

COMPENSATION COMMITTEE

The compensation committee has the responsibility of evaluating executive and director performance and establishing top-management compensation and benefit programs. To ensure against undue influence from management or executive directors, compensation committees are often composed solely of independent directors with sufficient knowledge in performance evaluation and adequate human resources experience in compensation and related issues. Compensation committees may hire outside compensation advisers to assist them in effectively fulfilling their responsibility. These advisers should report directly to and are compensated by the committee to ensure objectivity and independence from senior management.

Recent controversies over executive pay levels, expensing of stock-based compensation, and illegal backdating of executive stock options have generated considerable interest in the formation and function of compensation committees. The Obama Administration plans to limit executive compensation for those companies receiving bailout money and restrict severance packages. The SEC also appears determined to undertake initiatives improving compensation committee performance. Shareholders also believe in strengthening the link between executive pay and company financial performance. In addition, the growing gap between executive pay and average worker pay (275:1 as reported by the Economic Policy Institute in its report "The State of Working America" in 2007) creates a public impression of unbridled and misguided top-management compensation policies (Economic Policy Institute 2007).

To be effective, the compensation committee should be independent from management influence. To promote this ideal, the Internal Revenue Service (2007) requires that compensation committees be composed of two or more outside, independent directors for executive compensation to be tax deductible by the company. Stock exchange listing standards further require compensation committees to be composed solely of three or more independent directors with the primary responsibility of determining compensation for company directors and senior executives (NYSE 2004).

Compensation committee responsibilities include:

- Developing, approving, monitoring, and disclosing the company's executive pay philosophy, which considers the full range of pay components, desired mix of cash and equity awards, and relation of executive pay to compensation of other employees.
- Vigilantly overseeing all aspects of executive compensation for top executives including the company's chief executive officer (CEO), chief financial officer (CFO), and other highly paid executives of subsidiaries, special purpose entities, and other affiliates to ensure fair, nondiscriminatory, rewarding, and forward-looking pay.
- Implementing pay-for-performance executive compensation driven predominately by performance.
- Annually reviewing the performance of individuals in the oversight group (directors) and approving their bonuses, severance, equity-based awards, death/disability benefits, retirement benefits, termination with and without cause, changes of control agreements, and voluntary termination.
- Assuming accountability for the committee's operations, including attending all annual and special shareholder meetings, being available to respond directly to questions regarding executive compensation, reporting on its activities to the independent directors of the company's board, and preparing and being responsible for the compensation committee report included in the annual proxy materials.
- Assuming the responsibilities for hiring, retaining, and firing outside independent experts including legal counsel, financial advisers, and human resources consultants when negotiating contracts with executives.
- Disclosing all aspects of the company's executive compensation, fully and fairly, in the annual proxy statement to enable shareholders to clearly understand how and how much directors and executives are paid, including salary and short- and long-term incentive compensation.

Compensation Committee Report

The compensation committee should prepare an annual report that discloses its activities and accomplishments. In July 2006, the SEC (SEC 2006) adopted amendments that would refine current tabular compensation disclosure and combine it with an improved narrative disclosure to enhance the transparency of compensation disclosure. Public companies are required to provide compensation disclosure in the form of a "Compensation Disclosure and Analysis" (CD&A) that (1) specifies the objectives and implementation of executive compensation programs;

(2) addresses the most important factors underlying the compensation policies and decisions; (3) will be filed and be a part of disclosure subject to certification by the company's CEO and CFO; (4) will require a statement of whether the compensation committee has reviewed and discussed the CD&A with management and recommended that it be included in the company's annual report and proxy statement; (5) separates the performance graph from executive compensation disclosure and moves it to the section covering the market price of common equity and related matters; (6) organizes executive compensation disclosures into three broad categories (compensation over the past three years; holdings of outstanding equity-related interests received as compensation that are the source of future gains; and retirement plans, deferred compensation, and other post-employment benefits [OPEB]); and (7) provides in tabular and narrative disclosures columns for salary, bonus, stock, stock options, grant date fair value of option, a more complete picture of compensation (SEC 2006).

Determinants of Effective Compensation Committees

Rezaee (2007) suggests the following 12 best practice determinants of an effective compensation committee:

1. Public companies must have an independent compensation committee responsible for evaluating and compensating the company's senior executives and directors.
2. Members of the compensation committee must be independent directors who are not affiliated with and do not receive any other compensation or items of value from the company aside from board meeting or committee-related fees.
3. The compensation committee should have a charter stating its roles, responsibilities, and functions. The charter should be approved by the entire board of directors and fully disclosed to shareholders.
4. The compensation committee should have authority and budgetary resources to hire experts, advisers, and consultants as it deems necessary to design and implement executive compensation arrangements.
5. The compensation committee should set pay for performance goals for the company's executives, establish executive compensation plans to achieve the stated goals, evaluate executive performance, and revise compensation plans as necessary to provide incentives for high executive performance.
6. The compensation committee should ensure executive compensation disclosures are sufficient and in compliance with SEC disclosure requirements.
7. The compensation committee should ensure that executives repay to the company any portion of their compensation affected by restatements of the company's financial results.
8. The compensation committee should establish compensation policies addressing the appropriate mix of salary, bonuses, and long-term incentive compensation, including severance and retirement arrangements, which are fully disclosed to and approved by the shareholders.
9. The compensation committee should establish pay-for-performance metrics based on appropriate performance measures such as economic value added (EVA), shareholder value added (SVA), return on equity (ROE), return on

assets (ROA), residual income (RI), and earnings and cash flow growth (ECG). These performance measures should exclude any gains resulting from market-wide and/or industry-wide movements.

10. The compensation committee should strongly encourage executive stock ownership and promote equity-based compensation (stock options and restricted stock).
11. The committee should properly disclose its policies, procedures, composition, authority, resources, and responsibilities.
12. The committee should provide compensation in the form of a Compensation Disclosure and Analysis, which is included in the company's annual report on Form 10-K and proxy statements.

NOMINATING COMMITTEE

The nominating/governance committee is usually responsible for identifying, evaluating, and nominating new directors for the board; renominating existing directors; and facilitating the election of the new directors by shareholders. The nominating committee may seek advice from the CEO and/or use staffing support provided by the CEO in identifying and recruiting new members for the company's board of directors. An effective nominating committee can substantially reduce the traditional role played by the CEO in selecting new directors who may not be independent from management.

Responsibilities of the Nominating Committees

The nominating committee is responsible for:

- Assessing the qualifications and performance of the current directors.
- Determining the need for new directors, if any, and renomination of existing directors.
- Identifying the pool of candidates for board membership.
- Working with the CEO in determining the qualifications, skills, and background needs of the board.
- Evaluating the skills, background, diversity (gender, ethnic background, experience), and knowledge of candidates for the board.
- Assisting in the nomination and election of qualified new directors.
- Communicating with shareholders regarding board candidates and other shareholder concerns and issues.
- Leading the process for directors' assessment and election.

Selection and Nomination of New Directors

The nominating committee is responsible for selecting and nominating new directors and assisting shareholders in the election of new directors and reelection of existing directors. The company's CEO can assist the nomination committee in identifying and nominating a new director for membership. The nominating committee in cooperation with the company's CEO and/or by consulting with independent advisers should determine the independence, expertise, knowledge, and other attributes and qualifications including the gender and ethnic diversity needed on the board. The needs and desired profile of the company's board should be compared with the existing board profile in determining the number and attributes of new directors. The nominating committee should select a pool of candidates meeting the board's needed profile and assess the qualifications, backgrounds, and skills of these candidates. The entire board should approve the selected candidates before proposing them to shareholders for possible election at the company's annual meeting.

As indicated in the 2008 survey of the Spencer Stuart Board Index (SSBI 2008), the recruiting task of the board's nominating committee is expected to become more challenging and complex in the post-SOX era for five reasons:

1. The move toward supermajority independent directors (all independent directors except for the CEO) is gaining wider acceptance from public companies, demanded by investor activists, and supported by regulators and standard setters. In 2008, boards appointed 16 percent more independent directors to the board compared to 2007.
2. The pool of traditional candidates for directorship is shrinking as active senior executives (CEOs, corporate operating officers, and CFOs) now serve on no more than one outside corporate board. Active CEOs and chief operating officers (COOs) accounted for 31 percent of new board appointees, which is down from 48 percent in 1998. However, minorities still represent a small percentage. For example, women are underrepresented in most-senior corporate positions, holding only 6 percent of the highest-compensated positions.
3. There is a growing demand for specific director expertise to assist with the ever-increasing complex business issues such as cutting-edge manufacturing, corporate governance, and environmental expertise.
4. There is greater scrutiny and heightened sensitivity about the director selection process in order to avoid real or potential conflicts and improve the transparency of the nomination and election process. Companies are informing their shareholders about the nomination and election process and even disclosing in their proxy statements the sources of recommendations for new directors. In 2008, companies, on average, interviewed 20 to 25 candidates for the director position before developing a short list of the candidates to present to the nominating committee.
5. Boards increasingly rely on retired CEOs and COOs. The number of retired CEOs and COOs who were recruited has risen from 6 percent in 2005 to 16 percent in 2008.

Election of Directors

Upon the selection and approval of the director nominees, the nomination committee discloses the list of candidates in proxy materials to shareholders for their consideration and election of director candidates to the board of directors. The shareholders elect directors to represent their interests. After election at the annual meeting, directors complete their terms unless they are otherwise removed or forced to resign.

Recent corporate governance reforms suggest that in order to better represent shareholder interests, directors should be elected or reelected annually under a majority vote rule. Under the current plurality voting system, a director can be elected even if he only casts one vote for himself, as the plurality standard does not permit shareholders to vote against a director candidate. Under the plurality voting system, shareholders are only permitted to cast a symbolic withhold vote if they oppose the election of an individual director. Because of this limitation of the possibility of being elected with only one positive vote, many criticize the plurality standard as not being democratic. The move toward voluntarily adopting majority voting for the election of directors democratizes the public company director election process by making the corporate board more accountable to and more representative of shareholders. There has been continuing momentum by shareholders to encourage companies to voluntarily adopt a majority-vote standard for the election of directors. For example, the California Public Employees' Retirement System (CalPERS) board recently adopted a three-pronged plan to advocate for adoption of a majority-vote standard for the election of public company directors.

Nominating Committee Disclosures

In October 2003, the SEC proposed rule amendments that would, under certain circumstances, allow shareholders representing at least 15 percent of voting shares to include their own board nominees along with management's choices on the company's official ballot (SEC 2003c). The SEC adopted the proposal in May 2009 and released new proposed rules which allow shareholders, under certain conditions, to include their director nomination in the company's proxy statement (SEC 2009). The amendments expand the current proxy statement disclosure regarding a company's nominating or similar committee to include:

- Whether the company has a nominating or similar committee, and if not, the rationale behind the decision and who among the directors performs that duty.
- A copy of the nominating committee's charter or listing on its web site if it is available; if the charter is not available, why not; and if it does not exist, a statement to that fact.
- A statement as to the independence of the directors on the nominating committee.
- Whether the nominating committee has a policy with regard to the consideration of any director candidates recommended by security holders, and if so, the particulars of the policy.
- The minimum qualifications and skills necessary to be considered for nomination.
- How the nominating committee goes about nominating directors.
- The party that recommended the nominee.
- If a third party was involved and if any fees were paid.
- How to contact the board of directors and its committees, including the nominating committee.

OTHER BOARD STANDING COMMITTEES

The board of directors often establishes special committees to assist it with unusual matters and issues. The special committee process should be in place to ensure its due diligence and effectiveness in fulfilling the board's fiduciary duties. Public companies may form standing or special committees to deal with issues requiring particular expertise. The board can also establish special committees to handle emerging issues such as environmental issues, mergers, acquisitions, and investigation of alleged wrongdoing by directors and officers. The most common special committees are governance/strategic, litigation, and special investigation committees composed solely of independent directors.

Governance/Strategic Committee

The governance/strategic committee typically establishes the agenda for the company's board of directors to determine what issues the board should discuss with management and to what extent. Traditionally, management has controlled and dictated the board's agenda and the board has acted as a rubber stamp with inadequate discussions and often inevitable "yes" votes to ratify management's strategic recommendations. Many boards have not taken the initiative to direct management's strategic decisions. When the CEO dictates the board's agenda, it may cause board members to have inadequate information, short meetings, and less constructive discussions. The emerging corporate governance reforms require a higher level of accountability for the company's board of directors. The governance/strategic committee should collaborate with the company's CEO in designing a mutually agreed-upon agenda for board meetings. The governance committee should be formed to facilitate and coordinate the activities of the entire board and all other committees.

The governance/strategic committee should:

- Control the agenda and the meeting.
- Review the past agendas and minutes of meetings to ensure adequate time and discussion are devoted to each issue.
- Revise the agenda as necessary and set priorities for meetings.

Independent Lead Directors Committee

When the company's CEO also serves as the chair of the board of directors, the board should form an independent lead directors' committee to maintain the board's independence from management and the CEO. The composition of this committee should consist solely of nonexecutive directors and should engage in an oversight function. The entire board should elect the independent presiding or lead director of the board.

Executive Committee

The executive committee usually meets between board meetings to review and approve managerial decisions, plans, and actions on behalf of the entire board. Colley, Doyle, Stettinius, and Logan (2003) suggest using the executive committee to deal with an emerging or time-sensitive issue when gathering the entire board is difficult. Thus, an executive committee consisting of available independent directors can make decisions on behalf of the company's entire board of directors. The committee can be composed of the chairs of other committees to coordinate their activities and set an agenda for the entire board. The executive committee can act as a senior board to address all issues before they are presented to the entire board. In this situation, the executive committee serves best when the board of directors is large.

Disclosure Committee

The SEC (2002) recommends that public companies establish a disclosure committee to assist the company's executives (e.g., CEO and CFO) in complying with Section 302 of SOX (2002) internal control and financial statement certifications. A disclosure committee should consist of personnel who are knowledgeable of the company's periodic filing requirements, business and legal disclosure practices, and disclosure controls and procedures, such as the general counsel, chief accounting officer (CAE), controller, risk management officer, outside legal counsel, and investor relations manager. The responsibilities of the disclosure committee include, but are not limited to:

- Overseeing the appropriateness of all disclosures that are made publicly available and the process of disseminating public information.
- Assisting executives in the preparation of and compliance with SOX executive certification requirements.
- Assisting management in the assessment of the effectiveness of the design and operation of internal control over financial reporting.
- Ensuring compliance with laws, regulations, rules, and standards related to the company's periodic filings.
- Assisting management with the assessment of control deficiencies and their classifications as either substantial deficiencies that should be communicated to the audit committee or material weaknesses that should be disclosed in the SEC filings.

SUMMARY AND CONCLUSIONS

Effective compliance with new corporate governance reforms, complexity of business, globalization, and technological advances have encouraged boards of directors to establish subcommittees to best use the expertise, knowledge, and efforts of its directors. Several subcommittees of the board have emerged. The three mandatory subcommittees for listed companies are audit, compensation, and nominating committees. Some public companies may also establish other board subcommittees such as budget, finance, executive, special litigation, disclosure, or investment committees. Recent developments in corporate governance reforms have boosted the relevance, importance, and public profiles of all three mandatory subcommittees for public companies. The board normally forms subcommittees to assist in effectively fulfilling its fiduciary duty of protecting investor interests with the keen understanding that the entire board is responsible for the company's oversight function.

DISCUSSION QUESTIONS

1. Identify the three mandatory subcommittees for listed companies and briefly explain their roles and responsibilities.
2. Describe the modifications that audit committee regulations have undergone from late 1980s to the present time.
3. Based on the 12 best practices determinants of effective compensation committees, describe how a successfully structured compensation committee can help a business improve operations and sustain a healthy growth rate.
4. Explain the structure of the audit committee and provide an example.
5. What are major industry practices with respect to audit committee compensation packages?
6. What kind of special board committees exist and why are they needed?

REFERENCES

American Institute of Certified Public Accountants (AICPA). 2005. *Management override of internal controls: The Achilles' heel of fraud prevention*. February. www.aicpa.org/audcommctr/spotlight/achilles_heel.htm.

Blue Ribbon Committee (BRC). 1999. *Reports and recommendations of the Blue Ribbon Committees on improving the effectiveness of corporate audit committee*. New York: NYSE and NASD.

Colley, John, Jacqueline Doyle, Wallace Stettinius, and George Logan. 2003. *Corporate governance: The McGraw-Hill Executive MBA series*. New York: McGraw-Hill.

Economic Policy Institute. 2007. The state of working America. http://blogs.ft.com/gapperblog/files/2009/01/state-of-working-america.pdf.

Ernst and Young (E&Y). 2006. Audit committee survey and industry insights. http://www.ey.com/global/assets.nsf/Norway/Audit_committeesurvey_2006/$file/ME_AuditCommittee2006.pdf.

Federal Deposit Insurance Corporation (FDIC). 1991. Regulations on FDIC Improvement Act of 1991. U.S. Congress FDIC Corporate Improvement Act of 1991. http://www.fdic.gov/regulations/laws/rules/8000-2400.html.

Internal Revenue Service (IRS). 2007. Code Section. Trade or Business Expenses. Section 162 (m)(c)(i). www.irs.gov.

New York Stock Exchange. 2003. Listing Standards. www.nyse.com/about/listed/1101074746736.html.

———. 2004. Listing Standards. www.nyse.com/about/listed/1101074746736.html.

Public Company Accounting Oversight Board (PCAOB). 2007. Board proposes new ethics and independence rule concerning communications with audit committees and an amendment to its existing tax services rule and adjusts implementation schedule for tax services rule. July 24. www.pcaob.org/News_and_Events/News/2007/07-24.aspx.

Public Oversight Board (POB). 2000. Panel on Audit Effectiveness, Report and Recommendations, August 11, 2000. http://www.pobauditpanel.org/downloads/prefatory.pdf.

Rezaee, Zabihollah. 2006. Audit committee oversight effectiveness post-Sarbanes-Oxley Act. *Accounting Policy and Practice*, Portfolio 5401. Tax Management Inc., a BNA Company.

———. 2007. Board committees. In *Corporate governance Post-Sarbanes-Oxley: Regulations, requirements, and integrated processes*, Chapter 4. Hoboken, NJ: John Wiley & Sons.

Sarbanes-Oxley Act (SOX). 2002. *Public Company Accounting Reform and Investor Protection Act*. Public Law No. 107-204, 116STAT.745. July 30. www.sec.gov/about/laws/soa2002.pdf.

Securities and Exchange Commission (SEC). 2000. SEC Final Rule No. 34-42266. File No. S7-22-99 Audit Committee Disclosure. January 31, 2000. http://www.sec.gov/rules/final/34-42266.htm.

———. 2002. Certification of disclosure in companies' quarterly and annual reports. August 29. www.sec.gov/rules/final/33-8124.htm.

———. 2003a. Standards relating to listed company audit committees. Release 33-8220; 34-47654; IC-26001; File No. S7-02-03. April 25, 2003. http://www.sec.gov/rules/final/33-8220.htm.

———. 2003b. Disclosure required by Sections 406 and 407 of the Sarbanes-Oxley Act of 2002. SEC Release 33-8177; 34-47235; File No. S7-40-02. March 3, 2003. http//www.sec.gov/rules/final/33-8177.htm.

———. 2003c. Disclosure regarding nominating committee functions and communications between security holders and boards of directors. (November). www.sec.gov/rules/final/33-8340.htm.

———. 2006. SEC votes to adopt changes to disclosure requirements concerning executive compensation and related matters. July 26. http://www.sec.gov/news/press/2006/2006-123.htm.

———. 2009. SEC votes to propose rule amendments to facilitate rights of shareholder to nominate directors. Press release, May 20. http://www.sec.gov/news/press/2009/2009-116.htm.

Spencer Stuart Board Index (SSBI). 2008. The 2008 survey of the Spencer Stuart Board Index (SSBI). http://content.spencerstuart.com/sswebsite/pdf/lib/SSBI_08.pdf.

Treadway Commission. 1987. Report of the National Commission on Fraudulent Financial Reporting (NCFFR). New York: AICPA. http://www.coso.org/Publications/NCFFR.pdf.

ABOUT THE AUTHOR

Zabihollah Rezaee is the Thompson-Hill Chair of Excellence and professor of accountancy at the University of Memphis and served a two-year term on the Standing Advisory Group (SAG) of the Public Company Accounting Oversight Board (PCAOB). He received his BS from the Iranian Institute of Advanced Accounting, his MBA from Tarleton State University in Texas, and his PhD from the University of Mississippi. Professor Rezaee holds several certifications (CPA, CMA, CIA, CFE, CGFM, CSOXP, CGRCP and CGOVP) and has published more than 180 articles in a variety of accounting and business journals. He has also published six books: *Financial Institutions, Valuations, Mergers, and Acquisitions: The Fair Value Approach* (John Wiley & Sons, 2004); *Financial Statement Fraud: Prevention and Detection* (John Wiley & Sons, 2009); *U.S. Master Auditing Guide*, 3rd edition (Chicago: Commerce Clearing House, 2004); *Audit Committee Oversight Effectiveness Post-Sarbanes-Oxley Act* (BNA Tax & Accounting, 2006); *Corporate Governance Post-Sarbanes-Oxley: Regulations, Requirements, and Integrated Processes* (John Wiley & Sons, 2007); and *Corporate Governance and Business Ethics* (John Wiley & Sons, 2008).

CHAPTER 14

Executive Compensation: Incentives and Externalities

PHILIPP GEILER
Researcher, Tilburg University

LUC RENNEBOOG
Professor of Corporate Finance, Tilburg University and
European Corporate Governance Institute

INTRODUCTION

"No benevolent man ever lost altogether the fruits of his benevolence" (Smith 1790). With these words, Adam Smith dispelled the doubts of those who questioned the efficiency of the market. His economic principle of the *invisible hand*, a force which brings great benefits to a society, is still acclaimed by many economists despite some arguing that the market mechanism should operate with social corrections. Why not let the market decide about executive pay?

A well-debated question is whether executive pay is effective in stimulating rational managerial decision making that focuses on creating shareholder value while simultaneously preventing excessive rent extraction by executives. This chapter contrasts the classical corporate governance perspective on executive compensation that advances the view of executive remuneration as a *market mechanism* with more recent ideas such as the managerial self-serving and skimming nature of compensation contracts. A review of recently published empirical papers on executive compensation suggests that leaving market forces to shape compensation contracts does not decrease agency problems but rather amplifies them.

The remainder of this chapter consists of five sections. The next section illustrates the various pay components and their associated incentives followed by an international comparison of level and composition of CEO pay packages. The discussion then turns to providing the theoretical background behind a pay-setting process that provides incentives to CEOs to create shareholder wealth and that prevents rent extraction. The next segment discusses the theories behind the externalities of executive pay. The final section provides a summary and advances important policy recommendations as well as suggestions for further research.

Exhibit 14.1 Comparison of CEO Compensation in 2005–2006

The table shows estimates of typical CEO pay for companies with at least U.S. $500 million in worldwide sales. All figures are in (2005) U.S. dollars.

Pay Component		United States	United Kingdom
Short-term	Base salary	584,537	509,522
	Annual bonus	227,969	152,857
Long-term	Stock options, stocks	771,589	254,761
Additional	Benefits	129,897	225,138
	Perquisites	108,248	35,548
Total		2,164,952	1,184,936

Source: Towers Perrin's Worldwide Remuneration Survey 2005–2006.

PAY COMPONENTS AND INCENTIVES

The level and composition of top executive compensation as well as the pay-for-performance relation at many large companies raises questions about the effectiveness of remuneration policies at the corporate level. Compensation packages consist of base salary, annual bonus, stocks and stock options, insurance premiums, pension benefits, and severance pay. In the pay-setting process, the level and mix of executive remuneration is an important instrument for creating incentives, as well as aligning shareholders' and executives' interests. Exhibit 14.1 presents a comparison of chief executive officer (CEO) compensation packages in the United States and the United Kingdom. The table shows the short- and long-term components of pay along with additional pay components. The large difference in total compensation between U.S. and UK executives can be attributed to substantially greater use of equity-based compensation in the United States.

Exhibit 14.2 presents an example of a particularly valuable compensation package awarded to a CEO. The person in question was the highest-paid CEO of all British utilities in 2007, according to Manifest. He received a salary of around £1,305,000 (entirely paid in cash), a total bonus of £2,122,000 (partially paid in shares), and equity compensation of about £14,261,000 from a long-term incentive plan and a deferred bonus scheme. Leaving aside the increase in transfer value of his defined benefit pension scheme and additional payments for insurances and benefits, he received a total of about £17,700,000 (US $35,133,000) in 2007. While

Exhibit 14.2 Example of a CEO Compensation Package in 2007

Base salary	Total salary	£ 1,305,000
Short-term compensation	Total bonus	£ 2,122,000
Long-term compensation	2003 Long-term incentive plan	£ 12,334,000
	Deferred bonus scheme	£ 1,927,400
Others	Pension	£ 1,675,700
	Insurances, benefits	£ 23,500
Total		£ 19,387,600

Source: Data are extracted from Manifest.

an annual income of this size is exceptional for a European manager of a listed commercial or industrial firm, it occurs rather frequently in the United States. In addition, managers of investment funds or hedge funds often earn several times more than this compensation package.

Short-Term Components of Pay

Short-term compensation includes base salary and a bonus plan based on single-year performance. The *base salary* is set by the compensation committee (a subset of the board of directors), who take into account the specific tasks and challenges of top managers, their seniority and experience, and the salary earned by (industry) peers. Murphy (1999), among others, documents a strong correlation between salary and firm size. As Conyon and Murphy (2000) note, since the early 1990s, base salary accounts for a steadily declining percentage of total pay.

The determination of an executive's *annual bonus* follows a similar procedure to the one outlined for base salary. Annual incentive bonuses can be structured according to three basic components: performance measures, performance standards, and the structure of the pay-for-performance relation. In their performance assessment, the vast majority of companies rely on two or more performance measures using factors such as sales or revenues, earnings per share, and operating income or profit (Towers Perrin 2005).

While revenue is the most frequently used performance measure in the United States, it is net profit per share in the United Kingdom. Based on these performance measures, the final bonus can either be calculated by aggregating the outcomes (*additive approach*), or, less frequently, by multiplying the measures for different subcategories (*multiplicative approach*). Because researchers and others often criticize financial performance measures for their backward-looking approach and ease of manipulation, other nonfinancial measures (such as operational or strategic performance targets, quality improvements, and scorecard-based systems) may also be taken into account.

Long-Term Components of Pay

Long-term components of pay include stock options, restricted stock, and long-term incentive plans. *Stock options* have been an important part of executive pay since the 1950s, but beginning in the 1990s they accounted for an increasingly large part of executive pay (Frydman and Saks 2007). The basic idea behind the granting of options is to encourage managers to undertake (risky) investments that increase shareholder wealth. The options are usually issued at-the-money, meaning that the exercise price equals the current market price. The maturity of top executive's options is most frequently set at 10 years. Typically, such an option becomes vested (exercisable) after three years. However, in case of a change in corporate control (e.g., following a full or partial takeover), *accelerated vesting* may become possible. Moreover, accelerated vesting as a form of severance pay is possible.

In the United Kingdom, *performance-vested options* can be forfeited unless a performance trigger is hit. That is, executives cannot profit from options unless a certain threshold (e.g., of the stock price) is met. As for *purchase options*, the manager pays a fraction of the strike price when options are granted and has to pay the remainder (of the grant strike price) when exercising the option. Executives who fail to exercise the option lose the prepaid fraction of the strike price. In case of *reload options*, managers who exercise an option before maturity and pay for it with preowned shares receive an additional (*reload*) option. This reload option covers the same number of shares and has the same maturity as the exercised option and an exercise price equal to the market price of this exercised option. Thus, managers can lock in all future price appreciations of the stock on the full number of shares covered by the option.

In calculating the value of option grants, firms normally use the basic Black-Scholes (BS) formula for European options. The use of this formula in the context of management options bears several limitations: (1) It overstates the value of the option as it assumes that the option can only be exercised at the expiration date; (2) the formula may be, at best, a measure of the firm's cost of granting an option (Hall and Murphy 2000); (3) it assumes no restrictions on short-selling, while in practice executives are not allowed to trade or sell their options; and (4) executives forfeit options when they leave the firm, which again reduces the cost associated with granting the option and overstates the BS option value. As a result, the value of an executive stock option is less than that of a standardized financial option with the same underlying value, exercise price, volatility, and maturity. Moreover, risk-averse executives demand a premium for accepting risky options rather than safe base pay (Murphy 1999).

Compensation packages consisting of a large portion of stock options create a strong relationship between executive pay and firm performance (pay-for-performance) because the payout of an in-the-money option increases dollar-for-dollar with an increase in share price. However, executive stock options have many downsides. For example, issuing additional stock to grant options has a dilutive effect on the company's stock. In addition, options only reward stock price appreciation and not the total return to shareholders, as the latter also includes dividends. This implies that executive options may influence the payout policy of the firm. That is, managers holding stock options have strong incentives to repurchase shares rather than to pay out excess cash through the dividend channel (Renneboog and Trojanowski 2005). Dividend protection can be accomplished in three ways: automatically decreasing the stock option exercise price when dividends are paid out, restating stock prices on a predividend basis, and allowing executives to receive accumulated dividends at exercise of the options.

There are two additional drawbacks to using executive stock options. Management holding executive options may engage in riskier investments because an increase in the financial risk of the assets of the firm augments the value of the executive options. Jensen and Murphy (1990) suggest that option grants to executives only act as incentives if the granting of the options is conditional upon a firm performance criterion. In addition, Bolton, Scheinkman, and Xiong (2003) show that the presence of heterogeneous beliefs by managers and shareholders about firm value may induce a short-term orientation or myopic outlook among CEOs. In their model, stock prices reflect both the long-run fundamental value of the firm and a short-term speculative component, which reflects (some) investors' overconfidence. In the presence of large heterogeneity in beliefs, a CEO is (partially) incentivized to undertake inefficient projects to increase the stock price in the short-run. Bolton et al. claim that this calls for an intervention of the board toward a more long-term orientation.

The Popularity of Stock Options

As previously argued, stock options provide managers with the right incentives to focus on shareholder value, which hence aligns the interests of shareholders and managers. In addition, favorable taxation rules and the accounting treatment of stock options also contribute to their popularity. In the United States, the *tax treatment* depends on the type of option considered. Statutory options include incentive stock options and options granted under an employee stock purchase plan. For the holder of this *qualified* (statutory) option, taxation is deferred until the stock is sold. Then, the executive faces capital gains taxes on the gain in stock price since the time of grant. For the firm, the tax consequences are nil at both the granting date and the date when the stock is sold. If the fair market value at grant date of an exercisable stock option exceeds $100,000, it is treated by the fiscal authorities as a nonstatutory option.

Nonstatutory options (i.e., all options that do not qualify as statutory) are commonly referred to as *nonqualified stock options* (NQSOs). The holder of a NQSO faces tax consequences at two points in time: (1) when the option is exercised, and (2) when the stock is sold. At exercise, the holder has to pay income tax on the difference between stock price and exercise price of the option. When the stock is sold, a capital gains tax on the difference between the stock price when the option is sold and the exercise price of the option is due. Hence, the tax burden on NQSOs is higher than for qualified options for the manager.

In the United Kingdom, options granted to employees and directors are tax exempt up to a value of £30,000, calculated at the date of the grant, if these options belong to a discretionary Company Share Option Plan (CSOP). Gains on options that exceed this amount (and are thus not covered under an approved CSOP scheme) will be taxed at the income tax level according to the UK Income Tax Act 2003, Chapter 5 ("Share Options").

A second reason for the popularity of stock options has been the *accounting treatment* rule FAS No. 12, "Accounting for Stock-based Compensation," which did not specifically require U.S. firms to expense options. According to this procedure, companies only incurred an accounting charge equal to the spread between the current stock price and the grant-date exercise price if the exercise price and the expiration date had been predetermined. This implies no accounting charge for fair-market-value and premium options (Murphy 1999). The new relevant accounting treatment FAS123r (effective since 2005) requires that costs resulting from all share-based payment transactions be recognized in the financial statement and establishes fair value as the measurement objective. In the European context, compensatory stock options are treated under IFRS2. This stipulates that share-based payments without a vesting date are expensed at fair value as determined at the grant date. If share options have a vesting date, share-based payments have to be expensed gradually over the vesting period.

Restricted stock consists of shares that become transferable after meeting certain conditions or *restrictions*. Often these conditions simply refer to a period of time (commonly three to five years), though they also may be conditional upon reaching specific performance targets. Usually, executives receive restricted stock as part of their annual bonus compensation, but firms may also choose to pay part of the compensation in stocks under so-called long-term incentive plans (LTIPs). Under an LTIP, executives are typically awarded shares after a vesting period and when meeting multiple additional requirements. These requirements usually include specific firm performance criteria and the executive remaining in employment throughout the vesting period.

In the United Kingdom, the popularity of LTIPs has increased since the publication of the Greenbury Report on Directors' Remuneration. Here, firms adopt performance pay plans that only pay out in the event of good performance as compared to a peer group of competitors (Conyon and Schwalbach 2000). In the United States, LTIPs currently include restricted stock grants that vest over time, and bonus plans over multiple years based on either cumulative performance or rolling-average performance (Conyon and Murphy 2000).

Because executives must forfeit their restricted stock when leaving the company, this pay component could induce a more long-term commitment from the recipients. This possibility of forfeiture guarantees a favorable tax and accounting treatment. Under FAS123r, restricted stock is treated in the United States under the same accounting treatment as stock options, and nonvested equity shares granted to employees must be measured at their fair value at grant date. Yet some argue that stock awards provide a more efficient incentive mechanism for CEOs of high-growth firms than restricted stock as the latter provides relatively inefficient inducements for risk-averse CEOs to pursue risky, yet value-enhancing, investment projects (Bryan, Hwang, and Lilien 2000).

Additional Components and Severance Pay

Some companies offer their managers supplemental executive retirement plans (SERPs). Benefits are based on company performance or on the number of years served. Typically, the information disclosed in the annual report and accounts is insufficient to calculate the exact value of such plans, but the few cases with complete information show that the pension benefits could be substantial.

Beyond SERPs, executives can receive substantial pay through additional programs or components: compensation for loss of office, cash recruitment incentives, and relocation expenses. Other components of executive compensation may be severance pay and golden parachutes. The idea behind golden parachutes and severance agreements is to provide executives with the incentive to maximize shareholder wealth without any concern for job loss. However, severance pay is nothing less than assets leaking out of the firm as this type of remuneration cannot be related to future performance. Hence, the stock market may react negatively as severance pay may signal broader governance problems within a company. The counterargument is that severance pay is part of an efficient multiperiod incentive contract, which aims to maintain corporate secrets and avoid adverse publicity when a top manager leaves the company.

LEVEL AND MIX: AN INTERNATIONAL COMPARISON

Although some components of the top executive compensation packages have changed in similar ways across countries (e.g., the rise of long-term option grants), marked differences still exist. Exhibit 14.3 shows the evolution of average CEO compensation (in April 2005 USD) between 1997 and 2006 for firms with

The figure shows a comparison of the estimated compensation level in 22 countries in 1997 and 2005 for companies with at least US$500 million in worldwide annual sales. The amounts are inflated and expressed in April 2005 U.S. dollars. Total pay is calculated as a sum of salary, bonus, options/LTIPs, and other compensation. Salary represents the base salary including regular payments (vacation allowance, 13th month salary) and non-performance-related bonus; bonus includes target performance-based cash awards. Options/LTIPs includes the grant-date expected value of option grants and annualized targets from long-term incentive plans. Other compensation includes both compulsory and voluntary company contributions.

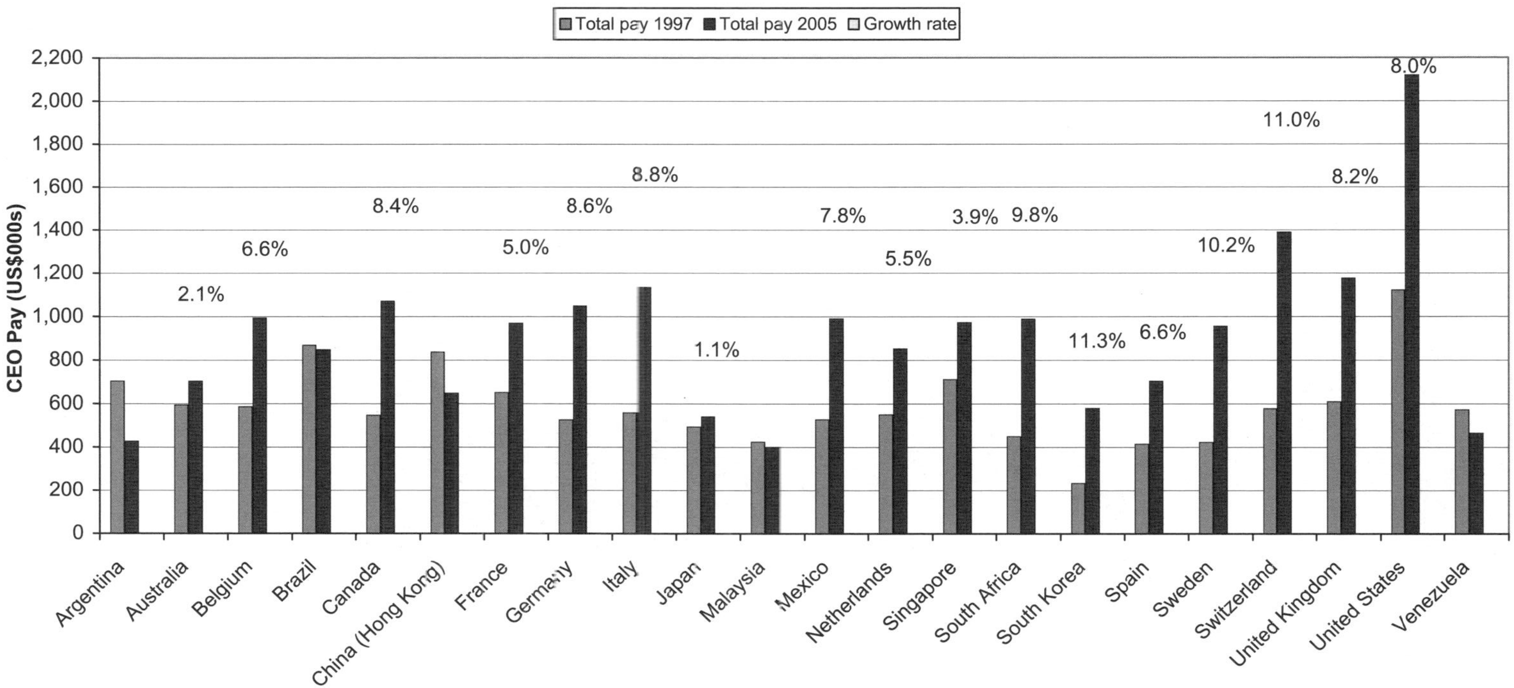

Exhibit 14.3 Total CEO Pay, 1997 versus 2005

Source: Data are extracted from both Murphy (1999) and Towers Perrin's 2005/06 Worldwide Total Remuneration Report.

approximately US$500 million in sales. The total pay is calculated as the sum of salary, bonus, options/LTIPs and other compensation. The graph exhibits the rising CEO compensation levels over time: The highest compensation is found in the United States and the lowest in Malaysia. Exhibit 14.3 also reveals that CEO pay levels have risen significantly. For example, since 1997, CEO pay in some European countries, the United Kingdom, the United States, South Africa, and South Korea has risen at a yearly growth rate of 8 percent or higher (in real 2005 USD terms). For a few countries, mainly in Asia and South America, CEO pay has decreased over the same period.

Exhibit 14.4 illustrates the level and composition of variable pay in CEO compensation. Two pay components are observed: variable bonus and long-term incentives as a percentage of annual basic compensation. The variable bonus includes all payments that are short-term and performance-related. Long-term incentives comprise stock options, restricted stock grants, and other awards. Several striking facts emerge. First, the figures show that the use of long-term compensation is highest in the United States, Singapore, and China, whereas in India, long-term components only account for a small part of variable pay. Second, the reliance on variable bonuses also differs widely across countries. For instance, South Africa and Germany rely heavily on performance-related payments whereas companies in Japan use variable bonuses only to a small extent.

Figure 14.5 presents a detailed picture of the level and mix of CEO compensation of firms with at least US$500 million in worldwide sales for 26 countries. U.S. CEOs receive the highest total pay with more than twice as much of their compensation arising from stock options relative to the other CEO-country combinations in the sample. Within Europe, the highest CEO compensation is found in Switzerland, the United Kingdom, France, and Germany. Several other countries, including Canada, but also Mexico, Brazil, Singapore, and South Africa, belong to the group with a high CEO pay-level. While Murphy (1999) noted in 1999 that stock options were absent in 9 of the 24 countries surveyed, stock options in 2005 make up part of CEO compensation in all but one country.

Concerns about standards of financial reporting and accountability, as well as the controversy over executive pay packages, have led to proposals to improve governance standards around the world. An important element in a law or code on corporate governance is the disclosure of managerial remuneration. In many countries, compliance with those codes is not mandatory: Often a distinction is made between nonbinding recommendations and the so-called comply-or-explain principle. Under comply-or-explain, firms must declare their degree of conformity with the code and their reasons for deviation from the code. However, this gives firms the opportunity not to reveal the actual level of executive pay. Given the cost of the compensation packages and the role that shareholders can play in verifying the incentive mechanisms embedded in compensation packages, further disclosure for all top management, officers, and directors should be made mandatory.

INCENTIVES

Corporate governance deals with the question of how to ensure investors receive a fair return on their investment. One of the solutions to this fundamental question is an (unavoidably) incomplete contract, which is set up to better align the interests of

The figure shows CEO level and composition of variable pay (i.e., variable bonus and long-term incentives) measured as a percentage of annual basic compensation in 2005. Variable bonus includes all payments that are (short-term) performance-related. Long-term incentives comprise stock options, restricted stock grants, and other awards.

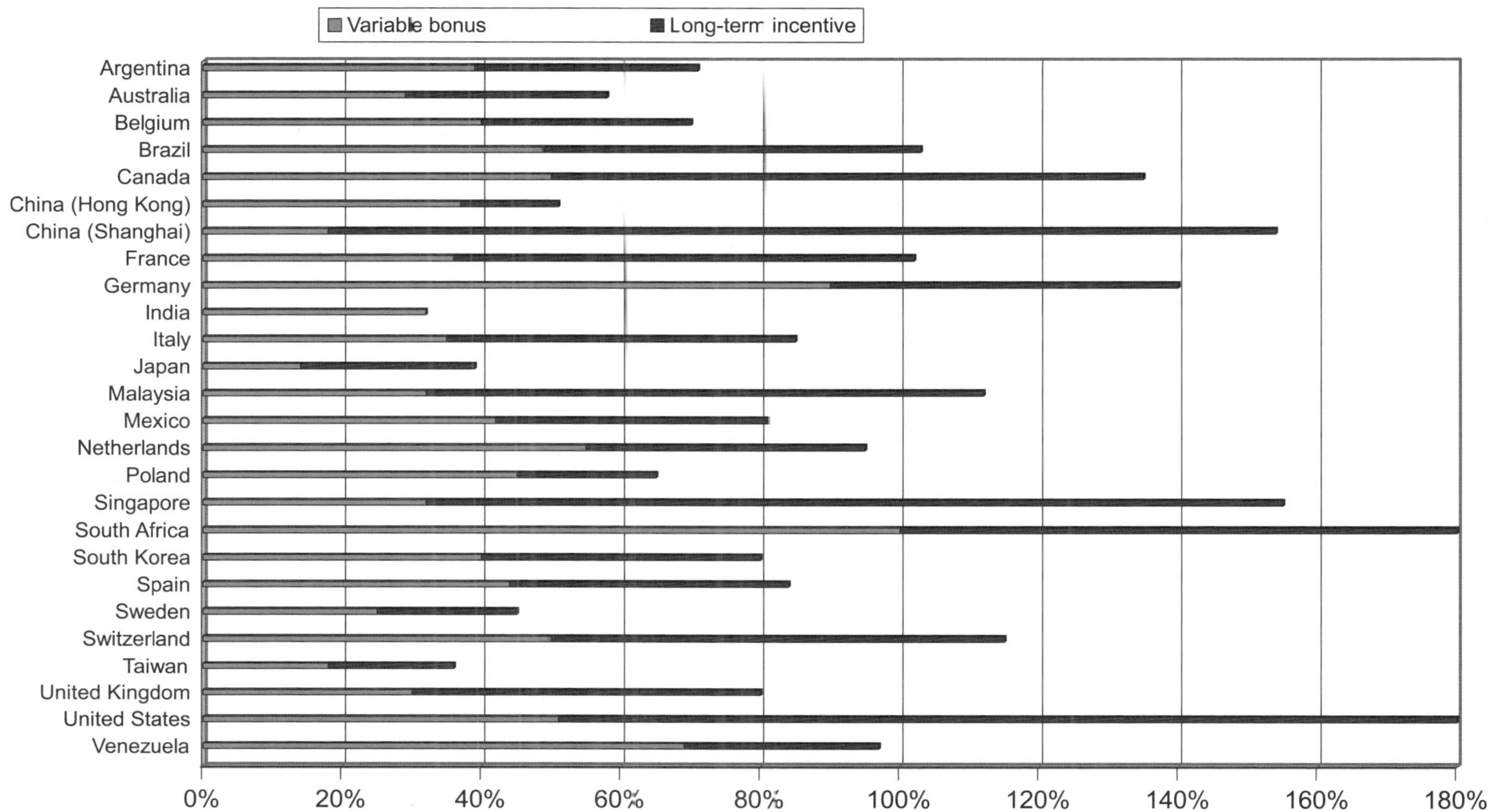

Exhibit 14.4 CEO Variable Pay

Source: Data are from Towers Perrin's 2005/06 Worldwide Total Remuneration Report.

The figure shows the estimated compensation level and mix for local employees of firms in 26 countries in 2005, with approximately US$500 million in worldwide sales. The amounts are expressed in US$ converted at the exchange rates of April 1, 2005. Salary represents the base salary including regular payments (vacation allowance, 13th month salary) and non-performance-related bonus; bonus includes target performance-based cash awards. Options/LTIPs includes the grant-date expected value of option grants and annualized targets from long-term incentive plans. Other compensation includes both compulsory and voluntary company contributions.

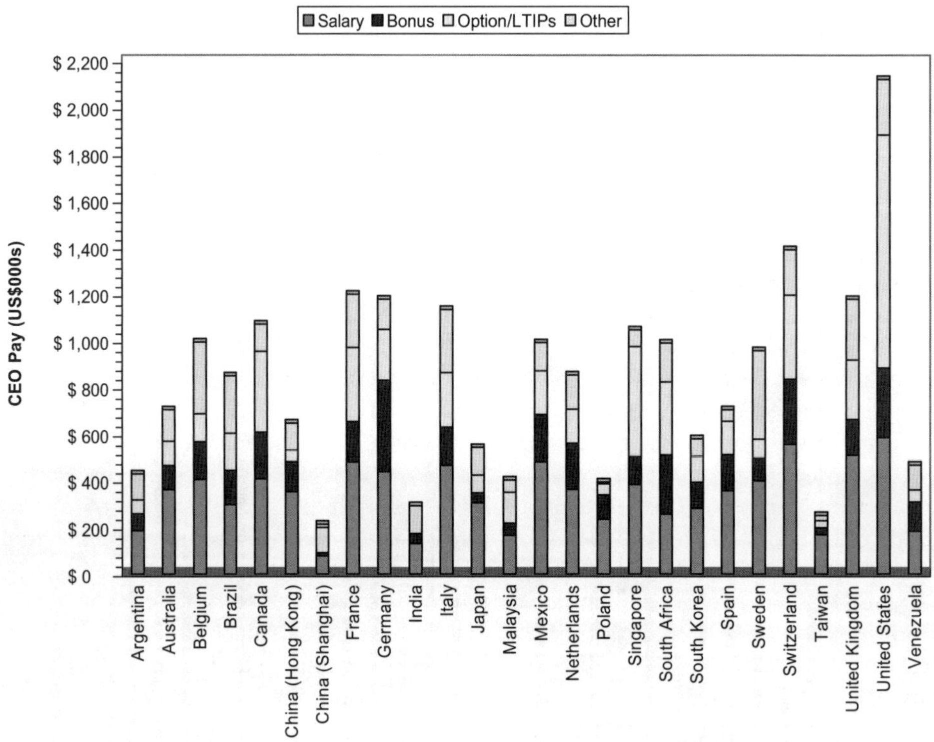

Exhibit 14.5 Level and Mix of CEO Pay: An International Comparison
Source: Data are from Towers Perrin's 2005/06 Worldwide Total Remuneration Report.

shareholders and executives. Such a contract typically includes share ownership, compensation, and the threat of dismissal, but leaves the executive with some residual control rights (i.e., the right to make decisions in the absence of a predefined rule). Decisions leading to managerial self-interest should be discouraged by corporate governance mechanisms, which instead incentivize managers to pursue actions that are beneficial to shareholders (Daily, Dalton, and Cannella 2003). This is the reason the principal-agent model and the stewardship/stakeholder perspective on executive compensation claim that effective remuneration contracts result from a market mechanism corrected by good corporate governance rules.

The Arm's-Length Contracting Model

Despite its theoretical limitations, the principal-agent framework has long been the dominant framework to analyze corporate governance problems in general and executive compensation problems in particular (Bruce, Buck, and Main 2005). At the heart of the agency problem is the separation of ownership and control (Jensen and Meckling 1976). The agency perspective on executive compensation is based on the standard principal-agent model of corporate governance, whereby shareholders are the principals and top managers are the agents. Shareholders need the expertise of the managers to generate the returns on invested capital. The agent and the principals have diverging interests and aim to maximize their own utilities, thus inducing agency problems. The question then becomes how to have self-interested managers maximize the wealth of the shareholders.

Advocates propose various governance mechanisms to protect shareholder interests, including increased shareholder monitoring and enhanced interest alignment. Close shareholder monitoring may encourage managers to act in the best interest of shareholders as their decisions will be observed constantly. However, monitoring is costly for the principal and will only generate a sufficient payoff if the shareholder has a large enough share stake. Firms can achieve interest alignment in various ways, but one of the easier methods is to fine-tune executive compensation schemes. The practical importance of corporate governance becomes evident in the pay-setting process by the board of directors, often referred to as *arm's-length contracting* between shareholders and managers.

Executive pay should be related to corporate performance: The pay-performance sensitivity (PPS) is the key metric that affects the outcome of the pay-setting process (Bruce et al. 2005). Firms can achieve PPS by means of an annual bonus on top of an executive's base salary or by stock ownership targets. In the words of Demsetz and Lehn (1985, 1156): "The more concentrated is ownership, the greater the degree to which benefits and costs are borne by the same owner." Core and Larcker (2002) find that the adoption of ownership targets is followed by a rise in stock price, indicating that markets are sensitive to the state of a firm's governance. The use of stock options is yet another possibility to create incentives for the executive to generate shareholder value.

The remaining divergences between shareholders and managers (not corrected by governance devices) result in a *residual loss* that contributes, along with monitoring costs, to the total agency costs. A reduction of agency costs may also occur as a consequence of a range of shareholder activism such as proxy proposals (Renneboog and Szilagyi 2008; Cziraki, Reneboog, and Szilagyi 2009), pressure on management by shareholder coalitions (Becht, Franks, Mayer, and Rossi 2009), and the threat of top management turnover as a consequence of a disciplinary takeover (Franks and Renneboog 2001). These mechanisms act jointly towards establishing a rational intention for managers to build up shareholder value and simultaneously prevent the excessive extraction of funds by executives.

However, the assumption that agents act in a completely rational manner and choose to maximize their individual utility is questionable. The principal-agent framework is also accused of hindering legal and academic thinking by assuming that the only issue to be taken into account is the relationship between principals and agents, and that creating shareholder value will solve all problems (Clarke 2007). Critics of agency theory have proposed several alternative theories such as the self-serving executive model, the stakeholder theory, and the stewardship theory.

Stewardship Theory

As opposed to the principal-agent theory, *stewardship theory* derives from the assumption that the interests of both parties (the management and the shareholders) do not necessarily diverge. In fact, stewardship theory describes situations in which managers' interests align with the objectives of shareholders (Davis, Schoorman, and Donaldson 1997). The reason lies in the manager, who acts on social norms and values. These manager-stewards derive a higher utility from collectivistic and pro-organizational behavior than they do from the maximization of their own wealth. Stewards act collectively because they want to further the objectives of the organization. They may be convinced that working toward collectivistic and organizational ends will, in the end, better serve their personal needs. A steward's behavior can be considered rational as his behavior may leave him with a higher utility. Consequently, a steward would decide to act cooperatively in a situation in which his interests are not aligned with the interests of the shareholders. A steward's performance is dependent on his structural situation. His autonomy should be empowered in order to maximize the benefits of his actions. Stewardship theory is more concerned with structures that empower than with monitoring. The difference in the behavior of a steward compared to that of an agent is based on the idea that the steward is more concerned with extrinsic values than with intrinsic rewards.

Under the stewardship theory, executives maximize shareholder value rather than pursuing their individual-utility-maximizing behavior. However, the implications of an empowerment of the CEO on the pay-setting process reveal the limited practical applicability of the stewardship theory. While risk-averse shareholders may be aware of the fact that a CEO may seek to further his individual utility, Davis et al. (1997, 26) note that establishing a stewardship structure may be analogous to "turning the hen house over to the fox."

The Arguments Pro Market

Where the compensation packages currently offered to top management are subject to substantial criticism (see the next section), it may be that market forces are determining the magnitude and composition of the remuneration. Furthermore, many good reasons exist to consider managerial stock options as an effective pay component. First, stock options provide the most direct link between firm performance and executive pay. Therefore, this pay component induces substantial managerial effort and encourages executives to make rational shareholder-oriented decisions. Moreover, stock options enable a firm to attract external managers and then motivate them to stay with the firm. However, risk-averse and undiversified executives may discount options because of the risk associated with this pay component. Corporations also may erroneously perceive options as cheap when relying on the Black-Scholes formula to calculate the opportunity cost of an option (Murphy 2002).

Second, although the practice of granting at-the-money options may facilitate excessive rent extraction, several optimal reasons exist for at-the-money option grants. As stock options induce more risk into managerial compensation, they may also lead to an increase of managers' effort incentives (Bryan et al. 2000). The grant price of an option induces these incentives. While in-the-money options lose their favorable tax treatment (as they do not qualify any longer as performance-based compensation and hence lose their status as statutory option), setting the exercise price at or below the market price of the grant date may be optimal (Murphy 2002). In the latter case, however, options incur some accounting charge in the United States, which may explain the commonly observed fact that options are granted at-the-money. Moreover, Hall and Murphy (2000) point out that setting the option exercise price equal to the granting-date share price may maximize the incentives for risk-averse and undiversified executives. Lastly, these at-the-money options should not be indexed as this would destroy any meaningful incentives. As Murphy (2002) notes, reload options that grant an additional option upon exercise of the original option are inefficient due to the high economic costs related to their granting, relative to their low value to the recipient.

Third, the criticism on the prima facie abuses of the use of stock options (mainly the repricing) can be overturned, as option repricing mainly takes place after market downturns. Kalpathy (2009) views repricing as being motivated by incentive alignment and retention, as there are no signs that internal governance problems or conflicts of interest drive repricing.

Finally, the self-serving argument concerning executive pay may be wrong because it predicts that excessive rents cannot be transferred to other firms. Fee and Hadlock (2003), however, show that when changing firms, executives receive option grants and stock awards that more than offset the losses incurred when leaving the old firm. Furthermore, Murphy and Zábojník (2004) provide a market-based explanation for self-dealing, which says that the level of CEO pay is determined by competition among firms for executives and depends upon the portion of the CEO's skills that is transferable across firms and industries. They argue that the fact that the general skills a manager ought to possess to run a modern corporation are in scarce supply can explain the increase in executive remuneration.

EXTERNALITIES

The following examples in the popular press cast doubt on the effectiveness of the market mechanism in determining executive pay.

> *... no matter what hare-brained ideas politicians come up with to curb controversial pay packets, bright minds in finance will find a way round them or exit the regulated part of the industry.* (Financial Times, *September 23, 2008)*

> *Anger rumbles on after the revelation that American International Group (AIG) paid millions in bonuses to employees at the unit that broke the giant insurer, which required a \$173 billion bailout. ("Rumbling on,"* Economist, *March 23, 2009)*

If executive pay is really the outcome of a market mechanism, then understanding why managers still receive bonuses in the wake of poor corporate performance (directly resulting from poor managerial decision making or risk management) is difficult. Also, if market mechanisms drive executive remuneration, the question arises as to why some firms still hide the actual amount and composition of managers' pay from shareholders.

The implementation of effective corporate governance mechanisms to create sufficient incentives for managers to create shareholder value and to prevent excessive extraction of rents by the managers from the firm can be hard. For example, the rationale is unclear whether larger shareholders function as an effective governance mechanism (Bertrand and Mullainathan 2000; Franks, Mayer, and Renneboog 2001) or whether institutional investors can affect pay setting (Cheffins and Thomas 2001). Equally, results are ambiguous as to the effects of separating the roles of CEO and chairman (Brickley, Coles, and Jarrell 1997; Adams and Ferreira 2005; Goyal and Park 2005; Faleye 2007), the optimality of board structure (Hermalin and Weisbach 2003; Linck, Netter, and Yang 2008), the establishment of remuneration committees (Gordon 2005; Conyon and Peck 1998), and the efficiency of the disciplinary turnover mechanism (Renneboog and Trojanowski 2005). To sum up, even in the presence of governance mechanisms, residual control rights may leave management with substantial scope to extract rents from the shareholders, possibly through the channel of executive compensation. Accordingly, some authors believe that top managers serve their own best interests (Bertrand and Mullainathan 2001; Bebchuk and Fried 2003).

Some boards of directors, especially their remuneration committees, probably do not function as efficient governance mechanisms. For instance, a director who is a friend of the CEO or who has been hired by the CEO may be unlikely to critically question the level and mix of the CEO's compensation. Furthermore, a director who is tough on pay may be considered a troublemaker by the managers of his firm and by the network of nonexecutive directors at large such that this director may therefore lose his position on other boards (Bhagat and Black 1999).

Managerial Power and Self-Dealing

The self-serving perspective of management, convincingly stated by Bebchuk, Fried, and Walker (2002) and Bertrand and Mullainathan (2001), proposes that executive directors extract funds from shareholders for their own benefit. According to this theory, managers may attempt to affect the terms of their compensation contracts for reasons of self-dealing. These authors also argue that managers' influence over their own pay may impose substantial costs on shareholders by diluting and distorting the incentives of managers with consequences for corporate performance (Bebchuk and Fried 2003). Various empirical findings suggest that the self-dealing of executives is a real problem. Yermack (1997), for example, finds that managers receive stock option grants shortly before good news announcements and delay such grants until after bad news announcements.

The managerial power approach to explaining executive compensation has two underlying building blocks: outrage costs/constraints and camouflage. *Outrage costs* are related to reputational harm to the firm and the loss of support from shareholders. As Bebchuk et al. (2002, 789) state, "outrage costs depend on the extent to which the rent extraction can be easily and distinctly identified." *Camouflage*, by contrast, refers to the practice of hidden rent extraction. This implies that managers may have a preference for compensation arrangements that enable them to extract funds from the shareholders in such a way that these compensation agreements can be camouflaged as optimal contracting. Bebchuk and

Fried (2003, 76) emphasize the importance of strict disclosure regulation: "... the transparency and salience of disclosure can have a significant effect on CEO compensation." Hidden compensation comes in forms such as perquisites, pension plans, and severance pay agreements (Jensen and Meckling 1976; Bebchuk and Fried 2003; Yermack 2006a). Moreover, Kuhnen and Zwiebel (2007) show that this hidden part of compensation increases with the noise in production process (as proxied in the variation of a firm's industry-adjusted return on assets) as well as the manager's outside option (as proxied by the strength of the CEO's ties with the firm, his age, and his education).

Bertrand and Mullainathan (2001) question the effectiveness of executive pay by showing that (windfall) earnings that are not a result of management's decisions affect CEO pay just as much as earnings that are a result of managements' decisions; thus, CEOs are paid for luck. Compensation contracts do not appear to be sophisticated because they do not filter out payment for luck. However, Bertrand and Mullainathan (2000) find that the presence of large shareholders moderates the increase in CEO pay and limits self-dealing. Some studies provide evidence consistent with the skimming view in the absence of large shareholders—that is, CEOs can capture the board and determine their own compensation at the expense of corporate profits. Bertrand and Mullainathan (1999) also show that when the introduction of antitakeover devices reduces a takeover threat to a firm, CEO pay still rises on average. The increase in CEO pay is highest in firms with no large shareholders, as large shareholders are instrumental in preventing excessive rent extraction.

An example of perquisite consumption by CEOs in major companies is the personal use of company aircraft (Yermack 2006b). Shareholders (and the market) penalize firms when such managerial fringe benefits are disclosed. When personal aircraft use by CEOs is first disclosed to shareholders, company stock prices drop by about 1.1 percent. Furthermore, firms permitting CEO aircraft use underperform market benchmarks by about 400 basis points per year, constituting a severe shortfall beyond the costs of the resources consumed. Particularly strong associations appear to exist between personal aircraft use and a CEO's golfing activity. These results indicate that the market is concerned that the agency costs in such firms far exceed the direct costs of all the managerial perks. Indeed, after the aircraft perk is first disclosed, firms release greater rates of bad news to shareholders in the form of write-offs and negative earnings surprises. These patterns are consistent with a hypothesis of strategic disclosure behavior whereby managers minimize the bad news flowing to the market until after they have secured access to desirable fringe benefits.

Options and Risk Taking

Several studies focus on the relation between stock option plans and management risk-taking. DeFusco, Johnson, and Zorn (1990) demonstrate that option-holding managers are incentivized to undertake risky projects. Rajgopal and Shevlin (2002) and Bulan, Sanyal, and Yan (2008) confirm that adding stock options to a manager/CEO pay package generally decreases his risk aversion due to downside protection.

Options-induced changes in managerial risk may also influence bondholder returns: An increase in asset risk can trigger a lower price for corporate bonds in the secondary market. Billett, Mauer, and Zhang (2006) show that the negative effect for bondholders is larger in firms where the agency costs are expected to be highest (when CEOs only hold a relatively low fraction of the firm's shares). Moreover, these negative effects are amplified when managerial power is high and shareholder rights weak.

Option Backdating

Option backdating refers to the practice in which management chooses the grant day of an option ex post, namely once they have the benefit of hindsight to identify a day in the past on which the stock price was particularly low. Thus, they can lock in the lowest exercise price, which immediately results in a more valuable option (Lie 2005; Ritter 2008).

Surprisingly, option backdating is legal in the United States provided that it is acknowledged when it occurs. This practice of backdating options is widespread and systematically applied to executive option grants in the United States (Heron and Lie 2007 and 2009). Narayanan, Schipani, and Seyhun (2006) estimate that the disclosure of option backdating results in an average of a 7 percent decrease of the stock price, which corresponds to about US$400 million in market value, while the gain to the individuals is only about US$500,000 per firm per year (Ritter 2008).

Repricing of Stock Options

In cases where the options' incentives to a manager disappear when the stock price drops below the exercise price (an *underwater option*), two possibilities exist to readjust lost incentives: (1) Options can be surrendered and replaced with new options with an exercise price equal to the current market price, or (2) the terms at which options were awarded can be adjusted. However, the practice of repricing (i.e., resetting the exercise price of options) is widely considered inappropriate for several reasons. First, options may be protected from general industry and market movements ex ante—in other words, options may be designed so that effects beyond management's control are screened out (Bebchuk et al. 2002). Second, repricing creates an incentive problem. If executives anticipate the repricing of options when share price collapses or moves down, then the option would no longer function as a strong incentive mechanism (Chance, Kumar, and Todd 2000). On the positive side, Kalpathy (2009) shows results consistent with the idea that firms use repricing to moderate CEOs' incentives to increase risk.

Repricing follows poor firm-specific performance and is commonly observed in small firms, often in industries where human capital is important (Carter and Lynch 2001; Kalpathy 2009). But is option repricing effective in (re)stimulating management to focus on shareholder value? Research indicates that poorly performing firms engaging in repricing activities manage to generate good performance after resetting the exercise price (Chance et al. 2000). However, this does not convince Bebchuk et al. (2002) who claim that the repricing of stock options is counterproductive. It is only in the best interest of management and not in the best interests of shareholders because managers benefit (perhaps unfairly) from large option gains in bull markets and (unjustly) justify option repricing in case of poor stock performance.

The Role of Compensation Consultants

Compensation consultants such as Towers Perrin, Watson Wyatt, or Hewitt Associates can support the board of directors in the pay-setting process with their knowledge about the design of pay packages in the industry and the company's peer group. In particular, they can offer advice and assistance in the design of compensation packages to compensation committees (Bender 2007). For the United Kingdom, Conyon, Peck, and Sadler (2006) show that almost all firms employ some form of compensation consultant. While these consultants promote pay packages to align managerial and shareholder interest, chief executive pay (and especially the equity-based component) is higher in firms with more consultants and with consultants that offer various services (Conyon et al. 2006; Conyon 2008; Armstrong, Ittner, and Larcker 2008). Wade, Porac, and Pollock (1997) find that companies with more concentrated and active outside owners are more likely to justify their pay practices by using the advice of compensation consultants. These findings are consistent with the argument that firms use compensation consultants to camouflage CEO pay and to enable the excessive extraction of funds (Bebchuk and Fried 2003).

Determining the level of pay relative to a peer group, a procedure commonly employed by compensation consultants, leads to what is commonly referred as *ratcheting up* of pay. The competition among pay consultants may drive this effect on CEO pay, suggesting that this is not in the shareholders' best interest (Minhat 2008). More importantly, the knowledge about the design of pay packages in the industry and the company's peer group may also be misleading. In particular, compensation consultants may spread deficiencies from one client firm to another client firm. A study by Cadman, Carter, and Hillegeist (2008) shows, however, that while compensation consultants enable the extraction of funds from the shareholders, this does not reduce the pay-for-performance sensitivity relation.

SUMMARY AND CONCLUSIONS

This chapter has contrasted the classical governance framework on the level and composition of executive pay and the managerial self-serving/skimming model. The principal-agent theory, stewardship theory, and the stakeholder theory claim that remuneration contracts result from a market mechanism. This mechanism is further corrected by good corporate governance rules, shareholder activism, shareholder coalitions that exercise pressure on management, and the threat of turnover to top management. The view on option compensation as a market-based mechanism assumes that there is an effective link between performance and executive pay. However, empirical evidence casts serious doubt on the effectiveness of executive pay as resulting from a market mechanism in general and the optimality of the use of stock options in particular.

The use of options may be subject to some severe problems. For example, firms overestimate the value of options to executives and erroneously take options as a cheap form of compensation. The strong reliance on stock options in compensation contracts is dubious, as one of the reasons for the reliance seems to be the favorable tax treatment of options. Furthermore, easily applicable mechanisms to filter out luck (dividend protection, indexing) are simply not implemented in executive stock options. The empirical results in relation to the repricing of options show that the costs associated with resetting the exercise price are too high to justify this practice and that the incentive effects are mitigated by the use of this type of equity-based pay. Moreover, stock options seem to have negative effects on bondholder wealth. The same holds true for severance pay: Including large bonuses in the compensation packages in case a CEO is forced to leave (often in the wake of poor corporate performance) establishes perverse incentives.

To sum up, the available empirical evidence indicates that managerial self-dealing and the skimming of corporate profits by managers through compensation packages create a real problem. Executive compensation often seems to be in conflict with shareholder value creation. This situation is further exacerbated by evidence suggesting that hidden compensation is used to transfer wealth to executives.

DISCUSSION QUESTIONS

1. What is the idea behind the market mechanism of pay?
2. What effect does the adoption of stock option programs have on executives?
3. What alternatives exist to option repricing?
4. What is the meaning of the term *skimming*?
5. What is the reason for pay-for-performance and does it work?

REFERENCES

Adams, Renée B., and Daniel Ferreira. 2005. A theory of friendly boards. Working paper, ECGI.

Armstrong, Chris, Christopher D. Ittner, and David F. Larcker. 2008. Economic characteristics, corporate governance, and the influence of compensation consultants on executive pay levels. Working paper, Wharton School, University of Pennsylvania.

Bebchuk, Lucian A., and Jesse M. Fried. 2003. Executive compensation as an agency problem. *Journal of Economic Perspectives* 17 (3): 71–92.

Bebchuk, Lucian A., Jesse M. Fried, and David I. Walker. 2002. Managerial power and rent extraction in the design of executive compensation. *University of Chicago Law Review* 69 (3): 751–846.

Becht, Marco, Julian Franks, Colin Mayer, and Stefano Rossi. 2009. Returns to shareholder activism: Evidence from a clinical study of the Hermes UK Focus Fund. *Review of Financial Studies* 22 (8): 3093–3129.

Bender, Ruth. 2007. Paying for advice: The role of the remuneration consultant in UK listed companies. Discussion paper, Cranfield University.

Bertrand, Marianne, and Sendhil Mullainathan. 1999. Corporate governance and executive pay: Evidence from takeover legislation. Working paper, MIT Department of Economics.

———. 2000. Do CEOs set their own pay? The ones without principals do. Working paper, NBER.

———. 2001. Are CEOs rewarded for luck? The ones without principals are. *Quarterly Journal of Economics* 116 (3): 901–932.

Bhagat, Sanjai, and Bernard S. Black. 1999. The uncertain relationship between board composition and firm performance. *Business Lawyer* 54 (3): 921–963.

Billett, Matthew T., David C. Mauer, and Yilei Zhang. 2006. Stockholder and bondholder wealth effects of CEO incentive grants. Working paper, University of Iowa.

Bolton, Patrick, Jose A. Scheinkman, and Wei Xiong. 2003. Executive compensation and short-termist behavior in speculative markets. *Review of Economic Studies* 73: 3, 577–610.

Brickley, James A., Jeffrey L. Coles, and Gregg Jarrell. 1997. Leadership structure: Separating the CEO and chairman of the board. *Journal of Corporate Finance* 3 (3): 189–220.
Bruce, Alistair, Trevor Buck, and Brian G. M. Main. 2005. Top executive remuneration: A view from Europe. *Journal of Management Science* 42 (7): 1493–1506.
Bryan, Stephen H., Lee-Seok Hwang, and Steven B. Lilien. 2000. Stock-based compensation: An empirical analysis of incentive-intensity, relative mix, and economic determinants. *Journal of Business* 73 (4): 661–693.
Bulan, Laarni T., Paroma Sanyal, and Zhipeng Yan. 2008. A few bad apples: An analysis of CEO performance pay and firm productivity. Working paper, Brandeis University.
Cadman, Brian D., Mary Ellen Carter, and Stephen A. Hillegeist. 2008. The role and effect of compensation consultants on CEO pay. Working paper, INSEAD.
Carter, Mary Ellen, and Luann J. Lynch. 2001. An examination of executive stock option repricing. *Journal of Financial Economics* 61 (2): 207–225.
Chance, Don M., Raman Kumar, and Rebecca B. Todd. 2000. The repricing of executive stock options. *Journal of Financial Economics* 57 (1): 129–154.
Cheffins, Brian R., and Randall S. Thomas. 2001. Should shareholders have a greater say over executive pay? Learning from the US experience. *Journal of Corporate Law Studies* 1 (2): 277–316.
Clarke, Thomas. 2007. *International corporate governance: A comparative approach.* New York: Routledge.
Conyon, Martin J. 2008. Compensation consultants and executive pay: Evidence from the United States and the United Kingdom. Working paper, ESSEC.
Conyon, Martin J., and Kevin J. Murphy. 2000. The prince and the pauper? CEO pay in the United States and United Kingdom. *Economic Journal* 110 (4):7, 640–671.
Conyon, Martin J., and Simon I. Peck. 1998. Board size and corporate performance: Evidence from European Countries. *European Journal of Finance* 4 (3): 291–304.
Conyon, Martin J., Simon I. Peck, and Graham V. Sadler. 2006. Compensation consultants and executive pay. Working paper, Wharton School.
Conyon, Martin J., and Joachim Schwalbach. 2000. Executive compensation: Evidence from the UK and Germany. *Long Range Planning* 33 (4): 504–526.
Core, John E., and David F. Larcker. 2002. Performance consequences of mandatory increases in executive stock ownership. *Journal of Financial Economics* 64 (3): 317–340.
Cziraki, Peter, Luc Renneboog, and Peter Szilagyi. 2009. Shareholder activism through proposals. The European perspective. Working paper, ECGI.
Daily, Catherine M., Dan R. Dalton, and Albert A. Cannella, Jr. 2003. Corporate governance: Decades of dialogue and data. *Academy of Management Review* 28 (3): 371–382.
Davis, James H., F. David Schoorman, and Lex Donaldson. 1997. Toward a stewardship theory of management. *Academy of Management Review* 22 (1): 20–47.
DeFusco, Richard A., Robert R. Johnson, and Thomas S. Zorn. 1990. The effect of executive stock option plans on stockholders and bondholders. *Journal of Finance* 45 (2): 617–627.
Demsetz, Harold, and Kenneth Lehn. 1985. The structure of corporate ownership: Causes and consequences. *Journal of Political Economy* 93 (6): 1155–1177.
Faleye, Olubunmi. 2007. Does one hat fit all? The case of corporate leadership structure. *Journal of Management & Governance* 11 (3): 239–259.
Fee, C. Edwards, and Charles J. Hadlock. 2003. Raids, rewards, and reputations in the market for CEO talent. *Review of Financial Studies* 16 (4): 1315–1357.
Franks, Julian, Colin Mayer, and Luc Renneboog. 2001. Who disciplines management in poorly performing companies? *Journal of Financial Intermediation* 10 (3-4): 209–248.
Frydman, Carola, and Raven E. Saks. 2007. Executive compensation: A new view from a long-term perspective, 1936–2005. Working paper, NBER.
Gordon, Jeffrey. 2005. Executive compensation: If there's a problem, what's the remedy? The case for compensation discussion and analysis. Working paper, Columbia Law School.

Goyal, Vidhan K., and Chul W. Park. 2005. Board leadership structure and CEO turnover. *Journal of Corporate Finance* 8 (1): 49–66.
Hall, Brian J., and Kevin J. Murphy. 2000. Stock options for undiversified executives. *Journal of Accounting and Economics* 33 (1): 3–42.
Hermalin, Benjamin E., and Michael S. Weisbach. 2003. Boards of directors as an endogenously determined institution: A survey of the economic literature. *Economic Policy Review* 9 (1): 7–26.
Heron, Randall A., and Eric Lie. 2007. Does backdating explain the stock price pattern around executive stock option grants? *Journal of Financial Economics* 83 (3) 271–295.
———. 2009. What fraction of stock option grants to top executives have been backdated or manipulated. *Management Science* 55 (4): 513–525.
Jensen, Michael C., and William H. Meckling. 1976. Theory of the girm: Managerial behavior, agency costs and ownership structure. *Journal of Financial Economics* 3 (4): 305–360.
Jensen, Michael C., and Kevin J. Murphy. 1990. Performance pay and top-management incentives. *Journal of Political Economy* 98 (2): 225–264.
Kalpathy, Swaminathan. 2009. Stock option repricing and its alternatives: An empirical examination. *Journal of Financial and Quantitative Analysis* 44: 1459–1487.
Kuhnen, Camelia M., and Jeffrey H. Zwiebel. 2007. Executive pay, hidden compensation and managerial entrenchment. Working paper, Stanford University.
Lie, Eric. 2005. On the timing of CEO stock option awards. *Management Science* 51 (5): 802–812.
Linck, James S., Jeffry M. Netter, and Tina Yang. 2008. The determinants of board structure. *Journal of Financial Economics* 87 (2): 308–328.
Minhat, Marizah. 2008. The role of compensation consultant in executive pay governance. Working paper, University of Stirling.
Murphy, Kevin J. 1999. Executive compensation. In *Handbook of Labor Economics*, ed. Orley Ashenfelter and David Card, 2485–2563. North-Holland: Elsevier.
———. 2002. Explaining executive compensation: Managerial power vs. the perceived cost of stock options. *University of Chicago Law Review* 69 (3): 847–869.
Murphy, Kevin J., and Jan Zábojník. 2004. CEO pay and appointments: A market-based explanation for recent trends. *American Economic Review* 94 (2): 192–196.
Narayanan, M. P., Cindy A. Schipani, and Hasan Nejat Seyhun. 2006. The economic impact of backdating of executive stock options. *Michigan Law Review* 105 (8): 1589–1642.
Rajgopal, Shivaram, and Terry Shevlin. 2002. Empirical evidence on the relation between stock option compensation and risk taking. *Journal of Accounting and Economics* 33 (2): 145–171.
Renneboog, Luc, and Peter G. Szilagyi. 2008. Corporate restructuring and bondholder wealth. *European Financial Management* 14 (4): 792–819.
Renneboog, Luc, and Grzegorz Trojanowski. 2005. The managerial labour market and the governance role of shareholder control structures in the UK. Discussion paper, Tilburg University.
Ritter, Jay R. 2008. Forensic finance. *Journal of Economic Perspectives* 22 (3): 127–147.
Smith, Adam. 1790. *Theory of moral sentiments*. London: A. Millar.
Towers Perrin. 2005. 2005 Annual incentive plan design survey findings report.
Wade, James B., Joseph F. Porac, and Timothy G. Pollock. 1997. Worth, words, and the justification of executive pay. *Journal of Organizational Behavior* 18 (S1): 641–664.
Yermack, David. 1997. Good timing: CEO stock option awards and company news announcements. *Journal of Finance* 52 (2): 449–476.
———. 2006a. Golden handshakes: Separation pay for retired and dismissed CEOs. *Journal of Accounting and Economics* 41 (3): 237–256.
———. 2006b. Flights of fancy: Corporate jets, CEO perquisites, and inferior shareholder returns. *Journal of Financial Economics* 80 (1): 211–242.

ABOUT THE AUTHORS

Philipp Geiler is a researcher and PhD candidate in finance at Tilburg University. He holds an MSc in international economics and business studies from the Erasmus University Rotterdam and an MPhil in finance from the Rotterdam School of Management. While at Tilburg University, he worked on remuneration contracting related to payout policy and spent several months as a visiting graduate student at the University of Oxford. His research interests are in corporate governance, corporate finance, behavioral corporate finance, and gender studies.

Luc Renneboog is professor of corporate finance at Tilburg University and a research fellow at CentER and the European Corporate Governance Institute (ECGI, Brussels). He graduated from the Catholic University of Leuven with degrees in management engineering (MSc) and in philosophy (BA); from the University of Chicago with an MBA; and from the London Business School with a PhD in financial economics. He held appointments at the University of Leuven and Oxford University, and visiting appointments at, among others, London Business School and HEC (Paris). He has published in the *Journal of Finance, Journal of Financial Intermediation, Journal of Law and Economics, Journal of Corporate Finance, Journal of Banking and Finance, Oxford Review of Economic Policy, Cambridge Journal of Economics, European Financial Management*, and others. He has co-authored and edited several books on corporate governance, dividend policy, and venture capital. His research interests are corporate finance, corporate governance, takeovers, dividend policy, insider trading, law and economics, and the economics of art.

CHAPTER 15

Compensation Consultants and Executive Pay

MARTIN J. CONYON
Professor, IE Business School

INTRODUCTION

Compensation consultants are firms or individuals who advise client organizations about executive pay practices (Bebchuk and Fried 2006; Conyon, Peck, and Sadler 2009a). Critics contend that consultants lead to excessive chief executive officer (CEO) pay and poorly designed contracts. As Crystal (1991, 9) notes, "Executive compensation in the United States did not go out of control simply through some random process; it went out of control because of the actions—or inactions—of a number of parties. The first culprits in what will be a litany of culprits are compensation consultants." An alternative perspective is that compensation consultants are experts who provide valuable information and data to busy boards of directors. Their presence ameliorates opportunistic behavior by CEOs and leads to well-structured optimal compensation contracts (Conyon et al. 2009a). Do pay consultants promote the best interests of the firm's owners or do they simply enrich entrenched CEOs?

This chapter has two objectives. First, it reviews whether compensation consultants enhance or encumber the effective governance of CEO pay in light of recent studies in the field. Second, the chapter provides new evidence on the association between CEO pay and consultants in a sample of publicly held firms in the United Kingdom.

CEOs in the United States can earn large sums of money (Conyon, Core, and Guay 2009; Conyon and Murphy 2000; Fernandes, Ferreira, Matos, and Murphy 2009). CEO pay in S&P 500 firms has increased substantially from about $3 million in 1993 to a peak of about $16 million in 2000. While it has fallen back in recent years, average CEO pay in 2006 still stood at more than $8 million (Kaplan 2008). Comparisons with other employees are also important to consider. Kaplan documents that American CEOs earn significantly more than the typical American household. As Kaplan notes, average total pay of CEOs was just under 100 times greater than median household income in 1993 but it was more than 200 times greater by 2006.

The high level of CEO pay is controversial and a common topic of media coverage. This is not surprising when set against the perceived lack of pay-for-performance, growing income disparities, the economic crisis, and putative declining ethical standards in company boardrooms. Some academics have been especially critical of executive pay, questioning whether current arrangements are consistent with shareholder interests (Bebchuk and Fried 2003, 2004, and 2006). Bebchuk and Fried (2004) provide an in-depth review of the problems surrounding CEO pay practices. However, not all academics are so critical of CEO compensation. Kaplan (2008), for example, provides a robust defense of CEO pay practices in the United States. He argues that CEO pay is tied to performance, boards are appropriately setting pay, and CEOs are subject to market forces. Other studies also examine whether the market power or efficient contracting approach is a more appropriate explanation for patterns of CEO pay (Core, Guay, and Thomas 2005; Conyon et al. 2009).

Until recently, the role of executive compensation consultants has been largely unexamined. These consultants often advise busy boards and compensation committees on the design of executive pay packages. As with CEO pay, consultants are controversial (Crystal 1991; Bebchuk and Fried 2003, 2004, and 2006; Waxman 2007). Critics argue that consultants are responsible for high levels of CEO pay and their poorly designed compensation packages include too many perks, hidden benefits such as golden parachutes or lucrative pension deals, and nondemanding performance criteria. Especially salient is the hypothesis that consultants are not sufficiently independent. Consultants suffer from conflicts of interest because they sell other services to their clients and are thus wary of provoking the CEO for fear of jeopardizing this other business (Bebchuk and Fried 2004; Waxman 2007).

This chapter contributes to a nascent literature on pay consultants. The remainder of the chapter has four sections. The first section discusses compensation consultants including disclosure rules, the role of consultants, and consultant independence. This section is followed by a review of existing studies. New empirical evidence on CEO pay and consultants is then presented. The final section contains a summary and conclusion.

COMPENSATION CONSULTANTS

This section discusses the role of compensation consultants in determining the level of CEO pay. Disclosure rules pertaining to consultants are discussed. A primer on the market for compensation consultants is provided, focusing on why firms use pay consultants and asking whether they are independent.

Disclosure Rules

Disclosure of information about executive compensation consultants is now required in the United States, the United Kingdom, and Canada. Each country stipulating disclosure requires firms to identify the pay consultant by name, but regulations in each dominion are nuanced so that information disclosure is appreciably different. For example, UK firms disclose whether the consultant engages in other noncompensation consulting business activities such as actuarial services with the client firm. This is not mandated in the United States but companies may voluntarily reveal this information. In Canada, firms sometimes separately reveal fee income paid to consultants for executive compensation services and non-executive-pay business. In the United States and the United Kingdom, this rarely happens.

Disclosure of compensation consultant information in the United States has been mandated by the Securities and Exchange Commission since 2007 (SEC 2007). New rules came into effect for companies filing with the SEC after December 2006. Item 407(e) of the new regulations requires firms both to identify the consultants and to disclose any role of compensation consultants in determining or recommending the amount or form of executive and director compensation. Disclosure happened earlier in the United Kingdom. The Directors' Remuneration Report Regulations (2002) mandated firms to disclose consultant information in the United Kingdom for accounting periods after December 2002. The firms must name any person who provided material advice or services to the compensation committee and must disclose whether services in addition to compensation advice were given (Bender 2008; Conyon et al. 2009a; Kabir and Minhat 2009). Disclosure in Canada has been required since 2005. On April 15, 2005, the Canadian Securities Administrators (CSA) issued National Instrument 58-101 that requires corporations to disclose whether a firm has used a compensation consultant (Canada 2005). Together, the United States, the United Kingdom, and Canada report sufficient information about compensation consultants to investigate their effect on CEO pay.

The Market for Executive Compensation Consulting Services

The market for executive compensation consulting services is an oligopoly. That is, a few prominent compensation consultants supply a range of services to a large number of client firms. Panel A of Exhibit 15.1 illustrates the basic market structure for the United States, the United Kingdom, and Canada. The "big six" consulting firms in the United States are Towers Perrin, Mercer Human Resource Consulting, Frederick W. Cook & Co., Hewitt Associates, Watson Wyatt Worldwide, and Pearl Meyer and Partners. Various studies document evidence of the dominance of the big six (Bebchuk and Fried 2004; Waxman 2007; Armstrong, Ittner, and Larcker 2008; Cadman, Carter, and Hillegeist 2009; Conyon et al. 2009a; Murphy and Sandino 2009). These major consulting firms are also prevalent in the United Kingdom (Bender 2008; Conyon et al. 2009a; Conyon, Peck, and Sadler 2009b; Kabir and Minhat 2009; Voulgaris, Stathopoulos, and Walker 2009) as well as in Canada (Murphy and Sandino 2009). Other important players in the UK market are New Bridge Street Consultants and Monks Partnership. The market is becoming more concentrated. Towers Watson was formed from a merger between Towers Perrin and Watson Wyatt in 2010.

Exhibit 15.1 shows the following noteworthy features of the market. First, six firms consulting on executive compensation dominate the market. The frequency distribution of client market shares is right-skewed such that the big six capture most clients but there is a long tail of other consulting firms. Second, consulting firms are ubiquitous. Most large publicly traded firms use compensation consultants. Third, pay consultants often supply additional services other than pay advice to client firms, such as actuarial or benefits advice. Various parties use these other services to measure whether the consultant has a potential conflict of interest with the client firm.

Why Do Firms Use Pay Consultants?

Compensation consultants are firms or individuals who provide client organizations with advice and information about executive pay. Why do firms use pay

Exhibit 15.1 Executive Compensation Consultants

This table shows the major compensation consultants used by firms in the United States, the United Kingdom, and Canada. The analysis is based on data from previous studies.

	United States[a]		United Kingdom[a]		Canada[b]	
	n	%	n	%	n	%
Panel A: Major Consultants						
Towers Perrin	95	23.8	68	29.4	45	36
Mercer Consulting	84	21.0	26	11.3	53	42
Frederic W. Cook & Co.	77	19.3	n/a	n/a	5	4
Hewitt Associates	66	16.5	13	5.6	9	7
Watson Wyatt Worldwide	31	7.8	30	13.0	6	5
Pearl Meyer	22	5.5	n/a	n/a	n/a	n/a
PricewaterhouseCoopers Monks	n/a	n/a	37	16.0	n/a	n/a
New Bridge Street Consultants	n/a	n/a	62	26.8	n/a	n/a
Panel B: Consultant Use						
No consultant used	125	14.2[c]	26	11.2[e]	41	20.5[f]
Two or more consultants used	181	17.0[d]	95	40.9[e]	n/a	n/a
Panel C: Potential Conflicts						
Consultant supplies other business to client firm	113	63.1[g]	106	45.9[h]	156	46.2[i]
Compensation committee retains consultant[j]	n/a	n/a	125	54.2	n/a	n/a
Ratio of fees for other services to fees for executive pay advice	n/a	11[g]	n/a	n/a[h]	n/a	13.4[i]

Notes: n = number; % = percentage.
[a] Based on Conyon et al. (2009a, 49, Table 1) using a sample of 400 U.S. firms and 231 UK firms.
[b] Based on Murphy and Sandino (2009, 42, Table 8, Panel B) using a sample of 200 Canadian firms.
[c] Based on Cadman et al. (2009, 29, Table 1) using a sample of 880 U.S. firms.
[d] Based on Murphy and Sandino (2009, 8) using a sample of 1,046 U.S. firms.
[e] Based on Conyon et al. (2009c, 36) using a sample of 232 UK firms.
[f] Based on Murphy and Sandino (2009, 26) using a sample of 200 Canadian firms.
[g] Based on Waxman (2007) using 2006 data on 179 firms from the Fortune 250 (information unavailable publicly). Murphy and Sandino (p. 27) report 11.7 percent.
[h] Based on Conyon et al. (2009b) using 231 UK firms.
[i] Based on Murphy and Sandino (2009, 27–28).
[j] This is an inverse measure of potential conflict.

consultants? Compensation consultants can form part of an optimal governance structure by providing information that can reduce agency costs and help boards arrive at the best compensation contract to offer the CEO on the behalf of shareholders. Consultants provide expert advice, salient information, data, and valuable analysis (Baker, Jensen, and Murphy 1988; Bebchuk and Fried 2004; Conyon et al. 2009a; Murphy and Sandino 2009). They are experts in helping boards and compensation committees understand the value of complex pay packages and associated tax, disclosure, and accounting issues. In this scenario, consultants are not controversial. Their use is warranted and defensible because consultants represent a low-cost (economic) solution for generating the optimal compensation contract and reducing moral hazard. Problems arise, as discussed next, if consultants are not independent or suffer from conflicts of interest.

Are Pay Consultants Independent?

Critics often contend that pay consultants face substantial conflicts of interest that impede their impartiality and independence (Crystal 1991; Bebchuk and Fried 2003 and 2006). Critics argue that executive compensation contracts will be suboptimal and favor the CEOs interests at the expense of the owners/shareholders. Three issues potentially compromise the consultant's independence and create a conflict of interest:

1. *Psychological bias*. In practice, the company, not the shareholders, hires the consultant. Consequently, the consultant may psychologically favor management's interests at the expense of shareholders' interests. This bias might be inadvertent or strategic. A consultant hired by the firm or CEO may feel psychologically obligated to the CEO (Bebchuk and Fried 2004; Core et al. 2005; Murphy and Sandino 2009). A type of gift exchange has occurred. The consultant having received a lucrative assignment by the client firm may reciprocate by recommending generous pay for the CEO. When management does the hiring, the consultant's incentives may be skewed in favor of the CEO's interests rather than those of the shareholders.
2. *Repeat business*. The prospect that the consultant's assignment may be terminated or not renewed may also distort incentives (Bebchuk and Fried 2004; Conyon et al. 2009a). This has been referred to as the *repeat business* hypothesis (Murphy and Sandino 2009). If the consultant recommends low CEO pay, then the probability of being terminated increases. The likelihood of getting business from other clients may also diminish (Bebchuk and Fried 2004). Consultants who fear being fired and losing repeat business are more likely to recommend pay contracts that favor the CEO at the expense of shareholders.
3. *Cross-selling of other services*. Compensation consultants often provide services in addition to advice about executive compensation (Armstrong et al. 2008; Cadman et al. 2009; Conyon et al. 2009a; Murphy and Sandino 2009). Such advice may involve actuarial assignments, benefits, accounting, and general management. Selling other services in addition to compensation advice potentially distorts the incentives. These additional services make consultants unwilling to attack a CEO's pay package for fear of putting this other business at risk. The extant literature hypothesizes that CEO pay is higher in client firms if the consultant provides business services other than executive compensation advice (Cadman et al. 2009; Conyon et al. 2009a; Murphy and Sandino 2009). As noted in Exhibit 15.1, the cross-selling of other services is a relatively common practice in the United States and the United Kingdom.

In summary, compensation consultants may be conflicted for the following reasons: (1) the psychological pressures that bond them closely to management (e.g., reciprocation and gift exchange); (2) the fear of losing future or repeat business;

and (3) the presence of other lucrative business opportunities. The result is that potentially conflicted consultants offer advice in favor of management rather than shareholders. One brake on opportunistic consultant behavior is the consultant's desire to maintain a high-quality reputation. A consultant exposed for colluding with management or recommending lucrative pay deals for poor performance will suffer a loss of reputation or risk termination by the client firm's board of directors. Maintaining and developing a good market reputation is therefore important for the consultant and ameliorates the tendency for consultants to side with management over shareholders. The effect of maintaining a good reputation works against finding a positive correlation between CEO pay and conflicted consultants.

LITERATURE REVIEW

Several recent research papers on pay consultants have emerged. The broad hypothesis tested in these papers is that compensation consultants are associated with higher CEO pay at client firms. These new studies generally use multivariate regression methods. The overall goal has been to determine whether pay consultants are operating in the best interests of shareholders or err on the side of management. Current evidence comes from three countries where disclosure rules permit data collection: the United States, the United Kingdom, and Canada. These are English legal origin countries (La Porta, Lopez-de-Silanes, and Shleifer 2008).

The emerging literature uses data from different countries. Two studies adopt a comparative methodology: Conyon et al. (2009a) focus on the United States and the United Kingdom while Murphy and Sandino (2009) study the United States and Canada. Other papers focus on single countries such as the United States (Armstrong et al. 2008; Cadman et al. 2009) or the United Kingdom (Bender 2008; Conyon et al. 2009b; Kabir and Minhat 2009; Voulgaris et al. 2009). Still other papers remark on compensation consultants but this is not the primary focus of the research design (Tosi and Gomez-Mejia 1989; Wade, Porac, and Pollok 1997; Bizjak, Lemmon, and Naveen 2008; Faulkender and Yang 2008).

Central to this new literature is how to measure the variable *consultant*. Researchers use many different measures, thus making direct comparisons across studies difficult. For example, studies use an indicator variable (1 = yes, 0 = no) for the presence of a compensation consultant (Armstrong et al. 2008; Conyon et al. 2009a and 2009b; Kabir and Minhat 2009; Voulgaris et al. 2009); the market share of the consultants (Kabir and Minhat 2009); proxies for conflicts of interest in the cross-selling of other services (Cadman et al. 2009; Conyon et al. 2009a and 2009b; Murphy and Sandino 2009); the ratio of fee income from additional non-compensation services divided by fees from executive pay advice (Murphy and Sandino 2009); and various indicator variables for individual specific consultants (Armstrong et al. 2008; Kabir and Minhat 2009).

Multicountry Studies

Conyon et al. (2009a) investigate the relation between CEO pay and compensation consultants in the United States and the United Kingdom. In the research design, they consider the two countries separately rather than pooling them into the same sample. Their econometric models use a sample of 308 U.S. firms from the S&P 500 in 2006 and 229 large UK firms in 2003. The sample size is small relative to other emerging studies in this field. The authors use ordinary least squares (OLS) methods on cross-section data. They measure CEO pay in a manner consistent with the extant executive compensation literature (Murphy 1999). The authors broadly calculate CEO compensation as the sum of salary, bonus, benefits, stock options, restricted stock, and other compensation. This measure reflects the expected cost to shareholders of granting equity and stock options. Granted stock options are valued using the Black-Scholes model where the price of a European call option on a dividend paying stock is

$$c = Se^{-qt}\mathrm{N}(d_1) - Xe^{-rt}\mathrm{N}(d_2)$$

where

$d_1 = \{\ln(S/X) + [(r-q) + \sigma^2/2]t\} \,/\, \sigma\sqrt{t}$
$d_2 = d_1 - \sigma\sqrt{t}$
S is the stock price
X is the exercise price
t is the maturity term
r is the risk-free interest rate
q is the dividend yield
σ is the volatility of returns
N(.) is the cumulative probability distribution function for a standardized normal variable (Black and Scholes 1973) and e is exponential function.

The source of the U.S. pay data is the ExecuComp database, and data for the UK firms are hand-collected from annual reports and accounts.

Conyon et al. (2009a) find the level of CEO pay is positively correlated with the presence of consultants (defined as a 0-1 binary variable) in both the United States and the United Kingdom. They also find that the mix of CEO pay, defined as the fraction of equity pay in total CEO compensation, is positively correlated to consultants. The latter suggests that consultants provide client CEOs with greater pay-at-risk, an outcome that is presumably in shareholder interests as it represents greater pay-for-performance. The results have implications for the interpretation of the positive association between the level of CEO pay and consultants. Risk-averse CEOs whose contracts contain more risky pay (for example, more stock options or other equity pay) will need to be compensated with greater expected levels of pay (Conyon et al. 2009; Fernandes et al. 2009). The findings imply that the higher levels of CEO pay associated with the presence of consultants may well be part of an efficient contract and not due to upward pay pressures promulgated by conflicted consultants. Further evidence in favor of this interpretation is the fact that the authors can measure directly conflicted consultants by an indicator variable of whether the consultant also supplies other business to the client firm. The variable is insignificant in their estimated OLS models.

Conyon et al. (2009a) also investigate whether CEO pay is related to potentially conflicted consultants. This is measured as a binary variable (= 1) if the consultant supplies other services to the firm. Firms are mandated to reveal this information in the report and accounts in the United Kingdom but not in the United States. Instead, for the United States, the authors use a dummy variable (= 1) if the firm uses consulting firm Pearl Meyer or Frederick W. Cook. This follows a strategy advocated by Cadman et al. (2009). Pearl Meyer and Frederick C. Cook do not provide other noncompensation services to clients and thus are less prone (relative to other consulting firms) to be potentially conflicted. Conyon et al. find no statistical relation between CEO pay in firms whose clients also supply other business.

Murphy and Sandino (2009) investigate the relation between CEO compensation and consultants in the United States and Canada. They focus explicitly on potentially conflicted consultants, rather than just the presence of a consultant. Murphy and Sandino (p. 30) find "marginally significant evidence in the U.S. that CEO pay is higher in firms where the consultants provide other services and that pay increases with the number of other services provided. Empirical analyses using data from Canada suggest that CEO pay is higher when the consultant provides other services, especially actuarial or benefits-administration services."

Murphy and Sandino (2009) use a snapshot of U.S. data on 1,341 S&P 500, S&P MidCap 400, and SmallCap 600 firms. The sample is larger than that used by Conyon et al. (2009a), who focus instead on constituents of the S&P 500. Murphy and Sandino measure the potential conflicts of interest faced by the compensation consultant in a two ways: whether the consultant offers a defined-benefit (DB) plan; and whether the consultant is also the actuary for the client firm. Using these measures, no statistical evidence exists of a positive correlation between potentially conflicted compensation consultants and CEO pay. Murphy and Sandino (p. 20) also investigate CEO pay in firms "whose compensation consultant provides other services to the company beyond (or in addition to) actuarial services, based on voluntary and self-reported disclosures by companies." In the United Kingdom, legal rules mandate this disclosure (Directors' Remuneration Report Regulations, 2002) but in the United States the information is voluntary. Importantly, the authors find a significantly positive correlation between CEO pay and the variable *consultant provides other services*.

Murphy and Sandino (2009) also test the relation between CEO pay and potentially conflicted compensation consultants using data on 120 Canadian firms. They find that CEO pay is higher in firms whose consultants supply other business to the firm. Especially important is the explanatory variable *fee ratio*, defined as the fees paid for non-executive-compensation services divided by the fees paid for executive compensation services. The fee ratio variable arguably captures the degree of incentive distortion that a consultant faces. If zero, the consultant cares only about compensation consulting fee incomes. The greater the ratio, the more the consultant cares about noncompensation service fees. The coefficient on the fee ratio variable is positive and significant in the regression models. The authors note, however, that outliers may drive this result because once they remove some extreme observations from their data, the significance of the finding erodes considerably. In principle the fee ratio seems to be a good measure of the temptation faced by consultants to side with management. As yet, this ratio is generally unavailable to researchers in the United States or the United Kingdom.

Single-Country Studies

Cadman et al. (2009) investigate whether U.S. compensation consultants' potential cross-selling incentives are positively correlated with CEO pay in client firms.

Specifically, they investigate 755 firms from the U.S. S&P 1500 for 2006. The sampling frame is akin to Murphy and Sandino (2009) and larger than that of Conyon et al. (2009a). Cadman et al. (p. 1) are "unable to find widespread evidence of higher levels of pay or lower pay-performance sensitivities for clients of consultants with potentially greater conflicts of interest. Overall, [they] do not find evidence suggesting that potential conflicts of interest between the firm and its consultant are a primary driver of excessive CEO pay." This finding is consistent with the results contained in Conyon et al. for the United States and the weakly significant U.S. results in Murphy and Sandino.

As with other U.S. studies, Cadman et al. (2009) find that consultants are ubiquitous (only about 14 percent of firms do not retain a consultant). Cadman et al. (p. 2) define potentially conflicted consultants as:

> *(1) client firms who affirmatively disclose that their compensation consultant provides non-EC services; (2) firms that are not clients of Frederic W. Cook or Pearl Meyer, large consultants that focus exclusively on executive compensation services and thus do not have cross-selling incentives; and (3) firms that hire their auditor for significant non-audit services, indicating a willingness to allow possible conflicts of interest among their professional service providers.*

There is little evidence that CEO pay is correlated with these different measures of conflict of interest. An important feature of the study is the recognition that the selection of the consultant is endogenous. The authors estimate a two-stage least squares (2SLS) regression, but the main results of the effect of consultants on CEO pay remain qualitatively unaltered.

Armstrong et al. (2008) investigate the relation between CEO pay and the use of compensation consultants in a sample of 2,116 U.S. firms in fiscal year 2006. The firms are effectively the constituents of the Russell 3000 and this sample is substantially larger than other U.S. studies. The authors define a binary variable (1 = yes, 0 = no) where the firm uses a compensation consultant for strategic compensation advice as opposed to no consultant or simple pay benchmarking.

Armstrong et al. (2008, 1) find that "CEO pay is generally higher in clients of most consulting firms, even after controlling for economic determinants of compensation." About 87 percent of participants in their sample use pay consultants. An important feature of their analysis is the propensity score matching methodology. This permits the authors to create statistically equivalent distributions for the users of consultants (the treatment group) and nonusers of consultants (the control group) based on a broad set of covariates (except CEO pay). This approach is compelling because it helps correct for the endogenous nature of the treatment variable in nonrandom data. In the empirical results, Armstrong et al. (p.1) find that when

> *... users and non-users are matched on both economic and governance characteristics, differences in pay levels are not statistically significant. These results are consistent with claims that compensation consultants provide a mechanism for CEOs of companies with weak governance to extract and justify excess pay.*

The authors investigate CEO pay in client firms across the different consultants. As with Cadman et al. (2009), Armstrong et al. find little support for the hypothesis that CEO pay is higher in firms using "conflicted" consultants who also offer additional non-compensation-related services (i.e., are not Pearl Meyer or Frederick W. Cook).

For UK firms, Kabir and Minhat (2009) and Minhat (2009) investigate the effect of pay consultants on executive pay using a sample of 175 companies for the period 2003–2006 (700 firm-year observations). Kabir and Minhat (p. 1) find "no support for the hypothesis that CEO pay is higher when firms employ multiple compensation consultants. Instead, [their] results show that the market share of compensation consultants is significantly related to CEO compensation." The authors interpret their finding as consistent with the idea that consultants do not want to lose business with client firms.

In Kabir and Minhat (2009), the primary measure of compensation consultant influence is the count of the number of consultants used by a firm. They measure executive compensation as total pay. Using OLS and panel data (random effects) methods, the authors find no statistical relation between CEO pay and the number of consultants used. However, a statistically positive correlation exists between CEO pay and the consulting firm's market share. The panel data methodology used in the study is attractive because such data methods attenuate persistent firm effects, capturing them in the error structure of the estimating equation. The study does not attempt to control for potentially conflicted consultants by investigating whether the CEO hired them or if the consultants provide any other noncompensation services.

Voulgaris et al. (2009) investigate the relation between CEO pay and compensation consultants in a cross-section of 2006 data. The sample consists of 500 UK firms from the FTSE 100, FTSE 250, and Small Cap indexes. Similar to other studies, the authors measure CEO pay as the sum of salaries, bonuses, long-term incentives, and stock option grants, where stock options are valued using the Black-Scholes method. Overall, they find that 134 firms (about 27 percent) do not have consultants, but larger and more complex firms are more likely to use consultants than smaller ones. In a regression model, Conyon et al. (2009b) also find a positive correlation between the use of consultants and firm size.

Voulgaris et al. (2009) find a positive correlation between CEO pay and the presence of a compensation consultant, which is consistent with the hypothesis that consultants raise pay. They also find that the ratio of equity pay to total pay is higher in firms using consultants and the ratio of salary to total pay is lower. This finding suggests that consultants not only raise the level of pay but also design contracts that contain more risk (equity pay) and less insurance (salary pay), consistent with shareholder goals. This result is consistent with Conyon et al. (2009a), who find a positive correlation between the equity pay mix and consultants in U.S. and UK firms. Another attractive feature of the Voulgaris et al. study is that it controls for the endogenous nature of the pay consultants. They reestimate their CEO pay models using 2SLS where the first stage is a probit selection model on the use of consultants. Importantly, they find that CEO pay is still greater, the salary pay mix is lower, and the equity pay mix is higher in firms using a compensation consultant.

Conyon et al. (2009b) investigate the relation between CEO pay and consultants in a set of 232 large UK firms in 2003. The authors discover a positive correlation between CEO pay and conflicted compensation consultants, measured as the consulting firm selling other business to the client firm. The result is marginally significant. Additionally, they find that CEO pay is positively correlated with CEO pay in peer firms who use the same consultant as the focal firm. Their results also show that the level of CEO compensation in the focal firm is positively related to the number of board interlocks created by both a shared director and a shared compensation consultant. As with Voulgaris et al. (2009) in the United Kingdom and Cadman et al. (2009) in the United States, Conyon et al. also model the selection of the compensation consultant. They find that firm size is a significant predictor variable of using a compensation consultant.

Bender (2008) provides a qualitative account of compensation consultants in the United Kingdom rather than using quantitative methods. She analyzes 12 (anonymous) companies from the UK FTSE 350 covering 40 individual and group interviews between 2001 and 2003. The author interviews CEOs, remuneration committee chairs, and five consultants advising those companies. Although firms choose consultants for their expertise, Bender (p. 11) finds that

> *There was no common thread to how the consultants had been engaged, other than the fact that the consultants' reputation was very important, and personal recommendations, for example from a board member who had worked with them before, were an advantage.*

Bender (p. 23) also reports that pay consultants themselves do recognize the potential for conflicts of interest:

> *... yes you [the consultants] do come across difficulties between the execs who have appointed you or the remuneration committee who have appointed you. And that's when you've got to know who appointed you. Because at the end of the day if there is a conflict, you've got to go back to the people who appointed you and say look I cannot advise both of you.*

Apparently, all parties (i.e., consultants and firms) tend to recognize this conflict and take steps to ameliorate it so as not to harm owner interests. In a similar vein, Murphy and Sandino (2009) report that pay consulting firms address their internal governance structures to avoid conflicts of interest by building formal divisions between different parts of the overall business.

Related Studies

Related studies also remark on the importance of compensation consultants (Baker et al. 1988). An early study by Tosi and Gomez-Mejia (1989) finds that consultants are important for determining CEO pay. The authors base their analysis on survey data. Wade et al. (1997) theorize that companies use consultants to justify and legitimize executive pay practices. Their results show that firms that pay their CEOs high salaries are more likely to explain this by reference to a compensation consultant in proxy statements. Faulkender and Yang (2008) study how peer group comparisons affect CEO pay. They find evidence that consultants can influence the choice of peer firms used in the benchmarking of CEO pay.

CONSULTANTS AND CEO PAY: UK EVIDENCE

This section provides new evidence on the relation between CEO pay and compensation consultants using UK data found in Conyon et al. (2009a). The main results are based on OLS estimates. Using insights from the prior literature, I estimate the relation between CEO pay and the compensation consultant by estimating a fairly standard CEO pay equation. Exhibit 15.2 contains the results. Columns 1 to 3 are based on measuring consultant use (1 = yes, 0 = no). Columns 3 to 6 are conditional on the firm using at least one consultant. These columns measure "conflicted" compensation consultants either as the consultant supplying other business to the client firm (1 = yes, 0 = no) or whether the compensation committee appoints the compensation consultant (1 = yes, 0 = no; this is an inverse measure of conflict).

CEO compensation is calculated as the sum of salary, bonus, benefits, stock options (using the Black-Scholes formula), restricted stock, and other compensation. The regression models contain economic and human capital control variables including the size of the firm (the log of firm sales), reflecting the returns to organizational complexity (Murphy 1985 and 1999; Core, Holthausen, and Larcker, 1999). The model includes company performance, reflecting the potential alignment of owner and manager interests (Murphy 1985 and 1999; Core et al., 1999) measured as total returns to shareholders (share price appreciation plus dividends). The book-to-market ratio is included as an (inverse) measure of growth opportunities within the firm (Core et al. 1999). The model contains a measure of stock volatility, measured as the standard deviation of annualized monthly stock returns over the prior calendar year to capture the idea that risk-averse executives require greater compensation in more risky corporate environments. The model includes human capital variables—CEO tenure and CEO age—to reflect the CEO's skill and experience. Finally, the regression model includes a set of industry indicator variables as controls for interindustry variation in the demand for executive talent (Core et al. 1999).

Columns 1 to 3 demonstrate a positive correlation between CEO total pay (including bonuses and options) and the use of consultants. CEO salary is also positively correlated with the presence of a consultant. Additionally, CEO equity pay mix (the amount of options and other equity expressed as a fraction of total pay) is greater in firms that use consultants. These results control for other economic determinants such as growth opportunities (book-to-market ratio), firm performance (shareholder returns), firm risk (stock price volatility), and demographic characteristics (CEO tenure and age), and agree with other work (Conyon et al. 2009a; Voulgaris et al. 2009). The coefficient estimates are all significant. Adjusted standard errors are reported based on clustering on the consulting firm because different consulting firms may offer different pay strategies and advice. For example, column 1 suggests that total CEO pay is approximately 26 percent higher in firms using consultants (calculated as $e^{0.23} - 1$). Similarly, CEO equity pay mix is about 14 percent higher in such firms. In columns 3 to 6, there is marginal evidence that CEO pay is higher in firms whose consultants supply other business. CEO salary is estimated to be about 7 percent higher in such firms (conditional on having hired a consultant). Although the coefficient estimates of the consultant effect on total CEO pay and the equity pay mix are positive, they are not significant

Exhibit 15.2 Consultants and CEO Pay: UK Regression Results

This table provides OLS estimates of the relation between CEO pay and compensation consultants in the United Kingdom. The analysis uses data from large publicly traded firms in the United Kingdom in 2003. The sample consists of 229 UK firms in 2003. *CEO pay* is the sum of salary, bonus, Black-Scholes value of stock option grants, restricted stock grants, and other pay. *Equity pay mix* is equity pay (the value of options and restricted stock) divided by CEO pay. *Consultant* is an indicator variable equal to 1 if the firm has a consultant and 0 otherwise. *Consultant supplies other business* and *Compensation committee appoints consultant* are also indicator variables. *Consultant supplies other business* is an indicator variable equal to 1 if the consultant provides services other than remuneration advice to the focal firm. *Log sales* is the log of firm sales revenues. *Book to market* is the book value of assets divided by the market value of the company. *Shareholder returns* are stock price appreciation plus dividends over three years. *Volatility* is the annualized standard deviation in stock prices. *Job tenure* is executive time in office (years). *CEO age* is the executives' age (years). Robust standard errors are in parentheses.

	(1)	(2)	(3)	(4)	(5)	(6)
Variables	**Log CEO Total Pay**	**Log CEO Salary**	**Equity Pay Mix**	**Log CEO Total Pay**	**Log CEO Salary**	**Equity Pay Mix**
Consultant	0.23**	0.08**	0.13***			
	(0.07)	(0.03)	(0.02)			
Consultant supplies other business				0.10	0.07*	0.01
				(0.09)	(0.03)	(0.03)
Compensation committee appoints consultant				0.08	0.05	0.04
				(0.10)	(0.05)	(0.02)
Log sales	0.26***	0.18***	0.02	0.24***	0.18***	0.02
	(0.04)	(0.01)	(0.01)	(0.04)	(0.02)	(0.01)
Book to market	−0.45**	−0.27*	−0.04	−0.45**	−0.30**	−0.04
	(0.13)	(0.11)	(0.05)	(0.13)	(0.12)	(0.06)
Shareholder returns	0.00	0.00	−0.00	0.00	0.00	−0.00
	(0.00)	(0.00)	(0.00)	(0.00)	(0.00)	(0.00)
Volatility	0.10	−0.09	0.08	−0.04	−0.15	0.02
	(0.18)	(0.13)	(0.07)	(0.08)	(0.11)	(0.06)
Job tenure	−0.00**	0.01*	−0.01***	−0.00	0.00	−0.01**
	(0.00)	(0.00)	(0.00)	(0.00)	(0.00)	(0.00)
CEO age	0.00	0.01*	−0.00	0.01	0.01**	−0.00
	(0.01)	(0.00)	(0.00)	(0.00)	(0.00)	(0.00)
Constant	5.15***	4.31***	0.30**	5.25***	4.28***	0.44***
	(0.22)	(0.26)	(0.10)	(0.19)	(0.28)	(0.09)
Industry dummies	Yes	Yes	Yes	Yes	Yes	Yes
Observations	229	229	229	209	209	209
R^2	0.325	0.501	0.138	0.318	0.520	0.088

*** $p < 0.01$, **$p < 0.05$, *$p < 0.10$.

at the 0.10 level. However, the insignificance may be due to the small sample size, so the sign of the coefficient is of interest.

One issue to note when interpreting such results is how the disclosure of information about consultants affects the dynamic estimation between CEO pay and measures of (conflicted) consultants. Typically, researchers estimate reduced-form econometric models using observed data rather than the underlying (true) parameters from a theoretical or structural equation. These estimates of the CEO pay and consultant relation could have changed when the disclosure policy changed. For example, in the predisclosure period, there might have been a positive correlation between CEO pay and consultants but the data were not publicly observable to the econometrician. However, when the policy changed, so that more information was disclosed, this may have modified agent behavior—for example, the previously conflicted pay consultants decided to no longer recommend lavish CEO pay. In consequence, the relation between CEO pay and consultant altered. This suggests that policy decisions based on reduced-form models could be misleading. Lucas (1976) discusses these types of policy issues.

In addition to the OLS results contained in Exhibit 15.2, I also carried out some sensitivity analysis using propensity score matching methods to investigate the relation between CEO pay and consultants (as in Armstrong et al. 2008). In principle, propensity score matching can alleviate selection biases arising from the nonrandom assignment of data (Rosenbaum and Rubin 1983; Heckman, Ichimura, and Todd 1997 and 1998; Rubin 2006). Propensity score does so by optimally matching firms that use consultants (the treatment condition) to firms that do not use consultants (the control condition). Using a nearest neighbor algorithm (Leuven and Sianesi 2003), a matched sample of firms was constructed between firms that use consultants (treatment) and those firms not using consultants (control). The results indicate that CEO pay in firms using consultants is no different from firms not using consultants. Further, CEO pay is not higher in firms using potentially conflicted consultants (i.e., those firms where the consultant supplied other business) compared to client firms using independent consultants. This illustrates that studies based on OLS methods alone might result in false inference if the characteristics of the two distributions (consultant versus no-consultant) are different. Propensity score methods can help considerably when using such nonexperimental data (Armstrong et al. 2008).

SUMMARY AND CONCLUSIONS

Changes in disclosure rules in the United States, the United Kingdom, and Canada have led to more available information about pay consultants for investors and researchers (Waxman 2007; Armstrong et al. 2008; Cadman et al. 2009; Conyon et al. 2009a; Murphy and Sandino 2009). Yet nuances exist in the information reported across countries. For example, in the United States, firms reveal the name of the consultant. In the United Kingdom, firms are also mandated to reveal whether the consultant supplies any other business. In Canada, although not mandated, firms may reveal fee incomes from noncompensation services as well as fees received from executive pay advice. Such enhanced disclosure provides traction on whether the consultant is subject to a potential conflict of interest. Overall, there is much more available information about pay consultants today than 10 years ago, but more low-cost transparency might be welcome.

A review of the existing evidence shows mixed findings of the effects of consultants on CEO pay. In general, a positive correlation exists between the level of CEO pay and the presence of consultants: Firms that use consultants pay their CEOs more. Interpreting this result is problematic because CEOs of firms using consultants may have more pay at risk in the form of options or restricted stock. If so, higher levels of CEO pay in firms using consultants might simply reflect a risk premium rather than a failure of compensation consultants to recommend contracts that are in the best interests of shareholders. Interpreting whether a positive correlation exists between CEO pay and the presence of a consultant as being necessarily bad for owners' interests is difficult.

A better approach is to measure directly whether the consultant has a potential conflict of interest. For example, such conflicts could arise by selling other services to the client firm or receiving high level of fees for such services relative to income from executive pay advice. Many studies use this strategy, including Cadman et al. (2009), Conyon et al. (2009a and 2009b), and Murphy and Sandino (2009). The current evidence has produced mixed evidence in support of the hypothesis that conflicted consultants lead to higher CEO pay. Murphy and Sandino find some evidence that conflicted consultants are associated with higher CEO pay in client firms in the United States. For Canada, they find stronger evidence that CEO compensation is higher in firms with conflicted consultants, especially for actuarial and benefits administration services. Conyon et al. (2009a) and Cadman et al. find little evidence of a relation between CEO pay and conflicted consultants measured inversely by whether the firm uses Frederick W. Cook or Pearl Meyer. In UK firms, studies find that CEO pay is greater in firms with consultants but weaker evidence that CEO pay is higher in firms with conflicted consultants such as cross-selling other services (Conyon et al. 2009a and 2009b; Kabir and Minhat 2009; Voulgaris et al. 2009). Thus, the existing empirical evidence does not universally support the hypothesis that conflicted consultants lead to higher CEO pay.

In summary, CEO pay is an important tool for aligning management and shareholder interests (Murphy 1999). Recently, researchers have hypothesized that pay consultants face conflicts of interest that lead to excessive CEO pay and poorly structured pay contracts. Studies are emerging to test this claim, but the available empirical evidence is not wholly supportive. An expanded set of studies is warranted to further test how pay consultants influence executive compensation.

DISCUSSION QUESTIONS

1. Why do firms use compensation consultants?
2. What are the main characteristics of the market for executive compensation consulting services?
3. Are compensation consultants sufficiently independent?
4. Does the current empirical evidence show that the use of consultants leads to excess CEO pay and/or poorly designed pay packages?
5. How should governments and policy makers respond to the fact that compensation consultants have potential conflicts of interest?

REFERENCES

Armstrong, Christopher S., Christopher D. Ittner, and David F. Larcker. 2008. Economic characteristics, corporate governance, and the influence of compensation consultants on executive pay levels. http://ssrn.com/abstract=1145548.

Baker, George P., Michael C. Jensen, and Kevin J. Murphy. 1988. Compensation and incentives: Practice vs. theory. *Journal of Finance* 43 (3): 593–616.

Bebchuk, Lucian A., and Jesse M. Fried. 2003. Executive compensation as an agency problem. *Journal of Economic Perspectives* 17 (3): 71–92.

———. 2004. *Pay without performance: The unfulfilled promise of executive remuneration.* Cambridge, MA: Harvard University Press.

———. 2006. Pay without performance: Overview of the issues. *Academy of Management Perspectives* 20 (1): 18–24.

Bender, Ruth. 2008. Paying for advice: The role of the remuneration consultant in UK listed companies. Working paper, Cranfield University.

Bizjak, John, Michael L. Lemmon, and Lalitha Naveen. 2008. Does the use of peer groups contribute to higher pay and less efficient compensation? *Journal of Financial Economics* 90 (2): 152–168.

Black, Fischer, and Myron Scholes. 1973. The pricing of options and corporate liabilities. *Journal of Political Economy* 81 (3): 637–654.

Cadman, Brian, Mary Ellen Carter, and Stephen Hillegeist. 2009. The incentives of compensation consultants and CEO pay. http://ssrn.com/abstract=1103682.

Canada. 2005. *Corporate governance rules.* http://www.osc.gov.on.ca/index_en.jsp?lang=en.

Conyon, Martin J., John E. Core, and Wayne R. Guay. 2009. Are US CEOs paid more than UK CEOs? Inferences from risk-adjusted pay. http://ssrn.com/abstract=907469.

Conyon, Martin J., and Kevin J. Murphy. 2000. The prince and the pauper? CEO pay in the United States and United Kingdom. *Economic Journal* 110 (467): 640–671.

Conyon, Martin J., Simon I. Peck, and Graham V. Sadler. 2009a. Compensation consultants and executive pay: Evidence from the United States and the United Kingdom. *Academy of Management Perspectives* 23 (1): 43–55.

———. 2009b. New perspectives on the governance of executive compensation: An examination of the role and effect of compensation consultants. *Journal of Management and Governance*, Published online, 15 October, 2009: DOI 10.1007/s10997-009-9117-6.

Core, John E., Wayne R. Guay, and Randall S. Thomas. 2005. Is U.S. CEO compensation inefficient pay without performance? *Michigan Law Review* 103 (6): 1142–1185.

Core, John E., Robert W. Holthausen, and David F. Larcker. 1999. Corporate governance, chief executive officer compensation, and firm performance. *Journal of Financial Economics* 51 (3): 371–406.

Crystal, Graef S. 1991. Why CEO compensation is so high. *California Management Review* 34 (1): 9–29.

Directors' Remuneration Report Regulations. 2002. http://www.opsi.gov.uk/si/si2002/20021986.htm.

Faulkender, Michael, and Yun Yang. 2008. Inside the black box: The role and composition of compensation peer groups. http://ssrn.com/abstract=972197.

Fernandes, Nuno G., Miguel A. Ferreira, Pedro P. Matos, and Kevin J. Murphy. 2009. The pay divide: (Why) are U.S. top executives paid more? http://ssrn.com/abstract=134163.

Heckman, James J., Hidehiko Ichimura, and Petra Todd. 1997. Matching as an econometric evaluation estimator: Evidence from a job training programme. *Review of Economic Studies* 64 (4): 605–654.

———. 1998. Matching as an econometric evaluation estimator. *Review of Economic Studies* 65 (2): 261–294.

Kabir, Rezaul, and Marizah Minhat. 2009. The effect of compensation consultants on UK CEO pay. Working paper, University of Stirling.

Kaplan, Steven N. 2008. Are U.S. CEOs overpaid? *Academy of Management Perspectives* 22 (2): 5–20.

La Porta, Rafael, Florencio Lopez-de-Silanes, and Andrei Shleifer. 2008. The economic consequences of legal origins. *Journal of Economic Literature* 46 (2): 285–332.

Leuven, Edwin, and Barbara Sianesi. 2003. PSMATCH2: Stata module to perform full Mahalanobis and propensity score matching, common support graphing, and covariate imbalance testing, Version 3.1.5. http://ideas.repec.org/c/boc/bocode/s432001.html (accessed May 2, 2009).

Lucas, Robert. 1976. Econometric policy evaluation: A critique. *Carnegie-Rochester Conference Series on Public Policy* 1 (1): 19–46.

Minhat, Marizah 2009. The role of CEO pay in corporate governance. Working paper, University of Stirling.

Murphy, Kevin J. 1985. Corporate performance and managerial remuneration: An empirical analysis. *Journal of Accounting and Economics* 7 (1–3): 11–42.

———. 1999. Executive compensation. In *Handbook of labor economics*, Volume 3, ed. Orley Ashenfelter and David Card, 2485–2563. Armsterdam: North Holland, Elsevier.

Murphy, Kevin J., and Tatiana Sandino. 2009. Executive pay and "independent" compensation consultants. http://ssrn.com/abstract=1148991.

Rosenbaum, Paul R., and Donald B. Rubin. 1983. The central role of the propensity score in observational studies for causal effects. *Biometrika* 70 (1): 41–55.

Rubin, Donald B. 2006. *Matched Sampling for Causal Effects*: Cambridge: Cambridge University Press.

Securities and Exchange Commission (SEC). 2007. *Executive compensation and related person disclosure* 2007. http://www.sec.gov/rules/final/2006/33-8732a.pdf.

Tosi, Henry L., and Luis R. Gomez-Mejia. 1989. The decoupling of CEO pay and performance: An agency theory perspective. *Administrative Science Quarterly* 34 (2): 169–189.

Voulgaris, Georgios, Konstantinos Stathopoulos, and Martin Walker. 2009. Compensation consultants and executive pay: U.K. evidence. Working paper, Manchester University.

Wade, James B., Joseph F. Porac, and Timothy G. Pollock. 1997. Worth, words, and the justification of executive pay. *Journal of Organizational Behavior* 18 (Special Issue): 641–664.

Waxman, Henry. 2007. Executive pay: Conflicts of interest among compensation consultants. Washington, DC: Unites States House of Representatives Committee on Oversight and Government Reform Majority Staff.

ACKNOWLEDGMENTS

The author thanks Simon Peck, Graham Sadler, Ruth Bender, Brian Cadman, Peter Cappelli, Mary Ellen Carter, John Core, Sourafel Girma, David Maber, Mark Muldoon, James Reda, Kym Sheehan, Randall Thomas, Steve Thompson, Sarah Wilson, and Vicky Wright (Watson Wyatt, CIPD) for discussions during the preparation of this paper, as well as seminar participants at Case Western Reserve University, EDHEC Business School, ESMT in Berlin, ESSEC, Georgetown University, Instituto de Empresa, Lehigh University, London School of Economics, Nottingham University, and the University of Stirling. Funding from the Wharton-SMU Research Center at Singapore Management University and the EU Marie Curie Fund is gratefully acknowledged. Practitioner colleagues at Mercer Human Resource Consulting, Towers Perrin, and Watson Wyatt provided helpful advice and comments. Finally, the author thanks Graham Sadler (especially) and

Wang Liao, Chloe Wayne, Teresa Baik, Sabina Tacheva, and Robert Clarke for research assistance in assembling the data.

ABOUT THE AUTHOR

Martin J. Conyon is a professor at IE Business School. He is also a senior fellow at the Wharton School, University of Pennsylvania. He has a PhD in economics from Warwick University and has held faculty posts at the Wharton School, University of Pennsylvania; as well as Warwick Business School, University of Warwick; and the Queen's College, University of Oxford. Professor Conyon is the author of more than 50 articles, book chapters, or reports relating to corporate governance. He has written extensively about boards and compensation. He serves on the editorial boards of various journals including the *Strategic Management Journal* and the *Journal of Business Finance and Accounting*. His research may be accessed at SSRN Author page http://ssrn.com/author=222606 or http://web.me.com/conyon/.

CHAPTER 16

Corporate Governance and Ownership Structure

JOHN J. McCONNELL
Emanuel T. Weiler Distinguished Professor of Management, Purdue University

STEPHEN B. McKEON
Ph.D. candidate, Purdue University

WEI XU
Visiting Assistant Professor of Finance, DePaul University

INTRODUCTION

This chapter addresses the question of whether who owns a corporation's shares influences the corporation's market value and/or its operating performance. The *who* in this question does not refer to specific individuals. It refers to classes or groups of individuals. These classes include atomistic anonymous outside shareholders. They include, as a separate group, managers and the members of the board of directors who are sometimes referred to as executive or inside shareholders. They include shareholders who own a large single block of shares. Such blockholders are sometimes insiders, or they can be outside blockholders.

Or they might be institutional shareholders, and the institutional shareholders might be subdivided into blockholders and atomistic shareholders. Or the class of shareholders might be a family, and families can be subdivided into those in which the family also holds significant management positions or those in which the family is merely another class of outside shareholders. And those can be divided into families in which the family founder continues to play a major managerial role and those in which the founder has passed from the scene but his heirs play a key managerial role.

Regardless of the classification of the shareholders, the question is whether the ownership structure *matters* in the sense of whether the various permutations of ownership either create (or reduce) value. If the ownership structure does matter, does it matter in specific circumstances?

The following section of this chapter outlines the theoretical underpinnings of various approaches that address this issue. Each approach begins with the presumption that the incentives of management of the firm are not perfectly aligned with those of nonmanagement shareholders. In these circumstances, managers are further presumed to sometimes make decisions that advance their own interests to the detriment of other shareholders. The theoretical studies then analyze various mechanisms through which the misalignment of managerial and other shareholders' interest can be resolved. The simplest of these is the direct ownership of shares by management. As it turns out, however, even that direct mechanism can create problems of its own.

With the theoretical foundations in place, the chapter then considers empirical studies that attempt to distinguish among the predictions that flow from the theoretical analyses. Given the heterogeneity among the various classes of ownership and the volume of empirical studies, the chapter begins with what is, perhaps, the broadest and simplest classification of ownership structure: inside (or managerial) shareholders and outside (or atomistic) shareholders.

One of the contentious issues in the empirical studies of the relation between ownership structure and corporate performance is whether any relation, if one is identified empirically, is reliable. More specifically, on the one hand, various studies have found a nonlinear relation between inside ownership and corporate value which has been put forward as evidence that ownership structure matters in the sense that who owns the shares influences corporate value, and that changing the ownership structure in a particular way can change that value.

On the other hand, other studies have argued that this empirical relation is spurious and arises because of misspecification of the empirical tests. This chapter gives particular attention to that issue in the review of studies that focus on the broad dichotomy of inside and outside shareholders. However, the issue, sometimes referred to as the *endogeneity* problem, pervades many of the empirical analyses of the relation between ownership structure and corporate performance regardless of the specific classes of shareholders examined, and many of these studies devote much of their attention to ensuring that the results reported are free of the concerns created by the potential endogeneity problem.

Following the in-depth discussion of the empirical studies that focus on the broad distinction between inside and outside shareholders, the chapter provides somewhat less detailed discussions of studies that focus on more narrowly defined classes of ownership, including institutional investors and family blockholders.

MANAGERIAL SHARE OWNERSHIP AND CORPORATE VALUE: THEORETICAL CONSIDERATIONS

Concerns about whether who owns the shares of a corporation influences its value and operating performance are often traced to Berle and Means (1932) who appear to be the first to have used the term *separation of ownership from control* to describe the large, *open* or publicly traded U.S. corporation. These authors were concerned about the rise of the large corporation as an instrumentality of commerce in the early twentieth century. Among other things, they argue that share ownership of the largest publicly traded U.S. corporations had become widely dispersed. Thus, for all intents and purposes, management, who often owned only a small fraction of the shares, could operate the firm unfettered by the concerns of share ownership.

Berle and Means (1932) certainly acknowledge the role of the board of directors as the nominal representatives of shareholders and the overseers of the corporation and, therefore, of management, but observe that candidates for board membership are typically identified by senior corporate management and the slate of directors typically runs unopposed in annual elections. In this setting, Berle and Means propose that the profit motive, which lies at the foundation of the capital market system, may no longer be presumed to be the driving force behind many large corporate enterprises. If so, they ask, what is the motivating force and what factors entice otherwise disinterested individuals to turn over control of their capital to managers over which they appear to have no control. According to Berle and Means (p. 9),

> *... the [business] organization under the system of private enterprise has rested upon the self-interest of the property owner—a self interest held in check only by competition and the conditions of supply and demand. Such self-interest has long been regarded as the best guarantee of economic efficiency.... In the quasi-public corporation, such an assumption no longer holds.... Those in control of that wealth, and therefore in a position to secure industrial efficiency and produce profits, are no longer, as owners, entitled to the bulk of such profits. Those who control the destinies of the typical modern corporation own so insignificant a fraction of the company's stock that the returns from running the corporation profitably accrue to them in only a very minor degree. The stockholders, on the other hand, to whom the profits of the corporation go, cannot be motivated by those profits to a more efficient use of the property, since they have surrendered all disposition of it to those in control of the enterprise.*

It is in this way that Berle and Means raise questions that still capture the attention of scholars who study what has come to be called the field of *corporate governance*.

Certainly scholars paid much attention to the questions raised by Berle and Means (1932) between the publication of their book in 1932 and 1976. However, much of the more recent literature in the field of corporate governance uses Jensen and Meckling (1976) as its starting point. Jensen and Meckling construct a model of the firm as a nexus of contracts among individuals who include shareholders, creditors, managers, nonmanaging employees, suppliers, customers, and others. In this contractual setting, the authors identify shareholders as residual risk bearers who have a principal-agent relationship with managers. In this relationship, managers, as the agents, are, at least nominally, contractually obligated to devote their efforts toward working in the best interests of the principals (i.e., the shareholders).

The Jensen and Meckling (1976) analysis begins with an owner-manager who owns 100 percent of the firm's equity. This owner-manager can devote all of the firm's resources to productive undertakings that lead to firm value maximization. Or he can consume some fraction of those resources as nonmarketable perquisites for which he pays the full cost. The situation changes once the owner-manager issues shares to outside shareholders. In that case, the owner-manager ostensibly bears only a fraction of the cost of the perquisites that he consumes and, thus, he will consume more such perquisites, which will, in turn, reduce the value of the firm.

Because outside shareholders will build the full cost of the incremental perquisite consumption into the up-front price that they pay for the shares, the owner-manager actually pays the full cost of his perquisite consumption at the time the shares are issued. It, therefore, behooves the owner-manager to take steps to assure outside investors that he will minimize his consumption of such perquisites. But he cannot write a contract that is perfectly enforceable and, despite any effort he makes to write such a contract, his actions are not perfectly observable. Thus, once the owner-manager issues shares to outside investors, the firm value declines by an amount that reflects the costs of outside shareholders monitoring the owner-manager plus a *residual* loss that reflects his inability to enter into a perfectly enforceable contract.

The perquisite consumption may include simple expenditures such as a larger-than-necessary office or a company-paid car, but may also encompass such costly undertakings as overpaying for an empire building acquisition or avoiding a potentially highly profitable, but also risky, project that could jeopardize the owner-manager's position. Or the perquisite consumption could take the form of shirking or simply choosing to enjoy the quiet life.

One question arising from Jensen and Meckling's (1976) analysis is whether there is an optimal fraction of equity that the owner-manager can issue to outside shareholders. Much of the empirical literature covered later in the chapter focuses on that question.

According to Manne (1965), one factor that can help mitigate the residual loss due to managerial perquisite consumption is the corporate takeover market. He argues that when managers undertake actions that deviate sufficiently far from value maximization, it will pay an outside investor, customarily thought of as another firm, to make a bid for the shares of the underperforming target. Once in control, the new owner can install a new management team to manage the firm so as to increase value. Manne's argument presumes that the owner-manager's fractional ownership of the underperforming firm is insufficiently large for the owner-manager to defeat a takeover attempt by an outside investor.

Morck, Shleifer, and Vishny (1988) argue that in circumstances such as those described by Manne (1965), two opposing forces may be at work. On the one hand, an increase in the fraction of shares owned by managers more closely aligns the interests of management with those of atomistic outside shareholders. On the other hand, an increase in the fraction of shares owned by management reduces the likelihood that a takeover attempt by an outside investor can be successful.

Morck et al. (1988) refer to the first of these two forces as the *convergence of interests* effect and the latter as the *entrenchment* effect. The authors propose that these effects can be at work over the entire range of managerial ownership (i.e., from 0 percent to 100 percent managerial ownership). Over some ranges, the convergence of interest effect can dominate, and over other ranges the entrenchment effect can dominate. Thus, Morck et al. propose that the relation between corporate value and managerial ownership can be positive over some ranges of managerial ownership and negative over other ranges and that identification of the relation is ultimately an empirical matter.

In a similar spirit, Stulz (1988) constructs a model in which the divergence of interests between management and outside shareholders arises solely because a successful hostile takeover affects managers and other shareholders differently. In his model, an outside bidder can gain control of the firm only by paying a premium. When managers own no shares, a hostile bidder can gain control by offering a small premium. As the fraction of shares owned by management increases, the premium required for an outsider to gain control increases. However, as the fraction of shares owned by management increases, the probability that a takeover attempt will be successful decreases. When management owns 50 percent or more of the firm's shares, the probability of a successful hostile takeover is zero.

Given that the value of the firm will reflect the likelihood of a hostile takeover offer being made and the premium required for the takeover attempt to be successful, the value of the firm will first increase and then decrease as the fraction of shares owned by management increases. At 50 percent managerial ownership, the value of the firm will be its *intrinsic* value absent any control premium. Thus, Stulz (1988) predicts a nonlinear relation between inside ownership and the value of the firm. He provides a specific prediction in which value initially increases and then falls as managerial share ownership increases up to 50 percent managerial ownership, at which point value is unaffected by any further increases in managerial share ownership.

MANAGERIAL SHARE OWNERSHIP AND CORPORATE VALUE: EMPIRICAL CONSIDERATIONS

Our brief review highlights some of the theoretical treatments of the interaction between corporate governance, corporate value, and ownership structure. We now turn to the empirical analyses that address the same questions.

Initial Evidence of a Nonlinear Relation between Managerial Ownership and Corporate Value

As previously noted, Morck et al. (1988) conclude that the relation between share ownership by insiders and the value of the firm is an empirical question. To answer the question, Morck et al. estimate a cross-sectional piecewise linear regression where the dependent variable is Tobin's q. In this analysis, Tobin's q is a proxy for firm value. This proxy is regressed against insider ownership and various control variables. The Morck et al. sample encompasses 371 of the Fortune 500 firms for the year 1980 and all of the variables are measured as of 1980.

Morck et al. (1988) measure Tobin's q as the ratio of the firm's market value of common stock plus preferred stock plus debt, divided by the estimated replacement cost of the firm's physical assets with data from the *Griliches R&D Database*. They measure inside ownership as the sum of the common stock ownership of all members of the board divided by total shares outstanding where the share ownership data are from Corporate Data Exchange. Their empirical methodology allows the data to identify the inflection points for changes in the slopes of the piecewise linear regression over various ranges of board ownership. They conclude that a specification in which the slope is positive over the range of 0 percent to 5 percent inside ownership, negative over the range of 5 percent to 25 percent inside ownership, and mildly positive above 25 percent inside ownership best fits the data. Morck et al. also estimate a piecewise linear regression in which the dependent variable is operating return on assets. They report that the same piecewise specification applies to these data.

Morck et al. (1988) interpret the initial positive slope between 0 percent and 5 percent as reflecting a convergence of interests, and the negative relation between 5 percent and 25 percent as the dominance of an entrenchment effect. They conclude that ownership structure matters for firm value and performance and that it matters in a specific way.

McConnell and Servaes (1990) also estimate a nonlinear relation between Tobin's q and insider ownership. Their analysis uses Stulz (1988) as their point of departure. McConnell and Servaes estimate a quadratic regression model which includes the percentage of shares owned by insiders, the percentage of shares owned by insiders squared, and various control variables. Their quadratic specification allows for a curvilinear relation of the type implied by Stulz, but does not rule out a nonlinear relation caused by an alignment of interest effect and an entrenchment effect of the types proposed by Morck et al. (1988).

McConnell and Servaes (1990) conduct their analysis with two samples of firms, one for 1976 and the other for 1986. The former sample includes 1,173 firms and the latter includes 1,093 firms. Both samples consist of New York Stock Exchange (NYSE) and American Stock Exchange (AMEX) listed firms. Like Morck et al. (1988), McConnell and Servaes measure Tobin's q as the market value of common stock plus the estimated market value of debt and preferred stock divided by the replacement value of assets. They estimate all components of the ratio using Compustat data.

McConnell and Servaes (1990) measure inside ownership as the sum of the shares owned by officers and directors as reported by *Value Line Investment Survey*. They report that for 1976, average inside ownership is 13.9 percent (median = 6 percent) and ranges from 0 to 90 percent. For 1986, average inside ownership is 11.84 percent (median = 5 percent) and ranges from 0 to 89 percent. With both the 1976 and 1986 data, the coefficient of the percentage of shares owned by insiders is positive and significant and the coefficient of the squared term is negative and significant. This significant curvilinear relation is broadly consistent with the predictions of Stulz (1988), but does not rule out the predictions in Morck et al. (1988).

McConnell and Servaes (1990) also replicate the piecewise linear specification of Morck et al. (1988) with their data. They find a positive and significant coefficient for inside ownership between 0 percent and 5 percent, but, in contrast to Morck et al., find that the slope over the range of 5 percent to 25 percent is also positive albeit not significant. As with Morck et al., McConnell and Servaes conclude that ownership structure matters and that it matters in a specific way. In particular, their evidence suggests that firm value is maximized when insiders hold between 30 and 40 percent of the firm's equity.

Hermalin and Weisbach (1991) estimate a piecewise linear regression using 134 NYSE firms. Rather than a cross-sectional regression for a single year, they use a panel of data encompassing the years 1971, 1974, 1977, 1980, and 1983. These authors distinguish between inside directors and outside directors and compile their ownership data directly from proxy statements. Because their ownership data are more granular, Hermalin and Weisbach can specify an additional breakpoint at 1 percent inside ownership. They also find a nonlinear relation between inside ownership and q, but one that differs from Morck et al. (1988). Specifically, they find a positive relation between q and inside ownership between 0 percent and

1 percent inside ownership, and a negative relation between 1 percent and 5 percent inside ownership. They conclude that the incentive alignment effect dominates over the range of 0 percent to 1 percent, but above 1 percent inside ownership the entrenchment effect more than offsets the incentive alignment effect.

McConnell and Servaes (1995) extend their 1990 results by separating their sample into low-growth and high-growth firms. This study is motivated by the observation that managers prefer to manage larger firms and, thus, may engage in empire building regardless of the implications for corporate value (Jensen 1986; Stulz 1990). As the existence of profitable growth opportunities declines, this empire-building behavior becomes increasingly detrimental to shareholder value as the only way to increase firm size is to undertake negative net present value projects. This observation gives rise to the prediction that if the allocation of equity ownership matters, it will be more important in firms with fewer growth opportunities. Consistent with this observation, McConnell and Servaes find that the coefficients on the ownership variables are typically larger for low-growth firms than for high-growth firms. The results weakly support the conjecture that the allocation of equity ownership among corporate insiders and other investors is more important in firms with fewer profitable investment opportunities. McConnell and Servaes conclude that ownership structure matters, but it matters more for firms in which the principal-agent problem identified by Jensen and Meckling (1976) is of greater consequence.

Holderness, Kroszner, and Sheehan (1999) assemble ownership data for a sample of 1,236 exchange-listed firms in 1935 and compare the fraction of share ownership by officers and directors with the fraction of share ownership by officers and directors of a sample of 3,759 exchange-listed firms in 1995. Their primary goal is to determine whether the separation of ownership from control has become more severe during the twentieth century. To the contrary, Holderness et al. find that share ownership by officers and directors actually increased from an average of 13 percent to 21 percent over that time period.

These authors also estimate a piecewise linear regression with the firm's market-to-book ratio of assets (as a proxy for Tobin's q) as the dependent variable and the percentage of shares owned by officers and directors as the key independent variable along with certain control variables. The coefficients of their regression with 1935 data are similar to those of Morck et al. (1988), who used 1980 data. With 0 percent to 5 percent inside ownership, the relation between q and inside ownership is positive; over the range of 5 percent to 25 percent, the relation is negative; and above 25 percent, the relation is negligible. Holderness et al. (1999) shy away from drawing a causal interpretation of this relation but observe that whatever the cause of the relation, it has not changed much over the twentieth century.

An Alternative Interpretation of the Empirical Relation between Managerial Ownership and Corporate Value

Demsetz (1983) can be viewed as tackling the premise that the value of a firm with diffuse share ownership that is controlled by managers who own but a few shares necessarily means that firm value is not maximized. He argues that the ownership structures that emerge across firms will be the endogenous outcome

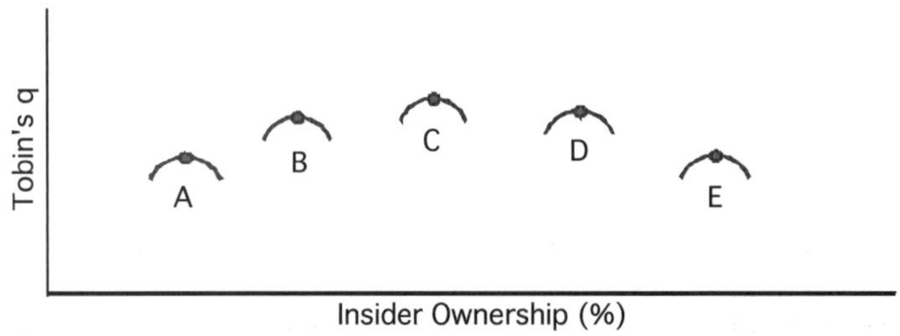

Exhibit 16.1 Possible Relations between Insider Ownership and Firm Value as in Demsetz (1983)

of a maximizing process among shareholders and managers. An implication of Demsetz's argument is that different ownership structures will be optimal for different firms. A further implication that has prompted much discussion and debate goes to the problem of empirically estimating a relation between corporate value and ownership structure. To understand the roots of the debate, consider Exhibit 16.1.

The vertical axis of Exhibit 16.1 represents corporate value and the horizontal axis represents the percentage of shares owned by management. Each of the convex curved lines represents an individual firm. Consistent with Morck et al. (1988) and Stulz (1988), the relation between firm value and the percentage of shares owned by managers is nonlinear, first increasing, then decreasing as the fraction of shares owned by management increases. According to Demsetz (1983), each firm will have an ownership structure that maximizes value for that firm. In this case, each firm will have the ownership structure that lies at the peak of its own curved line. (Of course, this figure is only representative of many possible characterizations across firms.)

The empirical problem arises when the data across the set of firms is combined into a single data set and a single empirical relation is estimated to represent all firms. Exhibit 16.2 shows how the observed data would likely look for the set of firms depicted in Exhibit 16.1.

Each dot in Exhibit 16.2 represents the optimal ownership structure for a firm from Exhibit 16.1. If a single cross-sectional regression is estimated using the values and ownership structures of all the firms from Exhibit 16.1, the observed empirical relation will be the curved line that connects the dots in Exhibit 16.2. Accordingly,

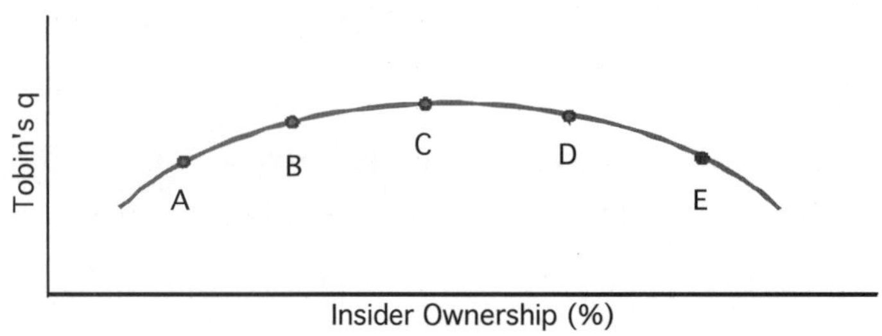

Exhibit 16.2 Spurious Outcome of a Cross-Sectional Regression Based on Exhibit 16.1

the relation between ownership structure and value may be nonlinear, but the estimated curved line just happens to be the spurious outcome of an improperly specified empirical analysis. Consequently, interpreting the results of that analysis as meaning that there is a single optimal ownership structure at the peak of the curved line is fallacious.

Demsetz and Lehn (1985) alter the direction of the debate. Rather than focusing on the relation between ownership structure and value, they focus on identifying the fundamental factors that differentiate among firms (or among industries) and investigate whether these factors influence ownership structure. They identify three factors that they deem to merit investigation: (1) value-maximizing size; (2) control potential, or, as they put it, "the profit potential from exercising more effective control"; and (3) systematic regulation or constraints on the scope of shareholder decisions.

Demsetz and Lehn (1985) estimate regression models that are directed at identifying the factors that determine ownership concentration where concentration is measured as the percentage of shares owned by the top 5 and the top 20 shareholders. Using a sample of 511 U.S. firms, they take their ownership data from the Corporate Data Exchange. As a proxy for size, they use total equity market capitalization. As proxies for control potential they use various measures of stock market volatility. They use indicator variables for public utilities and financial firms to identify systematic regulation. Demsetz and Lehn find that these variables are significant in explaining ownership concentration. Therefore, they conclude that ownership structure across firms is consistent with owners choosing an ownership structure that is value-maximizing for that firm.

Demsetz and Lehn (1985) then regress firms' profit rates against ownership concentration and find no significant relation using a linear specification. They conclude that firms do have optimal ownership structures and that firm owners choose the structures that maximize the values of their firms, but that optimal ownership structures differ across firms. In short, one interpretation of Demsetz and Lehn's work is that the nonlinear relation observed by Morck et al. (1988), McConnell and Servaes (1990), and Hermalin and Weisbach (1991) in the cross section of firms is due to happenstance.

A further implication is that, if all firms are at their endogenously determined value-maximizing ownership structures, a change in the fraction of shares owned by insiders would have no effect (or, perhaps, have a negative effect) on firm value. The alternative interpretation is that the nonlinear relation identified by Morck et al. (1988), McConnell and Servaes (1990), and Hermalin and Weisbach (1991) represents the relation between ownership and value such that a change in ownership that moves a firm along a line of the sort depicted in Exhibit 16.2 would be associated with an increase or decrease in value depending upon whether the change in ownership moves the firm toward or away from the value-maximizing ownership structure. The policy implication is that, after controlling for other factors that affect value, all firms should move along the line toward the universal optimal ownership structure. Of course, the alternative perspective is that each firm has already achieved its optimal ownership structure and perturbation of that structure will inevitably destroy value.

There is a second aspect of the endogeneity problem that requires discussion and that aspect has to do with the direction of causality. In cross-sectional regressions of the type conducted by Morck et al. (1988) and others, even if the empirical relation discovered is not spurious, it is unclear that ownership structure causes corporate value to rise and then fall as inside ownership increases. It could be that the relation runs from firm value to ownership, and the cross-sectional regressions cannot rule out that direction of causality.

Before moving on, it is worthwhile to comment upon the empirical analysis conducted by Demsetz and Lehn (1985). In contrast to Morck et al. (1988) and others, Demsetz and Lehn find no significant relation between operating profit and ownership concentration. There are at least three explanations for their results. First, the analysis of Morck et al. and others may be flawed. Second, instead of using the split of ownership between insiders and outside shareholders in their analysis, Demsetz and Lehn use the fraction of shares owned by the top 5 and top 20 shareholders. Thus, arguably, their analysis has nothing to say about the relation between corporate value and the split of shares between management and other shareholders. Third, they use only a linear specification in their analysis that could well cloud an actual nonlinear relation.

Do Misspecified Tests Explain the Observed Empirical Relation between Insider Ownership and Corporate Value?

Like Demsetz and Lehn (1985), Agrawal and Knoeber (1996), Loderer and Martin (1997), Cho (1998), and Demsetz and Villalonga (2001) conclude that the empirical relation reported in Morck et al. (1988) and others is likely to be the spurious result of misspecified tests. Each of these studies takes a slightly different approach to dealing with the endogeneity problem that is potentially latent in the cross-sectional regressions of Morck et al. and others.

The main premise of Agrawal and Knoeber (1996) is that corporate governance mechanisms aimed at limiting the principal-agent conflict that can arise when ownership and control are separated do not operate in isolation. Rather, firm owners employ various mechanisms to control the principal-agent conflict. This observation motivates the authors to study such mechanisms jointly. This is similar in spirit to the Demsetz (1983) argument. While Demsetz contends that insider ownership is chosen optimally given the firm's environment, Agrawal and Knoeber extend the argument to include three additional internal control mechanisms—(1) outside representation on the board, (2) leverage, and (3) reliance on external labor markets—and three external control mechanisms: (1) institutional shareholdings, (2) outside block ownership, and (3) activity in the market for corporate control.

They hypothesize that if the various control mechanisms are selected optimally, there should be no empirical relation between firm performance and the use of these mechanisms in the cross section of firms. To be clear, this is not the same as suggesting that the mechanisms do not matter. Rather, if the mechanisms are chosen optimally, then cross-sectional variation occurs simply due to environmental differences across firms. To the extent that an investigator can control for the sources of variation across firms, the relation between the governance mechanisms and firm performance should disappear.

Agrawal and Knoeber (1996) start with a data set of the largest 500 U.S. firms in 1987 as identified by *Forbes* and compile complete data for 383 firms. They obtain data on the ownership structure of each firm from Disclosure CD-ROM. The authors calculate Tobin's q using Compustat data. They define this measure as the market value of equity plus the approximated market value of preferred stock and debt, divided by book value of total assets.

Using ordinary least squares (OLS) regressions, Agrawal and Knoeber (1996) regress q against each control mechanism individually plus other variables. In a quadratic specification, as in McConnell and Servaes (1990 and 1995), insider ownership has a positive and significant coefficient while insider ownership squared has a negative, but insignificant, coefficient. Agrawal and Knoeber find a significantly negative relation between q and the percentage of board outsiders, use of debt, and acquisition probability. When the OLS specification includes all governance mechanisms, insider ownership loses its significance. Further, when modeled using simultaneous equations, each of the mechanisms except the percentage of outside directors loses its significance. Agrawal and Knoeber conclude that empirical evidence based upon using control mechanisms individually can be misleading.

Loderer and Martin (1997) study the relation between insider ownership and performance using corporate acquisitions as their setting. They use a simultaneous equations approach. Their sample includes 867 U.S. acquisitions that occurred between 1978 and 1988 as listed in *Mergers & Acquisitions*. The authors employ two measures of firm value. For q, they use the sum of market value of equity, book value of long-term debt, and book value of short-term debt, all divided by the book value of total assets. For their second measure of value, they use cumulative abnormal returns around the acquisition announcements, as measured from five days prior to announcement date through the announcement date. Using either measure of performance, the evidence from the simultaneous equation models indicates that causality runs from performance to ownership but not vice versa.

Cho (1998) hypothesizes that the relation between insider ownership and firm value documented by Morck et al. (1988) and McConnell and Servaes (1990) is driven by investment policy. He studies a cross section of 326 U.S. firms in 1991, with ownership data from Value Line, financial data from Compustat, and R&D data from the *BusinessWeek Annual R&D Scoreboard*. Cho notes that all three variables may be endogenously determined and estimates a simultaneous equations system of ownership structure, investment, and corporate value using two-stage least squares (2SLS) regressions. His evidence suggests that the variables are endogenously determined and that causality runs from q to ownership structure, rather than in the other direction.

Demsetz and Villalonga (2001) pay special attention to measurement issues that arise in firm performance and ownership structure. Specifically, most studies use q, which is forward-looking and determined by market participants, while the Demsetz and Lehn (1985) study employs historical accounting measures of performance, which are backward-looking. Further, Demsetz and Villalonga note that heterogeneity exists regarding the interests of various inside owners (i.e., a chief executive officer [CEO] versus a director representing a blockholder). They argue that studies consolidating director and managerial ownership into a single *insider ownership* variable implicitly assume that the interests of all insiders are homogeneous, which may not be the case in many instances.

Demsetz and Villalonga (2001) randomly sample 223 firms from the sample studied by Demsetz and Lehn (1985). In OLS regressions, they find evidence consistent with previous studies documenting a significant relation between ownership and performance; however, when reestimated using simultaneous equations in a two-stage least squares model, the relation disappears. They interpret their findings as supporting the view that optimal ownership structures are determined by market forces and differ across firms due to differences in each firm's contracting environment, particularly with regard to size, regulation, and risk.

CHANGES IN OWNERSHIP STRUCTURE AND CHANGES IN CORPORATE VALUE

Theories of the effect of ownership structure on corporate value and performance all begin with the premise that an agency conflict arises when the interests of managers and owners diverge and that an optimal ownership structure can alleviate this conflict. However, no consensus has been achieved regarding whether observed ownership structures represent the result of a value-maximizing choice by owners and managers as argued by Demsetz and Lehn (1985) or whether the ownership structures of certain firms are suboptimal. The latter interpretation implies that value can be created by adjusting the ownership structure toward its optimal mix, as implied by Morck et al. (1988) and McConnell and Servaes (1990 and 1995).

Himmelberg, Hubbard, and Palia (1999) propose a methodology to distinguish between the two alternative perspectives. They observe that, if all firm-specific factors that determine the firm-specific optimal ownership structure are controlled for and if ownership structure changes through time, the actual empirical relation between firm value and ownership structure should be observable. Their methodology proposes to accomplish this by using a panel of data along with a firm fixed effects regression. In this regression, the dependent variable is q and the independent variables include a zero/one indicator variable to identify each firm along with the percentage of shares owned by insiders and firm-specific control variables such as firm size, firm risk, profitability, and others. They argue that, with their procedure that controls for observable firm-specific factors and unobservable firm-specific factors through the firm-specific indicator variables, the remaining variation in q should be related to changes in the percentage of shares owned by insiders if the implication of the Morck et al. (1988) and McConnell and Servaes (1990) analyses is correct.

Himmelberg et al. (1999) estimate their model with a sample that includes 600 firms from the Compustat universe that have no missing data over the period 1982–1984. Their analysis encompasses the period 1982–1992. They find no significant relation between q and changes in the percentage of shares owned by insiders and conclude that their results are consistent with the propositions put forth by Demsetz (1983).

Zhou (2001) challenges the methodology of Himmelberg et al. (1999). Zhou shows that a fixed effects model that relies upon time series variation lacks power because most changes in ownership are small, and large changes are infrequent. Meanwhile, value may vary significantly for other reasons. Thus, with the fixed effects methodology, detecting a meaningful relation between ownership and performance, if one exists, is difficult. Zhou concludes that tests such as the ones employed by Himmelberg et al. do not constitute strong evidence against a causal relation between inside ownership levels and firm performance.

An alternative approach to control firm-specific effects is by examining the effect of concentrated changes in inside ownership on firm value. Two papers propose to do this: The first is by Core and Larcker (2002) and the second is by McConnell, Servaes, and Lins (2008).

Core and Larcker (2002) study firms' accounting and stock price performance following their adoption of target stock ownership plans. Such plans establish target levels of managerial stock ownership. Their sample encompasses 195 U.S. firms that adopted such plans over the period 1991–1995. Relative to the control sample, they find that firms adopting target ownership plans, on average, have lower managerial ownership before the plan adoption and that, over the two years after plan adoption, managerial share ownership increases. Core and Larcker also find that, relative to a control firm benchmark, these firms experience significantly improved stock price performance over the six months following plan adoption and improved accounting performance over the two years following plan adoption. Core and Larcker (p. 317) interpret their findings to mean that "increases in managerial equity ownership from suboptimal levels appear to result in improvements in firm performance."

McConnell et al. (2008) undertake an event study of stock price changes around announcements of large insider share purchases. In a regression model with announcement period abnormal returns as the dependent variable, their study implicitly preserves the fixed effects model which controls for endogeneity. Their sample encompasses 4,141 instances of large insider share purchases (i.e., share purchases of at least 10,000 shares) across 1,700 different firms over the period 1994–1999. The authors find that the coefficient of the change in ownership is positive, the coefficient of the change in insider ownership squared is negative, and the coefficient of the interaction is negative. These results are consistent with the curvilinear relation between insider ownership and firm value initially reported by McConnell and Servaes (1990). Their results are consistent with the view that firms do deviate from their optimal ownership structure and that changes in ownership structure do affect corporate value.

Kim and Lu (2009) take a different approach to address the question of whether changes in ownership structure can affect firm value. They examine the relation between ownership structure and firm value for two types of firms: (1) firms that operate under strong governance, proxied by strong product competition and higher institutional ownership, and (2) all other firms. Their sample consists of firms for which data on at least five top executives are available from S&P ExecuComp; the sample period is 1992 to 2006. They find that the inverted U-shape relation between firm value and insider ownership exists only in the set of firms with weak governance. The results of Kim and Lu are consistent with both Demsetz and Lehn (1985), Morck et al. (1988), and Agrawal and Knoeber (1996) in that it suggests that ownership structure should not be studied in isolation from the set of other governance mechanisms. When existing governance mechanisms are weak, changes in ownership structure help to alleviate the loss in value that can come about due to the agency conflict between management and other shareholders.

However, whether an optimal ownership structure exists in the presence of alternative strong governance mechanisms remains unclear.

Kim and Lu's results can be interpreted as suggesting that when strong governance mechanisms are in place, firms are more likely to be forced toward the optimal ownership structure. Alternatively, the results can be interpreted to mean that when other governance forces are strong enough to alleviate the agency conflict caused by the separation of ownership and control, ownership structure does not matter (i.e., there is no optimal ownership structure).

BLOCK SHAREHOLDERS, INSTITUTIONAL SHAREHOLDERS, AND FAMILY SHAREHOLDERS

This chapter first addressed the broad classification of shareholders as insiders and outsiders, or as managers and atomistic shareholders. The chapter now turns to other classifications of shareholders. Three such classifications are considered: blockholders, institutional investors, and family shareholders. The distinction among the three classifications is not clean. For example, family shareholders are most likely to be relevant as a class of shareholders only when the family owns a block of shares. Institutional investors might be relevant based upon their collective holdings, but it is also possible that a single institutional investor, such as a pension fund, is important because the fund holds a single large block of shares. Exhibit 16.3 provides a schematic portrayal of the way in which classes of shareholders can be considered.

Shleifer and Vishny (1986) put forward a theoretical model in which a takeover can be successful only when a bidder has already acquired a large minority ownership position in the firm. The potential takeover threat that the large blockholder represents works as an effective device for monitoring management. Thus, Shleifer and Vishny predict that the presence of a large blockholder will have a positive effect on the value of the firm.

Pound (1988) proposes three hypotheses to describe the relation between institutional ownership and corporate value. According to the first, the *efficient monitoring hypothesis*, institutional investors have greater expertise and can monitor management at lower cost than can atomistic shareholders. Thus, this hypothesis predicts a positive relation between institutional ownership and corporate value. According to the *conflict-of-interest hypothesis*, institutional investors are coerced into voting with management because of other profitable business relationships with the firm. According to the *strategic-alignment hypothesis*, institutional investors and managers find it mutually advantageous to cooperate. This cooperation reduces the beneficial effects that could arise from more efficient monitoring. Thus, the

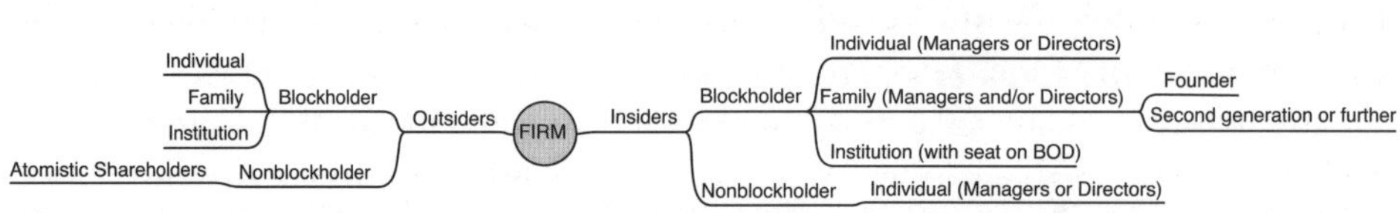

Exhibit 16.3 Ownership Class Taxonomy

conflict-of-interest and the strategic-alignment hypotheses both predict a negative relation between firm value and institutional ownership.

Anderson and Reeb (2003) summarize the theoretical discussions of the connection between corporate value and family ownership. The theory, which is still in its formative stages, proposes that family ownership can have either a positive or negative effect on firm value. On the one hand, a family usually controls a large block of shares because the progenitor of the family was the company's founder. In these instances, the current top management of the firm may have inherited their positions rather than have earned them by virtue of merit. In such cases, the firm's performance may suffer. In line with the arguments of Jensen and Meckling (1976), holding the title of CEO may be a nonmarketable perquisite associated with family control. Or the family more generally may come to view the firm as their personal piggy bank and extract resources that, arguably, belong to shareholders more generally. Both of these factors could lead to reduced value for the firm.

On the other hand, it is possible that a family whose members are descendants of the founder will have a vested interest in seeing that the firm performs well, especially if most of the family's wealth is tied up in the firm. Family members will be especially vigilant monitors of other family members. If management of the firm is entrusted to nonfamily members, the family can be in an especially strong position to monitor and discipline poorly performing nonfamily management.

The following discussion provides a brief presentation of the empirical findings regarding the relation between corporate value or performance and share ownership by the various classes of investors. The discussion comments upon which hypotheses the findings reject or support. The discussion does not elaborate upon concerns with the endogeneity problem as it relates to these empirical findings. Much of the preceding discussion regarding the endogeneity problem applies here as well.

In their cross-sectional regressions using 1976, 1986, and 1988 samples of exchange-listed U.S. firms, an innovation of McConnell and Servaes (1990, 1995) is to introduce the percentage of shares owned collectively by institutional investors and individually by the firm's largest nonmanagement blockholder, where a *blockholder* is defined as any shareholder who owns 5 percent or more of the firms shares. They report that of the 1,173 firms in their 1976 sample, 113 have at least one blockholder and the average blockholder owns 32.4 percent of the firm's shares. Of the 1,093 firms in their 1986 sample, 281 have at least one blockholder and the average blockholder owns 25.65 percent of the firm's shares. The statistics for their 1988 sample are similar to those for 1986.

In their cross-sectional regressions, McConnell and Servaes (1990 and 1995) find a positive and statistically significant relation between corporate value and the percentage of shares held by institutional investors and a positive, but not statistically significant, relation between corporate value and block ownership. They interpret their results as being consistent with the institutional investors, in the aggregate, serving as effective monitors.

In their two-stage cross-sectional model with data for 1987, Agrawal and Knoeber (1996) include six measures of corporate governance, including the percentage of shares owned by institutional investors and the percentage of shares owned in the aggregate by shareholders who own at least a 5 percent block of shares. Neither of these variables is significantly related to their measure of Tobin's q. They interpret their results as being consistent with the argument of Demsetz (1983) and Demsetz and Lehn (1985) that owners structure their share holdings such that each firm's ownership composition is optimal. If the regression analysis is properly specified, no relation will be apparent in the data.

In their cross-sectional regressions with data for the years 1971, 1974, 1977, 1980, and 1983, Hermalin and Weisbach (1991) include an indicator variable equal to 1 if any two directors of a firm are related. They call this variable *Family Company*. The coefficient of this variable is sometimes positive, sometimes negative, and rarely statistically significant.

Anderson and Reeb (2003) give specific attention to the role of founding-family ownership as a determinant of corporate value and performance among U.S. firms. Their sample comprises S&P 500 firms from 1992 to 1999. They identify a firm as a founding-family firm if members of the founder's family still retain an ownership interest in the shares of the company or the descendants of the founder are members of the board. In the typical year, the sample comprises 141 firms; family ownership averages 18 percent; in 15 percent of the firms, the founder is CEO; and in another 30 percent, a descendant of the founder is CEO.

With their panel of data, Anderson and Reeb (2003) estimate separate regressions with operating performance and q as the dependent variable. Their regressions include both family and nonfamily firms. In one set of regressions they include an indicator variable to identify whether the firm is a family firm, an indicator to identify a firm with a family member as CEO, an indicator to identify whether the founder is the CEO, and various control variables. In a second set of regressions, they include the percentage of shares owned by the family, the percentage of family-owned shares squared, and various control variables. Anderson and Reeb find that operating performance and q are higher in family firms than in nonfamily firms and higher still when the founder or a descendant of the founder is CEO. They also report a nonlinear relation between q and the percentage of shares owned by the family in which the coefficient of the percentage of shares owned is positive and significant and the percentage of shares owned squared is negative and significant. Anderson and Reeb conclude that family firms perform as well as or better than nonfamily firms, suggesting that family ownership is an effective mechanism for minimizing the loss in firm value due to the principal-agent conflict in large U.S. open corporations.

Villalonga and Amit (2006) observe that family ownership is different from family management of the firm. They further observe that different factors could be at work in the circumstances when family management and family ownership are distinct. They attempt to empirically distinguish between the two sets of circumstances using data for Fortune 500 firms for the period 1994–2000. To disentangle the effects, they estimate regressions in which they include variables to separate family ownership from family management. Villalonga and Amit conclude that family firms are more valuable than nonfamily firms, but only when the firm's founder remains as CEO, whereas second-generation CEOs reduce value. In sum, family control can be either a positive force or a negative force depending upon the role played by the family in managing the firm.

The study of the role and effect of family ownership and management on firm value and performance is still in its infancy. Undoubtedly, further studies on this topic will shed greater light on the extent to which family ownership and control influence corporate value.

SUMMARY AND CONCLUSIONS

Berle and Means (1932) present data to illustrate that during the early twentieth century, among large publicly listed U.S. corporations, control of the company had become increasingly separated from ownership of the shares. Under the presumption that separation of control from ownership is likely to dampen management's incentive to operate the firm to achieve its highest profit potential, the authors pose the question as to what forces are likely to propel the firm toward value creation and, in the absence of an ownership interest, what forces are likely to motivate managers to operate the firm efficiently. These questions gave rise to the scholarly field of corporate governance.

At its root, corporate governance is only a concern when ownership and control are separated. But someone must hold a firm's shares. The question then arises as to whether who owns the shares—where the *who* in this question refers to various classes or categories of shareholders including managers, atomistic outside or small shareholders, blockholders, institutional investors, and families—influences managerial behavior. An extensive literature has evolved that attempts to answer that question and the related question: If who owns the shares does matter, why does it matter?

This chapter reviews the extant literature and attempts to answer those questions. Perhaps surprisingly, there appears to have emerged a consensus that who owns the shares matters in the sense that there is an optimal ownership structure that can achieve greater value for the firm than can other ownership structures. The greater value is achieved by helping to alleviate the principal-agent conflict that arises when ownership and control are separated. Where the consensus breaks down is in efforts to estimate the precise relation between ownership structure and corporate value or performance. Various authors, but chief among them Demsetz (1983), argue that an optimal ownership structure will emerge for each firm as the endogenous outcome of an optimization process engaged in by shareholders and managers. As such, each firm's observed ownership structure will be optimal for that firm. The implication is that in a cross-sectional regression any observed relation between ownership structure and firm value is spurious.

Various approaches have been proposed to address this endogeneity problem. In the view of this chapter's authors, the most promising of these has been to examine instances wherein firms' ownership structures are significantly altered and to examine whether the value of the firm changes in a systematic way. Studies that have adopted this approach find that firm values do change in a systematic way when ownership structures are altered. A reasonable interpretation of this evidence is that while there may not be a single ownership structure that is universally optimal, there are instances where firms have strayed from their value-maximizing ownership structure. Thus, adjustments toward the optimum have implications for corporate value and performance.

Undoubtedly new theories will be put forth and new empirical methodologies will be used to further uncover the relation between corporate value and ownership structure. What is so far lacking is a consensus as to how to empirically identify an optimal ownership structure to guide owners and managers in moving toward that optimum. Would-be owners or would-be value-maximizing managers are not much helped by the advice that currently observed ownership structures must be optimal, otherwise they would not exist. Identifying that optimum is the empirical challenge that persists for financial scholars who hope to provide guidance to managers and investors.

DISCUSSION QUESTIONS

1. Some use the word *who* to denote various groups or classes of shareholders, arguing that who owns corporate shares can influence corporate value and performance. What are the origins of this view?
2. Early empirical studies by Morck, Shleifer, and Vishny (1988) and McConnell and Servaes (1990) find a nonlinear relation between corporate value and inside or managerial share ownership. How did the authors conduct these studies and interpret the results?
3. Describe the Demsetz (1983) argument and discuss its implications for the empirical work of Morck, Shleifer, and Vishny (1988) and McConnell and Servaes (1990).
4. What is the endogeneity problem in empirical analyses of the relation between corporate value and performance and corporate ownership structure? How do empirical studies such as Agrawal and Knoeber (1996), Himmelberg, Hubbard, and Palia (1999), and Demsetz and Villalonga (2001) propose to deal with this problem? What do these studies conclude?

REFERENCES

Agrawal, Anup, and Charles R. Knoeber. 1996. Firm performance and mechanisms to control agency problems between managers and shareholders. *Journal of Financial and Quantitative Analysis* 31 (3): 377–397.

Anderson, Ronald C., and David M. Reeb. 2003. Founding-family ownership and firm performance: Evidence from the S&P 500. *Journal of Finance* 58 (3): 1301–1328.

Berle, Adolf A., and Gardiner C. Means. 1932. *The modern corporation and private property*. New York: McMillan.

Cho, Myeong-Hyeon. 1998. Ownership structure, investment, and the corporate value: An empirical analysis. *Journal of Financial Economics* 47 (1): 103–121.

Core, John E., and David F. Larcker. 2002. Performance consequences of mandatory increases in executive stock ownership. *Journal of Financial Economics* 64 (3): 317–340.

Demsetz, Harold. 1983. The structure of ownership and the theory of the firm. *Journal of Law and Economics* 26 (2): 375–390.

Demsetz, Harold, and Kenneth Lehn. 1985. The structure of corporate ownership: Causes and consequences. *Journal of Political Economy* 93 (6): 1155–1177.

Demsetz, Harold, and Belén Villalonga. 2001. Ownership structure and corporate performance. *Journal of Corporate Finance* 7 (3): 209–233.

Hermalin, Benjamin, and Michael Weisbach. 1991. The effects of board compensation and direct incentives on firm performance. *Financial Management* 20 (4): 101–112.

Himmelberg, Charles P., R. Glenn Hubbard, and Darius Palia. 1999. Understanding the determinants of managerial ownership and the link between ownership and performance. *Journal of Financial Economics* 53 (3): 353–384.

Holderness, Clifford, Randall Kroszner, and Dennis Sheehan. 1999. Were the good old days that good? Changes in managerial stock ownership since the Great Depression. *Journal of Finance* 54 (2): 435–470.
Jensen, Michael. 1986. Agency costs of free cash flow, corporate finance, and takeovers. *American Economic Review* 76 (2): 323–329.
Jensen, Michael C., and William H. Meckling. 1976. Theory of the firm: Managerial behavior, agency costs and ownership structure. *Journal of Financial Economics* 3 (4): 305–360.
Kim, E. Han, and Yao Lu. 2009. CEO ownership and valuation. Working paper, University of Michigan.
Loderer, Claudio, and Kenneth Martin. 1997. Executive stock ownership and performance: Tracking faint traces. *Journal of Financial Economics* 45 (2): 223–255.
Manne, Henry. 1965. Mergers and the market for corporate control. *Journal of Political Economy* 73 (2): 110–126.
McConnell, John, and Henri Servaes. 1990. Additional evidence on equity ownership and corporate value. *Journal of Financial Economics* 27 (2): 595–612.
———. 1995. Equity ownership and the two faces of debt. *Journal of Financial Economics* 39 (1): 131–157.
McConnell, John, Henri Servaes, and Karl Lins. 2008. Changes in insider ownership and changes in the market value of the firm. *Journal of Corporate Finance* 14 (2): 92–106.
Morck, Randall, Andrei Shleifer, and Robert Vishny. 1988. Management ownership and market valuation: An empirical analysis. *Journal of Financial Economics* 20 (2): 293–315.
Pound, John. 1988. Proxy contests and the efficiency of shareholder oversight. *Journal of Financial Economics* 20 (2): 237–265.
Shleifer, Andrei, and Robert Vishny. 1986. Large shareholders and corporate control. *Journal of Political Economy* 94 (3): 461–488.
Stulz, René. 1988. Managerial control of voting rights: Financing policies and the market for corporate control. *Journal of Financial Economics* 20 (1): 25–59.
———. 1990. Managerial discretion and optimal financing policies. *Journal of Financial Economics* 26 (1): 3–27.
Villalonga, Belén, and Raphael Amit. 2006. How do family ownership, control and management affect firm value? *Journal of Financial Economics* 80 (2): 385–417.
Zhou, Xianming. 2001. Understanding the determination of managerial ownership and its relationship to firm performance: Comment. *Journal of Financial Economics* 62 (3): 559–571.

ABOUT THE AUTHORS

John J. McConnell is the Emanuel T. Weiler Distinguished Professor of Management at the Krannert Graduate School of Management at Purdue University, where he has been a faculty member since 1976. He has published more than 75 articles in leading finance, economics, and management journals on such topics as corporate governance, banking and financial intermediation, financial derivatives, and corporate valuation. He is a fellow of the Financial Management Association and was selected as a Distinguished Scholar by the Eastern Finance Association (2006).

Stephen B. McKeon is a PhD candidate in the Management Department (finance) at the Krannert School within Purdue University. He received his MS in economics from Purdue University and his BS in business administration (finance) from the Lundquist College of Business at the University of Oregon. Before his doctoral studies, he spent seven years as the chief financial officer and a member of the board of directors of Greenfield Wine Company in Napa Valley, California. His research interests include corporate governance, capital structure, and equity issuances.

Wei Xu is visiting assistant professor of finance at the Kellstadt Graduate School of Business at DePaul University. She was a senior financial analyst at Mathematica Capital Management from 2007 to 2009 and a senior economist at LECG from 2004 to 2007. Professor Xu earned her doctorate in quantitative methods at the Krannert School of Management at Purdue University in 2003. Her interests include risk management, investment management, and corporate finance. Her paper "Equity Returns at the Turn of the Month," published in the *Financial Analysts Journal*, won the Graham and Dodd Scroll Award presented by the CFA Institute in 2008.

CHAPTER 17

The Effects of Management Turnover on Firm Performance

MARK R. HUSON
Pocklington Professor of Private Enterprise and Associate Professor of Finance, University of Alberta

ROBERT PARRINO
Lamar Savings Centennial Professor of Finance, University of Texas at Austin

INTRODUCTION

Hiring and firing decisions are among the most important decisions made by a board of directors. The senior executives at a firm greatly influence the policies of the firm and are responsible for implementing them over an extended period of time. A highly capable manager can create considerable stockholder wealth, while a poor manager can destroy wealth on a large scale. Consequently, the study of the effects of management turnover on firm performance provides insights about the effectiveness of the board of directors as a governance mechanism.

This chapter discusses the academic research on the impact of management turnover on firm performance. Over the past 50 years, researchers have produced a substantial body of work in this area. The earliest research appeared in the sociology and management literatures during the 1950s, and for 30 years management turnover research was almost exclusively found in these literatures. Turnover research began to appear in accounting and finance journals during the 1980s and since then a substantial accounting and finance literature in this area has emerged.

Because the extensive quantity of research on the performance effects of turnover precludes discussing all of it in detail, this chapter focuses mainly on the related accounting and finance literatures. To provide background for this discussion, the chapter begins by describing the sociology and management literatures on management turnover from the 1950s through the 1980s. The discussion of the early research provides a useful perspective on the evolution of the literature on the effects of management turnover on firm performance and the interpretation of the more recent evidence. As will become apparent, the accounting and finance literatures owe much to research in sociology and management.

EARLY RESEARCH

The first efforts to empirically document the effects of management turnover on firm performance can be found in the sociology and management literatures of the 1950s and 1960s. Furtado and Karan (1990) and Kesner and Sebora (1994) provide comprehensive discussions of the major streams of the management turnover literature through the early 1990s. This early research establishes the theoretical foundation upon which much of the subsequent research has been based. The earliest empirical work mainly focuses on the relations between the frequency of turnovers within a firm and post-turnover performance, as well as between the characteristics of new managers and how firms perform under their direction.

Early empirical researchers quickly recognized the difficulties associated with isolating the effects of management turnover on firm performance from the effects of other factors that might affect performance. This has been the fundamental challenge in this literature from the beginning. To compare performance of a firm under the old manager (before the turnover) with performance under the new manager (after the turnover), a researcher must control for the other factors that affect firm performance. These factors might include changes in general economic conditions, industry and firm characteristics, consumer preferences, technological innovations, and so on.

Some of the early studies of post-turnover firm performance, such as Grusky (1963 and 1964) and Gamson and Scotch (1964), focus on manager turnover in major sports teams (initially baseball teams) as a means of simplifying the empirical challenges. Researchers can relatively easily measure performance of sports teams using simple, readily available metrics such as wins and losses. Controls for changes in economic and industry factors are less crucial than for a typical corporation. Furthermore, team-specific factors such as player turnover and salaries were not as much of a concern in the early 1960s as they would be today. These sports team studies examine the relation between the rate of turnover and post-turnover performance with inconclusive results. The evidence they report appears to be sample-specific.

Other non–sport team studies of management turnover from the 1950s and 1960s examine how the characteristics of incoming managers affect post-turnover performance. These studies, which often rely on small samples or individual organizations, find that factors such as whether the manager is from outside the firm, how well the manager fits with the organization, the political acumen of the manager, or the administrative style of the manager are all related to performance. Examples of these studies include Carlson (1961), Guest (1962), Grusky (1964 and 1969), Zald (1965), and Kotin and Sharaf (1967). However, they do not shed light on the effectiveness of boards as a governance mechanism because they do not address the question of whether boards select managers who have attributes that are correlated with strong post-turnover performance.

Much of the 1970s literature on the relation between management turnover and firm performance focuses on the impact of the new manager's status as an insider or an outsider (successor origin), as well as other manager characteristics. These studies include Helmich and Brown (1972), Lewin and Wolf (1974), and Helmich (1975). The studies from this period, principally in management journals, exploit larger samples that include more complex organizations than the earlier studies. The evidence on successor origin generally suggests that outsiders are associated with more organizational change and better post-turnover accounting performance than insiders when pre-turnover accounting performance is poor. Collectively, this evidence suggests that outsiders can serve as change agents when a change in corporate policies is desired. However, the studies from this period do not provide direct evidence on whether the turnover decisions made by boards result in performance improvements.

In the 1980s, the management turnover literature began to take advantage of new developments in empirical methods and the widespread availability of electronic data and low-cost computing power. For example, a relatively large number of studies from this period examine stock price reactions to chief executive officer (CEO) turnover announcements. Furtado and Karan (1990) as well as Kesner and Sebora (1994) provide detailed summaries of the evidence from these event studies. The motivation for this focus is the recognition that the stock price reaction to a turnover announcement reflects the market's expectations concerning the impact of management turnover on future firm performance. Unfortunately, the evidence from these event studies is mixed. While some document a positive average stock price reaction, others document a negative reaction. This inconclusive evidence arises because the stock price reactions to turnover announcements not only reflect investor expectations about how the turnover itself will affect firm performance but also reflect the potentially offsetting effect associated with other information contained in turnover announcements. These potentially confounding effects are discussed in detail later in this chapter.

The first studies of the performance consequences of turnover appeared in the accounting and finance literatures during the 1980s (see Johnson, Magee, Nagarajan, and Newman 1985; Reinganum 1985; Warner, Watts, and Wruck 1988; Weisbach 1988; and Bonnier and Bruner 1989). All of the finance and accounting studies from this period examine stock price reactions to turnover announcements as a means of assessing the impact of turnover on performance.

Several management studies in the 1980s also directly examine the relation between turnover and post-turnover performance. Like the studies from the 1960s that focus on manager turnover in sports teams, two of these studies report evidence from turnovers in football (Brown 1982) and basketball (Pfeffer and Davis-Blake 1986) teams. As with the earlier evidence from sports teams, the evidence from these studies is also inconclusive. No reliable relations are observed between turnover and performance.

Researchers also studied more complex organizations for evidence on the performance effects of management turnover during the 1980s. The evidence from these studies provides a richer understanding of the mechanisms by which management turnover affects firm performance as well as of the cross-sectional variation in performance effects. For example, studies from this period show that the type, timing, and nature of the turnover influences the ability of the new manager to succeed (Louis 1980); that performance improvements around turnover are related to strategic changes (Tushman, Virany, and Romanelli 1985); and that the frequency of failures among newspaper firms increases following founder deaths (Carroll 1984).

Investigations into the relation between manager origin and post-turnover performance also continued throughout the 1980s. Kesner and Sebora (1994) provide a detailed summary of the successor origin studies during this period. As with the earlier studies, Brady and Helmich (1982) find that top managers who are hired from outside the firm are associated with greater organizational change. In addition, researchers in the 1980s started to investigate how differences in post-turnover performance between insiders and outsiders varied depending on the pre-turnover performance of the firm. The evidence suggests that post-turnover performance is weaker following internal promotions at poorly performing firms and that it is stronger following outside succession at firms that are performing well (Chung, Lubatkin, Rogers, and Owers 1987; and Lubatkin, Chung, Rogers, and Owers 1989).

MORE RECENT EVIDENCE AND THE CURRENT STATE OF THE LITERATURE

This section discusses the more recent evidence on how management turnover affects firm performance, with a particular focus on the accounting and finance literatures. This discussion begins by identifying the factors that lead to management turnover. As suggested by earlier research, the outcome of a management turnover is likely to vary with its cause. Several theories of the effect of turnover on performance are then reviewed. Finally, the most recent evidence on the impact of turnovers on firm performance is discussed.

Antecedents of Management Turnover

Many studies of top-management turnover published since the 1980s distinguish between forced and voluntary turnover. Forced turnover occurs when the board of directors removes the top manager for poor performance. Voluntary turnover occurs when the departing manager steps down voluntarily. Voluntary turnovers include normal retirements as well as turnovers that take place because the incumbent manager becomes too ill to continue in the job, leaves to take a better industry job, pursues an alternative career, or assumes a position in government.

The evidence from numerous studies is consistent with the theory that boards of directors act to forcibly remove poorly performing managers. Early studies in the accounting and finance literatures that document a negative relation between stock returns and the likelihood of turnover include Coughlan and Schmidt (1985), Warner et al. (1988), and Weisbach (1988). Weisbach (1988) and Kang and Shivdasani (1995) report evidence of a negative relation between the likelihood of turnover and the firm's accounting performance.

While managers who are forcibly removed from office might be expected to be of relatively low ability or to have put forth little effort, there is no reason to expect this of managers who step down voluntarily. A turnover that is precipitated by mandatory retirement, illness, or the lure of an alternative job does not provide a clear signal about the exiting manager's ability. In fact, evidence in Denis and Denis (1995) and Huson, Malatesta, and Parrino (2004) shows that while forced turnovers tend to be preceded by substantial loss of shareholder wealth, there is no evidence of negative abnormal performance before voluntary turnovers. As discussed shortly, this difference in the pre-turnover performance of firms experiencing forced and voluntary turnover leads to different predictions for the performance changes associated with each type of turnover.

The evidence in the management literature on successor origin suggests that the impact of forced or voluntary turnover on post-turnover firm performance is also likely to depend on whether the new senior manager is promoted from within the firm or hired from outside. Recall that the early turnover research suggests that outsiders are associated with greater organizational change and are therefore more likely to change firm policies where such changes are necessary. Boards of directors appear to recognize and act on this characteristic of outsiders. Evidence from Huson, Parrino, and Starks (2001), among others, indicates that outsiders are more likely to be appointed to replace a CEO who is being fired than to replace one who is departing voluntarily. For example, Huson et al. (2001) find that over the 1988 to 1994 period, outsiders replace 21.2 percent of CEOs who depart voluntarily and 58.7 percent of CEOs who are forced from office.

Theories about the Impact of Management Turnover on Firm Performance

The impact of a management turnover on firm performance depends on the quality of the incoming manager relative to the incumbent and the disruption costs associated with the change in leadership. The difference in the quality between the new and old manager depends on the quality of the departing manager and the ability of the board to identify and hire a superior replacement. The firm incurs disruption costs as the new manager becomes familiar with the responsibilities of the job and develops the human capital and relationships necessary to operate effectively. The costs might result from actual business disruptions, lost opportunities, inefficiencies, and so on. Because disruption costs occur to some extent with all turnovers, the next subsection discusses these costs first, followed by a discussion of issues related to changes in manager quality.

Disruption Costs

All top-management turnovers are disruptive to some extent. This disruption might be relatively minimal if the turnover is voluntary and the baton is passed to an heir apparent in an orderly succession. However, if the successor in a voluntary turnover is chosen from among several internal candidates in what Vancil (1987) describes as a "horse race," disruption may be greater as unsuccessful candidates leave the firm and are replaced and the successful candidate learns the job. Of course, forced turnovers are often even more disruptive, especially if the new manager is from outside the firm and brings along a team of senior managers to replace the team that worked with the departing manager.

Although disruption accompanies turnover, there is little evidence on the magnitude of the actual costs arising from such disruptions because they are inherently difficult to measure. One study that attempts to quantify these costs is Taylor (2008). Using a sample of CEO turnovers at large firms from 1971 to 2006, Taylor estimates that the total disruption costs associated with CEO turnover equal approximately 6 percent of the typical firm's assets.

Fee and Hadlock (2004), building on the earlier management literature such as Helmich and Brown (1972), provide insights into disruption costs through an examination of turnover among executives below the CEO when the CEO changes. They examine turnover of the top five executives in a sample of 443 firms over the 1993 to 1998 period and find evidence that the dismissal rates of non-CEO top executives are higher in periods around CEO dismissals. This turnover across the hierarchy increases the learning costs associated with CEO turnover and disrupts the firm's normal operations.

While disruption costs can be nontrivial, they are largely a short-term phenomenon. The new manager and his team will normally develop the human capital and relationships necessary for the job in a relatively short period of time. Because of this, the change in manager quality, which has longer-term implications for firm performance, tends to be the dominant effect with regard to whether stockholder wealth is increased or decreased by turnover of the top manager.

Changes in Manager Quality

Since the change in manager quality is generally the key determinant of the impact of top-management turnover on stockholder wealth, turnover characteristics related to this change have received considerable attention. We next discuss issues that are related to the relative quality of the new and the old manager.

Voluntary versus Forced Turnover

The disparity in the quality between the new and old managers is likely to differ between voluntary and forced turnovers. The typical departing executive in a voluntary turnover is of considerably higher quality than the typical departing executive in a forced turnover. Because the departing executive in a voluntary turnover can be of very high quality, the most capable candidate might be of lower quality than the incumbent. Even if the board is subsequently able to hire the best possible candidate, there is no guarantee that manager quality will improve.

The evidence from Denis and Denis (1995) and Huson et al. (2004) indicates that forced turnover occurs after a board recognizes the low quality of the incumbent. The board then has an opportunity to install a new manager of higher quality. However, a board that is acting in the best interests of stockholders will weigh the value from the expected improvement in manager quality against disruption costs and will only replace the manager when the net benefit is positive. Grusky (1963) refers to this as the *common sense* theory of CEO replacement and predicts improved firm performance following forced CEO turnover.

In addition to the common sense theory, Grusky (1963) also proposes the *vicious circle* theory, which maintains that disruption costs outweigh any quality improvements and therefore performance tends to decline following turnover. This circle begins when low post-turnover performance is attributed to the replacement, who is then replaced with another manager, and so on. The *vicious circle* theory predicts worse firm performance after forced turnover.

Both the *common sense* and *vicious circle* theories attribute performance (net of disruption costs) to manager quality. However, events outside the manager's control, such as a meltdown in the financial markets, can also affect post-turnover performance. Such events can give rise to poor performance that is unrelated to managerial quality, suggesting that managers removed for poor performance could be scapegoats. The agency models of Mirlees (1976) and Holmstrom (1979) provide a theory that rationalizes *scapegoating* behavior.

This *scapegoat* theory, as first suggested by Gamson and Scotch (1964), assumes that quality does not vary across managers. Therefore, a credible threat of dismissal elicits identical levels of effort from managers and poor performance results only from bad luck. The theory goes on to state that while boards understand that quality does not vary across managers, they must fire managers of poorly performing firms to ensure a credible threat of dismissal. Hence, fired managers are scapegoats because randomly occurring outcomes cause turnover. The *scapegoat* theory predicts that in the absence of disruption costs, performance should improve following turnover as firm performance reverts to its mean.

Inside versus Outside Succession

Whether the new manager is an insider or an outsider is also likely to affect the change in manager quality. Although disruption costs associated with outsiders tend to be higher, the quality of an outsider who is hired to replace the incumbent is also expected to be higher than that of the inside candidates. Dalton and Kesner (1985) argue that boards consider the higher costs of hiring outsiders and will only hire an outsider if they expect a correspondingly large improvement relative to inside candidates. Chan (1996) argues that boards might award competitive handicaps to inside candidates when outsiders are competing for top-level positions in the firm. According to Chan, boards provide these handicaps to inside candidates in order to motivate them in the face of the increased competition that they must contend with when the pool of potential managers is expanded to include outsiders. The quality of any successful outside candidate must be high enough to overcome these handicaps. Because both disruption costs and the expected increase in manager quality are related to the origin of the successor, considering the origin of the successor is critical when evaluating the effect of management turnover on firm performance.

Evidence on the Impact of Management Turnover on Firm Performance

The evidence in the accounting and finance literatures on the effects of management turnover in business enterprises can be roughly divided into three categories. The first category consists of evidence on stock price reactions to turnover announcements. As discussed previously, the earliest studies of the effects of management turnover on firm performance in the accounting and finance literatures focus on stock price reactions to assess the net impact of management turnover on firm performance. The second category comes from later research which looks for evidence of changes in operating performance to assess the impact of turnover on performance. Finally, the third category consists of evidence on changes in the real activities of firms, such as divestitures, and changes in total employment, both of which provide insight on the impact of turnover on specific characteristics and activities of the firm. The following subsections summarize the evidence in each of these three areas.

Evidence from Event Studies

Early accounting and finance research on the performance effects of top-management turnover used event study methodology to measure the market's reaction to news about turnover events. As previously discussed, the idea behind these inquiries is that any improvement in managerial quality will be capitalized into the stock price at the time of the announcement and, therefore, improvements in expected performance should be reflected in a positive abnormal return.

Unfortunately, interpretation of stock price reactions to turnover announcements is not that simple. A turnover announcement provides information about the quality of the incumbent as well as information about potential changes in firm performance. If the turnover announcement reveals that past managerial decisions were misguided, then the market reaction to the turnover news could be negative, even if the market believes the successor is of superior quality and that performance will improve.

For example, the market might interpret the announcement that a CEO is being fired for poor performance as indicating that there will be an improvement in managerial quality. All else equal, this might be associated with an increase in the stock price. However, the revelation that the board needed to fire the CEO could signal to the market that conditions are worse at the firm than previously thought. This would have a negative effect on the stock price. In fact, this negative *information effect* could outweigh the positive *real effect* on the stock price that is due to the expected increase in management quality.

This mixed-signal problem of turnover announcements probably explains the range of evidence yielded by event studies. For example, in the accounting and finance literatures, Khanna and Poulsen (1995) report a significant negative reaction to the announcement of CEO turnover. This contrasts with the positive and significant stock price reactions documented by Weisbach (1988) and Bonnier and Bruner (1989). Finally, studies by Reinganum (1985) and Warner et al. (1988) report statistically insignificant price changes.

Despite the mixed-signal problem, some event studies do shed light on the impact of turnover on firm performance. For example, Bonnier and Bruner (1989) construct a sample of firms whose most recent reported quarterly earnings were negative and which had suspended their regular dividends. They argue that the *information effect* associated with such obviously distressed firms is likely to be relatively small. Therefore, the stock price reactions to turnover announcements at such firms are likely to mostly reflect the value associated with changes in anticipated performance: the *real effect*. Consistent with the theory that managers at distressed firms tend to be replaced by higher-quality managers, Bonnier and Bruner find that the average abnormal return around the turnover announcements for their sample of senior managers is positive and significant.

In addition to reporting evidence on the average overall stock price reaction to turnover announcements, Bonnier and Bruner (1989) also examine how the stock price reaction differs between announcements in which an insider is replacing the incumbent and those in which an outsider is appointed. They find that, on average, the stock price reaction is 1.99 percentage points greater when an outsider is appointed to a senior management position (chairman, CEO, or president) than when an insider is appointed. This is consistent with the idea that, on average, outsiders appointed at distressed firms are associated with better subsequent performance.

In another event study, Borokhovich, Parrino, and Trapani (1996) find, on average, positive and significant stock price reactions to forced turnover announcements when an outsider is appointed CEO (1.64 percent with a t-statistic of 3.37) and negative and significant stock price reactions when an insider is appointed (–0.85 percent with a t-statistic of –3.08). This evidence, combined with that from Bonnier and Bruner (1989), is consistent with the idea that either (1) outsiders (or the boards that appoint them) are more likely to change firm policies when such changes are needed, or (2) on average, the outsiders who are appointed CEO are of higher quality than the insiders who are appointed, or both.

The evidence on stock price reactions to turnover announcements from Bonnier and Bruner (1989) and from Borokhovich et al. (1996) suggests that, on average, investors believe that turnover at distressed firms will be followed by improved performance, especially when an outsider is appointed CEO.

The abnormal stock return at the time of a top-management turnover announcement reflects only the market's expectation about the effect of the turnover on firm performance, not what actually happens. The next subsection provides a discussion of the direct evidence on the impact of turnover on firm performance.

Evidence on Operating Performance

While many studies report evidence on the market reaction to the announcement of management turnover, there is surprisingly little direct evidence on the impact of turnover on firm performance. Evidence reported by Hotchkiss (1995), Perez-Gonzalez (2006), Denis and Denis (1995), and Huson et al. (2004) does provide some insights. Exhibit 17.1 summarizes the major findings of these papers.

All four studies in Exhibit 17.1 present evidence that performance improves following turnover. However, they differ in the generalizability of their findings. The evidence from the first three studies is limited to firms or turnovers with certain characteristics, and some of the evidence from the third study is specific to a period of time characterized by a very active market for corporate control. Only the sample studied by Huson et al. (2004) covers both a broad range of firms and a long (25-year) period.

In a study of firm performance following bankruptcy, Hotchkiss (1995) provides evidence on the relation between turnover and subsequent firm accounting performance. For a sample of 197 firms that are emerging from Chapter 11, Hotchkiss finds that 40 percent of the firms report operating losses in the three years following reorganization and that 32 percent either file for bankruptcy again or are involved in a distressed restructuring. Hotchkiss relates these outcomes to managerial turnover and finds that both the likelihood of poor performance and the likelihood of filing for a second bankruptcy are higher when the prebankruptcy management retains control of the firm. She also notes that 69 percent of new managers in firms that replaced the prebankruptcy managers are outsiders. Her evidence suggests that management turnover is associated with improved firm performance. The generalizability of Hotchkiss' results is unclear because her sample consists of firms that experience extremely poor performance.

Perez-Gonzalez (2006) presents evidence on the importance of CEO quality in determining the outcome of turnover. He studies a sample of 335 turnovers at firms with concentrated ownership or founding family involvement. In this sample, 122 of the successors appear to inherit their position as they are related by blood or

Exhibit 17.1 Studies Reporting Evidence on Post-Turnover Operating Performance

Study	Sample	Main Conclusions
Hotchkiss (1995)	197 U.S. firms that filed for Chapter 11 bankruptcy between October 1979 and September 1988 and that subsequently emerged from bankruptcy as public companies.	• There is a strong association between the retention of the prebankruptcy management team and poor post-bankruptcy performance.
Perez-Gonzalez (2006)	122 CEO turnovers in which the new CEO is related to the departing CEO, the founder of the firm, or a large stockholder (family successions), and 213 nonfamily CEO successions. All turnovers occurred in U.S. nonfinancial, nonutility firms between 1980 and 2001.	• Post-turnover performance of firms with family successions is poorer than that of firms with nonfamily successions. • Post-turnover performance of firms with family successions is poorer when successors have weaker educational backgrounds.
Denis and Denis (1995)	908 turnovers during the 1985 to 1988 period that involved senior managers at firms which are included in the *Value Line Investment Survey* as of the end of 1984. The sample includes 353 turnovers involving the top manager, of which 73 can be classified as forced and 58 can be classified as normal retirements.	• Forced resignations of the top manager follow declines in operating performance are followed by operating performance improvements. • No evidence of poor operating performance prior to voluntary top manager turnovers, but small operating performance improvement afterwards. • Abnormal stock returns are significant and positive following forced top manager turnovers and insignificantly different from zero following voluntary turnovers. • Firms significantly reduce the scale of their operations following forced turnovers and grow more slowly than their peers following voluntary turnovers.
Huson, Malatesta, and Parrino (2004)	1,344 CEO turnovers during the 1971 to 1995 period at firms listed in the *Forbes* annual compensation surveys during that period; 215 of the turnovers are classified as forced and 1,129 are classified as voluntary.	• Controlling for mean reversion in operating performance and survivor bias, the changes on pre- and post-turnover operating performance around forced turnovers are similar to those reported by Denis and Denis (1995). There is no significant improvement in operating performance after voluntary turnovers.

Exhibit 17.1 (*Continued*)

Study	Sample	Main Conclusions
		• The post-succession performance improvements around forced turnovers are only observed during the 1983 to 1994 subperiod. There is no evidence of improvement in the first half of the sample period. • The degree of performance improvement is positively related to institutional ownership, the presence of an outsider-dominated board, and the appointment of a CEO from outside the firm. • Turnover announcements are associated with significant positive abnormal stock returns and these returns are positively related to subsequent changes in operating performance. • Employee productivity improves following both forced and voluntary turnovers. • Evidence on scale of operations is similar to that reported by Denis and Denis (1995).

marriage to the departing CEO, founder, or largest shareholder. Perez-Gonzalez argues that the expected quality of heirs is lower than that of successors who are chosen competitively.

For his entire sample Perez-Gonzalez (2006) reports a statistically significant increase in industry- and performance-adjusted operating return on assets (OROA) over the period from one year before the turnover to three years after the turnover. The CEOs who were chosen competitively drive this result. There is no evidence of performance improvements following the appointment of heirs. The difference between the two groups' performance changes is statistically significant.

Perez-Gonzalez (2006) separates the heirs on the basis of their ability, which he estimates from the quality of their educational background. He finds that low-ability heirs significantly underperform their industry- and performance-matched peers. These results indicate that turnover-related performance improvements are not only predicated on the removal of poor performers, but also require the board to identify and hire high-ability replacements. While informative, the magnitudes of the estimates in this study are specific to cases where the new CEO is related to the departing CEO, the founder, or a large stockholder.

Denis and Denis (1995) examine a broader sample of 908 management turnover events over the 1985 to 1988 period. The sample consists of 353 turnovers involving the top executive and 555 changes involving other top managers. The authors categorize these turnovers as forced or voluntary based on statements made at the time of the turnover and characteristics of the incumbent and successor.

Consistent with the idea that poor performers tend to be removed in forced turnovers, Denis and Denis (1995) document a statistically significant average cumulative abnormal stock return (CAR) of –17 percent in the year leading up to forced turnover of top managers. The CAR preceding their sample of voluntary turnovers is also negative but not significantly different from zero, suggesting that, on average, voluntary turnovers are not predicated on prior performance. Denis and Denis also document significant positive CARs of 2.5 percent at the announcement of the forced turnover and an insignificant average market reaction to the announcement of voluntary turnover.

To gauge the impact of turnover on operating performance, Denis and Denis (1995) measure levels and changes in the operating return on total assets over a seven-year window centered on the year of the turnover. Data constraints at this stage of their analysis reduce their sample of top executive turnovers to 296, of which they can identify 73 as forced and 58 as normal retirements. The following discussion focuses on comparisons between these two groups of top-management changes.

Consistent with the evidence from the CARs, there are indications of poor operating performance before forced turnover in the Denis and Denis (1995) sample. The mean (median) industry-adjusted change in operating performance over the period from three years to one year before the turnover (–3, –1) is a statistically significant –1.7 percent (–3.8 percent). However, they find no evidence of poor operating performance preceding voluntary turnover. In fact, managers who leave voluntarily outperform their industry peers by 0.8 percent on average and 1.3 percent at the median over the three years leading up to their departure.

The evidence of changes in post-turnover operating performance comes from analysis of changes in OROA over the period from one year before the turnover to three years after the turnover (–1, +3). Three years following forced turnover, the mean and median unadjusted OROA is significantly higher by 2.7 (3.4) percentage points. The mean (median) changes in industry-adjusted OROA are 3.9 and 4.6 percentage points, respectively. These significant changes in operating performance are consistent with the evidence that forced turnovers improve the quality of management and suggest that the value realized from the improvements exceeds the disruption costs.

Denis and Denis (1995) observe no statistically significant change in the level of unadjusted OROA following voluntary turnovers. However, the industry-adjusted measures show significant performance improvement. The average industry-adjusted OROA three years after a voluntary turnover is 1.8 percentage points higher than the average measured in the year before the turnover. This improved performance is surprising as there is no evidence of poor performance before the voluntary turnover. If the typical CEO who leaves voluntarily is at least of average quality, the source of the improvement is not immediately clear.

Denis and Denis (1995) provide a potential explanation for performance improvements after voluntary turnover. They note that the incidence of corporate control activity following turnover is higher than normal. Based on results in Mitchell and Lehn (1990), Denis and Denis estimate that about 5.3 percent of firms should experience control activity in a given year. The actual rates of control activity in their sample are 22 percent per year after forced turnover and 9 percent following voluntary turnover. Denis and Denis suggest that the observed improvements in operating performance might be attributable to increased pressure from the market for corporate control rather than being directly related to the turnover.

Overall, the evidence reported by Denis and Denis (1995) indicates that operating performance improves following turnover. Their observation of improved operating performance and positive abnormal announcement returns for forced turnovers is consistent with the idea that the announcement return capitalizes the anticipated performance improvements. However, the heightened level of takeover activity during their sample period opens the possibility that the performance changes are not solely related to turnover.

Huson et al. (2004) extend the evidence on the outcome of CEO turnover in several ways. First, they report evidence from a large sample of 1,344 turnovers of top executives, including 215 forced turnovers. Second, their sample period is much longer than that in the Denis and Denis (1995) study. Huson et al. study turnovers during the 25-year period form 1971 to 1995. Third, Huson et al. provide evidence on the relation between post-turnover performance and firm-level takeover activity, institutional shareholdings, board composition, successor origin, and other public information available at the time of the turnover.

Like Denis and Denis (1995), Huson et al. (2004) examine changes in the OROA over the period from one year before the turnover to three years after the turnover (–1, +3). However, there are two key differences in their analysis. First, in addition to adjusting firm performance to control for industry effects, Huson et al. employ the performance-based control group matching method suggested in Barber and Lyon (1996). This matching method controls for potential mean reversion in the accounting measures of performance. Second, because some firms do not survive after turnover, Huson et al. use econometric techniques to control for survival bias.

Exhibit 17.2 presents plots of industry-adjusted OROA around CEO turnover from the Huson et al. (2004) sample. It summarizes their main findings on performance surrounding CEO turnover. The figure presents the median industry-adjusted OROA for their entire sample of turnovers and for subsamples partitioned by whether the turnover is forced or voluntary. The plots in this figure show the familiar pattern of deteriorating operating performance preceding forced turnover and no evidence of poor performance prior to voluntary turnover. Moreover, the figure shows substantial performance improvements following forced turnover.

Following forced turnover, the average changes in industry- and control group–adjusted OROA for the period (–1, +3) are 1.1 and 1.3 percentage points, respectively. Both are statistically significant. Huson et al. (2004) do not observe evidence of significant changes in industry-adjusted OROA after voluntary turnover, but do observe a statistically significant increase in the average control group–adjusted OROA of 0.9 percentage points.

Huson et al. (2004) also examine time series and cross-sectional variation in turnover-related performance changes. The time series analysis is motivated in part by their finding only modest increases in industry-adjusted OROA when compared with the evidence reported in Denis and Denis (1995). Huson et al. separate out all turnovers in their sample that occurred during the 1985 through 1988 period examined by Denis and Denis and compare evidence from this subsample to that from the turnovers in other years. They find that changes in industry-adjusted OROA are higher during the 1985 through 1988 subperiod than in the other years

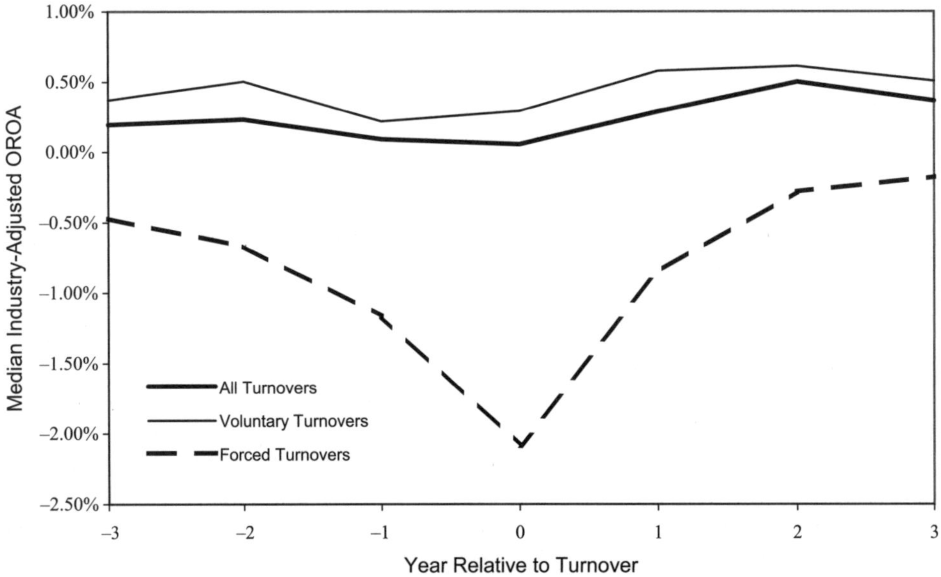

Exhibit 17.2 Median Industry-Adjusted Operating Return on Assets (OROA) around CEO Turnover
Source: Huson et al. (2004), Figure 2.

during the Huson et al. sample period. This suggests that the overall changes in industry-adjusted performance reported in Denis and Denis are unique to that period. Huson et al. note that while both industry- and control group–adjusted changes in OROA are larger in the 1985 through 1988 subperiod, their overall results are not driven by this subperiod.

Huson et al. (2004) also present evidence that performance changes following turnover are especially large during the second half of their sample period (1983 through 1994). In fact, they find no evidence of performance improvements during the first half of their sample period. They suggest that this difference might be related to a change in the nature of turnover decisions during the second half of the sample, which reflected contemporaneous changes in the characteristics of governance mechanisms, such as board composition and institutional ownership.

To provide evidence for this explanation, Huson et al. (2004) examine the cross-sectional determinants of performance changes following turnover. In univariate tests comparing performance changes across groups stratified on the basis of governance characteristics, they find that raw and industry-adjusted OROA are significantly higher for firms with outsider-dominated boards. Voluntary turnovers in their sample drive these results. They observe similar results when sorting firms into groups on the basis of pre-turnover exposure to corporate control activity and the origin of the successor. Firms subject to takeover pressure before the turnover and firms appointing outside successors have significantly higher raw and industry-adjusted changes in OROA. For the forced turnovers in the sample, the univariate comparisons only show evidence that the presence of institutional shareholders affects post-turnover performance. Overall, the univariate analysis provides relatively weak evidence that governance characteristics influence post-turnover performance changes.

Multivariate analysis of post-turnover performance changes yields similar results. In tests that control for changes in industry performance, Huson et al. (2004) find that post-turnover performance is higher at firms with outsider-dominated boards and at firms with higher levels of institutional ownership. When they include changes in the performance of control group firms in the analysis, only the fractional shareholdings of institutional investors is positively related to changes in performance following turnover.

As noted earlier, Huson et al. (2004) detect larger changes in performance following turnovers in the second half of their sample period than in the first half. Because changes in the effectiveness of governance mechanisms over time might have caused this difference, Huson et al. examine whether the relations between performance changes around turnovers and governance characteristics vary through time. Huson et al. find that the positive effect of institutional ownership on performance changes is constant over the sample period. They also observe that the role of outsider-dominated boards changed over the sample period. In the last six years of their sample period, firms with outsider-dominated boards have larger performance improvements following turnover than firms with outsider-dominated boards in earlier periods.

The multivariate analysis also reveals a strong positive relation between the announcement-period abnormal stock return and subsequent changes in operating performance. This result supports the idea that the abnormal return observed at the announcement reflects the expectation by investors that the turnover will affect operating performance. The positive and significant relation between announcement period returns and post-turnover performance changes is observed in regressions that control for governance characteristics and other variables that financial theory predicts will affect firm performance. This suggests that investors use information beyond that contained in those variables to forecast post-turnover performance changes.

Evidence of Post-Turnover Restructuring

The previously discussed significant improvements in operating performance following turnover raise the question of how the real activities within firms change following management turnover. Several studies provide evidence on this question. Huson et al. (2004) study changes in employee productivity while both Denis and Denis (1995) and Huson et al. examine post-turnover restructuring activity as measured by changes in total assets; property, plant, and equipment; capital expenditures; and employment. In addition, Denis and Denis as well as Weisbach (1995) examine publicly announced restructuring activity during the two years following turnover and the impact of turnover on divestiture decisions, respectively.

Huson et al. (2004) find evidence of increased productivity following turnover. Median industry- and control group–adjusted measures of sales per employee increase by 3.58 percent and 2.31 percent, respectively, following voluntary turnover. The corresponding increases following forced turnover, at 7.35 percent and 10.40 percent respectively, are significantly larger. The authors document similar results for the percentage increase in operating income per employee. This evidence suggests that part of the improved performance following turnover comes from improved operating efficiencies.

Both Denis and Denis (1995) and Huson et al. (2004) find that the book value of assets at firms experiencing top-management turnover grows more slowly than the book value of assets at their industry peers. This is true following both forced and voluntary turnover. Over the period from one year before to three years after the turnover, Denis and Denis report a median industry-adjusted percentage change in book assets of –29 percent following forced turnovers and –6 percent following voluntary turnovers. Huson et al. report similar declines of –29 percent and –7 percent and note that the difference is statistically significant.

The slower growth in the value of book assets following turnover appears to be related to reductions in capital expenditures. Denis and Denis (1995) report a median industry-adjusted percentage change in capital expenditures of –31 percent over the three-year period following forced turnovers. While this change is not statistically significant, Huson et al. (2004) report statistically significant median industry-adjusted changes in capital expenditures of –17 percent and –5 percent in the three years following forced and voluntary turnover, respectively.

The evidence also indicates that, relative to their industry peers, firms experiencing top-management turnover tend to reduce the number of employees during the ensuing three years. Denis and Denis (1995) find the median industry-adjusted percent change in employment is –33 percent following forced turnover and –11 percent following voluntary turnover. The corresponding values reported by Huson et al. (2004) are –21 percent and –4 percent, respectively. The evidence indicates a tendency for significant downsizing following turnover.

Denis and Denis (1995) augment their analysis of balance sheet data with evidence of restructuring activities from the *Wall Street Journal*. They collect all announcements of restructuring activity for the year of and two years following each turnover in their sample. An analysis of these announcements indicates that 59 percent of the firms experiencing forced turnover engage in asset sales following the turnover. The corresponding number after voluntary turnovers is 56 percent. The similar incidence of asset sales, combined with the evidence of greater reductions in the book value of assets following forced turnover, suggests that the asset sales following forced turnover are larger, or that firms experiencing voluntary turnover engage in more acquisition activity. Denis and Denis provide evidence of the latter. They report that the incidence of announced acquisitions and joint ventures is greater following voluntary turnover (75 percent of firms) than following forced turnover (32 percent of firms). While firms shed assets following forced turnover, they tend to shuffle assets more following voluntary turnover.

Weisbach (1995) provides more detailed evidence on the impact of management turnover on divestiture activity. He begins with a sample of 270 acquisitions that have a value of at least $100 million, in 1982 dollars. These acquisitions were made by 200 firms over the 1971 to 1982 period. He then identifies the CEO who made each of the acquisitions and examines what happens to the acquired asset when the acquiring CEO leaves office. Weisbach reports that the probability of a firm divesting a poorly performing acquisition rises following the departure of the CEO who was responsible for the acquisition. He estimates the probability that a firm divests an unsuccessful acquisition in nonturnover years to be 3.6 percent. Weisbach's estimate of this probability increases to 13.7 percent in turnover years, a statistically significant difference from the percentage in nonturnover years. Interestingly, Weisbach finds that both forced departures and voluntary retirements increase the probability of divesting poorly performing acquisitions. He suggests that turnover, both forced and voluntary, is part of an error-correction process that provides firms with the opportunity to correct managerial mistakes. This suggests that part of the performance change observed following turnover stems from restructuring activities.

Post-Turnover Stock Returns

Huson et al. (2004) present evidence that the abnormal stock returns around turnover announcements capture expectations about performance improvements following turnover. Denis and Denis (1995) suggest that the announcement returns seem small relative to the magnitude of the realized performance changes. One possible explanation for this is the mixed-signal problem discussed earlier. The negative *information effect* might offset the positive *real effect* attributable to expected performance improvements. This would result in announcement returns that seem small relative to the realized performance improvements. Another possible explanation is that the market does not fully anticipate the magnitude of the post-turnover performance changes. To the extent that the market systematically underestimates post-turnover performance, the expectation would be to observe significantly positive abnormal returns following turnover.

Denis and Denis (1995) examine cumulative market-adjusted returns over the two-year period following forced and voluntary turnover. Over the first six months following forced turnover, they find significant average market-adjusted returns of –6.1 percent. In addition, they find no evidence of abnormal market-adjusted returns following voluntary turnovers that are not associated with post-turnover control activity. None of their evidence is consistent with the market systematically underestimating the magnitude of performance changes.

Huson et al. (2004) also examine post-turnover stock performance using a different methodology and find similar evidence. They measure abnormal returns using the calendar-time portfolio techniques advocated by Mitchell and Stafford (2000) and control for the market as well as the size and market book factors. Huson et al. find no evidence of post-turnover abnormal market returns.

The absence of abnormal stock returns following turnover suggests that investors do not fail to fully incorporate anticipated performance improvements in stock prices. Rather, the announcement returns reflect an unbiased assessment of the performance change that is offset by confounding information revealed by the turnover announcement.

While management turnover does not appear to be followed by long-term abnormal returns, there is evidence that it is followed by increased volatility of stock returns. As previously discussed, turnover is associated with changes in productivity, the value of book assets, the composition of assets, and total employment. Uncertainty related to the magnitude and effectiveness of these changes appears to increase the volatility of returns.

Clayton, Hartzell, and Rosenberg (2005) suggest two possible ways that turnover might increase return volatility. The first has to do with strategy changes following turnover. They posit that volatility will increase more when there is a greater likelihood that the turnover will result in large changes in a firm's strategy.

Stock return volatility under this argument is related to uncertainty about the nature of the new strategy and its range of outcomes. Clayton et al. maintain that strategy shifts and therefore volatility increases will be larger for forced turnovers.

Clayton et al. (2005) also maintain that turnover might increase volatility because of the uncertainty about the ability of the successor. They suggest that return volatility will increase as investors learn about the ability of the new manager and capitalize revised expectations in the stock price. The authors argue that there will be greater uncertainty and more learning about the ability of outside successors.

Clayton et al. (2005) use a sample of 872 CEO turnovers that took place during 1979 to 1995 to test their predictions. In their analysis, they calculate the annualized standard deviation of returns over days –500 to –251, relative to the turnover announcement, and compare it to the annualized standard deviation of returns over days +1 to +500.

For their entire sample, Clayton et al. (2005) report a statistically significant increase in return volatility of 1.8 percentage points. Furthermore, volatility increases following both forced and voluntary turnovers and for both inside and outside successions. Consistent with their predictions, they observe the largest volatility increases after forced turnover (23 percent) followed by voluntary turnover with outside successors (14 percent). They find that stock return volatility decreases over time, but do observe significantly higher volatility for as many as three years after the turnover. The authors suggest these volatility changes, and therefore management turnover, might exacerbate agency relationships in the firm such as those between stockholders and bondholders.

SUMMARY AND CONCLUSIONS

Overall, the evidence on the effects of management turnover on firm performance suggests that management turnover can affect performance, but that the magnitude of this effect varies with the circumstances surrounding the turnover. Examples of these circumstances include whether the turnover is forced or voluntary, the characteristics of the new manager such as whether the manager is an insider or an outsider, and the opportunities for value-enhancing change. The ultimate effect of a turnover on firm performance depends on the extent to which the ability of the new manager exceeds the ability of the old manager, as well as the opportunities that are available for the new manager to make changes in firm activities that improve value. These opportunities depend on the condition of the firm at the time of the turnover as well as the ability of the board to identify managers of high ability, and the board's willingness to support changes in the real activities of the business.

The evidence from stock price reactions to turnover announcements, pre- versus post-turnover operating performance, and changes in real activities around turnover suggests that boards of directors do, on average, make turnover decisions that benefit stockholders. This appears to have been particularly true after the mid-1980s and at firms with outsider-dominated boards. Furthermore, there is evidence that institutional investors also influence turnover decisions in ways that benefit stockholders.

The effects of management turnover on firm performance have been the subject of academic research for 50 years. Yet relatively little direct evidence exists in the accounting and finance literatures on the magnitude of the changes that can be directly attributed to a new CEO, as opposed to the combined influence of the board and the top-management team, or on the real activities that lead to performance improvements. The evidence from Weisbach (1995), Denis and Denis (1995), and Huson et al. (2004) provides some insight on changes in real activities but is far from definitive. Furthermore, ongoing changes in corporate governance and turnover characteristics, such as the increase in institutional stockholder activism and the large increase in the incidence of forced turnover in recent years, are also likely to affect the impact of turnover on firm performance. These are just a few of the many fertile avenues for future research in this area.

DISCUSSION QUESTIONS

1. Why might a board replace a CEO even if it does not expect to find a replacement of higher quality? What are the implications of this for observed changes in firm performance?
2. Why might the results of event studies of the announcement of CEO turnover provide inconclusive or even misleading evidence about the impact of CEO turnover on firm performance? Do event studies of turnover announcements provide useful information about the effect of turnover on performance?
3. What are the costs and benefits of choosing a successor from outside the firm? Are external hires likely to be more prevalent after forced or voluntary turnovers?
4. What evidence indicates that successor choice is an important determinant of performance improvements associated with turnover?

REFERENCES

Barber, Brad M., and John D. Lyon. 1996. Detecting abnormal performance: The empirical power and specification of test statistics. *Journal of Financial Economics* 41 (3): 359–399.

Bonnier, Karl-Adam, and Robert F. Bruner. 1989. An analysis of the stock price reaction to management change in distressed firms. *Journal of Accounting and Economics* 11 (1): 95–106.

Borokhovich, Kenneth A., Robert Parrino, and Teresa Trapani. 1996. Outside directors and CEO selection. *Journal of Financial and Quantitative Analysis* 31 (3): 337–355.

Brady, Gene F., and Donald L. Helmich. 1982. The hospital administrator and organizational change: Do we recruit from the outside? *Hospital and Health Services Administration* 27 (1): 53–62.

Brown, M. Craig. 1982. Administrative succession and organizational performance: The succession effect. *Administrative Science Quarterly* 27 (1): 1–16.

Carlson, Richard O. 1961. Succession and performance among school superintendents. *Administrative Science Quarterly* 6 (2): 210–27.

Carroll, Glenn R. 1984. Dynamics of publisher succession in newspaper organizations. *Administrative Science Quarterly* 29 (1): 93–113.

Chan, William. 1996. External recruitment versus internal promotion. *Journal of Labor Economics* 14 (4): 555–570.

Chung, Kae H., Michael H. Lubatkin, Ronald C. Rogers, and James E. Owers. 1987. Do insiders make better CEOs than outsiders? *Academy of Management Executive* 1 (3): 323–329.

Clayton, Matthew C., Jay C. Hartzell, and Joshua Rosenberg. 2005. The impact of CEO turnover on equity volatility. *Journal of Business* 78 (5): 1779–1808.

Coughlan, Anne T., and Ronald M. Schmidt. 1985. Executive compensation, management turnover, and firm performance: An empirical investigation. *Journal of Accounting and Economics* 7 (1–3): 43–66.

Dalton, Dan R., and Idalene F. Kesner. 1985. Organizational performance as an antecedent of inside/outside chief executive succession: An empirical assessment. *Academy of Management Journal* 28 (4): 749–762.

Denis, David J., and Diane K. Denis. 1995. Firm performance changes following top management dismissals. *Journal of Finance* 50 (4): 1029–1057.

Fee, C. Edward, and Charles J. Hadlock. 2004. Management turnover across the corporate hierarchy. *Journal of Accounting and Economics* 37 (1): 3–38.

Furtado, Eugene P. H., and Vijay Karan. 1990. Causes, consequences, and shareholder wealth effects of management turnover: A review of the empirical evidence. *Financial Management* 19 (2) (Summer): 60–75.

Gamson, William A., and Norman A. Scotch. 1964. Scapegoating in baseball. *American Journal of Sociology* 70 (1): 69–72.

Grusky, Oscar. 1963. Managerial succession and organizational effectiveness. *American Journal of Sociology* 69 (1): 21–31.

———. 1964. Reply to "Scapegoating in baseball." *American Journal of Sociology* 70 (1): 72–76.

———. 1969. Succession with an ally. *Administrative Science Quarterly* 14 (2): 155–70.

Guest, Robert H. 1962. Managerial succession in complex organizations. *American Journal of Sociology* 68 (1): 47–54.

Helmich, Donald L. 1975. Corporate succession: An examination. *Academy of Management Journal* 18 (3): 429–41.

Helmich, Donald L., and Warren B. Brown. 1972. Successor type and organizational change in the corporate enterprise. *Administrative Science Quarterly* 17 (3): 371–81.

Holmstrom, Bengt. 1979. Moral hazard and observability. *Bell Journal of Economics* 10 (1): 74–91.

Hotchkiss, Edith. S. 1995. Postbankruptcy performance and management turnover. *Journal of Finance* 50 (1): 3–21.

Huson, Mark R., Paul H. Malatesta, and Robert Parrino. 2004. Managerial succession and firm performance. *Journal of Financial Economics* 74 (2): 237–275.

Huson, Mark R., Robert Parrino, and Laura T. Starks. 2001. Internal monitoring mechanisms and CEO turnover: A long term perspective. *Journal of Finance* 56 (6): 2265–2297.

Johnson, W. Bruce, Robert P. Magee, Nandu J. Nagarajan, and Harry A. Newman. 1985. An analysis of the stock price reaction to sudden executive deaths: Implications for the managerial labor market. *Journal of Accounting and Economics* 7 (1–3): 151–174.

Kang, Jung-Koo, and Anil Shivdasani. 1995. Firm performance, corporate governance, and top executive turnover in Japan. *Journal of Financial Economics* 38 (1): 29–58.

Kesner, Idalene F., and Terrence C. Sebora. 1994. Executive succession: Past, present and future. *Journal of Management* 20 (2): 327–72.

Khanna, Naveen, and Annette B. Poulsen. 1995. Managers of financially distressed firms: Villains or scapegoats. *Journal of Finance* 50 (3): 919–940.

Kotin, Joel, and Myron R. Sharaf. 1967. Management succession and administrative style. *Psychiatry* 30 (3): 237–248.

Lewin, Arie, and Carl Wolf. 1974. When the CEO must go. *Advanced Management Journal* 39 (3): 59–62.

Louis, Meryl R. 1980. Career transitions: Varieties and commonalities. *Academy of Management Review* 5 (3): 329–340.
Lubatkin, Michael H., Kae H. Chung, Ronald C. Rogers, and James E. Owers. 1989. Stockholder reactions to CEO changes in large corporations. *Academy of Management Journal* 32 (1): 47–68.
Mirlees, James. A. 1976. The optimal structure of incentives and authority within an organization. *Bell Journal of Economics* 7 (1): 105–131.
Mitchell, Mark, L., and Kenneth Lehn. 1990. Do bad bidders become good targets? *Journal of Political Economy* 98 (2): 372–398.
Mitchell, Mark L., and Erik Stafford. 2000. Managerial decisions and long-term stock price performance. *Journal of Business* 73 (3): 287–329.
Perez-Gonzalez, Francisco. 2006. Inherited control and firm performance. *American Economic Review* 96 (5): 1559–1588.
Pfeffer, Jeffrey, and Alison Davis-Blake. 1986. Administrative succession and organizational performance: How administrator experience mediates the succession effect. *Academy of Management Journal* 29 (1): 72–83.
Reinganum, Marc R. 1985. The effect of executive succession on stockholder wealth. *Administrative Science Quarterly* 30 (1): 46–60.
Taylor, Lucian A. 2008. Why are CEOs rarely fired? Evidence from structural estimation. Working paper. The Wharton School, University of Pennsylvania.
Tushman, Michael L., Beverly Virany, and Elaine Romanelli. 1985. Executive succession, strategic reorientations, and organizational evolution: The minicomputer industry as a case in point. *Technology in Society* 7 (2–3): 297–313.
Vancil, Richard F. 1987. *Passing the baton: Managing the process of CEO succession.* Cambridge, Massachusetts: Harvard Business School Press.
Warner, Jerold B., Ross L. Watts, and Karen H. Wruck. 1988. Stock prices and top management changes. *Journal of Financial Economics* 20 (1–2): 461–492.
Weisbach, Michael S. 1988. Outside directors and CEO turnover. *Journal of Financial Economics* 20 (1–2): 431–460.
———. 1995. CEO turnover and the firm's investment decisions. *Journal of Financial Economics* 37 (2): 159–188.
Zald, Mayer N. 1965. Who shall rule? A political analysis of succession in a large welfare organization. *Pacific Sociological Review* 8 (1): 52–60.

ABOUT THE AUTHORS

Mark R. Huson is the Pocklington Professor of Private Enterprise and associate professor of finance in the Department of Finance and Management Science in the School of Business, University of Alberta. Professor Huson joined the finance faculty at the University of Alberta School of Business in 1993. His research includes work on executive compensation, corporate governance, restructuring, financial reporting, and capital formation. Professor Huson has published his research in top finance and accounting journals and has presented it at seminars and conferences around the world. His research has been the subject of articles in the *Wall Street Journal* and *Chief Executive* magazine. Professor Huson is a co-founder of the Financial Research Association. In addition to the University of Alberta, he has been on the faculties of the University of Texas at Austin and the Richard Ivey School at the University of Western Ontario. Professor Huson holds a BS in finance from Canisius College as well as an MS in applied economics and PhD in finance from the University of Rochester.

Robert Parrino is the Lamar Savings Centennial Professor of Finance and Founding Director of the Hicks, Muse, Tate & Furst Center for Private Equity Finance in the Department of Finance, McCombs School of Business, University of Texas at Austin. A member of the finance faculty at the McCombs School of Business at the University of Texas at Austin since 1992, Professor Parrino's research includes work on corporate governance, financial policies, restructuring, and private equity markets. His research has been published in top finance journals and he has received a number of research awards. Professor Parrino is co-founder of the Financial Research Association and the Forum on Corporate Finance. In addition to the University of Texas, he has been on the faculty at the University of Chicago and IMADEC University in Vienna. Professor Parrino holds a BS in chemical engineering from Lehigh University, an MBA degree from the College of William and Mary, and MS and PhD degrees in applied economics and finance, respectively, from the University of Rochester.

PART THREE

External Governance

Nonexecutive Shareholders

Nonequity Stakeholders

Proxy Contests and Markets

Accounting, Legal, and Regulatory Intervention

CHAPTER 18

Corporate Monitoring by Blockholders

ISABELLE DHERMENT-FÉRÈRE
Assistant Professor of Finance, University of South-Toulon-Var

LUC RENNEBOOG
Professor of Corporate Finance, Tilburg University and European Corporate Governance Institute

INTRODUCTION

The purpose of this chapter is to investigate whether the role and effectiveness of blockholder monitoring as a corporate governance mechanism differ among countries. Specifically, the chapter examines control concentration and its nature as a mechanism to discipline poorly performing companies. The chapter also considers the role of the market in share blocks, the internal organization of boards of directors, and creditor monitoring as these alternative mechanisms may serve as substitutes to strong control concentration.

The generic classification of corporate governance regimes is the dichotomy of the market-oriented Anglo-American system and the blockholder-oriented system of Continental Europe and Japan. A different legal fundament underpins each of these regimes: common versus civil law. The United Kingdom serves as a representative country for the market-oriented system. Several features characterize this country's governance system including strong shareholder and creditor legal protection, a judicial system with efficient enforcement of legal rights in courts, and strong accounting standards (La Porta, Lopez-de-Silanes, Shleifer, and Vishny 2000).

With regard to the blockholder system, a distinction is made between corporate governance regimes based on German and French civil law. The analysis shows that the German system differs from the French system in many ways, such as the nature of ownership (type of blockholders), the use of bank finance, and the structure of the board of directors. Many differences exist even in countries belonging to the same (sub)type of corporate governance regime.

In terms of governance, Belgian firms are similar to French firms because of legal origin, unitary board structure, violation of the one-share-one-vote principle (arising from the widespread use of ownership pyramids), and the quality of accounting standards. Still, board structure differs in Belgium, as do the legal mechanisms to protect the rights of minority shareholders. Creditors in Belgium have better legal protection than in France, and the overall regulatory enforcement by the judicial system is better in Belgium than in France. Consequently, the chapter also investigates whether corporate governance differs among countries whose governance mechanisms are prima facia very similar. Henceforth, the chapter compares the corporate governance mechanisms of these four countries: Germany, France, Belgium, and the United Kingdom.

Because Continental European ownership structures are often complex and pyramidal, the chapter gives consideration to both direct and indirect control and analyzes whether control leverage using pyramidal structures dilutes corporate monitoring by blockholders. In addition, the chapter provides an analysis of the dynamics of ownership by studying whether a market for share blocks is triggered by poor corporate performance. If this is the case, such a market for share blocks can be considered as a (partial) market for control. Denis and Kruse (2000) find that even when merger and acquisition (M&A) activity slows, managerial disciplining does not decrease. The chapter also investigates the role of creditor monitoring and analyzes whether specific board compositions provide beneficial monitoring. Finally, the chapter examines which corporate governance mechanisms, if any, are responsible for managerial disciplining by country, where there is redundancy, and whether some forms consistently dominate others.

The remainder of this chapter has the following organization. The next section formulates the conjectures and relates these to the literature, followed by a presentation of the sample selection, data sources, and methodology. The subsequent two sections provide the stylized facts and a discussion of the main results of the multicountry analysis. The final section provides a summary and conclusions.

CONJECTURES AND RELATED LITERATURE

Corporate performance is a noisy measure of managerial performance, but also reflects the quality of monitoring by outside mechanisms such as blockholders or creditors and of internal corporate governance devices such as the board of directors. This chapter distinguishes between two types of directors and follows the European classification: executive directors, who are often called officers in the United States; and nonexecutive directors, who are often called directors in the United States. Because a firm usually does not disclose the outcome of board meetings and of shareholder-management convocations, the chapter necessarily focuses on visible corporate governance actions, namely, the managerial disciplining process in the wake of poor performance. Share price returns and accounting performance largely reflect managerial achievements, but both performance yardsticks encounter measurement problems when considering managerial quality. First, the correlation between performance-related management dismissal and past share price performance may be weaker than expected because past share prices may already have anticipated the beneficial impact of removing poorly performing management and replacing it with more competent successors. Second, incumbent management can temporarily manipulate accounting performance by income smoothing and the choice of accounting policies. Hence, when studying whether management is held responsible for poor performance, relating managerial turnover to various performance measures such as share price returns, operating and net accounting earnings, and changes in dividend policy is important.

Blockholder Monitoring

Two aspects of ownership are important in relation to corporate monitoring. First, control concentration is important because monitoring is only cost effective if a single party becomes large enough to internalize the costs of corporate control. Such costs are borne by the monitoring shareholders individually, but the financial benefits resulting from corporate governance actions are only reaped in proportion to their cash flow rights (Grossman and Hart 1988). Hence, small shareholders benefit when they shirk the effort to affect corporate actions and free-ride on the efforts of larger shareholders. Second, the nature of ownership concentration may also influence the degree of corporate control. This issue can be deduced from the fact that blocks are usually sold at a premium, suggesting the presence of private information or benefits, and from the fact that such gains vary across investors or ownership categories. The source of the control premium is the additional compensation and perquisites that the controlling security holders can accord themselves (Dyck and Zingales 2004). Evidence from the United States supports the fact that different classes of owners have different abilities to extract control rents (Barclay and Holderness 1991).

The reason the nature of ownership and control may be correlated to board restructuring depends upon the resources that blockholders have at their disposition to monitor and upon their private benefits of control. For example, corporate blockholders may acquire voting rights in order to hold a board seat at a supplier or customer company. Thus, the blockholder may influence and/or capitalize on the target firm's strategic decisions. Private benefits are potentially numerous for holding companies. For example, the cost of capital of the group members may be reduced if the holding company creates an internal market for funds or if tax deductions are captured by intercompany transfers. Likewise, a holding company may concentrate profit in wholly owned subsidiaries (where it owns 100 percent of the cash flow rights) by implementing a specific transfer pricing policy between subsidiaries with and without minority shareholders. Various empirical papers cast doubt on the governance role of such holding companies in Continental Europe. For example, Banerjee, Leleux, and Vermaelen (1997) examine France; Renneboog (2000) discusses Belgium; Volpin (2002) focuses on Italy; Franks and Mayer (2001) investigate Germany; and Johnson, La Porta, Lopez-de-Silanes, and Shleifer (2000) study Central Europe.

In contrast to other outside shareholders, little corporate monitoring is expected from institutional investors. Goergen and Renneboog (2001) report that UK institutions are passive shareholders because of the following: (1) They lack the resources to be involved in corporate strategies of all their portfolio companies; (2) their share stakes in individual firms are frequently modest in size; and (3) due to insider trading regulation, they abstain from collecting private information so as not to immobilize the liquidity of their portfolios. Finally, whereas nonexecutive-director blockholders should discipline poorly performing management, executive directors owning large blocks may be able to impede executive board restructuring. This group extracts different types of private benefits including cash and option-based compensation and possibly nonpecuniary benefits of being an executive director.

Thus, conjecture 1 states the following:

1a. In the wake of poor performance, the presence of large outside blockholders (corporations, holding companies, as well as families and individuals not related to a director) leads to higher executive board turnover.
1b. Executive directors controlling a high concentration of voting rights resist managerial disciplining.
1c. Conflicts of interest dissuade financial institutions to take disciplinary corporate control actions.

Given that the distribution of blockholdings across investor categories varies across Germany, France, Belgium, and the United Kingdom, the relation between blockholdings by type of owner and managerial disciplining may differ. As the most important shareholder categories in the United Kingdom are institutional investors and directors, there is unlikely to be clear evidence of shareholder monitoring in the United Kingdom. A priori, the predominance of large outside shareholders in France, Belgium, and Germany may lead to increased shareholder monitoring. Still, monitoring activity may be influenced by the fact that holding companies are more numerous in both Belgium and France than in Germany. If the studies cited earlier focusing on France and Belgium are correct, there should be less monitoring activity in these countries than in Germany. Furthermore, the notion that the German universal banks can exercise substantial control via their direct and indirect (via the *Depotstimmrecht*) voting stakes (Gorton and Schmid 2000) may also lead to more intensive managerial disciplining.

As Germany, France, Belgium, and most other Continental European countries widely use ownership pyramids or cascades for reasons of control leverage, true control is not found at the direct ownership tier (Faccio and Lang 2002; Faccio, Lang, and Young 2010). Hence, for each direct shareholding, constructing the ownership pyramid until reaching the ultimate shareholder (a family, individual, widely held company, or institutional investor) is important. Consequently, each direct share block can be classified in terms of who ultimately controls that particular block (see the later section "Data and Methodology" for the classification rules).

Because ultimate shareholders and not direct or intermediate investors make corporate governance decisions, the relation between turnover and concentration of voting rights held (directly or indirectly) by ultimate blockholders may be stronger than between turnover and direct share blocks. This qualifies conjecture 1 for Continental European countries only because pyramidal ownership structures are rare in the United Kingdom. Franks, Mayer, and Rossi (2009) provide more details and describe the historical evolution of ownership concentration.

The Market for Share Blocks

Poor corporate performance results, to a large extent, from poor managerial performance. Still, poor performance also reflects ineffective monitoring and control. Therefore, a market in blocks may be triggered by corporate underperformance such that high-quality monitors replace low-quality monitors. These blockholders are expected to discipline poorly performing management.

Bolton and von Thadden (1998) argue that the degree of voting right concentration acts as a commitment device to delegate a certain degree of authority from shareholders to management. They show that the use of equity implements state-contingent control. In states of the world with decreasing corporate profitability, close monitoring resulting from strong ownership concentration is desirable. In other states of the world, close monitoring may not be optimal as this may reduce managerial discretion and hence management's effort.

For the United States, Bethel, Liebeskind, and Opler (1998) find that activist purchases take place in poorly performing, diversified U.S. firms. Likewise, Jenkinson and Ljungqvist (2001) show that the acquisitions of important (hostile) share stakes are a substitute for the takeover market in Germany. Thus, poor performance gives rise to changes in the ownership structure which are, in turn, associated with higher managerial turnover (conjecture 2). Given the prevalence of nonfinancial outside shareholders in Continental Europe, the expectation is that a market of share blocks induced by corporate governance considerations is more likely to arise in Continental Europe than in the United Kingdom.

Creditor Monitoring

Creditor intervention is expected when the probability of defaulting on debt covenants increases or when the company needs to refinance. The choice of gearing (financial leverage) can be considered as a bonding mechanism for management. However, both total leverage and the composition of the debt portfolio are important. In contrast to the United Kingdom, the loans contracted by German firms are more concentrated with one universal bank, called the *Hausbank* (House bank), with which the firm has a long-term lending relationship (Köke 2004). This house bank may have substantial impact. It may hold a direct equity stake in a firm, obtain indirect voting power via the *Depotstimmrecht*, occupy a seat on the supervisory board, and provide the bulk of the bank loans. This is why the German corporate governance system is often called a *bank-oriented* system. High leverage or low interest coverage intensifies creditor monitoring and managerial disciplining (conjecture 3). This is more so for Germany than for Belgium, France, and the United Kingdom, given the important role of the Hausbanken in the former country.

Boards of Directors

The structure of the board should minimize the potential conflicts of interest among decision makers and residual risk bearers. Board composition could reduce the transaction or agency costs associated with the separation of management and ownership. An important task of the nonexecutive directors of a one-tier board and of a supervisory board is that of supervision. Nonexecutive directors have strong incentives to monitor for the following reasons. First, they are legally bound due to their fiduciary duty to represent large shareholders. From the perspective of fiduciary duties, nonexecutive blockholders in the United Kingdom are expected to be better monitors because these duties are wider and more developed than on the continent (Baums 2000). In the Continental European governance systems, most nonexecutives are appointed by and represent the dominant blockholders.

Second, nonexecutives have incentives arising from human capital considerations to develop reputations as decision control experts. Nonexecutive directors face an external labor market that provides some form of disciplining for passive leadership. Separating the roles of CEO and nonexecutive chairman can also strengthen the board's monitoring ability, as a nonexecutive chairman is more able to safeguard a higher degree of independence from management. Such recommendations have been formulated in the United Kingdom in the Combined Code of 1998 (consisting of the Cadbury Committee report of 1992, the Greenbury report of 1995, and the Hampel report of 1997), and in all the codes of good governance/corporate law in Continental Europe and the United States.

Consequently, the expectation is that the greater the proportion of nonexecutive directors, the higher the monitoring ability of the nonexecutive directors, which is reflected in increased executive turnover when performance is poor (conjecture 4). Whether nonexecutive directors are better monitors in Continental European governance regimes compared to the Anglophone system is an empirical matter. In the latter system, the fiduciary duties are more clearly and explicitly enshrined in corporate law, whereas in the former systems, nonexecutive directors may be incentivized by large blockholders whom they represent.

DATA AND METHODOLOGY

We first discuss the sample selection of our countries of interest and develop the empirical model. We subsequently discuss the main determinants of corporate monitoring (blockholders, the market for share blocks, creditors, and the board of directors).

Sample Selection and Data Sources

The sample consists of 361 German companies, representing almost all nonfinancial firms listed on the German stock exchanges. Financial companies (banks, insurance companies, and real estate) are excluded because their balance sheet data are not comparable with those of nonfinancial firms. The Belgian sample consists of all companies listed on the Brussels Stock Exchange, excluding the financial sector. The French sample consists of the 325 nonfinancial companies listed on the First Market of the Paris Stock Exchange. From all companies listed on the London Stock Exchange, a random sample of 250 nonfinancial companies is selected. All variables are, wherever possible, defined similarly and observations are chosen using comparable selection procedures. An assumption is that all managerial turnover is disciplinary unless the turnover is the result of age-related retirements (managerial age of at least 62 years), death, or illness (the so-called *natural turnover*).

German ownership, board structure, share price, and accounting information are collected from Hoppenstedt Guide of German Companies and the Capital Market Database. Belgian accounting and share data are collected from annual reports, the Central Depository of Balance Sheets, Datastream, the Brussels Stock Exchange, *Memento der Effecten*, and the Yearbook of Directors. French accounting, board structure, ownership, and share price data are from the DAFSA fiches, Fininfo, the *Statistiques Annuelles de la Société des Bourses Françaises* (SBF), and Banque de France. UK accounting and share price data are collected from Datastream and the London Share Price Database. Ownership and board data are from annual reports, Datastream, the *Financial Times*, and Nexus databases.

To determine the dominating ultimate blockholder requires using the following three rules. First, the *strong ownership rule* states that a chain of control is pursued to the next level if the shareholder being analyzed is owned with a share stake of 50 percent or more by a shareholder on the next level, while all other shareholders on the next level own less than 50 percent. Second, the *weak ownership rule* is used if rule 1 does not apply: A chain of control is pursued to the next level if the shareholder being analyzed is owned with a share stake of 25 percent or more by a shareholder on the next level, while all other shareholders on the next level own less than 25 percent. Finally, the *stop rule* is implemented if neither of the two previous rules applies; the chain of control is then not pursued any further. These rules guarantee that no more than one ultimate owner is identified for every

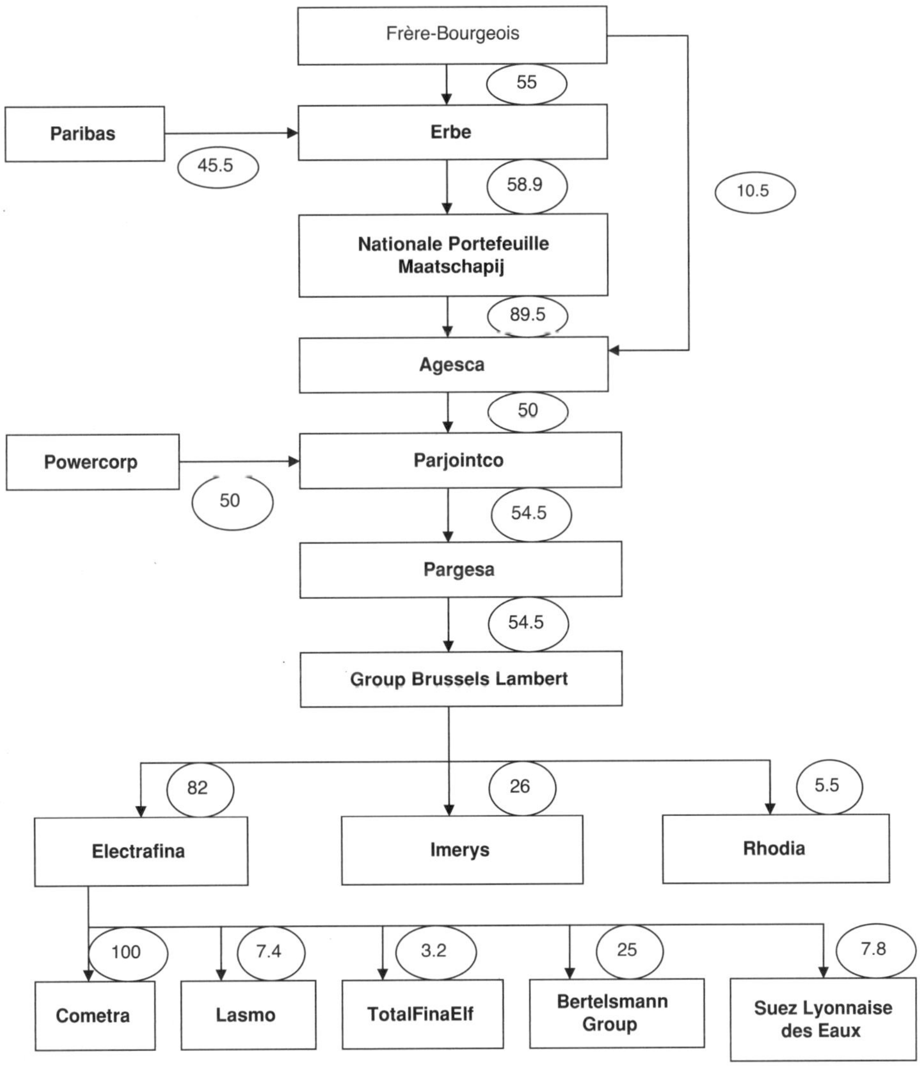

Exhibit 18.1 Ownership and Control Structure of the Group Brussels Lambert as of March 1, 2001
Source: Trends.

direct shareholder. If a shareholder has split his share stake in a particular company into several smaller stakes, these smaller stakes should be combined into a single block. After having identified all ultimate owners (for every direct share stake), the shareholder who ultimately controls the company can also be determined. When no shareholder fulfills these rules, the respective firm is considered widely held.

This criterion is illustrated with an example based on the (simplified) shareholding structure of the Belgian Group Brussels Lambert (GBL), as shown in Exhibit 18.1. Via the intermediate electricity holding Electrafina, GBL controls important share stakes in a Belgian-French energy holding company (TotalFinaElf), in a German media group (Bertelsmann), and in one of the largest French utilities (Suez). At the top of the pyramid, the Frère-Bourgeois family maintains absolute control via five intermediate-level holding companies, with a voting pact until 2017. The advantage of such an ownership structure is obvious. For example, Albert Frère controls a 25 percent block in the Bertelsmann Group but holds less than 0.88 percent of the cash flow rights. This study classifies the 25 percent stake in Bertelsmann not as a shareholding controlled by the utility Electrafina but as a block controlled by Albert Frère and hence belonging to the category "families or individuals, excluding directors."

Methodology and Variable Description

Four data panels are formed with eight years of data for Germany, six years for Belgium and the United Kingdom, and five years for France, with each firm-year representing a separate observation. The following relation is estimated for each country:

$$\begin{aligned}
\text{Turnover}_{i,t} &= \sum_{k=0}^{2} \beta_{c,k} \times \text{Perform}_{i,t-k} \\
&\quad \text{(Performance)} \\
&\quad + \sum_{l=1}^{4} \gamma_{c,l} \times \text{Block}_{i,l,t-1} + \sum_{l=1}^{4} \delta_{c,l} \times \text{Block}_{i,l,t-1} \times \text{Perform}_{i,l,t-1} \\
&\quad \text{(Ownership concentration, interaction)} \\
&\quad + \sum_{l=1}^{4} \pi_{c,l} \times \text{Purchase}_{i,l,t} + \sum_{l=1}^{4} \theta_{c,l} \times \text{Purchase}_{i,l,t} \times \text{Perform}_{i,l,t-1} \\
&\quad \text{(Market in share blocks, interaction)} \\
&\quad + \sum_{m=1}^{2} \phi_{c,m} \times \text{Debt}_{i,m,t-1} + \sum_{m=1}^{2} \eta_{c,m} \times \text{Debt}_{i,m,t-1} \times \text{Perform}_{i,m,t-1} \\
&\quad \text{(Control variables: Debt policy, interaction)} \\
&\quad + \sum_{n=1}^{2} \varphi_{c,n} \times \text{Board}_{i,n,t} + \sum_{n=1}^{2} \lambda_{c,n} \times \text{Board}_{i,n,t} \times \text{Perform}_{i,n,t-1} \\
&\quad \text{(Control variables: Board structure, interaction)}
\end{aligned}$$

$$+\theta_c \times \text{Size}_{i,t} + \sum_{p=1}^{86} \iota_p \times \text{Industry}_{i,t} + \sum_{q=1}^{7} \tau_q \times \text{Year}_{i,t} + \varepsilon_{i,t}$$

$$\text{(Control variables : Size, industry, and time)}$$

where

c = country (Belgium, France, Germany or the United Kingdom)
i = firm
t = year
k = lag of performance
l = class of owner
m = debt policy variable
n = board composition variable
p = country-specific industry
q = year

Other variables in this equation are defined as follows:

- *Turnover* stands for executive director turnover.
- *Perform* represents the performance variables measured by current and lagged (by one or two years) (1) ROA and (2) market-adjusted return. All accounting performance variables are corrected for their two-digit industry median by country.
- *Block* denotes control concentration by class of owner: (1) families and individuals, (2) financial institutions (banks, insurance companies, and investment and mutual funds), (3) industrial and commercial companies as well as industrial and financial holding companies, (4) government, (5) directors (and their families), and (6) the free-floating shares. Both the sum of the ownership and the percentage held by the largest blockholder (by category of owner) are collected. The direct shareholdings are reclassified according to the ultimate control criterion (discussed earlier).
- *Purchase* represents the acquisition of share blocks (in percentage) by old and new shareholders (combined), by category of owner.
- *Debt* denotes the debt structure: the ratio of long-term debt to total assets and interest coverage (EBIT/interest expenses). For Germany, the variable House bank debt/total debt is also used. This variable captures the bank debt granted by the large universal German banks or the so-called Hausbanken.
- *Board* stands for board size (for Germany only the number of the members of the management board) and board structure (the percentage of nonexecutive directors, for Germany). The number of directors in the *Aufsichtsrat* is divided by the combined number of directors in *Vorstand* and *Aufsichtsrat*.
- *Size* is the natural logarithm of total assets.

Tobit models are used because the dependent variable (turnover) is truncated at 0 and 1. All models include two-digit country-specific industry dummies and time dummies, which are not reported. Controlling for outliers involves winzorizing all performance variables at the 1 percent and 99 percent level. The models are also run with lagged ownership, debt, and board variables because managerial discipline may only take place after poor firm performance.

STYLIZED FACTS

Control concentration, board structure, and performance differ across countries, even across Germany, Belgium, and France, which belong to the same generic corporate governance system. This section highlights the main differences in corporate governance variables.

Blockholders

Total control concentration is remarkably different between Continental European countries and the United Kingdom. The combined blockholders (owning 5 percent of the voting equity or more) control two-thirds of the voting rights in French and German firms and more than 50 percent of the shares in Belgian firms (see Exhibit 18.2). In the United Kingdom, this sum is only 38 percent, even though the UK data overstate the relative ownership concentration as UK disclosure is based on a 3 percent threshold. The differences between the United Kingdom and the Continent are even more striking when considering the average largest share block. The main UK shareholder holds a share stake of about 15 percent whereas the dominant shareholder in Germany controls an absolute majority of voting rights

Exhibit 18.2 Control Concentration by Country

This table shows the average control concentration of all large share stakes for Germany, Belgium, France, and the United Kingdom by category of owner. Large share stakes are defined (in line with the local disclosure regulation) as 5 percent for France, Belgium, and Germany and 3 percent for the United Kingdom. *Sum* stands for the sum of the large share stakes by category of owner; *largest* represents the largest share stake by category. The data reflect the averages over the 1990s for Germany, Belgium, France, and the United Kingdom. The share stakes are classified by category of owner by using the ultimate control criterion. The number of observations is 2,377 for Germany, 727 for Belgium, 1,255 for France, and 1,071 for the United Kingdom.

Control Concentration by Category of Owner		Germany	Belgium	France	United Kingdom
Families and individuals	Largest	17.9	11.6	11.8	1.6
	Sum	33.0	12.1	20.6	2.4
Financial institutions	Largest	8.2	2.1	10.7	11.3
	Sum	8.9	5.1	14.8	18.4
Holding companies	Largest	2.4	12.9	12.9	—
	Sum	2.4	23.3	14.7	—
Nonfinancial firms	Largest	20.8	7.9	2.5	5.1
	Sum	21.6	9.1	3.3	5.8
State	Largest	1.9	2.4	9.8	0.1
	Sum	2.0	2.5	12.6	0.1
Directors	Largest	—	—	—	8.1
	Sum	—	—	—	11.2
Total control concentration	Sum	67.9	52.2	66.0	38.0

and his counterparts in Belgium and France control 35 percent and 45 percent, respectively. These data are in line with the information collected by the European Corporate Governance Institute (ECGI) and disclosed in Barca and Becht (2001).

Exhibit 18.2 also reveals that the nature of control concentration differs across the four countries. The most important shareholder category in Germany is families and individuals, with nonfinancial firm (industrial and commercial) a close second. The blockholders of these categories control in aggregate 33 percent and 22 percent of the voting rights. The average stake of German financial institutions is modest (9 percent), including banks controlling 7 percent (not shown). However, the proxy votes of shareholders depositing their shares with a bank may yield the banks substantially more voting power (Böhmer 2000). For Belgium, industrial firms and holding companies combined also control about one third of the voting rights; the other important class consists of families and individuals. The picture for France bears some resemblance to Germany with block-holding families controlling more than one-fifth of the voting rights. Expectedly, financial institutions hold, in aggregate, most of the share blocks in the United Kingdom, although the true ownership by institutions is substantially higher (by about three times) because many of their stakes are below the disclosure threshold of 3 percent. Directors are the second most important shareholder category with an average of 11.2 percent.

The Market for Share Blocks

Initiating a hostile raid on German, French, and Belgian firms is in most cases nearly futile because one party controls the majority of voting rights. Nevertheless, a market for share blocks exists in these countries. When studying the number of share blocks acquired by different classes of shareholders by quintile of performance (e.g., ROA), the results indicate that corporations acquire relatively more share blocks in German companies that substantially underperform the ROA of their industry (see Exhibit 18.3). The next section investigates whether this increase in control is related to increased managerial disciplining. If this is the case, the market for share blocks can be considered as a disciplinary corporate governance mechanism.

For French and Belgian companies, the results indicate a higher frequency of block purchases by corporations in the worst-performing companies (Exhibit 18.3). Investment by institutions does not seem to be related to performance in Belgian and French firms. For the United Kingdom, financial institutions acquire relatively more share blocks in well-performing firms. There is no linear relation between performance and share block acquisitions by directors. They invest in control relatively more frequently in average-performing firms. Outside shareholders comprising corporations and families also seem to focus their control acquisition efforts on poorly performing firms. When using market-adjusted share price returns (instead of ROA) to create quintile portfolios, these conclusions remain valid.

Executive Board Turnover and Board Characteristics

Board structure differs substantially across the four countries. In the United Kingdom, Belgium, and France, one body combines both management and nonexecutive directors whereas in Germany, executive and nonexecutive functions are

Exhibit 18.3 Purchases of Share Blocks by Quintile of Performance (ROA_{t-1})

This table shows the number of purchases of large share blocks (> 5%) by new shareholders and by quintile of performance. Performance is the lagged industry-adjusted return on assets. The percentages express how the number of purchases is spread over the quintiles.

	Quintile 1: Low Performance		Quintile 2		Quintile 3		Quintile 4		Quintile 5: High Performance		Total # Block Purchases	Test:
Number of Block Purchases	N	%	N	%	N	%	N	%	N	%	N	Q1 vs. Q5
Germany												
Changes by type of owner												
Families	29	25.9	29	25.9	24	21.4	12	10.7	18	16.1	112	0
Financial institution	19	20.0	20	21.1	18	18.9	16	16.8	22	23.2	95	0
Corporations	72	38.7	46	24.7	23	12.4	29	15.6	16	8.6	186	**
State	6	20.0	8	26.7	14	46.7	2	6.7	0	0.0	30	0
All	126	29.8	103	24.3	79	18.7	59	13.9	56	13.2	423	**
Belgium												
Changes by type of owner												
Families	11	28.9	9	23.7	8	21.1	6	15.8	4	10.5	38	0
Financial institution	4	14.8	9	33.3	4	14.8	8	29.6	2	7.4	27	0
Corporations	38	39.6	19	19.8	18	18.8	7	7.3	14	14.6	96	*
State	3	33.3	2	22.2	2	22.2	2	22.2	0	0.0	9	0
All	56	32.9	39	22.9	32	18.8	23	13.5	20	11.8	170	*

France												
Changes by type of owner												
Families	4	26.7	2	13.3	6	40.0	3	20.0	0	0.0	15	0
Financial institution	39	17.1	36	15.8	47	20.6	58	25.4	48	21.1	228	0
Corporations	55	32.9	29	17.4	33	19.8	27	16.2	23	13.8	167	**
State	3	33.3	2	22.2	2	22.2	2	22.2	0	0.0	9	0
All	101	24.1	69	16.5	88	21.0	90	21.5	71	16.9	419	0
United Kingdom												
Changes by type of owner												
Families	12	29.3	13	31.7	9	22.0	5	12.2	2	4.9	41	*
Financial institution	86	15.7	98	17.9	126	23.0	114	20.8	124	22.6	548	0
Corporations	46	47.4	18	18.6	18	18.6	6	6.2	11	11.3	97	**
State	0	0.0	1	33.3	1	33.3	0	0.0	1	33.3	3	0
Directors	13	17.3	18	24.0	26	34.7	9	12.0	9	12.0	75	0
All	157	29.1	148	27.4	180	33.3	134	24.8	147	27.2	764	0

***,**,* denote statistical significance at the 0.01, 0.05, and 0.10 level, respectively. Zero denotes no significant difference.

Exhibit 18.4 Board Composition and Turnover

This table shows the board characteristics: board size (for Germany, of the management and supervisory boards separately); whether the CEO is also the board chairman (1 = yes); the percentage of nonexecutive directors on board (for Germany this is taken as the percentage of supervisory board members on management and supervisory boards); and percentage of representatives of the shareholders, of the debtholders, or of the founders on the board (and of the management and supervisory boards for Germany), if applicable. This table also shows the average yearly turnover of the CEO and the executive directors. The turnover data are corrected for natural turnover (retirement, death, and illness).

	Germany	Belgium	France	United Kingdom
Board composition				
Board structure	2-tier	1-tier	1-tier	1-tier
Board size	12.7	9.4	9.5	9.5
Supervisory board size	9.2			
Management board size	3.5			
Fraction of executives (%)	28.2	26.1	14.6	60.5
CEO = Chairman (yes = 1) (%)	0.0	35.2	85.9	32.7
Percent of shareholders' representatives	63.2		12.0	
Percent of debtholders' representatives			9.3	
Percent of founders' representatives			3.9	
Turnover data				
CEO turnover (%)	15.1	7.4	18.4	12.5
Executive director turnover (%)	12.2	19.6	10.9	9.0

separated in a management board (*Vorstand*) and supervisory board (*Aufsichtsrat*). Still, Exhibit 18.4 shows that the board sizes are similar across countries. The average French, Belgian, and UK listed firm reports approximately 9.5 directors, with medians of 8 (Belgium) and 9 (France and the United Kingdom). The combined number of directors on the German supervisory and management boards amounts to 12.7 with a median of 9 (6 supervisory directors and 3 executive directors).

There are marked differences regarding the separation of the role of chairman and CEO among the countries under consideration. In Germany, the functions of CEO and chairman of the board are de facto separated given the two-tier board system. In the majority of French firms, the functions of CEO and chairman are combined by a powerful *Président Directeur Generale* (PDG) (Dherment-Férère and Renneboog 2002). In the United Kingdom and Belgium, one person holds the combined function of CEO and chairman of the board in only about one-third of listed firms (see Exhibit 18.4). The number of firms with unitary board control in these countries has been decreasing to currently less than 20 percent as a consequence of the codes of best corporate governance practice.

In Germany and Belgium, the average proportion of nonexecutive directors amounts to 71.8 percent and 73.9 percent, respectively, as shown in Exhibit 18.4. The nonexecutive directors overwhelmingly dominate (in numbers) French boards. There are frequently only two executive directors on the board (one of which is the PDG). In contrast, in the average listed UK firm, executive directors form a board majority with, on average, 60.5 percent of the board seats. While large dominating shareholders usually have board representatives in Continental Europe, the nonexecutive directors of UK boards' fiduciary duty extends to all shareholders such that they are obliged to take an arm's-length position with respect to the dominating shareholders. In Germany, supervisory board representation of shareholders and employees is enshrined in corporate law. Goergen and Renneboog (2003) and Goergen, Martynova, and Renneboog (2005) provide details about co-determination.

Annual CEO turnover in Belgium amounts to 7.4 percent (as shown in Exhibit 18.4), less than that of the United Kingdom (12.5 percent), Germany (15.1 percent), or France (18.4 percent). Exhibit 18.5 shows executive director turnover by quintile of performance and by ownership concentration. The evidence shows that for Germany, Belgium, and the United Kingdom, executive director turnover is significantly larger in the lowest quintile of performance, which implies that part of the turnover is disciplinary. The only exception is France where turnover does not differ significantly across performance quintiles. For Germany, Belgium, and the United Kingdom, the results indicate that the relation between turnover and performance also depends on the presence of controlling share blocks, especially those owned by corporations and families. The following section investigates whether these results hold in a multivariate framework.

DISCUSSION OF RESULTS

This section investigates whether existing blockholders and new blockholders monitor companies and discipline the management of poorly performing firms in each of four countries with a different corporate governance regime. This section also investigates whether alternative governance mechanisms such as board structure or creditors perform this monitoring task more effectively.

Do Large Shareholders Monitor?

Exhibit 18.6 shows evidence of managerial disciplining by major shareholders for Germany. When corporations and families hold large control stakes, there is an increase in executive director turnover. Furthermore, the negative interaction term of performance and control by corporations indicates that board restructuring is particularly high in poorly performing companies. Control held by families, financial institutions, or the government appears not to be used for disciplinary activities when earnings are low. These findings support conjectures 1a (outsider monitoring) and 1c (no monitoring by institutions) for Germany.

In contrast, the monitoring role of major shareholders is not supported for listed Belgian and French firms. Share stakes held by the Belgian government even make managers more immune against replacement. The presence of large corporations in France leads to a higher level of dismissal of executive directors, but not more so in poorly performing firms, which suggests that large corporate blockholders restructure the board for reasons other than poor performance. In firms with low ROA, governmental control also seems to ensure that managers stay in place. Thus, for Belgium and France, there is only support for conjecture 1c (the lack of institutional shareholder activism).

Finally, Exhibit 18.6 provides no evidence that major shareholders actively monitor poorly performing firms in the United Kingdom, although the presence of

Exhibit 18.5 Executive Director Turnover and Performance (ROA) for Firms Controlled by Families, Institutions, Companies, and Directors by Country

This table reports the average annual turnover of executive directors by quintile of performance. Performance is return on assets (EBIT/total assets) adjusted for the industry mean. A two-tailed t-test on the differences between turnover in the lowest and the highest quintiles of performance is calculated. A firm is controlled by a specific category of owner when the dominant blockholder belongs to that particular category. The classification of share blocks by type of owner was based on the ultimate control criterion (the category of the ultimate shareholder on top of the ownership pyramid).

	Quintile 1: Low Performance		Quintile 2		Quintile 3		Quintile 4		Quintile 5: Best Performance		
Average Annual Executive Turnover	**% Turnover**	**# of Firms**	**% Turnover**	**# of Firms**	**% Turnover**	**# of Firms**	**% Turnover**	**# of Firms**	**% Turnover**	**# of Firms**	**Test: Q1 vs. Q5**
Germany											
All firms	18.2	(476)	12.2	(476)	11.5	(476)	8.1	(475)	11.1	(475)	**
Firms controlled by:											
Families	18.0	(203)	15.7	(196)	16.2	(243)	9.5	(217)	12.2	(198)	***
Financial institution	12.5	(45)	10.4	(69)	10.5	(29)	6.7	(76)	12.7	(80)	0
Corporations	20.5	(206)	13.8	(196)	14.8	(184)	11.3	(177)	10.6	(172)	**
State	6.9	(22)	15.6	(15)	10.2	(20)	5.5	(6)	9.4	(26)	0
Belgium											
All firms	27.7	(132)	16.8	(131)	15.3	(131)	17.9	(131)	16.9	(131)	***
Firms controlled by:											
Families	22.6	(13)	19.4	(27)	13.8	(25)	18.9	(23)	17.5	(14)	0
Financial institution	10.9	(35)	14.2	(24)	10.7	(10)	15.6	(14)	8.4	(27)	0
Corporations	24.6	(80)	19.4	(74)	14.0	(89)	17.5	(91)	19.6	(84)	*
State	28.6	(4)	16.5	(6)	18.4	(7)	10.4	(3)	25.2	(6)	0

France											
All firms	12.8	(252)	10.1	(252)	11.5	(252)	9.2	(252)	10.8	(252)	0
Firms controlled by:											
Families	13.9	(34)	10.0	(21)	15.8	(28)	7.7	(31)	14.8	(21)	0
Financial institution	8.2	(50)	11.1	(57)	10.1	(41)	9.7	(37)	14.1	(43)	*
Corporations	14.4	(142)	12.2	(143)	8.8	(166)	9.9	(160)	11.0	(171)	0
State	18.1	(26)	9.0	(31)	7.4	(17)	12.6	(24)	9.4	(17)	*
United Kingdom											
All firms	16.1	(215)	9.4	(214)	8.1	(214)	4.2	(214)	7.6	(214)	***
Firms controlled by:											
Families	15.1	(24)	8.8	(19)	7.4	(21)	7.1	(22)	6.6	(15)	**
Financial institution	15.8	(106)	14.1	(117)	10.5	(122)	6.5	(114)	12.4	(128)	0
Corporations	19.5	(35)	10.5	(31)	9.5	(29)	6.4	(39)	13.1	(30)	*
State	22.7	(4)	14.5	(6)	12.8	(3)	9.0	(4)	9.5	(1)	0
Directors	8.9	(46)	5.8	(41)	7.3	(39)	3.3	(35)	5.7	(40)	0

***, **, and * denote statistical significance at the 0.01, 0.05, and 0.10 level, respectively. Zero denotes no significant difference.

Exhibit 18.6 Tobit Relation between Executive Turnover, Ownership, and Performance (ROA)

This table shows Tobit regression results explaining executive turnover, which is measured as the number of leaving executive directors to the number of all executive directors. Performance is lagged return on assets (EBIT/total assets) adjusted for the industry mean. The definition of variables is presented in the chapter text. Intercept, time dummies as well as two-digit country-specific industry dummies are included but not reported.

	Germany		Belgium		France		United Kingdom	
	Coefficient	**p-value**	**Coefficient**	**p-value**	**Coefficient**	**p-value**	**Coefficient**	**p-value**
Performance at t	0.061	0.55	−0.015	0.78	**−0.165***	0.10	**−0.431*****	0.01
Performance at t–1	**−2.664***	0.06	0.537	0.53	−0.514	0.56	−0.167	0.77
Performance at t–2	−0.103	0.53	−0.339	0.19	−0.215	0.63	0.152	0.36
Ownership variables:								
Blockholder: families	**0.002***	0.09	−0.005	0.13	−0.001	0.73	**−0.004****	0.01
Blockholder: financial institution	0.001	0.34	0.004	0.35	−0.001	0.74	−0.003	0.30
Blockholder: corporations	**0.004***	0.05	0.006	0.62	**0.003***	0.08	0.001	0.42
Blockholder: government	0.001	0.89	**−0.009***	0.07	0.001	0.69	−0.016	0.44
Blockholder: directors	—		—		—		**−0.073****	0.02
Interaction term: Control and lagged performance								
Families × Performance	0.014	0.18	0.016	0.50	0.016	0.75	−0.009	0.25
Financial Institution × Performance	0.015	0.43	0.062	0.12	0.028	0.44	−0.011	0.35
Corporations × Performance	**−0.021***	0.08	**0.028***	0.05	0.026	0.32	−0.003	0.83
Government × Performance	−0.033	0.32	0.019	0.63	**0.081***	0.04	−0.140	0.67
Directors × Performance	—		—		—		−0.015	0.39
Controlling variables:								
Log(assets)	−0.028	0.15	−0.029	0.26	0.001	0.86	**−0.057****	0.04
Industry dummies	Yes		Yes		Yes		Yes	
Time dummies	Yes		Yes		Yes		Yes	
Log likelihood	−22.730		−17.530		5.260		−12.520	
Number of observations	2340		710		1238		1064	

***, **, and * denote statistical significance of 0.01, 0.05, and 0.10, respectively.

large blocks held by families is positively related to increased executive turnover regardless of corporate performance. However, when directors own substantial share stakes, the lower levels of board restructuring suggest that even in the wake of poor performance, directors successfully impede their departure. This supports conjecture 1b (director resistance against monitoring) for the United Kingdom. All in all, with the exception of Germany, there is little evidence that incumbent shareholders take on a disciplinary task.

Is the Market in Share Blocks a Corporate Governance Mechanism?

Although not shown, the results also indicate that the acquisition of share blocks by corporations goes hand in hand with increased dismissal of top management in Germany, Belgium, and France. This finding supports conjecture 2. In the former two countries, the market in share blocks seems to function as a corporate governance device because the increases in control by corporations are followed by higher, performance-induced levels of top management dismissal. Köke (2004) confirms that block transfers in Germany coincide with poor performance and are followed by increased layoffs of employees and board restructuring. Still, the subsequent performance increase is only modest. In the United Kingdom, the strengthening of directors' voting power results in lower levels of dismissal. This finding does not come unexpectedly as several U.S. and UK studies such as Denis, Denis, and Sarin (1997) and Franks, Mayer, and Renneboog (2001) document managerial entrenchment and its adverse consequence on corporate value.

Alternative Governance Devices

The monitoring efficiency by blockholders may also depend upon the regulatory framework in which corporate governance devices are embedded. Investigating the importance of two alternative governance devices is relevant for firms that lack strong (new) outside shareholders (such as corporations or families): namely the role of creditors and the (supervisory) board of directors.

Creditors

For Germany, data are collected for the proportion of the debt provided by the four main Hausbanken. A high ratio of debt provided by one of these universal banks indicates that the potential influence of the Hausbank is likely to be high. Across all German firms, the four main universal banks hold 29 percent of all debt. The Continental European firms are more levered than those in the United Kingdom. The interest coverage is highest for the United Kingdom (5.2) and is lowest for French firms (3.1), reflecting their higher leverage and lower profitability.

The analysis unveils no relation between the debt/equity ratio or interest coverage and the incidence of turnover in Belgium, France, and the United Kingdom. For Germany, however, the results show that a high ratio of universal bank loans goes hand in hand with increased board restructuring, a relation which is intensified for poorly performing firms. In addition, the evidence shows that interest coverage and its interaction term with poor performance are significant, implying that low interest coverage and poor performance also increase turnover. This provides some evidence that creditors (in this case, the Hausbanken) may play an important role in disciplining management in Germany especially when the threat is imminent that the debt covenants will be violated (low interest coverage). Thus, conjecture 3 is supported for Germany but not for the other countries.

Board of Directors

For Germany, the functions of CEO and chairman of the supervisory board are legally separated. For France, the CEO often also exerts the function of chairman of the (unitary) board. Hence, only the effect of separation for the United Kingdom and Belgium can be studied. The results show that a larger board in Germany, Belgium, and the United Kingdom facilitates the removal of executive directors in all firms, not just the poorly performing ones. This finding suggests that a large board may provide a pool of successors for departing executives or has a better network to attract new top managers (Yermack 1996). Following conjecture 4, the expectation is that a large proportion of nonexecutive directors (shareholder representatives as well as independent ones) fosters the degree of independence from management. The results show that this is the case in Belgium, but cannot support this conjecture for German and French firms. For UK companies, the evidence demonstrates that a large proportion of independent directors even reduces executive turnover, which is in line with Franks et al. (2001) who document that nonexecutive directors seem to support the incumbent executive directors even in the wake of poor performance. Separating the functions of CEO and chairman reduces the former's grip on the board in both the United Kingdom and Belgium, especially in poorly performing companies.

SUMMARY AND CONCLUSIONS

This chapter investigates the role of monitoring mechanisms and their effect on managerial discipline in countries with different corporate governance regimes (Germany, France, Belgium, and the United Kingdom). The expectation is that differences in the institutional and regulatory framework influence the efficiency of corporate governance. First, large blockholders may exert a corporate monitoring task provided their ownership stakes are sufficiently large to internalize the costs of monitoring. Relating these blockholdings with past performance enables investigating whether executive turnover is connected to past managerial underperformance. Second, this chapter investigates whether a market in share stakes operates as a partial corporate control market. This is the case if blockholders accumulate control in the wake of poor performance and subsequently force management to resign. A third mechanism consists of monitoring by creditors, who are expected to dismiss management not only when performance is poor, but also when leverage is high or interest coverage is low. Fourth, board structure and composition—measured by the percentage of nonexecutive directors, separation of control, and board representation—may be a proxy for the degree of independence of the nonexecutive directors.

The evidence shows substantial differences across countries. Executive turnover (corrected for natural turnover such as retirement and illness) is strongly related to past performance in Germany, Belgium, and the United Kingdom but not in France. Overall, there is little evidence that existing blockholders play an active role in disciplining underperforming management. The strongest evidence of disciplinary actions against underperforming management is found for Germany. Management board restructuring in the wake of poor performance is high when the largest blockholder is a corporation. The evidence does not find shareholder activism by corporations in France. Managers of government-controlled companies in France and Belgium do not seem to be disciplined when they underperform. In UK firms, executive directors with voting blocks appear to be successful in impeding executive board restructuring and, hence, in defending their private benefits, even when the share price returns and accounting returns of their firms are substandard. Blockholdings are calculated and categorized, taking into account the pyramidal ownership structures for Germany, Belgium, and France. The question of whether large control leverage through long chains of ownership weakens the effectiveness of corporate governance actions of existing and new shareholders in Germany and Belgium is answered negatively.

Evidence also shows that part of the market for blockholdings can be considered a corporate governance market in Germany and Belgium. First, nonfinancial companies in Germany, Belgium, and France obtain or increase control power when a target firm performs poorly. Second, a significant relation exists between the acquisition of share blocks and increased managerial turnover in poorly performing German and Belgian firms. In contrast, the markets for share blocks in the United Kingdom are not related to managerial disciplining.

There is no evidence of creditor monitoring in Belgium, France, and the United Kingdom. In contrast, for Germany, the Hausbanken play an important role in disciplining management, especially when the threat is imminent that the debt covenants will be violated.

A large proportion of nonexecutive directors fosters the degree of independence from management. The results show that this is the case in Belgium, but there is no support for this conjecture in German and French firms. For the UK companies, the evidence indicates that when the firm has a large proportion of independent directors executive turnover is even reduced. This result is in line with Franks et al. (2001), who document that nonexecutive directors seem to support the incumbent executive directors, even in the wake of poor performance. Separating the functions of CEO and chairman reduces the former's grip on the board in both the United Kingdom and Belgium, especially in badly performing companies in which top management removal is necessary. Finally, in Germany, Belgium, and the United Kingdom, a large board seems to facilitate managerial disciplining. This relation might arise because there is a higher probability that the board comprises a potential successor to a departing CEO.

The overall conclusion is that the German corporate governance system seems to better undertake its disciplinary role than the Belgian, French, or British systems.

German corporations with substantial voting control and/or those acquiring new share blocks remove underperforming management. Pyramidal ownership structures do not hinder the exertion of control power by the ultimate blockholders. In addition, when a firm has contracted a substantial amount of debt with the German universal banks, managerial disciplining occurs more frequently. Although poor performance is correlated to higher managerial turnover, there is no strong evidence that disciplining is taking place by large blockholders in the United Kingdom. Directors owning large stakes are entrenched, even in the wake of poor performance. In the Belgian corporate governance system, the corporations and the nonexecutive directors adopt a monitoring and disciplinary role. In contrast, the French system does not seem to be adept at removing poorly performing executive directors as the CEO dominates the board. There is little evidence that board structure and composition are related to disciplining underperforming management. Moreover, control by holding companies and the government entrenches the management of poorly performing firms. In conclusion, the impact and effectiveness of blockholders depends on the whole corporate governance regime consisting of board structure and independence, creditor monitoring, the market for shareblocks, and the regulatory framework.

DISCUSSION QUESTIONS

1. Why are only sufficiently large blockholders expected to monitor management?
2. Whereas the United States and the United Kingdom have a large and active takeover market, this is much less the case for Germany and most Continental European countries. Explain why this situation exists.
3. Are institutional investors such as banks or investment funds expected to be good monitors? Explain why or why not.
4. Why do blockholders create ownership pyramids?

REFERENCES

Banerjee, Saugata, Benoit Leleux, and Theo Vermaelen. 1997. Large shareholdings and corporate control: An analysis of stake purchases by French holding companies. *European Financial Management* 3 (1): 23–43.

Barca, Fabrizio, and Marco Becht. 2001. *The control of corporate Europe*. Oxford: Oxford University Press.

Barclay, Michael J., and Clifford G. Holderness. 1991. Negotiated block trades and corporate control. *Journal of Finance* 46 (3): 861–878.

Baums, Theodor. 2000. Corporate governance in Germany—system and current developments. Working paper, University of Osnabrück.

Bethel, Jennifer E., Julia Porter Liebeskind, and Tim Opler. 1998. Block share purchases and corporate performance. *Journal of Finance* 53 (2): 605–634.

Böhmer, Ekkehart. 2000. Industry groups, bank control, and large shareholders: An analysis of German takeovers. *Journal of Financial Intermediation* 9 (2): 117–148.

Bolton, Patrick, and Ernst-Ludwig von Thadden. 1998. Blocks, liquidity and corporate control. *Journal of Finance* 53 (1): 1–25.

Denis, David J., Diane K. Denis, and Atulya Sarin. 1997. Ownership structure and top executive turnover. *Journal of Financial Economics* 45 (2): 193–221.

Denis, David J., and Timothy A. Kruse. 2000. Managerial discipline and corporate restructuring following performance declines. *Journal of Financial Economics* 55 (3): 391–424.

Dherment-Férère, Isabelle, and Luc Renneboog. 2002. Share price reactions to CEO resignations and large shareholder monitoring in listed French companies. In *Convergence and diversity of corporate governance regimes and capital markets*, ed. Luc Renneboog, Joe McCahery, Piet Moerland, and Theo Raaijmakers, 297–324. Oxford: Oxford University.

Dyck, Alexander, and Luigi Zingales. 2004. Private benefits of control: An international comparison. *Journal of Finance* 59 (2): 537–600.

Faccio, Mara, and Larry H. P. Lang. 2002. The ultimate ownership of Western European corporations. *Journal of Financial Economics* 65 (3): 365–395.

Faccio, Mara, Larry H. P. Lang, and Leslie Young. 2010. Pyramiding versus leverage in corporate groups: International evidence. *Journal of International Business Studies* 41, 88–104.

Franks, Julian, and Colin Mayer. 2001. Ownership and control of German corporations. *Review of Financial Studies* 14 (4): 943–977.

Franks, Julian, Colin Mayer, and Luc Renneboog. 2001. Who disciplines management in poorly performing companies? *Journal of Financial Intermediation* 10 (3–4): 209–248.

Franks, Julian, Colin Mayer, and Stefano Rossi. 2009. Ownership: Evolution and regulation. *Review of Financial Studies* 22, 4009–56.

Goergen, Marc, and Luc Renneboog. 2001. Strong managers and passive institutional investors in the UK. In *The control of corporate Europe*, ed. Fabrizio Barca and Marco Becht, 259–284. Oxford: Oxford University Press.

———. 2003. The discrepancy of ownership and control concentration in German and UK firms: Evidence from initial public offerings. *Journal of Law, Economics and Organization* 3 (2): 379–400.

Goergen, Marc, Marina Martynova, and Luc Renneboog. 2005. Corporate governance convergence: Evidence from takeover regulation reforms. *Oxford Review of Economic Policy* 21 (2): 243–268.

Gorton, Gary, and Frank A. Schmid. 2000. Universal banking and the performance of German firms. *Journal of Financial Economics* 58 (1–2): 29–80.

Grossman, Sanford J., and Oliver D. Hart. 1988. One share, one vote, and the market for corporate control. *Journal of Financial Economics* 20 (1): 175–202.

Jenkinson, Tim, and Alexander Ljungqvist. 2001. The role of hostile stakes in German corporate governance. *Journal of Corporate Finance* 7 (4): 397–446.

Johnson, Simon, Rafael La Porta, Florencio Lopez-de-Silanes, and Andrei Shleifer. 2000. Tunnelling. *American Economic Review* 90 (2): 22–27.

Köke, Jens. 2004. The market for corporate control in a bank-based economy: A governance device? *Journal of Corporate Finance* 10 (1): 53–80.

La Porta, Rafael, Florencio Lopez-de-Silanes, Andrei Shleifer, and Robert Vishny. 2000. Investor protection and corporate governance. *Journal of Financial Economics* 58 (1–2): 3–27.

Renneboog, Luc. 2000. Ownership, managerial control and the governance of poorly performing companies listed on the Brussels Stock Exchange. *Journal of Banking and Finance* 24 (12): 1959–1995.

Volpin, Paolo F. 2002. Governance with poor investor protection: Evidence from top executive turnover in Italy. *Journal of Financial Economics* 64 (1): 61–90.

Yermack, David. 1996. Higher market valuation of companies with a small board of directors. *Journal of Financial Economics* 40 (2): 185–212.

ABOUT THE AUTHORS

Isabelle Dherment-Férère graduated from Toulouse Business School and from the University of Aix-en-Provence with a master's degree in computing and with a PhD in management. Currently, she is an assistant professor at the University of South-Toulon-Var where she is also academic director of the master's program in corporate finance and auditing. Her research interests are value creation of corporate governance and information systems. She has published in the *Finance Contrôle Stratégie*, *Revue Française de Gestion*, *Banque et Marchés*, and *Revue Management et Avenir*. Professor Dherment-Férère has published the book *Maîtrise d'ouvrage et ERP: Processus Logistiques, Comptables et Financiers* (Hermes-Lavoisier Editions, 2007).

Luc Renneboog is professor of corporate finance at Tilburg University and a research fellow at CentER and the European Corporate Governance Institute (ECGI, Brussels). He graduated from the Catholic University of Leuven with degrees in management engineering (BSc and MSc) and in philosophy (BA); from the University of Chicago with an MBA; and from the London Business School with a PhD in financial economics. He held appointments at the University of Leuven and Oxford University, and visiting appointments at London Business School, HEC (Paris), and others. He has published in such journals as the *Journal of Finance*, *Journal of Financial Intermediation*, *Journal of Law and Economics*, *Journal of Corporate Finance*, *Journal of Banking and Finance*, *Oxford Review of Economic Policy*, *Cambridge Journal of Economics*, and *European Financial Management*. He has co-authored and edited several books on corporate governance, dividend policy, and venture capital. His research interests are corporate finance, corporate governance, takeovers, dividend policy, insider trading, law and economics, and the economics of art.

CHAPTER 19

The Governance of Family Firms

MORTEN BENNEDSEN
André and Rosalie Hoffmann Chaired Professor in Family Enterprise and Professor of Economics, INSEAD

FRANCISCO PÉREZ-GONZÁLEZ
Assistant Professor of Finance, Stanford University and Faculty Research Fellow, National Bureau of Economic Research (NBER)

DANIEL WOLFENZON
Stefan H. Robock Professor of Finance and Economics, Columbia University and Research Associate, National Bureau of Economic Research (NBER)

INTRODUCTION

Corporate governance deals with collective action problems facing a firm's alternative stakeholders. To address these conflicts, firms often rely on large shareholders, who combine substantial ownership and control rights to affect decisions. Around the world, the most common large shareholders are families (La Porta, Lopez-de-Silanes, and Shleifer 1999; Morck, Stangeland, and Yeung 2000; Claessens, Fan, and Lang 2000; Faccio and Lang 2002; Anderson and Reeb 2003a; Villalonga and Amit 2006). The prevalence of family firms has sparked a growing body of research that focuses on the governance of these firms. This chapter attempts to summarize the main issues in this literature and to highlight its future potential.

The chapter emphasizes four main issues. First, family firms are a promising area of research. Family businesses play a prominent role in the allocation of resources that is still understudied by a literature that historically views such businesses as an anomaly. Family firms are widespread around the world and are also correlated with significantly more variation than other firms in measures of economic output. The literature does not currently provide a comprehensive understanding of the governance mechanisms that drive these extreme outcomes or that explain why family firms are the dominant form of organization in the world.

Second, an important challenge in the advancement of this area of research is the lack of a clear definition of a family firm. Different researchers define family firms in various ways, but the definition used is crucial to (1) understand the many seemingly unrelated stylized facts documented in the literature, and (2) flesh out the specific governance challenges facing these firms. This chapter provides a narrow definition of family firms and then uses it to make an array of empirical predictions that distinguish family from other firms.

Third, in terms of corporate governance, a major challenge has been to identify the distinguishing characteristics of family firms relative to other firms. Family businesses, like other corporations with ownership concentration, typically have a dominant shareholder. As a result, the common agency conflict that plagues widely held firms is often superseded by the conflict of interests between controlling and noncontrolling shareholders.

So why are family firms different? Family firms are unique because a family is at the apex of the firms' governance institutions. The most important voice in governance is, in consequence, not necessarily exercised by an individual but rather by a group of people who are linked to each other by blood or marriage relations. As a result, the allocation of power within the family, the family governance institutions, the interaction between family members and other stakeholders, as well as family characteristics (such as size, age, and talent) are likely to have a determining impact on firms' outcomes.

The arguments for the overlap of family and business structures often rely on market imperfections that make arm's-length contracts unattractive, or on private benefits that reduce family participation costs. In terms of market frictions, within-family labor or capital provision may be less exposed to information asymmetry or opportunistic behavior. Multiple family interactions may facilitate screening and enforcement of contracts, firm-specific investments, and reputation building. The joint maximization of family and business objectives, however, may also entail significant distortions to firms.

The central objective of family-firm governance research is, therefore, to understand how family firms balance the protection that the controlling family brings to the firm with the challenges this structure imposes on minority shareholders. The existing literature provides few clues into the specific ways in which family firms use their characteristics or structure to affect value. Direct tests on the effect of family characteristics on performance are rare in the literature, yet they provide the distinguishing mark and the future of this area of research.

The fourth main issue examined by this chapter is that family firms can provide an attractive laboratory for addressing several research questions of general interest. Empirical work in corporate governance is plagued with endogeneity and omitted variables concerns. Causal relationships are difficult to establish. Nevertheless, variation in family firm decision making may result from family, not firm, characteristics. These traits can potentially be exogenous to firms' prospects. As a result, family firm research can be a fruitful avenue to addressing central questions in financial economics.

In sum, the future of family firm governance research seems intrinsically linked to family governance. To this end, detailed data sets are increasingly being put together by researchers all over the world, including data sets from the United States (Pérez-González 2006; Villalonga and Amit 2006 and 2009; Miller, Le Breton-Miller, Lester, and Cannella 2007); Denmark (Bennedsen, Nielsen, Pérez-González, and Wolfenzon 2007; Bennedsen, Pérez-González, and Wolfenzon 2009); Italy (Cucculelli and Micucci 2008); Japan (Mehrotra, Morck, Shim, and Wiwattanakantang 2009); Thailand (Bunkanwanicha, Fan, and Wiwattanakantang 2008; Bertrand,

Johnson, Samphantharak, and Schoar 2008); and Singapore, Hong Kong, and Taiwan (Fan, Jian, Jin, and Yeh 2009). This trend is likely to continue in the future.

A cautionary caveat applies. The format and size restrictions of this chapter limit the scope and scale of analysis. The chapter focuses on the empirical governance literature and emphasizes governance problems facing minority shareholders. It stresses firm-level governance mechanisms and devotes substantial attention to identification problems that affect applied research. The chapter is, therefore, not a review on the vast family firm literature. Particular papers are only introduced insofar as they enter the discussion of what the authors consider are the main issues and the most prominent topics for future research. As a result, the chapter does not make due consideration to all the excellent papers written on this topic.

The remainder of the chapter is organized as follows. The next section provides the motivation for focusing on family firms. Following that, a definition of family firms is presented. The chapter then analyzes the ownership and control characteristics of family firms, and their governance challenges, in two separate sections. The chapter also includes a methodology section that highlights common empirical challenges in corporate governance research and why family firms can provide a solution to inference problems. The final section concludes.

WHY FAMILY FIRMS?

This section summarizes the main arguments that make the governance of family firms a promising area of research. They include their prevalence, wide dispersion in performance measures, current intergenerational challenges, and potential macroeconomic effects.

Prevalence, Data, and Persistence

Family firms have historically been underrepresented in the literature for at least three reasons. First, research has traditionally focused on the widely held paradigm of firms (Berle and Means 1932). Second, data on family firms are generally harder to obtain because they are disproportionately private, smaller in size, and prevalent in developing economies. Third, family firms are often perceived as an anachronism in modern market economies. Recent studies are overcoming these barriers and challenging such conventional wisdom about family firms.

As argued previously, recent papers have shown that the majority of firms around the world have, as a large shareholder, a founder or the founder's family. La Porta et al. (1999) document that families control over 53 percent of publicly traded firms with at least $500 million in market capitalization in 27 countries. Additional evidence of the prominent role of families in large firms has been provided by Anderson and Reeb (2003a) and Villalonga and Amit (2006) for the United States; Morck et al. (2000) for Canada; Faccio and Lang (2002) for Europe; Claessens, Djankov, Fan, and Lang (2002) for East Asian countries; and many others. Also, detailed data sets on governance and family characteristics are increasingly being developed all over the world. The availability of private firm data and of ownership and family characteristics is often superior outside the United States, particularly in Europe, the East, and Southeast Asia. These data sets provide fertile ground for original and potentially influential research.

Finally, recent work by Franks, Mayer, and Rossi (2009) and Mehrotra et al. (2009) challenge the perception that family firms are destined to disappear in developed economies. These studies show that other than in the United Kingdom, family firms are persistent over time.

Dispersion in Performance

The rise to prominence of corporate governance research is heavily influenced by the observation and strong empirical case of the idea that governance is vital in explaining dispersion in measures of economic output. Within this literature, family firms have been shown to be particularly prevalent at the extremes of the performance distribution. For example, Anderson and Reeb (2003a), Villalonga and Amit (2006), and Sraer and Thesmar (2007), document their superiority in terms of market-to-book valuations and profitability. In contrast, Morck et al. (2000), Pérez-González (2006), and Bennedsen et al. (2007) provide evidence of underperformance. Specifically, they find that firms managed by family chief executive officers (CEOs) significantly underperform. Similarly, Bloom and Van Reenen (2007) document that family-managed firms are among the least productive firms in Western Europe and that these firms may help to explain the observed productivity gap between this region and the United States.

Why do such disparate outcomes exist? The evidence suggests that the definition of family firm used and sample selection play an important role in explaining these estimated results. For example, the positive effect of family firms has been largely explained by large founder-led firms. Random subsets of family firms do not overperform (Miller et al. 2007). Yet Bennedsen et al. (2007) establish a significant family-CEO underperformance result that is unlikely to be driven by sample selection. They find an arguably causal link between family CEOs and lower performance.

Overall, governance and firms' outcomes of family and other firms may differ for many reasons. The biggest challenge is, therefore, establishing direct causal links between family governance characteristics and firm outcomes. Overcoming these obstacles provides ample opportunities for future research.

Generational Transfers

An added rationale for focusing on family firms is the massive intergenerational transfer of assets that is currently under way around the world. Aging demographic statistics imply that a large fraction of these firms will be subject to leadership and wealth transfer challenges. Survey data from the United States, for example, indicates that 40 percent of the business owners expect to retire within a decade and the majority of them expect control to remain within the family (MassMutual 2007). Family firms may be particularly vulnerable around succession events because governance institutions are often underdeveloped or centralized. Further work is needed to understand the challenges facing these firms and the potential consequences for resource allocation. Yet recent evidence by Ellul, Pagano, and Panunzi (2009) and Tsoutsoura (2009) suggests that, for example, inheritance regulations can significantly affect firm investment and performance.

Macroeconomic Implications and Political Connections

Another strand of the literature has explored the macroeconomic consequences of having a corporate sector dominated by family firms. These firms have been argued to be second-best solutions that arise due to the underdevelopment of market institutions (Khanna and Yafeh 2007). On an aggregate level, these nonmarket institutions have been alleged to hinder growth prospects due to distortions in the allocation of human capital (Caselli and Gennaioli 2003) and financing efficiency (Almeida and Wolfenzon 2006).

A related line of research analyzes the consequences of political connections on firms (Fisman 2001; Faccio 2006). While these papers do not focus on family firms per se, they do document that connections tend to be particularly stronger for these firms (Faccio and Parsley 2009). Various scholars argue that these connections retard growth through their impact on the development of market institutions (Morck et al. 2000; Morck, Wolfenzon, and Yeung 2005).

Cross-country evidence is suggestive that some of these forces may be at work (Morck et al. 2000; Bertrand and Schoar 2006). Yet countries differ in many dimensions and, as a result, interpreting these results as causal is difficult.

WHAT IS A FAMILY FIRM?

As previously argued, researchers have used several and often broad definitions of family firms. This section develops a narrow definition of family firms, which serves as the basis for discussing the main characteristics and governance challenges facing these firms. Following this narrow approach seems a fruitful avenue to advance this area of research.

A *family firm* is herein defined as an organization that shares four common traits:

1. *Family.* Two or more members of the same family (blood or marriage) are direct participants in the firm's formal governance institutions such as management and the board of directors.
2. *Ownership.* The family owns a significant fraction of the shares in the firm. Using classic portfolio theory as a benchmark, a *significant* threshold is defined as an investment exceeding the firms' share in the overall market portfolio. In other words, this threshold is not necessarily related to a fraction of shares held.
3. *Control rights.* Members of the family exert significant control rights in the firm, where the control threshold is at least as large as the fraction of ownership rights held.
4. *Preference for within-firm intergenerational transfers.* Families attach value to retaining their ownership and control rights within the family firm across generations.

Defining family firms as those organizations that meet these four traits necessarily implies that many firms that other researchers, practitioners, or owners describe as family firms would not be considered as such. In particular, entrepreneurial firms such as Microsoft are often classified as family firms even if the crucial family component is missing. The preceding definition, however, captures the main traits that most family firms share.

OWNERSHIP AND CONTROL: FAMILY AND NONFAMILY BLOCKHOLDERS

This section stresses the role of ownership and control concentration in family firms and compares the resulting issues to the ownership concentration literature at large. It highlights the common ingredients between these two literatures and the empirical challenges in establishing causal ownership and control effects on performance.

Ownership

From the point of view of diversification, concentrated portfolio exposures are puzzling, particularly when individual human capital is also exposed to a firm. Why hold such exposures? Rationality implies that such exposures result from the existence of counterbalancing benefits.

Private benefits of control may be one such benefit. In consequence, family firms tend to be more prevalent in settings with large private benefits or large amenity values, such as in sport firms (Demsetz and Lehn 1985). Some of these benefits, such as the value of running a newspaper founded by one's grandfather, are unlikely to be valued by other market participants. Other benefits such as the prestige attached to ownership may be marketable.

Standard portfolio logic implies, however, that family firms' survival rates would tend to be lower when exposed to significant diversifiable shocks. Total risk exposure would put owners at a disadvantage. Similarly, family firms would be induced to engage in diversification, leading to, for example, business group creation. Consistent with these ideas, Faccio, Marchica, and Mura (2009) show that shareholders' diversification affects firms' risk-taking behavior. Anderson and Reeb (2003b), however, do not find evidence for this notion in S&P 500 U.S. firms.

An alternative route for keeping private benefits while minimizing portfolio costs is separating ownership and control rights. Not surprisingly, family firms have been found to control firms using dual-class shares with differential voting rights (Villalonga and Amit 2009) and pyramidal ownership structures (Morck et al. 2005).

In terms of governance, ownership concentration may alleviate the agency problems from dispersed shareholdings. The challenge is that families may steer firms toward decisions that favor them at the expense of minority shareholders. This large shareholder risk has been previously examined in the literature and it is therefore not unique to family firms (Shleifer and Vishny 1986 and 1997; Becht, Bolton, and Roell 2003).

The empirical record linking family ownership and firm value is mixed. Most studies that focus on large firms document a positive correlation between family ownership and performance (Anderson and Reeb 2003a; Villalonga and Amit 2006). This evidence is, however, difficult to interpret as results may be driven by selection. Consistent with this concern, random samples do not exhibit such an overperformance result (Miller et al. 2007).

Selection is hardly surprising because families determine when they sell their ownership stakes. Average performance may be insufficient to warrant concentrated ownership positions. Families may, as a result, prefer to diversify their positions. The resulting samples would indicate that family ownership is positively correlated with performance even when the relevant counterfactuals (i.e., the performance of the family firm without family ownership or the performance of nonfamily firms with family owners) would be difficult to predict.

More generally, the family ownership literature faces the same inference challenges as the older ownership concentration studies. As highlighted by Himmelberg, Hubbard, and Palia (1999), ownership is endogenous. As a result, establishing the direct ownership effects on performance is difficult. Overall, while ownership concentration provides important insights on the characteristics and challenges facing family firms, it does not, by itself, provide a compelling case for an independent literature on family businesses.

Control

In terms of control rights, the literature has emphasized that control matters in settings of contract incompleteness (Williamson 1985). In these settings, stakeholders may not ex ante invest in efficient tasks (Grossman and Hart 1986; Hart and Moore 1990) or would strategically invest in value-destroying projects (Shleifer and Vishny 1989). Similarly, ex post bargaining may be affected by, for example, free-rider problems (Grossman and Hart 1980) or wealth constraints (Aghion and Bolton 1992). In terms of optimal organizational design, the literature is interested in understanding the circumstances under which family control is efficient.

Firm control, for example, would tend to reside with the family whenever family firm-specific, noncontractible investments are important. The exact nature of these investments in industries as disparate as construction or malt beverage manufacturing, where family firms prevail, is difficult to spell out and is a source of debate in the literature. Following this logic, family control may be inefficient in rapidly evolving industries where strategic investments are difficult to predict. Tight family control would discourage other stakeholders' investments (Burkart, Gromb, and Panunzi 1997). Consistent with this idea, family control is rare in research and development intensive industries (Pérez-González 2006; Villalonga and Amit 2008).

The focus on family control may lead families to separate cash flows and voting rights to achieve diversification or to fund large-scale projects. Such separation tends to be priced: Investors would pay less for limited control rights. An empirical challenge of this observation is that family excess control would occur only in firms where the distortions generated by control dilution are outweighed by their perceived benefits, at least from the perspective of the family.

In practice, establishing causal control (not ownership) effects on firm performance or valuation has been difficult in the governance literature at large. Despite this fact, the family firm literature has examined the specific mechanisms used to retain family control and the mostly cross-sectional differences between family control and firm value.

La Porta et al. (1999) and Morck et al. (2005) show international evidence that family firms exert disproportionate control relative to cash-flow rights through the use of pyramids and active participation in management positions. Villalonga and Amit (2009) document that families in the United States retain control through dual-class shares, excess board representation, and voting agreements. Pyramids are rare in the United States. Similarly, Bennedsen and Nielsen (2009) show a widespread use of dual-class shares in Western Europe.

An alternative way to document family control is to compare the probability of takeovers for family and other firms. Morck, Shleifer, and Vishny (1989) document that hostile takeovers are more infrequent for firms run by a member of the founding family, and Slovin and Sushka (1993) show founders' deaths lead to increases in the probability of control contests.

Studies that have examined the effect of family control on firm value have documented a strong positive correlation (McConaughy, Walker, Henderson, and Mishra 1998; Villalonga and Amit 2006). These results suggest that family control may increase efficiency. Yet these findings are also subject to the selection concerns that plague ownership studies. Recent studies that estimate the value of control document significant premiums for insiders, particularly in settings of poor investor protection (Nenova 2003; Dyck and Zingales 2004). As a result, the verdict is still out in terms of the net effect of family control concentration and minority shareholder value.

Family firms are similar to other firms with concentrated ownership because decision making is often concentrated in a few hands. Large shareholders and CEOs are often the same person. As a result, changes in common governance mechanisms often fail to bring about substantial effects on outcomes.

A board of directors, for example, even if nominally independent may not discipline management when the largest owner is the manager herself. Such an independent board *de jure* may not be *de facto* independent. Similarly, the market for corporate control may not discipline managers when they themselves are the large owners. In consequence, changes in governance mechanisms may still matter, as Anderson and Reeb (2004), Anderson, Duru, and Reeb (2009), and others have shown, but the scope for intervention may be limited relative to other settings.

So what distinguishes family firms from other firms with concentrated ownership? The family is the *sine qua non* or indispensible condition of any study in this area of research. Surprisingly, family analysis is often underemphasized in empirical tests. Families are not distinguished from other groups of individuals or they are frequently assumed to be monolithic entities. The next section examines these key distinguishing traits.

INSIDE THE FAMILY FIRM: FAMILY INFLUENCE AND INTERGENERATIONAL ISSUES

Building on the idea that even small changes in family governance can bring about large effects for firm outcomes, this section emphasizes the role of the family behind the family firm.

Mixing Family and Business

Starting with the seminal work of Becker (1981), economists have viewed families as entities that produce and organize multiple activities. Families make decisions that maximize the welfare of the family. But the joint maximization of family and business objectives often entails gains in one sphere at the expense of the other. Given these distortions, finding that most firms around the world are exposed to such problems is surprising. Not surprising, however, is that these distortions are typically accompanied by benefits favoring the family firm organizational form.

The arguments for mixing family with business transactions often rely on market imperfections that make arm's-length contracts expensive. For example, within-family labor or capital provision may be less exposed to information asymmetry or opportunistic behavior than hired inputs. Multiple family interactions facilitate screening and contract enforcement, leading to higher levels of trust.

Advantageous features also include similarity in preferences. Ex post inefficiencies, for example, may be reduced if the preferences of relatives are closer to each other than the preferences of nonfamily members. Hansmann (1996) provides compelling evidence that agents with disparate preferences rarely share control.

Similarly, if family ties are stronger than nonrelatives links ("blood is thicker than water"), higher separation costs for relatives may lead to greater commitment, higher ex ante investments, and longer maturity in investments. These investments may be crucial in firms that thrive on firm-specific knowledge. The apprentice system, where younger generations learn the intricacies of business from their elders, is easier to sustain in such conditions.

Private benefits associated with working for a business that carries one's name or that was founded by an ancestor may lead to lower participation costs for relatives. Similar private benefits may be derived from working with relatives. In some cases, these forces are so strong that the firm may be an extension of the family and an integral part of the family identity.

The superiority of family firms may also result from their culture or reputation. The family may provide a focal point for a corporate culture that minimizes transaction costs (Kreps 1990). Families have the reputation to establish a credible commitment that authority will be consistently used. For example, if a family enjoys a reputation for integrity, other stakeholders may expect the firm to follow that principle. Strong reputations can smooth transactions in most market interactions. They also facilitate social network development and political connections.

Joint family and firm optimization, however, may result in substantial costs. The potential inconsistency of family norms with business rationale may lead to epic and emotional rivalries. Families tend to favor equality among members, while productive organizations base rewards on productivity. Hiring based on blood and not on merit considerations hinders efficiency. Needless to say, firing and comforting one's child may be difficult. Furthermore, some of the attractive features of family firms require undisputed family control. As a result, family firms may also be at a disadvantage when financing large projects or at hiring talented employees.

The preceding discussion suggests that family characteristics, such as family size and talent, and resources can have an important impact on firms' outcomes. If, for example, costly external financing is a crucial friction in the marketplace, the ability of the firm to overcome this friction may depend on the depth of the family's pockets.

The analysis provides an array of predictions in terms of the settings where family firms would be expected to flourish, including countries where market institutions are poorly developed (Burkart, Panunzi, and Shleifer 2003) or where family trust relative to nonfamily trust is disproportionate (Banfield 1958). Other settings involve industries where implicit contracts are important or firms whose products or corporate culture are intricately linked to the reputation of a family.

The arguments also provide a benchmark for a critical assessment of the family firm. The path of least resistance is, in many firms, preserving the status quo, where family labor and financial resources are by default allocated to the firm. Such practices do not need to maximize family or firm value. Unleashing family resources, through family offices or by inducing relatives to find productive matches for their talent, could potentially add value even for nonfamily investors. An extreme version of this analysis may lead to the decision to exit the business.

Succession

Succession is perhaps the most visible test of the quality of firms' ongoing governance institutions. Succession is a crucial concern for family members, practitioners, and family firm researchers. Succession may take many forms, such as family, ownership, board, management, and wealth succession. Succession is a powerful force that seems to preserve an instinctual drive.

Family firms typically have strong preferences for family continuity. Such preferences may be the result of private benefits derived from having close relatives influencing decisions. If children are the closest relatives, then the family would tend to focus on the future. Alternatively, family members often view themselves as the stewards of their firms (Davis, Schoorman, and Donaldson 1997). Within-family-specific stewardship leads to similar predictions with regard to the future. Empirically, separating between these arguments is difficult.

Intergenerational preferences also imply large trade-offs for family firms. Dynastic motives may facilitate long-term investments, help overcome asset substitution conflicts (Jensen and Meckling 1976), or provide incentives to develop a family reputation. The family willingness to invest for the long run may explain family firm prevalence in reputation-intensive industries such as in media outlets. It may also translate into stronger labor relations (Sraer and Thesmar 2007) or lower financing costs (Anderson, Mansi, and Reeb 2003).

Within-family intergenerational preferences may, in contrast, lead to nepotism in management or board representation; to an inability to hire or retain nonfamily talent; to inefficient strategic investments that reinforce the likelihood of a family succession; or to political activism to block growth-enhancing reforms.

Family Governance: Open Issues and Recent Evidence

In terms of governance, the previously described arguments indicate that the family organization can play a crucial role in decision making. At the most general level, family governance determines the type of interactions between the family and the firm (such as ownership, board of directors, and management) and the rules that guide those interactions.

In a broad sense, few systematic studies provide direct tests on the specific channels through which family structure affects value. There is hardly any evidence on family, not firm, board (family council) effects: the effect of its composition and size on decisions and outcomes. Little is known about the selection processes or incentive contracts to induce family member participation, or about family rules that guide participation. How do families make decisions? How do families with complicated family trees reduce or manage the level of complexity? How do families prevent inefficient participation from unqualified relatives? How does the family isolate the business from unexpected family shocks? How does the family protect the relatives' standard of living from drastic changes in firm profitability? Should family governance institutions be concerned about these otherwise personal issues? Under what circumstances does family governance become active and contentious? What is the interaction between liquidity (ex dividend) policies and family governance? What family arrangements induce relatives to exit the business? When does the family exit the business?

The empirical governance literature has, to date, only scratched the surface of the family characteristics that may provide answers to these questions. It has thus far mostly focused on family effects with regard to management and investment. The focus on these issues is partly data driven but as detailed data sets become available, the room for sharper analyses and more ambitious tests grows.

With regard to managerial succession, Pérez-González (2006) shows that a proxy for managerial talent of family heirs (the selectivity of the college attended) can have a large and significant effect on firm performance. Within the pool of incoming family CEOs, the differential performance gap between talented and less talented family CEOs is at least 15 percent of firm value. He finds no such difference for incoming nonfamily CEOs.

Bennedsen et al. (2007) provide stark evidence that the characteristics of the family behind the firm can affect succession decisions and performance. Using data from Denmark they show that the gender of the first child of a family CEO affects the probability of observing a family CEO (if male, higher than if female) and that succession decisions affect profitability (family CEOs lead to lower profitability). As discussed in the next section, this evidence provides perhaps the cleanest evidence to date that family characteristics affect performance. The random assignment of gender to firms provides a compelling argument for a causal negative family-CEO effect on performance.

Two related studies are Bloom and Van Reenen (2007) and Mehrotra et al. (2009). Bloom and Van Reenen show that Western European firms that select CEOs based on primogeniture rules exhibit lower levels of managerial practices and productivity than other firms. Mehrotra et al. show that small changes in the quality of the family talent pool of Japanese firms can have positive effects on performance. In-laws or other adopted sons, who are often selected based on managerial talent, outperform blood relatives. The implication of this result is that giving priority to firm considerations when evaluating prospective partners in arranged marriages settings can significantly affect firm performance.

The results of these papers cast doubt on the benefits of succession policies that select CEOs at birth (e.g., primogeniture) and suggest that an important subsample of family firms around the world may benefit from limiting the family interaction to ownership and board representation. Whether family firms can retain their effectiveness without the top management positions (i.e., without the negative costs on management) is an open research question.

In terms of investment, Bertrand et al. (2008) use data from Thailand to show that the number of founder's sons affects how assets are divided within the family. They also show that the number of sons is negatively related to business groups' recovery from the financial crisis of the late 1990s. Bunkanwanicha et al. (2008) show that marriages in Thailand are a common way to establish business networks and that these marriages can affect firm valuation.

Ellul et al. (2009) and Tsoutsoura (2009) demonstrate that family inheritance regulations and taxes can negatively affect investment. Ellul et al. find that countries that tend to force equal inheritances have lower investment rates after succession. Tsoutsoura studies the effect of personal wealth transfer taxes on the investment decisions of Greek family firms. Using a tax reform as a laboratory for analysis and the first-born approach of Bennedsen et al. (2007), she finds that wealth transfer taxes affect the probability of observing family successions and investment decisions. These two papers show that the separation between firms' decisions and personal characteristics predicted by Fisher (1930) does not hold empirically.

In sum, this section has emphasized the importance of family governance as the key determining factor in the governance of the family firm. It described the main arguments that favor the development of family firms and the conditions that challenge their existence. The discussion highlighted the role of succession as a crucial governance event. Lastly, this section stressed that the empirical literature currently provides few answers regarding the effectiveness of the family as the main governance institution of the family firm.

FAMILY FIRMS AND RESEARCH DESIGN

This section emphasizes that family firms may generate variation in firm decision making that can potentially be used to establish causal relationships. The discussion is organized around the challenges faced when assessing a specific research question: the impact of family CEOs on firm performance

Research Design: From Randomization to Family Firms

Researchers are ultimately interested in establishing causal links. With this objective in mind, randomized experiments are the natural approach to establishing cause-and-effect relationships. Yet randomized experiments are rarely an option in corporate governance research. Furthermore, because firms do not randomly make decisions, empirical corporate governance research tends to be plagued with endogeneity and omitted variables concerns.

In general terms, endogeneity challenges imply that demonstrating whether a governance variable causes the observed effect on performance or, alternatively, whether performance drives governance outcomes is difficult. Concerns with omitted variables arise when a variable of interest, often unobserved, is omitted from the analysis, and other variables that are included as controls capture the variation of this omitted control. As a result, establishing a direct effect from the control variables reported is challenging.

Adding more covariates may be counterproductive in these settings if these variables are themselves outcome variables of the problem under examination. For example, the size or composition of the board may vary in preparation for the appointment of a family CEO. Consequently, board characteristics should not be assumed to be exogenous and should not be included as controls.

How can governance researchers overcome these empirical challenges? Instrumental variables provide one potential solution to endogeneity and omitted variables concerns (Angrist and Pischke 2009). A valid instrumental variable (IV) must be correlated with the key control variable (family CEOs) but it cannot be correlated with the error term in the variable of interest (performance equation). Such an IV generates variation in the key control variable (family CEO) that is likely to be exogenous, overcoming inference problems. This clean source can potentially allow researchers to estimate the causal effect of the control variable (family CEOs) on the outcome variable (performance). In practice, however, finding instruments that meet these two basic criteria is difficult. This section illustrates how a family characteristic, such as the gender of the first child of a founder, can potentially be used as a valid instrumental variable.

Instrumental Variables: An Example

Suppose that firm performance is given by $Q + I$, where Q is a firm characteristic that affects performance, such as the quality of the firm's new projects, and I is related to the identity of a CEO. Assume that CEOs can be of two types: family or unrelated. Let $I = f$ when the incoming CEO is related to the outgoing CEO and $I = u$ when the incoming CEO is unrelated or nonfamily. In terms of inference, researchers are interested in estimating $f - u$, the direct effect of family CEOs. Suppose there is heterogeneity in the quality of firms' new projects around succession decisions that the econometrician cannot observe or control. Specifically, the quality of a firm's new projects can be high (q_H), medium (q_M), or low (q_L), each with a probability of one-third.

A standard ordinary least squares specification would yield $f - u$ directly if family and unrelated CEOs were randomly assigned to firms. However, firms are unlikely to follow random assignment of CEO positions. In fact, Pérez-González (2006) and Bennedsen et al. (2007) document that firms that select family versus nonfamily CEOs differ along several observable and likely unobservable characteristics. In other words, they highlight that the assumption that CEO promotions are random is strong.

To stress the effect of nonrandom assignment, and in the spirit of Hermalin and Weisbach (1998), suppose that the higher the quality of the firm's prospects, the more powerful the departing CEO and the more likely he selects a family CEO. Also, suppose that for non-firm-related reasons (e.g., family tradition) the likelihood of a family succession is higher when the CEO's firstborn child is male. Exhibit 19.1 shows a decision rule that satisfies these conditions.

Standard least squares estimates compare firms according to the *observed* outcomes: family versus unrelated succession. If male and female firstborn

Exhibit 19.1 Relationship between Investment Opportunities and CEO Selection Decisions

This table describes a decision rule that leads to the appointment of a family (unrelated) chief executive officer (CEO) as a function of the firms' unobserved investment opportunities to illustrate the potential advantage of using an exogenous family characteristic for overcoming omitted variables and endogeneity concerns. Specifically, the table indicates that whenever investment opportunities are above (below) average, or "high" ("low"), family firms would appoint family CEOs (unrelated CEOs). When investment opportunities are moderate ("medium"), firms tend to select a family CEO if the first child of the founder is male but an unrelated CEO if the first child is female. Assuming the variation from the gender of the first child is random, researchers may use this variation to test for the impact of family CEOs on firm performance.

Investment Opportunities	Gender of First Child: Male	Gender of First Child: Female
High	Family CEO ($q_H + f$)	Family CEO ($q_H + f$)
Medium	Family CEO ($q_M + f$)	Unrelated CEO ($q_M + u$)
Low	Unrelated CEO ($q_L + u$)	Unrelated CEO ($q_L + u$)

children occur with equal probability, the difference in performance in these two groups is

$$1/3(q_H - q_L) + 1/2(f - u)$$

Clearly, the standard least squares estimated coefficients would reflect not only the true effect of family CEOs but also a selection bias, which would then be incorrectly attributed to CEO characteristics. In consequence, the estimate would have an upward bias. In other words, family CEOs would look better than unrelated CEOs because family CEOs receive the best firms.

Instrumental variables, in contrast, starts by using information on all CEO successions conditional on the gender of the firstborn child and then compares the outcome of CEO successions as a function of the IV. Intuitively, this is equivalent to comparing the outcomes of all CEO transitions in Exhibit 19.1 and calculating the difference in performance across columns. Mathematically, this difference is $1/3(f - u)$.

The IV estimator uses only the information of the group with medium investment prospects, which is the variation that is not contaminated by differences in investment opportunities. Other than the fact that family transitions are more common in male firstborn firms, firms falling in each of the two columns are likely to have similar characteristics. The effect of unobserved variables on performance then cancels out when the difference across groups is taken. Indeed, Bennedsen et al. (2007) show that when firms are classified by the gender of the firstborn child of the CEO, their characteristics are remarkably similar, suggesting the gender of a firstborn child is randomly distributed across firms.

Lessons of General Interest

Given that family firms are subject to variation in family characteristics, some of which are determined by nature, and as a result exogenous to firm investment opportunities, research based on these firms can potentially shed light on important questions in financial economics.

As previously discussed, Bennedsen et al. (2007) use the gender of the first child born of a departing CEO to establish that family CEOs negatively affect performance. This result, however, also highlights that nonfamily CEOs provide valuable services to the organizations they head. This direct test is important because finding convincing evidence that CEOs add value in organizations has historically been difficult.

In a more recent paper, Bennedsen et al. (2009) test for the importance of CEO focus for performance. Using variation in CEO attention that results from deaths in his immediate family (such as spouse, children, and parents), they show that CEOs significantly affect firm outcomes. This result has broad implications in corporate governance research because it provides direct evidence that CEO actions can have a meaningful impact on performance.

In sum, family businesses are a fruitful area of research. Family firms are relevant and understudied in the literature. Furthermore, they can also provide an attractive laboratory for addressing central questions of general interest in financial economics.

SUMMARY AND CONCLUSIONS

The focus on family firm research is relatively new in the financial economics literature. The interest in understanding the governance institutions of family firms is motivated by recent evidence documenting that the majority of firms around the world are owned by members of the founding family of the corporation. This chapter studies the governance mechanisms of family firms; it examines the main issues and challenges in the existing literature and then highlights a number of promising lines of research.

The analysis emphasizes four broad issues. First, family-firm research provides a fertile ground for corporate governance research. Family businesses are prevalent around the world and they are also correlated with significantly more dispersion in measures of economic output than other firms. The corporate governance mechanisms that allow for such extreme outcomes in performance are currently only partially understood. More data will be needed to investigate these issues. Recent research, however, shows that detailed data sets can be constructed to provide novel answers to these questions.

Second, moving this research agenda forward requires sharper definitions of family firms. This chapter provides one such definition and then stresses its main governance implications. A large number of stylized facts that have been found in the literature are direct implications of a simple characterization of these firms. For empirical researchers, such observation implies that arguing that governance, investment, financial, or succession decisions are exogenous with regard to other characteristics is difficult.

Third, family firms are unique because the governance of these firms is largely determined by the governance of the family behind the family firm. Market imperfections often introduce a wedge between family and arm's-length transactions, favoring the within-family allocation of resources. As a result, the collective action problems that characterize family decision making and family relationships in the context of nonrelative relationships may differ in systematic ways. Understanding these relationships is crucial for the development of this area of research.

Fourth, family firms may provide an attractive laboratory for addressing important research questions in financial economics. Family-firm decisions that result from family, not firm, characteristics provide researchers with the opportunity to overcome endogeneity and omitted variables concerns that plague corporate governance research. Further work is needed to understand how family firms balance the protection that the controlling family brings to the firm with the challenges this structure imposes on minority shareholders.

DISCUSSION QUESTIONS

1. Discuss two explanations for why founding families hold concentrated ownership stakes in a publicly traded firm. Describe two potential distortions that such holdings may introduce in firm behavior.
2. Why may such common corporate governance mechanisms as the board of directors, compensation, and market for corporate control be ineffective in disciplining family firms?
3. Discuss two potential governance benefits and two potential governance costs that are unique to family firms.
4. From the perspective of corporate governance researchers, why are family firms a promising laboratory to empirically examine questions of general interest in financial economics?

REFERENCES

Aghion, Philippe, and Patrick Bolton. 1992. An incomplete contracts approach to financial contracting. *Review of Economic Studies* 59 (3): 473–494.

Almeida, Heitor, and Daniel Wolfenzon. 2006. Should business groups be dismantled? The equilibrium costs of efficient internal capital markets. *Journal of Financial Economics* 79 (1): 99–144.

Anderson, Ronald, Augustine Duru, and David M. Reeb. 2009. Founders, heirs, and corporate opacity in the U. S. *Journal of Financial Economics* 92 (2): 205–222.

Anderson, Ronald, Satter A. Mansi, and David M. Reeb. 2003. Founding-family ownership and the agency cost of debt. *Journal of Financial Economics* 68 (2): 263–285.

Anderson, Ronald C., and David M. Reeb. 2003a. Founding-family ownership and firm performance: Evidence from the S&P 500. *Journal of Finance* 58 (3): 1301–1328.

———. 2003b. Founding-family ownership, corporate diversification, and firm leverage. *Journal of Law and Economics* 46 (2): 653–687.

———. 2004. Board composition: Balancing family influence in S&P 500 firms. *Administrative Science Quarterly* 49 (2): 209–237.

Angrist, Joshua D., and Jorn-Steffen Pischke. 2009. *Mostly harmless econometrics: An empiricist's companion.* Princeton: Princeton University Press.

Banfield, Edward. 1958. *The moral basis of a backward society*. New York: Free Press.
Becht, Marco, Patrick Bolton, and Ailsa Roell. 2003. Corporate governance and control. In *Handbook of the economics of finance*, ed. George M. Constantinides, Milton Harris, and René Stulz, Vol. 1: 1–109, Amsterdam: Elsevier, North-Holland.
Becker, Gary. 1981. *A treatise on the family*. Cambridge, MA: Harvard University Press.
Bennedsen, Morten, and Kasper M. Nielsen. 2009. Incentive and entrenchment effects in European ownership. *Journal of Banking and Finance*, forthcoming.
Bennedsen, Morten, Kasper M. Nielsen, Francisco Pérez-González, and Daniel Wolfenzon. 2007. Inside the family firm: The role of families in succession decisions and performance. *Quarterly Journal of Economics* 122 (2): 647–691.
Bennedsen, Morten, Francisco Pérez-González, and Daniel Wolfenzon. 2009. Do CEOs matter? Working paper, Stanford University.
Berle, Adolf A., and Gardiner C. Means. 1932. *The modern corporation and private property*. New York: Macmillan.
Bertrand, Marianne, Simon Johnson, Krislert Samphantharak, and Antoinette Schoar. 2008. Mixing family with business: A study of Thai business groups and the families behind them. *Journal of Financial Economics* 88 (3): 466–498.
Bertrand, Marianne, and Antoinette Schoar. 2006. The role of family in family firms. *Journal of Economic Perspectives* 20 (2): 73–96.
Bloom, Nick, and John Van Reenen. 2007. Measuring and explaining management practices across firms and countries. *Quarterly Journal of Economics* 122 (4): 1351–1408.
Bunkanwanicha, Praumuan, Joseph Fan, and Yupana Wiwattanakantang. 2008. Why do shareholders value marriage? ECGI Working paper 227.
Burkart, Mike, Denis Gromb, and Fausto Panunzi. 1997. Large shareholders, monitoring, and the value of the firm. *Quarterly Journal of Economics* 112 (3): 693–728.
Burkart, Mike, Fausto Panunzi, and Andrei Shleifer. 2003. Family firms. *Journal of Finance* 58 (5): 2167–2202.
Caselli, Francesco, and Nicola Gennaioli. 2003. Dynastic management. NBER Working paper 9442.
Claessens, Stijn, Simeon Djankov, Joseph P. H. Fan, and Larry H. P. Lang. 2002. Disentangling the incentive and entrenchment effects of large shareholdings. *Journal of Finance* 57 (6): 2741–2771.
Claessens, Stijn, Joseph P. H. Fan, and Larry H. P. Lang. 2000. The separation of ownership and control in East Asian corporations. *Journal of Financial Economics* 58 (1–2): 81–112.
Cucculelli, Marco, and Giacinto Micucci. 2008. Family succession and firm performance: Evidence from Italian family firms. *Journal of Corporate Finance* 14 (1): 17–31.
Davis, James H., David Schoorman, and Lex Donaldson. 1997. Toward a stewardship theory of management. *Academy of Management Review* 22 (1): 20–47.
Demsetz, Harold, and Kenneth Lehn. 1985. The structure of corporate ownership: Causes and consequences. *Journal of Political Economy* 93 (6): 1155–1177.
Dyck, Alexander, and Luigi Zingales. 2004. Private benefits of control: An international comparison. *Journal of Finance* 59 (2): 537–600.
Ellul, Andrew, Marco Pagano, and Fausto Panunzi. 2009. Inheritance law and investment in family firms." Working paper, Indiana University.
Faccio, Mara. 2006. Politically connected firms. *American Economic Review* 96 (1): 369–386.
Faccio, Mara, and Larry H. P. Lang. 2002. The ultimate ownership of Western European corporations. *Journal of Financial Economics* 65 (3): 365–395.
Faccio, Mara, Maria-Teresa Marchica, and Roberto Mura. 2009. Large shareholder diversification and corporate risk-taking. Working paper, Purdue University.
Faccio, Mara, and David C. Parsley. 2009. Sudden deaths: Taking stock of geographic ties. *Journal of Financial and Quantitative Analysis* 33 (3): 683–718.
Fan, Joseph P. H., Ming Jian, Li Jin, and Yin-Hua Yeh. 2009. Succession: The roles of specialized assets and transfer costs. Working paper, Chinese University of Hong Kong.

Fisher, Irving. 1930. *The theory of interest as determined by impatience to spend income and opportunity to invest it*. New York: Macmillan Company.

Fisman, Ray. 2001. Estimating the value of political connections. *American Economic Review* 91 (4): 1095–1102.

Franks, Julian, Colin Mayer, and Stefano Rossi. 2009. Ownership: Evolution and regulation. *Review of Financial Studies* 22 (10): 4009–4056.

Grossman, Sanford, and Oliver S. Hart. 1980. Takeover bids, the free-rider problem, and the theory of the corporation. *Bell Journal of Economics* 11 (1): 42–64.

———. 1986. The costs and benefits of ownership: A theory of vertical and lateral integration. *Journal of Political Economy* 94 (4): 691–719.

Hansmann, Henry. 1996. *The ownership of enterprise*. Cambridge, MA: Belknap Press of Harvard University Press.

Hart, Oliver S., and Moore John. 1990. Property rights and the nature of the firm. *Journal of Political Economy* 98 (6): 1119–1158.

Hermalin, Benjamin E., and Michael S. Weisbach. 1998. Endogenously chosen boards of directors and their monitoring of the CEO. *American Economic Review* 88 (1): 96–118.

Himmelberg, Charles, Glenn Hubbard, and Darius Palia. 1999. Understanding the determinants of managerial ownership and the link between ownership and performance. *Journal of Financial Economics* 53 (3): 353–384.

Jensen, Michael C., and William H. Meckling. 1976. Theory of the firm: Managerial behavior, agency costs and ownership structure. *Journal of Financial Economics* 3 (4): 305–360.

Khanna, Tarun, and Yishay Yafeh. 2007. Business groups in emerging markets: Paragons or parasites? *Journal of Economic Literature* 45 (2): 331–372.

Kreps, David. 1990. Corporate culture and economic theory. In *Perspectives on positive political economy*, ed. James Alt and Kenneth Shepsle, 90–143. New York: Cambridge University Press.

La Porta, Rafael, Florencio Lopez-de-Silanes, and Andrei Shleifer. 1999. Corporate ownership around the world. *Journal of Finance* 54 (2): 471–517.

MassMutual Financial Group, Kennesaw State University, and Family Firm Institute. 2007. *American family business survey*. http://www.massmutual.com/mmfg/pdf/afbs.pdf.

McConaughy, Daniel L., Michael C. Walker, Glenn Henderson Jr., and Chandra S. Mishra. 1998. Founding family–controlled firms: Efficiency and value. *Review of Financial Economics* 7 (1): 1–19.

Mehrotra, Vikas, Randall Morck, Jungwook Shim, and Yupana Wiwattanakantang. 2009. Adoptive expectations: Rising sons in Japanese family firms. Working paper, University of Alberta.

Miller, Danny, Isabelle Le Breton-Miller, Richard H. Lester, and Albert A. Cannella. 2007. Are family firms really superior performers? *Journal of Corporate Finance* 13 (5): 829–858.

Morck, Randall, Andrei Shleifer, and Robert W. Vishny. 1989. Alternative mechanisms for corporate control. *American Economic Review* 79 (4): 842–852.

Morck, Randall K., David A. Stangeland, and Bernard Yeung. 2000. Inherited wealth, corporate control and economic growth: The Canadian disease? In *Concentrated corporate ownership*, ed. Randall K. Morck, 319–369. Chicago: University of Chicago Press.

Morck, Randall, Daniel Wolfenzon, and Bernard Yeung. 2005. Corporate governance, economic entrenchment, and growth. *Journal of Economic Literature* 43 (3): 655–720.

Nenova, Tatiana. 2003. The value of corporate votes and control benefits: A cross-country analysis. *Journal of Financial Economics* 68 (3): 325–351.

Pérez-González, Francisco. 2006. Inherited control and firm performance. *American Economic Review* 96 (5): 1559–1588.

Shleifer, Andrei, and Robert W. Vishny. 1986. Large shareholders and corporate control. *Journal of Political Economy* 94 (3): 461–488.

———. 1989. Management entrenchment: The case of manager-specific investments. *Journal of Financial Economics* 25 (1): 123–139.
———. 1997. A survey of corporate governance. *Journal of Finance* 52 (2): 737–783.
Slovin, Myron B., and Marie E. Sushka. 1993. Ownership concentration, corporate control activity, and firm value: Evidence from the death of inside blockholders. *Journal of Finance* 48 (4): 1293–1321.
Sraer, David, and David Thesmar. 2007. Performance and behavior of family firms: Evidence from the French stock market. *Journal of the European Economic Association* 5 (4): 709–751.
Tsoutsoura, Margarita. 2009. The effect of succession taxes on family firm investment: Evidence from a natural experiment. Working paper, Columbia University.
Villalonga, Belén, and Raphael Amit. 2006. How do family ownership, control, and management affect firm value? *Journal of Financial Economics* 80 (2): 385–417.
———. 2008. Family control of firms and industries. Working paper, Harvard Business School.
———. 2009. How are U.S. family firms controlled? *Review of Financial Studies* 22 (8): 3047–3091.
Williamson, Oliver E. 1985. *The economic institutions of capitalism: Firms, markets and relational contracting*. New York: Free Press.

ABOUT THE AUTHORS

Morten Bennedsen is the Hoffmann Chair of Family Business Management and professor in economics at INSEAD. His main area of research is the governance of family firms and other closely held corporations. His work has been published in many top finance and economics journals such as the *Journal of Political Economy*, *Quarterly Journal of Economics*, and *Journal of Financial Economics*, among others. He has a PhD in economics from Harvard University, a master's degree from the London School of Economics, and a bachelor of arts degree from the University of Copenhagen.

Francisco Pérez-González is assistant professor of finance at Stanford University and a faculty research fellow of the National Bureau of Economic Research. His research is in the intersection of corporate finance and organizational economics, with particular emphasis on family firms. His work has been published in top economics journals such as the *American Economic Review* and *Quarterly Journal of Economics*. He received a bachelor's degree in economics from ITAM in Mexico and earned both a master's and a PhD in economics from Harvard University.

Daniel Wolfenzon is the Stefan H. Robock Professor of Finance and Economics at Columbia University and a research associate of the National Bureau of Economic Research. His research interests are in corporate finance and organizational economics. He has studied control sharing in small firms, the effects of investor protection on ownership concentration, and the structure of business groups around the world. He has also performed extensive work related to family firms. His work has been published in top economic and finance journals such as the *Quarterly Journal of Economics*, *Journal of Finance*, and *Journal of Financial Economics*. He received a master's and a PhD in economics from Harvard University and holds a BS in economics and a BS in mechanical engineering from MIT.

CHAPTER 20

Institutional and Other Shareholders

CHRIS MALLIN
Professor of Corporate Governance and Finance, and Director of the Centre for Corporate Governance Research, Birmingham Business School

INTRODUCTION

Corporate governance has gained an increasingly high profile over the past two decades. Financial scandals and collapses occur around the globe in companies of all sizes and types: Enron, Worldcom, Shell, China Aviation Oil, Société Générale, Northern Rock, and many more. These incidences have affected confidence in the market. The global financial crisis sent capital markets into a free fall and caused questions to be asked about the fundamental strengths and weaknesses of corporate governance systems worldwide.

Over the years, institutional shareholders such as pension funds, insurance companies, and mutual funds have become increasingly influential. In addition, other shareholders including hedge funds, private equity, sovereign wealth funds, and banks were seen as powerful players in the investment world. Various corporate governance codes and guidelines emphasized the rights and responsibilities of share ownership. Many institutional shareholders have their own set of corporate governance principles based on national and international corporate governance guidance.

Given that institutional shareholders have cross-border portfolio investments, their influence extends well beyond their home countries. However, institutional shareholders tend to have the most influence in the United Kingdom and the United States. Thus, much of the discussion in this chapter focuses on these two countries.

Institutional shareholders generally agree on the core principles of corporate governance and what might be deemed to be good corporate governance. Such practices include disclosure, transparency, accountability, and a responsible approach to business. Occasionally, institutional shareholders may work together to try to ensure that companies in their portfolio improve their governance structures or to challenge extremely generous remuneration packages for executive directors.

The Organisation for Economic Co-operation and Development (OECD) (2004, 37) expressed the sentiments of many when it stated in its Principles of Corporate Governance:

> *The effectiveness and credibility of the entire corporate governance system and company oversight will, therefore, to a large extent depend on institutional investors that can make informed use of their shareholder rights and effectively exercise their ownership functions in companies in which they invest.*

The OECD emphasizes both the informed use of shareholder rights and the effective exercise of ownership functions.

This chapter proceeds as follows. First, it identifies institutional shareholders and then discusses the growth of these shareholders, particularly in the United Kingdom and the United States. It then discusses some influential organizations such as the Association of British Insurers (ABI) and the National Association of Pension Funds (NAPF) in the United Kingdom, and organizations such as the Council of Institutional Investors (CII) in the United States. The role of influential organizations such as the International Corporate Governance Network (ICGN) is also discussed. The chapter highlights some of the tools of governance that institutional shareholders have at their disposal including constructive dialogue, voting, focus lists, and shareholder proposals (resolutions), and gives examples of how leading institutional investors use these tools. Hot issues for institutional shareholders are identified. Finally, the chapter concludes with comments on how the future role of institutional shareholders may change, given the perception that they should be more involved in the corporate governance of their investee companies.

WHO ARE INSTITUTIONAL SHAREHOLDERS?

Institutional shareholders are generally understood to be large investors such as pension funds, insurance companies, and mutual funds. In countries such as the United Kingdom and the United States, share ownership is concentrated in the hands of this type of investor. There has been a corresponding decline in share ownership by individuals. Although institutional shareholders tend to display a home bias, they also have substantial international diversification in their portfolios. Thus, the influence of institutional shareholders carries beyond their home country to cross-border investments.

Countries that have liberalized their markets and undergone privatization programs often find that institutional shareholders play an important role. Developing countries seeking foreign direct investment also attempt to attract institutional shareholders. These shareholders are generally looking for familiar standards of corporate governance. Therefore, countries seeking to attract institutional shareholders usually try to ensure that they have a corporate governance code that embodies internationally recognized corporate governance principles and is appropriately supported by a sound regulatory regime. The influence of institutional investors is persuasive in many countries and in companies with a range of ownership structures.

In addition to the institutional shareholders identified thus far, there are other important players including banks, sovereign wealth funds, private equity firms, and hedge funds. Banks play a key role in various countries including Japan and Germany where they often hold seats on the board. Japanese banks have traditionally had a close relationship with firms from prewar Zaibatsu groupings to latter-day *keiretsu* networks (Mallin 2006). Although banks' traditional relationships have come under pressure in recent years, change is slow and banks are still able to exert an influence on companies. In Germany, many view banks as playing an important role on the supervisory boards of German companies although, as in Japan, this attitude may change over time.

Sovereign wealth funds are funds owned by governments and these funds often tend to be very large and influential. The United Arab Emirates, China, Singapore, and Saudi Arabia all have large sovereign wealth funds that sometimes make strategic infrastructure and other investments in foreign countries. Examples of investing in the infrastructure of a country include investments in airports, harbors, and road networks. Given that sovereign wealth funds are often opaque, some view such strategic investments with unease.

The International Working Group of Sovereign Wealth Funds (IWG) (2008), with a membership of 26 countries that have sovereign wealth funds, was established in May 2008. In 2008, the IWG published the Santiago Principles, designed as a set of generally accepted accounting principles (GAAP) that properly reflects its investment practices and objectives. These principles should lead to improved disclosure and transparency, sound governance structures, accountability, and more confidence in sovereign wealth funds and their activities.

Private equity funds may be broadly defined as funds that invest in equity not publicly traded on a stock exchange. Private equity firms sometimes acquire large, well-known High Street or brand-name companies. Institutional shareholders may fund these types of deals. Private equity investments may include activities such as venture capital, buyouts, acquisitions of large or controlling positions in more mature companies, investments in financially distressed companies, or investments in companies with unrealized value that the private equity fund can realize. Private equity funds cause some concern because they typically do not disclose much information about their operations.

In the United Kingdom, the Walker Working Group (2007) published *Guidelines for Disclosure and Transparency in Private Equity*. These voluntary guidelines are aimed at private equity firms and place an onus on private equity funds to provide more details about the financial performance of companies they acquire. The new rules require private equity companies to publish accounts for large companies that they own no later than six months after financial year-ends.

Hedge funds were originally investment funds that sought to hedge or offset potential losses by hedging their investments through a variety of methods. Originally, hedge funds tended to be more risk averse but today they often use hedging methods such as short-selling to increase rather than reduce risk, hoping for a higher return.

The OECD (2008a and 2008b) also published two documents in relation to private equity firms and hedge funds: *Codes and Industry Standards Covering the Behaviour of Alternative Investors*, a list of private-sector initiatives aimed at addressing policy issues; and *The Role of Private Equity and Activist Hedge Funds in Corporate Governance–Related Policy Issues*. The latter document concludes that private equity firms and activist hedge funds often act as informed owners and are more active in monitoring the performance of companies and their management than other institutional investors. The report also concludes that any corporate governance concerns that relate to governance practices by private equity firms and activist hedge funds are best addressed within the framework of the existing OECD Principles.

GROWTH IN INSTITUTIONAL SHAREHOLDERS

The previous section identified the institutional shareholders. This section examines the growth in corporate governance in the context of providing a background for the development of institutional shareholders and their perceived influence.

Rise of Corporate Governance

What led to the growth in interest in corporate governance from various parties including directors, shareholders, government, and trade unions? A combination of several key drivers has stimulated the growth in corporate governance. First, over a number of years a series of corporate scandals and collapses took place that shook the investment community and led to the establishment of corporate governance committees in various countries. The leading proponents in the early 1990s were arguably the UK Committee on the Financial Aspects of Corporate Governance, chaired by Sir Adrian Cadbury, and the Bosch Committee in Australia. Both committees produced insightful reports that laid the foundations for the development of corporate governance in many countries around the world. These reports emphasized the role of institutional investors in trying to ensure that the companies in which they invested (investee companies) had good corporate governance.

As more codes were introduced, both of a country-specific nature and with international applicability, these codes tended to recognize the role that institutional investors could play in helping to encourage the adoption of good corporate governance practices. Even in countries where institutional investors were not dominant, companies wanting to raise new capital would often look to foreign investors to provide this capital and, in turn, the foreign investors would look for certain standards of corporate governance. Therefore, committees established in various countries around the world recognized the importance of institutional investors. In turn, institutional investors seeking to diversify and invest in a portfolio of international equities emphasized the corporate governance principles with which they were familiar.

This increased emphasis on corporate governance has resulted in several fundamental implications for companies. Practical structural effects include the following:

- The establishment of key board committees such as the audit committee (to manage the relationship with the external auditor), remuneration or compensation committee (to set the remuneration of the executive directors or managers), and nomination committee (to provide a transparent process for the nomination and appointment of directors).

- The separation of the roles of chair and chief executive officer (CEO) to avoid any single individual wielding too much power.
- The presence of a balanced board, comprised of executive and independent nonexecutive directors, each with the relevant skills and experience to make an appropriate contribution to the business.

Implications have also arisen for how companies manage their relationships with investors and particularly the relationship with large shareholders. The next section highlights the growth of institutional shareholders and develops the relationship between corporate governance codes and the role of institutional shareholders.

Trends in Share Ownership

A sea change has occurred in share ownership in many countries in the past 40 years. In the United Kingdom and the United States, this has resulted in share ownership moving away from individuals and into the hands of institutional shareholders. Institutional shareholders own around 65 percent of U.S. equity. In the United Kingdom, the Office of National Statistics provides an analysis of share ownership, as shown in Exhibit 20.1.

As Exhibit 20.1 shows, at the end of 2008 institutional shareholders (pension funds and insurance companies) owned 26 percent of UK equity, overseas shareholders (predominately institutional investors) owned 42 percent, and individual shareholders owned just over 10 percent. Comparing these percentages to data from 1963 shows that major changes have occurred as share ownership has moved away from individuals who used to own 54 percent of UK equity and into the hands of insurance companies, pension funds, and overseas investors who once owned 7 percent but now own 42 percent. Many of the overseas investors are U.S. institutional investors who tend to be more active in pushing for better

Exhibit 20.1 Main Categories of Share Ownership in the United Kingdom, 1963–2008

This table presents the change in the levels of share ownership by various types of investor over the period 1963–2008. The most striking changes are the decline in individuals' share ownership and the increase in ownership by institutional investors and overseas investors. (Other categories owning shares include investment trusts, public sector, industrial, and commercial companies.)

Type of Investor	1963 (%)	2008 (%)
Individuals	54	10
Insurance companies	10	13
Pension funds	6	13
Banks	1	4
Unit trusts	1	2
Overseas	7	42

Source: Based on Office of National Statistics (ONS) Share Ownership 2010.

corporate governance. This has implications for UK companies and UK institutional investors because U.S. investors tend to vote more and may be more inclined to intervene in companies. Both of these aspects are much more of a regular part of the U.S. investor/company scene than in the United Kingdom.

This analysis clearly shows that institutional ownership in the United Kingdom has increased over time. Of course, this trend is not unique to the United Kingdom. According to Becht, Bolton, and Roell (2002), the growth in pension plans in many countries has led to more money being invested in pension funds and mutual funds, thus helping to create large influential institutional investors.

The OECD (2006) introduced *Guidelines on Pension Fund Asset Management*. The OECD recognized that pension funds were one of the most important players in the financial markets of the OECD countries, managing more than $15 trillion of assets in 2003 and representing more than 80 percent of the OECD's area gross domestic product (GDP). The OECD guidelines serve to show that institutional investors are recognized as key players globally.

Using a comprehensive data set of equity holdings from 27 countries over the period 2000–2005, Ferreira and Matos (2008, 28) find that institutions are becoming prominent shareholders in companies worldwide and that "all institutional investors seek large firms and firms with strong governance indicators ... there is some hope for a 'good firm' in a 'bad' country." Furthermore, their findings suggest that some institutional groups are effective monitors of the firms in which they invest.

CORPORATE GOVERNANCE AND INSTITUTIONAL INVESTORS

Corporate Governance Codes

In the United Kingdom, successive corporate governance codes have recognized the role played by institutional investors in trying to ensure good governance in the companies in which they invest. Given the size of their shareholders, the power and influence that institutional investors can exercise is substantial. They may exercise this power in various ways including one-to-one meetings between institutional investors and company directors, voting their shares at the company's annual general meeting, and through focus lists and shareholder proposals or resolutions.

Reviewing the UK corporate governance codes can prove helpful to highlight the emphasis given to the role of institutional investors. In 1992, the Committee on the Financial Aspects of Corporate Governance, chaired by Sir Adrian Cadbury, produced a report with recommendations on corporate governance best practices in the United Kingdom. The Cadbury Committee, as it became widely known, was formed after various financial scandals and collapses started to affect confidence in financial reporting and accountability. In relation to institutional investors, the Cadbury Committee (1992, 52) stated: "we look to the institutions in particular ... to use their influence as owners to ensure that the companies in which they have invested comply with the Code."

The subsequent Greenbury Committee (1995, 19), chaired by Sir Richard Greenbury and established to provide recommendations on directors' remuneration disclosure, states that "the investor institutions should use their power and influence to ensure the implementation of best practice as set out in the Code." Similarly, the Hampel Committee (1998, 40) states "it is clear ... that a discussion of the role of shareholders in corporate governance will mainly concern the institutions."

These governance codes established an emphasis on the role of institutional investors in UK corporate governance. The Combined Code (1998), which brought together the recommendations of the three aforementioned Committees, carried on this trend by emphasizing the role of institutional investors as its principles of good governance. The Combined Code contains a section headed "Institutional Investors" covering three areas:

1. *Shareholder voting*. Institutional shareholders have a responsibility to make considered use of their votes.
2. *Dialogue with companies*. Institutional shareholders should be ready, where practical, to enter into a dialogue with companies based on the mutual understanding of objectives.
3. *Evaluation of governance disclosures*. When evaluating companies' governance arrangements, particularly those relating to board structure and composition, institutional investors should give due weight to all relevant factors.

The Combined Code was revised in 2003, 2006, and 2008. In relation to institutional investors, the same emphasis remains in terms of the expectation that institutional investors will enter into a dialogue based on the mutual understanding of objectives; will appropriately evaluate governance disclosures; and will make considered use of the votes attaching to their shareholdings.

The phrase "mutual understanding of objectives" is an important one and can be traced back to the Myners Report (1995) on *Developing a Winning Partnership*, which looked at how companies and institutional investors could work together. The report was the result of a joint city/industry working group (where *city* is used as a metonym for the financial services sector) established under the chairmanship of Paul Myners, then at Gartmore plc, with the support of the UK Department of Trade and Industry. The Myners Report (p. 4) states that "... the quality of the relationships between companies and their institutional shareholders plays an important part in encouraging managers to invest for the long-term ... drawing on best practice from a variety of sources, we have developed a 'model' listed company and a 'model' institutional investor to demonstrate how that partnership might work." The Myners Report mentions structured meetings, with an agenda and knowledge of the institution's investment objectives, as vital for the investor/company relationship.

The Trustee Relationship

One area that has been garnering more attention in the context of pension funds is the relationship among the trustee board, the institutional investors, and the ultimate beneficiaries. The term *ultimate beneficiary* may have different meanings depending on the context, but in this case the term means the person who eventually has the benefit of the invested funds. This area relates to pension fund institutional shareholders who are appointed by the board of trustees after taking the advice of specialist consultants. These pension fund institutional investors manage the funds that are invested on behalf of the pension fund beneficiaries, the ultimate beneficiaries.

In recent years the Trade Union Congress (TUC) has focused its activities on highlighting this aspect of the employee pension provision and has drawn attention to the role of the trustees of pension funds. In the wider corporate governance arena, there has been additional emphasis on institutional shareholders acting more as shareowners and exercising their rights on behalf of the ultimate beneficiaries. Yet a fundamental gap exists as the institutional shareholders state that their responsibility is to the trustees of the pension fund when reporting back on their approach to investing and the investments' performance and not to the members (ultimate beneficiaries of the pension fund).

The Myners Report (1995, 19) concludes that

> *Pension fund managers take direction from the trustees of the pension fund who therefore play a key role in the chain that directs money from pension contributions to long-term investment in industry [and] trustees have an important part to play in enhancing the relationship between institutional investors and industry.*

In 2001, Myners (2001) issued a report reviewing institutional investment in the United Kingdom. This was a wide-ranging and comprehensive review that examined, for example, issues associated with the trustee aspects of institutional investment and the legal requirements relating thereto with the aim of raising the standards of institutional investment and promoting greater shareholder activism. According to the Myners report of 2001, many trustees have little in-depth knowledge of investments and are dependent on advisers. In fact, the report finds that 62 percent of trustees have no professional qualifications in finance or investments; 77 percent of trustees have no in-house professionals to assist them; more than 50 percent of trustees receive less than three days' training when they became trustees; and 49 percent of trustees spend three hours or less preparing for pension investment matters. Larger pension schemes have more resources to invest in the recruitment and training of trustees and so can appoint more knowledgeable trustees or can provide appropriate training to give them the skills they require.

Dangers clearly arise when pension fund trustees are too dependent on external advice. Myners (2007) identifies two such dangers. First, a lack of a mandate for decisive action on the part of the trustees exists because trustees believe they lack the expertise to give such a mandate. In addition, the advisers believe they lack the power to make decisions. Second, decisions about where to invest the pension fund's assets are fundamental to the trustees' role, and trustees should at least be able to critically assess the advice they are being given. Myners (p. 17) also states that "managers would routinely consider the possibility of intervening in investee companies as one of the means of adding value, and would account to their clients for their strategies in doing so." Thus, strong encouragement exists for institutional investors to take a more proactive approach and engage in investee companies as a means of increasing shareholder value.

In the spring of 2005, the UK government approached the Pensions Management Institute (PMI) to coordinate the establishment of an independent Trustee Panel to be composed of trustees nominated by the PMI, the National Association of Pension Funds (NAPF), the TUC, and the Occupational Pensions Defence Union

(OPDU). Through this means, the Pensions Minister maintains regular contact with trustees who have experience with a range of different pension funds.

In recent years, the TUC has become much more proactive in the corporate governance arena using a number of approaches. The TUC has three nominees on the Trustee Panel (established in 2005) and trustees can e-mail concerns or comments on any issue to these three members. Although most schemes currently do not experience difficulties recruiting trustees, some believe that trustees may become harder to recruit in the future if the role of the trustees becomes more difficult.

In 2007, the NAPF published the results of its review of the extent to which pension fund trustees were complying with the recommendations (principles) of Myners (2001). The NAPF (2007, 5) stated that "the recommendations set out in this report provide a framework for developing further the Principles so that they remain relevant for the world in which pension fund trustees operate today." Her Majesty's Treasury (2008) published *Updating the Myners Principles: A Response to Consultation*. This report identifies six principles: (1) effective decision making, (2) clear objectives, (3) risk and liabilities, (4) performance assessment, (5) responsible ownership, and (6) transparency and reporting. The report emphasizes greater industry ownership of the principles and places the onus on trustees to report on their own practices.

INSTITUTIONAL INVESTOR REPRESENTATIVE GROUPS

Institutional investors, through their equity holdings, have the ability to wield much power and influence in the corporate governance arena. The institutional investors in the United Kingdom are represented by a number of professional bodies or investor representative groups who, for example, publish guidance on various corporate governance issues or offer (proxy) voting services. These groups include the Association of British Insurers (ABI), the National Association of Pension Funds (NAPF), the Association of Investment Companies (AIC), the Investment Management Association (IMA), and the Institutional Shareholders' Committee (ISC). The ISC acts as a forum for the aforementioned groups that make up its constituent members.

The Association of British Insurers (ABI)

The ABI represents the collective interests of the United Kingdom's insurance industry. The ABI has around 440 companies in membership, providing some 95 percent of domestic insurance services sold in the United Kingdom. It is funded by the subscriptions of member companies and acts as a spokesperson on issues of common interest. The ABI also participates in debates on public policy issues.

The ABI has substantial influence as the United Kingdom insurance industry is the largest in Europe and the third largest in the world. ABI's web site (www.abi.org.uk) states "the popularity of insurance as a savings vehicle—as well as its valuable protection role—gives the UK the highest per capita insurance expenditure in the European Union and the second highest in the world. UK premium income as a percentage of GDP is the highest in Europe and second in the world rankings." As such, the ABI has large investments in the UK stock market with its members owning some 15 percent of UK equity, according to data from the Office of National Statistics (2007).

The ABI has produced various corporate governance guidelines, some jointly issued with the NAPF. The guidelines can be accessed on the Institutional Voting Information Service (IVIS) web site. IVIS is produced by the ABI and was developed to advise Association members on aspects of corporate governance in the UK companies in which they invest. IVIS reviews UK companies' annual reports and accounts to assess whether they comply with the Combined Code (2008) and with ABI Guidelines. Each IVIS report comprises the following: (1) a Proxy Report with IVIS's detailed review of a company's executive remuneration and all other proposed resolutions analyzed in line with the ABI Guidelines; (2) an Environmental, Social, and Governance (ESG) Report that monitors a company's compliance with the ABI Guidelines on Responsible Investment Disclosures; (3) a Combined Code Report that indicates how a company has applied the Combined Code's principles; and (4) a color coding that may be a Blue Top, Green Top, Amber Top, or Red Top.

Color coding is based on evaluating each resolution on the company's meeting agenda and then coding as follows: Red indicates the strongest concern, followed by Amber Top. A Blue Top indicates no areas of major concern and a Green Top report indicates an issue that has now been resolved. Selvaggi and Upton (2008) explain which types of situation may result in the issue of the different colored tops. For example, a Red Top may be triggered by a board of directors where none of the nonexecutive directors meets the independence criteria laid down in the Combined Code, or where an executive director is a member of the audit or remuneration committee. Amber Tops may be triggered by abnormal salary or bonus increases for executive directors. Matters of concern are dealt with in liaison with ABI members who tend to be major shareholders in the companies monitored.

The National Association of Pension Funds (NAPF)

The NAPF is the principal UK organization representing the interests of the employer-sponsored pensions group. Its members include large and small companies as well as local authority and public-sector bodies, which together provide pensions for more than 10 million employees and 5 million people in retirement. NAPF members also include those providing professional services to pension funds such as investment services, consultancy, trustee, and actuarial advice.

Through the NAPF's Corporate Governance Policy, which is firmly based on the provisions of the Combined Code, the NAPF aims to protect the interests of its members as shareholders and to provide guidance to companies on corporate governance matters. The NAPF regularly engages with and is consulted by companies on corporate governance matters such as board structures and executive remuneration. Over the years, the NAPF has published various corporate governance guidelines, some jointly issued by ABI.

Association of Investment Companies (AIC)

Formed in 1932, the AIC is the trade body of the closed-ended investment trust industry. It represents a broad range of closed-ended investment companies, incorporating investment trusts, offshore investment companies, and venture capital trusts (VCTs), which are traded on the London Stock Exchange, AIM, and Euronext. The AIC (2007) issued the *Corporate Governance Guide for Investment Companies* in 2007. The guide is aimed at its members and lists each Combined Code requirement and describes its relevance and applicability to investment companies.

Investment Management Association (IMA)

The IMA is the trade body for the United Kingdom's £3,000 billion asset management industry. The money managed by its members is in various investment vehicles including authorized investment funds, pension funds, stocks, and shares. The IMA represents the asset management industry and seeks to promote high standards.

The Institutional Shareholders Committee

The Institutional Shareholders Committee (ISC) comprises members from the ABI, the NAPF, the AIC, and the IMA. In late 2002, the ISC issued a statement recommending that institutional investors should have a clear policy statement on activism and how it will discharge its responsibilities as shareowners. The ISC also recommended that institutional investors should monitor performance of their investee companies, which should be a regular process, clearly communicable, and checked periodically for effectiveness. Further, the ISC advocates that institutional investors intervene when necessary. For example, intervention is appropriate when the ISC has concerns about independent directors failing to hold executive management properly to account; internal controls failing; inadequate succession planning; an unjustifiable failure to comply with the Combined Code; inappropriate remuneration packages; and the company's approach to corporate social responsibility. Finally, institutional investors should evaluate and report on the outcomes of their shareholder activism.

The ISC (2002, 2) stated that the policies on activism that it describes "do not constitute an obligation to micromanage the affairs of investee companies, but rather relate to procedures designed to ensure that shareholders derive value from their investments by dealing effectively with concerns over underperformance. Nor do they preclude a decision to sell a holding, where this is the most effective response to such concerns." The aim of the ISC statement was to substantially enhance how institutional shareholders discharge their responsibilities in relation to the companies in which they invest. Some saw the statement as an encouragement to institutional investors to be aware of their responsibilities towards investee companies and to be proactive.

In 2005, the ISC (2005) published a review of its 2002 statement of principles on the responsibilities of institutional shareholders and their agents. The review monitored the progress of the statement for the two years since its launch in 2002 and concluded that there had been a general increase in the level of engagement with investee companies. The ISC (2007) further reviewed and updated the Statement of Principles in 2007, resulting in a recommendation for institutional investors to publish a policy on voting disclosure. The ISC states that the most cost-effective method of disclosure is usually via a web site. Unlike a number of companies in the United States, it states that disclosure should take place only after the relevant general meeting to avoid the possibility of jeopardizing the creation of value through engagement with investee companies.

In June 2009, the ISC (2009) issued a report entitled *Improving the Institutional Investors' Role in Governance*, which contains proposals designed to make engagement by investors more effective in the wake of the banking crisis. This document covers five areas:

1. Fund managers should be given clear mandates as to the type of commitment to corporate engagement that is expected of them.
2. There should be regular dialogue between institutional investors and companies which, although usually conducted on an individual basis, may benefit from a collective approach where the former is failing. Such a collective approach might include sovereign wealth funds and foreign investors.
3. When dialogue fails, shareholders should be prepared to exercise their full range of powers including voting. Boards could be made more accountable by having the chairs of key board committees (such as audit and remuneration) standing for reelection each year.
4. The ISC will review its publication, *The Responsibilities of Institutional Shareholders and Agents: Statement of Principles* (ISC 2007) and designate it as a Code to which institutional investors can sign up.
5. Various suggestions were made to enhance the quality of the dialogue between companies and investors.

Council of Institutional Investors

In the United States, the Council of Institutional Investors (CII) is a nonprofit association of public, union, and corporate pension funds with combined assets that exceed $3 trillion. Member funds are major long-term shareowners with a duty to protect the retirement assets of millions of American workers. The CII strives to educate its members, policy makers, and the public about good corporate governance, shareowner rights, and related investment issues, and to advocate on its members' behalf. The CII provides information on key governance issues including accounting and auditing, broker voting, executive compensation, independent board chair, international convergence, legal issues, majority voting for directors, and proxy access.

The CII has a focus list of five large companies, which it states have consistently low stock performance and persistently high total CEO pay relative to peer companies. For a company to be eligible for the focus list, it had to be a Standard & Poor's (S&P) 500 company that (1) underperformed the S&P 500 index and the median total stock returns for its industry group over the one-, three-, and five-year periods ended June 30, 2008; and (2) had total CEO pay exceeding the median total CEO pay of its peer group in the past one-, three-, and five-year periods. The Council is not making the focus list public in order to encourage companies on the list to discuss their compensation practices with Council members. The focus list is a good example of one of the tools of governance in action and is used where dialogue has failed and the board of directors is unresponsive to shareholders' concerns.

International Corporate Governance Network

The International Corporate Governance Network (ICGN) (2007) produced a *Statement of Shareholder Responsibilities* that set out the ICGN's view of the responsibilities of institutional shareholders, both in relation to their external role as owners of company equity and also in relation to their internal governance. Both of these areas are of interest to beneficiaries and other stakeholders. Ownership of equity carries important responsibilities, and the rights attached to share ownership must be exercised responsibly. Responsible ownership requires high standards of transparency, probity, and care on the part of institutions.

More recently, following the global financial crisis, the ICGN (2009, 3) notes that

> *... institutional shareholders must recognize their responsibility to generate long-term value on behalf of their beneficiaries, the savers and pensioners for whom they are ultimately working, and shareholders should take governance factors into account and consider the riskiness of a company's business model as part of their investment decision making. Governance should not be a parallel activity. It needs to be integrated into investment.*

TOOLS OF GOVERNANCE

The tools of governance can be identified as constructive dialogue, (proxy) voting, shareholder proposals (resolutions), and focus lists.

Constructive Dialogue

Institutional investors in countries such as the United Kingdom and the United States have enormous power and influence. Because companies generally recognize this, they engage in constructive dialogue with these investors. Companies are expected to be responsive to investor requests for information and to react to any issues about which institutional investors are unhappy. Further, companies are expected to have open communication channels for investors through the forum of the annual general meeting (for all investors) and one-on-one meetings for institutional investors.

Voting

Rights of investors should be respected and companies should ensure that there are no barriers to the exercise of investor rights; for example, no barriers to voting. In many cases, the process of voting, at least in theory, is relatively straightforward especially in the United Kingdom and the United States, which use electronic voting systems. The decision as to how to vote on any given resolution is often more difficult as resolutions need to be carefully examined. Years ago, most votes would more or less automatically go with incumbent management as institutional shareholders were more passive. In the United Kingdom, many did not vote their shares. This latter point contrasts with the United States which has traditionally had higher levels of voting, partly because of the Employee Retirement Income Security Act (ERISA) (1974) mandating private pension funds to vote. Public pension funds tended to follow suit. Consequently, voting levels of more than 80 percent are not uncommon in the United States whereas in the United Kingdom voting levels were as low as 32 percent in the mid-1990s. More recently, voting levels in large companies in the United Kingdom have approached 65 percent.

In some countries, barriers still exist to voting, which may affect institutional shareholders' ability to vote cross-border. Such barriers include share blocking, whereby shares have to be deposited with a central depository, public notary, or depositary named by the company and may not be traded for a period around the annual general meeting. Other barriers may include a requirement to be physically present at the meeting to vote and language problems when the proxy voting information is in a foreign language. Still other barriers may involve timing problems, both in terms of short turnaround times and the incidence of many meetings on the same day (for example, in Japan where the majority of meetings are held on the same day in June), or meetings being held at inconvenient times or in remote locations.

Currently, institutional shareholders seem more inclined to abstain (withhold their vote) or vote against management on certain issues. A case in point has been the recent outcry at the size of executive remuneration (compensation) packages, which some perceive as being overly generous and not appropriately related to firm performance. Also, there has been much concern around executive directors receiving large payoffs or *golden goodbyes* for poor performance.

Shareholder Proposals

In the United Kingdom, unease over executive directors' compensation has led to a higher incidence of another tool of governance, the shareholder proposal (resolution). Unlike in the United States, where shareholders put forward around 800 to 900 shareholder proposals per year, this tool has traditionally not been well used in the United Kingdom. This is because of the difficulty in meeting the criteria for putting forward a shareholder proposal, which can be put forward by members owning 5 percent of the voting power of the company or by 100 or more shareholders whose paid-up share capital averages at least £100 each. The resolution may be circulated at the expense of the members making the request, unless the company resolves otherwise. Nonetheless, from 2008 through 2009, shareholder proposals in the United Kingdom have substantially increased as concerns over executive compensation have become more commonplace.

Focus Lists

Some institutional investors have established focus lists whereby they target underperforming companies and include them on a list of companies that have underperformed a benchmark index such as Standard and Poor's 500. The companies are included on the focus list when dialogue has failed. The focus list highlights underperforming companies and can often lead to major changes in board structure—for example, the removal of nonperforming board directors. Once focus list firms make such changes, they often substantially outperform the market.

INSTITUTIONAL INVESTOR EXAMPLES

Two examples of large proactive institutional investors are Hermes and the California Public Employees' Retirement System.

Hermes

Hermes is a large and influential institutional investor based in the United Kingdom. Hermes focuses on pension fund investment, is active in corporate governance matters, and is a leader in the field of engagement with its investee companies. In 2002, Hermes issued its Hermes Principles. The first principle was that "companies should seek an honest, open, and ongoing dialogue with shareholders." This reflects the spirit of the various United Kingdom corporate governance codes that have recommended that institutional investors have an ongoing dialogue with their investee companies. The other principles cover various aspects of the relationship between Hermes and its investee companies.

Hermes (2006) issued its Hermes Corporate Governance Principles (HCGP) that form the basis of its engagement with the companies in which it or its clients invest. The two parts of the HCGP focus on global principles and regional principles. The former is based on the Statement on Global Corporate Governance Principles issued by the ICGN and also draws on UK corporate governance guidelines. However, the global principles should be read in conjunction with the regional principles which cover additional issues that may be specific to certain regions or markets or emphasize certain points or Hermes' preferred approach.

Hermes states that it interprets the HCGP pragmatically and takes into account individual company circumstances including the legal and financial environments. Hermes' overriding objective of its stewardship activities is maximizing long-term returns for its clients.

As mentioned, Hermes is proactive and engages with its investee companies to try to improve their corporate governance. Is there any financial benefit to this engagement? A study carried out by Becht, Franks, Mayer, and Rossi (2006) seems to show a benefit. Hermes gave the researchers unlimited access to its resources including letters, memos, minutes, presentations, transcripts or recordings of telephone conversations, and client reports, all of which documented its work with the companies in which Hermes' UK Focus Fund invested in a period over five years (1998–2004). Becht et al. reviewed all forms of public and private engagement with 41 companies and found that when the engagement objectives led to actual outcomes, there were economically large and statistically significant positive abnormal returns around the announcement date. On the basis of the findings, Becht et al. conclude that shareholder activism can produce corporate governance changes that generate significant returns for shareholders.

California Public Employees' Retirement System (CalPERS)

The California Public Employees' Retirement System (CalPERS) provides retirement and health benefits to more than 1.6 million public employees, retirees, and their families and more than 2,500 employers. It is the largest U.S. public pension fund, with assets totalling $165 billion that span domestic and international markets. According to CalPERS (http://www.calpers-governance.org),

> *[G]ood corporate governance leads to better performance. We seek corporate reform to protect our investments. The corporate governance team challenges companies and the status quo—we vote our proxies, we work closely with regulatory agencies to strengthen our financial markets, and we invest with partners that use corporate governance strategies to earn value for our fund by turning around ailing companies.*

In March 2009, CalPERS published its *Global Principles of Accountable Corporate Governance*. The Principles create the framework by which CalPERS executes its proxy voting responsibilities. In addition, the Principles provide a foundation for supporting the system's corporate engagement and governance initiatives to achieve long-term sustainable risk-adjusted investment returns.

CalPERS operates a focus list whereby it identifies annually about 15 to 20 companies in the domestic internal equity portfolio that exhibit poor economic performance and corporate governance. CalPERS focuses on reforming the company's governance practices with an emphasis on accountability, transparency, independence, and discipline in an attempt to positively impact shareowner wealth.

In reporting on the "CalPERS Effect," Junkin and Toth (2009, 9) conclude that

> *CalPERS' approach to improving portfolio returns by engaging management of poorly performing companies to rethink governance and strategy continues to work. Despite underperforming their respective benchmarks by 84.2 percent for the five years up to CalPERS' shareholder activism, the 139 companies that were targeted by the System from 1987 to the fall of 2007 have outperformed by 15.4 percent over the subsequent five-year period.*

HOT ISSUES

The hot issues in corporate governance will inevitably include executive directors' remuneration (compensation) packages that many see as being too generous. Some banks are still being criticized for not having learned their lesson from the global financial crisis as they continue to offer huge remuneration packages. Institutional shareholders will also be looking for better risk management in investee companies, for a balanced board with no one individual being too powerful, and for better succession planning. Issues relating to ethical, environmental, and social aspects are also likely to be the focus of more attention in the future.

SUMMARY AND CONCLUSIONS

This chapter has focused on highlighting the important role that institutional investors play in corporate governance, the means that they have at their disposal to influence corporate governance outcomes in companies, and the issues that will be particularly important to them in the future. The world expects institutional shareholders to engage with companies, to monitor companies, and to intervene when appropriate. Some institutional shareholders already play an activist role, and these institutions will lead the way for other institutions that have yet to act more as shareowners rather than just shareholders.

DISCUSSION QUESTIONS

1. Critically discuss the responsibilities of institutional investors in corporate governance and the extent to which the investors are able to meet them.
2. To what extent should institutional investors intervene in a company? Include the following areas: succession planning, board remuneration, and the corporate social responsibility policies of the company.
3. What tools of governance are available to institutional investors? How effective are these tools? What are their limitations?
4. What corporate governance issues might be associated with some of the new players such as sovereign wealth funds and private equity funds?

REFERENCES

Association of Investment Companies. 2007. *Corporate governance guide for investment companies*. AIC: London.

Becht, Marco, Patrick Bolton, and Ailsa Roell. 2002. Corporate governance and control. Finance working paper 02/2002, ECGI.

Becht, Marco, Julian Franks, Colin Mayer, and Stefano Rossi. 2006. Returns to shareholder activism: Evidence from a clinical study of the Hermes U.K. Focus Fund. Finance Working Paper No. 138/2006, ECGI.

Cadbury Committee. 1992. *Report of the Committee on the financial aspects of corporate governance*. London: Gee Publishing Ltd.

California Public Employees Retirement System (CalPERS). 2009. *Global principles of accountable corporate governance*. Sacramento: CalPERS.

Combined Code. 1998. *The combined code on corporate governance*. London: Gee Publishing Ltd.

———. 2008. *The combined code on corporate governance*. London: Financial Reporting Council.

Employee Retirement Income Security Act (ERISA). 1974. Washington DC: United States Department of Labor.

Ferreira, Miguel A., and Pedro Matos. 2008. The colors of investors' money: The role of institutional investors around the world. *Journal of Financial Economics* 88 (3): 499–533.

Greenbury Committee. 1995. *Directors' remuneration*. London: Gee Publishing Ltd.

Hampel Committee. 1998. *Committee on corporate governance: Final report*. London: Gee Publishing Ltd.

Her Majesty's Treasury. 2008. *Updating the Myners principles: A response to consultation*. London: Her Majesty's Treasury.

Hermes. 2002. *The Hermes principles*. London: Hermes Investment Management Ltd.

———. 2006. *The Hermes corporate governance principles*. London: Hermes Investment Management Ltd.

Institutional Shareholders' Committee (ISC). 2002. *The responsibilities of institutional shareholders and agents: Statement of principles*. London: ISC.

———. 2005. *Review of the institutional shareholders' committee statement of principles on the responsibilities of institutional shareholders and agents*. London: ISC.

———. 2007. *The responsibilities of institutional shareholders and agents: Statement of principles*. London: ISC.

———. 2009. *Improving the institutional investors' role in governance*. London: ISC.
International Corporate Governance Network. 2007. *Statement of shareholder responsibilities*. London: ICGN.
———. 2009. *Second statement on the global financial crisis*. London: ICGN.
International Working Group of Sovereign Wealth Funds (IWG). 2008. *Sovereign wealth funds, generally accepted principles and practices: Santiago principles*. IWG http://www.iwg-swf.org/.
Junkin, Andrew, and Thomas Toth. 2009. *The "CalPERS effect" on targeted company share prices*. Santa Monica, CA: Wilshire Associates.
Mallin, Christine A. 2006. *Corporate governance*. Oxford: Oxford University Press.
Myners Report. 1995. *Developing a winning partnership: How companies and institutional investors are working together*. London: Joint City/Industry Working Group.
Myners, Paul. 2001. *Myners report on institutional investment*. London: HM Treasury.
———. 2007. *Review of the impediments to voting U.K. shares*. London: Investment Management Association.
National Association of Pension Funds (NAPF). 2007. *Institutional investment in the UK: Six years on*. London: National Association of Pension Funds.
Office of National Statistics. 2010. *Share ownership: A report on ownership of shares as at 31 December 2008*. Norwich: HMSO.
Organisation for Economic Co-Operation and Development (OECD). 2004. *Principles of corporate governance*. Paris: OECD.
———. 2006. *Guidelines on pension fund asset management*. Paris: OECD.
———. 2008a. *Codes and industry standards covering the behaviour of alternative investors*. Paris: OECD.
———. 2008b. *The role of private equity and activist hedge funds in corporate governance–related policy issues*. Paris: OECD.
Selvaggi, Mariano, and James Upton. 2008. *Governance and performance in corporate Britain*. ABI Research Paper 7. Report from the ABI Research and Investment Affairs Departments, London.
Walker Working Group (Private Equity Working Group on Transparency and Disclosure). 2007. *Guidelines for disclosure and transparency in private equity*. London.

ABOUT THE AUTHOR

Chris Mallin is professor of corporate governance and finance and founder and director of the Centre for Corporate Governance Research at the Birmingham Business School in the United Kingdom. She is a member of the International Corporate Governance Network (ICGN) and has been on two of the ICGN's working parties established to draft guidelines on international corporate governance principles, and on global voting, and a member of the United Kingdom's Shareholder Voting Working Group chaired by Paul Myners. She was a director (2000–2006) and chair of the Audit and Risk Management Committee (2004–2006), of the Aston Reinvestment Trust (chaired by Sir Adrian Cadbury), which was launched in 1997 as a pioneer of social investment. She was the editor of *Corporate Governance: An International Review* from 2000 to 2007. She has published widely on corporate governance issues in both academic and professional journals. The third edition of her book *Corporate Governance* will be published by Oxford University Press in 2009.

CHAPTER 21

The Politics of Shareholder Activism

DONALD NORDBERG
Senior Lecturer, Westminster Business School

INTRODUCTION

By the middle of 2008, big institutional investors had grown uneasy about their investments in the German carmaker Volkswagen AG (VW). Owning the shares had become too political. Porsche Automobil Holding SE held more than 30 percent of the shares. VW's supervisory board chairman, Ferdinand Piëch, was a member of the family that controls Porsche, which had become something of a corporate governance pariah by refusing to accept the unofficial norm of quarterly financial reporting in Germany. Porsche had also irritated the country's Social Democrats by dropping the *Aktiengesellschaft* legal form in favor of the new European Union *Societas Europeas* form that allowed Porsche to reduce representation of German workers on the supervisory board. Moreover, Piëch had ousted the VW chief executive in 2006 and then entered a court battle with the company's second largest shareholder: the state of Lower Saxony that held more than 20 percent of VW's equity. Lower Saxony also benefited from a special law giving it veto power over important managerial and board decisions, a statute recently reinforced by the German parliament after the European Court of Justice ruled parts of the old law illegal. The European Commission had said that the new version of what German news media called the "VW law" was illegal and Porsche agreed. But attempts at VW's annual meeting by other shareholders—including activist institutional investors—to challenge Porsche's creeping control of its rival carmaker fell on deaf ears (Milne 2005 and 2006; Milne, Williamson, and Tait 2008).

Within a few months Porsche used a derivative instrument known as a *contract for difference* to acquire an economic interest equivalent to about 75 percent of the stock. Although Porsche had not directly purchased 75 percent of the shares, under German law, the company was able to keep this fact a secret. Speculators, including hedge funds that had expected a fall in the price of VW and sold short, soon faced a mad scramble to cover their positions. VW shares soared by 400 percent, briefly making it the most valuable company in the world. Newspaper reporters began to liken Porsche itself to a giant hedge fund with a small carmaker attached (Schäfer and Mackintosh 2009).

Shareholder activism is fundamentally a battle for power acted out in a political landscape that stretches from boardrooms through national legislatures and encompasses supranational organizations. The exercise of power by shareholders shapes and is shaped by the political force fields of corporate governance. When public policy concerning private-sector companies is set, some shareholders make their voices heard as well. Sometimes the goal is to ensure that shareholder power over management is strengthened. Sometimes it is to avoid the erosion of power to employees or outside lobbies. Often, however, the goal is to wrest power away from other shareholders.

An obvious and occasionally overlooked question when considering the forces that shape corporate governance is: What is in the shareholders' best interests? The interests of one shareholder often do not coincide with those of others. Most of the time, diverging shareholder interests do not matter because shareholders are not often able to vote on matters of corporate policy. But for directors with their fiduciary responsibility to look after shareholder interests, understanding what is in the shareholders' best interests represents an important question. The competing interests of shareholders arise from different stances that investors take to their investments.

Shareholder interests constitute a complex picture of rivalry for the high ground. The rivalry shapes the way shareholders vote at company annual meetings, how they vie for directors' attention, and how they seek to influence the public policy debate on the enterprise's future. The discussion of activism focuses mainly on the approaches that institutional investors take. They dominate the investment landscape, even in the United States, where private persons—retail investors—give a greater sense of democracy to shareholder capitalism than in many other countries around the world. These private individuals, unless extremely wealthy and willing to take risks, are rarely able to gain a voice in the political debate that sets the policy of individual companies and the framework of laws and regulations in which boards operate.

The purpose of this chapter is to describe the role that shareholder activism plays in corporate affairs. The first section gives a history of activism, showing how the practice has changed, especially as hedge funds have become activist investors, and discussing the issues that type of activism raises. The next two sections develop a model called the *shareholder stance*. They explore how different shareholders' interests can collide and how coalitions of shareholders can develop over issues, despite the different approaches to their investments. The next section shows how these differing stances can lead to conflict over policy decisions, leading to conclusions that suggest the difficulty in identifying what *shareholder value* means when activism is viewed as a political process.

ISSUES IN SHAREHOLDER ACTIVISM

Many people, including policy makers in major countries, believe that shareholders ought to actively engage with the managements and boards of the companies in which they invest. In Britain, for example, the government has encouraged institutional investors, who collectively own more than 80 percent of the equity in UK listed companies, to vote their shares. Pension funds have been under pressure to publish their voting records so that beneficiaries can judge their performance. But in the minds of many corporate executives, a difference exists between shareholders being active and being activists. From its origins in the efforts of small shareholders not to be overlooked, the evolution of shareholder activism has resulted in institutional investors ousting management, changing a firm's strategic direction, or altering a company's direction. With the addition of activist hedge funds to the mix in the past few years, some writers such as Lipton (2008) now see a condition in which shareholder activism is on steroids.

Naming and Shaming

The practice of naming and shaming began in the United States during the 1940s when a change in securities regulation gave shareholders the right to offer resolutions for consideration at corporate annual meetings. However, there were restrictions: Proposals had to be "proper subject for action by securities holders" (for elaboration, see Gillan and Starks [2007, 56]). In the 1970s, many such resolutions were the product of a handful of *gadfly* investors, private investors including Lewis and John Gilbert and Evelyn Davis. These gadfly investors demanded higher dividends or other shareholder-friendly changes in company policy through a combination of direct agitation at annual meetings and skillful use of the media to publicize their efforts. Other activists came from religious groups and from those espousing political causes, often adopting the techniques of the gadflies (Marens 2002).

In the mid-1980s came the addition of research-led programs, backed by pension funds and other institutional investors to seek out underperforming companies and effect changes in direction. Robert Monks used his LENS asset management company and his research firm, Institutional Shareholder Services, to identify issues with corporate governance practices in companies. He built coalitions of investors including large, public-sector pension funds such as the California Public Employees Retirement System (CalPERS) to demand changes from corporate managements as well as legislative and regulatory actions that would give shareholders a bigger say in setting corporate policy and selecting directors.

Ward, Brown, and Graffin (2009) found that naming and shaming poor performers had an effect on share prices, as institutional investors reacted to a reputable signal—in their case, the Council of Institutional Investors and its focus list. But they found the investors' reaction was less pronounced in the case of companies with boards that were seen as independent of management. Those boards responded to the signal by changing management incentives to favor a change in direction.

These efforts are often confrontational as these activists frequently use the media to challenge corporate decisions and muster support for their positions from other investors. By contrast, much of this form of shareholder activism in Europe takes place behind closed doors. Asset managers occasionally join together to discuss issues with companies in their portfolios. Asset managers, however, must bear in mind the rules about not acting so closely together that they might be deemed to be "acting in concert" and thus be forced to make a takeover bid. The Association of British Insurers and the National Association of Pension Funds in the United Kingdom, whose members have investments in financial markets around the world, will sometimes organize meetings with company executives and directors to seek to resolve issues or change the board's thinking. Seldom do these encounters reach the glare of public attention. "If our engagement ever reaches the front page of the *Financial Times*," one pension fund manager states, "that is because it has failed" (from a private conversation with the author).

A somewhat different approach can be seen in perhaps the most vocal of European investment institutions, Hermes. Similar to CalPERS, the UK asset management firm Hermes, owned by the old British Telecommunications pension fund and the largest pension fund manager in the country, set up a special unit to conduct activist campaigns. Because of its size and its actuarial needs, Hermes invests across the entire UK market. Hermes justifies its activism as the only way to improve the performance of its investments. Again like CalPERS, Hermes has a subsidiary to target underperforming companies, takes very large stakes, and then presses management for changes in policy and personnel—often in private but occasionally in public. A study of Hermes' performance by Becht, Franks, Mayer, and Rossi (2009) shows abnormally high returns on its portfolio through engagement activities. The lesson: Activism pays. Its success in the United Kingdom led Hermes to move into Continental European and U.S. markets.

Hedge Fund Activism

Actions such as those undertaken by CalPERS and Hermes have become in many ways the model for a new form of shareholder activism. Activist hedge funds use detailed analysis of a company's business to identify weaknesses. They then build large equity stakes to force management to listen. The biggest difference between the older-style activists, such as Monks and his allies, and the newer-style activists, such as hedge funds, is that the hedge funds exploit very high leverage. They also build positions in options and other derivative instruments that traditional asset managers would not be willing or allowed to use. As a result, hedge funds potentially seek policy changes designed to affect shorter-term performance than their more traditional counterparts. This short-term orientation frequently allows the popular press to portray hedge funds as rapacious. In Germany, a politician once likened them to "locusts" (see the later section on "Shareholder Politics and Markets"). Are hedge funds, especially the activist ones, the devil described in popular accounts? They may be aggressive, but do they justify the fear that corporate managers often show?

In the United States, Klein and Zur (2006) find that hedge funds took quite a different activist approach than traditional activist investors. Instead of targeting underperforming companies and seeking changes in direction, these funds sought to extract cash from generally well-performing companies.

Activist strategies among hedge funds have gained support, albeit based on data during the heady days in investment markets in the mid-2000s. Brav, Jiang, Thomas, and Partnoy (2006) find hedge funds working in ways often prescribed to large blockholders: friendly interaction with management in striving for better financial performance. At other times, hedge funds may confront management that they see as entrenched. Importantly, Brav et al. find that the performance improvements they sought persist after the hedge funds have exited their positions. As Brav et al. (p. 37) note, "Unlike traditional institutional investors, hedge fund managers have very strong personal financial incentives to increase the value of their portfolio firms, and do not face the regulatory or political barriers that limit the effectiveness of these other investors."

Clifford (2008) reports that target companies of hedge funds pursuing activist agendas perform better than a control group of investments that hedge funds passively held. But Clifford's evidence suggests that the funds seek a greater liquidity buffer for activist portfolios. That is, the lock-in periods for activist funds are typically longer than the lock-in periods that the hedge funds manage without engagement. By examining the record of voting, litigation, and change of control contests, Partnoy and Thomas (2006) find that hedge fund activism is more effective in inducing change in corporations than engagement by traditional institutional investors.

Moreover, Haarmeyer (2007) believes that activism by hedge funds has accelerated the distribution of corporate cash in mature businesses, through dividends and share buybacks. According to Haarmeyer (p. 38), "Hedge fund activists become catalysts for initiating and helping to execute the painful but critical process that moves resources into more productive uses and thus drives shareholder value creation and economic prosperity."

Issue-Based Activism

A more limited form of activism comes in agitation over particular issues either in corporate policy or in company law and regulation. A topical case is the growing calls for new ways to address the persistent problem—as seen from the perspective of investors—of giving shareholders a *say on pay* for senior management. Since 2002, shareholders in the United Kingdom have had an advisory vote on compensation policy, an example where voice has made some difference.

Practitioners argue that such efforts—copied in some other European and Australian jurisdictions and a matter of heated debate in the United States—could undermine the board's discretion in setting pay levels. Keith Johnson, a former Wisconsin state pension fund manager, and Daniel Summerfield from USS, the United Kingdom's second largest pension fund, argue that giving shareholders a direct voice on pay should empower the board, rather than undermine it. As Johnson and Summerfield (2008, 3) remark, "Say on Pay leaves boards with full control over executive compensation while giving them increased support for a display of backbone when needed! ... Muddling through is no longer an option." Johnson and Summerfield see the move at many U.S. companies for majority voting, instead of plurality voting, as a step to create greater shareholder voice on pay.

A study of the outcome of the UK experience by Ferri and Maber (2008) gives a more qualified view of the success that shareholder votes on pay might have on the level of executive pay. Their analysis suggests that say on pay increased the sensitivity to pay levels of executives in poorly performing companies, and especially among those that had high compensation before introduction of the law. Still, giving shareholders a voice had little effect on the overall levels of pay.

Giving shareholders greater rights is only one part of the activist equation. For a director seeking to act in shareholder interests there is another question. What is it that interests shareholders?

DIMENSIONS OF SHAREHOLDER POLITICS

Many factors contribute to the interests that a single shareholder might have in the board's decision making. A shareholder may be more interested in receiving dividends than capital gains or want the board, for example, to avoid investments in genetically modified crops. Shareholders from one country may bring with them preconceptions about the best way to organize a business when they invest in a company based in a different country. These factors all contribute to the content of any recommendations that shareholders make to the board. Taking a step back from the content of their interests, one can assess their political stance across three dimensions: (1) their attitude toward the stock, (2) their approach to engagement and activism, and (3) their investment horizons.

Attitude

At any given time, shareholders have a simple view of each stock in their portfolio or watch list: They buy, sell, or hold. Investment analysts use a wider variety of categories in their research recommendations and these nomenclatures vary somewhat between investment banks. In the wake of the dot-com collapse in 2000–2001, investment banks and the analysts they employed faced criticism for their use of arcane classification systems and for making recommendations where the intended advice meant something different from the words themselves (Dreman 2000). Legislation, litigation, and new codes of ethics for research around the world ensued (for an example, see CFA Institute [2005]).

For many asset managers, the investment decision rarely involves massive shifts toward or away from a particular stock. Consequently, a more nuanced version of the old "buy-sell-hold" mantra has emerged: Investors might *accumulate*, *reduce*, or *maintain* their exposure to a particular security.

Participation

Investors can take three participatory stances toward their investments, either as a general inclination toward their entire portfolio or toward a specific stock. Investors may be *docile*, passive in their approach to the company, its strategy, and its management. This may involve routinely voting with management at shareholder meetings or perhaps not voting at all. This is frequently the stance of index-tracking funds, which are explicitly designed as low-cost operations. These funds seek to avoid the cost of voting and trading the shares they hold.

A second approach is the *walkers*, invoking a notion sometimes called the "Wall Street Walk" (Admati and Pfleiderer 2007). If unhappy with a company's direction, investors will sell their shares to avoid future price declines or to seek greater returns in an alternative investment. They can also walk into an investment. That is, investors buy when seeing a strategic decision they like or a change in the business environment that might be favorable to a particular stock or industry. Traditional active portfolio managers, who seek to outperform the index or benchmarks by intelligent stock selection, often adopt this stance. A wide range of other investors use this approach, whether they are the traditional long-only asset management firms that buy and sell actively, individual investors looking for a gain, or leveraged investors seeking to turbocharge their holdings by buying stock on margin.

Walkers can affect corporate policy and therefore governance. If the stock price is depressed by their decisions to sell, then the company may have difficulty raising capital in debt and equity markets. The resulting increase in the cost of capital, so the theory goes, makes the company less competitive, putting pressure on profitability and on management to change direction. Some writers such as Coffee (1991) find this an inefficient way of monitoring and controlling corporations. Such writers argue that the role should fall to certain types of investors, particularly pension funds and closed-end collective investment funds.

Edmans (2009), however, has modeled situations in which the use of exit rather than voice can itself be a form of activism. Studies by Edmans and Manso (2009) and Edmans (2009) consider companies in which investors' stakes are too small to influence the company by either gaining a seat on the board or getting their concerns heard by management. These investors' stakes are large enough that staying informed about the company's business and monitoring management performance, and then using the threat of an exit to gain attention, is worthwhile. Edmans' work suggests that using exit as a form of voice need not lead to a short-term management focus. The signals sent through activism-with-your-feet could even stimulate boards and managements to take a long-term focus.

There are funds that are neither passive nor walkers but take a different approach with at least some of their investments. *Activist* shareholders seek to influence the direction of the companies in which they invest. They often use their voting rights to indicate displeasure with strategy or management, while lobbying occasionally with directors and senior management for a change in policy. Activists come in a variety of flavors. Some advocate specific policy changes on ethical grounds. This approach was commonplace as shareholder activism gained ground in the 1960s and 1970s as individual shareholders, churches, and charities used their votes to force changes in policy of companies toward investments in munitions and tobacco or on trade with the apartheid regime in South Africa. Indeed, much of the early effort in the United States to develop corporate governance research arose from churches who sought to use their votes at shareholder meetings to express their displeasure with U.S. foreign policy and military actions in Vietnam.

Other activists seek changes in management or shifts in strategy in poorly performing companies. Others lobby for actions to give shareholders greater rights—for example, to oversee executive pay policy or to vote on potential acquisitions. Still others may seek to oust the board of directors and impose a new board and new management or push through a merger or acquisition by another company hostile to the incumbent management and board.

Some, by dint of the size of their holdings, can get private access to senior managers or members of the board to make their opinions known. Others, generally the smaller ones, resort to *megaphone diplomacy* as a way to be heard. A few, notably large pension funds in the United States and United Kingdom, combine the two, using the latter when attempts with the former have shown few results. What these activists share is their active use of voting rights and often other ways of expressing their voice on policy. But they share something else as well. All seek to assert what they see as their rights *as owners* to influence decision making with the board and management (Davis, Lukomnik, and Pitt-Watson 2006).

Horizon

Shareholders' intentions toward a stock also vary over time. Stocks held today are ones that shareholders might be inclined to buy again or sell at some time in the future. Beyond that lies a general inclination toward the process of buying and selling. Index-tracking funds, for example, hold shares for as long as the company is a constituent of the index they track. Their actions are dictated by index decisions. Only those on the cusp of the index are ever likely to be traded. Thus, for most of the investments of these managers, the time horizon of the investment is quite long. Pension funds, looking to achieve sufficient yields over the lifetime of their beneficiaries, share a long-term orientation toward the market in general although some may choose to manage their portfolios more actively. They tend to be long-term investors despite sometimes having a short-term horizon for an individual stock.

The investment literature, similar to the tax code in some jurisdictions, draws a distinction between long- and short-term investing. The latter is more speculative in nature. For tax purposes, capital gains and losses might be treated more like earned income for individuals or income from operations for corporate entities rather than savings. Both academics and the taxman often set an arbitrary threshold to distinguish between the short and long term—for example, one year. In practice, differentiating between an investment of 13 months, of 11 months, or even decades can be quite difficult.

From a corporate governance perspective, long-term investors sometimes expect different treatment from the companies, even if their attitude toward the stock might involve an inclination to sell. There has been a growth of speculative, short-term investing among traditional, long-only funds as institutional investors seek to build their businesses by outperforming rivals as a result of beating their quarterly benchmarks. In turn, this has put pressure on corporate managements to strive for better short-term performance, often at the expense of strategic decision making (Tonello 2006).

A third stance exists under the rubric of horizon—the *perverse* orientation toward an investment. The horizon in this case is often short-term, though it need not be. One version of this stance might involve buying and selling simultaneously but with differing time horizons for the two actions. For example, otherwise long-term investors seeking to achieve capital gains but avoid dividend income often take this stance. They will sell the stock on a cash basis over the dividend record or payment date, having arranged ahead of time to buy the stock back *forward* at a predetermined price. These stock lending activities have counterparties. Sometimes the counterparties are investors seeking dividends to boost the yield of a portfolio that pledges its beneficiaries a regular stream of income. These investors then capture the dividend in exchange for an interest payment to the lender. Depending on their separate tax positions, these approaches can produce benefits for both sides.

Corporate governance implications arise when these arrangements cover voting periods at the company's shareholder meeting. Who is the real owner? When both tend to be long-term in orientation, the governance implications might not be particularly large. Given the broad diversification of assets in many institutional portfolios, the borrower might well be a holder or even a lender of the same stock it has borrowed, so the implications for voting and corporate governance are perhaps of greater theoretical than practical concern.

Other types of borrowers such as short-sellers with non-neutral intentions may hold the stock. These shorts borrow the stock so they can deliver it to someone to whom they have sold it. The intention in a short sale is to buy the stock back at some point in the future before the prearranged return sale to the original lender. If the stock falls in the meantime, the short-seller makes a gain on the difference less the fee paid for having borrowed the stock in the first place. As a result, short-sellers can benefit from a fall in share price or a collapse of the company. During the period in which they maintain the short position, they are, in a technical sense, the holder of the shares. For these reasons, various countries ban short-selling and others restrict its use. Before the banking crisis hit in the second half of 2008, many countries had begun to give short-sellers a freer hand. In 2004, the U.S. Securities and Exchange Commission (SEC) experimented with a new rule to lift the requirement that a short sale could only take place when the previous transaction in that stock was at a higher price than the one before, called the *uptick* rule (SEC 2004).

Hong Kong, a market with a history of stock trading almost as old as London and New York, introduced short selling subject to an uptick rule in 1994. It allowed *naked* short sales—when the seller does not first borrow the stock—a year later and then removed the uptick rule. After a cascading sell-off in the Asian markets in 1998 the uptick came back, only to be repealed again in 2007. McKenzie and Henry (2007) believe short-selling is broadly neutral over time as heavy selling in one period reverses in the next.

In the United Kingdom, the Financial Services Authority (FSA) broadly backs short-selling. Yet incidents in the early months of 2008 led it to adopt a temporary measure to tighten reporting requirements when companies were in the process of issuing new capital through *rights* issues (FSA 2008). Australia, which had some curbs on the practice, sought market opinion in 2008 about how to tighten short-selling regulations (ASX 2008). In the weeks after the collapse of Lehman Brothers in September 2008, authorities in many jurisdictions, including the United States, moved to curtail short-selling in the stocks of financial companies. The SEC quickly rescinded the U.S. ban; Christopher Cox, the outgoing chairman of the SEC, even called the ban the "biggest mistake" of his tenure (Paley and Hilzenrath 2008). Constraints in other countries stayed in place for many months.

In the past several years, the perverse stance has added a layer of complexity. Through the use of derivative instruments, including a device called a *contract for difference* (CFD), an investor may have a large economic interest—whether the share rises or falls—without actually buying or selling the shares themselves. This can pose governance issues for the companies involved because CFDs can be linked with an implicit commitment on the part of the counterparty such as an investment bank to hold the equivalent number of shares and even vote them on the instruction of the derivative holder.

An example of a governance problem in this type of perverse relationship is the Mylan Laboratories bid in 2004 to acquire King Pharmaceutical in the United States, which resulted in so-called *empty voting*. The hedge fund Perry was a major shareholder of King and stood to benefit from the transaction. However, shareholders in Mylan needed to approve the transaction, and opposition to the deal arose from some large shareholders including the activist investor Carl Icahn. To push the deal through, Perry bought a stake in Mylan, simultaneously hedging the investment with an equity swap with two investment banks. Indeed, the swaps more than covered Perry's exposure and gave Perry 9.9 percent voting rights at a time when it had a net negative economic interest in Mylan (Hu and Black 2006; Kahan and Rock 2006).

SHAREHOLDER POLITICS AND MARKETS

Because investors take these different stances, traders can make a market in company shares. Buyers need sellers, and even long-term investors sometime sell. Differences of tax positions can lead otherwise like-minded investors to take opposite stances towards the same stock. Even short-sellers, who are the most perverse of the perverse stance, perform a valuable function in providing sellers when others seek to buy. When coupled with an activist stance, actions of short-sellers can raise serious governance concerns. Evidence exists that short-selling helps the market achieve the best price for corporate equity (for recent examples, see Charoenrook and Daouk [2005]; Bris, Goetzmann, and Zhu [2007]; Chang, Cheng, and Yu [2007]; McKenzie and Henry [2007]; Curtis and Fargher [2008]). Indeed, Cohen, Diether, and Malloy (2007) show that in markets with poor disclosure regimes, short-selling provides a useful mechanism for the transmission of private information. Bris et al. (2007) present a more nuanced picture. By looking at dual-listed shares that trade on markets that either permitted or restricted short-selling, they find evidence supporting the notion that price discovery was better with short-selling. Although short-selling does not cause a crash, their results indicate that it may affect the magnitude of a crash.

Exhibit 21.1 summarizes the variety of possible approaches along these three dimensions. A complex picture emerges indicating the difficulty for investors or any individual to know what constitutes *shareholder value* when shareholder interests fundamentally diverge on structural grounds, irrespective of differences on companies' business policies and future cash flows.

The balance between investors' different interests will change over time for both individual companies and the market as a whole. For example, the growth of passive investment through index-tracking funds has led to an expansion of funds that seek to maintain their stakes in companies over a long time horizon. To keep costs down, many of these funds are docile and vote with management if they vote at all. With the rise of index funds has come a relative decline in the strength of traditional long-only, actively managed asset management firms that were the backbone of the walkers and activists taking a long-term approach to the horizon.

While the growth of hedge funds in the 1990s and the early years of the new century vastly expanded the number of managers taking a short-term view of their investments, hedge funds probably still represent a small proportion of equity ownership. Data concerning the size and shape of hedge fund investing are fragmentary at best. The industry is secretive and lightly or unregulated in many jurisdictions. Early versions of hedge fund strategies often speculated on intraday price movements with any associated risk hedged through the use of derivatives.

The shareholder stance is a tool to evaluate what a particular shareholder's interest involves. It has three dimensions: the attitude toward the stock (accumulate, maintain, and reduce), its participation in company affairs (docile, walkers, and activists), and the investor's general investment horizon (long-term, short-term, or perverse).

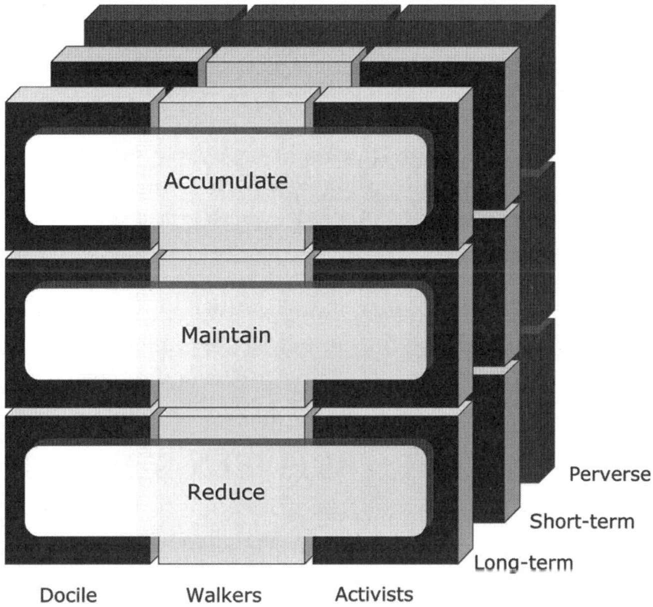

Exhibit 21.1 Shareholder Stance (© Donald Nordberg).

These trades had little to do with the governance of the company. What created a new governance relationship and a new set of politics to go with it was the development of hedge fund activism: asset managers taking a large, often highly leveraged stake in a company and holding it while agitating for a change in policy.

Perhaps the most celebrated case in the brief history of hedge fund activism is the move by a fund with the cuddly name The Children's Investment Fund (TCI). TCI rocked the tradition-bound world of German equities when Deutsche Börse, the German stock exchange company, tried to take over the London Stock Exchange in 2004. TCI sensed an opportunity to prevent the merger and generate a higher share price for Deutsche Börse. The shares of bidding companies often fall during or after a takeover, reflecting the premium paid for the acquired company. In cases of contested takeovers, the premium is likely to be even higher. TCI sensed that if it could thwart the merger, then Deutsche Börse's share price would increase. TCI acquired a substantial stake and agitated for a change in direction through contesting the reelection of directors at the exchange company's 2005 annual meeting. The move attracted other hedge funds to follow suit, and soon UK-based and U.S.-based hedge funds held a large portion of the shares in this German institution. The tactic succeeded to a greater extent than almost anyone had imagined possible. Deutsche Börse not only abandoned its bid but also dismissed the chairman of its supervisory board, its chief executive officer, and its chief financial officer (Nordberg 2005). Germany's vice chancellor then famously warned about "locusts" invading the capital markets (Bovensiepen and Blechschmidt 2005) and a new term—*hedge fund activism*—entered the corporate governance lexicon (Achleitner and Kaserer 2005).

TCI's intervention in the case of Deutsche Börse was in the spirit of much of the activism of corporate raiders in the 1980s and 1990s. That is, this intervention used leverage to invest heavily in a company and then used its voting power and appeal to persuade other investors to seek a change in strategic direction. Whether the campaign ultimately created value is unclear because so many other changes in the company and its competitive landscape have ensued. TCI attracted support from other traditional, long-term investors more associated with walking rather than activism, suggesting that TCI's interest was not *perverse*. But the approach to get their slate of directors elected rather than following the company's plan of action shows that TCI's engagement was a play for power with the board and management of Deutsche Börse, the German government, and the trade unions to defend the status quo.

POWER AND POLITICS BETWEEN SHAREHOLDERS

The array of potential political stances that shareholders take shows how the lines of conflict potentially develop around company-specific issues, corporate control, and law. Four examples help to illustrate the point.

1. *Entrance versus exit.* A venture capital fund is typically an investor with a long-term horizon. Its interests differ fundamentally from those of another long-term investor, such as a pension fund, in the period shortly after a company issues stock on a public exchange. The venture capital firm wants to sell its stake soon and uses its seat on the board to agitate for policy that would maximize cash flows and enhance short-term performance. The interest of the pension fund, a large but distant investor with little voice and perhaps even a docile approach to participation, would be better served by a policy of investment in research and development aimed at providing sustainable profits.
2. *One share, one vote.* The founder maintained supermajority voting rights when his company went public 25 years ago. The founder's shares carry five times the voting strength of those held by others. The founder only owns 10 percent of the cash-flow rights but has 50 percent of the voting rights. The founder retires. The institutions that bought the lower-voting shares now argue that because of the founder's retirement, the disproportionate voting rights should be abandoned. Because the matter cannot be resolved in the boardroom or the annual meeting, the institutional investors take their case to the government, seeking a new law banning disproportionate rights. Having been rebuffed by government, they then turn to a supranational body, urging it to propose a new legislative mandate to be imposed by all member governments.

3. *One share, more votes.* Aware of the rise of hedge fund activism and the perverse horizon incentives of many hedge funds, pension and insurance funds argue empty voting could lead to decision making that would damage the economic interests of the company and perhaps even the sustainability of the business. They argue, first with the board, then at the shareholder meeting, and later with the government, for long-term investors to be given superior voting power over mere speculators.
4. *Director nominations.* To avoid the practice of a powerful chairman-CEO creating a board of cronies, institutional investors agitate—first with the board and then at the shareholder meeting—for a change in the articles of association that provides shareholders a voice in nominating candidates to the board. Unsuccessful, they turn to the securities market regulator for a rule opening the proxy statement. A lobbying organization representing CEOs makes representations about how damaging such a measure would be. Opening the nominations process would make companies subject to an assault from single-issue lobbying organizations that would seek to get their own board members elected, who would pursue their own agendas rather than those of the company. The regulator considers the arguments and proposes that only shareholders representing at least 5 percent of the equity should be allowed the right to nominate directors.

These are not far-fetched examples. Each is drawn from a real-life example of politics in action in corporate governance. Each case involves the assertion by one party that its interests are more important or even more legitimate that those of other shareholders. Each actor in the political system seeks to use its power to enforce its view on the board's decision, the shareholders' decision, or the macro-political decision. In these disputes, each side has a legitimate point even when those points are sometimes in conflict. Resolving these conflicts without resorting to physical force requires that the exercise of power depends crucially on its perception of legitimacy.

SUMMARY AND CONCLUSIONS

The changing nature of shareholder activism has led some to argue that activists should be subject to more rigorous public scrutiny and accountability. Anabtawi and Stout (2008) argue that an increase in shareholder power should accompany an increase in fiduciary responsibility on activist fund managers. For its part, the International Corporate Governance Network (ICGN), a loose association of long-term, traditional asset management firms with a bent towards activism, has recognized the problem. Perhaps to head off too much intervention from the government, the ICGN set itself the task of reforming the governance approaches of the firms themselves (Cadbury and Millstein 2005).

Such calls indicate potential concerns with the power that institutional investors hold. Weber (1922/1947), a sociologist, identified three bases for legitimacy in the exercise of power. Legitimacy arises in a pure way either through tradition, by an appeal to reason and legality, or in the charisma of the leader. The power of the chairman or CEO in dealing with activist investors comes mainly from charisma entrenched with a dose of legality as boards invoke company law to limit shareholder involvement in the day-to-day affairs and management decisions. Tradition looms large in persistence of the unequal voting rights in many established Continental European companies.

But what provides the basis for legitimacy by one type of shareholder—long-term, activist asset management firms—that corporate boards and management should ignore the wishes of another type of shareholder—the perverse activist? Those long-term activists may be outnumbered in voting strength by the perverse activists and the long-term, docile investors who lent them stock, and other long- and short-term investors who have chosen to walk. Whose rights are more legitimate and on what basis?

In these circumstances, legitimacy involves an appeal to reason. As these investors plead with boards of individual companies and with governments, should companies act in the interests of the holders of a majority of the shares when those interests are perverse? Is it not better under all circumstances, they say, to heed the wishes of the long-term investor, even if the short-term and perverse ones have control? Company policy cannot be set for all investors equally. Even determining where the majority interest lies is hard enough when investors take differing stances and use their power in differing and even perverse ways to influence company policy. How should managements and boards take account of the interests of the docile, long-term institutional investor who has lent its stock to a short-seller?

There is another approach, another political channel to explore. It involves appealing beyond the circle of shareholders, to government or another authority with political legitimacy, to impose accountability on the asset management industry such as through mandatory share voting or mandatory reporting of how they voted their shares.

Legitimacy helps. Legitimacy allows corporations to enjoy the trust of the investment community with the benefit of lowering investors' perceived risk and the cost of capital. The company becomes more competitive with economic benefits for the whole economy. But as the VW/Porsche case shows, in a crunch, the decisions that boards adopt come back to raw power—legitimate or otherwise—and its skilful deployment in the politics of shareholder activism.

DISCUSSION QUESTIONS

1. For different classes or types of shareholders, describe how their stance might be classified using the framework suggested in the chapter.
2. How can shareholders' interests coincide even though they take different stances toward the company?
3. How can shareholders' interests differ even when their orientations mainly agree?
4. If directors cannot work in the interests of all shareholders, how can they decide which shareholders to prefer?
5. When might directors justifiably ignore the interests of shareholders?
6. If some shareholders should be ignored, some might argue that *shareholder value* itself is an invalid principle for corporate decision making. If so, what alternatives are there? Discuss how to assess their validity.

REFERENCES

Achleitner, Ann-Kristin, and Christoph Kaserer. 2005. *Private equity funds and hedge funds: A primer*. Center for Entrepreneurial and Financial Studies, Technische Universität München: SSRN. http://ssrn.com/paper=1109100.

Admati, Anat R., and Paul C. Pfleiderer. 2007. The "Wall Street walk" and shareholder activism: Exit as a form of voice. Working paper, Stanford University Graduate School of Business. https://gsbapps.stanford.edu/researchpapers/library/RP1918R2.pdf.

Anabtawi, Iman, and Lynn A. Stout. 2008. Fiduciary duties for activist shareholders. http://ssrn.com/paper=1089606.

ASX. 2008. Short selling: Asx public consultation. ASX Australian Stock Exchange, Sydney. http://www.asx.com.au/about/pdf/short_selling_public_consultation_paper.pdf.

Becht, Marco, Julian Franks, Colin Mayer, and Stefano Rossi. 2009. Returns to shareholder activism: Evidence from a clinical study of the Hermes UK Focus Fund. *Review of Financial Studies* 22 (8): 3093–3129.

Bovensiepen, Nina, and Peter Blechschmidt. 2005. Müntefering kritisiert Manager: Bei manchen Unternehmern stimmt die Ethik nicht. In *Süddeutsche Zeitung*, Munich. http://www.sueddeutsche.de/deutschland/artikel/468/51417/.

Brav, Alon, Wei Jiang, Randall S. Thomas, and Frank Partnoy. 2006. Hedge fund activism, corporate governance, and firm performance. http://ssrn.com/paper=948907.

Bris, Arturo, William N. Goetzmann, and Ning Zhu. 2007. Efficiency and the bear: Short sales and markets around the world. *Journal of Finance* 62 (3): 1029–1079.

Cadbury, Adrian, and Ira Millstein. 2005. A new agenda for the ICGN. International Corporate Governance Network. http://www.icgn.org/conferences/2005/documents/cadbury_millstein.pdf.

CFA Institute. 2005. Code of ethics and standards of professional conduct. New York: CFA Institute. http://www.cfapubs.org/doi/pdf/10.2469/ccb.v2005.n8.4568.

Chang, Eric C., Joseph W. Cheng, and Yinghui Yu. 2007. Short-sales constraints and price discovery: Evidence from the Hong Kong market. *Journal of Finance* 62 (5): 2097–2121.

Charoenrook, Anchada, and Hazem Daouk. 2005. A study of market-wide short-selling restrictions. http://papers.ssrn.com/sol3/papers.cfm?abstract_id=687562.

Clifford, Christopher P. 2008. Value creation or destruction? Hedge funds as shareholder activists. *Journal of Corporate Finance* 14 (4): 323–336.

Coffee, John C., Jr. 1991. Liquidity versus control: The institutional investor as corporate monitor. *Columbia Law Review* 91 (6): 1277–1368.

Cohen, Lauren, Karl B. Diether, and Christopher J. Malloy. 2007. Supply and demand shifts in the shorting market. *Journal of Finance* 62 (5): 2061–2096.

Curtis, Asher, and Neil L. Fargher. 2008. Does short-selling amplify price declines or align stocks with their fundamental values? http://ssrn.com/paper=817446.

Davis, Stephen, Jon Lukomnik, and David Pitt-Watson. 2006. *The new capitalists: How citizen investors are reshaping the corporate agenda*. Boston: Harvard Business School Press.

Dreman, David. 2000. The contrarian: When buy means sell. In *Forbes*. http://www.forbes.com//forbes/2000/1113/6613386a.html.

Edmans, Alex. 2009. Blockholder trading, market efficiency, and managerial myopia. *Journal of Finance*, forthcoming.

Edmans, Alex, and Gustavo Manso. 2009. Governance through exit and voice: A theory of multiple blockholders. Working paper, Wharton School of Management. http://ssrn.com/abstract=1102730. Accessed March 20, 2009.

Ferri, Fabrizio, and David Maber. 2008. Say on pay vote and CEO compensation: Evidence from the UK. http://ssrn.com/paper=1169446.

FSA. 2008. Short selling instrument. London: Financial Services Authority. http://www.fsa.gov.uk/pubs/press/PN0572008_instrument.pdf.

Gillan, Stuart, and Laura Starks. 2007. The evolution of shareholder activism in the United States. *Journal of Applied Corporate Finance* 19 (1): 55–73.

Haarmeyer, David. 2007. The revolution in active investing: Creating wealth and better and better governance. *Journal of Applied Corporate Finance* 19 (1): 25–41.

Hu, Henry T., and Bernard S. Black. 2006. Empty voting and hidden (morphable) ownership: Taxonomy, implications, and reforms. *Business Lawyer* 61 (3): 1011–1070.

Johnson, Keith L., and Daniel Summerfield. 2008. Shareholder say on pay—ten points of confusion. Cambridge, MA: Harvard Law School. http://blogs.law.harvard.edu/corpgov/files/2008/11/say-on-pay-ten-points.pdf.

Kahan, Marcel, and Edward B. Rock. 2006. Hedge funds in corporate governance and corporate control. http://ssrn.com/paper=919881.

Klein, April, and Emanuel Zur. 2006. Entrepreneurial shareholder activism: Hedge funds and other private investors. *NYU Law and Economics Research Paper No. 06/41*. http://ssrn.com/paper=913362.

Lipton, Martin. 2008. Shareholder activism and the "eclipse of the public corporation": Is the current wave of activism causing another tectonic shift in the American corporate world? *Corporate Governance Advisor* 16 (5): 1–7.

Marens, Richard. 2002. Inventing corporate governance: The mid-century emergence of shareholder activism. *Journal of Business & Management* 8 (4): 365–89.

McKenzie, Michael, and Ólan T. Henry. 2007. The determinants of short selling in the Hong Kong equities market. Melbourne: University of Melbourne Economics Department. http://www.economics.unimelb.edu.au/SITE/research/workingpapers/wp07/1001.pdf.

Milne, Richard. 2005. Investors open fire on VW's deal with Porsche. *Financial Times*. London. October 19, 32.

———. 2006. A chairman with no desire to leave office. *Financial Times*. London. December 18, 27.

Milne, Richard, Hugh Williamson, and Nikki Tait. 2008. Bitter fight for control of VW moves to the courts. *Financial Times*. London. May 28, 28.

Nordberg, Donald. 2005. Governance lesson as heads roll at Deutsche Börse. London: The Board Agenda. http://www.edgevantage.co.uk/categories/article.asp?i=2457.

Paley, Amit R., and David S. Hilzenrath. 2008. SEC chief defends his restraint. Washington: *Washington Post*. http://www.washingtonpost.com/wp-dyn/content/article/2008/12/23/AR2008122302765.html.

Partnoy, Frank, and Randall S. Thomas. 2006. Gap filling, hedge funds, and financial innovation. Vanderbilt University Law School Law and Economics Working paper 0621. http://ssrn.com/paper=931254.

Schäfer, Daniel, and James Mackintosh. 2009. Hedge funds may sue Porsche over VW. Longon: *Financial Times*. http://www.ft.com/cms/s/0/ac72c164-1188-11de-87b1-0000779fd2ac.html.

SEC. 2004. 17 Cfr Parts 240, 241, and 242: Short Sales; Final Rule and Notice "Regulation SHO." Washington, DC: U.S. Securities and Exchange Commission. http://www.sec.gov/rules/final/34-50103.pdf.

Tonello, Matteo. 2006. Revisiting stock market short-termism. The Conference Board. http://www.conference-board.org/Publications/describe.cfm?id=1116.

Ward, Andrew J., Jill A. Brown, and Scott D. Graffin. 2009. Under the spotlight: Institutional investors and firm responses to the council of institutional investors' annual focus list. *Strategic Organization* 7 (2): 107–35.

Weber, Max. 1922/1947. *The theory of social and economic organization*, trans. A. M. Henderson and Talcott Parsons. New York: Oxford University Press.

ABOUT THE AUTHOR

Donald Nordberg is a senior lecturer in strategy and corporate governance at Westminster Business School and honorary visiting professor of journalism at City University, London. In a career in financial journalism and investor relations, he has been a correspondent and senior editorial executive for Reuters in Germany, Switzerland, the United Kingdom, and the United States and served as senior adviser to The Conference Board in Europe. He has degrees from the University of Illinois and Warwick Business School in England. His articles have appeared in the *Journal of General Management, Journal of Financial Regulation and Compliance, Journalism: Theory, Practice and Criticism*, and others.

CHAPTER 22

Executive Behavior: A Creditor Perspective on Managerial Ownership

RONALD ANDERSON
Professor of Finance, American University

SATTAR MANSI
Associate Professor of Finance, Virginia Tech

DAVID REEB
Professor of Finance and Accounting, Temple University

INTRODUCTION

Management researchers suggest that executive equity ownership acts as an important governance device, portraying it either as a control mechanism (agency) or as an identification mechanism (stewardship). Agency theorists argue that managers exercise substantial control and influence in allocating firm resources and can use their discretion to divert assets for private benefit at the expense of the firm's investors (Berle and Means 1932). In an effort to remedy this concern, firms often provide managers an equity stake in the firm that potentially aligns their interests with those of investors (Anderson and Reeb 2003). Stewardship theorists, in contrast, contend that managers often possess sufficient self-motivation to act in the best interests of all firm stakeholders (Davis, Schoorman, and Donaldson 1997). In this setting, managerial ownership improves identification with the firm and increases organizational commitment, leading to a greater emphasis on protecting corporate assets (Sundaramurthy and Lewis 2003). Agency theorists thus portray managerial equity holdings as an adversarial governance mechanism that limits opportunistic behavior, while stewardship theorists suggest that it acts as a relational governance device that increases managerial commitment and identification with the organization.

Considerable debate in the empirical governance literature also arises over the effects of managerial equity stakes. Hoskisson and Turk (1990) suggest that chief executive ownership improves firm performance and reduces managerial incentives to engage in value-decreasing diversification. Hall and Liebman (1998) report that firm performance is positively related to managerial holdings. Yet, in a large-scale, multicountry study, Gugler, Mueller, and Yurtoglu (2004) examine managerial ownership and firm performance and find that executive equity stakes supply few, if any, tangible benefits to the firm. In contrast, Salancik and Pfeffer (1980) describe how greater chief executive ownership insulates managers from dismissal when firms perform poorly. Dalton, Daily, Certo, and Roengpitya (2003) incorporate the results of several studies into their meta-analysis and conclude that managerial ownership provides little benefit to shareholders. Overall, academic research yields no consensus on the benefits or costs generated by managers holding an equity stake in the firm (Coles, McWilliams, and Sen 2001).

Both theoretical and empirical studies on the role of managerial ownership focus primarily on its impact on equity holders. However, shareholders represent only one type of stakeholder or investor in the firm. Mizruchi and Stearns (1994) observe that companies often obtain a substantial portion of their capital from debt, depending on a variety of economic and organizational factors. S&P 500 companies, for instance, raise nearly one-third of their long-term investment needs from debt. Creditors, or debtholders, are concerned with the organizational structure of the firm and face many of the same issues that shareholders encounter; including governance problems, environmental uncertainty, and organizational failure (Anderson, Mansi, and Reeb 2003). Because creditors receive payment before shareholders but from the same stream of funds as shareholders, they show great concern over characteristics that affect firm health and viability (Donaldson 1961).

This chapter departs from the extant literature by examining the relation between managerial ownership and the returns demanded by debtholders. The chapter argues from a conceptual perspective that equity holdings provide managers with incentives that influence executive effort and increase managerial commitment to the firm. As a stakeholder sensitive to firm performance, creditors account for the incentive and commitment effects of managerial ownership and accordingly adjust the returns (or interest rate) on the capital they provide to the firm. This chapter contends that corporate creditors show great concern for managerial ownership because it may affect executive behavior and thus the value of the firm's underlying assets.

The chapter also explores whether managerial ownership influences creditor demand or the need for other governance mechanisms. Firms do not typically employ a single governance instrument but rather use bundles of devices to affect managerial actions (Coles et al. 2001). Beyond equity ownership, executives confront (among other devices) boards of directors, large-block shareholders, and equity-based compensation that potentially affect the quality of corporate governance (e.g., Anderson, Mansi, and Reeb 2004; Donoher, Reed, and Storrud-Barnes 2007). Based on the unique nature of creditors' claims, this chapter argues that agency and stewardship models of managerial behavior yield distinct and differing theoretical predictions on the interaction of chief executive ownership and other governance devices.

This study provides several important implications. First, creditors perceive that executive equity ownership influences managerial effort and opportunistic behavior. Expanding the discussion of managerial ownership beyond shareholders to include other stakeholders in the firm provides a broader backdrop to explore its impact on managerial behavior. Second, agency theory appears to explain the role of managerial ownership as a governance device from a creditor perspective. The concurrent use of managerial ownership with other governance devices appears to limit managerial opportunism, with creditors viewing them as substitutes. Third, the analysis suggests that stock-option holdings and equity holdings provide differing incentives to managers. Equity ownership appears to provide managers with incentives to protect firm assets while option ownership provides incentives to assume more risk. Fourth, firms with strong governance practices during the marked uncertainty of the late 1990s and early 2000s accrued substantial benefits. Based on the theoretical framework developed in this chapter, these implications suggest that equity holdings play an important role in mitigating opportunistic behavior.

The remainder of the chapter consists of four sections. The first section develops hypotheses—using agency and stewardship theory—on the relation between debtholders and managerial equity holdings. The second section describes the sample, variables, and econometric method used in the empirical analysis. The next section provides the results of the empirical analysis. The final section provides a discussion of the results and limitations of the study.

DEBTHOLDERS: ANOTHER STAKEHOLDER IN THE FIRM

Firms raise external capital from two primary sources: debt and equity. Debtholders possess a fixed claim that promises payment of interest and repayment of principal before other claimants can receive profits or funds from the firm. Prior research examines the determinants of corporate borrowing and suggests that organizational factors such as managerial values, competitor choices, and firm social ties are important in shaping financing decisions (Donaldson 1961). For instance, Mizruchi and Stearns (1994) argue that board composition and CEO educational background influence the firm's capital structure choice.

This chapter takes a different tack and asks whether governance choice affects the returns or yields demanded by the firm's investors (rather than the amount of debt the firm uses). Each investor group—debtholders and shareholders—confronts different risks arising from firm and managerial choices, and thus requires different rates of return for the use of their capital. The primary risk borne by equity holders arises over a firm's ability to earn economic profits on invested capital (Jensen and Meckling 1976). Debtholders bear the risk that firms cannot meet interest payments and/or repayment of principal (Donaldson 1961). As the likelihood of default increases on debt payments, creditors demand greater compensation for bearing greater risk; debtholders earn greater compensation by requiring firms to pay higher rates of interest (Smith and Warner 1979). Shareholders and debtholders face many of the same factors that potentially jeopardize their returns on invested capital, including governance problems, poor economic conditions, and marketing failures. From a practical perspective, debt represents a central and vital form of financing for most firms. S&P 500 firms, for instance, obtain over one-third of their long-term capital from debt. On a combined basis, current and long-term debt provides nearly 65 percent of large firms' total capital requirements.

Focusing on how executive behavior can affect other important stakeholders in the firm, this chapter examines organizational structure, executive ownership, and the returns demanded by debtholders. As residual claimants, shareholders are responsible for establishing the bundle of governance mechanisms that control managerial actions and choice (Devers, Canella, Reilly, and Yoder 2007). Although shareholders set the types and levels of control devices to maximize their returns, other stakeholders in the firm potentially capture or garner benefits from the same devices (Schneper and Guillen 2004). Governance systems affecting managerial effort or avarice, for instance, arguably generate greater returns for shareholders but also potentially limit the risk borne by debtholders. By bearing less risk, debtholders require less compensation and thereby require lower returns (lower interest rates) for the use of their capital (Smith and Warner 1979).

Opportunism, Commitment, and Debtholder Returns

Berle and Means (1932) characterized the largest U.S. firms as being run by professional managers with many small and poorly informed investors who supplied the firm's capital. Agency theory revolves around a simple question about such an organizational structure: How can atomistic investors ensure that managers do not expropriate or waste the supplied capital? Early economists argued that professional managers would be less diligent than owners in decision making and may also select projects and investments that provide personal benefits, rather than benefits to the suppliers of capital (Berle and Means 1932). Managers can waste or expropriate firm wealth in several ways, including producing fraudulent or inaccurate accounting reports (WorldCom and Enron), confiscating corporate funds (Tyco and Adelphia), engaging in nepotism (Rite-Aid), and setting transfer prices to companies owned by the manager (Hollinger International). Recent passage of the Sarbanes-Oxley Act in 2002 by the U.S. Congress indicates that a manager's misrepresentation and obfuscation of corporate activities and reports has been a particularly prevalent form of the principal-agent conflict over the past decade.

Prior research posits that supplying equity stakes to managers can alleviate the classic principal-agent conflict (Jensen and Meckling 1976). Equity stakes arguably provide monetary incentives for managers to improve firm performance and increase firm cash flows, thereby benefiting investors (Donoher et al. 2007). Jensen and Meckling's model indicated that a manager's incentive to expropriate or waste firm wealth depends on the cost for misbehaving relative to the benefits accrued from consuming firm resources. The author's model shows that managers incur greater costs from misconduct as their ownership stake in the firm increases. Misconduct becomes especially costly as managers' human capital and wealth become increasingly undiversified in the firm. As Stein (1989) shows, equity ownership mitigates myopic investment decisions and provides incentives for managers to invest for the long term. Agency theory specifies that equity stakes mitigate managerial incentives to waste and expropriate firm resources and thus lead to lower risk premiums on the capital supplied by investors.

Although agency theory provides perhaps the most common structure for investigating corporate governance issues, stewardship theory depicts an alternative model of managerial behavior. Stewardship theory focuses on empowering managers and fostering their commitment and identification with the firm.

More specifically, stewardship focuses on the idea that managers can identify with the firm and internalize the organization's mission, leading to a collaborative management approach (Sundaramurthy and Lewis 2003). Stewards of corporate assets eschew purely self-serving behavior that harms the firm and instead focus on promoting group interests because they inherently seek to do a good job (Donaldson and Davis 1991). The theory first stressed that managers maintain incentives that benefit all stakeholders, not simply to provide benefits to themselves or shareholders.

Davis et al. (1997) note that firms developing organizational structures that foster long-term relationships and high levels of trust also tend to develop steward relationships between managers and investors. In this context, managerial identification with the firm leads to a situation in which managers incorporate firm well-being into their utility function. Pierce, Rubenfeld, and Morgan (1991) argue that ownership among the firm's employees yields marked attitudinal and behavioral effects, suggesting a relation between managerial ownership and steward-like behavior. Rousseau and Shperling (2003) argue that ownership plays a key role in developing managerial identification with the firm, while Brouthers and Bamossy (2006) observe that processes or mechanisms that facilitate a relationship between managers and the firm are important to firm success. Consequently, to enhance the steward relationship with the firm, Sundaramurthy and Lewis (2003) prescribe providing managers with an equity stake because it encourages firm identification and assists in developing long-term relationships. Similarly, Hambrick and Jackson (2000) advocate meaningful equity stakes to increase identification with the firm, encouraging collective behavior and strengthening commitment. Stewardship theory thus suggests that as equity stakes become larger, managers become better stewards of corporate wealth.

Using agency and stewardship arguments, the prior discussion suggests that corporate debtholders show great concern with managerial ownership. Because behavior that reduces or enhances the value of the firm's underlying assets similarly affects the value of creditors' claims on the firm, the compensation (interest rate) that debtholders require from the firm will potentially exhibit a relation to managerial ownership. If equity stakes control managerial opportunism (agency view) or promote greater managerial commitment (stewardship view), then debtholders bear less risk and thus require less compensation on their invested capital. The specific hypothesis pertaining to agency and stewardship theory is:

Hypothesis 1 (H1): The greater the percentage of managerial ownership in public firms, the lower the compensation required by debtholders (i.e., the lower the cost of debt financing).

Increasing Levels of Chief Executive Ownership

Prior research from an agency theoretic view suggests that the alignment or incentive effects of managerial ownership change as the level of holdings increases (Morck, Shleifer, and Vishny 1988). Specifically, at low levels of holdings, ownership provides monetary incentives to managers that align their interests with those of shareholders. Yet, as executive ownership continues to increase, managers arguably become both increasingly risk averse and powerful, suggesting an ability to entrench themselves in their positions and/or expropriate firm resources to their private benefit (Jensen and Meckling 1976). Prior agency research as such posits a curvilinear relation (an inverted U-shape) between managerial ownership and firm performance.

Stewardship models of managerial decision making also potentially indicate a nonlinear relation between chief executive ownership and firm performance. Formal equity holdings and feelings of ownership (psychological ownership) represent two distinct aspects of ownership, with equity holdings recognized by legal systems and psychological ownership generated *within* by the manager (Pierce et al. 1991). Although a congruent relation potentially exists between these two ownership forms, possible divergences also exist (Pierce, Kostova, and Dirks 2001). On the one hand, once managers reach the point where they view the firm as an extension of themselves (Belk 1988), additional chief executive holdings in the firm may have little impact on their commitment or decision making, suggesting diminishing returns to chief executive ownership. On the other hand, psychological ownership and firm identification may affect managerial control and power within the firm (Wilpert 1991). If low levels of equity holdings provide relatively little power and control, but higher levels grant greater authority, then a non-monotonic relation potentially exits between ownership and managerial identification with the firm. This leads to the second hypothesis, based on both agency and stewardship models of managerial decision making, which is:

Hypothesis 2a (H2a): At low levels of managerial holdings, the greater the ownership of managers, the lower is the risk premium required by debtholders.

Hypothesis 2b (H2b): At high level of managerial holdings, the greater the ownership of the managers, the higher is the risk premium required by debtholders.

Ownership, Other Governance Mechanisms, and Debtholder Returns

The following subsections explore whether creditors perceive alternative governance mechanisms as substitutes in controlling managerial actions or whether these alternative devices limit or diminish managerial commitment to the firm. Although this chapter's adversarial- and relational-based arguments make similar inferences on the association between managerial ownership and the cost of debt, both agency theory and stewardship theory potentially yield distinct and unique predictions on the relation between debt costs and additional or multiple governance devices.

Agency Theory, Debt Returns, and Internal Monitoring

Agency theory suggests that equity ownership provides incentives that align managers' interests with those of shareholders, thereby potentially improving firm performance. Although creditors maintain a senior claim on the firm relative to equity holders, they still face many of the same risk factors as shareholders. Debtholders are thus greatly concerned over activities that increase firm risk and affect the value of their investments and wealth (Smith and Warner 1979). Agency costs produce such risks. Managerial expropriation of firm assets, for example, draws valuable resources away from investments and increases the probability that firms will be unable to service debt payments. Executives who expend less effort (shirking) on decision making and oversight also increase the probability that firms will experience problems, thereby affecting debtholder wealth. Overall, the nature of the debt claims suggests that creditors greatly value devices that promote beneficial executive behavior and decision making.

Equity ownership, as outlined earlier, provides one method of lessening the principal-agent problem by aligning managerial interests with those of the shareholders. Yet other governance systems potentially restrict managerial actions, suggesting a further mitigation of risk factors—thereby better protecting debtholders' investments. Internal monitoring arguably functions as such an additional governance layer. Internal monitoring can arise from boards of directors and large shareholders. Prior research generally hypothesizes that boards, independent from senior management, provide objectivity and expertise that limits managerial opportunism and expropriation (Hambrick and Jackson 2000; Anderson and Reeb 2004). Likewise, large shareholders maintain substantial economic incentives to monitor managers and possess the power to ensure that managers act in investors' best interests (David, Hitt, and Gimeno 2001; Anderson, Duru, and Reeb 2009). Jensen and Meckling (1976) suggest that large shareholders provide perhaps the most direct way to mitigate conflicts of interest between managers and investors. Internal monitoring thus potentially provides an additional layer of governance beyond equity ownership that further mitigates firm risk.

A substitution effect potentially exits between managerial ownership and other governance devices. Most researchers approach the substitution hypothesis from the perspective of transaction cost economics (TCE). TCE suggests shareholders will only introduce governance mechanisms to the extent that these devices reduce significant exchange hazards. Once absent these hazards, shareholders incur no further costs in governing the exchange (Williamson 1991). Strong boards of directors, for example, may sufficiently control managerial actions, indicating that shareholders have less need to rely on equity ownership to affect executives' effort. Although shareholders bear the direct cost of governance devices, bondholders bear an opportunity cost from the implementation of these mechanisms. Resources spent on governance systems, for instance, could alternatively have been invested in research and development, advertising, or other projects that increased firm value and thereby reduced bondholder risk. Because creditors potentially benefit from shareholder-implemented governance devices and bear an implicit cost, bondholders (similar to shareholders) could potentially view these mechanisms as substitutes to one another.

In summary, internal monitoring devices could lead to a lower cost of debt. However, from an agency-based perspective, these additional mechanisms potentially exert a moderating effect on the relation between managerial ownership and debt costs (a positive coefficient estimate on the interaction of ownership and the other governance devices).

Hypothesis 3a (H3a): The greater the level of managerial ownership and the greater the level of internal monitoring in publicly traded firms, the lower is the cost of debt financing.

Hypothesis 3b (H3b): Managerial ownership and internal monitoring systems function as substitutes to one another in explaining the cost of debt financing.

Stewardship Theory, Debt Returns, and Internal Monitoring

Despite agency theoretic reasoning to view equity ownership and internal monitoring as substitutes for one another from a creditor perspective, stewardship theory and relational governance provide compelling arguments for an alternative view. As noted earlier, stewardship theory focuses on developing organizational structures that foster long-term relationships and high levels of trust (Davis et al. 1997). Managerial equity stakes arguably give rise to this trust and commitment. Prior research generally views greater trust levels as obviating or diminishing the need for other governance mechanisms (Dyer and Singh 1998; Malhotra and Murnighan 2002). For instance, steward-based or trust-based relationships potentially replace formal governance systems such as internal monitoring that rely on restricting and controlling managerial actions. Other research from a stewardship perspective suggests that implementing governance mechanisms potentially has a detrimental effect upon managerial effort. Specifically, because governance mechanisms limit managerial authority, executive motivation suffers and negatively affects organizational wealth (Tosi, Brownlee, Silva, and Katz 2003). Firm performance depends on organizational structures that, rather than limiting executive discretion, grant greater authority and freedom and thereby empower managers (Davis et al. 1997; Donaldson and Davis 1991). Accordingly, Lee and O'Neill (2003) suggest that firms waste valuable capital by requiring governance systems that limit managerial discretion and power. Pierce et al. (2001) argue that a loss of power over what managers view as *theirs* can have severe psychological and behavioral effects. In this setting, internal monitoring and equity ownership do not serve the same function; managerial ownership increases commitment and influence, while monitoring diminishes commitment and influence.

The previous stewardship-based arguments suggest that internal monitoring systems act to limit or diminish managerial commitment and identification with the firm. If so, board of director independence and large-shareholder presence arguably has a moderating effect on managerial ownership. More importantly, however, if these alternative governance devices diminish managerial commitment and identification, then these devices potentially lead to a higher cost of debt financing. This leads to the final stewardship hypothesis.

Hypothesis 4a (H4a): The greater the level of internal monitoring devices in public firms, the weaker is the effect of managerial ownership on debt costs.

Hypothesis 4b (H4b): The greater the use of internal monitoring devices in the firm, the higher is the cost of debt financing.

METHOD

Sample, Variables, and Econometric Technique

For a firm to be included in the sample, it must be covered by both the Lehman Brothers Fixed Income database (LBFI) and the S&P 500 Industrial Index as of December 31, 1992. The LBFI provides security-specific information on firms' outstanding publicly traded debt; specifically, coupon rates, bond yields (market interest rate), time to bond maturity, credit ratings from Moody's and S&P, and bond prices. Although the database does not contain the universe of publicly traded debt, the authors have no reason to suspect any systematic bias with the sample. Financial and utility firms are excluded from the sample because of potential regulatory effects on the cost of debt financing.

Information on managerial ownership, board of director structure, and family ownership is manually collected from corporate proxy statements. Firm-specific financial data not already included in the LBFI is garnered from the Compustat Industrial Files and the Mergent Bond Record. Combining these databases, information from corporate proxy statements, and data from the Compustat Industrial Files yields a sample of 1,906 firm-year observations on 278 firms for the period 1993 through 2004.

The dependent variable in the empirical analysis—the risk premium on debt financing—is measured as the difference between the firm's cost of debt financing less the cost of debt financing on a U.S. Treasury security with an equivalent duration (or effective maturity). In debt markets, U.S. Treasury securities are typically assumed to be the least risky debt investment available to bondholders and as such provide the lowest return to holders. By differencing each firm's cost of debt financing with that of an equivalent-duration U.S. Treasury security, a measure is obtained of the additional return that a bondholder earns for holding a corporate debt security, above and beyond that of a U.S. Treasury. This measure reduces concerns of serial correlation and economy-wide changes in interest rates.

A two-way fixed effects model (panel data) is used for the regression analysis; the fixed effects are dummy variables for each year of the sample and for each two-digit standard industrial classification (SIC) code. The construction of the dependent variable (differencing the firm's cost of debt with that of a U.S. Treasury) mitigates concerns of serial correlation. In robustness testing, several different econometric techniques are used to examine the relation between debt costs and equity ownership (fixed effect at the firm level, random effect at the firm level, mean regressions, and median regressions). All of these techniques yield estimates consistent with the primary specifications.

Independent Variables

The term *managerial* or *executive* ownership is ambiguous. Some researchers interpret the term *manager* to mean the firm's chief executive officer (CEO) and note that decision-making authority rests with the CEO (Hall and Liebman 1998). However, other researchers note that other top managers have the ability and incentives to expropriate or to be stewards of firm resources (Dalton et al. 2003). U.S. regulators also tend to support this view by requiring that firms disclose information on the firm's five highest-paid employees. This analysis considers both approaches. As CEO ownership perhaps provides the cleanest test of agency and stewardship theories of managerial behavior, the primary measure of managerial equity ownership is defined as the percent of equity held by the firm's top executive or CEO. The percent equity holdings of the firm's top five managers are used as an alternate measure of managerial ownership. The measures of CEO ownership and top management ownership exclude stock options holdings, which are included in a later defined variable.

Internal monitoring of managers can arise from several sources, including boards of directors, other senior managers, institutional shareholders, large-block shareholders, and auditors. Two proxies, board of director independence and founding-family ownership, are employed for internal monitoring.

A three-tier system is used for board of director classification: independent, affiliated, and insiders. Directors employed by the firm, retired from the firm, or who are immediate family members are insiders. Affiliate directors are directors with potential or existing business relationships with the firm but who are not full-time employees. Consultants, lawyers, financiers, and investment bankers are examples of affiliate directors. Independent directors are individuals whose only business relationship to the firm is their directorship. The fraction of independent directors on the board is used as the measure of board independence. Specifically, board independence equals the number of independent directors on the board divided by total board size.

This study proxies for large shareholder presence by using the fractional equity holdings of founding-family shareholders. Anderson et al. (2003) note that family shareholders provide oversight and monitoring of the firm that leads to better firm performance and lower debt costs. Following their definition, family ownership is measured as the fractional equity holdings of the founding family as reported in annual corporate proxy statements. For firms with multiple share classes, total firm voting power is used as the proxy for family ownership. Binary variables are also introduced that denote the type of CEO serving in family firms (i.e., founder, founder descendant, or hired manager).

Equity-based compensation, particularly stock options, receives substantial interest from academics and practitioners because of its potential to align managers' and shareholders' interests (Devers et al. 2007). Stock option holdings are measured in a similar fashion to equity holdings. Specifically, the number of unexercised options (both exercisable and nonexercisable) held by the manager is divided by the number of outstanding shares. The resulting number gives the percent of equity—in stock option form—held by the CEO or the top management team. Compensation data come from S&P's ExecuComp Database.

Several control variables are introduced into the analysis to account for firm- and security-specific characteristics. Firm size is measured as the natural log of total assets. Firm risk is calculated by using the standard deviation of stock returns for the previous 36 months. Firm profitability or performance is measured as the return on assets calculated as earnings before interest, taxes, depreciation, and amortization, divided by total assets. Firm leverage is the ratio of long-term debt divided by the sum of equity and debt invested in the firm. The fractional equity holdings of institutional investors come from Thomson Financial.

The analysis includes four control variables that are specific to debt securities. First, because not all debt expires on the same date, duration is introduced to control for differences. Duration is computed as:

$$\text{Duration} = \Sigma\ (t \times CF_t)/P\ (1 + Y)^t$$

where

CF_t is the cash flow (coupon or principal) at time t
t is the number of periods until the cash flow
P is the market price of the bond
Y is the bond's yield to maturity

The second security-specific variable, credit ratings, controls for differences in default risk for each firm's bonds. Credit ratings are measured as the average of Moody's and S&P bond ratings. Bond ratings are computed using a conversion process in which AAA-rated bonds are assigned a value of 22 and D-rated bonds receive a value of 1. For example, a firm with A1 rating from Moody's and an A+ rating from S&P would receive an average score of 18. To mitigate the possibility that credit rating may already incorporate the impact of managerial ownership, a measure of credit ratings is developed without the managerial ownership component (Anderson et al. 2003). This is achieved by regressing credit ratings (dependent variable) on managerial ownership (independent variable). The error term from this regression incorporates the credit rating information without the influence of managerial ownership. The error term from this regression is labeled as Credit and is used as the primary measure of credit ratings.

The third debt-specific control variable, bond liquidity, accounts for differences in the speed and ease with which a bond can be converted to cash. Bond age is used as the measure of liquidity (Sarig and Warga 1989). Bond age is the number of years that a bond has been outstanding or publicly traded. Finally, credit ratings may exhibit nonlinearities as many institutions are barred from holding securities below a certain grade. Therefore, a binary variable, Nonlinear Credit Rating, is included in the analysis to denote those firms with non-investment-grade debt.

RESULTS

Summary Statistics

Exhibit 22.1 presents means, medians, standard deviations, and minimum and maximum values for each variable in our sample of firms. The first row of Exhibit 22.1 shows the dependent variable, the debt risk premium or the additional return that bondholders require for investing in corporate debt securities

Exhibit 22.1 Descriptive Statistics for Variable Measures (n = 1,906)

Variable	Mean	Median	Standard Deviation	Minimum	Maximum
Spread (basis points)	171.89	122.14	192.84	2.24	1,146.75
CEO equity (%)	0.75	0.11	2.10	0.00	57.04
Top management equity (%)	1.35	0.27	4.57	0.00	57.07
Family ownership (%)	5.10	0.00	12.76	0.00	87.01
Stock option holdings (%)	0.60	0.41	0.64	0.00	4.74
Institutional ownership (%)	63.02	64.01	14.97	0.01	99.37
Board independence (%)	64.69	66.67	17.93	0.00	93.75
Bond duration (years)	6.46	6.46	2.46	0.08	14.10
Credit rating	15.67	16.00	3.27	1.00	22.14
Ln (Total assets)	9.10	8.90	1.21	4.40	13.53
Bond age (years)	3.82	3.51	2.43	0.01	25.65
Risk (%)	0.09	0.08	0.03	0.04	0.27
Leverage (%)	22.56	21.60	12.59	0.00	92.29
Performance (%)	14.45	13.84	8.63	−19.20	69.47

relative to investing in a U.S. Treasury security of the same maturity. Debtholders, on average, demand an additional 171.89 basis points (100 basis points = 1.0 percent) for holding corporate bonds versus holding a U.S. Treasury. CEOs hold, on average, about 0.75 percent of the firm's outstanding equity while the firm's top management team (top five executives) owns 1.35 percent of the firm's stock. Average board independence is 64.7 percent. CEOs, on average, hold option portfolios that represent 0.60 percent of the firm's outstanding shares, which is slightly less than one-half the size of their equity ownership positions.

Multivariate Results

Hypothesis 1a predicts that debt costs decrease as CEO (top management) equity ownership increases. In particular, a negative relation exists between the cost of debt financing and managerial ownership. The results in Exhibit 22.2 support this hypothesis. CEO ownership bears a significant and negative relation to debt risk premia. Economically, the coefficient estimate on CEO equity indicates that the cost of debt decreases by 28.35 basis points for a one standard deviation increase in CEO equity holdings (one standard deviation equals 2.10 percent). The cost savings from such an increase in CEO ownership is nearly \$22.9 million per year for the average firm in the S&P 500. This savings is calculated as follows:

$$\begin{aligned}\text{Cost savings} &= \text{Coefficient estimate} \times \text{one standard deviation of CEO equity}\\ &\quad \times \text{average debt level of S\&P 500 firms}\\ &= -.001350 \times 2.10 \times \$8.087 \text{ billion}\\ &= \$22.9 \text{ million}\end{aligned}$$

Column 4 of Exhibit 22.2 shows the results of the analysis when using top management equity holdings—the firm's top five executive officers—as the independent variable. Consistent with the prior regression, equity holdings exhibit a significant and negative relation to debt costs. The magnitude of the coefficient, although less than with CEO ownership, indicates that the average firm in the S&P 500 would create annual cost savings of about \$15.3 million by increasing top management equity holdings by one standard deviation (one standard deviation of top management ownership equals 4.57 percent). Again, this is calculated as:

$$\begin{aligned}\text{Cost savings} &= \text{coefficient estimate} \times \text{one standard deviation in top}\\ &\quad \text{management equity} \times \text{average debt level of S\&P 500 firms}\\ &= -0.000415 \times 4.57 \times \$8.087 \text{ billion}\\ &= \$15.3 \text{ million}\end{aligned}$$

As Neubaum and Zahra (2006) note, the collapse of the dot-com bubble in 2001 led many industry and legal analysts to the collective belief that a governance crisis was occurring in America. Consequently, the late 1990s and early 2000s represent a particularly robust environment to examine the efficacy of executive ownership in mitigating agency problems and creating a steward relationship with the firm. If equity incentives failed to align managerial interests with those of the firm,

Exhibit 22.2 Yield Spread and CEO Ownership (n = 1,906)

This table reports multivariate regression results of yield spreads (debt costs) on CEO ownership and top management ownership.

	Dependent Variable = Debt Costs				
	(1)	(2)	(3)	(4)	(5)
Intercept		671.99**	680.50**	579.18**	579.15**
		(8.35)	(9.74)	(7.52)	(7.51)
CEO equity	?	−13.50**	−10.15*	—	—
		(3.87)	(1.99)		
(CEO equity)^2	?	—	−0.25	—	—
			(0.97)		
Top management equity	?	—	—	−4.15*	−4.52
				(2.07)	(1.78)
(Top management equity)^2	?	—	—	—	0.01
					(0.25)
Board independence		−439.54**	−454.14**	−269.07**	−267.57**
		(5.40)	(7.01)	(4.11)	(3.99)
Family ownership		−80.60**	−81.49**	−53.10**	−52.55**
		(4.91)	(6.52)	(3.86)	(3.58)
Option holdings	+	21.03**	19.52**	17.82**	17.78**
		(4.26)	(4.71)	(3.18)	(3.17)
Institutional ownership		−136.82**	−139.27**	−122.57**	−122.31**
		(3.46)	(3.93)	(3.09)	(3.06)
Duration	−	−1.53	−2.00	−2.21	−2.22
		(0.68)	(1.14)	(0.96)	(0.97)
Bond Age	+	7.54**	7.39**	7.41**	7.41
		(4.25)	(4.86)	(4.15)	(4.15)
Firm Size	+	−15.99*	−15.36**	−20.75**	−20.86
		(2.24)	(3.10)	(3.06)	(3.09)
Credit Rating	−	−18.73**	−18.93**	−10.89**	−10.80**
		(5.36)	(6.94)	(4.23)	(4.05)
Performance	−	−172.26**	−164.45**	−255.30**	−256.48**
		(2.58)	(3.38)	(3.83)	(3.83)
Leverage	−	257.62**	257.01**	309.24**	309.90**
		(3.33)	(4.25)	(4.08)	(4.11)
Firm Risk	+	18.46**	18.32**	17.13**	17.08**
		(6.06)	(6.76)	(5.82)	(5.73)
Nonlinear Credit Rating	+	117.20*	103.59*	165.11*	165.27*
		(2.03)	(2.09)	(3.01)	(3.02)
Adjusted R^2		0.464	0.461	0.452	0.451

**, * Indicates significance at the 0.01, 0.05 level or better, respectively. The t-values, given in parenthesis below each estimate, are corrected for heteroskedasticity. Serial correlation is controlled for in the construction of the yield spread and by including fixed effects for both industry and time.

then either no relation or a weakened relation is suggested between equity stakes and debt returns during this period. Alternatively, equity ownership potentially played a more important role during the crisis, indicating an incrementally stronger relation between equity stakes and debt returns. Because no specific dates exist to define the apparent crisis, regressions are run on a year-by-year basis to examine the relation between debt costs and CEO equity holdings. The results are shown in Exhibit 22.3. To conserve space, only the variables of interest are reported; however, all control variables were included in the regressions.

From 1993 through 1999, the analysis reveals a fairly stable but significant relation between managerial holdings and debt costs. Debt costs decrease, on average, about 9.7 basis points for each 1 percent of equity held by the CEO. This is calculated as an arithmetic average from 1993 through 1999. However, the following three years—2000, 2001, and 2002—reveal a vastly more sensitive relation between equity ownership and debtholder returns. For each 1 percent of equity held by the CEO during this period, debt costs on average decrease by 53.7 basis points (this as an arithmetic average across 2000, 2001, and 2002). The magnitude of the relation from pre-crisis (1993 through 1999) to crisis (2000 through 2002) increases by a factor of 5, and F-tests ($F = 6.21$) indicate that this difference is significant at the 0.01 level. For 2003 and 2004, the relation between debt costs and equity ownership returns to pre-crisis levels. F-tests indicate that the years 1993 through 1999 are not significantly different from 2003 and 2004.

Exhibit 22.3 also provides the coefficient estimates of the other key governance variables in the analysis. Interestingly, board independence, family ownership, and institutional ownership exhibit substantially heightened sensitivities to debt cost during the alleged crisis period relative to pre- or post-crisis. Based on these traditional governance measures, the analysis indicates that firms with better governance practices accrued substantial financial benefits via lower debt costs. Yet firms with poorer practices paid substantially higher rates for their borrowed capital. Consequently, corporate governance appeared to be highly valued during the collapse of the Internet bubble.

Increasing Levels of Chief Executive Ownership

Morck et al. (1988) suggest that the incentive effects of managerial ownership may change as executives come to own larger and larger fractions of the firm's outstanding shares. Consistent with this proposition, Hypotheses 2a and 2b predict a curvilinear relation (an inverted U-shape) between debt costs and managerial ownership. To empirically examine whether a curvilinear relation describes the relation between debt costs and equity ownership, ownership and the square of ownership are included in the regression model. Column 3 of Exhibit 22.2 shows the results for CEOs and Column 5 presents the results for the top management team. In both cases—CEOs and top management—the coefficient estimates for ownership are marginally significant but the estimates for the square of ownership are insignificant, suggesting that a curvilinear relation does not explain the link between managerial ownership and debt costs. Rather, as shown in the earlier regressions, a simple linear model appears to best describe the relation between debt costs and executive behavior, indicating from a creditor's perspective that

Exhibit 22.3 Yield Spread and CEO Ownership on a Year-by-Year Basis

This table provides regression results of yield spreads (debt costs) on CEO ownership and other important governance mechanisms for each year of the sample period. The control variables are included in each regression but not reported to conserve space.

	Dependent Variable = Debt Costs											
	1993	1994	1995	1996	1997	1998	1999	2000	2001	2002	2003	2004
CEO Equity	−15.78**	−8.09**	−9.49**	−10.56**	−9.12**	−9.39**	−11.57**	−64.06**	−51.84**	−45.16**	−16.63**	−13.23**
	(4.02)	(2.65)	(3.66)	(2.76)	(3.76)	(3.38)	(3.11)	(2.78)	(4.20)	(4.73)	(3.88)	(2.39)
Board	−377.91**	−179.89*	−240.45**	−279.78**	−260.20**	−234.15**	−302.24**	−1,596.13**	−1,287.65**	−1,012.36**	−558.62**	−588.70**
independence	(3.95)	(2.08)	(3.77)	(3.46)	(4.15)	(3.37)	(3.05)	(2.64)	(4.26)	(3.76)	(4.68)	(3.87)
Family	−57.11**	−38.05*	−47.45**	−85.98**	−56.73**	−54.28**	−61.94**	−304.56**	−215.38**	−165.81**	−87.18**	−98.06**
ownership	(2.75)	(2.01)	(3.77)	(4.15)	(4.34)	(4.66)	(2.70)	(2.80)	(4.29)	(3.54)	(3.17)	(2.74)
Option holdings	−5.87	−3.81	15.74	19.16	15.80**	11.29	42.11**	−27.20	52.56**	46.51**	28.98**	14.81
	(0.38)	(0.26)	(1.42)	(1.83)	(2.21)	(1.34)	(3.51)	(0.80)	(1.98)	(3.77)	(4.51)	(1.27)
Institutional	−42.40	−43.98	−73.15*	−134.38**	−37.75*	−137.54**	−51.26	−367.26	−384.60	−155.62	25.03	−10.73
ownership	(0.87)	(1.14)	(1.99)	(2.56)	(1.98)	(3.52)	(1.31)	(1.83)	(1.93)	(1.28)	(0.39)	(0.10)
Adjusted R^2	0.525	0.502	0.481	0.490	0.60	0.588	0.631	0.441	0.610	0.597	0.684	0.534
Observations	188	184	176	187	181	175	144	133	138	137	138	125

All control variables are included but are not shown (intercept, institutional ownership, duration, bond age, firm size, credit rating, performance, leverage, firm risk, Nonlinear credit rating, one-digit SIC code).

**, * Indicates significance at the 0.01 and 0.05 level or better, respectively.

greater levels of ownership mitigate managerial opportunism (agency perspective) and/or promote greater managerial commitment (stewardship view).

Managerial Ownership, Internal Monitoring, and Debtholder Returns

The results from the prior sections are consistent with both agency and stewardship arguments on the role that equity ownership plays in aligning managerial incentives with those of the firm's stakeholders. Yet other governance mechanisms beyond equity ownership affect managerial actions. To attempt to differentiate between these arguments, the analysis empirically investigates the joint effect of equity ownership with two other important internal governance devices: board independence and large, concentrated shareholder presence. The following regression equation is used:

$$\begin{aligned}\text{Debt Costs} = {} & \beta_0 + \beta_1\,(\text{CEO Equity}) + \beta_2\,(\text{Internal Monitoring Device}) \\ & + \beta_3\,(\text{CEO Equity} \times \text{Internal Monitoring Device}) + \beta_4\,(\text{Controls})\end{aligned} \quad (22.1)$$

Without the interaction term, β_1 is interpreted as the unique effect of CEO equity on debt costs. The introduction of the interaction term indicates that the unique effect of CEO equity on debt costs is not limited to β_1, but also depends on the value of the interaction term, β_3, which represents the marginal effect of internal monitoring on debt costs as a function of the CEO's equity stake in the firm. Finally, β_2 provides the unique effect of the alternative governance device(s) on the cost of debt.

The agency-based hypothesis on the joint effect of managerial ownership and internal monitoring systems suggests a substitution effect. Specifically, from an empirical perspective, a positive coefficient estimate on the interaction term would be indicative of a substitution between managerial holdings and the respective governance device. The agency predictions further indicate negative coefficient estimates on the stand-alone internal monitoring devices (board independence and family ownership).

The stewardship hypothesis also indicates a positive coefficient estimate on the interaction term. More importantly, the stewardship-based arguments indicate that internal monitoring diminishes or weakens managerial commitment. If so, bondholders potentially require higher interest rates in the presence of these alternative mechanisms, indicating positive coefficient estimates on the stand-alone terms for the internal monitoring devices. In summary, the expectations of the coefficient estimates are as follows:

Variable	Indicative of Agency Arguments	Indicative of Stewardship Arguments
CEO Equity	−	−
Internal Monitoring Device	−	+
CEO Equity × Internal Monitoring Device	+	+

Column 1 of Exhibit 22.4 presents the regression results examining the joint effect of managerial ownership and board independence on debt costs. Consistent with the prior analysis, CEO holdings (β_1) continue to exhibit a negative and significant relation to debt costs. The interaction term between CEO ownership and board independence (β_6) is positive and significant, which suggests that board independence attenuates the relation between managerial holdings and debt costs. Specifically, the results suggest a substitution effect and indicate that managerial ownership plays a less influential role as boards become progressively more independent. However, the coefficient estimate on the stand-alone board independence term indicates that bondholders deem greater levels of board independence as

Exhibit 22.4 Yield Spread, CEO Ownership, and Internal Corporate Governance

This table reports multivariate regression results of yield spreads (debt costs) on the interaction of CEO ownership and each of board independence, family presence, and CEO stock option holdings.

	Dependent Variable = Debt Costs					
	(1)	(2)	(3)	(4)	(5)	(6)
β_0 (Intercept)	684.29**	673.39**	656.78**	675.47**	671.99**	683.27**
	(8.44)	(9.66)	(7.77)	(9.76)	(9.62)	(9.78)
β_1 (CEO equity)	−23.33**	−15.04**	−12.64*	−15.88**	−13.50**	−16.73**
	(4.75)	(2.52)	(1.99)	(2.65)	(4.56)	(6.18)
β_2 (Board independence)	−454.59**	−439.90**	−402.49**	−452.91**	−439.55**	−447.77**
	(5.54)	(6.82)	(5.24)	(7.07)	(6.84)	(6.97)
β_3 (Family firm)	−81.39**	−81.07**	−77.42**	−80.77**	−80.60**	−80.46**
	(4.95)	(6.27)	(3.53)	(6.20)	(6.45)	(6.42)
β_4 (Option holdings)	19.42**	21.13**	21.43**	23.53**	21.03**	16.58**
	(4.07)	(5.03)	(4.27)	(5.25)	(5.02)	(3.60)
β_5 (CEO equity × Board independence)	21.94**	—	—	—	—	—
	(2.54)					
β_6 (CEO equity × Family firm)	—	14.37**	15.13*	16.53**	—	—
		(2.40)	(2.24)	(2.73)		
β_7 (CEO equity × Option holding)	—	—	—	—	—	4.52**
						(2.43)
β_8 (Founder CEO)	—	—	—	−96.42**	—	—
				(3.20)		
β_9 (Family descendant CEO)	—	—	—	0.55	—	—
				(0.04)		
Adjusted R^2	0.466	0.464	0.460	0.466	0.464	0.464
Observations	1,906	1,906	1,509	1,906	1,906	1,906

All control variables are included but are not shown (institutional ownership, duration, bond age, firm size, credit rating, performance, leverage, firm risk, nonlinear credit rating, one-digit SIC code).

**, * Indicates significance at the 0.01 and 0.05 level or better, respectively. The t-values, given in parenthesis below each estimate, are corrected for heteroskedasticity. Serial correlation is controlled for in the construction of the yield spread and by including fixed effects for both industry and time.

better able to protect their investment, consistent with an agency theoretic explanation. This result is inconsistent with the stewardship ideal of empowering managers in order to create greater organizational commitment.

Column 2 of Exhibit 22.4 examines the joint effect of managerial ownership and the second measure of internal monitoring: founding family ownership. For this analysis, three different specifications are examined because of the effects of founder-CEOs and founder-descendant CEOs on firm performance (Anderson et al. 2003). Column 2 shows a regression that includes the level of family ownership without regard to CEO type. Column 3 presents a specification that excludes observations where a family member (founder or founder-descendant) serves as CEO of the firm. Column 4 shows the results with all firms but binary variables are introduced that denote whether a founder or a founder-descendant serves as CEO.

All three specifications provide relatively similar results on family ownership. First, the analysis indicates that CEO holdings (β_1) continue to exhibit a negative and significant relation to debt costs. Next, the interaction term between family ownership/presence and CEO ownership bears a positive and significant relation to debt costs, suggesting managerial ownership plays a less important role in controlling executive effort/actions in the presence of a large, committed investor. Third, the stand-alone family variable(s) bears a significantly negative relation to the debt costs. This last result supports an agency theoretic view in that bondholders appear to value large-shareholder monitoring that limits or diminishes CEO discretion and influence.

Overall, the results indicate that from the debtholders' perspective, managerial ownership and internal monitoring (board independence and large shareholders) act as substitutes to one another. The agency and stewardship hypotheses both suggest this moderating effect. Yet board independence and large shareholder presence, as stand-alone terms, continue to be associated with lower costs of debt. This finding indicates that bondholders view these mechanisms as better able to protect their investment in the firm. The results on the relation between executive ownership and internal monitoring provide evidence generally consistent with an agency explanation on the role of equity ownership in managerial behavior.

An Alternative Test: The Role of Equity-Based Compensation

Managers often obtain at least a portion of their ownership stakes from stock-option pay, which suggests that equity compensation plays an important role in affecting executive behavior and in understanding the implications of this chapter's earlier results (Devers et al. 2007). Sanders (2001) and Hanlon, Rajgopal, and Shevlin (2004) find that stock options and equity ownership do not provide congruent incentives to managers. Specifically, options appear to increase risk-taking behavior and stock ownership tends to increase risk aversion. Greater managerial risk-taking could arguably lead to greater shareholder wealth. However, this increased risk-taking behavior can decrease the value of bondholders' stakes depending on the manner in which managers increase risk.

From an agency theoretic perspective, stock options potentially provide executives with incentives to transfer wealth from bondholders to stockholders via asset substitution, excessive dividend payouts, or more general risk shifting (Jensen and Meckling 1976). Option-based compensation also potentially induces managers to manipulate earnings or commit fraud (Donoher et al. 2007), which would also increase the risk to bondholders. Similarly, option compensation may provide executives with incentives to manage accounting reports (Devers et al. 2007) that are used in debt covenants to monitor firm activity. If option pay creates incentives for executives to increase their wealth at the expense of debtholders, the cost of debt (interest rate) should increase along with managers' stock option holdings. This evidence is consistent with an agency theoretic explanation.

However, stewardship theory provides an alternative prediction on the relation between stock option compensation and debt costs. Because corporate stewards maintain incentives that benefit all stakeholders in the firm (Donaldson and Davis 1991), managers potentially refrain from activities that transfer wealth from debtholders to creditors. Even in the presence of option pay, managers eschew self-serving behavior and promote both stockholder and bondholder interests—that is, managers seek methods of increasing risk that do not harm creditor interests. Further, if equity pay enhances the underlying value of the firm's assets, debtholders potentially benefit because their claim on the firm becomes less risky and more valuable. From a stewardship perspective, bondholder returns potentially exhibit no relation or a negative relation to managerial option holdings.

Column 5 of Exhibit 22.4 investigates the effect of executive stock option holdings on the firm's cost of debt. The analysis provides strong support, at least from a debtholder's perspective, that equity ownership and stock options do not provide the same incentives to managers. The coefficient estimate on CEO holdings (β_1) remains negative and significant. However, stock-option holdings (β_4) exhibit a significantly positive relation to debt costs, suggesting that as managers hold more and more options, debtholders bear greater risk and thus demand higher returns on their investment. Column 6 shows an alternative specification with an interaction term between option holdings and equity ownership. The results indicate a moderating effect on CEO ownership and suggest that stock options partially offset or diminish the beneficial (debt cost reducing) aspects of executive equity ownership. Overall, the analysis suggests that creditors view option pay as a mechanism that generates incentives for managers to transfer wealth from bondholders to shareholders. This evidence is consistent with an agency explanation.

SUMMARY AND CONCLUSIONS

The chapter's findings provide a new perspective on the role that managerial ownership plays in corporate governance and firm performance. Rather than using traditional stock-based or accounting-based measures of firm performance to examine executive behavior, this study focuses on corporate creditors, another important stakeholder. Because debtholders receive payment before shareholders and from the same stream of funds as shareholders, their claim on the firm potentially exhibits greater sensitivity to factors influencing firm performance than shareholders' claims.

From an agency perspective, managerial equity ownership presumably provides executives with strong monetary incentives to improve firm performance (Devers et al. 2007). Likewise, stewardship theory also indicates that equity ownership enhances executive commitment and identification with the organization and thereby improves organizational wealth (Donaldson and Davis 1991).

Extending both agency and steward theory, the chapter's central premise suggests that creditors demand a lower return on their capital as CEO equity ownership increases. The results of the empirical analysis indicate that increasing management ownership appears to affect managerial behavior and results in creditors requiring less compensation from the firm.

The chapter also examines the importance of equity ownership in aligning managers' and investors' interests during a markedly volatile and uncertain period of American corporate history, specifically the late 1990s and early 2000s (Neubaum and Zahra 2006). The results indicate that during this perceived corporate governance crisis, debtholders became particularly sensitive to equity ownership in affecting managerial behavior. Before the crisis, debt costs decreased by about 10 basis points when CEOs held 1 percent of a firm's equity. During the crisis, the relation intensified to suggest that a 1 percent equity stake diminished debt cost by 54 basis points. Further, although not the primary focus, the results indicated that debtholders became highly sensitive to other forms of corporate governance during the late 1990s and early 2000s. Small changes in board independence, institutional ownership, family ownership, and managerial option holdings were associated with large changes in firms' cost of debt. At least from a creditors' perspective, corporate governance systems played an important role in affecting managerial behavior during the turbulent years of 2000, 2001, and 2002.

This chapter also contributes to the organization and governance literature by finding fairly strong evidence that some governance forms act as substitutes for each another in affecting or controlling managerial behavior. Both agency- and stewardship-based arguments were developed to predict a moderating relation between managerial ownership and the cost of debt financing in the presence of other governance devices. However, from an agency theoretic viewpoint, debtholders arguably bear less risk in the use of governance devices to limit managerial discretion and will thus require lower returns, which suggests these devices are related to lower debt costs. Alternatively, from a stewardship perspective, managerial ownership increases managers' commitment to the firm, while other governance devices act to weaken this commitment. This evidence indicates that these internal monitoring devices are related to higher debt costs.

The results suggest that greater internal monitoring (board independence and family ownership) significantly mitigates the impact of managerial ownership on debt costs. Additionally, creditors apparently view CEO holdings as an alternate governance device for independent boards and the presence of large, concentrated shareholders, suggesting a substitution effect consistent with an agency explanation for the role of equity ownership.

The analysis also provides new insights on the role that stock options play in providing managerial incentives. Much of the prior literature in management, finance, and economics assumes that options and stock ownership provide the same incentives to managers—that is, maximizing shareholder wealth. This chapter indicates that creditors view these two governance mechanisms as imparting different incentives to managers. Ownership reduces creditor risk. Stock options increase creditor risk. Although both of these effects potentially lead to shareholder value maximization, the results indicate that stock options and equity ownership operate through different channels in affecting executive behavior.

Finally, the chapter adds to the growing literature on board of director effectiveness. Prior studies report little empirical evidence to support the hypothesis that greater board independence leads to better firm performance (Hambrick and Jackson 2000). The results from this analysis indicate that, at least from a creditor's perspective, board structure plays a valuable role in monitoring managers when managers maintain small equity stakes in the firm. However, as these equity stakes increase, boards appear to have a weakened effect on debt costs. Furthermore, consistent with the hypothesis that family shareholders act as monitors of firm management, the analysis suggests family presence has the greatest influence on debt costs when managers hold small equity stakes in the firm. The family's influence on debt costs appears to weaken as managers hold continually larger stakes in the firm. This evidence indicates that managerial ownership acts as a substitute for the monitoring role of large, concentrated shareholders.

This study broadens the debate on the influence of equity ownership on firm performance by exploring the incentive effects of managerial holdings using data from publicly traded corporate debt. The analysis indicates that chief executive equity holdings exhibit a negative and significant relation to the cost of debt, suggesting that executive ownership provides incentives to managers that affect firm performance. Additional testing indicates that larger executive equity stakes mitigate the need for board and shareholding monitoring, indicating a substitution effect among managerial control devices. These findings imply that creditors view chief executive holdings as increasing managerial effort and reducing opportunistic behavior.

DISCUSSION QUESTIONS

1. Managers, rather than shareholders or boards of directors, make day-to-day operating decisions for most companies. What are some of the mechanisms that shareholders and boards can use to ensure that managers make decisions in the best interests of shareholders?
2. From the perspective of agency theory, why would equity ownership influence corporate executives' actions?
3. From the perspective of stewardship theory, why would equity ownership influence corporate executives' actions?
4. Unlike shareholders, debtholders have a fixed and legally enforceable claim on the firm for payment of interest and principal. Consequently, why would debtholders care about managerial equity ownership or other corporate governance devices?

REFERENCES

Anderson, Ronald C., Augustine Duru, and David M. Reeb. 2009. Founders, heirs, and corporate opacity in the United States. *Journal of Financial Economics* 92 (2): 205–222.

Anderson, Ronald C., Sattar A. Mansi, and David M. Reeb. 2003. Founding family ownership and the agency costs of debt. *Journal of Financial Economics* 68 (2): 263–285.

———. 2004. Board characteristics, accounting report integrity, and the cost of debt. *Journal of Accounting and Economics* 37 (3): 315–342.

Anderson, Ronald C., and David M. Reeb. 2003. Founding family ownership and firm performance: Evidence from the S&P 500. *Journal of Finance* 58 (3): 1301–1328.

———. 2004. Board composition: Balancing family influence in S&P 500 Firms. *Administrative Science Quarterly* 49 (2): 209–237.

Belk, Russell W. 1988. Possessions and the extended self. *Journal of Consumer Research* 15 (2): 139–168.
Berle, Adolf A., and Gardiner C. Means. 1932. *The modern corporation and private property*. New York: MacMillan.
Brouthers, Keith D., and Gary J. Bamossy. 2006. Post-formation processes in eastern and western European joint ventures. *Journal of Management Studies* 43 (2): 203–229.
Coles, Jerily W., Victoria B. McWilliams, and Nilanjan Sen. 2001. An examination of the relationship of governance mechanisms to performance. *Journal of Management* 27 (1): 23–51.
Dalton, Dan R., Catherine M. Daily, S. Trevis Certo, and Rungpen Roengpitya. 2003. Meta-analyses of financial performance and equity: Fusion or confusion? *Academy of Management Journal* 46 (1): 13–26.
David, Parthiban., Michale A. Hitt, and Javier Gimeno. 2001. The influence of activism by institutional investors on R&D. *Academy of Management Journal* 44 (1): 144–157.
Davis, James H., F. David Schoorman, and Lex Donaldson. 1997. Toward a stewardship theory of management. *Academy of Management Review* 22 (1): 20–47.
Devers, Cynthia E., Albert A. Canella, Gregory P. Reilly, and Michele E. Yoder. 2007. Executive compensation: A multidisciplinary review of recent developments. *Journal of Management* 33 (6): 1016–1072.
Donaldson, Gordon. 1961. *Corporate debt capacity: A study of corporate debt policy and the determination of corporate debt capacity*. Cambridge, MA: Harvard University, Division of Research.
Donaldson, Lex, and James H. Davis. 1991. Stewardship theory or agency theory: CEO governance and shareholder returns. *Australian Journal of Management* 16 (1): 49–64.
Donoher, William J., Richard Reed, and Susan F. Storrud-Barnes. 2007. Incentive alignment, control, and the issue of misleading financial disclosures. *Journal of Management* 33 (4): 547–570.
Dyer, Jeffrey H., and Harbir Singh. 1998. The relational view: Cooperative strategy and sources of interorganizational competitive advantage. *Academy of Management Review* 23 (4): 660–679.
Gugler, Klaus, Dennis C. Mueller, and B. Burcin Yurtoglu. 2004. Corporate governance and the returns on investment. *Journal of Law and Economics* 47 (2): 589–633.
Hall, Brian J., and Jeffrey B. Liebman. 1998. Are CEOs really paid like bureaucrats? *Quarterly Journal of Economics* 113 (3): 653–691.
Hambrick, Donald C., and Eric M. Jackson. 2000. Outside directors with a stake: The linchpin in improving governance. *California Management Review* 42 (4): 108–127.
Hanlon, Michelle, Shiviram Rajgopal, and Terry J. Shevlin. 2004. Large sample evidence on the effect of stock option compensation on risk taking and future operating performance. Working paper, University of Michigan.
Hoskisson, Robert E., and Thomas A. Turk. 1990. Corporate restructuring: Governance and control limits of the internal capital market. *Academy of Management Review* 15 (3): 459–477.
Jensen, Michael C., and William H. Meckling. 1976. Theory of the firm: Managerial behavior, agency costs and ownership structure. *Journal of Financial Economics* 3 (4): 305–360.
Lee, Peggy M., and Hugh M. O'Neill. 2003. Ownership structures and R&D investments of U.S. and Japanese firms: Agency and stewardship perspectives. *Academy of Management Journal* 46 (2): 212–225.
Malhotra, Deepak, and J. Keith Murnighan. 2002. The effects of contracts on interpersonal trust. *Administrative Science Quarterly* 47 (3): 534–559.
Mizruchi, Mark S., and Linda Brewster Stearns. 1994. A longitudinal study of borrowing by large American corporations. *Administrative Science Quarterly* 39 (1): 118–140.

Morck, Randall, Andrei Shliefer, and Robert W. Vishny. 1988. Management ownership and market valuation: An empirical analysis. *Journal of Financial Economics* 20 (1): 239–258.
Neubaum, Donald O., and Shaker A. Zahra. 2006. Institutional ownership and corporate social performance: The moderating effects of investment horizon, activism, and coordination. *Journal of Management* 32 (1): 108–131
Pierce, Jon L., Tatiana Kostova, and Kurt T. Dirks. 2001. Toward a theory of psychological ownership in organizations. *Academy of Management Review* 26 (2): 298–310.
Pierce, Jon L., Stephen A. Rubenfeld, and Susan Morgan. 1991. Employee ownership: A conceptual model of process and effects. *Academy of Management Review* 16 (1): 121–144.
Rousseau, Denise M., and Zipi Shperling. 2003. Pieces of the action: Ownership and the changing employment relationship. *Academy of Management Review* 28 (4): 553–570.
Salancik, Gerald R., and Jeffrey Pfeffer. 1980. Effects of ownership and performance on executive tenure in U.S. corporations. *Academy of Management Journal* 23 (4): 653–664.
Sanders, William Gerard. 2001. Behavorial responses of CEOs to stock ownership and stock option pay. *Academy of Management Journal* 44 (3): 477–492.
Sarig, Oded, and Arthur Warga. 1989. Bond price data and bond market liquidity. *Journal of Financial and Quantitative Analysis* 24 (3): 367–378.
Schneper, William D., and Mauro F. Guillen. 2004. Stakeholder rights and corporate governance: A cross-national study of hostile takeovers. *Administrative Science Quarterly* 49 (2): 263–295.
Smith, Jr., Clifford, and Jerold B. Warner. 1979. On financial contracting: An analysis of bond covenants. *Journal of Financial Economics* 7 (2): 117–161.
Stein, Jeremy C. 1989. Efficient capital markets, inefficient firms: A model of myopic corporate behavior. *Quarterly Journal of Economics* 104 (4): 655–669.
Sundaramurthy, Chamu, and Marianne Lewis. 2003. Control and collaboration: Paradoxes of governance. *Academy of Management Review* 28 (3): 397–415.
Tosi, Henry L., Amy L. Brownlee, Paula Silva, and Jeffrey P. Katz. 2003. An empirical exploration of decision-making under agency controls and stewardship structure. *Journal of Management Studies* 40 (8): 2053–2071.
Williamson, Oliver E. 1991. Comparative economic organization: The analysis of discrete structural alternatives. *Administrative Science Quarterly* 36 (2). 269–296.
Wilpert, Bernhard. 1991. Property, ownership, and participation: On the growing contradictions between legal and psychological concepts. *International Handbook of Participation in Organizations* 149–164.

ABOUT THE AUTHORS

Ronald Anderson is a professor of finance and real estate at the Kogod School of Business at American University in Washington, D.C. He earned a BSE in engineering from the University of Pittsburgh, an MBA from the University of Pittsburgh, and his PhD in finance from Texas A&M University in 1997. Professor Anderson's teaching interests lie in the field of corporate finance with a particular emphasis on understanding the relation between managerial actions and firm value. He continues to follow an active research agenda with publications in the leading academic journals in business (*Journal of Finance, Journal of Financial Economics, Journal of Accounting and Economics, Journal of Law and Economics, Administrative Science Quarterly, Financial Management*, and *Journal of Financial and Quantitative Analysis*), with a special emphasis on family ownership of publicly traded companies.

Sattar Mansi is an associate professor of finance at Virginia Tech's Pamplin School of Business. He has over 20 years of research and private-sector experience. Professor Mansi is well published in the most influential journals in finance, accounting, law, international business, and marketing. His articles appear in such scholarly journals such as the *Journal of Finance, Journal of Financial Economics, Review of Financial Studies, Journal of Accounting and Economics, Journal of Accounting Research, Journal of Law and Economics, Journal of International Business Studies,* and *Journal of Marketing Research.*

David Reeb's research centers on corporate governance and disclosure policy. His research has been published in such leading academic business journals as the *Journal of Finance, Journal of Financial Economics, Journal of Accounting and Economics, Accounting Review, Journal of Law and Economics, Administrative Science Quarterly, Journal of International Business Studies,* and *Journal of Financial and Quantitative Analysis.* Professor Reeb's research has been featured in the *Wall Street Journal, BusinessWeek,* the *Economist, Forbes,* the *Financial Times,* the *International Herald Tribune, Inc.* magazine, *SmartMoney*, MSNBC, and several major newspapers and business magazines in the United States, Canada, and Australia.

CHAPTER 23

Governance of Banking Institutions

RENÉE BIRGIT ADAMS
Professor of Finance, University of Queensland

INTRODUCTION

Bank governance has been blamed to varying degrees for the recent financial crisis. For example, the Organisation for Economic Co-operation and Development (OECD) Steering Group on Corporate Governance argues that board failures in financial firms are a major cause of the financial crisis (Kirkpatrick 2009) and has launched an action plan to improve their governance. Similarly, the UK government has commissioned a former financial services regulator, Sir David Walker, to recommend measures to improve board-level governance at banks. In the United States, outrage over levels of executive pay at financial firms has led Congress to enact restrictions on pay for financial firms receiving funds from the government under the Troubled Asset Relief Program. These developments highlight the importance, both for research and policy making, to review the current state of bank governance.

This chapter focuses primarily on boards and executive compensation because these have been at the center of the recent reform debate, but it also discusses merger and acquisition (M&A) activity and ownership structure. These are of interest because they have implications for board-level governance. Because financial firms around the world have different activities and structures and face different regulatory constraints, providing an exhaustive discussion of bank governance across multiple countries is a complex task that is beyond the scope of this chapter. Consistent with the literature, the chapter concentrates primarily on publicly traded banks because better data are available for them. Furthermore, such banks represent the majority of the industry's assets. Adams (2009) estimates, for example, that the 93 public banks in her sample have assets comprising 49.8 percent of total U.S. commercial bank assets in 2007. However, the number of publicly traded banks is small. According to the Federal Deposit Insurance Corporation (FDIC), in 2007 there were 7,282 FDIC-insured commercial banks in the United States, while data from Osiris, a database of publicly quoted companies, indicates that there were 678 public banks in 2007, 205 of which were traded over-the-counter. DeYoung, Spong, and Sullivan (2001) and Cooper (2009) describe some governance features of closely held banks.

Bank boards have the same legal responsibilities as boards of nonfinancial firms: the duty of care and loyalty. As discussed later, there are almost no explicit regulatory constraints on boards of publicly traded banks. Additionally, almost no theoretical papers argue that bank governance should be fundamentally different from the governance of nonfinancial firms, except possibly to point out that regulation may substitute or complement other governance mechanisms. Thus, the empirical literature on bank governance generally focuses on the same measures of "good governance" as the literature on nonfinancial firms, such as the proportion of independent directors, board size, and sufficient pay-for-performance sensitivity (Mishra and Nielsen 2000). Several factors complicate understanding what constitutes an effective governance structure for a financial firm, such as regulation, the nature of banks' business, and organizational structure. As both Adams and Mehran (2003) and Adams (2009) document, board structures in bank holding companies (BHCs) differ substantially from board structures in nonfinancial firms. This finding suggests that these factors may affect traditional governance measures and their impact on organizational outcomes in systematic ways.

Regulation may affect governance because the objectives of regulators probably differ from those of shareholders. Because regulators care about financial stability, they pressure bank boards to act to ensure the safety and soundness of the financial institution through both direct and indirect restrictions. Consistent with the idea that regulators' and owners' interests may diverge, Laeven and Levine (2008) find that the impact of regulation on bank risk taking depends on a bank's ownership structure. Out of concern for investor protection, regulators have historically restricted the types of activities in which banks could engage as well as their locations. These restrictions affect bank governance by affecting competition and the market for corporate control.

The presence of a regulator raises the question of whether regulatory scrutiny complements or substitutes for board-level governance. In addition, the identity of a bank's regulator varies according to its charter type. This raises the question of whether regulators differ in the intensity with which they scrutinize the boards of the firms they examine. Some argue that regulators may engage in a race to the bottom to attract banks with lax restrictions (Rosen 2003; Whalen 2002). Thus, some regulators are possibly more lenient in evaluating bank board behavior than others. Heterogeneity in regulators suggests that governance may not be the same across all types of banks.

Changes in regulation also affect bank governance. By easing the task of engaging in merger and acquisition (M&A) activity, deregulation was a leading cause of consolidation in the banking industry in the 1990s. M&A activity affects board governance in several ways. First, acquiring firms commonly add target-firm directors to their boards, particularly in friendly acquisitions—the form of most bank acquisitions (Adams and Mehran 2008). Second, M&A activity may have disciplining effects even if the acquisition is friendly. Thus, the existence of an active market for corporate control may lead to general improvements in board effectiveness (James 1984; Schranz 1993). Yet bank managers may engage in mergers to protect their own interests, such as to obtain higher compensation (Bliss and Rosen 2001) or because of their too-big-to-fail status (Penas and Unal 2004). In the 1990s, regulators increasingly allowed banks to engage in investment banking activities. In 1999, the passage of the Gramm-Leach-Bliley Act formally abolished all restrictions on such activities. This may have influenced bank boards by changing both the nature of the competitive environment and the expertise required for directors.

The activities in which banks engage also influence board governance in several ways. According to the Federal Reserve Bank of Atlanta (2002, 47) bank directors often represent some of the best customers of the bank. Such directors are by definition not independent. Whether their presence reduces the monitoring capability of the board, as often argued for nonfinancial firms, is unclear. Because banks operate trust departments, they have the ability to own and vote their own shares, unlike nonfinancial firms. This clearly has important implications for managerial power and may also affect board composition. For example, Adams and Santos (2006) find that trust officers often sit on the boards of their sample banks.

Finally, organizational structure has important governance implications for banks. Banks are either stand-alone or organized as bank or financial holding companies. In the holding company, each subsidiary bank or BHC is separately chartered with its own board. This differs from most nonfinancial firms that are organized along functional or divisional lines and whose subsidiaries often do not have separate legal identities. The implication of this structure for BHCs appears to be that activities of subsidiaries are influenced through their boards. For example, directors of the parent BHC will often sit on the boards of subsidiaries. This has consequences for several aspects of board governance including composition and pay. It also suggests that the number of links between BHCs and their customers can be large if a BHC has many subsidiaries with boards. When considering the governance of publicly traded banks in particular, BHC structure offers another channel through which regulation may affect governance. Virtually all publicly traded banks are organized as BHCs, which are regulated by the Federal Reserve. This implies the likelihood of little variation in the role of regulation within a sample of BHCs. Still, regulation affects the subsidiaries in the holding company, which may in turn have implications for the governance of the BHC.

This chapter has the following organization. It begins with a discussion of legal and regulatory influences on governance. The chapter then provides a discussion of bank boards before reviewing ownership structure and executive compensation. For ease of exposition, the term *bank holding company* is used both for BHCs and financial holding companies, which are BHCs that received permission to engage in nontraditional financial activities. Finally, the chapter provides a summary and conclusion.

LEGAL AND REGULATORY INFLUENCES ON GOVERNANCE

Characterizing how regulation and the law affect bank governance is difficult because of limited literature on this topic. Regulators may exert pressure on bank governance that is hard to measure. Also unclear is the extent to which existing regulations are enforced. Nevertheless, several features of the institutional environment are likely to influence bank governance through requirements or expectations on their boards, by affecting the market for corporate control and competition and by influencing banks' organizational structure.

Bank Board Regulations

Since the National Bank Act of 1864, the United States has been characterized by a dual federal and state banking system. Banks in the federal system have a federal charter and are overseen by a federal supervisor, the Office of the Comptroller of the Currency (OCC), as well as members of the Federal Reserve System. Banks in the state system are state chartered and operate subject to state law and state supervision. State banks that elect to become members of the Federal Reserve System are subject to Federal Reserve regulations. The Federal Reserve also supervises the BHCs and financial holding companies but subsidiary banks are supervised according to their charters. All banks with FDIC-insured deposits are subject to FDIC regulations. Because banks can choose to have a national or state charter and whether to be a member of the Federal Reserve, they effectively choose their regulatory authority. Thus, the banking industry consists of four (or five, counting financial holding companies separately) different types of banks: national, state, state member, and bank holding companies. Each of these is subject to its own set of regulations, which are in addition to restrictions imposed by the Sarbanes-Oxley Act (SOX) and exchange listing standards for publicly traded banks. Because these regulations affect board structure and enforcement may differ across regulators, governance may vary across institutions by type.

BHC boards are probably the least regulated. If a BHC is troubled, it must submit written notice to the Federal Reserve Board 30 days before adding or replacing members of its board. Otherwise the only formal restriction is that a director of a BHC may not be a director of another BHC in the same city, town, or relevant metropolitan statistical area (RMSA). A director of a BHC with more than $2.5 billion in total assets may not be the director of another BHC with over $1.5 billion total assets (Federal Reserve Regulation L).

State member banks are subject to these same two restrictions except that Regulation L refers to directorships in state member banks. In addition, both state member and nonmember banks are subject to state banking law in the state in which they are chartered. Among others, these laws may impose state residency or U.S. citizenship requirements, require directors to own stock in the bank, and impose restrictions on the operation or structure of the board. For example, New York State Banking Law requires that bank boards consist of between 5 and 15 members, half of whom must be U.S. citizens. In addition, bank boards must hold regular monthly meetings at least 10 times a year. Alabama Banking Law requires that bank directors hold stock in the bank or parent holding company and that bank boards hold bimonthly meetings.

National banks are governed by the National Banking Act in Title 12 of the U.S. Code. Title 12 specifies that national banks must have between 5 and 25 directors who must be U.S. citizens and a majority of whom must reside in the state, territory, or district of the bank or within 100 miles of it for at least a year before and during their term. Directors must take an oath upon election or appointment, must hold stock in the bank or parent holding company, and may not serve longer than three years. The president of the bank is a member of the board and the chair, unless the board appoints another director as chair. The OCC has jurisdiction over governance issues and may grant waivers to these laws.

In addition to these formal requirements, regulators provide guidance to bank boards in the form of Supervision and Regulation (SR) letters and examination manuals. Regulators expect bank boards to help ensure the safety and soundness of the bank. Adams and Mehran (2003) provide some examples of additional expectations that regulators impose on bank boards for this purpose, including the adoption of real estate appraisal and evaluation policies (the *Federal Reserve Board Commercial Bank Examination Manual*), the annual approval of bank risk management policies (the *Federal Reserve Board Trading Activities Manual*), and the approval of short-term business plans (the *OCC's Director's Book*).

These regulations and expectations may not always be enforced in practice. For example, even though Federal Reserve Banks in theory penalize directors for poor attendance, Adams and Ferreira (2008) find that the attendance behavior of BHC directors is worse than in nonfinancial firms. One reason may be competition among regulators. In New York, for example, the Banking Board allows for exceptions to the mandated minimum number of 10 board meetings because it recognizes that this places state banks at a competitive disadvantage vis-à-vis national banks in finding qualified individuals to serve as directors (see http://www.banking.state.ny.us/legal/66amd.htm). Nevertheless, bank boards may still have strong incentives to fulfill regulatory expectations because bank directors are subject to greater liability risk than are directors of nonfinancial institutions (Macey and O'Hara 2003). Bank regulators can impose higher civil money penalties on bank directors than can the Securities and Exchange Commission (SEC), and director and officer (D&O) liability insurance for bank directors regularly includes exemptions denying coverage for violations of banking law (Subrahmanyam, Rangan, and Rosenstein 1997).

Several features of bank board regulation help explain why bank directors may appear to have limited expertise, as argued for example by the OECD (Kirkpatrick 2009). The Clayton Act prohibits directors of both financial and nonfinancial firms from sitting on the boards of competitors. But the restriction on interlocks in Federal Reserve Regulation L is more stringent. As Subrahmanyam et al. (1997) and Guerrera and Larsen (2008) point out, banks often have a difficult time identifying good candidates for directors because they cannot recruit anyone who is affiliated with other banks or investment banks. Furthermore, some candidates with banking experience prefer not to join a bank board because this limits their ability to work with other banks. The restriction on residences of national bank directors may make the task of finding good directors even more difficult. As discussed later, many directors of BHCs sit on subsidiary boards. When the subsidiary is a national bank, they are subject to the restrictions on national bank directors. Thus, restrictions on the pool of candidates at the bank level may also increase the difficulty for BHC boards to identify the number and type of directors they prefer. For public banks, these problems may be further exacerbated by the independence requirements in SOX.

Market for Corporate Control and Competition

Until 1994, regulations prohibiting interstate banking restricted the market for corporate control and competition. Until 1999, legal restrictions prohibited banks from engaging in investment banking activities. Although these restrictions may no longer seem relevant, they provide important insights into understanding bank governance before the twenty-first century. Also, these restrictions may still affect bank governance today. For example, the literature on the effects of bank mergers has produced inconsistent and sometimes puzzling results. In particular, little evidence indicates that the market expects bank mergers to create value. Delong and DeYoung (2007) put forth that because mergers are still a relatively new phenomenon, bank managers may lack expertise in carrying them out and the market may have difficulties valuing them. This is consistent with Subrahmanyam et al.'s (1997) observation that because national banks are prohibited from having investment bankers on their boards, they are restricted in their access to M&A expertise. Following the financial crisis, the banking industry is likely facing a period of more intense regulation. Thus, understanding the evolution of regulation of the industry is important.

The dual banking system is one source of regulatory restrictions on the market for corporate control and competition. Before the establishment of national banks, all banks were state chartered, and until 1975 no state allowed interstate banking (Savage 1993). The MacFadden Act of 1927 sought to give national banks competitive equality with state-chartered banks by letting national banks branch to the extent permitted by state law, but at the same time it prohibited interstate branching. Until the mid-1950s, BHCs could own subsidiaries in more than one state but the passage of the Bank Holding Company Act in 1956 rendered this nearly impossible. Although states began eliminating restrictions on interstate banking starting in 1975, it was not fully deregulated until the passage of the Riegle-Neal Interstate Banking and Branching Efficiency Act of 1994. Thus, for much of the twentieth century the market for corporate control in banking was restricted.

Before 1975, there were two primary ways of obtaining control over a commercial bank: through the acquisition of a controlling interest in the bank or through a merger. The BHC Act of 1956 limited the acquisition of control in commercial banks to BHCs. This Act applied nationwide but the regulations on the number of banks each BHC could control varied across states. Differences in state laws on branching also affected the likelihood that a bank became the target of a merger. A bank located in a state with statewide or restricted branching was arguably more likely to be acquired than a bank located in a unit banking state because it could be operated as a branch afterwards. By allowing full nationwide banking, regardless of state law (except for state restrictions on branching), the Riegle-Neal Act (along with prior state-level interstate banking laws) was a major cause of consolidation in the banking industry. Jones and Critchfield (2005) show, for example, that the number of banks dropped from 14,884 in 1984 to 7,842 in 2003.

Another source of restrictions on the market for corporate control was regulators' desire to avoid investor abuse. As Kroszner and Rajan (1994) describe, banks became increasingly involved in the securities underwriting business after World War I. This led to widespread concern that banks could exploit their informational advantage from preexisting lending relationships with underwritten firms and harm outside investors. The Glass-Steagall Act of 1933 was enacted to prohibit commercial banks from engaging in investment banking activities. The BHC Act of 1956 further restricted bank activities by prohibiting them from engaging in the insurance business. But following increased pressure by commercial banks, the Gramm-Leach-Bliley Act (GLB) lifted these prohibitions in 1999. The passage of GLB had a substantial influence on merger activity in the financial services industry (Yildirim, Kwag, and Collins 2006). Yet, unlike the Riegle-Neal Act, the GLB did not have a major effect on the number of banking institutions. GLB allows banks to engage in cross-industry mergers with investment banks and insurance companies, which does not lead to the elimination of bank charters. Nevertheless, GLB increases the amount of competition banks face in nonbanking industries, which could have governance effects.

Organizational Structure

Banking distinguishes itself from other nonfinancial industries in the United States because almost all large and many small banks are organized as holding companies. This organizational structure evolved in large part as a response to regulation but was also influenced by the nature of banks' business. Originally, holding companies were one way of circumventing restrictions on interstate banking. Although the 1956 BHC Act was designed to limit BHCs' ability to expand (to prevent the creation of monopoly power), it applied only to BHCs controlling more than one bank. Thus, many large banks chose to form one-bank holding companies during the 1960s. Chase and Mingo (1975) describe that by 1973, BHCs accounted for 65.5 percent of all commercial bank assets.

Although one-bank holding companies were still subject to restrictions on interstate banking, they enabled banks to circumvent other aspects of regulation. For example, because a one-bank holding company was not technically a bank, it could engage in nonbank activities. Chase and Mingo (1975) describe that by 1974, one-bank holding companies could engage in 14 permissible nonbank activities including leasing, data processing, and management consulting. Moreover, these activities were not subject to geographical restrictions. Bankers at the time argued that the ability to engage in nonbank financial activities without geographical restrictions represented an important avenue both for growth and diversification of banks (Bunting 1969). BHCs also had greater flexibility in liability management because they were less restricted in their issuance of debt securities than were banks. Moreover, they had greater flexibility in the design of stock option plans, which Bunting argued was helpful in attracting better managers than at commercial banks.

Although the Riegle-Neal Act and GLB removed many of the regulatory obstacles that drove banks to adopt the BHC form, few statistics indicate that the BHC form has become less popular. Moreover, most large banks today are still organized as BHCs. Few studies examine reasons for the persistence of this organizational form. A study by Kroszner and Rajan (1997), however, suggests that regulation alone is not the only factor influencing banks' choice of organizational form. They document that before the Glass-Steagall Act, banks that organized their securities underwriting business in separate affiliates with their own boards of directors, as opposed to internal departments, obtained higher prices for their issues. Moreover, these prices increased with the independence of the affiliates' boards. Kroszner and Rajan argue that banks with separate securities affiliates were better able to dispel the impression that they would exploit their informational advantage to the detriment of customers. Thus, even before banks were so heavily regulated, they naturally gravitated toward an organizational form that resembles a BHC.

From a governance perspective, the BHC organizational form is important for two main reasons. First, BHC subsidiaries are separately chartered. As Kroszner and Rajan (1997) suggest, this means that activities of subsidiaries are not as completely controlled by the parent as internal divisions might be. The issue of how activities among subsidiaries are coordinated in a BHC is important. As Adams and Mehran (2008) argue, the boards of subsidiaries are likely to play an important role in this respect. Second, BHCs have the same type of organizational structure as business groups in other countries (Khanna and Yafeh 2007). Thus, understanding the governance of BHCs may also be useful for understanding nonfinancial business groups.

BANK BOARDS

This section provides a brief comparison of BHC boards to boards of nonfinancial institutions. It then argues that some of the regulatory and institutional features of banking described thus far affect board governance. The section then turns to a brief discussion of the impact of bank board governance on outcomes. Data from Adams and Mehran (2003 and 2008) (henceforth Adams-Mehran data) are used to illustrate some of the arguments and discussions. The data consist of detailed board information for a random sample of 35 large publicly traded BHCs from 1986 to 2000. The data are extended using additional information from proxy statements.

Bank Board Basics

Although virtually no legal and regulatory restrictions exist on BHC board composition, in practice they look different than the boards of other types of corporations. Although many papers note the differences, such as Kroszner and Strahan (2001), they are documented most systematically in Adams and Mehran (2003) and Adams (2009). Adams and Mehran compare their BHC data to data on manufacturing firms. They document that BHCs have significantly larger boards, more independent directors, and more committees than nonfinancial firms. Using the Riskmetrics director database from 1996 to 2007, Adams shows that, controlling for the natural logarithm of assets as a proxy for firm size, bank boards are significantly larger, are less independent, and have lower average numbers of outside directorships per director, and lower director compensation than nonfinancial firms. The latter finding is consistent with Becher, Campbell, and Frye (2005) who document that bank directors received significantly less total and equity-based compensation relative to nonfinancial firms from 1992 to 1999. Although they argue that deregulation was narrowing the difference, Adams finds that bank directors still receive significantly lower total compensation in 2007. Although banks boards seem relatively large, Adams and Mehran (2008) show, using a 40-year data period, that bank boards were historically much larger and that their size has trended downward over time relative to manufacturing firms.

Bank Board Influences

This section provides a brief discussion of several internal and external factors affecting the structure and operation of bank boards. Important internal factors are bank activities and organizational structure. An important external factor is regulation.

The Nature of Banks' Business

Although bank activities have a potentially important impact on board governance, obtaining data on their influence is difficult. Thus, this section focuses on lending relationships and trust operations.

Bank directors often represent some of the best customers of the bank. The appointment of such customer-directors may explain why bank boards were much larger in the past. They may still be as important today, although they may be primarily represented on subsidiary boards rather than on parent holding company boards.

Determining which directors are customer-directors is difficult. Although publicly traded BHCs are supposed to disclose related-party transactions, they generally do not disclose details of lending relationships with directors' employers, except to state that they are not made on preferential terms.

Customer-directors are likely to have different incentives and motivations than other outside directors. To correctly measure board independence requires identifying them, but this is virtually impossible. Moreover, such lending relationships may be large enough to affect independence. For example, First Union Corporation's proxy for 2000 (p. 36) states that "the aggregate monthly outstanding principal balances of loans made by our bank to such directors and officers, including certain of their related interests, ranged from a high of approximately $3.6 billion to a low of approximately $2.9 billion." This means that measures of board independence in banking are potentially overstated, which could lead to biased inference in regression analysis. However, whether the presence of customer-directors reduces the monitoring capability of the board is unclear. Similar arguments have been made in the related lending literature (Halling and Stomper 2009). Thus, measured board independence may not be the most appropriate proxy for the monitoring intensity of bank boards.

The Influence of Organizational Structure and Regulation

Given that banking law and regulation impose virtually no explicit restrictions on BHC boards, whether regulation should affect BHC board structure is not obvious. Thus, this section documents that organizational structure influences board structure. Organizational structure provides a channel through which regulation affects BHC boards. For example, regulatory restrictions on boards of subsidiary national and state banks may influence the BHC board because directors from the subsidiary boards may also sit on the parent BHC board.

Adams and Mehran (2008) document the relationship between BHC organizational structure and board structure. They argue that organizational structure matters for governance because activities can be coordinated through boards of subsidiaries and the parent BHC board. The parent BHC board can also delegate duties to boards of subsidiaries, which is more likely the more important the subsidiary. Consistent with these ideas, they show that bank boards became smaller when banks adopted the holding company form. Moreover, both the number of subsidiaries and the relative size of the lead bank (the largest bank in the first tier of the holding company) are negatively correlated with parent BHC board size.

This section provides complementary evidence that organizational structure matters by presenting some data on the extent to which BHC directors sit on the board of what can be considered a lead bank or important subsidiary of the

BHC. The case of Chase Manhattan Corporation (CMC) permits obtaining detailed information on directors of CMC sitting on the board of the lead bank, the Chase Manhattan Bank, and vice versa from 1969 to 1996. These data illustrate that subsidiary directorships can be common. Data from 1969 to 1985 and earlier are from Wilson (1986); all other data on lead bank directorships, except for missing data in year 1986, are from Moody's Bank and Finance Manuals for 1987–1996 and proxy statements.

In 1955, the Bank of Manhattan (BM) merged with the Chase National Bank (CNB) to form the Chase Manhattan Bank (CMB). The Chase Manhattan Bank became a national banking association in 1965, and a wholly owned subsidiary of the Chase Manhattan Corporation, a one-bank holding company, during reorganization in 1969.

In 1955, directors from both BM and CNB sat on the newly formed CMB board. Directors from BM sat on CMB's board for 13 years, making up 21.8 percent of its board on average, ranging from a high of 37.0 percent to a low of 7.4 percent. Directors from CNB sat on CMB's board for 16 years, making up 21.1 percent of its board, ranging from a high of 55.6 percent to a low of 3.5 percent. Upon formation of the holding company in 1969, CMC's board consisted of 21 of the 28 directors on the board of CMB. CMC continued to share directors with CMB until the acquisition of CMC in 1996. During this time period, the average size of CMC's (CMB's) board was 23.9 (24.3) directors. On average, 90.0 percent of the BHC directors sat on the board of the bank and 92.6 percent of the bank's directors sat on the board of the BHC. From 1977 until 1992, all of the bank's directors sat on the board of the BHC, but not vice versa.

This particular example suggests that the practice of bank directors sitting on BHC boards may have originated because historically banks often predated the holding company. The practice still persists. Although obtaining data on the extent to which bank directors sit on their parent holding company boards is difficult, saying something about the extent to which BHC directors sit on their lead bank boards using data from proxy statements is possible. The data in the Adams-Mehran sample were obtained for 7,796 director firm-year observations. Of these, 3,944 observations or 49.3 percent of BHC directors are classified as also sitting on important subsidiary boards. Of inside directors, 49.3 percent sit on lead bank boards. Of nonexecutive directors, 50.7 percent sit on lead bank boards. On average, 51.1 percent of a BHC's board overlaps with its lead bank board. These numbers represent a lower bound for subsidiary memberships because whether they are always disclosed is unclear; for example, in only 17.2 percent of firm-years are no lead bank directorships disclosed for First Union Corporation. In 28.7 percent of firm-years, the entire BHC board also sits on the board of the bank. This is the case, for example, for Bank of Hawaii Corporation and J.P. Morgan.

The results in Adams and Mehran (2008) suggest that organizational structure affects the extent to which these board overlaps occur. More research needs to be done to analyze such overlaps. What is clear at this point is that they are frequent. They may also affect BHC board characteristics. For example, in 58.1 percent of firm-year observations, BHC proxy statements indicate that directors are paid to attend meetings of subsidiary boards. This means that measuring the total compensation a director receives from a BHC if he also sits on the board of a subsidiary may be difficult.

Perhaps most importantly, board overlaps can serve as a channel through which regulation can affect board functioning. Generally, directly measuring the influence of regulators is hard. Determining the extent to which regulations are enforced is also difficult. For example, Title 12 of the U.S. Code states that national banks are required to have a board of between 5 and 25 directors. Furthermore, the Code was only amended to allow the OCC to make exceptions to this rule in 2000. Yet the example of Chase Manhattan Bank illustrates that the OCC may not have been strictly enforcing this particular aspect of Title 12 for many years prior. Although Chase Manhattan Bank was always a national bank, its board exceeded the 25-director limit for 20 out of the 41 years from 1955 to 1995.

Bank director expertise is an important policy concern. Hau and Thum (2009) provide some evidence that expertise matters. They find that financial expertise of bank directors in Germany is negatively related to losses incurred by German banks in the recent financial crisis. One aspect of regulation may play an important role in restricting the pool of potential directors from which a BHC may choose. The requirement for national banks is that a majority of bank directors must reside in the state, territory, or district of the bank or within 100 miles. State laws may also impose similar restrictions for state banks. If most of the lead bank directors must be local to fulfill this aspect of regulation and if the board of the bank overlaps with the BHC board, then the BHC will also be constrained in its choice of directors.

To examine whether such geographic restrictions on banks affect BHC boards, the geographic distance between nonexecutive directors' employers and the BHC is analyzed. Data are collected on director employers for the Adams-Mehran sample from proxy statements. For 5,484 nonexecutive directors, the location of directors' employers is determined from proxy statements (52.8 percent of the sample) and the remainder are identified using other sources including the Internet, ExecuComp, and Lexis-Nexis. Based on a U.S. Geological Service Web-based tool, the distance is calculated between the BHC location and directors' employers' locations.

Many nonexecutive directors work in the same city as the BHC (36.8 percent) and a majority work within 101 miles of the BHC (61.2 percent). Because regulatory restrictions on geography are at the bank level, the expectation is that BHC directors are more likely to sit on the lead bank board if their workplace is closer. Column 1 of Exhibit 23.1 provides a simple firm fixed effect regression of a dummy variable indicating whether a nonexecutive BHC director sits on the bank board as a function of employer distance. The result indicates that directors whose workplaces are closer to the BHC are more likely to sit on the bank board. Column 2 shows a regression of the average nonexecutive employer distance at the BHC level on the average fraction of nonexecutive BHC directors who sit on the bank board. The results suggest that as the overlap between BHC board and bank board increases, the average employer distance on the BHC board decreases. These results illustrate that organizational structure can be a channel through which regulation affects BHC boards.

The Influence of M&A Activity on BHC Boards

Acquirers of any type may add directors of targets to their boards following a merger or acquisition. Once the market for corporate control in banking became deregulated, banks also adopted this practice. Exhibit 23.2 shows the average

Exhibit 23.1 Firm Fixed Effect Regressions Illustrating the Relation between Organizational Form and Director Employer Distance

Column 1 of this table contains a firm fixed effect regression of the dummy variable "BHC Director Sits on Lead Bank Board," which is equal to 1 if a nonexecutive director sits on the board of the BHC's lead bank and 0 otherwise, on the distance of the director's employer to BHC headquarters. Column 2 contains a firm fixed effect regression of the average distance of nonexecutive BHC directors' employers to BHC headquarters on the average fraction of nonexecutive BHC directors who sit on the lead bank board. The latter is a measure of the extent to which the lead bank board overlaps with the BHC board. The data set is an extended version of the data in Adams and Mehran (2003 and 2008) and consists of data on 35 BHCs from 1986 to 2000. The data in column 1 are at the director-firm-year level. The data in column 2 are at the firm-year level.

	BHC Director Sits on Lead Bank Board	Average Employer Distance
Employer distance	−2.580e-5** (3.51)	
Average fraction of BHC directors on lead bank board		−74.491* (1.74)
Constant	0.460** (111.69)	295.986** (13.52)
Observations	5,104	429

** indicates statistical significance at the 0.01 percent level, * indicates significance at the 0.10 level.

fraction of directors added after a merger (merger-directors) on BHC boards for the Adams-Mehran sample from 1986 to 2000. The fraction is only 6 percent in 1986 but, reflecting increasing consolidation in the industry, it increases to 20 percent in 2000.

One possible reason merger-directors may be more important in banking than in nonfinancial companies is because of organizational structure. When banks are acquired, they may remain as subsidiaries with their own boards. To facilitate coordination, directors from the subsidiary may be appointed to the BHC board. To examine whether this explanation is plausible, data are collected for 2,113 director-firm years on subsidiary board memberships other than lead-bank board memberships. The analysis indicates that 43.4 percent of merger-directors sit on subsidiary boards. Perhaps not surprisingly, most inside merger-directors (59.0 percent) sit on subsidiary boards. But the percentage of nonexecutive merger-directors sitting on subsidiary boards is also high (33.8 percent). Furthermore, the likelihood of sitting on the board of a subsidiary other than the lead bank is significantly (at greater than the 0.01 level) higher for merger-directors of any type. This suggests that M&A activity has a significant influence on BHC board composition and that one channel through which it operates is organizational structure.

Outcomes

Following the financial crisis, a temptation arises to look to performance regressions to identify those aspects of bank board structure that appear to be suboptimal and would benefit the most from reform. Although numerous studies relate bank governance to acquisition outcomes (see the comprehensive summary in Jones and Critchfield [2005]), relatively few studies relate BHC board structure to

Exhibit 23.2 Average Fraction of Board Added Following Mergers

This table shows the average fraction of both inside and nonexecutive directors who were added to the board after a merger or acquisition across all BHCs for each year from 1986 to 2000. The data are an extended version of the data in Adams and Mehran (2003 and 2008), which involve 35 BHCs from 1986 to 2000.

Year	Fraction of Board Added after a Merger
1986	0.06
1987	0.07
1988	0.10
1989	0.11
1990	0.11
1991	0.11
1992	0.14
1993	0.15
1994	0.15
1995	0.16
1996	0.18
1997	0.17
1998	0.18
1999	0.19
2000	0.20

nonacquisition outcomes, such as performance. Pi and Timme (1992), Mishra and Nielsen (2000), Sierra, Talmor, and Wallace (2006), and Adams and Mehran (2008) examine board structure and performance. Pathan (2009) examines board structure and risk. According to these studies, board features that may have a negative effect on outcomes for nonfinancial firms need not have the same effect for financial firms. For example, Adams and Mehran do not find that the larger board size in banks has a negative effect on performance, as documented for nonfinancial firms. Outcome regressions may be particularly problematic for banks because of regulatory and institutional features earlier identified in this chapter. Because these may also affect performance, if they are not properly accounted for, performance regressions will be biased. For example, Adams and Mehran argue that organizational structure affects both board structure and performance and, in addition, show that accounting for organizational structure in performance regressions affects the coefficient estimates on board structure variables.

BANK OWNERSHIP

In many countries outside the United States, families and states own banks (Caprio, Laeven, and Levine 2007; Laeven and Levine 2008). The data in Caprio et al. indicate that 90 percent of large U.S. BHCs are widely held. Thus, large blockholders are unlikely to be important governance mechanisms for U.S. banks. Instead, institutional and managerial ownership may be more important. Adams and Mehran (2003) find that institutional ownership in banks is significantly lower than in nonfinancial firms. Furthermore, bank CEOs have lower ownership than CEOs of nonfinancial firms. Nevertheless, several papers find that managerial ownership affects bank performance, risk taking, and M&A activity (Gorton and Rosen 1995; Hadlock, Houston, and Ryngaert 1999).

An infrequently studied feature of bank ownership structure may have a substantial effect on both the measurement of managerial control and its impact. Because banks operate trust departments, they have the ability to own and vote their own shares, unlike nonfinancial firms. Adams and Santos (2006) document, in a sample of banks from 1966, that control accumulated through this mechanism can have a significant impact on bank performance. For more recent data, determining how much control banks accumulate through their trust departments is difficult. Some data indicating that it may be significant can be found in a UBS Warburg (2001) study documenting the top three institutional ownership stakes for BHCs in the UBS Bank Index in 2001. By matching on names, the study indicates that 22 out of 48 BHCs in the UBS Warburg bank index are among the top three institutional holders of their own shares, with 13 BHCs having the largest owners and three BHCs having the second largest owners. Furthermore, the stakes BHCs hold in themselves through subsidiaries may be large relative to the stakes of other institutions. For example, with a stake of 12.9 percent, Synovus Financial Corporation was the largest institutional owner of its own shares. FMR Corporation held the second largest stake of only 3.8 percent.

EXECUTIVE COMPENSATION

Although critics put much blame for the financial crisis on incentive structures in banks, several studies document that historically CEO total pay (Houston and James 1995), CEO equity pay (Adams and Mehran 2003), and CEO pay-performance sensitivities (Fields and Fraser 1999; John and Qian 2003) are lower in banking than in other industries. Although deregulation may have narrowed the gap, Adams (2009) finds that even in 2007, the fraction of equity-based pay and size-adjusted total CEO pay are lower in banks. The difficulty of measuring CEO total pay in banking may be complicated if CEOs receive separate compensation for service on subsidiary boards. For 56.9 percent of 1,752 insider firm years in the Adams-Mehran sample, insiders of the BHC also hold a title in the lead bank. Insiders may also hold positions in other subsidiaries. More research needs to be done to determine the optimality of executive compensation contracts in banking.

SUMMARY AND CONCLUSION

Bank governance differs from the governance of nonfinancial firms in several aspects. The structures of boards of banks and nonfinancial firms vary. CEO compensation and ownership structures also differ. This chapter depicts some of these differences and argues that many may be due to regulation and the law. For example, the chapter provides evidence that is consistent with the idea that regulations and laws concerning director residences at the bank level influence the choice of

BHC directors at the BHC level. Pay is often lower in regulated industries, which may explain why CEO pay is lower in banking. Other features of bank governance are influenced by the ways in which banks conduct their business, in particular their choices of activities (e.g., trust activities) and their organizational form. Because many of the factors shaping bank governance are thus specific to banking, simply applying governance standards developed from studying nonfinancial firms to banks without further research would be a mistake. In particular, bank boards seem to have a unique role in linking subsidiaries to parents. Thus, different factors may improve bank boards than those that improve boards of nonfinancial firms.

This is bad news for policy makers, because it means that implementing good bank governance reform in the near future may be difficult. But it is good news for researchers because many important topics remain to be studied. One reason relatively little is known about bank governance is because of the difficulty of collecting data on boards. Perhaps a worthwhile policy goal in the near future would be to ask banks to provide a reasonable amount of governance data as part of their regulatory data provision.

DISCUSSION QUESTIONS

1. In what ways do bank boards differ from boards of nonfinancial firms?
2. What are some of the key institutional features influencing bank board governance?
3. Why might determining the effect of bank board structure on bank performance be difficult?
4. Does regulation substitute or complement corporate governance? Explain.

REFERENCES

Adams, Renée B. 2009. Governance and the financial crisis. Finance working paper 248/2009, ECGI.

Adams, Renée B., and Daniel Ferreira. 2008. Does regulatory pressure provide sufficient incentives for bank directors? Evidence from directors' attendance records. Working paper, University of Queensland.

Adams, Renée B., and Hamid Mehran. 2003. Is corporate governance different for bank holding companies? *Economic Policy Review* 9 (1): 123–142.

———. 2008. Corporate performance, board structure and its determinants in the banking industry. Federal Reserve Bank of New York Staff Report No. 330.

Adams, Renée B., and Joao A.C. Santos, 2006. Identifying the effect of managerial control on firm performance. *Journal of Accounting and Economics* 41 (1): 55–85.

Becher, David A., Terry L. Campbell, and Melissa B. Frye. 2005. Incentive compensation for bank directors: The impact of deregulation. *Journal of Business* 78 (5): 1753–1777.

Bliss, Richard T., and Richard J. Rosen. 2001. CEO compensation and bank mergers. *Journal of Financial Economics* 61 (1): 107–138.

Bunting, Jr., John. 1969. One-bank holding companies: A banker's view. *Harvard Business Review* 47 (3): 98–106.

Caprio, Gerard, Luc Laeven, and Ross Levine. 2007. Governance and bank valuation. *Journal of Financial Intermediation* 16 (4): 584–617.

Chase, Jr., Samuel B., and John J. Mingo. 1975. The regulation of bank holding companies. *Journal of Finance* 30 (2): 281–292.

Cooper, Elizabeth Webb. 2009. Monitoring and governance of private banks. *Quarterly Review of Economics and Finance* 49 (2): 253–264.
Delong, Gayle, and Robert DeYoung. 2007. Learning by observing: Information spillovers in the execution and valuation of commercial bank M&As. *Journal of Finance* 62 (1): 181–216.
DeYoung, Robert, Kenneth Spong, and Richard J. Sullivan. 2001. Who's minding the store? Motivating and monitoring hired managers at small, closely held banks. *Journal of Banking and Finance* 25 (7): 1201–1243.
Federal Reserve Bank of Atlanta. 2002. *The director's primer*. Atlanta: Federal Reserve Bank of Atlanta.
Fields, Laura P., and Donald R. Fraser. 1999. On the compensation implications of commercial bank entry into investment banking. *Journal of Banking and Finance* 23 (8): 1261–1276.
First Union Corporation. 2000. "Form DEF14A–Definitive proxy statement."
Gorton, Gary, and Richard Rosen. 1995. Corporate control, portfolio choice, and the decline of banking. *Journal of Finance* 50 (5): 1377–1420.
Guerrera, Francesco, and Peter Thal Larsen. 2008. Gone by the board? Why bank directors did not spot credit risks. *Financial Times*, June 25. http://www.ft.com/cms/s/0/6e66fe18-42e8-11dd-81d0-0000779fd2ac.html.
Hadlock, Charles, Joel Houston, and Michael Ryngaert. 1999. The role of managerial incentives in bank acquisitions. *Journal of Banking and Finance* 23 (2–4): 221–249.
Halling, Michael, and Alex Stomper. 2009. Related lending: Boards matter. http://ssrn.com/abstract=1343822.
Hau, Harald, and Marcel Thum. 2009. Subprime crisis and board (in-)competence: Private vs. public banks in Germany. http://ssrn.com/abstract=1360698.
Houston Joel, and Christopher James. 1995. CEO compensation and bank risk: Is compensation in banking structured to promote risk taking? *Journal of Monetary Economics* 36 (2): 405–431.
James, Christopher. 1984. An analysis of the effect of state acquisition laws on managerial efficiency: The case of the bank holding company acquisitions. *Journal of Law and Economics* 27 (1): 211–226.
John, Kose, and Yiming Qian. 2003. Incentive features in CEO compensation in the banking industry. *Economic Policy Review* 9 (1): 109–121.
Jones, Kenneth D., and Tim Critchfield. 2005. Consolidation in the U.S. banking industry: Is the "long, strange trip" about to end? *FDIC Banking Review* 17 (4): 31–61.
Khanna, Tarun, and Yishay Yafeh. 2007. Business groups in emerging markets: Paragons or parasites? *Journal of Economic Literature* 45 (2): 331–372.
Kirkpatrick, Grant. 2009. The corporate governance lessons from the financial crisis. *Financial Markets Trends* 96 (1): 52–81.
Kroszner, Randall S., and Raghuram G. Rajan. 1994. Is the Glass-Steagall Act justified? A study of the U.S. experience with universal banking before 1933. *American Economic Review* 84 (4): 810–832.
———. 1997. Organization structure and credibility: Evidence from commercial bank securities activities before the Glass-Steagall Act. *Journal of Monetary Economics* 39 (3): 475–516.
Kroszner, Randall, and Philip E. Strahan. 2001. Throwing good money after bad? Board connections and conflicts in bank lending. NBER Working Paper Series No. 8694.
Laeven, Luc, and Ross Levine. 2008. Bank governance, regulation, and risk taking. NBER Working Paper No. 14113.
Macey, Jonathan, and Maureen O'Hara. 2003. The corporate governance of banks. *Economic Policy Review* 9 (1): 91–107.
Mishra, Chandra S., and James F. Nielsen. 2000. Board independence and compensation policies in large bank holding companies. *Financial Management* 29 (3): 51–69.
Pathan, Shams. 2009. Strong boards, CEO power and bank risk-taking. *Journal of Banking & Finance* 33 (7): 1340–1350.

Penas, María Fabianam, and Haluk Unal. 2004. Gains in bank mergers: Evidence from the bond markets. *Journal of Financial Economics* 74 (1): 149–79.
Pi, Lynn, and Stephen G. Timme. 1992. Corporate control and bank efficiency. *Journal of Banking and Finance* 17 (2–3): 515–530.
Rosen, Richard. 2003. Is three a crowd? Competition among regulators in banking. *Journal of Money, Credit, and Banking* 35 (6): 967–998.
Savage, Donald T. 1993. Interstate banking: A status report. *Federal Reserve Bulletin* 79 (12): 1075–1089.
Schranz, Mary. 1993. Takeovers improve firm performance: Evidence from the banking industry. *Journal of Political Economy* 101 (2): 299–326.
Sierra, Gregory E., Eli Talmor, and James S. Wallace. 2006. An examination of multiple governance forces within bank holding companies. *Journal of Financial Services Research* 29 (2): 105–123.
Subrahmanyam, Vijaya, Nanda Rangan, and Stuart Rosenstein. 1997. The role of outside directors in bank acquisitions. *Financial Management* 26 (3): 23–36.
UBS Warburg, LLC. 2001. *Money in the bank*. New York: UBS Warburg, LLC.
Whalen, Gary. 2002. Charter flips by national banks. OCC Economic and Policy Analysis Working Paper 2002–1.
Wilson, John D. 1986. *The Chase: The Chase Manhattan Bank, N.A., 1945–1985*. Boston: Harvard Business School Press.
Yildirim, H. Semih, Seung-Woog Kwag, and M. Cary Collins. 2006. An examination of the equity market response to the Gramm-Leach-Bliley Act across commercial banking, investment banking, and insurance firms. *Journal of Business Finance & Accounting* 33 (9): 1629–1649.

ABOUT THE AUTHOR

Renée Birgit Adams joined the University of Queensland as professor of finance in 2006 after previous appointments at the Federal Reserve Bank of New York and the Stockholm School of Economics. She has published in the area of corporate governance in such journals as the *Journal of Accounting and Economics*, *Journal of Finance*, *Journal of Financial Economics*, and *Review of Financial Studies*. Together with Michael Weisbach and Benjamin Hermalin, she is a co-author of a forthcoming survey of the literature on boards of directors in the *Journal of Economic Literature*. Professor Adams is also a research associate at the European Corporate Governance Institute (ECGI). She received a PhD in economics from the University of Chicago in 2001.

CHAPTER 24

Corporate Governance: Nonequity Stakeholders

MARC GOERGEN
Professor of Finance, Cardiff Business School and European Corporate Governance Institute (ECGI)

CHRIS BREWSTER
Professor of International Human Resource Management, Henley Business School, University of Reading

GEOFFREY WOOD
Professor of Human Resource Management, University of Sheffield Management School

INTRODUCTION

Understandings of corporate governance that are concerned only with the rights of owners and shareholders and the relationship between them and the management of the business are inevitably limited. Organizations are complex bodies and have many other parties involved, including regulators, customers, suppliers, and local citizens. The salience of these parties and their stake in the organization varies markedly depending on the type of business, the sector and country in which it operates, and its success. The mainstream finance literature often assumes that the relationship between ownership and other stakeholder rights is a zero-sum game: Should the former be stronger, the latter will inevitably be weaker, and vice versa (Djankov, Glaeser, La Porta, Lopez-de-Silanes, and Shleifer 2003). In contrast, the varieties of capitalism (VOC) literature argues that the rights of stakeholders are potentially reconcilable, through the operation of complementarities, with sets of practices and relationships working better together than they do on their own (Hall and Soskice 2001). This chapter explores the extent of nonowner stakeholder rights in different contexts and focuses specifically on a core *insider* stakeholder group: employees.

For all organizations, a key and influential stakeholder is the people working in the business. These are employees, contractors, consultants, agency staff, and others who may be important in particular circumstances. In some countries, almost all these employees are likely to be in trade unions; in other countries, trade unions are illegal. In most developed countries, however, trade unions and collective representation play an important part in most large organizations. The factors influencing that role are determined by the relationship among institutions, corporate governance, and union power. A key issue is the degree of employer-employee interdependence, including employment security and the nature and extent of training and development (Whitley 1999). This chapter examines that relationship using evidence from a large-scale comparative survey of organizations.

Shareholder rights have been the focus of much of the literature on corporate governance (La Porta, Lopez-de-Silanes, Shleifer, and Vishny 1997 and 1998). This literature has been developed to explore the relationship between these shareholder rights and the way in which various forms of market, including labor markets, are regulated (Djankov et al. 2003; Botero, Djankov, La Porta, Lopez-de-Silanes, and Shleifer 2004). For example, Botero et al. analyze the link between laws on collective action and investor protection. Yet the mainstream finance literature remains dominated by rational hierarchical approaches that see institutional effects primarily in terms of constraints on rational actors, focusing on the relative strength of property rights, and looking at the effects of law, constitutions, and politics (Djankov et al.).

In reaction, an emerging body of socioeconomic literature has provided criticisms of such approaches on four fronts:

1. Owner and stakeholder behavior may not simply reflect state-regulatory pressures or the absence thereof: Institutional pressures operate at a wide range of levels and domains, encompassing markets, civil society, and organizations (Boyer 2006).
2. This implies that the rights of shareholders and their relationship with other key stakeholders will vary either from one state-regulatory system to another or perhaps between systems with different approaches to shareholder rights. This relationship is not a zero-sum game (Hall and Soskice 2001).
3. Institutional complementarity may not necessarily emerge from mutually supportive features but may, in fact, arise from contradictions (Crouch 2005). In turn, mutually beneficial complementarities are likely to reinforce specific industrial relations practices even if, over time, both will be subject to redefinition and change (Höpner 2005). Hence, strong ownership rights may not necessarily preclude strong employee rights and, indeed, strong employee rights may not be inimical to effective organizational performance.
4. Employees and managers are not passive subjects of external institutional forces but make choices of their own, molding organizational outcomes and affecting the relative powers of owners (Gospel and Pendleton 2004). This reflects a key difference in underlying assumptions: Rational-incentive approaches focus on the manner in which individuals seek to maximize their own benefit. In contrast, socioeconomic accounts give a central place to the issue of relationships (encompassing both individuals and associations) and the manner in which such relationships are regulated (Hall and Gingerich 2004).

Despite these criticisms, there is little systematic comparative evidence of the relationship among the relative strength of trade unions at the firm level, the dominant national corporate governance regime, and economic performance. Ezzamel and Reed (2008) note that evaluating and critiquing the full range of different accounts on corporate governance and firm behavior is of value both in understanding what firms do and in developing alternative, critical, and more explicitly multidimensional alternatives. This chapter provides a systematic assessment and critique of the predictions of rational hierarchical approaches to corporate governance on the relative strength of employees and their collectives in different national and organizational settings. The chapter also critically reappraises the implications thereof, and the relevance of alternative approaches within the heterodox socioeconomic tradition.

The chapter has the following organization. The next section reviews the various rational-incentives approaches to corporate governance systems and institutional settings. This is followed by a discussion of the socioeconomic alternatives such as the varieties of capitalism literature. The next section explains the data and methodology. The penultimate section interprets and discusses the findings of the empirical analysis, and the final section draws some conclusions.

RATIONAL-INCENTIVES APPROACHES

The rational-incentives approaches to institutions and their corporate governance can be summarized briefly. Many finance and economic scholars see institutions as constrainers on or incentive providers for rational profit-maximizing individuals in making optimal decisions (North 1990; Powell and DiMaggio 1991; Shleifer and Vishny 1997). Ezzamel and Reed (2008, 611) note that such approaches combine "the neo-rationalist emphasis on rational calculation and action with more recent theoretical reinterpretations that give greater emphasis to the strategic role of political and cultural power in reshaping modes of collective regulation," and hence, individual choices and actions.

These approaches are generally concerned specifically with the issue of property rights and have been particularly influential in the literature on finance and corporate governance (Djankov et al. 2003), but also in strands of the international management literature. In practice, the rational-incentives approaches assign paramount importance to hierarchies with dominant relations imposing isomorphism (Boyer 2006). The role of owners is privileged in these analyses; other stakeholders are treated as potential hinderers or, at best, facilitators on the effective operation of markets (North 1990). The assumption is that when hierarchies do not operate effectively, the system does not work optimally. Institutional settings create a particular process of decision making, leading to optimal or suboptimal outcomes.

Rational Incentive Accounts of the Relationship between the Firm and its Stakeholders

Fundamental to these concepts is the view of shareholders as the only stakeholders with sunk funds in the firm (Shleifer and Vishny 1997). Hence, some contend that the firm's sole objective should be the maximization of their wealth. Roe (2003) believes that improving the conditions of workers merely worsens the classical agency problem between managers and shareholders and prevents the separation of ownership and control. The classical agency problem consists of managers' tendency to focus on corporate growth rather than shareholder value. The suggestion is that both managers and employees prefer larger and growing firms, the former in the interests of empire building and the latter as larger firms tend to provide better working conditions and job security. Hence, as Roe notes, in countries with left-wing governments, ownership and control will remain concentrated to counteract managers' tendency toward empire building. Conversely, countries with right-wing governments favor investors over professional managers and workers, so ownership is separate from control as investors are well protected by law from abuses by corporate managers.

Stakeholder Power and Politics

Developments and extensions of rational-incentive approaches have, of course, factored in the impact of institutions, but only in terms of being providers of incentives or disincentives on rational actors. Pagano and Volpin (2005) hypothesize that the type of electoral system, whether a proportional or majoritarian electoral system, is the main determining factor of the levels of protection that employees and investors have. Whereas a majority of votes ensure victory in a proportional system, one needs to win a majority of districts in a majoritarian system. Pagano and Volpin argue that proportional systems make politicians focus on social groups with homogeneous preferences—workers and their unions and managers—at the expense of owners. Therefore, a proportional system produces stronger workers' rights but weaker investor protection. A majoritarian system produces the exact opposite outcome.

Type of Legal System

La Porta et al. (1997) distinguish between common law and civil law. Common law—the legal system of the United States, the United Kingdom, and most Commonwealth countries—accords an important role to the judges who make law in the courts by setting precedents. In contrast, civil law, the foundation of the legal systems of Continental Europe and most of the rest of the world, is based on extensive codes of law—having their origins in Roman law—and the role of the judges is limited to interpreting these codes in the courts. La Porta et al. argue that, given its higher flexibility and better enforcement, common law provides stronger investor protection than civil law. Further, among the civil law family, French law provides the weakest shareholder protection, followed by German law and then Scandinavian law. In recent developments of their argument, La Porta and colleagues claim that legal systems shape the regulation of a wide range of markets, including labor markets (Botero et al. 2004), and that civil law countries have direct regulation by governments of all these markets. This direct regulation of markets includes stronger job protection, which, in turn, is likely to affect the extent to which a firm invests in its people.

Summarizing Rational-Hierarchical Approaches

This literature advocates the maximization of shareholder value, privileging the role of the owners of the business who have sunk funds in the firm. Owner and employee rights are seen as a zero-sum game: If one is stronger, the other will be weaker and vice versa. Hence, Ezzamel and Reed (2008, 612–613) assume that "carefully devised laws and sanctions . . . as well as carefully drafted employment contracts are necessary to provide the necessary carrots and sticks for workers to act in the interests of owners." There are counter views, however. Goergen (2007) argues that workers and suppliers also have sunk investments in the firms they deal with and that they are equally likely to lose these investments when the firm disappears. Hence, the question of employee rights is not simply a matter of something that negatively or positively affects the manner in which the firm can be governed. It is central to the analysis of the nature of corporate governance. Labor is not simply another commodity that can be purchased and discarded. Recent work on corporate governance has focused on this lacuna and sought to explain how specific ownership regimes affect both managers and labor. Such work also examines the manner in which employees and their collectives influence both owners and managers (Gospel and Pendleton 2003 and 2004).

SOCIOECONOMIC ALTERNATIVES

Institutional features that are seemingly at odds with each other may in fact generate complementarities in compensating or balancing contrasting components, according to recent critiques. As an example, industry-relevant skills may offset pressures toward low labor mobility in other areas (Crouch 2005). In practice, institutional pressures operate at a wide range of levels and domains (Boyer 2006).

These socioeconomic alternatives make three fundamental critiques about the rational-hierarchical approaches that deserve further exploration.

1. Are the rational-hierarchical approaches to analyzing institutional effects sufficient for understanding managerial choices and, in turn, the relative power of shareholders in relation to employees and their collectives?
2. What is the relationship between shareholder powers and trade unions? The *mixed* approach to understanding institutional effects highlighted by Crouch (2005) emphasizes that strong shareholder powers do not necessarily make for weak unions. The relative strength of employee collectives may depend on complementarities elsewhere in the system: the relative strength of civil society and a wide range of non-shareholder-framed enablers and constraints on managerial behavior.
3. What is the relationship between relative shareholder power and the nature and extent to which firms invest in their people? Are there similar variations in employment security?

In contrast to the rational-incentive approaches, and starting from a heterodox point, a burgeoning body of socioeconomic literature (Whitley 1999; Dore 2000; Hall and Soskice 2001) locates institutions in terms of webs of relationships rather than individual selfish action (Ezzamel and Reed 2008). Hall and Gingerich (2004, 7) note that in order to effectively manage their people, firms "have to engage with multiple spheres of the political economy."

According to the varieties of capitalism (VOC) literature, not all forms of capitalism are the same. A key distinction arises between liberal market economies

(LMEs) that privilege the rights of shareholders and the coordinated market economies (CMEs) that balance shareholder rights with the rights of other stakeholders. Examples of LMEs would be Britain and the United States while examples of CMEs would be found in northwestern Continental Europe. This literature highlights the continued viability and distinct paths of alternatives to lightly regulated liberal markets. In nearly all varieties of capitalism, there are highly successful multinational corporations (MNCs). As relationships may make for mutually beneficial complementarities, there is no inherent reason employee and owner well-being should be antagonistic or mutually exclusive. Some argue that CMEs provide a more sustainable basis for prosperity through mutually beneficial trade-offs and compromises between key stakeholders (Lincoln and Kalleberg 1990; Dore 2000). The effects of the recent economic crisis seem to provide some support for that notion.

While the limits of rational-incentive approaches to understanding the position of stakeholders in corporate governance may be immediately evident, the VOC literature is not without problems. A two-archetype model (LME and CME) discounts important differences that exist within the coordinated market economies and the importance of other types of capitalism such as the Mediterranean variety (Boyer and Hollingsworth 1997; Amable 2003). Again, there are differences between Scandinavia and many Rhineland economies. For example, in countries such as Denmark and Norway, flexicurity policies are in operation, which combine some degree of job security with job market flexibility. This makes such approaches only of limited utility in seeking to understand the differences in stakeholder positions in practice in, for example, Continental Europe.

Such approaches in common with rational-incentive approaches assume that national institutional frameworks are deeply embedded and unlikely to change significantly over time (Boyer 2006). Alternative approaches to understanding institutions from regulationist and historical institutionalist starting points share the VOC literature's focus on relationships, associations, and informal and formal rules. As Boyer notes, the regulationist literature has stressed the temporary and inherently unstable nature of institutional mediation and the uneven nature of systemic evolution and change. The historical institutionalist literature assumes that institutions are flexible and dynamic although, at specific times, coherences will be evident at national and regional levels (Lane and Wood 2009). Attempts have also been made to broaden the range of capitalist archetypes from a simple LME/CME dichotomy. This has involved identifying, among other things, differences within the European coordinated market category, adding Far Eastern alternatives (Whitley 1999), and differentiating between Scandinavia and Continental Europe (Amable 2003). The accounts by Whitley and Amable rely much less on shareholder rights, which are not the focus of corporate governance in these non-LME countries, and give much more detailed attention to the types of difference in industrial relations that are likely to be encountered in different contexts; both identify unionization as a key dimension.

DATA AND METHODOLOGY

This chapter reports on a test of the veracity of the claims of the rational incentive approaches and explores the extent to which any limitations of these approaches may be accounted for within the literature on comparative capitalism (Goergen, Brewster, and Wood 2009a). The research uses longitudinal data sourced from the Cranet database. The surveys cover many countries across different years and are broadly representative for each year for organizations with more than 100 employees.

The influence of trade unions is measured as the proportion of the total number of employees in each company that are members of a trade union. Central to the strength of unions is an ability to draw members into the fold and organize them: Unions only exist wherever workers are unionized (Kelly 1998; Hyman 2002). In the survey questionnaire, the variable is ordinal in nature (0 if a firm has 0 percent of union membership; 1 if it is between 1 and 10 percent; 2 if it is between 11 and 25 percent; 3 if the proportion is between 26 and 50 percent; 4 if it is between 51 and 75 percent; and 5 if it exceeds 75 percent) and reflects the firm's ability to attract and retain workers (Checchi and Visser 2005).

Four separate ordered logit regressions are run using the pooled company-level data for 1995, 1999–2000, and 2003–2004. The first logit is a test of La Porta et al.'s (1997) legal theory. The second and third logit regressions test Roe's (2003) politics theory, using politics indexes from Cusack and Engelhardt (2006). RILE is a measure of the political orientation of the party in power based on its views on a wide range of economic and social issues (Roe 2003). The fourth logit regression is based on Pagano and Volpin's (2005) proportionality index. Thereafter, using cluster analysis, the differences between liberal market economies (LME) and coordinated (CME) ones are explored by examining training and development policies. Given that both the finance literature and the variety of socioeconomic approaches suggest that the relative degree of coordination in the category of the CMEs varies, further attention is devoted to exploring the differences between individual coordinated markets (Amable 2003). Drawing on the approach devised by Chiu et al. (2001), a two-step cluster analysis identifies relatively homogeneous groups of firms based on a range of specific characteristics. The clusters drawn are compared with the two archetypes, CMEs and LMEs, and the nature and extent of diversity in each category. This is supplemented when appropriate with the usage of analysis of variance (ANOVA).

EMPIRICAL EVIDENCE

Union Power

Exhibits 24.1 to 24.3 report the results for the various ordered logits. These tables present the regressions based on the proportion of employees who are members of a trade union. Exhibit 24.1 shows the results for the logit examining the proportion of employees in the trade union using La Porta et al.'s (1997) legal families. The threshold variables in the ordered logit are all highly significant. This suggests that an ordered logit is the appropriate estimation technique. The various pseudo R-squares are also relatively high. The dummies for the three families of common, German, and Scandinavian law are all highly significant. As hypothesized, the coefficient on the common law dummy is negative, suggesting that trade union penetration is lower in countries of the common law family. Contrary to La Porta et al. (1997, 1998, and 2000) and Botera et al. (2004), union membership is

Exhibit 24.1 La Porta, Lopez-de-Silanes, Shleifer, and Vishny's Legal Families: Proportion of Employees in Trade Union

The dependent variable (propunion) in the ordered logit is an ordinal variable which equals 0 if the proportion of employees who are members of trade unions is 0 percent; 1 if it is between 1 and 10 percent; 2 if it is between 11 and 25 percent; 3 if the proportion is between 26 and 50 percent; 4 if it is between 51 and 75 percent; and 5 if it exceeds 75 percent. Common law, German law, and Scandinavian law are dummy variables which equal 1 if the firm in question is from a country with common law, German law, and Scandinavian law, respectively, and equal 0 otherwise. All Wald tests have one degree of freedom.

Panel A. Regression Results

						95% Confidence Interval	
		Estimate	**Standard Error**	**Wald Test**	**Significance**	**Lower Bound**	**Upper Bound**
Threshold	(propunion = 0.00)	−1.404	0.123	129.208	0.000	−1.646	−1.162
	(propunion = 1.00)	0.213	0.122	3.056	0.080	−0.026	0.452
	(propunion = 2.00)	1.018	0.122	69.110	0.000	0.778	1.257
	(propunion = 3.00)	2.155	0.124	301.184	0.000	1.911	2.398
Location	Common law	−0.102	0.048	4.472	0.034	−0.196	−0.007
	German law	0.306	0.057	28.843	0.000	0.194	0.417
	Scandinavian law	2.663	0.061	1887.214	0.000	2.543	2.783
	IND2	0.421	0.158	7.055	0.008	0.110	0.731
	IND3	0.515	0.146	12.508	0.000	0.230	0.801
	IND4	0.309	0.125	6.109	0.013	0.064	0.555
	IND5	0.566	0.126	20.269	0.000	0.320	0.813
	IND6	0.069	0.150	0.214	0.643	−0.225	0.363
	IND7	−0.907	0.133	46.331	0.000	−1.169	−0.646
	IND8	0.257	0.144	3.183	0.074	−0.025	0.540
	IND9	−0.976	0.130	56.080	0.000	−1.232	−0.721
	IND10	−0.750	0.224	11.155	0.001	−1.190	−0.310

IND11	0.929	0.142	43.080	0.000	0.651	1.206
IND12	−0.164	0.157	1.091	0.296	−0.473	0.144
IND13	1.026	0.154	44.655	0.000	0.725	1.327
IND14	1.309	0.145	81.307	0.000	1.024	1.593
IND15	1.074	0.165	42.596	0.000	0.751	1.396
IND16	−0.201	0.134	2.234	0.135	−0.464	0.062
IND17	2.664	0.645	17.067	0.000	1.400	3.927
year95	0.175	0.049	12.573	0.000	0.078	0.271
year99	0.087	0.051	2.938	0.087	−0.012	0.186

Panel B. Pseudo R^2

Cox and Snell	Nagelkerke	McFadden
0.338	0.353	0.131

higher in countries with German law (the coefficient on the German law dummy is significant and positive) and highest in those with Scandinavian law (the dummy is significant and even higher) relative to countries of French law (the base case).

Virtually all industry dummies are significant and positive, suggesting that unionization varies across industries as well as across the various legal families, reflecting industry-specific variations in work organization and the relative centralization of bargaining (Boyer and Hollingsworth 1997). The year dummies are significant and positive with the year dummy for 1995 having the highest coefficient. This reflects the fact that the proportion of employees who are members of a trade union dropped steadily between 1995 and 2003–2004 in many national contexts. In turn, this would reflect the general weakening in the influence of unions that has followed the long period of prosperity and growth that ended in the early 1970s and the structural changes in the global economy that followed it (Western 1993; Kelly 1998; Checchi and Visser 2005).

Exhibit 24.2 tests Roe's (2003) politics theory using the Cusack and Engelhardt (2006) politics index RILE, which covers the government's orientation in terms of a wide range of social and economic issues. All of the threshold variables are significant. The coefficient on RILE is significantly negative, which suggests that the influence of trade unions, as measured by the proportion of employees who have membership, is lower in countries with right wing governments. This provides support for Roe's politics thesis. The findings also echo those of Checchi and Visser (2005) that the efforts of right wing governments to curtail union power negatively affected union density. Western (1993) suggests, however, that these effects may be lagged. In comparison with Exhibit 24.1 and the regressions based on La Porta et al. (1998), the values for the pseudo R-squares tend to be lower (by as much as a factor of about 3) and most of the industry dummies are significant.

In contrast to Exhibit 24.1, not all of the significant industry dummies are positive. In particular, the industry dummies for sectors providing services to public institutions are highly significant and positive, perhaps reflecting the privatization of central and local government services in Europe over the period of study. Private-sector organizations taking over the provision of public services may have inherited workers with high trade union representation (Dibben, Roper, James, and Wood 2007). Again, the dummy for the year 1995 is significantly positive, suggesting a decreasing trend in union membership over the period 1995 to 2003–2004.

Exhibit 24.3 reports on Pagano and Volpin's (2005) index of proportionality in electoral systems as the principal cause of union membership. The evidence shows that workers appear more unionized in countries with more proportional representation electoral systems. The pseudo R-squares are relatively high. The exhibits show a relative decline of union power since the mid-1990s. Industry variations cut across the different national systems.

In summary, based on the pseudo R-squared regression results, Pagano and Volpin's (2005) approach appears to be the most valuable in explaining the extent of union influence. Also, while the legal system seems to affect union strength, the results are not the same as would be suggested by La Porta et al. (1997). More specifically, French law, which according to La Porta et al. provides the lowest level of investor protection, is not associated with particularly strong unions, even if unions may have significant political clout. Some evidence supports Roe (2003), but it is not as strong as that in support of Pagano and Volpin (2005).

Exhibit 24.2 Roe's Politics Index: Proportion of Employees in Trade Union

The dependent variable (propunion) in the ordered logit is an ordinal variable which equals 0 if the proportion of employees who are members of trade unions is 0 percent; 1 if it is between 1 and 10 percent; 2 if it is between 11 and 25 percent; 3 if the proportion is between 26 and 50 percent; 4 if it is between 51 and 75 percent; and 5 if it exceeds 75 percent. RILE ranges from –100 (extreme left) to +100 (extreme right). The index measures the political orientation of the party in power based on its views on a wide range of economic and social issues. All Wald tests have one degree of freedom.

Panel A. Regression Results

						95% Confidence Interval	
		Estimate	Standard Error	Wald Test	Significance	Lower Bound	Upper Bound
Threshold	(propunion = 0.00)	−1.745	0.117	222.482	0.000	−1.974	−1.515
	(propunion = 1.00)	−0.297	0.115	6.659	0.010	−0.522	−0.071
	(propunion = 2.00)	0.370	0.115	10.324	0.001	0.144	0.595
	(propunion = 3.00)	1.253	0.116	117.340	0.000	1.027	1.480
Location	RILE	−0.003	0.001	20.306	0.000	−0.004	−0.001
	IND2	0.362	0.152	5.694	0.017	0.065	0.660
	IND3	0.281	0.140	4.015	0.045	0.006	0.556
	IND4	0.137	0.120	1.291	0.256	−0.099	0.373
	IND5	0.377	0.121	9.738	0.002	0.140	0.614
	IND6	0.051	0.144	0.127	0.722	−0.231	0.334
	IND7	−0.731	0.129	32.264	0.000	−0.983	−0.479
	IND8	0.434	0.138	9.881	0.002	0.163	0.704
	IND9	−0.926	0.126	53.987	0.000	−1.173	−0.679
	IND10	−0.386	0.217	3.154	0.076	−0.812	0.040

(Continued)

Exhibit 24.2 (*Continued*)

Panel A. Regression Results

					95% Confidence Interval	
	Estimate	**Standard Error**	**Wald Test**	**Significance**	**Lower Bound**	**Upper Bound**
IND11	0.640	0.135	22.401	0.000	0.375	0.905
IND12	−0.073	0.151	0.233	0.629	−0.369	0.223
IND13	0.724	0.146	24.576	0.000	0.438	1.010
IND14	1.262	0.137	85.169	0.000	0.994	1.530
IND15	1.091	0.154	50.004	0.000	0.788	1.393
IND16	−0.188	0.130	2.102	0.147	−0.442	0.066
IND17	1.906	0.648	8.653	0.003	0.636	3.176
year95	0.364	0.048	58.040	0.000	0.271	0.458
year99	−0.063	0.049	1.649	0.199	−0.158	0.033

Panel B. Pseudo R^2

Cox and Snell	Nagelkerke	McFadden
0.111	0.116	0.037

Exhibit 24.3 Pagano and Volpin's Proportionality Index: Proportion of Employees in Trade Union

The dependent variable (propunion) in the ordered logit is an ordinal variable which equals 0 if the proportion of employees who are members of trade unions is 0 percent; 1 if it is between 1 and 10 percent; 2 if it is between 11 and 25 percent; 3 if the proportion is between 26 and 50 percent; 4 if it is between 51 and 75 percent; and 5 if it exceeds 75 percent proportionality index. The index, which is available for 1985–2002, is equal to zero if none of the seats are assigned via a proportionality rule, 1 if a minority of seats are assigned by such a rule, 2 if the majority of seats are assigned by this rule, and 3 if all of the seats are assigned proportionally. All Wald tests have one degree of freedom.

Panel A. Regression Results

						95% Confidence Interval	
		Estimate	Standard Error	Wald Test	Significance	Lower Bound	Upper Bound
Threshold	(propunion = 0.00)	−0.784	0.120	42.389	0.000	−1.020	−0.548
	(propunion = 1.00)	0.792	0.120	43.854	0.000	0.558	1.027
	(propunion = 2.00)	1.518	0.120	159.092	0.000	1.282	1.753
	(propunion = 3.00)	2.487	0.122	416.518	0.000	2.249	2.726
Location	PROPVOT	0.561	0.015	1339.102	0.000	0.531	0.591
	IND2	0.384	0.153	6.316	0.012	0.085	0.684
	IND3	0.301	0.141	4.549	0.033	0.024	0.578
	IND4	0.320	0.121	6.991	0.008	0.083	0.558
	IND5	0.617	0.122	25.567	0.000	0.378	0.856
	IND6	0.162	0.145	1.244	0.265	−0.123	0.447
	IND7	−0.555	0.129	18.382	0.000	−0.809	−0.301
	IND8	0.519	0.139	13.865	0.000	0.246	0.792
	IND9	−0.799	0.127	39.714	0.000	−1.048	−0.551
	IND10	−0.386	0.219	3.109	0.078	−0.816	0.043

(Continued)

Exhibit 24.3 (*Continued*)

Panel A. Regression Results

					95% Confidence Interval	
	Estimate	Standard Error	Wald Test	Significance	Lower Bound	Upper Bound
IND11	0.933	0.137	46.274	0.000	0.664	1.202
IND12	0.254	0.153	2.779	0.095	−0.045	0.554
IND13	1.246	0.149	69.652	0.000	0.953	1.538
IND14	1.537	0.140	121.208	0.000	1.263	1.810
IND15	1.231	0.157	61.261	0.000	0.923	1.539
IND16	−0.168	0.130	1.654	0.198	−0.423	0.088
IND17	3.153	0.647	23.732	0.000	1.884	4.421
year95	0.311	0.048	42.079	0.000	0.217	0.405
year99	−0.135	0.050	7.387	0.007	−0.232	−0.038

Panel B: Pseudo R^2

Cox and Snell	Nagelkerke	McFadden
0.225	0.235	0.081

Employer Employee Interdependence—Training and Turnover

The next issue investigated involves employer-employee interdependence. Because neither the finance literature nor the dichotomous VOC approaches can explain this interdependence, the multi-variety model of Amable (2003) is used. This model draws a further distinction between the coordinated social democratic economies of Scandinavia and those of Rhineland/Continental Europe. Amable also argues that Mediterranean capitalism retains distinct features based on specific state and firm traditions, which affect present-day corporate governance. This approach particularly lends itself to cluster analysis. At the same time, reference is made to La Porta et al. (1997 and 1998) and the broader rational hierarchical finance tradition when relevant.

First, as a base for the clusters, country of origin (as a categorical variable), job band (managerial, professional/technical, clerical, and manual), the length of training provided (i.e., average number of training days), the percentage of wages spent on training, and the percentage of annual staff turnover are used. Exhibit 24.4 depicts the results of the analysis that yields four distinct clusters. Exhibit 24.5 reports the centroids based on average days of training, percentage of staff turnover, and proportion of wages spent on training. Most of the firms (71 to 99 percent) fall into a single cluster. The first cluster, which is totally at odds with what would be suggested by La Porta et al., (1997), Roe (2003), or Pagano and Volpin (2005), brings together the United Kingdom and Ireland, Finland, and Sweden. Amable (2003) notes, however, these are all countries with historically weak commitments to vocational training. Indeed, the cluster has significantly below-average days of training for all four job categories identified. Firms in these countries also spend significantly less on staff training but have above-average staff turnover rates.

Cluster 3 brings together a mix of Mediterranean (Greece, Portugal, and Spain) and northern European (Netherlands, Norway, and Denmark) economies. Such countries have close to the average training duration, training expenditures, and staff turnover rates. The three northern European economies (Netherlands, Norway, and Denmark) are all those with flexicurity systems that provide state-sponsored training schemes. Such systems provide some state relief for the training burden at firm level. While job security is less than in the bulk of Continental Europe, it is still more than what would typically be encountered in a liberal market setting. Mediterranean economies tend to have weak training systems, requiring much additional training by firms; at the same time, limited firm capacities would mitigate against overly high investment rates.

Cluster 4 encompasses the main continental European economies that have less flexible labor markets, reflected in lower staff turnover rates. Training spending and durations, however, may be spread over many years, given high levels of mutual organizational commitment.

Cluster 2 brings together a minority of firms from Scandinavia and Mediterranean Europe. Most of these firms are from four industry groups: agriculture, hunting, forestry, and fishing; metal manufacture; other manufacturing; and other services. There are also higher percentages of firms in cluster 2 with their headquarters abroad (51 percent compared to 33 percent for the entire sample)—in other

Exhibit 24.4 Cluster Analysis Based on Average Days of Training, Percentage of Staff Turnover, and Proportion of Wages Spent on Training

This table reports the results from a two-step cluster analysis. Based on the log-likelihood distance as a measure of similarity and Schwarz's Bayesian information criterion (BIC) to determine the optimal number of clusters, the analysis identified four different clusters. For each cluster, the table reports the frequency and percent of firm-year observations per country.

	Cluster									
	1		2		3		4		Combined	
	N	%	N	%	N	%	N	%	N	%
United Kingdom	624	92.4	51	7.6	0	0.0	0	0.0	675	100.0
France	0	0.0	12	6.2	0	0.0	182	93.8	194	100.0
Germany	0	0.0	17	5.6	0	0.0	286	94.4	303	100.0
Sweden	177	87.6	25	12.4	0	0.0	0	0.0	202	100.0
Spain	0	0.0	41	28.9	101	71.1	0	0.0	142	100.0
Denmark	0	0.0	10	4.4	219	95.6	0	0.0	229	100.0
The Netherlands	0	0.0	6	2.4	243	97.6	0	0.0	249	100.0
Italy	0	0.0	2	8.7	0	0.0	21	91.3	23	100.0
Norway	0	0.0	19	9.4	183	90.6	0	0.0	202	100.0
Switzerland	0	0.0	1	1.3	78	98.7	0	0.0	79	100.0
Ireland	144	95.4	7	4.6	0	0.0	0	0.0	151	100.0
Portugal	0	0.0	12	24.5	37	75.5	0	0.0	49	100.0
Finland	250	92.9	19	7.1	0	0.0	0	0.0	269	100.0
Greece	0	0.0	12	29.3	29	70.7	0	0.0	41	100.0
Austria	0	0.0	8	7.8	0	0.0	95	92.2	103	100.0
Belgium	0	0.0	25	10.2	0	0.0	219	89.8	244	100.0
Iceland	0	0.0	8	20.0	0	0.0	32	80.0	40	100.0

words, most are subsidiaries of multinationals. Such firms are also prone to higher staff turnover rates, training expenditure, and training duration, perhaps reflecting greater organizational resources and the effects of relocations across subsidiaries within the firm and country of origin.

Turning to tenure and the extent to which employees are willing and able to remain in their jobs over extended periods of time, Exhibit 24.6 depicts staff turnover rates. The following patterns emerge. First, as anticipated, staff turnover rates are relatively low in most Continental European and social democratic economies. Two notable exceptions are the flexicurity economies of Denmark and the Netherlands, where staff turnover rates tend to rise, reflecting the gradual development and extension of flexicurity over recent few years. Generally low turnover rates mean that, as noted earlier, training costs can be spread over many years, making expenditure per employee per annum lower than would otherwise be the case.

The ANOVA in Exhibit 24.7 confirms the patterns. The Continental European economies have significantly lower staff turnover than all the other groups. Indeed, their annual percentage staff turnover is only 6.1 percent. The social democratic

Exhibit 24.5 Centroids Based on Average Days of Training, Percentage of Staff Turnover, and Proportion of Wages Spent on Training

This table reports the characteristics (in terms of mean values and standard deviations) of the four clusters identified in the two-step cluster analysis reported in Exhibit 24.4.

	Cluster									
	1		2		3		4		Combined	
	Mean	Standard Deviation	Mean	Standard Deviation	Mean	Standard Deviation	Mean	Standard Deviation	Mean	Standard Deviation
Days training for managerial employees	5.114	3.107	13.182	8.010	5.528	3.157	5.076	3.028	5.914	4.392
Days training for professional and technical employees	5.119	3.020	14.096	9.471	5.857	3.540	4.617	2.819	5.966	4.807
Days training for clerical employees	3.310	2.118	10.018	7.700	3.381	2.188	3.011	1.874	3.829	3.556
Days training for manual employees	3.297	2.532	10.007	9.212	3.612	2.878	2.691	2.121	3.804	4.111
Percent of salaries and wages spent on training	2.042	1.752	5.298	8.600	2.219	1.868	1.898	1.437	2.334	3.138
Percent of staff turnover per year	7.529	3.002	15.565	24.799	7.411	6.722	4.883	4.972	7.496	10.155

The figure reports average annual percentage staff turnover rates across the four Cranet surveys for 1991, 1995, 1999–2000, and 2003–2004.

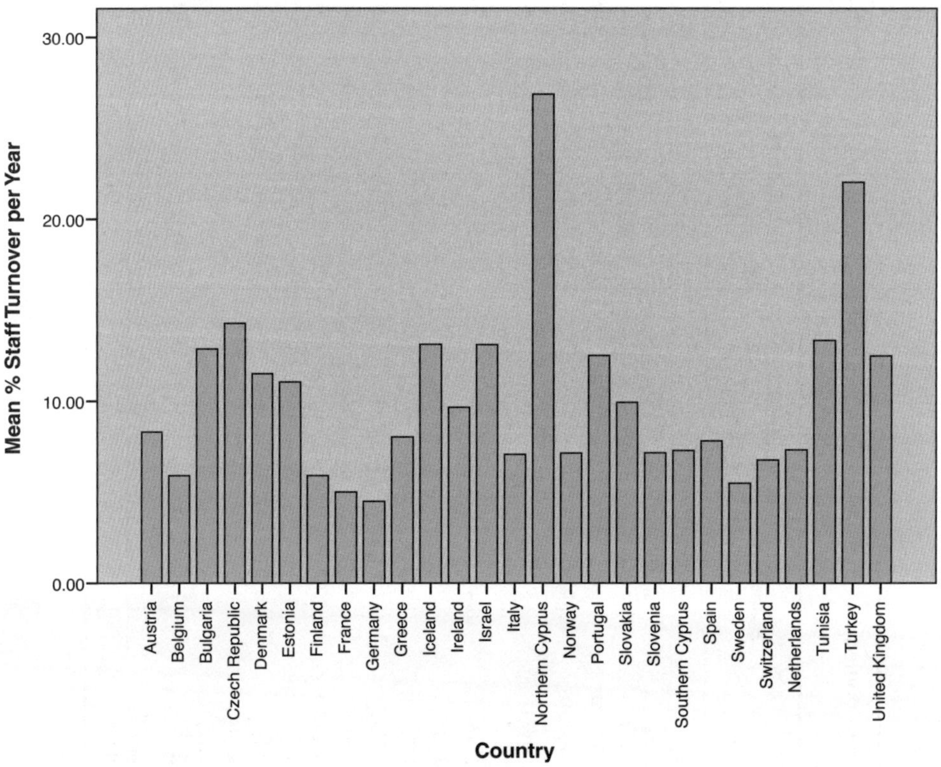

Exhibit 24.6 Average Annual Staff Turnover

countries follow with a significantly higher turnover rate by about 1 percent. Conversely, LMEs (United Kingdom and Ireland) have significantly higher staff turnover (11.6 percent) than the Continental European and the Southern European countries (8.5 percent). This would reflect both the buoyant job market (before 2008) in the former countries and weak employment protection under the law (Djankov et al. 2003). In contrast, while job security in Southern Europe may also be relatively weak (in practice, if not in the law), an inhospitable external labor market discouraged employees, comparatively, from leaving their jobs unless forced to do so.

Exhibit 24.8 depicts the main influences in defining training needs in 2003–2004. The figure distinguishes between four main types of influence: the individual, the line managers, the human resource management (HRM) department, and the trade union. The role of the individual seems particularly strong in the United Kingdom and Iceland, in the flexicurity economies of the Netherlands and Denmark, and in the social democracies with relatively weak vocational training systems, such as Sweden and Finland. In the case of the flexicurity economies, individuals have strong incentives to ensure that they are well equipped with up-to-date marketable skills and access to relevant training to remain marketable

Exhibit 24.7 Analysis of Variance: Staff Turnover

The table reports the annual percentage staff turnover rates for the four pooled survey waves. The figures in parentheses behind the name of each group of countries are the mean for that group.

(I)	(J)	Mean Difference (I–J)	Standard Error	Significance	95% Confidence Interval Upper Bound	95% Confidence Interval Lower Bound
1.00 Continental Europe (6.1399)	2.00 LME	−5.466*	0.289	0.000	−6.277	−4.656
	3.00 Social democratic	−1.104*	0.233	0.000	−1.757	−0.452
	4.00 South European	−2.345*	0.455	0.000	−3.621	−1.069
	5.00 Transitional	−6.174*	0.403	0.000	−7.304	−5.044
2.00 LME (11.6064)	1.00 Continental Europe	5.466*	0.289	0.000	4.656	6.277
	3.00 Social democratic	4.362*	0.314	0.000	3.483	5.242
	4.00 South European	3.122*	0.501	0.000	1.717	4.527
	5.00 Transitional	−0.707	0.455	0.721	−1.981	0.567
3.00 Social democratic (7.2440)	1.00 Continental Europe	1.104*	0.233	0.000	0.452	1.757
	2.00 LME	−4.362*	0.314	0.000	−5.242	−3.483
	4.00 South European	−1.241	0.471	0.082	−2.561	0.080
	5.00 Transitional	−5.070*	0.421	0.000	−6.250	−3.890
4.00 South European (8.4848)	1.00 Continental Europe	2.345*	0.455	0.000	1.069	3.621
	2.00 LME	−3.122*	0.501	0.000	−4.527	−1.717
	3.00 Social democratic	1.241	0.471	0.082	−0.080	2.561
	5.00 Transitional	−3.829*	0.574	0.000	−5.439	−2.219
5.00 Transitional (12.3137)	1.00 Continental Europe	6.174*	0.403	0.000	5.044	7.304
	2.00 LME	0.707	0.455	0.721	−0.567	1.981
	3.00 Social democratic	5.067*	0.421	0.000	3.890	6.250
	4.00 South European	3.829*	0.574	0.000	2.219	5.439

*The mean difference is significant at the 0.05 level.

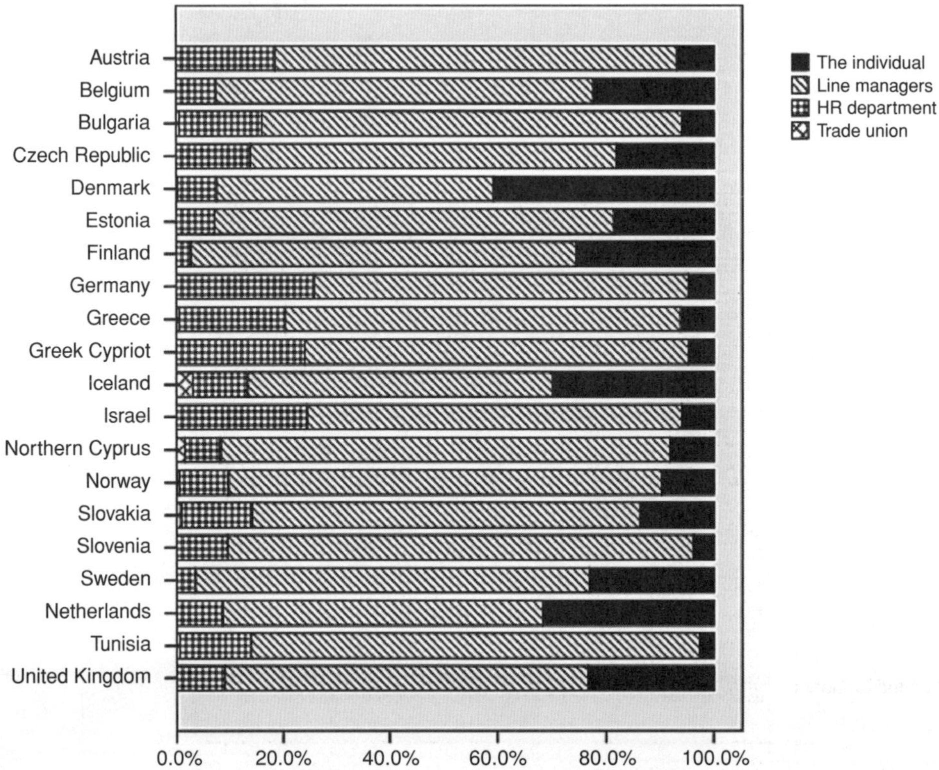

Exhibit 24.8 Main Influences on Defining Training Needs, 2003–2004

(Bredgaard, Larsen, and Madsen 2005). In contrast, the role of the individual is much smaller in Continental European economies such as Germany and Norway. This reflects both the closer links between industry-specific vocational training and industry needs and, more broadly speaking, the bargained nature of training provision in such contexts (Harcourt and Wood 2003). Iceland's exceptionalism is likely to be due to the relative degree of deregulation of its financial markets, and, more importantly, the high degree of internal diversity in its economy (e.g. the aluminum smelting industry versus the more traditional primary, fish processing and agriculture sectors).

The key characteristic of Southern European and transitional economies is that the role of HRM departments is relatively prominent. A case can be made for HRM departments to become more prominent in times of organizational crisis or transformation, given the linkage between high commitment and performance (Storey 2001; Martin 2006). A tradition of central managerial autocracy is hence likely to be diluted by the increased need for specialists to manage difficult transitions. Apart from a small percentage of companies in the Nordic social democratic countries and transitional economies, trade unions do not tend to be the main influence on defining training needs, reflecting the general trend toward more decentralized collective bargaining.

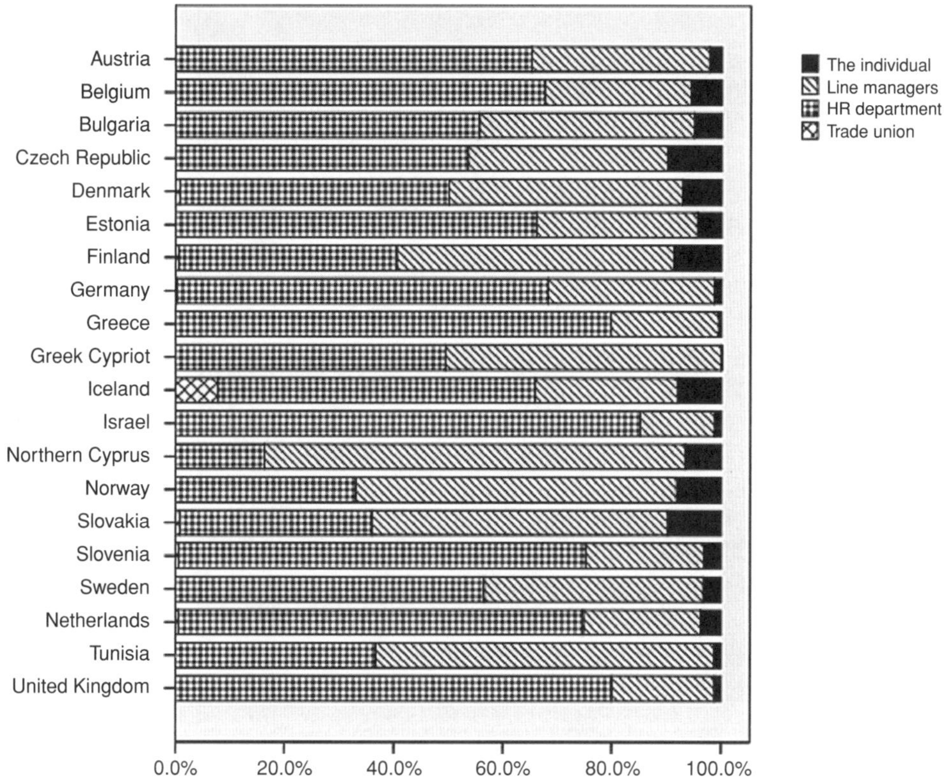

Exhibit 24.9 Main Influences on Designing Training Activities, 2003–2004

Exhibit 24.9 depicts the main influences in designing firm-sponsored and implemented training activities. Here a much more complex picture emerges. Across the board, the role of both individuals and unions is relatively weak with HRM or line managers dominating decision making in this area. Within social democratic and Continental European economies, centralized neo-corporatist deals may place some broader pressures on firms to take stronger account of the interests and well-being of employees (as opposed to immediate organizational needs) than would otherwise be the case (Kelly and Frege 2004; Turner 2004).

Considerable variation exists in the relative importance of the HRM department and the line manager, given differences as to whether the HRM department plays a more strategic or operational role. In the case of the former, line managers are typically entrusted to much more day-to-day responsibility for handling the implementation of HRM systems, leaving the specialist department freer to engage at the policy level (Goergen, Brewster, and Wood 2007). Trade unions are relatively unimportant as they are the main influence in only a small percentage of companies from some social democratic and Continental European countries, and some transitional economies.

Exhibit 24.10 summarizes the main influence on implementing training activities. A noticeable trend is the prominent role played by HRM departments in most transitional economies and in LMEs. Brewster et al. (2006) find that when

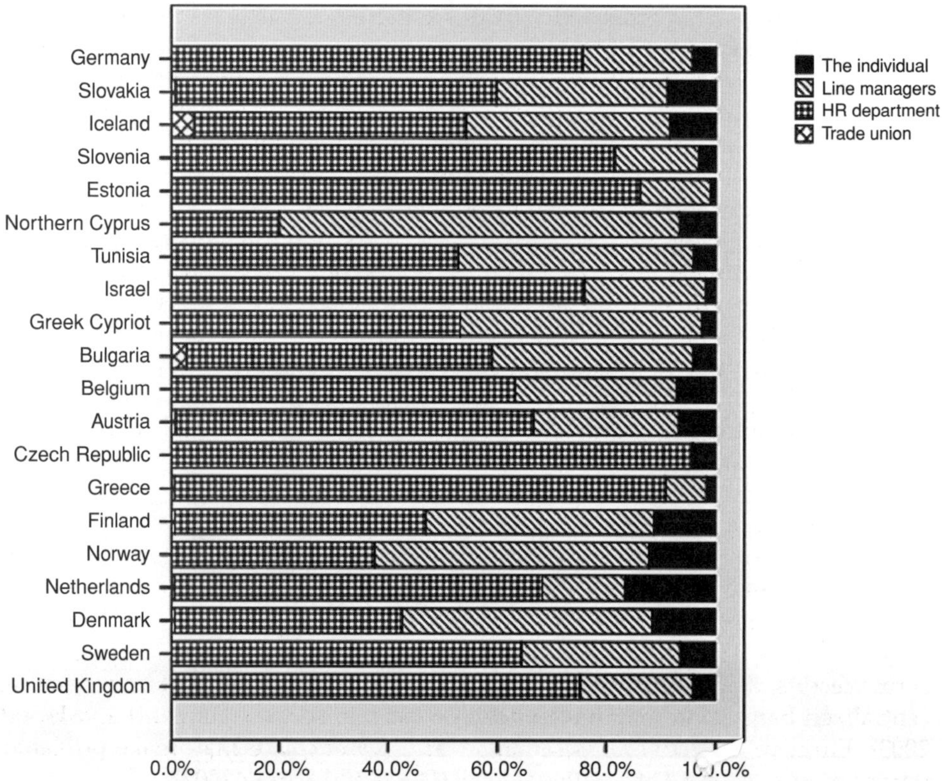

Exhibit 24.10 Main Influences on Implementing Training Activities, 2003–2004

employment relations are standardized through collective trade union–regulated contracts, HRM departments tend to be smaller. In contrast, they tend to be larger in situations, such as in the case of LMEs, when unions are weaker and individual contracts more common. Larger HRM departments are more likely to be encountered in organizations that have undergone substantial downsizing, which, in turn, is more likely to be the case in LMEs.

SUMMARY AND CONCLUSIONS

How does stakeholder power differ according to context? The survey findings indicate that national legal tradition is the strongest determinant of union power. Contrary to the predictions of the finance literature that unions would be strongest where owners are the weakest, the results show that unions within the Scandinavian and German legal traditions are stronger than those under French law. La Porta et al.'s (1997) index of shareholder protection and their later study on employee rights suggest that the converse should be the case (Botero et al. 2004).

This finding suggests that the relationship between owner and stakeholder rights is not strictly dichotomous. Rather, it may represent the product of the specific nature of employment law and the complementarities at work between this and actual firm practices. For example, if shareholder rights are weak, managers may have considerable autonomy in this regard but their freedom to act may be constrained or enhanced by the actions and interactions of other stakeholder groupings (e.g., civil society and industrial associations). Hence, in various civil law countries, employee rights are not that closely related to ownership protection. More broadly speaking, there is much more to national legal traditions than simple investor protection. The manner in which stakeholders seek to secure their rights is an open-ended process with real strategic choices open. That is, the results of such a process are not always predictable. The civil law systems category is a diverse one and the relative strength of owner rights in some contexts has proved compatible with cooperative industrial relations and strong unions (Jackson 2004).

Conversely, common law systems do not always work better for employers. Employee rights may be weaker but employment relations in such systems tend to be more litigious, imparting an element of uncertainty to the operationalization of the employment contract (Colvin 2006). Moreover, while weak on collective rights, common law systems often are associated with strong individual rights which may, when enforced, have a collective benefit (Wood, Harcourt, and Harcourt 2004).

The Pagano and Volpin (2005) model also appears to provide some useful insights. Greater investor power in majoritarian systems may enable companies to take a harder line against unions and external stakeholders generally. The evidence shows, however, that within national contexts, union power and influence vary across sectors, demonstrating that other factors also have an impact. For example, centralized bargaining may have uneven effects on sectors (Harcourt and Wood 2003). Effective collective representation at the workplace may make pro-labor parties more successful at a national level (D'Art and Turner 2007).

A somewhat weaker predictor is the Cusack and Engelhardt (2006) index of left- or right-wing government. While, as suggested by the literature, unions generally do worse under right-wing governments, this relationship does not appear to be a totally direct one. Centralized bargaining within specific sectors may, for example, better equip unions to withstand government hostility. Conversely, the decline of the union social democratic party relationship traditionally encountered in social democracies increases the difficulty of predicting that left-wing governments may be consistently union-friendly (McIlroy 1998; Valenzuela 2002). Additionally, different state traditions may result in a range of other external stakeholder groupings (e.g., community associations and employer organizations) having entrenched powers, limiting what governments can do (Turner 2004). This may explain why legal traditions are a stronger predictor of union strength. Still, concluding that when other stakeholders are more powerful, owners are worse off would be wrong. In Scandinavia, a tradition of consensus and compromise has made for sound economic performance for many years, a performance often superior to many liberal market economies (Arestis and Marshall 1995). This would suggest that understanding corporate governance is more than the relative strength of owner rights: Stakeholder relations may make for trade-offs and compromises in the better interests of a wider range of parties, owners included.

In looking at employee-employer interdependence and, more specifically patterns regarding the nature and extent of training, who promotes it, and job turnover rates, national variations are again apparent and clusters of countries emerge. In other words, there is no evidence of diffuse diversity. The patterns that emerge do not sit well with the predictions of the finance literature. Instead, fundamental differences emerge between the flexicurity/social democratic economies and the coordinated economies of Continental Europe. Mediterranean capitalism represents a complex phenomenon in its own right, reflecting differences in firm type, ownership, and distinct historical traditions (Amable 2003). Here, the evidence shows that Amable's multi-variety archetypes of capitalism (rooted with the socioeconomic tradition) provide the best explanation. Yet, the fit is not precise; differences that emerge reflect real institutional and ownership variations.

The findings reveal no linkage between weak stakeholder rights and strong economic performance. There appears to be much more to corporate governance than a zero-sum game, centering on investor rights. Rather, as suggested by the VOC literature, the possibility arises of complementarity in stakeholder rights with mutual gains. Where the VOC literature falls short is in the simplicity of analytical categories. The findings indicate that the dividing lines between VOCs are not as sharp as the existing literature suggests, and that much more diversity exists within national contexts.

DISCUSSION QUESTIONS

1. Are shareholder rights necessarily undermined if other stakeholders in the firm are given more voice? Explain why or why not.
2. What are the limitations of Hall and Soskice's (2001) two-archetype model to understanding differences in stakeholder rights in different contexts?
3. What are the limitations of the Cusack and Engelhardt (2006) index of left- or right-wing government in determining stakeholder rights?
4. Which theoretical framework provides the most convincing explanation for differences in stakeholder rights in different national contexts? Explain why.

REFERENCES

Amable, Bruno. 2003. *The diversity of modern capitalism*. Oxford: Oxford University Press.

Arestis, Philip, and Mike Marshall. 1995. Obstacles to and strategies for the achievement of full employment. In *The political economy of full employment: Conservatism, corporatism and institutional change*, ed. Philip Arestis and Mike Marshall, 1–25. Aldershot: Edward Elgar.

Botero, Juan C., Simeon Djankov, Rafael La Porta, Florencio Lopez-de-Silanes, and Andrei Shleifer. 2004. The regulation of labor. *Quarterly Journal of Economics* 119 (4): 1339–1382.

Boyer, Robert. 2006. How do institutions cohere and change. In *Institutions, Production and Working Life*, ed. Geoffrey Wood and Phil James, 13–61. Oxford: Oxford University Press.

Boyer, Robert, and J. Rogers Hollingsworth. 1997. From national embeddedness to spatial and institutional nestedness. In *Contemporary Capitalism: The Embeddedness of Institutions*, ed. J. Rogers Hollingsworth and Robert Boyer, 433–484. Cambridge and New York: Cambridge University Press.

Bredgaard, Thomas, Flemming Larsen, and Per K. Madsen. 2005. The flexible Danish labour market: A review. CARMA research paper, Aalborg University.

Brewster, Chris, Geoffrey Wood, Michael Brookes, and Jos van Ommeren. 2006. What determines the size of the HR function? A cross-national analysis. *Human Resource Management,* 45 (1): 3–21.

Checchi, Daniele, and Jelle Visser. 2005. Pattern persistence in European trade union density. *European Sociological Review* 21 (1): 1–21.

Chiu, Tom, Dong Ping Fang, John Chen, Yao Wang, and Christopher Jeris. 2001. A robust and scalable clustering algorithm for mixed type attributes in large database environment. *Proceedings of the 7th ACM SIGKDD International Conference on Knowledge Discovery and Data Mining,* 263–268.

Colvin, Alexander J. S. 2006. Flexibility and fairness in liberal market economies: The comparative impact of legal environment and high performance work systems. *British Journal of Industrial Relations* 44 (1): 73–97.

Crouch, Colin. 2005. Three meanings of complementarity. *Socio-Economic Review* 3 (2): 359–363.

Cusack, Thomas R., and Lutz Engelhardt. 2006. Parties, governments and legislatures data set. http://www.wz-berlin.de/mp/ism/people/misc/cusack/d_sets.en.htm#data.

D'Art, Daryl, and Thomas Turner. 2007. Trade unions and political participation in the European Union. *British Journal of Industrial Relations* 45 (1): 103–126.

Dibben, Pauline, Ian Roper, Philip James, and Geoffrey Wood (eds.). 2007. *Modernizing work and employment in public services.* London: Palgrave.

Djankov, Simeon, Edward L. Glaeser, Rafael La Porta, Florencio Lopez-de-Silanes, and Andrei Shleifer. 2003. The new comparative economics. *Journal of Comparative Economics* 31 (4): 595–619.

Dore, Ron. 2000. *Stock market capitalism: Welfare capitalism.* Cambridge: Cambridge University Press.

Ezzamel, Mahmoud, and Mike Reed. 2008. Governance: A code of multiple colours. *Human Relations* 61 (5): 597–615.

Goergen, Marc. 2007. What do we know about different systems of corporate governance? *Journal of Corporate Law Studies* 8 (1): 1–15.

Goergen, Marc, Chris Brewster, and Geoffrey Wood. 2007. Corporate governance regimes, investments in human capital and economic growth. Working paper, Management School, University of Sheffield.

———. 2009a. Corporate governance regimes and employment relations in Europe. *Industrial Relations/Relations Industrielles* 64 (4), 620-640.

———. 2009b. Corporate governance and training. *Journal of Industrial Relations* 51 (4): 461–489.

Gospel, Howard, and Andrew Pendleton. 2003. Finance, corporate governance and the management of labor: A conceptual and comparative analysis. *British Journal of Industrial Relations* 41 (3): 557–582.

——— (eds.). 2004. *Corporate governance and labor management: An international comparison.* Oxford: Oxford University Press.

Hall, Peter A., and Daniel W. Gingerich. 2004. Varieties of capitalism and institutional complementarities in the macroeconomy: An empirical analysis. MPIfG discussion paper 04/5.

Hall, Peter A., and David Soskice. 2001. An introduction to the varieties of capitalism. In *Varieties of capitalism: The institutional basis of competitive advantage,* ed. Peter A. Hall and David Soskice, 1–70. Oxford: Oxford University Press.

Harcourt, Mark, and Geoffrey Wood. 2003. Under what circumstances do social accords work? *Journal of Economic Issues* 37 (3): 747–767.

Höpner, Martin. 2005. What connects industrial relations and corporate governance? Explaining institutional complementarity. *Socio-Economic Review* 3 (2): 331–58.

Hyman, Richard. 2002. What is industrial relations. In *Industrial relations: Critical perspectives on business and management*, Volume 1, ed. John Kelly, 50–68. London: Routledge.
Jackson, Gregory. 2004. Toward a comparative perspective on corporate governance and labor management: Enterprise coalitions and national trajectories. In *Corporate governance and labor management: An international comparison*, ed. Howard Gospel and Andrew Pendleton, 284–309. Oxford: Oxford University Press.
Kelly, John. 1998. *Rethinking industrial relations: Mobilization, collectivism and long waves*. London: Routledge.
Kelly, John, and Carola M. Frege. 2004. Conclusions: Varieties of unionism. In *Varieties of unionism*, ed. John Kelly and Carola M. Frege, 181–196. Oxford: Oxford University Press.
Lane, Christel, and Geoffrey Wood. 2009. Capitalist diversity and diversity within capitalism. *Economy and Society* 38 (4), 531–551.
La Porta, Rafael, Florencio Lopez-de-Silanes, Andrei Shleifer, and Robert Vishny. 1997. Legal determinants of finance. *Journal of Finance* 52 (3): 1131–1150.
———. 1998. Law and finance. *Journal of Political Economy* 106 (6): 1113–1155.
———. 2000. Investor protection and corporate governance. *Journal of Financial Economics* 58 (1–2): 3–27.
Lincoln, James R., and Arne L. Kalleberg. 1990. *Culture, control and commitment: A study of work organization in the United States and Japan*. Cambridge: Cambridge University Press.
Martin, Graeme. 2006. *Managing people in organizations in changing contexts*. London: Butterworth-Heinemann.
McIlroy, John. 1998. The enduring alliance? Trade unions and the marking of new labor, 1994–1998. *British Journal of Industrial Relations* 36 (4): 537–564.
North, Douglass C. 1990. *Institutions, institutional change and economic performance*. Cambridge: Cambridge University Press.
Pagano, Marco, and Paolo Volpin. 2005. The political economy of corporate governance. *American Economic Review* 95 (4): 1005–1030.
Powell, Walter W., and Paul J. DiMaggio. 1991. *The new institutionalism in organizational analysis*. Chicago: University of Chicago Press.
Roe, Mark. 2003. *Political determinants of corporate governance*. Oxford: Oxford University Press.
Shleifer, Andrei, and Robert Vishny. 1997. A survey of corporate governance. *Journal of Finance* 52 (2): 737–783.
Storey, John. 2001. Looking to the future. In *Human resource management*, ed. John Storey, 364–367. London: Thomson Learning.
Turner, Lowell. 2004. Why revitalize? Labor's urgent mission in a contested global economy. In *Varieties of unionism*, ed. John Kelly and Carola M. Frege, 1–10. Oxford: Oxford University Press.
Valenzuela, Samuel J. 2002. Trade unions and political systems: Some variations. In *Industrial relations: Critical perspectives on business and management*, Volume 3, ed. John Kelly, 243–275. London: Routledge.
Western, Bruce. 1993. Postwar unionization in eighteen advanced capitalist countries. *American Sociological Review* 58 (2): 266–282.
Whitley, Richard. 1999. *Divergent capitalisms: The social structuring and change of business systems*. Oxford: Oxford University Press.
Wood, Geoffrey, Mark Harcourt, and Sondra Harcourt. 2004. The effects of age discrimination legislation on workplace practice. *Industrial Relations Journal* 35 (4): 359–371.

ACKNOWLEDGMENTS

Some of the arguments contained in this chapter are developed in Goergen et al. (2007, 2009a, and 2009b).

ABOUT THE AUTHORS

Marc Goergen holds a BA in economics from the Free University of Brussels; an MBA from Solvay Business School, Brussels; and a DPhil in economics from Oxford University. Professor Goergen holds a chair in finance at Cardiff Business School, Cardiff University. His previous appointments have been at UMIST, the University of Manchester, Reading University, and the University of Sheffield. Professor Goergen's research interests are in corporate finance, specifically initial public offerings, corporate governance, mergers and acquisitions, managerial compensation, private equity, and insider trading. His research has been published in various academic journals including *European Financial Management*, *Journal of Corporate Finance*, *Journal of Finance*, and *Journal of Law, Economics and Organization*. He is also a research associate of the European Corporate Governance Institute (www.ecgi.org).

Chris Brewster is a professor of international human resource management at Henley Business School, University of Reading, in the United Kingdom. Before becoming an academic, he worked for a trade union, a government department, in the construction and air transport industries as a human resources management (HRM) officer, and as a journalist and consultant on HRM. He has conducted extensive research in the field of international and comparative HRM, written or edited more than 20 books, and written or contributed to more than 100 articles. He has been awarded an honorary doctorate by the University of Vaasa and the Georges Pepitas prize for his contribution to international HRM by the practitioner body the World Federation of Personnel Management Associations.

Geoffrey Wood is a professor in human resource management in the School of Management at the University of Sheffield, and an overseas associate of the University of Witwatersrand, South Africa. He has authored, co-authored, or edited seven books and more than 100 hundred articles in peer-reviewed journals including journals. Examples of these journals include *Work and Occupations*; *Work, Employment and Society*; *Organization Studies*; *International Journal of Human Resource Management*; *British Journal of Industrial Relations*; *Review of Radical Political Economics*; *Journal of Economic Issues*; *Labor Studies Journal*; and *Human Resource Management*. He has received numerous research grants from funding councils, government departments (e.g., U.S. Department of Labor), charities (e.g., Nuffield Foundation), and the labor movement (e.g., the International Transport Workers Federation). Professor Wood's current research interests center on the systematic testing and development of contemporary institutional theory in the light of large-scale survey evidence.

CHAPTER 25

Proxy Contests

PETER G. SZILAGYI
Lecturer in Finance, Judge Business School, University of Cambridge

INTRODUCTION

While proxy contests are a formidable tool of shareholder activism and traditionally attract much media interest, their relevance in corporate governance as a disciplinary mechanism has been subject to much debate. In principle, proxy contests offer shareholders a valuable alternative to takeovers for removing the incumbent board and management as they do not require costly share acquisitions and cannot be blocked using antitakeover devices. Nonetheless, they remained relatively rare throughout the 1980s and 1990s, even as a wave of antitakeover laws and charter amendments rendered firms very well-protected against hostile takeovers. With the rise of hedge funds and technological advances, proxy contests finally staged a remarkable comeback in the 2000s. Georgeson (2009a) reports that the number of contested solicitations doubled between 2005 and 2008, with high-profile campaigns such as those against H. J. Heinz, Time Warner, and Yahoo! regularly dominating the headlines.

This chapter reviews the role and effectiveness of proxy contests as a corporate governance mechanism, discussing past academic research as well as recent and imminent developments. Manne (1965) argues that while proxy contests are certainly dramatic and well-publicized corporate events, they tend to both be prohibitively costly for dissident shareholders and have limited success. Pound (1988) attributes this to management's unfair advantage in proxy solicitation, asymmetric information about dissident quality, and inefficient or conflicted voting by the voting shareholders. According to Bebchuk and Hart (2002), the biggest challenge faced by dissidents is the need to persuade other shareholders that their victory would be beneficial. The empirical governance literature gives little evidence that other shareholders do benefit. Unless subsequently sold, target firms typically underperform their peers both before and after proxy interventions (Ikenberry and Lakonishok 1993; Mulherin and Poulsen 1998).

The proxy contests of the 2000s nonetheless appear to be both different and more effective than their predecessors. While interventions used to be waged by individual dissidents, including former managers seeking board control, interventions are now dominated by hedge funds pursuing governance arbitrage using innovative campaign strategies. According to Genkin (2008), hedge funds have also enjoyed the support of independent proxy advisory firms and won two-thirds of their proxy contests since 2001. Whether this latest wave of interventions will be sustained in the long run depends primarily on changes under way in the corporate governance environment, and especially on the new voting and proxy access rules proposed by the Securities and Exchange Commission (SEC) in response to the financial crisis. While these new rules are specifically designed to empower shareholders, they may ultimately make formal proxy contests largely redundant as a means to contest director elections.

The remainder of this chapter is set out as follows. The next section describes the mechanics of proxy contests and discusses the inefficiencies of the proxy system. This is followed by an overview of the empirical literature, which covers contests waged between the 1950s and the 1990s. Next discussed is the current wave of proxy interventions with a detailed overview of recent or imminent changes in voting and proxy access rules. The final section offers some concluding remarks.

THE MECHANICS OF PROXY CONTESTS

Dodd and Warner (1983) describe proxy contests, also known as proxy fights or proxy battles, as dramatic corporate events occurring when a "dissident" or "insurgent" shareholder attempts to obtain seats on the board of directors by soliciting other shareholders' proxy votes. The dissident, which may be another firm, an institutional investor, or an individual, including a former manager or director, typically claims that incumbent management is ineffective and does not maximize firm value. A proxy intervention achieves a wholesale change in corporate governance by changing the board itself, which is the highest authority in the firm and holds the power to appoint and remove managers. As such, proxy contests have traditionally been viewed as a useful alternative to takeovers in the market for corporate control, which provides the means to oust incumbent management without costly share acquisitions.

Not formally defined in federal law, proxy contests actually include solicitations against incumbent management over any particular corporate issue, provided that the dissident distributes its own proxy statement to shareholders rather than place a shareholder proposal in the firm's proxy materials. Nonetheless, most proxy contests do occur over directorships because the SEC does not allow shareholder access to the firm's proxy for the purpose of director nominations. Manne (1965) compares the process of proxy solicitation to a political campaign. The dissident sends a formal notice to management about its intention to solicit shareholder proxies, and both parties distribute their own proxy materials, also filed with the SEC, to the voting shareholders. The dissident and management then both embark on a publicity campaign, often complete with advertising and the use of professional proxy solicitors such as Georgeson, Innisfree M&A, or MacKenzie Partners. Shareholders can vote their shares by signing and returning the proxy card of the preferred party; Internet and telephone voting are now also permitted. Unless settled or withdrawn, the contest typically culminates at the firm's annual meeting because shareholders are not allowed to call special meetings or act by written consent unless the firm's charter or bylaws state otherwise.

Whether dissidents can successfully contest board seats largely depends on the firm's voting rule in place for director elections. Many firms use simple plurality to elect directors, whereby shareholders either vote to affirm or withhold their vote to reject each director nominee, and the available directorships are simply granted to the nominees who have received the most votes. Under this scheme, the dissident is likely to need a voting majority to win, but this is not necessarily the case. The two alternative voting rules are cumulative voting and actual majority voting. Cumulative voting maintains plurality, but shareholders get votes equal to the number of their shares multiplied by the available directorships, which can then be cast in any way across nominees, including on a single nominee. Cumulative voting helps minority interests elect at least some nominees of their own but is permitted by few firms. The majority voting rule formally prescribes that nominees must receive the majority of the total votes, and therefore presents the greatest challenge to dissidents in contested elections. Nonetheless, this scheme has been gaining wide acceptance in recent years because in the absence of an alternative slate of director nominees, it helps shareholders prevent incumbent nominees from being elected.

Inefficiencies of the Proxy System

While proxy contests are a traditional form of shareholder voice, Pound (1988) finds that due to various inefficiencies of the proxy system, shareholders have historically used them as a last resort. A first problem is that dissidents are at an unfair disadvantage to management in distributing proxy materials to and soliciting the votes of shareholders, the costs of which can run into millions of dollars. To facilitate the solicitation process, the SEC allowed shareholders to directly communicate with each other in 1992. Moreover, it adopted an e-proxy rule in 2006, which provides that rather than sending out paper copies, dissidents can post and notify shareholders of their proxy materials over the Internet using a *notice and access* system. Nonetheless, incumbent management is inevitably better equipped in maintaining shareholder lists, soliciting votes, and building relationships with uninformed shareholders. This is most apparent in large firms with dispersed ownership and high stock turnover, with shareholder registration laws already increasing the difficulty of determining who possesses the right to vote at any time. Dissidents are also at a great disadvantage when they seek to counter-solicit against managerial initiatives, because the time available for counter solicitation is set by management under state law and can be as short as 10 days.

A second problem is that dissidents must actually convince shareholders that their victory would be beneficial, which requires the use of costly signaling strategies. Dissidents can have legitimate reasons to contest board seats such as when they seek a takeover, management is protected by antitakeover devices, or they pursue specific operational or policy changes that would enhance shareholder value. However, dissidents may simply have self-serving agendas or a lack of confidence in their own capabilities, and thus may be reluctant to make the wealth commitment a takeover demands. According to Pound (1988) and Bebchuk and Hart (2002), high-quality dissidents can only separate themselves from low-quality ones by acquiring greater wealth exposure to the value of the firm; that is, by increasing their equity stake or launching a tender offer contingent on the contest outcome. These signaling strategies indeed make sense for potential bidders who can thereby take control of the board to remove antitakeover devices, use the proxy contest as a preliminary vote on a takeover bid, and possibly reduce the takeover premium they would otherwise have to pay. Other than that, the signaling cost represented by the wealth commitment is likely to diminish any comparative advantages a proxy contest would have as an alternative to a takeover bid.

A final problem with the proxy system is that small, fragmented shareholders tend to view themselves as inefficient monitors and so have little incentive to make informed voting decisions. Therefore, no matter how well dissidents try to signal their quality, the votes of these shareholders mostly end up supporting incumbent management if only due to the fact that brokers tend to vote uninstructed voting positions in management's favor. Pound (1988) argues that ultimately, the marginal voters in proxy contests tend to be institutional investors and large blockholders. However, these informed investors can also fail to support dissidents. McCahery, Sautner, and Starks (2009) find that institutional investors often abstain from voting and sell their shares rather than actively participate. Moreover, the voting decisions of both institutional investors and large blockholders may be driven by conflict-of-interest motivations. Blockholders can have strategic alliances with incumbent management, in which case they are unlikely to back a proxy contest. According to Brickley, Lease, and Smith (1988), institutional investors such as insurance companies and banks' trust departments are also pressure-sensitive due to their existing or potential business relationships with the firms in which they invest. Pound (1988) concludes that proxy contests are most likely to succeed when the marginal voters are pressure-insensitive institutional investors such as pension funds, investment funds, and independent investment advisers. Nonetheless, these investors are also not immune to concerns of conflicted voting, which prompted the SEC's mutual fund proxy vote disclosure rule in 2003 (Cremers and Romano 2007).

EMPIRICAL EVIDENCE ON PROXY CONTESTS

Despite the inefficiencies of the proxy system, proxy contests received considerable attention in the 1980s and 1990s as an alternative to takeovers in replacing inefficient management. This was bolstered by the fact that after a series of antitakeover laws and charter amendments following the 1980s hostile takeover wave, most firms became very well protected against takeover threat (Danielson and Karpoff 1998; Becht, Bolton, and Röell 2003). Indeed, by 1990, the 1,500 firms tracked by the proxy advisory firm RiskMetrics used an average 9 of the 24 antitakeover devices included in Gompers, Ishii, and Metrick's (2003) Governance Index, and two of the six most important provisions included in Bebchuk, Cohen, and Ferrell's (2009) Entrenchment Index—poison pills, classified boards, golden parachutes, limits to both bylaw and charter amendments, and supermajority provisions for mergers. Exhibit 25.1 shows that since the early 1990s, the use of poison pills and classified boards has remained largely unchanged at around 51 percent and 57 percent of firms, respectively, but the use of golden parachutes has continued to increase from 50 percent of firms in 1990 to 78 percent in 2006.

Whether proxy contests became more relevant after the late 1980s in the market for corporate control is strongly debatable. Exhibit 25.2 shows the number of contested solicitations, hostile takeovers, and nonhostile but unsolicited takeovers launched between 1981 and 2008. The data suggest that until the late 1990s hostile takeover activity and proxy contests actually exhibited similar cyclical patterns, falling dramatically after 1988 and recovering somewhat for the mid-1990s. In the

This figure summarizes the use of the six antitakeover devices included in Bebchuk, Cohen, and Ferrell's (2009) Entrenchment Index between 1990 and 2006. The left axis depicts the percentage of firms using each device. The right axis depicts the average number of devices used.

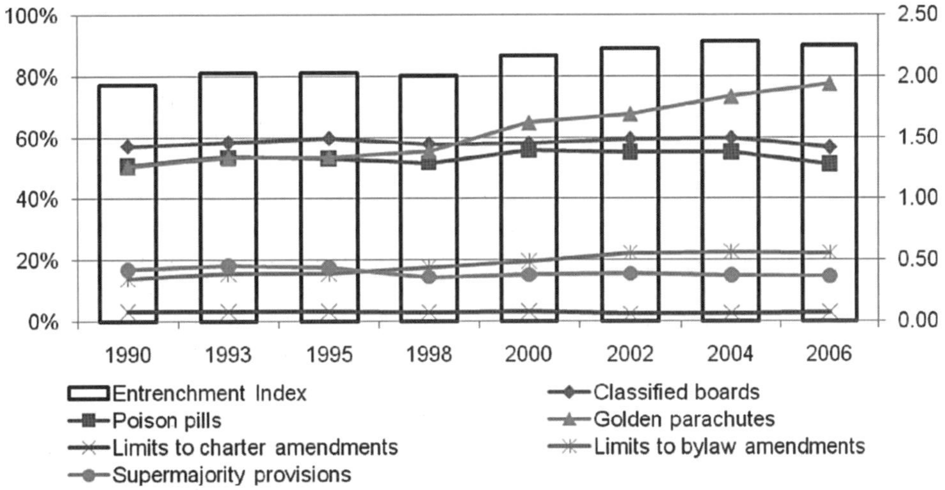

Exhibit 25.1 The Use of Antitakeover Devices
Source: RiskMetrics.

2000s, the number of proxy contests finally took off, more than doubling between 2005 and 2008. However, as discussed later in this chapter, this latest wave of proxy interventions is very different from previous ones.

Unfortunately, the corporate governance literature has yet to examine the 2000s wave of proxy contests and therefore provides a fairly dated account of the role of proxy interventions in corporate governance. The remainder of this section summarizes the main results of the literature so far, which focuses on proxy contests for board seats exclusively. Duvall and Austin (1965) provide the first empirical analysis of 65 contests initiated between 1956 and 1960. This is followed by the 1980s studies of Dodd and Warner (1983) on 96 contests in 1962–1978; DeAngelo (1988) on 86 contests in 1970–1983; DeAngelo and DeAngelo (1989) on 60 contests

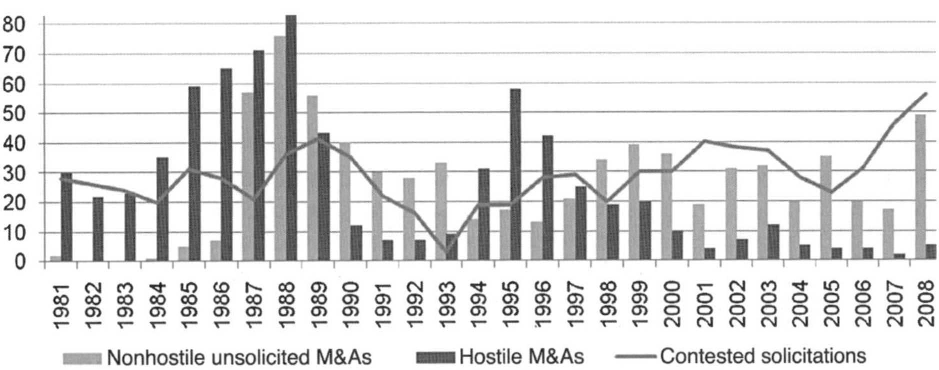

Exhibit 25.2 The Market for Corporate Control in 1981–2008
Source: Thomson ONE Banker; Georgeson.

in 1978–1985; and Pound (1988) on 66 contests in 1981–1985. The 1990s literature includes Borstadt and Zwirlein (1992) on 142 contests in 1962–1986; Ikenberry and Lakonishok (1993) on 97 contests in 1968–1987; and Mulherin and Poulsen (1998) on 270 contests in 1979–1994. Faleye (2004) provides the only major empirical study of the 2000s, examining 98 contests launched between 1988 and 2000.

The Dissidents

Highlighting a key difference between proxy contests and takeover bids, Dodd and Warner (1983) as well as DeAngelo and DeAngelo (1989) report that around 80 percent of proxy interventions are launched by individual investors rather than corporate entities. Dodd and Warner find that 42 percent of dissidents are shareholder groups led by former managers or directors, mostly initiating control contests for majority control of the board. DeAngelo and DeAngelo detect less involvement by former incumbents, noting that while 50 percent of dissident leaders have prior experience in the target's line of business, only 17 percent are former managers or directors. Nonetheless, the evidence shows that proxy contests can be linked to competition in the managerial labor market. At the same time, dissidents often appear to possess managerial or technological expertise specific to the target firm. However, they are either unable or unwilling to launch a formal takeover bid due to personal wealth constraints, the target's use of antitakeover devices, informational asymmetries, or other considerations.

According to DeAngelo and DeAngelo (1989), the reason rival firms rarely use proxy contests is that they prefer to make takeover bids unless they are prevented from doing so. The authors suggest that dissident firms are typically motivated by capacity constraints rather than antitakeover devices that prohibit a formal takeover bid. First, dissident firms are, on average, half the size of their targets in terms of equity value, whereas takeover bidders tend to be considerably larger. Second, dissident firms tend to have fairly concentrated ownership structures, which they are presumably reluctant to dilute with an equity tender offer.

Several studies nonetheless confirm that dissidents tend to make a reasonably significant wealth commitment to proxy contests and thus appear to have strong economic incentives to remove incumbent management. On one hand, the average size of dissident ownership ranges from 12.0 percent in Pound (1988) to 15.5 percent in Borstadt and Zwirlein (1992). On the other hand, Mulherin and Poulsen (1998) note that 43 percent of proxy contests are accompanied by a formal takeover bid contingent on victory.

The Targets

When embarking on a proxy campaign, dissidents tend to compile multiple facts that collectively raise concerns about the quality and competence of the incumbent board and management. Unsurprisingly, the main area of criticism is the firm's operating performance, measured through simple accounting-based indicators such as earnings or return on equity. DeAngelo and DeAngelo (1989) find that poor performance is cited in 68 percent of proxy contests, followed by an outright recommendation to sell the firm in 47 percent. These arguments still dominate in Faleye (2004), but they are used somewhat less, by 53 percent and 21 percent of dissidents, respectively. In both studies, around a quarter of dissidents seek some sort of restructuring such as divestitures, acquisitions, or changes to divisional operations or product lines. The firm's financial and payout policy is also targeted in 28 percent and 14 percent of proxy contests, respectively. Finally, DeAngelo and DeAngelo observe that most dissidents criticize management's competence and integrity, mostly with reference to its use of antitakeover devices and excessive compensation.

The empirical literature confirms that firms involved in proxy contests are performing poorly. Duvall and Austin (1965) and DeAngelo (1988) find that their return on equity is below market average, while Ikenberry and Lakonishok (1993) show that in the five years up to being targeted, firms underperform their size and industry peers in the growth of sales, operating income, net income, and cash flow, as well as dividends. Surprisingly, there is no evidence that proxy contests are launched after prolonged periods of poor stock price performance. Dodd and Warner (1983) and DeAngelo (1988) find insignificantly positive abnormal stock returns up to two years before dissident activity. Moreover, the literature does not examine whether poor operating performance is caused by generally poor governance structures such as inefficient boards or entrenched managers. Ikenberry and Lakonishok (1993) as well as Mulherin and Poulsen (1998) find that classified boards and poison pills are used by 31 percent and 39 percent of proxy contest targets respectively, but neither study draws comparisons with either nontarget firms or firms targeted by hostile takeover bids. Given the statistics in Exhibit 25.2, insufficient evidence exists to conclude that dissidents wage proxy interventions when poor governance quality demands a change in control.

Faleye (2004) is the first to analyze the target selection process in a multivariate setting, using logistic regressions and a control group of size and industry peers. The author does not consider target selection in proxy contests versus takeovers or analyze the influence of operating performance or governance quality. Nonetheless, he makes two important contributions to the literature. First, the probability of a proxy intervention decreases in managerial ownership and increases in outside block ownership. This implies that before deciding on a contest, dissidents study the potential outcome by examining the voting shareholders. Second, firms targeted by proxy contests hold 23 percent more cash than do comparable firms, and the probability of a contest significantly increases in excess cash holdings. This may indicate that proxy interventions are motivated by free cash flow concerns. According to Faleye (2004), however, this evidence shows that target firms tend to have entrenched managers protected from hostile takeover threat because they can use cash holdings to fend off hostile bids by repurchasing shares, acquiring a competitor, or acquiring the bidder itself (Stulz 1988; Dann and DeAngelo 1988; Bagwell 1991; Heron and Lie 2006).

The Success of Proxy Contests

Exhibit 25.3 summarizes the literature's findings on the success of proxy contests. The table partitions contest outcomes by type and shows that about two-thirds of proxy contests waged for board seats are *control contests* where the dissident seeks majority control of the board, and one-third are *participation contests* for minority board representation.

Exhibit 25.3 Proxy Contest Outcomes

		All			Control Contests			Representation Contests	
Study	**Sample Period**	**N**	**Dissidents Win Majority**	**Dissidents Win Seats**	**N**	**Dissidents Win Majority**	**Dissidents Win Seats**	**N**	**Dissidents Win Seats**
Duvall and Austin (1965)	1956–1960	64			45	15		19	9
Dodd and Warner (1983)	1962–1978	96	18	56	71	18	45	25	11
DeAngelo (1988)	1970–1983	86	24	28					
DeAngelo and DeAngelo (1989)	1978–1985	60	21	16					
Pound (1988)	1981–1985	66			42	17		22	17
Borstadt and Zwirlein (1992)	1962–1986	142			95	32		47	28
Ikenberry and Lakonishok (1993)	1968–1987	97	27	22					
Mulherin and Poulsen (1998)	1979–1994	270		140	184			86	
Faleye (2004)	1988–2000	98							

The data show that proxy contests tend to succeed in securing board representation for the dissident, with 44 to 77 percent of both control and participation contests winning at least one directorship. Yet only 25 to 40 percent of control contests achieve their actual objective of taking full control of the board. Pound (1988) attributes this to the fact that control contests carry relatively high ex post risk to the voting shareholders. In his view, shareholders are comfortable giving minority representation to dissidents because they view them as useful monitors, but shareholders are reluctant to give dissidents full control due to concerns over substantial changes in corporate policies. Nonetheless, Ikenberry and Lakonishok (1993) show that even participation contests are often won simply because the target firm allows cumulative voting, with dissidents winning 72 percent of contests under cumulative voting but only 41 percent under the simple plurality scheme.

The empirical evidence suggests that multiple factors drive contest success. Duvall and Austin (1965) demonstrate the relevance of the target firm's operating performance, showing that dissidents are more likely to win against firms that underperform in terms of return on equity, profit margin, and dividend payout. Accordingly, DeAngelo (1988) finds that managers often manipulate earnings during proxy campaigns, typically reporting an unexpected accrual of some 2 percent of total assets without a corresponding increase in operating cash flow.

Pound (1988) confirms that the success of a proxy contest also depends on the dissident's wealth commitment, with dissidents more likely to win when they hold considerable equity as well as when they make a simultaneous tender offer. The dissident's equity holding not only serves as a signal to the voting shareholders but also provides the dissident with actual voting rights. Pound finds that the identity of the voting shareholders is also important but that contest success decreases in cases of ownership by both institutional investors and outside blockholders. The author offers two explanations for this. On the one hand, these informed investors may vote strategically rather than make informed voting decisions, as per the conflict-of-interest motivations discussed earlier. On the other, their presence as owners and efficient monitors may simply render proxy interventions unnecessary such that the contests that are launched are likely to be crank bids or otherwise redundant in disciplining management.

Pound (1988) finally shows that management's comparative advantage in proxy solicitation has a nontrivial impact on contest success. On the one hand, the probability of the dissident winning is negatively related to the number of the firm's shareholders, an appropriate measure of proxy solicitation costs. On the other, contest success is positively related to the length of time between the contest's initiation and the shareholder vote, which is the time the dissident's proxy solicitor has to contact and lobby shareholders.

Corporate Changes after Proxy Contests

Shleifer and Vishny (1986) argue that given their limited success in assuring board control, proxy contests are unlikely to be effective in exerting discipline from a corporate governance perspective. However, the empirical literature often observes major changes in corporate control even after contests that are deemed unsuccessful. Dodd and Warner (1983) and Borstadt and Zwirlein (1992) attribute this to the fact that dissidents winning minority representation on the board already earn some influence. Moreover, the fact that a contest has occurred is likely to prompt both shareholders and the market to closely monitor management in order to determine whether a change in control is in fact warranted.

Indeed, DeAngelo and DeAngelo (1989) report that while incumbent managers have a 57 percent survival rate immediately after a proxy contest, only 28 percent stay on after one year and 18 percent after three years. The authors find that 28 percent of firms are sold and 3 percent are liquidated either during the proxy campaign or shortly thereafter. Interestingly, these events mostly occur when the dissident has won a minority of the board seats, which shows that the dissident can still force the sale or liquidation of the firm when it is valuable to do so. The authors observe resignations in top management after more than half of those interventions that have not achieved board control.

Other studies similarly find that once a dissident challenge materializes, it imposes a much greater threat to incumbent management than is implied by its immediate success. Borstadt and Zwirlein (1992) report a control change after 71 percent of proxy contests with 22 percent being management resignations without the dissident taking control or the firm being sold. Ikenberry and Lakonishok (1993) find management turnover within two years after 58 percent of contests in which the dissident has won a minority of the board seats and 24 percent of contests in which the dissident has won no board seats at all. More recently, Mulherin and Poulsen (1998) observe that 23 percent of firms are sold during or shortly after a proxy contest, with 59 percent of the remaining firms seeing management resignations within three years and 42 percent also being subjected to restructuring or liquidation.

Few studies examine the post-contest operating performance of target firms. DeAngelo (1988) shows that proxy contests that win majority board control are often followed by an earnings bath, whereby new management reduces earnings via discretionary noncash write-offs. The author observes that 64 percent of firms with a control change have major write-offs such as asset writedowns and gains or losses from discontinued operations, whereas their unexpected cash flows are positive and significantly different from zero. This evidence suggests that these firms experience an immediate increase in profitability but they do not report it initially so that management can deliver an improvement later.

Ikenberry and Lakonishok (1993) investigate how firms perform in the five years after being involved in a proxy contest. After a failed intervention, firms go on to perform in line with their size and industry peers. This is unsurprising to the extent that if management has previously underperformed, the threat of another hostile attempt is likely to exert discipline. Strikingly, Ikenberry and Lakonishok find that when the dissident has won one or more board seats, firms continue to perform disappointingly across a variety of performance measures. This underperformance is particularly pronounced for firms in which the dissident has won minority board representation. For example, these firms deliver 32 percent less growth in net sales, 99 percent less in cash flow, 79 percent less in operating income, and 73 percent less in dividends compared to their size and industry peers. The authors find that these results cannot be explained by asset restructuring or downsizing and are otherwise in line with Collins and DeAngelo's (1990) observation that security analysts provide overly optimistic earnings estimates for these firms. The finding that firms continue to underperform after a successful proxy contest remains unchallenged by the more recent literature.

The Stock Price Effects of Proxy Contests

Exhibit 25.4 summarizes the empirical evidence on the stock price effects of proxy contests. The table shows the abnormal stock returns reported in the literature around contest announcements, during proxy campaigns, during proxy contests as a whole from announcement to resolution, and after the conclusion of contests.

According to Exhibit 25.4, the market generally responds favorably to contest announcements, which suggests that it attributes nontrivial control benefits to proxy interventions. The announcement period abnormal returns are always positive and significant at the 0.01 level, ranging from 18.8 percent in DeAngelo and DeAngelo (1989) to 5.2 percent in Faleye (2004). The size of the returns is largely a function of the event window used because substantial dissident activity often precedes formal announcements. There is some evidence that proxy campaigns induce negative abnormal returns, which are significant in Dodd and Warner (1983) and insignificant in Mulherin and Poulsen (1998). Nonetheless, the returns remain positive and mostly significant at the 0.01 level for contests as a whole from announcement to resolution. This implies that the market already anticipates the contest outcome and is largely unaffected by new information disclosed during the campaign.

Exhibit 25.4 reveals interesting variations in the market reactions by partitioning the abnormal returns by contest characteristics. Dodd and Warner (1983) find that the market receives control contests more favorably than participation contests upon their announcement, with the positive abnormal returns only significant for control contests in the [−60, 0] time window. While the returns are significant for both control and participation contests for the full contest period, they remain higher for control contests at 8.8 percent and 6.3 percent, respectively.

Dodd and Warner (1983), DeAngelo and DeAngelo (1989), and Mulherin and Poulsen (1998) provide evidence that the market anticipates the correct contest outcome. All three studies find that the announcement period abnormal returns are higher for contests that later win board representation. Surprisingly, this result does not always hold post-campaign. DeAngelo and DeAngelo find that for contests as a whole, the returns are only significantly positive for those achieving a minority of the board seats. Meanwhile, Ikenberry and Lakonishok (1993) only report significant price effects for unsuccessful interventions. These results presumably suggest that proxy campaigns can reveal negative information about dissidents seeking full board control. Nonetheless, Ikenberry and Lakonishok's findings are curious because their sample period overlaps with those of the other studies.

Finally, DeAngelo and DeAngelo (1989) and Mulherin and Poulsen (1998) find that the market responds more favorably to contests followed by the sale of the target firm or accompanied by a tender offer. This implies that the positive abnormal returns at least in part reflect an anticipated takeover premium. Renneboog and Szilagyi (2009) also report similar results for shareholder-initiated proxy proposals targeting antitakeover devices.

Exhibit 25.4 Stock Price Effects of Proxy Contests

Study	Sample Period		N	Announcement	Post-Announcement	Full Contest Period	Post-Contest Period
Dodd and Warner (1983)	1962–1978	All	96	11.9***	−4.3***	8.2***	
		Control contests	71	14.2***	−5.5***	8.8**	
		Participation contests	25	5.2	−0.0	6.3	
		Dissidents win seats	56	14.1***	−5.9**	8.1**	
		Dissidents do not win seats	40	8.6**	−1.8	8.2	
				(−60,0)	*(+1,resolution)*	*(−60,resolution)*	
DeAngelo and DeAngelo (1989)	1978–1985	All	60	4.85***		6.0***	
		Dissidents win majority	21	6.5***		9.5	
		Dissidents win seats	16	4.0***		30.1***	
		Dissidents do not win seats	23	3.9***		−14.8	
				(−1,0)		*(−40,resolution)*	
		All	60	18.8***		6.0***	
		Target is acquired	15	22.4***		15.2***	
		Target is not acquired	45	17.6***		2.9**	
				(−40,0)		*(−40,resolution)*	
Borstadt and Zwirlein (1992)	1962–1986	All	142			11.4***	−7.4
		Dissidents win majority	32			7.8**	−22.8**
		Dissidents do not win majority					
		Subsequent takeover	34			7.8***	17.2**
		No subsequent takeover	71			13.1***	−5.9
						(−60,resolution)	*(24 months)*

Ikenberry and Lakonishok (1993)	1968–1987	All	95			4.3**	−17.2**
		Dissidents win seats	50			3.4	−28.6***
		Management turnover	29			4.2	−20.3
		No management turnover	21			2.4	−40.1***
		Dissidents do not win seats	45			5.2**	−3.9
		Management turnover	11			1.6	−4.4
		No management turnover	34			6.4	−4.2
						(month 0)	*(months 5 to 24)*
Mulherin and Poulsen (1998)	1979–1994	All	270	7.4***	−4.7	2.9***	−4.8*
		Contests with a takeover bid	116	9.9***	−1.4	8.7***	−4.7
		Target is acquired	63	13.5***	6.65***	20.1***	12.4*
		Target is not acquired	53	5.7***	−10.8**	−4.8	−23.7***
		Contests without a takeover bid	154	7.3***	−4.1	3.3***	0.5
		Dissidents win seats	85	8.0***	−3.2	4.9***	−1.7
		Management turnover	68	7.6***	1.9	9.6***	2.6
		No management turnover	17	9.4**	−24.6***	−13.8	−18.5**
		Dissidents do not win seats	69	6.4***	−5.1	1.3	3.3
		Management turnover	25	9.1**	−4.0	5.1	31.3***
		No management turnover	44	4.9**	−5.8	−0.9	−12.7
				(−20,5)	*(6,resolution)*	*(−20,resolution)*	*(1 year)*
Faleye (2004)	1988–2000	All	98	5.2***			
				(−1.1)			

*, **, and *** denote significance at the 0.10, 0.05, and 0.01 level, respectively.

Only a few studies analyze the post-contest stock price performance of target firms. Remarkably, the results show that despite the initial optimism, firms significantly underperform the market in the two years following a proxy contest. Borstadt and Zwirlein (1992) as well as Ikenberry and Lakonishok (1993) find that this underperformance is most pronounced when the dissident has taken full control of the board. Meanwhile, Mulherin and Poulsen (1998) report negative abnormal returns when the contest was not accompanied by a tender offer and incumbent management has not been replaced. These results correspond to Ikenberry and Lakonishok's observation that after successful control contests, firms deliver poor operating performance in the five years after being targeted. Overall, these results seriously question the effectiveness of proxy contests as a disciplinary device in the market for corporate control.

Mulherin and Poulsen (1998) provide further evidence that the positive announcement period stock price effects are partly driven by a future takeover premium anticipated by the market. The authors find that after contests accompanied by a tender offer, acquired firms deliver further abnormal price gains, whereas those not acquired do not experience a major abnormal loss. Borstadt and Zwirlein (1992) report similar results with the abnormal returns positive in the event of a takeover and insignificantly negative otherwise. These findings suggest that rather than attributing superior management qualities to dissidents, the market simply views them as a means to facilitate the sale of underperforming firms.

THE CURRENT ROLE OF PROXY CONTESTS IN CORPORATE GOVERNANCE

Recent Trends in Proxy Contests

While the academic literature provides empirical evidence on the corporate governance role of proxy contests in the 1970s and 1980s, much of this evidence is now probably outdated. As Exhibit 25.2 shows, proxy contests have gained much economic importance over the past decade. In 1998, TIAA-CREF became the first pension fund to win a contest over board control, demonstrating the growing power of institutional activists (Goodman, Olson, and Fontenot 2009). Since then, proxy interventions have staged a major surge, with Georgeson (2009a) reporting a more than twofold increase in the number of contested solicitations between 2005 and 2008. Several high-profile cases have also received substantial media coverage, such as Trian Fund Management's intervention at H. J. Heinz, or the billionaire Carl Icahn's campaigns against Motorola, Time Warner, and Yahoo!

The most recent rise in proxy contests is widely attributed to two key factors. First, due to technological advances, dissidents can now more easily and cheaply start and publicly communicate proxy contests. The Internet has been particularly instrumental in disseminating information, getting more shareholders involved, and increasing general awareness about shareholder rights (Knowledge@Wharton 2008). As an example, Gordon (2008) finds that the SEC's e-proxy rule alone has allowed dissidents to cut the costs of distributing proxy materials by more than 90 percent. Second, the growth and proliferation of hedge funds have made them formidable players in proxy interventions in recent years, with their controversial activist strategies already receiving much attention in the media and the academic literature (Brav, Jiang, Partnoy, and Thomas 2008; Becht, Franks, Mayer, and Rossi 2009; Greenwood and Schor 2009; Klein and Zur 2009; Bradley, Brav, Goldstein, and Jiang 2010). Laide and Mallea (2009) note that having suffered historical losses, the financial crisis has only made hedge funds even more willing to escalate activist campaigns into formal proxy contests.

Exhibit 25.5 shows some of the more interesting contested solicitations reported by Georgeson (2009a) for the 2008 proxy season. The data confirm that throughout the season, hedge funds were the main sponsors of proxy contests, accounting for more than half of all interventions launched. This is in sharp contrast with the academic literature discussed earlier which shows the dominance of individual dissidents. The activist strategies of hedge funds have also redefined the use of proxy contests in corporate governance, traditionally viewed as a means to replace the board and oust incumbent management.

Hedge funds tend to concentrate their investment and have large equity stakes, but they mostly pursue short-term gains and rarely seek full control of the board. Therefore, they typically launch participation contests with a short slate of director nominees and no accompanying tender offer. Rather than devise detailed business plans for their targets, hedge funds also tend to have event-driven objectives such as takeovers, spin-offs, share repurchases, or dividend payouts. Hu and Black (2006) and Nathan and Craythorn (2008) add that hedge funds often employ innovative strategies, such as wolf-pack coordination with other funds to quickly rearrange the target firm's shareholder base, and the use of stock lending and swaps to accumulate hidden voting power. According to Genkin (2008), hedge funds have won two-thirds of their proxy contests since 2001. This success is no doubt aided by the fact that proxy advisory firms such as RiskMetrics and Glass Lewis also tend to make voting recommendations at least partially in their favor.

The Road Ahead

While the rise of hedge funds has given proxy contests renewed relevance in recent years as a corporate governance tool, whether this will be sustained in the long run is unclear. As the new faces of shareholder activism, activist funds will continue to play a formidable role in disciplining poorly performing management. However, Laide and Mallea (2009) find that activist funds are already giving fewer advance notices of proxy contests than they did in 2008, which may be because pursuing takeovers or dividend payouts is impractical in the current environment.

Looking ahead, the future of proxy contests will no doubt also be affected by recent or imminent changes in voting and proxy access rules, prompted by exacerbated concerns over shareholder rights and director accountability as a result of the financial crisis. In a move that is likely to boost the success of proxy interventions, the SEC is banning discretionary broker votes on uninstructed voting positions as of the 2010 proxy season. Dissident shareholders have long blamed broker votes for skewing director elections in favor of incumbent nominees, by between 5 percent and 25 percent of the total vote. Thus, the elimination of these votes is a major victory because it gives much additional voting power to activists and the institutional clients of proxy advisers (Chung 2009).

However, other changes equally designed to empower shareholders should actually reduce dissidents' incentives to launch full-blown proxy contests in the

Exhibit 25.5 Proxy Contests in the 2008 Proxy Season

This table shows a list of contested solicitations in the 2008 proxy season.

Firm	Dissident	Contested Issue	Winner
1st Century Bancshares Inc.	Palisair Capital Partners LP	Director	Management
A Schulman Inc.	Ramius Capital Group LLC	Directors	Dissident
Alaska Air Group Inc.	Stephen Nieman	Directors	Management
ASA Limited	Laxey Partners Ltd.	Directors	Dissident
Bassett Furniture Industries Inc.	Costa Brava Partnership III LP	Directors	Settled
Biogen Idec Inc.	Carl Icahn et al.	Directors	Management
Charming Shoppes Inc.	Crescendo Partners; Myca Partners	Directors	Settled
Cliffs Natural Resources Inc.	Harbinger Capital Partners	Vote for control share acquisition	Management
Coinstar Inc.	Shamrock Activist Value Fund LP	Directors	Settled
CSX Corporation	Children's Investment Fund Management LLP, 3G Capital Partners Ltd.	Directors	Dissident
Emageon Inc.	Oliver Press Partners LLC	Director	Settled
EnPro Industries Inc.	Steel Partners II LP	Director	Settled
FNB Corp.	FNB Corp. SH Committee	Vote against merger	Management
Footstar Inc.	Outpoint Capital LP	Director	Management
Furniture Brands International Inc.	Sun Capital Partners	Directors	Dissident
Gencor Industries Inc.	Lloyd I Miller III	Director	Dissident
Hexcel Corp.	OSS Capital Management LP	Directors	Management
InSite Vision Inc.	Pinto Technology Ventures LP	Directors	Dissident
Luby's Inc.	Ramius Capital Group	Directors	Management
Media General Inc.	Harbinger Capital Partners	Directors	Dissident
MedQuist Inc.	Costa Brava Partnership III LP	Directors	Management
MMC Energy Inc.	Energy Holdings Limited LLC	Directors	Management
National Fuel Gas Co.	New Mountain Vantage Advisers	Directors	Settled
Phoenix Companies Inc.	Oliver Press Partners	Directors	Settled
Point Blank Solutions Inc.	Steel Partners II LP	Directors	Dissident
Prudential Bancorp Inc. of Pennsylvania	Joseph Stilwell	Withhold campaign	Management
Quality Systems Inc.	Ahmed Hussein	Directors	Management
Rackable Systems Inc.	Richard L. Leza Jr.	Directors	Management
SCPIE Holdings Inc.	Joseph Stilwell	Vote against merger	Management
Sierra Bancorp	Patricia Childress	Director	Management
Steak n Shake Co.	The Lion Fund	Directors	Dissident
Team Financial Inc.	Keith B Edquist	Directors	Settled
TVI Corporation	Allen E Bender	Directors	Management
VAALCO Energy Inc.	Nanes Delorme Partners I LP	Directors	Settled
Vineyard National Bancorp	Jon W. Salmanson	Directors; consent to amend bylaws	Dissident
Yahoo! Inc.	Carl Icahn et al.	Directors	Settled

Source: Georgeson (2009a).

future. First, majority voting is quickly becoming the norm in director elections, having been adopted by 66 percent of Standard and Poor's 500 firms by 2007, compared with 16 percent in 2005 (Allen 2007). The majority voting rule lends greater power to shareholders in rejecting incumbent director nominees and has been a key demand of activists submitting proxy proposals and targeting director elections with "just vote no" campaigns (Del Guercio, Seery, and Woidtke 2008; Renneboog and Szilagyi 2009). Nonetheless, the majority voting rule prescribes that dissidents must also achieve a full voting majority to install their own nominees, thereby reducing their chances of success. Verret (2007) argues that this disparity could be resolved by adopting cumulative voting for contested elections, but no corporate or regulatory advances have been made in this regard.

Second, the utility of proxy contests is likely to be reduced by new proxy access rules proposed by the SEC to facilitate director nominations by shareholders. Under the new Rule 14a-11, shareholders could include their own nominees in the firm's proxy materials for up to 25 percent of the available directorships, subject to eligibility conditions such as minimum ownership rules and a minimum holding period of one year. The rule, which may well be effective by the 2010 proxy season, would not apply to firms that prohibit shareholder nominations either under state laws or under their own governing documents. However, a revision to the existing Rule 14a-8(i)(8) would simultaneously authorize shareholders to submit proxy proposals seeking bylaw changes with respect to nominating procedures, which the SEC prohibited in 2007 (Georgeson, 2009b).

The proxy access amendments proposed by the SEC mirror and actually seek to federalize similar efforts already instituted in Delaware to support director nominations by shareholders. In April 2009, the state authorized firms to adopt bylaws that allow shareholders access to their own proxy statements and provide for the reimbursement of shareholders for their proxy solicitation costs. Hanley (2009) points out that these changes are partly of emphasis because whether firms in Delaware or elsewhere could not previously adopt such bylaws is by no means clear. Nonetheless, these changes should generally increase pressure on firms to make director nominations open to shareholders, which should in turn make formal proxy contests for minority board representation largely redundant.

SUMMARY AND CONCLUSIONS

While proxy contests are dramatic corporate events traditionally attracting considerable media interest, their role and effectiveness in corporate governance remains subject to much uncertainty. Thus far, empirical studies have found that firms targeted by proxy interventions tend to be poorly performing. Yet there has been no evidence that such firms would otherwise have poor governance structures or that they would perform significantly better after being targeted. Nonetheless, proxy contests have changed remarkably over the past decade. The interventions examined in the literature were relatively infrequent and mostly waged by individual shareholders. Conversely, the 2000s have experienced a new wave of successful interventions, waged by hedge funds aggressively pursuing governance arbitrage and using innovative campaign strategies. The wealth and performance effects of these contests have yet to be investigated.

Today, questions are also being raised about the future practicality of proxy contests. The financial crisis and loss of investor confidence have prompted regulatory efforts to increase director accountability and shareholder oversight. To that effect, new proxy access rules allowing shareholders to add their own director nominees to the firm's proxy materials should certainly increase shareholder control over the board. However, these rules should also reduce dissident incentives to wage expensive proxy contests in the coming years.

DISCUSSION QUESTIONS

1. To what extent do proxy contests serve as an alternative to takeovers?
2. How successful are proxy contests, and what is their impact on corporate performance?
3. How is the most recent wave of proxy contests different from previous ones?
4. How will the new voting and proxy access rules proposed by the SEC affect the use of proxy contests?

REFERENCES

Allen, Claudia H. 2007. Study of majority voting in director elections. Chicago: Neal, Gerber & Eisenberg LLP.

Bagwell, Laurie S. 1991. Share repurchase and takeover deterrence. *Rand Journal of Economics* 22 (1): 72–88.

Bebchuk, Lucian Arye, Alma Cohen, and Allen Ferrell. 2009. What matters in corporate governance? *Review of Financial Studies* 22 (2): 783–827.

Bebchuk, Lucian Arye, and Oliver Hart. 2002. Takeover bids vs. proxy fights in contests for corporate control. ECGI Law working paper 4.

Becht, Marco, Patrick Bolton, and Ailsa Röell. 2003. Corporate governance and control. In *Handbook of the Economics of Finance* 1A, ed. George Constantinides, Milton Harris, and René Stulz, 1–110. Amsterdam: Elsevier.

Becht, Marco, Julian Franks, Colin Mayer, and Stefano Rossi. 2009. Returns to shareholder activism: Evidence from a clinical study of the Hermes U.K. Focus Fund. *Review of Financial Studies* 22 (8): 3093–3129.

Borstadt, Lisa F., and Thomas J. Zwirlein. 1992. The efficient monitoring role of proxy contests: An empirical analysis of post-contest control changes and firm performance. *Financial Management* 21 (3): 22–34.

Bradley, Michael H., Alon Brav, Itay Goldstein, and Wei Jiang. 2010. Activist arbitrage: A study of open-ending attempts of closed-end funds. *Journal of Financial Economics* 95 (1): 1–19.

Brav, Alon, Wei Jiang, Frank Partnoy, and Randall S. Thomas. 2008. Hedge fund activism, corporate governance, and firm performance. *Journal of Finance* 63 (4): 1729–1775.

Brickley, James A., Ronald C. Lease, and Clifford Smith, Jr. 1988. Ownership structure and voting on antitakeover amendments. *Journal of Financial Economics* 20 (1–2): 267–291.

Chung, Joanna. 2009. SEC scraps brokers' discretionary votes in corporate director elections. *Financial Times*, July 2, 1.

Collins, Daniel W., and Linda DeAngelo. 1990. Accounting information and corporate governance: Market and analyst reactions to earnings of firms engaged in proxy contests. *Journal of Accounting and Economics* 13 (3): 213–247.

Cremers, K. J. Martijn, and Roberta Romano. 2007. Institutional investors and proxy voting: The impact of the 2003 mutual fund voting disclosure regulation. ECGI Law working paper 83.

Danielson, Morris G., and Jonathan M. Karpoff. 1998. On the uses of corporate governance provisions. *Journal of Corporate Finance* 4 (4): 347–371.
Dann, Larry Y., and Harry DeAngelo. 1988. Corporate financial policy and corporate control: A study of defensive adjustments in asset and ownership structure. *Journal of Financial Economics* 20 (1–2): 87–128.
DeAngelo, Harry, and Linda DeAngelo. 1989. Proxy contests and the governance of publicly held corporations. *Journal of Financial Economics* 23 (1): 29–59.
DeAngelo, Linda. 1988. Managerial competition, information costs, and corporate governance: The use of accounting performance measures in proxy contests. *Journal of Accounting and Economics* 10 (1): 3–36.
Del Guercio, Diane, Laura Seery, and Tracie Woidtke. 2008. Do boards pay attention when institutional investor activists "just vote no"? *Journal of Financial Economics* 90 (1): 84–103.
Dodd, Peter, and Jerold B. Warner. 1983. On corporate governance: A study of proxy contests. *Journal of Financial Economics* 11 (1–4): 401–438.
Duvall, Richard M., and Douglas V. Austin. 1965. Predicting the results of proxy contests. *Journal of Finance* 20 (3): 464–471.
Faleye, Olubunmi. 2004. Cash and corporate control. *Journal of Finance* 59 (5): 2041–2060.
Genkin, Barry H. 2008. Hedge fund activism. Presented at the SEC Hot Topics Institute, September 24. New York: Blank Rome LLP.
Georgeson. 2009a. 2008: Annual corporate governance review. New York: Georgeson.
———. 2009b. Corporate governance commentary. *Proxy Access Bulletin* 3. New York: Georgeson.
Gompers, Paul A., Joy L. Ishii, and Andrew Metrick. 2003. Corporate governance and equity prices. *Quarterly Journal of Economics* 118 (1): 107–155.
Goodman, Amy L., John F. Olson, and Lisa Fontenot. 2009. *Practical guide to SEC proxy and compensation rules*. New York: Aspen Publishers.
Gordon, Jeffrey N. 2008. Proxy contests in an era of increasing shareholder power: Forget issuer proxy access and focus on e-proxy. *Vanderbilt Law Review* 61 (2): 475–496.
Greenwood, Robin, and Michael Schor. 2009. Investor activism and takeovers. *Journal of Financial Economics* 92 (3): 362–375.
Hanley, Dean F. 2009. 2009 Updates to Delaware general corporation law—part 3: Improved shareholder access to proxy materials—Now, what will the SEC do? Boston: Foley Hoag LLP.
Heron, Randall A., and Erik Lie. 2006. On the use of poison pills and defensive payouts by takeover targets. *Journal of Business* 79 (4): 1783–1807.
Hu, Henry T., and Bernard Black. 2006. The new vote buying: Empty voting and hidden (morphable) ownership. *Southern California Law Review* 79 (4): 811–908.
Ikenberry, David, and Josef Lakonishok. 1993. Corporate governance through the proxy contest: Evidence and implications. *Journal of Business* 66 (3): 405–435.
Klein, April, and Emanuel Zur. 2009. Entrepreneurial shareholder activism: Hedge funds and other private investors. *Journal of Finance* 64 (1): 187–229.
Knowledge@Wharton. 2008. Winners and losers in the rising tide of proxy wars. knowledge.wharton.upenn.edu.
Laide, John, and Jim Mallea. 2009. 2008 Year end review: New highs set for unsolicited M&A and proxy fights. www.sharkrepellent.net.
Manne, Henry G. 1965. Mergers and the market for corporate control. *Journal of Political Economy* 73 (2): 110–120.
McCahery, Joseph A., Zacharias Sautner, and Laura T. Starks. 2009. Behind the scenes: The corporate governance preferences of institutional investors. Working paper, University of Amsterdam.
Mulherin, J. Harold, and Annette B. Poulsen. 1998. Proxy contests and corporate change: Implications for shareholder wealth. *Journal of Financial Economics* 47 (3): 279–313.

Nathan, Charles, and Dennis Craythorn. 2008. The 2009 proxy season and the year of investor anger. *New York Law Journal*, November 17.
Pound, John. 1988. Proxy contests and the efficiency of shareholder oversight. *Journal of Financial Economics* 20 (1–2): 237–265.
Renneboog, Luc, and Peter G. Szilagyi. 2009. Shareholder activism through the proxy process. Working paper, University of Cambridge.
Shleifer, Andrei, and Robert W. Vishny. 1986. Large shareholders and corporate control. *Journal of Political Economy* 94 (3): 461–488.
Stulz, René. 1988. Managerial control of voting rights: Financing policies and the market for corporate control. *Journal of Financial Economics* 20 (1–2): 25–54.
Verret, J. W. 2007. Pandora's ballot box, or a proxy with moxie? Majority voting, corporate ballot access and the legend of Martin Lipton reexamined. *Business Lawyer* 62 (3): 1007–51.

ABOUT THE AUTHOR

Peter G. Szilagyi has been at the University of Cambridge since 2007, having completed his PhD at Tilburg University and worked as a research fellow at the University of Oxford as member of the European Corporate Governance Training Network. His research interests include corporate finance, corporate governance, international finance, and financial market development. He has published in finance, economics, and statistics journals, and co-edited a special issue of *European Financial Management* as well as volumes for Elsevier and John Wiley & Sons. He previously worked for the BBC World Service and contributed to consulting projects for the Asian Development Bank.

CHAPTER 26

Corporate Takeovers and Restructurings

MIKE STEGEMOLLER
Associate Professor of Finance, Baylor University

INTRODUCTION

This chapter examines mergers and acquisitions (hereafter referred to as *takeovers*) as well as subsidiary sales, spin-offs, equity carve-outs, and targeted stock (hereafter, *restructurings*). A key question addressed in this chapter is: How do corporate takeovers and restructuring activities mitigate the principal-agent conflict within the firm?

The short answer to this question is that these transactions reorganize assets to more efficient uses. This reorganization is accomplished via external markets that serve as a monitoring mechanism to the firm. Takeovers provide a market for corporate control in which managers compete for the right to oversee a firm's resources, presumably in efficiency-promoting ways. Restructuring unshackles a firm's subsidiary operations from that of the parent so that the information contained in equity market prices about the parent, subsidiary, or both becomes less asymmetrical, thereby correlating more closely the actions of managers to the value of the firm.

The long answer to this question is more nuanced. For example, some observers suggest that the question of how takeovers and restructurings mitigate the principal-agent conflict is a presumptuous one because the question assumes that these transactions accomplish mitigation of the agency problem. Indeed, others suggest that some of these transactions exacerbate or take advantage of the principal-agent problem. Therefore, this nonexhaustive chapter provides the brevity of a short answer and some of the nuances of a long answer.

While external markets influence the internal governance structure of the firm, the importance of the market's role separates this chapter from other chapters in this book that primarily deal with a firm's internal governance. In takeovers and restructurings, the mitigation of the principal-agent conflict is dependent on some party or mechanism that is external to the firm to facilitate a change in governance. The outside party is an acquirer in the case of takeovers and subsidiary sales and the external party is an active equity market in the case of spin-offs, equity carve-outs, and targeted stock issuances. While those who incite these transactions can be from within the firm (for example, the firm's own management or angry shareholders), they are dependent on external markets for the resolution of their initiatives. Further, these transactions are unlike other external but direct means of governance. Law and regulation are examples of external governance mechanisms which intend to directly influence the monitoring of firms. The Sarbanes-Oxley Act of 2002 and state bankruptcy law are examples of direct, external governance. Thus, takeovers and restructurings are a form of indirect external governance.

Unlike direct governance mechanisms, indirect governance mechanisms do not explicitly monitor the firm's managers. So the role of takeovers and restructurings in mitigating the principal-agent conflict is in contrast to, for example, the role of the board of directors which explicitly functions as a monitor and adviser. The ensuing changes in corporate governance from takeovers and restructurings are often a by-product of a transaction intended to move assets to their best use. So, in an efficient market, when managers act rationally, takeovers and restructurings will increase the value of the firm or firms by better employing assets, perhaps by replacing underperforming managers or by incorporating synergies between the merging firms.

The indirect mitigation of the principal-agent conflict can be observed by examining takeovers in which there are numerous motivations that do not treat the internal governance of the firm as something of first-order importance. For example, an oft-stated reason for mergers and acquisitions is the creation of synergies from merging two firms. While the governance of one, if not both, of the firms must change in such transactions, the intention is not explicitly to change governance, but to create efficiencies by combining the firms. Also, the rationale for restructuring may center on changing a firm's culture or streamlining the parent in the case of a spin-off (Lublin 2009) or providing liquidity to the parent in the case of a subsidiary sale (Officer 2007). Nevertheless, these changes in efficiency, culture, or focus may require large changes in the governance structure of the firm.

There are several similarities between takeovers and restructurings including, but not limited to, being external and indirect methods of corporate governance. One commonality is that even if the explicit purpose of the transaction is not to change the firm's internal governance characteristics (i.e., the board of directors, compensation of management, the firm's capital structure, and its bylaws and charter provisions), both takeovers and restructurings achieve this end. In the case of takeovers and subsidiary sales, the target takes on the entirely new governance characteristics of the acquirer, though this diminishes if the target is relatively bigger in comparison to the acquirer. Generally, for spin-offs and equity carve-outs, the subsidiary takes on its own governance characteristics. In all of these transactions, the principal-agent conflict is always altered and is generally believed to be lessened. The breadth of internal governance changes as a result of takeover and restructuring is unrivaled in comparison to other corporate events.

Another common characteristic of these transactions is the speed with which the change in governance occurs. Although the effects of takeovers and restructurings on firm governance depend upon the type of transaction (e.g., takeover or spin-off), the relative severity of the restructuring (e.g., relatively small acquisitions versus mergers of equals), and the party examined (e.g., the target in a takeover or the parent in a carve-out), all of these transactions represent a relatively quick method of changing the entirety of how the firm is governed. Ignoring the time commitment of due diligence, most takeovers and restructuring activities generally take less than a year from the time a firm announces them until completion. For example, Time Warner announced on May 28, 2009, its plans to spin off AOL by the end of the year.

The purpose of this chapter is to examine these intriguing transactions and how they might serve to reduce the conflict between shareholders and those who oversee their investments. The remainder of this chapter is organized as follows. The first section discusses takeovers and how they can both act as a market for corporate control, which mitigates agency problems, and also be a source of agency problems. The next section discusses restructuring transactions. The final section summarizes the chapter and provides some concluding thoughts.

TAKEOVERS: MERGERS AND ACQUISITIONS

This section examines the motivations for takeovers and then turns to takeovers and the principal-agent relationship.

Motivations for Takeovers

The section begins by clarifying some terminology and examining some of the main motivations for takeover activity. The term *merger* connotes two firms, sometimes of similar size, entering into an agreement to pool their assets by one firm swapping its stock for the other firm's stock. The transaction is characterized by negotiations over top executive positions, board seats, the name of the new firm, and other matters. The term *acquisition* connotes deals in which one firm buys the other and there is a clear bidder and target. The term *takeover* includes mergers and acquisitions and is essentially a general term for a transaction in which one firm buys another. In this chapter, reference is made to bidders (or acquirers) and targets as if each party within a takeover is always well defined, but in many instances it is unclear.

The motives for takeovers are numerous. Some of these motives include capacity expansion (Gort 1969), asset reallocation due to economic shocks (Mitchell and Mulherin 1996), equity overvaluation (Shleifer and Vishny 2003), hubris (Roll 1986), agency problems (Jensen 1986), the creation of market power (Jensen and Ruback 1983), target mispricing (Jarrell, Brickley, and Netter 1988), the seemingly catch-all category of *synergies* (Bradley, Desai, and Kim 1983), and market discipline (Manne 1965), among others. These rationales can be more generally characterized and, indeed, Martin and McConnell (1991) choose only two. They state that acquisitions are undertaken either for the creation of synergies or to discipline the managers of the target firm. This categorization leaves out non-value-maximizing reasons (i.e., empire building) and mispricing motives for acquisitions.

While this chapter is mainly concerned with the disciplinary role of takeovers, one must acknowledge the other roles as they likely exist simultaneously in the same deal. Although the problem of confounding motivations is not specific to takeovers, this issue seems to be particularly relevant when analyzing takeovers. Therefore, an analysis of how takeovers mitigate the principal-agent conflict must consider the wide range of motivations to better discern the possible motivations at work in a specific takeover. This difficulty is especially problematic because many motivations have similar outcomes. For example, the short-run acquirer announcement returns of an acquisition undertaken for disciplinary reasons may have the same outcome (positive returns) as an acquisition undertaken for reasons related to market power. Further, even within a single transaction, these motivations are not mutually exclusive. Lastly, and in the context of takeovers mitigating principal-agent conflicts, there is no generally accepted measure of the severity of principal-agent problems. Indeed, specific firm characteristics, such as the number of insiders on the board of directors, are believed by some to exacerbate the principal-agent conflict and are viewed by others as important for exploiting valuable inside information and giving advice (for a broader discussion of this issue, see Bauguess and Stegemoller 2008). These issues make characterizing the influence of takeovers on the mitigation of the principal-agent conflict problematic.

An example of the complexities of takeover analysis may be instructive. Consider that an acquirer can correctly identify a firm with management that is destroying value and the acquirer successfully acquires and replaces the target's poorly performing managers. This is an example of an acquisition resulting from market discipline. The managers of the acquiring firm may also perform poorly for reasons arising from the principal-agent conflict, thereby adding another rationale for the acquisition: acquirer managerial incompetence. As a further complication, both firms in the transaction may exhibit operations that can improve with synergies. Thus, discussing takeovers mitigating the principal-agent conflict requires placing takeovers within the context of other likely motivations.

Despite the complexity of studying individual takeovers, these transactions represent a unique opportunity to observe a specific corporate investment associated with massive governance changes. Indeed, the span of changes in the internal governance structure of the firm is larger in takeovers than in any other corporate event. In an acquisition in which the acquirer is large (e.g., $1 billion) and the target is small (e.g., $10 million), the acquirer will likely see no significant change in any of its internal governance mechanisms, while the target's governance structure is likely to bear no resemblance to its pre-takeover structure. In this example, the target's capital structure, charter provisions, bylaws, and board of directors will be replaced by those characteristics of the acquirer. Likewise, managerial compensation will, at least, have a different metric for calculating compensation (e.g., the stock of the bidder replaces the stock of the target). However, as the target becomes large relative to the acquirer, the governance of the merged firms will become an increasingly larger part of negotiations. In the extreme case of a merger of equals, many of these mechanisms may change for both parties.

Takeovers and the Principal-Agent Conflict

Takeovers potentially represent sources of and solutions to the principal-agent conflict within the firm. This section first provides an examination of how takeovers mitigate the agency problems within the firm, and then shows the rationale behind how takeovers might be a source of agency problems.

How Takeovers Mitigate the Principal-Agent Conflict

Understanding how takeovers might mitigate the principal-agent conflict is perhaps best illustrated by an example. Consider two firms that are identical except for their management teams: Z Corp. is run by managers who largely look to the interests of the firm's shareholders when making investment decisions, and B Corp. is run by managers who largely look after their own interests, not those of the shareholders. If the managers of B Corp. pursue investment strategies that benefit themselves at the expense of shareholders, then the value of B Corp. will fall. In a well-functioning market, as the share price of the mismanaged firm falls, other managers with access to capital will begin to calculate the net present value (NPV) of purchasing B Corp. When purchasing B Corp. becomes profitable to Z Corp., it will buy B Corp., fire the managers, and replace them with its own managers.

If the scenario of Z Corp. buying B Corp. frequently occurs, then the knowledge that such transactions occur produces a threat to underperforming managers. As the frequency of acquisitions lessens, poorly performing managers begin to feel more secure in their jobs, knowing that the probability of being acquired and fired is low (Mikkelson and Partch 1997). This threat is an important factor in the market for corporate control—the market where managers compete for the right to manage the resources of other firms (Jensen and Ruback 1983). Thus, takeovers and the accompanying threat of takeovers allow the market for corporate control to act as a governance mechanism to publicly traded firms.

One well-known characteristic of the market for corporate control is that it is more active in some periods than in others (see, for example, Mitchell and Mulherin [1996]; Andrade and Stafford [2004]). Further, beneath the cycles of takeover activity is a change in the nature of this activity. The threat associated with an active market for corporate control and the perception of takeovers as an effective governance mechanism appears to be period specific (Holmstrom and Kaplan 2001; Netter, Poulsen, and Stegemoller 2009), functioning as an active source of discipline in times when internal governance mechanisms are weak (Kini, Kracaw, and Mian 2004). Even though detailed information about takeover activity really only begins in the 1970s, changes in the nature of takeover activity are evident in the span of just a few decades.

In the 1980s, the evidence suggests takeovers were largely in response to inefficient conglomerates run by management teams with little incentive to improve shareholder wealth. For example, less than a quarter of CEO compensation was tied to the firm's stock price, according to Hall and Liebman (1998). These takeovers largely took the form of going-private transactions in which the conglomerate was purchased, taken private, busted up, and sold back to shareholders in an initial public offering (Muscarella and Vestuypens 1990). In some sense, takeovers were the predominant source of the governance of firms. Managers could either behave or become the target of a hostile takeover.

In the mid- to late 1990s and into the first decade of this century, the nature of takeovers changed. The hostility in takeover bids was approximately cut in half from that of the 1980s (Andrade, Mitchell, and Stafford 2001; Holmstrom and Kaplan 2001) along with a rapid decline in the use of leverage. In addition, there was a shift in governance from the external to the internal. Managerial compensation became increasingly equity-based and the focus on corporate governance largely shifted to mechanisms within the firm. Takeovers were not seen as much as tools of correction (Netter, Poulsen, and Stegemoller 2009) and became friendlier and, in some cases, even became evidence of poor governance.

So far, this chapter has shown that the market for corporate control is an important form of external governance and that it has changed dramatically over the past 30 or so years. What then is the evidence concerning the influence of the market for corporate control on the principal-agent conflict within firms?

One area to search for evidence is the turnover of target and potential target managers in poorly performing firms. For example, Martin and McConnell (1991) find that the turnover of the top managers of acquired firms is higher than in nonacquired firms. Further, they report that top managers fired in target firms were not performing as well as their industry peers. Further, Agrawal and Walkling (1994) find that fired target CEOs generally do not obtain a senior executive–level job within three years of the acquisition. Thus, these two studies suggest that bad managers get acquired, fired, and have difficulty finding another top-level job. This is an indication that the market for corporate control is effective at mitigating agency problems.

The previous two studies suggest that the mere threat of takeover will influence the actions of the firm. Indeed, the findings of Mikkelson and Partch (1997) provide evidence that firms that are not targets pay attention to takeover activity. They show that when the market for corporate control is active, poorly performing firms have double the amount of CEO turnovers as in the years when the takeover market is not as active. Similarly, Denis and Kruse (2000) examine managerial discipline and restructuring events of poorly performing firms in two different takeover periods. They find more disciplinary actions and restructuring during the active period of takeovers and a lower incidence of such events during the less active period of takeovers. Thus, these studies suggest that the threat of takeover plays an important role in disciplining the behavior of poorly performing managers even if their firms are not acquired. Interestingly, Karpoff, Malatesta, and Walkling (1996) find evidence suggesting that proxy proposals, another threat to managers, do not have the same effect that an active takeover market does.

More recent evidence further highlights the principal-agent conflict in target firms during the negotiation process. Hartzell, Ofek, and Yermack (2004) find evidence that last-minute negotiation between the target and acquirer changes the golden parachutes of target CEOs by adding millions of dollars to their payouts, possibly at the expense of target shareholders in the form of a reduction in the premium paid for the target. Similarly, Moeller (2005) shows that CEOs having large share ownership in the target firm may negatively influence the premiums received by target shareholders, possibly in exchange for incentives provided by the bidder. Harford (2003) finds evidence suggesting that a potential target's outside directors—the directors most aligned with shareholders—may have less incentive to align themselves with target shareholders than does an executive with a golden parachute. These directors face the loss of future cash flows associated with a board seat due to the high probability of losing a board seat if acquired. All of these studies suggest not only a divergence in the incentives of target managers and board members but also that acquirers facilitated the bad behavior is in some ways.

Finally, in a study that highlights the influence of acquirer and target governance structure on the gains to takeover, Wang and Xie (2009) find that the combined returns of the target and acquirer are greater when the acquirer's shareholder rights are stronger than those of the target. Wang and Xie (p. 831) conclude that one source of gains from mergers is the "improvement in corporate governance effected by changes in control." In summary, the studies in this section show the importance of takeover activity in mitigating the principal-agent conflict in target and nontarget firms.

Takeovers and the Avoidance of Takeovers as a Source of Agency Problems

Much can be learned from market reactions to takeovers. Target shareholders react positively to acquisition announcements because the bidder almost always buys the target at a premium. However, the reaction of the acquiring-firm shareholders is much more difficult to interpret. For example, the reaction is typically small, may not be a surprise, and targets may be large relative to bidders. The change in acquirer value around acquisition announcements (of all target types) exhibits a normally distributed pattern of returns with a mean close to zero but positive. When restricting the transactions to takeovers between publicly held firms, the mean becomes negative (see Fuller, Netter, and Stegemoller 2002; Moeller, Schlingemann, and Stulz 2004; Netter, Stegemoller, and Wintoki 2009). Further, Netter et al. (2009) report that about 45 percent of all transactions have negative wealth effects at the time of the acquisition announcement. Moeller, Schlingemann, and Stulz (2005) provide evidence of very large losses to some takeovers. While remembering that most deals are not characterized by downward stock price revisions is important, the fact of many large investments by the firm appears to be bad news about the firm's prospects.

One set of explanations for such negative returns suggests that the bad news is largely explained by non-value-maximizing actions of the acquirer's managers. The managerial characteristics that might lead to an exacerbation of the principal-agent conflict in the context of mergers and acquisitions are well characterized by what Mulherin and Boone (2000) call *nonsynergistic* theory. They include agency problems of hubris, overconfidence, managerial entrenchment, and empire building. They all predict a negative market reaction to the bid. Still, examining the motives of managers can be problematic. A classic work discussing the less-than-good motivations for acquisitions is the hubris hypothesis by Roll (1986). His paper provides some context to these explanations. Roll (p. 214) notes that "management intentions may be fully consistent with honorable stewardship of corporate assets, but actions need not always turn out to be right." This statement suggests that managers may make mistakes in the acquisition process while fully intending to do well by the firm's shareholders. The opposite is also true—bad managers can be lucky. Therefore, balancing the claim of bad intentions with the knowledge that intentions are almost impossible to discern in the context of takeovers is important.

According to Netter et al. (2009), 45 percent of acquisitions do not increase the value of the firm. One response to this fact is that takeovers are simply zero NPV projects: Some slightly increase the value of the firm while some decrease the value of the firm, but on average there is no change in firm value (Andrade et al., 2001). Another response sets up the relation between corporate takeovers and corporate governance as a very odd one, which may be characterized by a conflicting rationale for takeover activity. Specifically, one way to realign the incentives of management is to gain control of the firm and then replace bad managers. However, one of the primary pieces of evidence of a looming problem between the principal and the agent is the presence of takeover activity.

Two studies highlight this latter view. Morck, Shleifer, and Vishny (1990) provide evidence that some poorly performing acquisitions are driven by deals in which managers diversify and deals in which the acquirer was performing poorly before the acquisition. Thus, managers that either underperform or appear to be interested in reducing their own risk exacerbate the principal-agent problem when they make acquisitions. In Gompers, Ishii, and Metrick (2003), the number of acquisitions a firm makes is highly related to its governance index, indicating that poorly governed firms make more acquisitions than firms that are better-governed. Though they do not interpret these findings as evidence of empire building on the part of acquiring-firm managers, Gompers et al. conclude that poorly governed firms engage in large amounts of inefficient investment.

If takeovers are not a source of the principal-agent conflict, then the compensation of the acquirer's managers would be expected to reflect the value-adding nature of their acquisitions. Harford and Li (2007) find that CEOs do not lose wealth following poor acquisitions: The wealth losses associated with poor stock performance are canceled out with additional stock grants to the CEO. Further, CEO wealth increases when he undertakes acquisitions that increase the value of the firm. In other words, their findings suggest that CEOs do not lose when making bad acquisitions, but gain when they make good acquisitions. Relating the degree of equity-based compensation before an acquisition to the short-run acquirer announcement returns, Datta, Iskandar-Datta, and Raman (2001) find that firms with a high degree of equity-based compensation experience positive acquisition announcement returns. Firms with a low degree of equity-based compensation experience negative announcement returns and post-acquisition performance. These findings suggest that when the incentives of executives are properly aligned with shareholders, they make better acquisitions, and when they are not aligned, the principal-agent conflict is likely worsened by the managers' acquisitiveness.

There is also a voluminous literature on what some believe is the outcome of entrenched management: antitakeover devices. These provisions in the corporate charter provide substantial frictions against the fluid functioning of the market for corporate control. Essentially, these devices create difficulties in replacing incumbent managers who greatly value the personal benefits of control. Such devices include but are not limited to dual-class recapitalizations, supermajority voting for merger approval, classified boards, golden parachutes, and poison pills. Indeed, such devices are important factors in the composition of popular indexes designed to measure the level of managerial entrenchment (see Gompers et al. 2003; Bebchuk, Cohen, and Ferrell 2009). As previously mentioned, Gompers et al. specifically link firms with the fewest shareholder rights (so-called *dictator* firms) to inefficient investment in acquisitions. Further, Masulis, Wang, and Xie (2007) find evidence that these antitakeover devices serve to entrench managers. They report a negative relation between acquisition announcement returns and the number of antitakeover devices used by the acquirer. According to Masulis et al., this is evidence that these devices only serve to entrench managers by excluding them from the market for corporate control. Two studies that do not support the spirit of these findings are those of Bates, Becher, and Lemmon (2008) and Bauguess and Stegemoller (2008). These studies find that some antitakeover devices do not serve to entrench management at stockholder expense.

Thus, the following irony exists: The market for corporate control that aims to eliminate one set of agency problems often initiates another set of agency problems (for a more thorough discussion see Robinson [2009]). Takeovers done in the name of governance may be examples of poor governance themselves. If managers are overconfident in their ability to recognize inefficient asset use due to managerial incompetence, then their acquisitions will largely be an example of the behavior for which governance is intended.

Two studies provide evidence of this circularity in the role of takeovers by suggesting that the market for corporate control disciplines managers who make poor acquisitions. Mitchell and Lehn (1990) find an active market for corporate control for bad acquirers: Acquirers that make value-destroying acquisitions are more likely to be acquired themselves. Since this study, however, internal governance structures have risen in prominence and antitakeover devices have flourished, possibly deteriorating the effectiveness of the presence of the market for corporate control. Lehn and Zhao (2006) find that takeovers still discipline errant acquirers alongside bankruptcy and internal governance mechanisms. Lehn and Zhao (p. 1761) conclude that "corporate governance and the external market for corporate control generally work well in disciplining managers who pursue acquisitions to the detriment of their stockholders." Thus, the evidence is not contradictory that acquisitions both mitigate and exacerbate the principal-agent conflict.

Whether takeovers mitigate or exacerbate the principal-agent conflict is an empirical question, and the evidence suggests both mitigation and exacerbation occur. The broad evidence shows that takeover activity is at least efficient on the whole. Netter et al. (2009) find that mergers and acquisitions lawfully occur every week of the year and that short-run returns around acquisition announcements do not, on average, destroy wealth. According to Mitchell and Mulherin (1996), these transactions appear to be related to major structural changes within the industries in which they occur.

As previously stated, the evidence shows the following: An acquirer's stock returns around an acquisition announcement are, on average, slightly positive and normally distributed around the mean. This empirical fact is indicative that there are both good and bad deals done for both good and bad reasons. Yet overall acquisitions serve their purpose as the driver of the market for corporate control, which keeps errant managers somewhat uncomfortable about their job security and mitigates the principal-agent conflict.

SUBSIDIARY SALES, SPIN-OFFS, EQUITY CARVE-OUTS, AND TARGETED STOCK

This section defines several restructuring events and discusses how restructuring mitigates the principal-agent relationship. The final part of this section examines the empirical evidence on restructuring.

Defining Restructuring Events

This section provides a discussion of four types of restructuring transactions in which a parent reorganizes its operations in order to divest itself of, or in some way to separate itself from, a particular subsidiary. The four restructuring transactions in this section are subsidiary sales, spin-offs, equity carve-outs, and targeted stock issuances.

A subsidiary sale, also called asset sales or subsidiary acquisitions, occurs when another firm buys a subsidiary operation from the parent firm. These transactions are the most frequent among the four restructuring transactions in this section. For the years 1990 through 1995, Officer (2007) reports 1,208 subsidiary sales and Gilson, Healy, Noe, and Palepu (1998) report only 146 spin-offs, carve-outs, and targeted stock offerings combined. Subsidiary sales shift the governance of the subsidiary from the previous parent to a new parent and are a source of liquidity to the selling parent. Some examples are PepsiCo buying Tropicana from Seagram's, and General Motors buying Land Rover from BMW.

In a spin-off, the parent proportionately distributes new shares in the subsidiary to all existing shareholders. The new firm is an independent entity with its own operations and management. Until large secondary market equity sales occur, the shareholders of the parent and the newly spun-off firm are identical. An example of a spin-off is PepsiCo Inc.'s divestiture of Taco Bell, KFC, and Pizza Hut. In the spin-off, PepsiCo Inc. shareholders received one share in Tricon Global Restaurants (the new holding company) for every 10 shares of PepsiCo Inc. they owned.

An equity carve-out is an initial public offering (IPO) of the stock of a subsidiary by the parent. In most cases, the parent is the majority owner of the carved-out firm. Thus, carve-outs create new equity holders and raise cash for the parent. The parent usually sells only a small proportion of the subsidiary—on average, 32 percent according to Benveniste, Fu, Seguin, and Yu (2008)—thereby retaining majority control of the newly public firm. An example of an equity carve-out is DuPont selling 30 percent of Conoco in 1998 in what was at the time one of the largest IPOs in U.S. history.

When a firm issues targeted stock (or tracking stock), it essentially divests a subsidiary without losing control of the unit. New shares are issued and earnings for the subsidiary are reported independently of the parent, but the parent retains control of the unit and raises cash from the issuance. The shareholders of the targeted stock do not own the subsidiary, but rather the parent. In this way, the targeted stock resembles a common stock of the subsidiary. Targeted stock does not mimic common stock, because it does not have distinct cash flow and control rights tied directly to the subsidiary. An example of a targeted stock issuance is that of AT&T Corp.'s AT&T wireless, at the time one of the largest U.S. IPOs ever, raising about $10 billion for AT&T.

How Restructuring Mitigates the Principal-Agent Conflict

The common result of these four restructuring events is that the parent becomes less complex, causing its stock price to better reflect the value of managerial decisions. In all of the transactions except a subsidiary sale, the subsidiary obtains a new stock price, which increases the monitoring ability of the market and the incentive of the firm's managers. Thus, restructuring events serve to alleviate asymmetric information about the parent and the subsidiary. These transactions also allow the subsidiary to operate either more independently (i.e., spin-offs, carve-outs, and targeted stock) or under some other governance structure, which will presumably be better able to employ the subsidiary's assets (i.e., subsidiary sale).

In a firm with a single segment, the products or services are highly related. The manager of the single-segment firm is mainly concerned with how to allocate resources to similar projects with varying NPVs. Importantly, the stock price of the single-segment firm reflects the changes in expected cash flows as a result of the manager's ability to invest wisely. The firm's stock price will reflect any change in expectations about cash flows, thereby both providing feedback to managers about the value of their proposed projects and serving as an incentive mechanism to the firm's managers (see Kau, Linck, and Rubin 2008).

In contrast to the single-segment firm, investment within a multisegment firm is more complex and projects of different types will compete for the same scarce resources. This complexity exacerbates the principal-agent conflict in several ways. First, intrafirm competition for scarce resources across a diversity of products or services may lead managers to invest within their expertise at the expense of higher-NPV projects. The more investment occurring within the expertise of a specific manager, the more difficult the manager is to replace because the value of the firms is largely dependent on the manager's expertise. These actions serve to entrench the manager, enabling him to extract unjustifiable wages and perquisites (Shleifer and Vishny 1989). Absent managerial entrenchment, the more diverse the parent's operations become, the less likely the firm's managers can efficiently allocate internal capital to the firm's best use (Stein 1997). Thus, no matter the intention of management, information asymmetries about the firm will reduce the value of the firm, and a multisegment firm should be lower in value than the sum of its segments relative to single-segment firms. This difference in value between diversified and focused firms is called the *diversification discount*. Evidence suggests that such a discount exists: Diversified firms have lower q (Lang and Stulz 1994), lower market values (Berger and Ofek 1995), and lower stock returns (Comment and Jarrell 1995) than more focused firms. The more unrelated segments that a firm has, the more inefficient is its investment allocation (Rajan, Servaes, and Zingales 2000).

The second way that firm complexity exacerbates the principal-agent conflict is based on the relation between the incentives of managers and the firm's stock price. The stock price of the multisegment firm reflects the expected cash flow changes resulting from the investment decisions of all of the firm's segments. Thus, the market and managers have greater difficulty in relating those cash flows to the specific but varied investment decisions across the units of the firm. The managers of subsidiaries involved in spin-offs, equity carve-outs, and targeted stock issuances have greater incentives to increase the value of the firm due to the newly formed relation between the merit of their investment decisions and the firm's new stock price. The new subsidiary stock price allows the subsidiary managers' compensation to be tied to their performance and also subjects the firm to the market for corporate control.

Consider an example. In a firm with two dissimilar segments, A and B, the changes in expectations about cash flows are high from segment A and low from segment B. This relation results in no movement in stock price and provides comparatively less information to managers about market expectations due to the intermingling of the cash flow expectations of both segments. This intermingling creates difficulty in using the firm's stock price as an incentive for managers, especially if each segment has a chief officer who is in turn overseen by a chief officer of the parent. In the multisegment firm, if both segment chiefs are compensated partially through the firm's stock price, then the chief officer of segment A will be undercompensated and the officer of segment B will be overcompensated, which will provide disincentives to both managers. Thus, to the extent that restructuring separates A and B, it will mitigate the principal-agent conflict by revealing the performance of the firm's managers to shareholders and possible acquirers.

Empirical Evidence on Restructuring

While subsidiary sales, spin-offs, carve-outs, and targeted stock all reduce the parent company's complexity and result in the divestiture of the subsidiary, the degree to which these mechanisms accomplish these goals varies widely even within a particular type of restructuring event. For example, subsidiary sales and spin-offs remove an entire unit from the parent in a relatively uniform fashion, but there is wide variation in the separation of parent and subsidiary governance in equity carve-outs. In an examination of 11 carve-outs by Thermo Electron, Allen (1998) concludes that the governance of the firm is greatly decentralized and is put into the hands of the managers of the carved-out firm, while in some carve-outs, the governance structure of the subsidiary remains that of the parent (Benveniste et al. 2008). Equity carve-outs are also transitory in nature because they are often repurchased by the parent or fully sold off within a few years of the IPO (Perotti and Rossetto 2007). Further, this difference in control within equity carve-outs seems to be related to firm performance. For example, Boone, Haushalter, and Mikkelson (2003) find that the extent to which the parent relinquishes ownership in the subsidiary is positively related to performance of the parent after the carve-out.

Increasing the focus of the parent is a common outcome of subsidiary sales, spin-offs, and carve-outs. The empirical evidence on these focus-increasing events of the parent shows significant value improvements to the parent. There are positive abnormal announcement returns associated with subsidiary sales (Lang, Poulsen, and Stulz 1994), spin-offs (Schipper and Smith 1983), and equity carve-outs (Allen and McConnell 1998). Ahn and Denis (2004), among others, show that the diversification discount associated with parent firms is reduced or eliminated when the firm divests a subsidiary. John and Ofek (1995) provide evidence of a positive relation between focus-increasing subsidiary sales and the parent's returns around the announcement of the sale. Together, this evidence is consistent with either lessening managerial entrenchment (thus mitigating the principal-agent conflict) or reducing the inefficient allocation of resources within the parent.

Increasing the scrutiny of the subsidiary via its own stock price mitigates the principal-agent conflict by providing managers with both the incentive and information to make value-maximizing decisions and reduces the amount of asymmetric information about the firm, thereby increasing the monitoring ability of the market. The empirical evidence suggests an improvement in information revelation and accuracy resulting from the creation of a new stock price for the subsidiary. Both analyst coverage and the accuracy of analysts' forecasts increase in spin-offs, equity carve-outs, and targeted stock offerings (Gilson, Healy, Noe, and Palepu 2001; Chemmanur and Paeglis 2001), which is consistent with greater monitoring of the firm. Krishnaswami and Subramaniam (1999) show that firms engaging in spin-offs have more asymmetric information about the firm than similar firms that do not. They show a positive relation between the amount of asymmetric information and spin-off announcement returns. This result is consistent with spin-offs creating value by allowing markets to better monitor the actions of the firm, thereby mitigating the principal-agent conflict. Lastly, D'Souza and Jacob (2000) find positive abnormal stock returns around the announcement of targeted stock offerings and attribute this to the increase in monitoring and resulting motivational effects of the subsidiary's managers.

Finally, an additional benefit from the creation of a new stock price is that the new firms (both the parent and the subsidiary) resulting from spin-offs and carve-outs become subject to the market for corporate control. The presence of this new external governance mechanism provides firms' managers with the incentive to act in the interest of shareholders, further mitigating the principal-agent conflict. In addition, as separate entities, both firms' assets are more easily transferable to a bidder. This conjecture is supported by the findings of Cusatis, Miles, and Woolridge (1993) showing that both subsidiaries and parents experience an unusually high level of takeover after the spin-off. They further indicate that the abnormally high performance of spin-offs is only associated with the spin-offs that are subsequently acquired.

In summary, the bulk of the empirical evidence on restructurings, as that of takeovers, suggests that a firm's restructuring activities are actions that mitigate the principal-agent conflict, thereby creating value for the stockholders of the parent and subsidiary.

SUMMARY AND CONCLUSIONS

What conclusions can be drawn about the influence of takeovers and restructuring events on the principal-agent conflict? Overall, these transactions, on average, change for the better the way in which a firm's operations are governed, but there is great variation in the outcomes. Takeovers serve as the single largest and quickest way in which the governance of a firm can change. This fact, coupled with their history of replacing poorly performing managers, enables takeovers to function as a market for corporate control that mitigates the principal-agent conflict. Restructuring events lessen the principal-agent conflict within the firm by offering an avenue to more clearly convey information about the firm. This clarity is brought by focusing the parent and providing a stock price for the subsidiary. These changes motivate managers by better tying their compensation to the value of the firm and by enabling the market to serve as a more informed monitor.

This previous point is the summary of the chapter and its main conclusion. However, there are two additional relevant conclusions that might guide future research. First, takeovers as a means of indirect, external governance appear to be growing less meaningful. Indirect external governance implicitly attempts to mitigate the principal-agent problem by making managers' investment decisions better reflected in stock prices and by replacing those managers who underperform. Thus, takeovers and restructurings provide both carrots and sticks. However, the stick of external governance appears to be weakening. Hostile takeovers are vanishing. In deals where target managers are replaced, the target managers receive sizeable payouts. Simultaneously, there has been a major increase in regulation of the firm's internal governance structure. Thus, one reasonable conclusion is that the stick of the market for corporate control may be giving way at the expense of onerous and costly regulation. Certainly, recent history provides numerous anecdotes of the movement of market functions into the hands of government.

Second, behind all of the attempts to mitigate the principal-agent conflict, whether through regulation, markets, or internal governance structure, is a basic attempt to change the actions of managers without directly addressing the morals of managers. While this point may seem obvious or irrelevant, many market observers, participants, and regulators seem to believe that an endless tweaking of governance will eventually produce managers with whom shareholders and regulators can be satisfied. Yet this pursuit is undertaken without regard to the single greatest influence on the behavior of management: what they hold as right and wrong, good and evil. Therefore, the agency problem is very much like a bull in a china shop. The approach thus far has been to spend an exorbitant amount of time and money herding the bull and erecting better corrals, while attention should perhaps be on finding out what makes a bull appreciate fine dinnerware.

DISCUSSION QUESTIONS

1. What are the motives for undertaking mergers and acquisitions? Which motives for takeovers are in apparent conflict?
2. Compare and contrast subsidiary sales, spin-offs, equity carve-outs, and targeted shares.
3. What is the market for corporate control and how has it changed over time?
4. What makes stock prices important to managers?
5. Why might intrafirm diversification affect firm value?

REFERENCES

Agrawal, Anup, and Ralph Walkling. 1994. Executive careers and compensation surrounding takeover bids. *Journal of Finance* 49 (3): 985–1014.

Ahn, Seoungpil, and David Denis. 2004. Internal capital markets and investment policy: Evidence from corporate spinoffs. *Journal of Financial Economics* 71 (3): 489–516.

Allen, Jeffrey. 1998. Capital markets and corporate structure: The equity carve-outs of Thermo Electron. *Journal of Financial Economics* 48 (1): 99–124.

Allen, Jeffrey, and John McConnell. 1998. Equity carve-outs and managerial discretion. *Journal of Finance* 53 (1): 163–186.

Andrade, Gregor, Mark Mitchell, and Erik Stafford. 2001. New evidence and perspectives on mergers. *Journal of Economic Perspectives* 15 (2): 103–120.

Andrade, Gregor, and Erik Stafford. 2004. Investigating the economic role of mergers. *Journal of Corporate Finance* 10 (1): 1–36.

Bates, Tom, David Becher, and Mike Lemmon. 2008. Board classification and managerial entrenchment: Evidence from the market for corporate control. *Journal of Financial Economics* 87 (3): 656–677.

Bauguess, Scott, and Mike Stegemoller. 2008. Protective governance choices and the value of acquisition activity. *Journal of Corporate Finance* 14 (5): 550–566.

Bebchuk, Lucian, Alma Cohen, and Allen Ferrell. 2009. What matters in corporate governance? *Review of Financial Studies* 22 (2): 783–827.

Benveniste, Lawrence, Huijing Fu, Paul Seguin, and Xiaoyun Yu. 2008. On the anticipation of IPO underpricing: Evidence from equity carve-outs. *Journal of Corporate Finance* 14 (5): 614–629.

Berger, Philip G., and Eli Ofek. 1995. Diversification's effect on firm value. *Journal of Financial Economics* 37 (1): 39–66.
Boone, Audra, David Haushalter, and Wayne Mikkelson. 2003. An investigation of the gains from specialized equity claims. *Financial Management* 32 (3): 67–83.
Bradley, Michael, Anand Desai, and E. Han Kim. 1983. The rationale behind interfirm tender offers: Information or synergy? *Journal of Financial Economics* 11 (1): 183–206.
Chemmanur, Thomas, and Imants Paeglis. 2001. Why issue tracking stock? Insights from a comparison with spin-offs and carve-outs. *Journal of Applied Corporate Finance* 14 (2): 102–114.
Comment, Robert, and Greg Jarrell. 1995. Corporate focus and stock returns. *Journal of Financial Economics* 37 (1): 67–88.
Cusatis, Patrick, James Miles, and Randall Woolridge. 1993. Restructuring through spinoffs: The stock market evidence. *Journal of Financial Economics* 33 (3): 293–312.
Datta, Sudip, Mai Iskandar-Datta, and Kartik Raman. 2001. Executive compensation and corporate acquisition decisions. *Journal of Finance* 56 (6): 2299–2336.
Denis, David, and Timothy Kruse. 2000. Managerial discipline and corporate restructuring following performance declines. *Journal of Financial Economics* 55 (3): 391–424.
D'Souza, Julia, and John Jacob. 2000. Why firms issue targeted stock. *Journal of Financial Economics* 56 (3): 459–483.
Fuller, Kathleen, Jeffry Netter, and Mike Stegemoller. 2002. What do returns to acquiring firms tell us? Evidence from firms that make many acquisitions. *Journal of Finance* 57 (4): 1763–1793.
Gilson, Stuart, Paul Healy, Christopher Noe, and Krishna Palepu. 1998. Information effects of spin-offs, equity carve-outs, and targeted stock offerings. Working paper, Harvard University.
———. 2001. Analyst specialization and conglomerate stock breakups. *Journal of Accounting Research* 39 (3): 565–582.
Gompers, Paul, Joy Ishii, and Andrew Metrick. 2003. Corporate governance and equity prices. *Quarterly Journal of Economics* 118 (1): 107–155.
Gort, Michael. 1969. An economic disturbance theory of mergers. *Quarterly Journal of Economics* 83 (4): 624–642.
Hall, Brian, and Jeffrey Liebman. 1998. Are CEOs really paid like bureaucrats? *Quarterly Journal of Economics* 113 (3): 653–691.
Harford, Jarrad. 2003. Takeover bids and target directors' incentives: The impact of a bid on directors' wealth and board seats. *Journal of Financial Economics* 69 (1): 51–83.
Harford, Jarrad, and Kai Li. 2007. Decoupling CEO wealth and firm performance: The case of acquiring CEOs. *Journal of Finance* 62 (2): 917–949.
Hartzell, Jay, Eli Ofek, and David Yermack. 2004. What's in it for me? CEOs whose firms are acquired. *Review of Financial Studies* 17 (1): 37–61.
Holmstrom, Bengt, and Steven Kaplan. 2001. Corporate governance and merger activity in the United States: Making sense of the 1980s and 1990s. *Journal of Economic Perspectives* 15 (2): 121–144.
Jarrell, Greg, James Brickley, and Jeffry Netter. 1988. The market for corporate control: The empirical evidence since 1980. *Journal of Economic Perspectives* 2 (1): 49–68.
Jensen, Michael. 1986. Agency costs of free cash flow, corporate finance, and takeovers. *American Economic Review* 76 (2): 323–329.
Jensen, Michael, and Richard Ruback. 1983. The market for corporate control: The scientific evidence. *Journal of Financial Economics* 11 (1): 5–50.
John, Kose, and Eli Ofek. 1995. Asset sales and increase in focus. *Journal of Financial Economics* 37 (1): 105–126.
Karpoff, John, Paul Malatesta, and Ralph Walkling. 1996. Corporate governance and shareholder initiatives: Empirical evidence. *Journal of Financial Economics* 42 (3): 365–395.

Kau, Jim, Jim Linck, and Paul Rubin. 2008. Do managers listen to the market? *Journal of Corporate Finance* 14 (4): 347–362.

Kini, Omesh, William Kracaw, and Shehzad Mian. 2004. The nature of discipline by corporate takeovers. *Journal of Finance* 59 (4): 1511–1552.

Krishnaswami, Sudha, and Venkat Subramaniam. 1999. Information asymmetry, valuation, and the corporate spin-off decision. *Journal of Financial Economics* 53 (1): 73–112.

Lang, Larry, Annette Poulsen, and René Stulz. 1994. Asset sales, firm performance, and the agency cost of managerial discretion. *Journal of Financial Economics* 37 (1): 3–37.

Lang, Larry, and René Stulz. 1994. Tobin's q, corporate diversification and firm performance. *Journal of Political Economy* 102 (6): 1248–1280.

Lehn, Kenneth, and Minxhin Zhao. 2006. CEO turnover after acquisitions: Are bad bidders fired? *Journal of Finance* 56 (4): 1759–1811.

Lublin, Joann. 2009. Firm offers blueprint for makeover in a spinoff. *Wall Street Journal*. June 29, B4.

Manne, Henry. 1965. Mergers and the market for corporate control. *Journal of Political Economy* 73 (1): 110–120.

Martin, Kenneth, and John McConnell. 1991. Corporate performance, corporate takeovers, and management turnover. *Journal of Finance* 46 (2): 671–687.

Masulis, Ron, Cong Wang, and Fei Xie. 2007. Corporate governance and acquirer returns. *Journal of Finance* 62 (4): 1851–1889.

Mikkelson, Wayne, and Megan Partch. 1997. The decline of takeovers and disciplinary managerial turnover. *Journal of Financial Economics* 44 (2): 205–228.

Mitchell, Mark, and Kenneth Lehn. 1990. Do bad bidders become good targets? *Journal of Political Economy* 98 (2): 372–398.

Mitchell, Mark, and Harold Mulherin. 1996. The impact of industry shocks on takeover and restructuring activity. *Journal of Financial Economics* 41 (2): 193–229.

Moeller, Sara, Frederik Schlingemann, and René Stulz. 2004. Firm size and the gains from acquisitions. *Journal of Financial Economics* 73 (2): 201–228.

———. 2005. Wealth destruction on a massive scale? A study of acquiring firm returns in the recent merger wave. *Journal of Finance* 60 (2): 757–782.

Moeller, Thomas. 2005. Let's make a deal! How shareholder control impacts merger payoffs. *Journal of Financial Economics* 76 (1): 167–190.

Morck, Randall, Andrei Shleifer, and Robert Vishny. 1990. Do managerial objectives drive bad acquisitions? *Journal of Finance* 45 (1): 31–48.

Mulherin, Harold, and Audra Boone. 2000. Comparing acquisitions and divestitures. *Journal of Corporate Finance* 6 (2): 117–139.

Muscarella, Chris, and Michael Vestuypens. 1990. Efficiency and organizational structure: A study of reverse LBOs. *Journal of Finance* 45 (5): 1389–1413.

Netter, Jeffry, Annette Poulsen, and Mike Stegemoller. 2009. The rise of corporate governance in corporate control research. *Journal of Corporate Finance* 15 (1): 1–9.

Netter, Jeffry, Mike Stegemoller, and Jide Wintoki. 2009. A study of 250,000 mergers from 1992 to 2009. Working paper, Texas Tech University.

Officer, Micah. 2007. The price of corporate liquidity: Acquisition discounts for unlisted targets. *Journal of Financial Economics* 83 (3): 571–598.

Perotti, Enrico, and Silvia Rossetto. 2007. Unlocking value: Equity carve-outs as strategic real options. *Journal of Corporate Finance* 13 (5): 771–792.

Rajan, Raghuram, Henri Servaes, and Luigi Zingales. 2000. The cost of diversity: The diversification discount and inefficient investment. *Journal of Finance* 55 (1): 35–80.

Robinson, David. 2009. Size, ownership, and the market for corporate control. *Journal of Corporate Finance* 15 (1): 80–84.

Roll, Richard. 1986. The hubris theory of corporate takeovers. *Journal of Business* 59 (2): 197–216.

Schipper, Karen, and Abbie Smith. 1983. Effects of recontracting on shareholder wealth: The case of voluntary spinoffs. *Journal of Financial Economics* 12 (4): 437–467.
Shleifer, Andrei, and Robert Vishny. 1989. Managerial entrenchment: The case of manager–specific investments. *Journal of Financial Economics* 25 (1): 123–139.
———. 2003. Stock market driven acquisitions. *Journal of Financial Economics* 70 (3): 295–311.
Stein, Jeremy. 1997. Internal capital markets and the competition for corporate resources. *Journal of Finance* 52 (1): 111–133.
Wang, Cong, and Fei Xie. 2009. Corporate governance transfer and synergistic gains from mergers and acquisitions. *Review of Financial Studies* 22 (2): 829–858.

ABOUT THE AUTHOR

Mike Stegemoller is an associate professor of finance at Baylor University. He is the author of several articles on mergers and acquisitions, which have been published in the *Journal of Finance, Journal of Financial Economics, Financial Management, Journal of Corporate Finance,* and *Review of Finance.* Professor Stegemoller holds a BS from Abilene Christian University, an MBA from Baylor University, and a PhD from the University of Georgia.

CHAPTER 27

Corporate Takeovers and Wealth Creation

MARINA MARTYNOVA
Associate, Cornerstone Research and Research Fellow, Tilburg University

LUC RENNEBOOG
Professor of Corporate Finance, Tilburg University

INTRODUCTION

Mergers and acquisitions (M&As) come in waves. Thus far, the literature documents five waves: the early 1900s, the 1920s, the 1960s, the 1980s, and the 1990s. Of these, the most recent wave of the 1990s was particularly remarkable in terms of size and geographical dispersion. For the first time, European firms were as eager to participate in takeovers as their U.S. counterparts. In fact, M&A activity in Europe hit levels similar to those experienced in the United States. Still, M&A activity collapsed in the middle of 2000 and remained substantially below the peak of 1999–2000 until the end of 2003. Subsequently, the takeover market picked up but slowed down once more in 2007 due to the worldwide subprime and credit crisis.

The high incidence and volume of mergers and acquisitions highlights their importance to the corporate world. Companies are keen to participate in M&As because by combining their assets with the assets of another firm they can achieve operating and financial synergies. Operating synergies arise through realization of economies of scale and scope, elimination of duplicate activities, vertical integration, increased market power, and increased utilization of the bidder's management team. Operating synergies mainly arise when the merging firms operate in the same or related industries. Firms forming a conglomerate tend to benefit from financial synergies. These may include improved cash flow stability, lower bankruptcy probabilities and increased market value of debt, cheaper access to capital, a larger internal capital market, and the use of underutilized tax shields.

Another type of takeover synergies discussed in the academic literature results from the improvement of the target firms' corporate governance. These synergies typically occur in hostile takeovers in which the bidding firm bypasses the management of the target firm and makes a direct offer to the target firm's shareholders to buy their shares. If the offer is successful, the target's incumbent management team is replaced. Jensen (1988) defines this activity as the market for corporate control, where management teams compete with one another for the right to manage the assets owned by shareholders. The team that offers the highest value to the shareholders acquires the right to manage the assets until another management team that can realize a higher value of the assets replaces the existing management. Hostile takeovers are expected when the target firm performs poorly and its internal corporate governance mechanisms fail to discipline managers. A hostile acquisition can thus be considered as an important corporate governance mechanism that corrects opportunistic managerial behavior.

In contrast, M&A activity is sometimes also mentioned as the outgrowth of corporate governance failure. This is because numerous empirical studies show that a substantial proportion of M&As destroy corporate value. Shleifer and Vishny (1991) cite agency problems between management and shareholders as the main driver of such value-destroying acquisitions. Self-interested managers may engage in M&A activity to achieve their personal objectives, such as building an empire, at the expense of shareholder value (Jensen 1988 and 2005).

Overall, corporate takeovers are expected to create value by achieving operating, financial, or corporate governance synergies. However, some transactions may result in value destruction if they occur as a result of the conflict of interest between management and shareholders of the bidding firm.

The remainder of this chapter focuses on the review of empirical evidence on value creation in takeovers. The review begins by providing an overview of the wealth effects of takeovers throughout history, starting with the second takeover wave in the beginning of the twentieth century, and ending with the fifth wave. Next, the chapter details the possible determinants of wealth creation as found in U.S. and European literature and distinguishes between characteristics of the takeover bid, of the bidder and target firms, and of the legal environment of bidder and target. Third, we provide a detailed analysis of the most recent wave. The chapter partly hinges on the work by Martynova and Renneboog (2006, 2008a, and 2010).

TAKEOVER PROFITABILITY: TAKEOVER VALUE AND ITS DETERMINANTS

In this section, we discuss how the stock market reacts to the announcement of a takeover announcement and examine the value drivers in mergers and acquisitions. We conclude this section by focusing on the impact of corporate governance regulation on takeover profitability.

Takeover Value: Short-Term Wealth Effects

The empirical literature is unanimous in its conclusion that takeovers create value for the target and bidder shareholders combined as reflected in the announcement abnormal returns. However, the vast majority of the gains accrue to the target shareholders. The evidence on the wealth effects for the bidder shareholders is mixed; some reap small, positive abnormal returns while others suffer (small) losses. Exhibit 27.1 gives an overview of studies dealing with the abnormal returns around takeover announcements. The findings in the table refer to successful domestic M&As between nonfinancial companies.

Target-Firm Stockholder Return

For all merger waves, Exhibit 27.1 shows that the share prices of target firms significantly increase at, and around, the announcement of a bid. Martynova and Renneboog (2008a) provide a more detailed table. For instance, for target firms acquired during the 1960–1970s, Eckbö (1983) as well as Eckbö and Langohr (1989) report significant positive cumulative average abnormal returns (CAARs) on the announcement day and the subsequent day. They show that these CAARs amount to a 6 percent increase for the United States and a 16 percent increase for France (panel A of Exhibit 27.1). Higher CAARs, of at least 16 percent, are reported for U.S. target firms in the 1980s and 1990s (panels B–D). Schwert (1996) shows that the share price reactions of target shareholders are not limited to the announcement day but commence 42 working days before the initial public announcement of the bid. Indeed, the price run-up is substantial and often exceeds the announcement effect itself: The run-up premium amounts to between 13.3 percent and 21.8 percent measured over a period of one month before the bid. These preannouncement returns imply that the market anticipates bids as a result of rumors, information leakages, or insider trading.

Exhibit 27.1 also reports that the abnormal returns of target firms measured over a holding period of two weeks surrounding the announcement date range from 14 percent to 44 percent. However, the two-week abnormal returns vary significantly through the decades. Bradley, Desai, and Kim (1988) and Bhagat, Dong, Hirshleifer, and Noah (2005) show that these returns amount to 18 to 19 percent over the 1960s, increase to 32 to 35 percent over the 1980s, and further increase to 32 to 45 percent over the 1990–2001 period. Changes in insider-trading laws and takeover regulation introduced in the United States in the late 1960s and 1980s may partially account for these differences.

Overall, empirical research shows that the shareholders of target firms accumulate significant positive CAARs in the period around the bid announcement. These CAARs can be partitioned into those realized before the bid announcement, the announcement returns, and those realized after the bid announcement. Whereas the announcement and post-announcement CAARs are similar across the takeover waves, the preannouncement CAARs (and hence the total CAARs) have been significantly different over time. The total takeover returns to the target firm shareholders have been increasing over the takeover waves.

Bidding-Firm Stockholder Returns

The contrast between the large takeover returns to target firms and the frequently negligible returns to bidding firms is striking. On average, bidder shareholders earn announcement abnormal returns that are statistically indistinguishable from zero. For takeovers during the 1960s and 1970s, Eckbö (1983) reports positive abnormal returns of 0.2 percent and 0.1 percent, respectively (panel A of Exhibit 27.1); for the late 1970s and the 1980s, Byrd and Hickman (1992) and Chang (1998) report negative abnormal returns ranging from –2.5 percent to –0.7 percent (panel B); and for takeovers occurring in the 1990s, the findings of 13 studies are split almost evenly between positive and negative returns (panel C). The fact that all these gains

Exhibit 27.1 Short-term Effects around M&A Announcements

This table presents the market reaction to M&A announcements. The results are for successful domestic takeovers between nonfinancial firms. The following notation is used.

Types of mergers and acquisitions: TO = tender offer, M = merger, MA = M&As, HMA = horizontal M&A, VMA = vertical M&A, RMA = related M&A (nonconglomerate), UMA = unrelated M&A (conglomerate or diversification), A = acquisition, FA = friendly acquisition, HA = hostile acquisition, Stock = all-stock offer, Cash = all-cash offer, Mixed = combination of stock and cash offer, Public (Pub) = Target company is public, Private (Priv) = Target company is private.

Benchmark Return Models: MM = Market model; MAM = Market-adjusted model; CAPM = Capital asset pricing model; BMCP = Beta-matched control portfolio (CRSP); FFM = Fama-French model; VPE = Valuation prediction error; PSM = Probability scaling method; TTA = Thin-trade adjusted; EV/PA = The ratio of the change in the bidder equity value to the acquisition price; SBM = size and book-to-market ratio matched portfolio, following the Barber and Lyon (1997) methodology. *Close* refers to the date when the target is delisted from trading on public exchanges.

Sample size: T/B/C stands for the number of observations for target firms/bidding firms/combined firms, respectively. If the three samples have the same number of observations, only one number is reported. (*Source:* Martynova and Renneboog 2008a.)

Significance level: * = significance is not reported; a/b/c = statistical significance at 0.01, 0.05, and 0.10 levels, respectively.

Study, Sample Country	Sample Period	Benchmark Return Model	Event Window (Days)	Sample Size: T/B/C	Type of M&A	CAARs Target %	CAARs Bidder %	CAARs Combined %
Panel A. Second and Third Takeover Waves, 1910s–1929 and 1950s–1973								
Eckbö (1983), U.S.	1963–1978	MM	(−1, +1)	57/102	HM	+6.24[a]	+0.07	
			(−20, +10)	57/102		+14.08[a]	+1.58	
Dennis and McConnell (1986), U.S.	1962–1980	MAM	(−19, 0)	76/90	M	+16.67[a]	+1.07	
			(−6, +6)			+13.74[b]	+3.24[a]	
Lang, Stulz, and Walkling (1989), U.S.	1968–1986	MM	(−5, +5)	87	TO	+40.30[a]	+0. 01	+11.31[a]
Franks and Harris (1989), UK	1955–1985	MM, MAM, CAPM; results for MAM, TTA	(0, +20)	1,693/1,012	TO	+24.0[b]	+1.2[b]	
				121/46	M	+14.8[b]	−3.6[b]	
Eckbö and Langohr (1989), France	1966–1982	MM	(0, +5)	90/52	TO, public	+16.48[a]	−0.29	

Panel B. Fourth Takeover Wave, 1981–1989

Franks, Harris, and Titman (1991), U.S.	1975–1984	MM	(−5, +5)	399	All MA	+28.04[a]	−1.02[c]	+3.90[a]
				156	Cash	+33.78[a]	+0.83	+6.41[a]
				128	Stock	+22.88[a]	−3.15[a]	+0.42
				114	Mixed	+25.81[a]	−1.18	+4.38[a]
				93	HA	+39.49[a]	−1.35	+8.91[a]
				306	FA	+24.57[a]	−0.92[c]	+2.41[a]
Servaes (1991), U.S.	1972–1987	MM	(0, close)	577/307/307	FA	+21.89[a]	−0.16	+3.29[a]
				125/77/77	HA	+31.77[a]	−4.71	+5.08[c]
Kaplan and Weisbach (1992), U.S.	1971–1982	MM	(−5, +5)	209/271/209	M&TO	+26.9[a]	−1.49[a]	+3.74[a]
Healy, Palepu, and Ruback (1992), U.S.	1979–1984	MAM	(−5, close)	50	Largest A	+45.6[a]	−2.2	+9.1[a]
Byrd and Hickman (1992), U.S.	1980–1987	MM	(−1, 0)	128	TO		−1.23	
Schwert (1996), U.S.	1975–1991	MM	(−42, −1)	959	M	+11.90[b]	+1.4*	
			(−42, −1)	564	TO	+15.60[b]	+1.70*	
			(0, close)	959	M	+4.90[b]	−3.4*	
			(0, close)	564	TO	+20.10[b]	+2.5*	
Chang (1998), U.S.	1981–1992	MM	(−1, 0)	101	Public, cash		−0.02	
				154	Public, stock		−2.46[a]	
				131	Private, cash		+0.09	
				150	Private, stock		+2.64[a]	
Franks and Mayer (1996), UK	1985–1986	MAM	(0, +20)	34	FA	+18.44[a]		
				32	HA	+29.76[a]		
Danbolt (2004), UK	1986–1991	Size—decile, MAM, MM, CAPM	(0, +20)	514	Domestic deals	+18.76[a]		
			(−2, +1)			+20.64[a]		
			(+1, +5)			−1.85[a]		
Doukas, Holmen, and Travlos (2002), Sweden	1980–1995	MM	(−5, +5)	46	RMA		+2.74[a]	
				46	UMA		−2.37[c]	

(continued)

Exhibit 27.1 Short-term Effects around M&A Announcements (*Continued*)

Study, Sample Country	Sample Period	Benchmark Return Model	Event Window (Days)	Sample Size: T/B/C	Type of M&A	CAARs Target %	CAARs Bidder %	CAARs Combined %
Panel C. Fifth Takeover Wave, 1993–2001								
Datta, Iskandar-Datta, and Raman (2001), U.S.	1993–1998	MM	(−1, 0)	1577	M		+0.003	
				142	TO		+0.23	
				337	Cash		+0.52[a]	
				1382	No cash		−0.10	
Moeller, Schlingemann, and Stulz (2004), U.S.	1980–2001	MM	(−1, +1)	4862	Cash		+1.38[a]	
				2958	Stock		+0.15[a]	
				4203	Mixed		+1.45[a]	
				2642	Public		−1.02[a]	
				5583	Private		+1.49[a]	
Fuller, Netter, and Stegemoller (2002), U.S.	1990–2000	MAM	(−2, +2)	456	Public		−1.00[b]	
				2060	Private		+2.08[a]	
Sudarsanam and Mahate (2003), UK	1983–1995	4 methods, results are for MAM	(−1, +1)	519	All deals		−1.39[a]	
			(+2, +40)				+0.14	
Faccio and Stolin (2006) and Faccio, McConnell, and Stolin (2006), Europe	1996–2001	MAM	(−2, +2)	735	Public, all		−0.38	
				436	Public, cash		+0.30	
				189	Public, stock		−1.81[b]	
				110	Public, mix		−0.66	
				3694	Private, all		+1.48[a]	
				2876	Private, cash		+1.17[a]	
				201	Private, stock		+3.90[a]	
				617	Private, mixed		+2.14[a]	

Goergen and Renneboog (2004), Europe	1993–2001	6 methods, results are for MM (TTA)	(−2, +2)	40/41	M	+12.62[a]	+4.35[a]	
				53/55	FA	+11.33[a]	+1.94[a]	
				28/32	HA	+17.95[a]	−3.43[a]	
				88/86	Cash	+13.56[a]	+0.90[c]	
				30/33	Stock	+11.38[a]	+2.57[a]	
				18/23	Mixed	+13.24[a]	+0.22	
Campa and Hernando (2004), EU	1998–2000	CAPM	(−1, +1)	182	Domestic deals	+3.86[b]	+0.61	+1.33[b]
Martynova and Renneboog (2006, 2010), Europe	1993–2001	6 methods, results are for MM (TTA)	(−5, +5)	259/1659	M	+6.25[a]	+1.07[a]	
				380/329	FA	+20.19[a]	−0.29	
				123/120	HA	+22.36[a]	−0.18	
				405/754	Cash	+20.17[a]	+1.03[a]	
				185/285	Stock	+11.10[a]	+0.66	
				92/412	Mixed	+17.48[a]	+1.03[c]	
				525/1334	RMA	+15.16[a]	+0.98[a]	
				234/774	UMA	+17.36[a]	+0.45	
Holmen and Knopf (2004), Sweden	1985–1995	MM	(−5, +5)	121	TO	+16.99[a]	+0.32	+4.12[a]
Schaik and Steenbeek (2004), Japan	1993–2003	MM	(−1, +1)	136	All deals		+0.57	
Bae, Kang, and Kim (2002), Korea	1981–1997	MM	(−5, +5)	107	M all		+2.666[b]	
				66	RMA		+3.904[a]	
				41	UMA		+0.672	

(continued)

Exhibit 27.1 Short-term Effects around M&A Announcements (*Continued*)

Study, Sample Country	Sample Period	Benchmark Return Model	Event Window (Days)	Sample Size: T/B/C	Type of M&A	CAARs Target %	CAARs Bidder %	CAARs Combined %
Panel D: Takeover Waves Comparison								
Bradley, Desai, and Kim (1988), U.S.	1963–1968	MM	(−5, +5)	51	TO	+18.92[a]	+4.09[a]	+7.78[a]
	1968–1980			133		+35.29[a]	+1.30	+7.08[a]
	1981–1984			52		+35.34[a]	−2.93[a]	+8.00[a]
	1963–1984			236		+31.77[a]	+0.97[b]	+7.43[a]
Andrade, Mitchell, and Stafford (2001), U.S.	1973–1979	MM	(−1, +1)	598	All deals	+16.0[b]	−0.3	+1.5
	1980–1989			1226	All deals	+16.0[b]	−0.4	+2.6[b]
	1990–1998			1864	All deals	+15.9[b]	−1.0	+1.4[b]
	1973–1998			3688	All deals	+16.0[b]	−0.7	+1.8[b]
	1973–1998			2194	Stock	+13.0[b]	−1.5[a]	+0.6
	1973–1998			1494	No stock	+20.1[a]	+0.4	+3.6[b]
Moeller and Schlingemann and Stulz (2005), U.S.	1980–1990	MM	(−1, +1)	448	All deals		+0.64	
	1991–2001			1519			+1.20[*]	
	1998–2001			729			+0.69[*]	
Moeller and Schlingemann (2005), U.S.	1985–1990	MAM	(−1, +1)	1214	Domestic deals		+0.44[a]	
	1990–1995			2832			+1.49[c]	
Bhagat, Dong, Hirschleifer, and Noah (2005), U.S.	1962–1968	MM; results differ when new PSM is applied	(−5, +5)	71	TO	+17.96[a]	+3.29[a]	+7.45[a]
	1968–1980			176		+27.97[a]	+0.05	+6.40[a]
	1981–1984			45		+31.90[a]	−1.42[c]	+8.12[a]
	1985–1988			214		+25.61[a]	−0.49	+5.19[a]
	1989–1992			84		+29.08[a]	−1.78[a]	+3.59[a]
	1993–1996			139		+31.92[a]	+0.98	+5.05[a]
	1997–2000			210		+33.18[a]	+0.97[c]	+4.61[a]
	2000–2001			79		+44.78[a]	−0.81	+3.57[a]

and losses are statistically insignificant and do not differ across takeover waves is confirmed by the comparative study of Andrade, Mitchell, and Stafford (2001).

The one-month share price run-up before a takeover announcement is mostly insignificant for bidder shareholders. For instance, Dennis and McConnell (1986) report that the abnormal bidder gains in the third wave are close to zero (panel A). Schwert (1996) arrives at a similar (insignificant) result (1.7 percent) for tender offers during the fourth takeover wave (panel B).

In sum, the evidence suggests that shareholders of the bidding firm earn insignificant CAARs before and at the announcement of a takeover. This holds for each takeover wave and there are no significant differences in the preannouncement and announcement bidder CAARs across waves. The differences emerge when post-announcement and total returns are scrutinized. There was a substantial decrease in the returns during the third takeover wave but an increase during the fourth one. The next section shows that most of these changes in CAARs across waves can be attributed to differing takeover bid characteristics within each wave.

The Determinants of Takeover Value

Theoretical and empirical M&A literature show that a variety of factors affect takeover announcement returns. Empirical studies document that changes in the bidder-firm and target-firm share prices at the announcement of the M&A depend on the attributes of the transaction and the characteristics of the bidding and target firms. Bruner (2004) and Martynova and Renneboog (2006 and 2010) provide a detailed overview.

Takeover Characteristics

The following transaction attributes are likely to affect the takeover returns of bidders and targets:

- The geographical scope of the bid (domestic versus cross-border M&A).
- The form of and the attitude toward the bid (hostile versus unopposed bids, and negotiated deals versus tender offers).
- The legal status of the target firm (public versus privately held).
- The industry relatedness of the bidding and target firms (a focus versus diversification strategy of the bidder).
- The type of acquisition (full versus partial acquisitions).
- The means of payment (all cash, all equity, mixed offer).

Bidding and target firms participating in *cross-border mergers and acquisitions* are likely to benefit by taking advantage of imperfections in international capital, factor, and product markets, by internalizing the research and development (R&D) capacity of foreign target companies, and by expanding their businesses into new markets (as a response to globalization). As these synergies are unavailable to firms involved in domestic M&As, the takeover wealth effect may *ceteris paribus* be higher in cross-border deals. However, Schoenberg (1999) argues that regulatory and cultural differences between the bidder's and target's countries may induce difficulties in the post-merger consolidation process and result in a failure to achieve the envisaged merger synergies. Anticipating such difficulties in cross-border bids, the market may discount the expected takeover gains. Conn, Cosh, Guest, and Hughes (2005) and Moeller and Schlingemann (2005) provide evidence consistent with this latter prediction.

Hostile takeovers (opposed bids) generally target poorly performing firms and create value by improving the corporate governance of these firms (i.e., by replacing their management). Despite the expected gains from the improved corporate governance of target firms, hostile takeovers are frequently associated with lower wealth effects to the bidder's shareholders (see, for example, Franks and Mayer [1996]; Goergen and Renneboog [2004]). Shareholders of bidding firms fear their firm will offer too high a premium if the target opposes the bid or if the bidder makes an offer directly to the target's shareholders (bypassing the board of directors). The anticipated upward revisions in the offer premium may erode the takeover gains accruing to the bidder's shareholders. Conversely, the higher wealth effects for the targets reflect the fact that opposition against the bid may be a profitable bargaining strategy to extract a higher offer price.

Takeover bids on privately held companies may lead to bidders' returns exceeding those obtained in the bids on public firms (see, for example, Faccio, McConnell, and Stolin [2006]). The shares of privately held firms are by definition illiquid, which may create a price discount. Also, takeover negotiations with the owners of private firms may have a better chance of succeeding than when a public tender offer has to be launched for a widely held firm. However, the acquisition of a private firm may also entail considerably more risk due to the potential unreliability of the available information about the firm's true value and growth potential.

Although *diversifying* (or *conglomerate*) acquisitions are expected to create operational and financial synergies, the creation of diversified firms is associated with various negative attributes such as rent-seeking behavior by divisional managers (Scharfstein and Stein 2000), bargaining problems within the firm (Rajan, Servaes, and Zingales 2000), or bureaucratic rigidity (Shin and Stulz 1998). These disadvantages of diversification may outweigh the alleged synergies and result in wealth destruction for the bidder's shareholders. Diversifying mergers may be an outgrowth of agency conflicts between managers and shareholders (Shleifer and Vishny 1991). As such, M&As between companies operating in unrelated industries are expected to trigger lower takeover returns to the bidder's shareholders than M&As between firms in related industries. Conversely, the wealth effects to the shareholders of the target firm are likely to be higher in diversifying M&As. The reason is that investors expect bidders pursuing diversification strategies to bid more aggressively and hence pay higher takeover premiums than bidders adhering to a focus strategy.

Partial acquisitions of less than 100 percent of the equity are likely to lead to lower takeover returns to the target's shareholders than acquisitions in which a bidder obtains full control. Bidding firms may use partial acquisitions as an instrument to transfer wealth from the target's minority shareholders to themselves, potentially by using pyramidal control chains (Bertrand and Mullainathan 2003). The incidence of partial acquisitions depends on the extent to which legal and judiciary systems tolerate the extraction of private benefits. The highest incidence of partial acquisitions is expected in countries that provide little legal or regulatory protection to minority shareholders—in other words, where private benefits of control are high.

The *means of payment* is another important transaction characteristic that influences the short-term wealth effects of a takeover. All-cash takeovers are expected to generate higher returns to the bidder's and target's shareholders than all-equity deals (see, for example, Moeller, Schlingemann, and Stulz [2004]; Martynova and Renneboog [2009b]). The dominant explanation is that investors consider an equity offer as a signal that the bidder's shares are overpriced and hence adjust the share price downward. This is in line with the notion that managers attempt to time equity issues to coincide with surging stock markets or even with the peak of the stock market cycle. The market interprets a cash offer as a positive signal about the target firm's quality as the bidding firm is buying out the target's shareholders and is therefore not willing to share future value increases with them. As such, the wealth effect to the bidder's and target's shareholders is higher in all-cash takeovers than in takeovers involving equity payments.

Characteristics of Bidding and Target Firms

The bidder's characteristics that are likely to influence short-term wealth effects are firm size, Q-ratio, leverage, cash flows, and the preannouncement share price run-up. The *size of the bidder* is considered a proxy for managerial hubris (Roll 1986), as larger acquirers tend to overpay in takeovers (Moeller et al. 2004). Therefore, the bidder's takeover returns are expected to decrease with firm size. The *bidder's Q-ratio* is a proxy for the firm's growth potential and the quality of internal corporate governance. Lang, Stulz, and Walkling (1989) and Servaes (1991) document higher returns for bidders with higher Q-ratios. In contrast, Moeller et al. (2004) find a negative relationship between bidder's returns and Q-ratios for their sample of U.S. takeovers conducted in the 1990s. Therefore, the expected effect of the bidder's Q-ratio on returns is ambiguous. A significant relationship is expected between the bidder's takeover returns and *cash flows* and *leverage*, as these characteristics should discern the acquisitions driven by agency problems (free cash flow). Bidders with high cash flow and low leverage are more likely to make value-destroying acquisitions. Finally, the market reaction to the takeover announcement may depend on the bidder's prior share performance as measured by the bidder's *preannouncement share price run-up*.

Beyond the bidder's leverage and cash flows influencing short-term wealth effects, the leverage and cash flows of the target also play a role. Specifically, bidders are likely to pay a higher premium for a target with low leverage and high cash flows. The shareholders of target firms with high growth opportunities (high Q-ratio) and good prior share performance are also likely to earn higher returns.

Uncertainty about the target's true market value implies a higher probability that a bidder may incur substantial losses in the case of a post-acquisition adverse revaluation of the acquired assets. The magnitude of the potential revaluation losses to the bidder increases with the *target firm's relative size*. Therefore, the bidder's announcement returns are expected to decrease with the relative size of the target.

Bidders can make substantial profits on the *toehold stake* built up before the takeover. The larger the toehold, the lower the number of shares for which the bidder pays the full takeover premium (Grossman and Hart 1980; Shleifer and Vishny 1986). Therefore, the larger the toehold stake before the bid, the lower the average takeover price a bidder will have to pay—that is, the bidder's returns increase with the toehold and the target's returns decrease.

Corporate Governance Environment

English-origin countries (such as the United States and the United Kingdom) and Continental European countries represent two different types of *corporate governance regimes*: the market-based and the blockholder-based systems, respectively (McCahery and Renneboog, 2002). The market-based system of English-origin countries relies on legal rules, largely resulting from case law, and on the effective legal enforcement of shareholder rights. The blockholder-based system of Continental Europe relies on codified law and emphasizes rules protecting stakeholders such as creditors and employees. A growing body of literature advocates that the U.S. and UK corporate governance systems ensure better investor protection and stronger corporate focus on shareholder value than the corporate governance regimes of the Continental European countries (La Porta, Lopez-de-Silanes, Shleifer, and Vishny 1997). Recent empirical research documents that better investor protection and a more shareholder-oriented corporate governance focus results in lower agency costs and higher company valuations and growth potential (Levine 1999). Extending these arguments to M&As, takeovers by UK and U.S. firms likely yield higher returns to the bidders' and targets' shareholders than takeovers by Continental European firms.

DATA SOURCES AND METHODOLOGY

In this section, we report the sample selection and the event study methodology used for the empirical part of this chapter.

Sample Selection

To illustrate the relation between the determinants of value in takeovers as derived from economic theory and earlier empirical research, Martynova and Renneboog (2010) create a sample of European M&A announcements consisting of 2,419 deals involving firms from 28 European countries. The sample consists of European acquisitions undertaken during the fifth takeover wave (1993–2001) from the Mergers and Acquisitions Database of the Securities Data Company (SDC).

Methodology

Takeover announcement returns are the sum of daily abnormal returns realized in the period starting one day before and ending one day after the event day. Considering longer event windows within the (–60, +60) interval is necessary to capture the preannouncement and post-announcement effects. Daily abnormal returns are computed as the difference between realized and market model benchmark returns, which proxy for the returns that would be generated in case the takeover bid would not have taken place. The market model uses the MSCI-Europe Index and the parameters are estimated over 240 days, starting 300 days before the acquisition announcement. The estimates of the abnormal returns are robust with respect to different choices of the market index (local, European-wide, and worldwide index) and the estimation model of the benchmark returns (the estimated beta is adjusted for mean-reversion and nonsynchronous trading). In the multivariate analysis, Martynova and Renneboog (2010) model the market reaction to takeover announcements consisting of two components: the pre-event days (period [–60, –2]) and the announcement effect (the three days around the bid announcement).

MARKET REACTION TO TAKEOVER ANNOUNCEMENTS

This section contains the results of the univariate analyses of bidder's and target's cumulative average abnormal returns (CAARs) realized in intra-European M&As. The CAARs are related to the various characteristics of target and bidding firms and of the bid itself (Martynova and Renneboog 2009a, 2009b, and 2010).

Univariate Analysis

Target versus Bidding Firms

As a bidding firm is expected to create substantial corporate value when it acquires a target firm, the target shareholders will only be interested to sell their share stakes if they are offered a substantial premium. This premium should be immediately reflected in the target firms' share prices. Exhibit 27.2 depicts that the announcement of a takeover bid causes substantial positive abnormal returns for the target shareholders: An abnormal return of 9 percent is realized on the event day. In addition, the target firm's share price significantly increases over a period of two months (about 40 trading days) before the initial public announcement. On average, investors who own shares in the target firm for a period starting two months before the event day and sell their shares at the end of the event day earn a return of 21 percent. After about 25 trading days following the event day, the CAAR decreases by 2 percent. This decrease is due to the fact that some bidders withdraw their offers as a consequence of successful opposition by the target's board of directors, or as a result of delays in takeover negotiations that raise investors' concerns about the ultimate success of the bid.

In comparison to the target CAARs, the price reactions for the bidding firms are modest: Exhibit 27.3 shows a small but statistically significant at the 1 percent level abnormal return of 0.5 percent. Over a 10-day window centered on the event day, the statistically significant CAAR amounts to 0.8 percent. Strikingly, the CAARs of the bidding firm generated over a three-month period (–3 percent) after the bid are significantly negative. This negative pattern in post-announcement abnormal returns is mainly due to the collapse of the M&A market that followed the burst of the technology bubble in 2000. Given that the target shareholders capture most of the anticipated wealth creation, the remainder of this section mainly provides a discussion of the target CAARs.

Hostile Bids versus Friendly Mergers and Acquisitions

Martynova and Renneboog (2009a, 2009b, and 2010) partition all bids into three groups based on the target firm's attitude toward the bid (hostile versus friendly)

This figure shows the market reaction to the announcement of M&A transactions for target firms as well as the CAARs before and after the event (day 0). The benchmark used in the market model is the MSCI-Europe index returns; the model parameters are estimated over 240 days starting 300 days before the acquisition announcement.

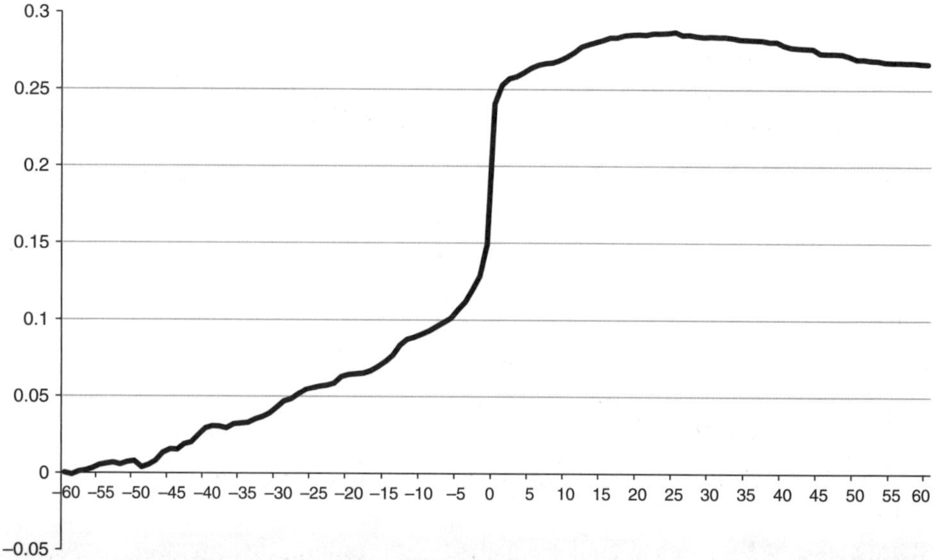

Exhibit 27.2 Target CAARs around the M&A Announcement
Source: Martynova and Renneboog (2006).

This figure shows the market reaction to the announcement of M&A transactions for bidding firms as well as the CAARs before and after the event (day 0). The benchmark used in the market model is the MSCI-Europe index returns; the model parameters are estimated over 240 days starting 300 days before the acquisition announcement.

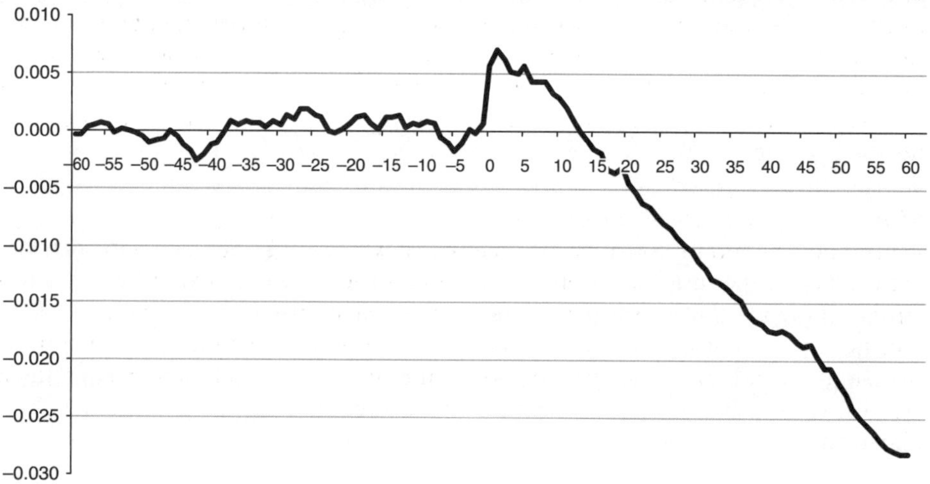

Exhibit 27.3 Bidder CAARs around the M&A Announcement
Source: Martynova and Renneboog (2006).

This figure shows the evolution of the market reaction to the announcement of M&A transactions for target firms by bid attitude and by form of the bid. The sample of hostile acquisitions includes deals in which the target firm's board opposes the takeover and deals in which a competing bidder was present. The benchmark used in the market model is the MSCI-Europe index returns; the model parameters are estimated over 240 days starting 300 days before the acquisition announcement.

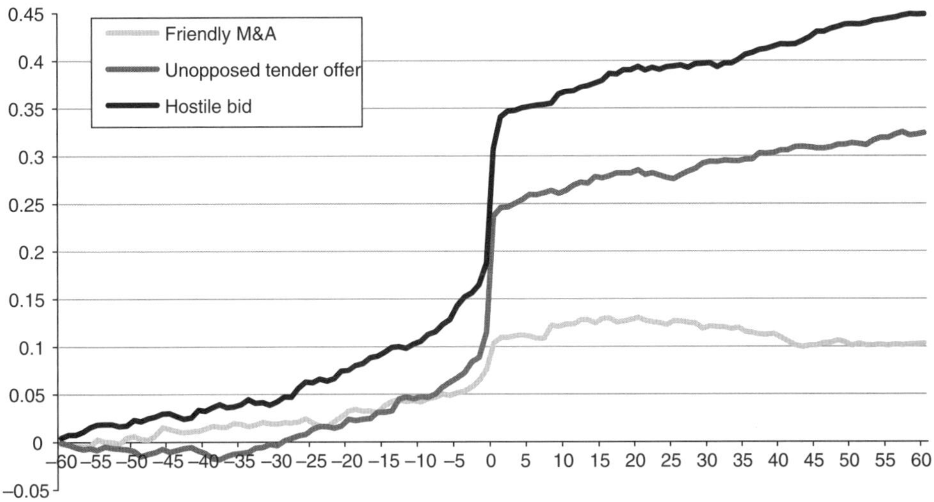

Exhibit 27.4 Target CAARs by Bid Attitude (Friendly vs. Hostile) and by Form of the Bid (Tender Offer vs. Negotiated M&As)
Source: Martynova and Renneboog (2006).

and by the form of the bid (tender offer versus negotiated M&A). For all bid types, a strong positive increase in the target's share price arises at the time of bid announcement, as shown by Exhibit 27.4. Expectedly, hostile bids generate the largest abnormal returns (15 percent) to the target shareholders on the announcement day. The returns of hostile takeover bids are significantly higher than the ones for friendly M&As (3 percent) and unopposed tender offers (12 percent). Exhibit 27.4 also demonstrates that there are large differences in the share price run-ups between friendly and hostile takeover bids, suggesting that the market anticipates hostile takeovers.

Means of Payment in Takeover Bids

Researchers generally consider the means of payment to be an important signal of the quality of the target firm or the potential synergy value. Exhibit 27.5 reports strong evidence that the target's share price reaction is indeed sensitive to the means of payment in a takeover bid. All-cash offers as well as bids combining cash, equity, and loan notes trigger substantially higher target's abnormal returns (12 percent and 10 percent, respectively, at the announcement) than all-equity bids (7 percent).

UK versus Continental European Bids

In comparison with their UK peers, Continental European companies operate in an environment with weaker investor protection (La Porta et al., 1997). A

This figure shows the market reaction to the announcement of M&A transactions for target firms by means of payment employed in the transaction: all-cash, all-equity, and mixed cash/equity, or offers of which the payment was not disclosed (and remains unknown to date). The benchmark used in the market model is the MSCI-Europe index returns; the model parameters are estimated over 240 days starting 300 days before the acquisition announcement.

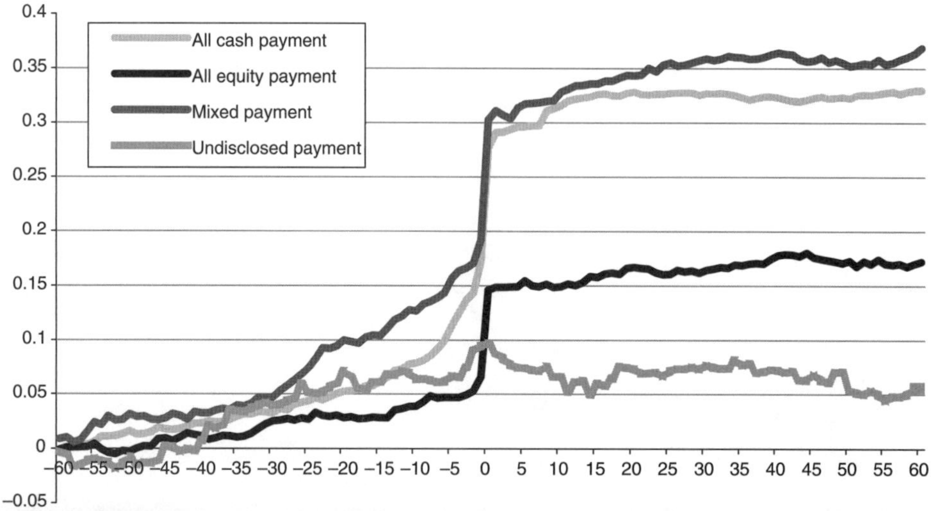

Exhibit 27.5 Target CAARs by Means of Payment
Source: Martynova and Renneboog (2006).

growing body of literature advocates that weaker investor protection results in higher agency costs, lower company valuations, and poorer growth potential (La Porta et al. 2002; Himmelberg, Hubbard, and Love 2002). Extending these arguments to M&As, Martynova and Renneboog (2010) expect takeovers by Continental European firms to yield lower returns to the target's shareholders than takeovers by UK firms. In line with this prediction, the announcement effect is substantially larger for the UK target firms in both domestic and cross-border bids (13.7 percent and 13.8 percent, respectively) than for Continental European targets (4.5 percent and 5.9 percent, respectively). See Exhibit 27.6.

Legal Origin of the Bidding and Target Firms

Although the difference in CAARs between Continental Europe and the United Kingdom is remarkable, some variation also occurs in the market reaction to takeovers within the Continental European countries. Differences in laws and their subsequent enforcement may explain a part of this variation (Bris and Cabolis 2007 and 2008; Rossi and Volpin 2004). For instance, evidence shows that takeover premiums are higher in countries with better shareholder protection and in countries where the law enforces mandatory bid requirements. The mandatory bid rule requires the acquirer to make a tender offer to all the shareholders once he has accumulated a certain percentage of the shares. In the United Kingdom, for example, when a shareholder acquires a share stake of 30 percent, he is required to make an offer to buy out all remaining shares (Goergen, Martynova, and Renneboog, 2005).

The figure shows the market reaction to the announcement of domestic and cross-border M&A transactions for UK and Continental European target firms. The benchmark used in the market model is the MSCI-Europe index returns; the model parameters are estimated over 240 days starting 300 days before the acquisition announcement.

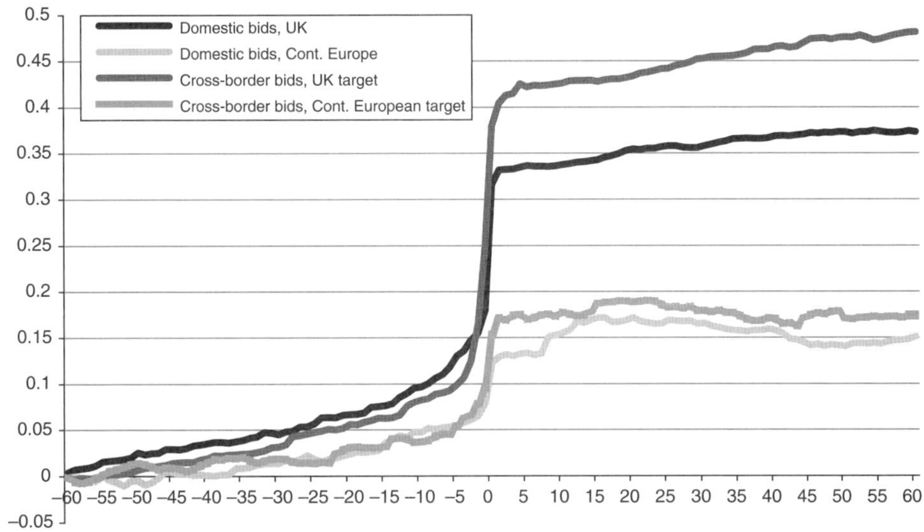

Exhibit 27.6 Target CAARs, United Kingdom versus Continental European Targets
Source: Martynova and Renneboog (2006).

The ownership threshold triggering a mandatory bid varies by country (Faccio and Lang, 2002).

To measure the impact of the legal environment on takeover premiums, Martynova and Renneboog (2010) classify all acquisitions into five groups according to the legal origin of the target firms. As documented earlier, the target firms of English legal origin experience very large wealth effects (of 27.9 percent over the event day and the price run-up period). Notably, target firms in Scandinavian countries, with similar corporate governance legislation and financial institution features as the United Kingdom (LaPorta, Lopez-de-Silanes, Shleifer, and Vishny 1998) also exhibit positive CAARs (21 percent). Target firms based in countries of the European Union enlargement of 2004 and 2007 experience the lowest announcement effect (–0.5 percent). Target firms of French and German legal origin also experience particularly low CAARs (1.7 percent and 2.3 percent, respectively). See Exhibit 27.7.

Focused Strategies versus Diversification Strategies

Exhibit 27.8 compares the CAARs of target firms in diversifying takeovers to firms in industry-related M&As. The target shareholders earn significantly larger returns (by 2.4 percent) in M&As by bidders operating in unrelated industries. Regardless of the length of the window, diversifying takeovers beat M&As with a focus strategy in the short run. This suggests that bidders overpay for target firms from unrelated industries as they tend to engage in more aggressive bidding strategies.

This figure shows the market reaction to the announcement of domestic M&A transactions for target firms by legal origin. Countries are grouped according to their legal origin following the classification by LaPorta et al. (1998) and according to the EU enlargement process. Countries are grouped as follows: English legal origin (Republic of Ireland and the United Kingdom), German legal origin (Austria, Germany, Switzerland), French legal origin (Belgium, France, Greece, Italy, Luxembourg, the Netherlands, Portugal, Spain), Scandinavian legal origin (Denmark, Iceland, Finland, Norway, Sweden), the EU enlargement consists of Czech Republic, Cyprus, Estonia, Hungary, Latvia, Lithuania, Poland, Slovak Republic, Slovenia, Bulgaria, Romania. The benchmark used in the market model is the MSCI-Europe index returns; the model parameters are estimated over 240 days starting 300 days before the acquisition announcement.

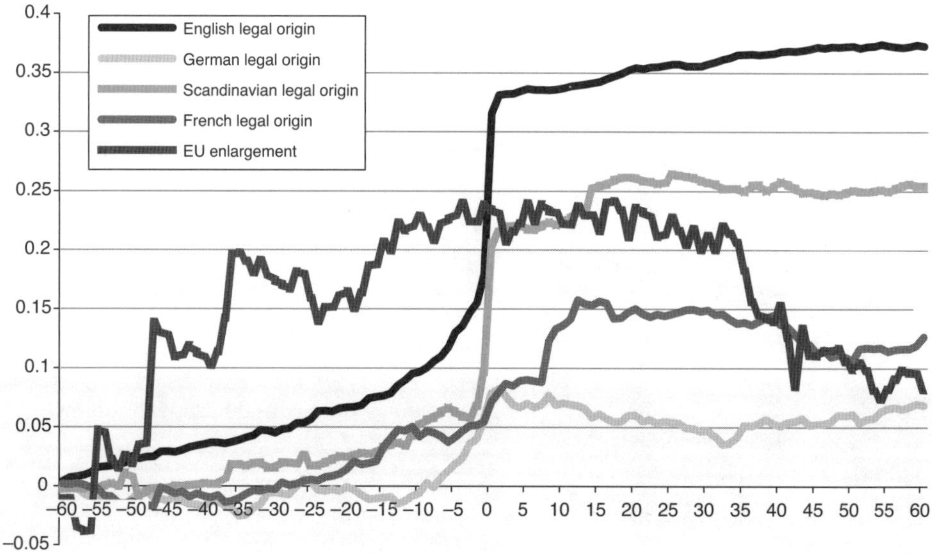

Exhibit 27.7 Target CAARs in Domestic Bids by Legal Origin
Source: Martynova and Renneboog (2006).

Public versus Private Target Firms

Acquisitions of privately held companies account for more than 60 percent of intra-European acquisitions. Theoretical and empirical literature suggests that bids for such firms may lead to bidder returns that exceed those obtained in bids for public firms. The announcement of an acquisition of a private firm causes significantly positive abnormal returns of 0.8 percent to the bidder's shareholders, whereas the announcement of a bid for a public firm results in an (insignificantly) negative return of –0.1 percent.

Multivariate Analysis of the Anticipated Takeover Gains

The results of the univariate analysis suggest that the market reaction to takeover announcements varies across takeover bids with different characteristics. Martynova and Renneboog (2010) explore which of the effects documented in the previous section dominates in a multivariate framework. The authors first run the regressions of the target's CAARs measured over the (–1, +1) window on the characteristics of bidding firms, target firms, and of the takeover deal. In line with the results of the univariate analysis, multivariate regression analysis shows that

This figure shows the market reaction to the announcement of M&A transactions for target firms by takeover strategy (focus versus diversification). A takeover strategy is considered to be focus-oriented if the two-digit SIC codes of the bidding and target firms coincide, and to be diversification-oriented if this is not the case. The benchmark used in the market model is the MSCI-Europe index returns; the model parameters are estimated over 240 days starting 300 days before the acquisition announcement.

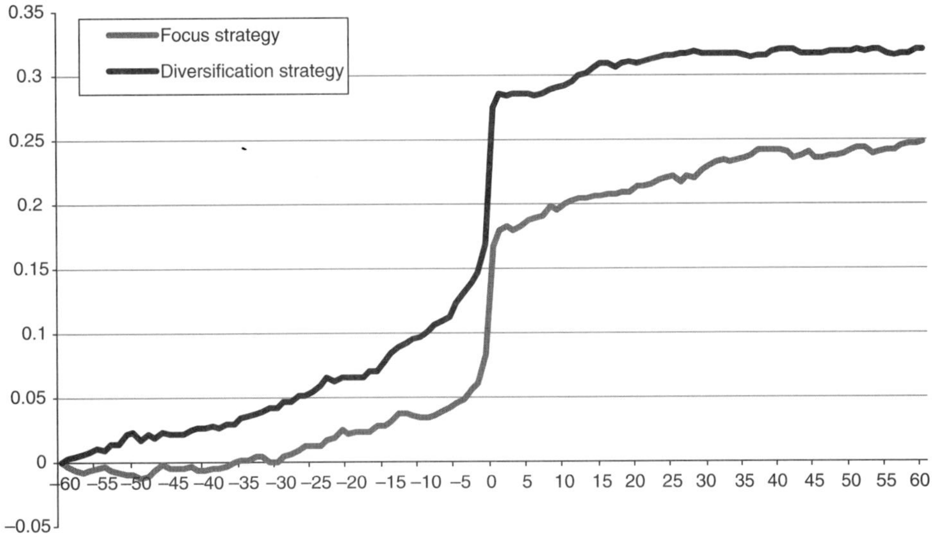

Exhibit 27.8 Target CAARs by Corporate Strategy, Focus versus Diversification
Source: Martynova and Renneboog (2006).

the target's shareholders obtain significantly higher returns at the announcement of opposed (hostile) bids and unopposed tender offers. Lower target announcement returns are observed in M&As with equity payments and in deals with undisclosed transaction terms. Target companies from the United Kingdom earn markedly higher announcement premiums than Continental European targets. Cross-border and diversifying takeovers trigger significant share price increases for Continental European target firms and have no significant impact on share price reaction for UK firms. When a UK company is acquired, the relative size of the transaction matters: An increase in the relative size leads to a reduction in the target's announcement returns.

In addition to these results, the multivariate analysis also reveals a significantly positive relation between the share price run-up and the announcement returns of Continental European target firms. Remarkably, the results do not show such a relation for UK targets. The significant relation between announcement and run-up returns of Continental European targets suggests that the share price run-up, frequently caused by insider trading, is harmful to bidding firms as it significantly raises the price to be paid to acquire control. Another feature of M&As involving Continental European targets is the negative relation between the bidder's toehold and announcement returns accruing to the target's shareholders. A larger toehold implies a relatively lower total takeover price paid by the bidder. Interestingly, the relation between the toehold and the announcement effect is insignificant for UK firms.

Running similar regressions for the bidder's CAARs measured over the (–1, +1) shows, as in the case of the target's CAARs, that most of the results from the multivariate regression are consistent with those of the univariate analyses. Specifically, the results reveal that the announcement of a hostile takeover or a tender offer triggers significantly lower bidder's returns. Higher returns arise for bids for private targets and acquisitions of full control, while an all-equity offer forces investors to adjust bidder's returns downwards. UK bidders experience significantly lower announcement returns compared to Continental European bidders. This result is rather surprising because the law and finance literature predicts an opposite relation (La Porta et al. 1997 and 2002). The evidence suggests that Continental European investors expect their firms to capture higher profits in takeovers relative to their UK peers.

Martynova and Renneboog (2006 and 2010) provide a more detailed discussion of the results of pre- and post-announcement returns. A discussion of the financing decisions in takeovers can be found in Martynova and Renneboog (2009b); of the impact of financial regulation, in Goergen, Martynova, and Renneboog (2005) and Martynova and Renneboog (2008b and 2009a); and of the long-term operating performance, in Martynova, Oosting, and Renneboog (2007).

SUMMARY AND CONCLUSIONS

This chapter examines the market reaction to the announcements of corporate takeovers. It documents that the majority of takeover deals are expected to generate synergy value: takeovers trigger substantial share price increases at the announcement, most of which are captured by the target firm's shareholders. This is valid for all past research surveyed in this chapter as well as for a large sample of intra-European takeovers. Martynova and Renneboog (2010) find large announcement effects (9.13 percent) for the target firms compared to an announcement effect of merely 0.53 percent for the bidding firms.

The evidence shows systematic variation in the valuation effects of different types of takeovers. The takeover announcement returns are lower for bidders but higher for targets in hostile takeovers and tender offers. Acquisitions of private firms trigger significantly higher abnormal returns for the bidder's shareholders. Further, investors adjust both bidder's and target's share prices downwards at the announcement of all-equity offers. Also, Martynova and Renneboog (2010) demonstrate that takeovers occurring when takeover activity is slowing down trigger lower returns to both the bidder's and target's shareholders than deals at the beginning or peak of the wave.

When comparing UK and Continental European takeovers, the following additional results emerge. Shareholders of UK target firms are able to pocket significantly higher returns than their Continental European peers. This may be caused by differences in the corporate governance systems. This also may explain lower returns to UK bidders relative to Continental European bidders. Thus, the results point out that the differences in corporate governance systems may have significant impact on takeover profitability.

DISCUSSION QUESTIONS

1. Takeovers can be an important corporate governance device as they can discipline the management of a poorly performing target company. What synergies can be achieved in this type of takeover? What is the empirical evidence on the profitability of disciplining takeover?
2. The legal origin of the bidder and target firms has an impact on the returns in acquisitions. Why would the differences in legal origin and the differences in corporate governance regulation matter?
3. Diversifying takeovers are frequently associated with negative announcement returns to the bidders. Why would the market expect diversifying M&As to destroy value?
4. Empirical results show that bidding firms experience negative abnormal returns at the announcement of M&As paid with equity. Should one interpret this result as evidence that equity-paid M&As destroy wealth of the bidder's shareholders? Explain why or why not.

REFERENCES

Andrade, Gregor, Mark Mitchell, and Erik Stafford. 2001. New evidence and perspectives on mergers. *Journal of Economic Perspectives* 15 (2): 103–120.

Bae, Kee-Hong, Jun-Koo Kang, and Jin-Mo Kim. 2002. Tunneling or value added? Evidence from mergers by Korean business groups. *Journal of Finance* 57 (6): 2695–2740.

Barber, Brad M., and John D. Lyon. 1997. Detecting long-run abnormal stock returns: the empirical power and specification of test statistics. Journal of Financial Economics 43 (3): 341–372.

Bertrand, Marianne, and Sendhil Mullainathan. 2003. Pyramids. *Journal of the European Economic Association* 1 (2–3): 478–483.

Bhagat, Sanjai, Ming Dong, David Hirshleifer, and Robert Noah. 2005. Do tender offers create value? New methods and evidence. *Journal of Financial Economics* 76 (1): 3–60.

Bradley, Michael, Anand Desai, and E. Han Kim. 1988. Synergistic gains from corporate acquisitions and their division between the stockholders of target and acquiring firms. *Journal of Financial Economics* 21 (1): 3–40.

Bris, Arturo, and Christos Cabolis. 2007. Corporate governance convergence through cross-border mergers: The case of Aventis. In *Corporate governance and regulatory impact on mergers and acquisitions: Research and analysis on activity worldwide since 1990*, ed. Gregoriou Gregoriou and Luc Renneboog, 71–101. Boston Massachusetts: Elsevier.

———. 2008. The value of investor protection: Evidence from cross-border mergers. *Review of Financial Studies* 21 (2): 605–648.

Bruner, Robert F. 2004. Does M&A pay? In *Applied Mergers and Acquisitions*, ed. Robert F. Bruner, 11–15. Hoboken, NJ: Wiley Finance.

Byrd, John, and Kent A. Hickman. 1992. Do outside directors monitor managers? Evidence from tender offer bids. *Journal of Financial Economics* 32 (2): 195–214.

Campa, Jose M., and Ignacio Hernando. 2004. Shareholder value creation in European M&As. *European Financial Management* 10 (1): 47–81.

Chang, Saeyoung. 1998. Takeovers of privately held targets, methods of payment, and bidder returns. *Journal of Finance* 53 (2): 773–784.

Conn, Robert C. L., Andy Cosh, Paul M. Guest, and Alan Hughes. 2005. The impact on U.K. acquirers of domestic, cross-border, public and private acquisitions. *Journal of Business Finance and Accounting* 32 (5–6): 815–870.

Danbolt, Jo. 2004. Target company cross-border effects in acquisitions into the UK. *European Financial Management* 10 (1): 83–108.
Datta Sudip, Mai Iskandar-Datta, and Kartik Raman. 2001. Executive compensation and corporate acquisition decisions. *Journal of Finance* 56 (6): 2299–2336.
Dennis, Debra K., and John J. McConnell. 1986. Corporate mergers and security returns. *Journal of Financial Economics* 16 (2): 143–187.
Doukas, John A., Martin Holmen, and Nickolaos Travlos. 2002. Diversification, ownership and control of Swedish companies. *European Financial Management* 8 (3): 281–314.
Eckbö, Espen B. 1983. Horizontal mergers, collusion, and stockholder wealth. *Journal of Financial Economics* 11 (1–4): 241–274.
Eckbö, Espen B., and Herwig Langohr. 1989. Information disclosure, method of payment, and takeover premiums: Public and private tender offers in France. *Journal of Financial Economics* 24 (2): 363–403.
Faccio, Mara, and Larry H. P. Lang. 2002. The ultimate ownership of Western European corporations. *Journal of Financial Economics* 65 (3): 365–395.
Faccio, Mara, John McConnell, and David Stolin. 2006. Returns to acquirers of listed and unlisted targets. *Journal of Financial and Quantitative Analysis* 41 (1): 197–220.
Faccio, Mara, and David Stolin. 2006. Expropriation vs. proportional sharing in corporate acquisitions. *Journal of Business* 79 (3): 1413–1444.
Franks, Julian R., and Robert S. Harris. 1989. Shareholder wealth effects of corporate takeovers: The U.K. experience 1955–1985. *Journal of Financial Economics* 23 (2): 225–249.
Franks, Julian, Robert Harris, and Sheridan Titman. 1991. The postmerger share-price performance of acquiring firms. *Journal of Financial Economics* 29 (1): 81–96.
Franks, Julian, and C. Mayer. 1996. Hostile takeovers and the correction of managerial failure. *Journal of Financial Economics* 40 (1): 163–181.
Fuller, Kathleen, Jeffry Netter, and Mike Stegemoller. 2002. What do returns to acquiring firms tell us? Evidence from firms that make many acquisitions. *Journal of Finance* 57 (4): 1763–1793.
Goergen, Marc, and Luc Renneboog. 2004. Shareholder wealth effects of European domestic and cross-border takeover bids. *European Financial Management* 10 (1): 9–45.
Goergen, Marc, Marina Martynova, and Luc Renneboog. 2005. Corporate governance convergence: Evidence from takeover regulation reforms. *Oxford Review of Economic Policy* 21 (2): 243–268.
Grossman, Sanford J., and Oliver D. Hart, 1980. Takeover bids, the free-rider problem and the theory of the corporation. *Bell Journal of Economics* 11 (1): 42–64.
Healy, Paul M., Krishna Palepu, and Richard. S. Ruback. 1992. Does corporate performance improve after mergers? *Journal of Financial Economics* 31 (2): 135–175.
Himmelberg, Charles, R. Glenn Hubbard, and Inessa Love. 2002. Investor protection, ownership, and the cost of capital. World Bank Working Paper Series 2834.
Holmen, Martin, and John Knopf. 2004. Minority shareholder protections and the private benefits of control for Swedish mergers. *Journal of Financial and Quantitative Analysis* 39 (1): 167–91.
Jensen, Michael C. 1988. Takeovers: Their causes and consequences. *Journal of Economic Perspectives* 2: 21–48.
———. 2005. Agency costs of overvalued equity. *Financial Management* 34 (1): 5–19.
Kaplan, Steven N., and Michael S. Weisbach. 1992. The success of acquisitions: Evidence from divestitures. *Journal of Finance* 47 (1): 107–138.
Lang, Larry H. P., René M. Stulz, and Ralph Walkling. 1989. Managerial performance, Tobin's q, and the gains from successful tender offers. *Journal of Financial Economics* 24 (1): 137–154.
La Porta, Rafael, Florencio Lopez-de-Silanes, Andrei Shleifer, and Robert W. Vishny. 1997. Legal determinants of external finance. *Journal of Finance* 52 (3): 1131–1150.
———. 1998. Law and finance. *Journal of Political Economy* 106 (6): 1113–1155.
———. 2002. Investor protection and corporate valuation. *Journal of Finance* 57 (3): 1147–1170.

Levine, Ross. 1999. Law, finance, and economic growth. *Journal of Financial Intermediation* 8 (1–2): 8–35.

Martynova, Marina, and Luc Renneboog. 2006. Mergers and acquisitions in Europe. In *Advances in Corporate Finance and Asset Pricing*, ed. Luc Renneboog, 13–75. Amsterdam: Elsevier.

———. 2008a. A century of corporate takeovers: What have we learned and where do we stand? *Journal of Banking and Finance* 32 (10): 2148–2177.

———. 2008b. Spillover of corporate governance standards in cross-border mergers and acquisitions. *Journal of Corporate Finance* 14 (3): 200–223.

———. 2009a. A corporate governance index: Convergence and diversity of national corporate governance regulations. AEA 2009 Meeting Paper.

———. 2009b. What determines the financing decisions in corporate takeovers: Cost of capital, agency problems, or the means of payment. *Journal of Corporate Finance* 15 (3): 290–315.

———. 2010. The performance of the European market for corporate control: Evidence from the 5th takeover wave. *European Financial Management*, forthcoming.

Martynova, Marina, Sjoerd Oosting, and Luc Renneboog. 2007. Long-term performance of European mergers and acquisitions. In *International mergers and acquisitions activity since 1990: Quantitative analysis and recent research*, ed. Gregoriou Gregoriou and Luc Renneboog. Boston: Elsevier.

McCahery, Joe, and Luc Renneboog. 2002. Recent developments in corporate governance. In *Convergence and diversity of corporate governance regimes and capital markets*, ed. Joe McCahery, Piet Moerland, Theo Raaijmakers, and Luc Renneboog. Oxford: Oxford University Press.

Moeller, Sara B., and Frederik P. Schlingemann. 2005. Global diversification and bidder gains: A comparison between cross-border and domestic acquisitions. *Journal of Banking and Finance* 29 (3): 533–564.

Moeller, Sara B., Frederik P. Schlingemann, and René M. Stulz. 2004. Firm size and the gains from acquisitions. *Journal of Financial Economics* 73 (2): 201–228.

———. 2005. Wealth destruction on a massive scale? A study of acquiring-firm returns in the recent merger wave. *Journal of Finance* 60 (2): 757–782.

Rajan, Raghuram, Henri Servaes, and Luigi Zingales. 2000. The cost of diversity: The diversification discount and inefficient investment. *Journal of Finance* 55 (1): 2537–2564.

Roll, Richard. 1986. The hubris hypothesis of corporate takeovers. *Journal of Business* 59 (2): 197–216.

Rossi, Stefano, and Paolo F. Volpin. 2004. Cross-country determinants of mergers and acquisitions. *Journal of Financial Economics* 74 (2): 277–304.

Scharfstein, David S., and Jeremy C. Stein. 2000. The dark side of internal capital markets: divisional rent-seeking and inefficient investment. *Journal of Finance* 55 (6): 2537–2564.

Schoenberg, Richard. 1999. Cultural compatibility in international acquisitions. In *International business organization: Subsidiary management, entry strategies and emerging markets*, ed. Fred Burton, Malcolm Chapman, and Adam Cross, 294–306. New York: St. Martin's Press.

Schwert, William G. 1996. Markup pricing in mergers and acquisitions. *Journal of Financial Economics* 41 (2): 153–162.

Servaes, Henri. 1991. Tobin's q and the gains from takeovers. *Journal of Finance* 46 (1): 409–419.

Shin Hyun-Han, and René M. Stulz. 1998. Are internal capital markets efficient? *Quarterly Journal of Economics* 113 (2): 531–552.

Shleifer, Andrei, and Robert Vishny. 1986. Large shareholders and corporate control. *Journal of Political Economy* 94 (3): 461–488.

———. 1991. Takeovers in the '60s and the '80s: Evidence and implications. *Strategic Management Journal* 12, Winter special issue, 51–59.

Sudarsanam, Sudi, and Ashraf A. Mahate. 2003. Glamour acquirers, method of payment and post acquisition performance: The UK evidence. *Journal of Business Finance and Accounting* 30 (1–2): 299–342.

Van Schaik, Dimitri, and Onno W. Steenbeek. Price and volume effects on merger bids in Japan. Working paper, Erasmus University. Available at http://papers.ssrn.com/sol3/papers.cfm?abstract_id=592081.

Van Schaik and Steenbeek (2004), Japan.

ABOUT THE AUTHORS

Marina Martynova is an associate at Cornerstone Research, the leading financial litigation company in the United States. Before moving to the United States, Martynova held posts as an assistant professor of finance at Sheffield University (United Kingdom) and research fellow at Tilburg University (Netherlands). She also participated in the European Commission research project "New Forms of Governance." Her expertise is in corporate finance and corporate governance. She specializes in mergers and acquisitions, leveraged financing, equity issues, financial and accounting reporting, corporate governance regulation, and applied econometrics. Her research has been published in highly ranked academic journals such as *Journal of Corporate Finance, Journal of Banking and Finance,* and *Oxford Review of Economic Policy*. Dr. Martynova has been invited to give presentations at numerous conferences and seminars, including annual meetings of American and European finance associations. She also acts as a referee for major journals in the field of finance. Martynova holds a PhD in financial economics from Tilburg University.

Luc Renneboog is professor of corporate finance at Tilburg University and a research fellow at CentER and the European Corporate Governance Institute (ECGI) in Brussels. He graduated from the Catholic University of Leuven with degrees in management engineering (MSc) and in philosophy (BA); from the University of Chicago with an MBA; and from the London Business School with a PhD in financial economics. He held appointments at the University of Leuven and Oxford University, and visiting appointments at, among others, London Business School, and HEC (Paris). He has published in the *Journal of Finance, Journal of Financial Intermediation, Journal of Law and Economics, Journal of Corporate Finance, Journal of Banking and Finance, Oxford Review of Economic Policy, Cambridge Journal of Economics, European Financial Management*, and others. He has co-authored and edited several books on corporate governance, dividend policy, and venture capital. His research interests are corporate finance, corporate governance, takeovers, dividend policy, insider trading, law and economics, and the economics of art.

CHAPTER 28

Corporate Governance and Accountability

RENEE M. JONES
Associate Professor, Boston College Law School

INTRODUCTION

Corporate governance consists of a set of internal procedures, laws, and informal guidelines that govern how corporate officials make decisions and who bears responsibility for harms, losses, or injuries that flow from such decisions (Iksander and Chamlou 2000; Monks and Minow 2004; Thomsen 2008). The objective of the system is to ensure that corporate decisions are made with the best interests of the corporation and its stakeholders in mind and that corporate officials speak truthfully when communicating with investors and the public (Sale 2004).

The principal challenge for corporate governance is to create a system that holds decision makers accountable while according proper respect to their authority over the corporation. The standard accountability mechanisms are the market, shareholder voting, and civil and criminal liability. In theory, these mechanisms work together to create incentives for responsible decision making and to deter self-dealing or other forms of misconduct. In reality, however, each of these accountability mechanisms contains flaws that allow corporate officials to sometimes exercise an unreasonable degree of discretion when making decisions that affect the fortunes of so many. When governance systems fail, the impact can be devastating for investors, employees, and the economy. Recent corporate scandals and the near-collapse of the global financial system all demonstrate the importance of maintaining an effective corporate governance regime.

This chapter begins with a description of the principal sources of corporate governance standards. It then provides a detailed examination of federal oversight of financial reporting, and identifies significant problems within the oversight system. Next, it describes prospective corporate governance reforms proposed in response to the 2008 financial crisis. The final section offers summaries and conclusions.

SOURCES OF CORPORATE GOVERNANCE STANDARDS

In the United States, corporate governance standards arise from an amalgam of state law, federal law, and stock exchange standards, as well as guidelines and principles devised by private organizations. Together these laws, listing standards, and informal guidelines create a structure designed to provide accountability for corporate decision makers.

State Law

The base layer of corporate law rules are set at the state level through statutes and case-by-case decision making in the common law tradition. Under the internal affairs doctrine, the law of the state of incorporation governs disputes that arise between corporate officials, shareholders, or creditors. By choosing a state of incorporation, corporate managers select the law that governs the substance of their relationship with creditors, shareholders, and the state. Delaware has long been the leading choice for state of incorporation for large publicly traded corporations, leading many to argue that Delaware has led a race to the bottom in corporate law (Cary 1974; Nader, Green, and Seligman 1976). Others maintain such competition has instead created to a race to the top for optimal legal standards in corporate law (Winter 1977; Romano 1993).

Under state law, a corporation's directors are charged with managing the business and affairs of the corporation (Delaware General Corporation Law 2002, § 141). Directors delegate this authority to executives who manage the day-to-day affairs of the firm. Ostensibly, shareholders elect directors at the annual meeting. As Bebchuk (2007) and others indicate, however, the board of directors tends to be a self-perpetuating body and shareholders have little practical ability to displace directors when dissatisfied with their performance.

State corporate statutes provide little guidance regarding a director's duties. Instead, the contours of these duties have developed through common law decision making in courts. Through common law doctrine, courts have established that directors and officers owe fiduciary duties to their corporations. These obligations include duties of care, loyalty, candor, and good faith, which require directors to manage the corporation with diligence and to advance the interests of the corporation rather than their own (*Guth v. Loft* 1939).

The shareholder lawsuit is the principal mechanism for enforcing fiduciary duties. In a derivative lawsuit, shareholders may sue directors or officers on the corporation's behalf for breach of fiduciary duty. Shareholders can also sue directly when they suffer direct harm as a result of directors' decisions (Clark 1986). But shareholders' ability to enforce fiduciary duties is hampered by several formidable doctrinal and procedural hurdles.

First, under the business judgment rule, courts defer to directors' judgment on most substantive corporate decisions. Courts focus instead on assessing the process by which a decision was reached. In *Smith v. Van Gorkom* (1985), for example, the directors' failure to adequately inform themselves before approving a merger led the court to set aside the business judgment rule and require that the challenged transaction be assessed for its fairness to the stockholders.

The business judgment rule is also set aside when a conflict of interest exists between a corporation and its officers or directors, such as when a director stands on both sides of a transaction. When such a conflict exists, courts will scrutinize the challenged transaction for fairness. However, statutory and doctrinal rules restore the business judgment rule when a conflict transaction is approved by disinterested directors or shareholders (*Oberly v. Kirby* 1991).

Recent decisions in Delaware such as *In re Walt Disney Co. Derivative Litigation* (2006), *Stone v. Ritter* (2006), and *Lyondell Chemical Co. v. Ryan* (2009) have elevated the doctrinal significance of the duty of good faith. After the Delaware Supreme Court revived a lawsuit against Disney's directors in 2003, Sale (2004) and Griffith (2005) speculated that "good faith" might become a tool that judges use to discipline errant directors, especially during times of scandal. Subsequent Delaware Supreme Court decisions in *Disney*, *Stone*, and *Lyondell* have undermined the disciplinary threat that the newly revived "good faith" standard had implied. These more recent rulings firmly ensconce good faith within the duty of loyalty rubric, making clear that only sustained dereliction of duty or an act intended to harm the corporation will lead to personal liability for independent directors (*Stone v. Ritter* 2006).

Special procedural burdens associated with derivative litigation such as the demand requirement and special litigation committees further ensure that directors can avoid liability for errors in judgment or neglect of their duties (Jones 2006). Finally, exculpation, insurance, and indemnification provide additional protection to corporate officials by covering litigation costs and most judgments and settlements. The cumulative result of these doctrinal and procedural protections is that outside directors almost never pay personally for the breach of their duties to shareholders (Black, Cheffins, and Klausner 2006). The absence of an effective enforcement mechanism for fiduciary duties has led many to conclude that state corporate law may be best understood as providing merely aspirational guidelines for how directors should manage a corporation's affairs (Rock 1997; Stout 2003).

Federal Securities Law

The federal securities laws provide an important supplement to state corporate governance standards. These laws require corporations to disclose financial and other business information to investors and the public on an ongoing basis. Under the Securities Act of 1933 (the 1933 Act) and the Securities Exchange Act of 1934 (the 1934 Act), a corporation must provide investors with detailed information whenever it proposes to sell securities to the public or if its securities trade in a public market.

Although disclosure rules are the dominant feature of the federal securities laws, Seligman (2003) and others have pointed out that some of the 1934 Act's most significant provisions govern corporate conduct. For example, the conduct of the shareholder meetings is dictated largely by the requirements of the Exchange Act and stock exchange listing standards with state law requirements playing a supporting role. More importantly, many disclosure requirements addressing compensation, conflicts of interest, and the like are simply regulators' attempts to indirectly influence corporate conduct.

Unlike state-based duties that are notoriously difficult to enforce, corporations and their officials face significant liability for making false or misleading statements to investors or failing to disclose material facts when a duty to disclose exists. Securities law liability extends to the corporation, its officers and directors, accountants, underwriters, promoters, and even its attorneys and bankers (Securities Act of 1933, §§11, 12(a)(2); Securities Exchange Act of 1934, Section §10(b), Rule 10b-5). All of these officials face the prospect of draconian liability for violating securities laws.

Enforcing the Securities Laws

The securities laws are subject to multiple enforcement mechanisms including private lawsuits, SEC enforcement actions, and criminal prosecutions by the U.S. Department of Justice. In recent years, state authorities have become more active in enforcing state securities statutes, introducing another layer of oversight into the system.

The private class action lawsuit presents the most significant liability threat. The aggregate value of settlements for securities class action lawsuits reach into the billions of dollars each year (Ryan and Simmons 2008). The largest settlements involving Enron, WorldCom, and Cendant were $7.1 billion, $6.1 billion, and $3.5 billion, respectively. In addition to the prospect of astronomical settlements, securities litigation is costly and complex and can consume a disproportionate amount of management resources and time. These costs and aggravations have led to concerns about the efficiency and fairness of the shareholder liability regime.

Alexander (1991), Grundfest (1994), and Pritchard (2008) have all targeted the open-market securities fraud class action under Exchange Act Rule 10b-5 as an unjustified aspect of the securities regime. In a fraud action under Rule 10b-5, plaintiffs can recover damages whenever a corporation's stock price drops due to false or misleading disclosures by the issuer or its executives (*Basic Inc. v. Levinson* 1988). Critics charge that the astronomical amount of potential damages creates skewed incentives for plaintiff attorneys who file speculative suits on a contingent basis in the hope of securing a quick and lucrative settlement (U.S. House of Representatives 1995).

According to these critics, private attorneys function as public policemen but they are free from effective discipline or oversight mechanisms to prevent them from advancing their own interests at the expense of the plaintiff class. In response to concerns about the plaintiff bar's extortionary power, Congress adopted the Private Securities Litigation Reform Act of 1995 (PSLRA). Among other reforms, the PSLRA created heightened pleading standards for Rule 10b-5 claims, stayed discovery pending a defendant's motion to dismiss, and replaced a system of joint and several liability with a proportionate liability regime for most unknowing violations of the securities laws.

The PSLRA increased the costs of shareholder suits while reducing the chances that such claims would survive a preliminary motion. Coffee (2002) and Cunningham (2003) suggest that by discouraging securities lawsuits and reducing litigation risks, the PSLRA may have contributed to a business environment in which fraud could thrive unchecked. Scholars have attempted to assess the impact of the PSLRA on securities filing and settlement trends. Choi's (2007) study concludes that the statute not only has deterred frivolous claims (as intended), but also has discouraged lawyers from filing meritorious claims. Johnson, Pritchard, and Nelson (2006) reach a similar conclusion.

SEC Enforcement

Some critics of the shareholder litigation regime assert that limiting private lawsuits is justified in light of the SEC's ability to enforce the securities laws. They assert that the SEC's public mission and its political accountability make it a more trustworthy advocate for shareholder interests than the private plaintiffs' bar. SEC enforcement efforts can deter fraud through monetary penalties, disgorgement, and other sanctions. The SEC also has power to compensate investors through Sarbanes-Oxley's "FAIR funds" provision, which allows the SEC to return penalties collected from defendants to shareholders harmed by their fraud (Sarbanes-Oxley 2002, § 108).

Although some view the SEC as the most appropriate agent for vindicating shareholder interests, the effectiveness of SEC enforcement has been seriously questioned (Poser 2009; Fisch 2009). Macey (1994) and Pritchard (2005), among others, have long charged that the SEC is subject to industry capture, such that it affords powerful business interests with high-priced legal representation advantages that are not available to ordinary citizens. There is some evidence to support this capture perspective. For example, Cox and Thomas (2003 and 2009) find that the SEC concentrates its enforcement efforts on smaller companies and typically allows larger firms to settle claims by paying small fines and agreeing to minor sanctions.

A recent report by the SEC's Inspector General (SEC 2008a) lends further support to the capture paradigm. The Inspector General found that lawyers at a large New York law firm enjoyed special access to senior SEC enforcement staff and awareness of such access may have impeded the progress of an ongoing investigation against a senior Wall Street official. Moreover, Jones (2004) and Macey (2004) note that the SEC lagged behind state regulators in high-profile investigations involving investment analyst conflicts, mutual fund market timing, and, more recently, abuses in marketing auction rate securities to investors.

Despite these shortcomings in the agency's enforcement program, many scholars including Seligman (2003), Langevoort (2006), and Prentice (2006) reject the capture narrative. Instead, these scholars view the SEC as an institution that balances competing interests of investors, issuers, and financial intermediaries rather than serving a monolithic corporate interest. Although the capture scenario is likely too simplistic, recent history suggests that the SEC is a less than perfect enforcer of the securities laws.

Another difficulty with relying exclusively on public enforcement of the securities laws is the concern that the SEC has not been sufficiently aggressive in pursuing corporate fraud. In the post-Enron era, the SEC became more aggressive in its enforcement practices, but retreated dramatically under Chairman Christopher Cox's leadership. In a recent report, the U.S. Government Accountability Office (GAO) (2009) noted that the aggregate amount of SEC penalties fell from $1.59 billion in 2005 (the beginning of Chairman Cox's term) to $256 million in 2008.

Many suspect that new SEC policies contributed to this decline. In 2006, the Commission adopted a policy that seemed to question the appropriateness of corporate-level penalties. Then in 2007, the SEC initiated a "Pilot Program" requiring enforcement staff to consult with the Commission before engaging in settlement discussions with corporate counsel (Nagy, Painter, and Sachs 2008). The GAO concluded that these policies and practices caused the enforcement staff to retreat in its pursuit of corporate penalties due to the Commission's unwillingness to accept staff recommendations on sanctions. SEC chair Mary Schapiro announced the end of the Pilot Program in 2009, and pledged to work to address enforcement staff concerns about their autonomy and authority (Schapiro 2009a and 2009b).

Criminal Enforcement

In addition to civil enforcement by private citizens and the SEC, the U.S. Justice Department pursues criminal violations of the securities laws. High-profile frauds at Enron and WorldCom led to criminal convictions of Kenneth Lay, Jeff Skilling, and Bernard Ebbers. All of these men received long prison sentences for their roles in their corporations' frauds.

Other Sources of Corporate Governance

Other important sources of corporate governance standards are the U.S. stock exchanges and nonbinding pronouncements developed by private entities. Stock exchange listing standards cover such governance issues as director independence, audit committee composition, shareholder voting in mergers, executive compensation, brokers' discretion to vote for their clients, and many other key areas of corporate governance. These rules are subject to SEC approval and the agency can amend exchange rules as it deems necessary and appropriate in furtherance of the purposes of the Exchange Act (Securities Exchange Act of 1934, § 19(c)).

Among the most influential privately generated governance standards are the American Law Institute's (ALI) *Principles of Corporate Governance* (1994). The ALI Principles offer directors and officers guidance in the conduct of corporate affairs beyond what is provided by corporate law doctrine. Other important purveyors of governance standards (sometimes called *best practices*) include the National Association of Corporate Directors and the Business Roundtable.

FEDERAL OVERSIGHT OF FINANCIAL REPORTING

The federal securities laws provide significant discipline for corporate officers and directors. The financial reporting system forms the backbone of this accountability system. Under the 1934 Act, public corporations must file periodic reports of financial results with the SEC. These reports include the annual report on Form 10-K, quarterly reports on Form 10-Q, and interim reports on Form 8-K which must be filed upon the occurrence of specified material events.

Investors rely on the information in these reports to evaluate a company's business prospects and make investment decisions. Although investors value the historical information included in SEC filings, they are much more interested in estimates of future performance from a firm's management or professional analysts. These forecasts and earnings estimates have a large impact on stock price, and missed estimates (reporting actual earnings below analysts' consensus estimate) often lead to a sharp decline in stock price.

In addition to the required SEC filings, companies communicate with investors on a more informal basis through press releases, speeches, and conference calls. One purpose of these informal communications is to manage investors' expectations with respect to future performance. Managers are keenly aware of the close connection between earnings projections and stock price and seek to ensure that financial analysts' published estimates are reasonable in light of management's own internal projections. Achieving such harmony requires managers to communicate regularly with the financial analyst community.

During the 1990s, SEC chair Arthur Levitt expressed concerns about the common practice in which financial officers would "whisper" earnings estimates to analysts to ensure that published estimates were in line with reality (Levitt 2002). To curtail this practice, the SEC adopted Regulation F-D, which prohibits selective disclosures to investment professionals. Under Regulation F-D, whenever a company discloses material information to analysts or investors, it must simultaneously disclose the information to the public at large (SEC 2000).

Financial Reporting Standards

The securities laws grant the SEC authority to develop standards for financial reporting. Since its inception, the agency has looked to private standards setters to generate generally accepted accounting principles (GAAP). Through its professional organization, the American Institute of Certified Public Accountants (AICPA), the accounting profession played a leading role in establishing the GAAP framework (Bratton 2007). Concerns with the potential distortions associated with allowing the accounting profession to set accounting standards led the AICPA to cede direct authority over GAAP to an independent body.

In 1973, acting with SEC support, the profession created the Financial Accounting Standards Board (FASB) to oversee GAAP. Until 2002, the FASB was funded through the sales of publications and voluntary contributions from public accounting firms. This funding arrangement proved problematic as the board found it awkward to adopt accounting standards opposed by audit firms and their clients while depending on those same firms for its operating funds (Nagy 2005). With the Sarbanes-Oxley Act of 2002 (SOX), Congress quashed this arrangement by requiring any standard setter designated by the SEC to be funded by fees collected by the federal government from filing companies (Sarbanes-Oxley § 109).

Concerns with the FASB's independence were more than theoretical. As Herwitz and Barrett (2006) explain, the FASB proposed a number of controversial accounting pronouncements during the 1990s that reporting companies resisted because they prohibited the accounting treatments they preferred. The FASB's efforts to adopt new reporting standards for employee stock options are emblematic of this tension.

In 1993, the FASB proposed rules to require companies to treat stock options as a compensation expense rather than a charge to capital on the balance sheet. The major audit firms and the high tech industry led private-sector opposition to this standard. Critics argued the rule would unreasonably burden start-up firms that relied on options to attract and retain management talent and appealed to the SEC and Congress for support. At the behest of these advocates, several congressmen, including Senator Joseph Lieberman, introduced bills to prevent the FASB from adopting the standard (Levitt 2002). In response to this pressure, the FASB relented and adopted FAS 123 which encouraged, but did not require, companies to expense options. Similar controversies surrounded FASB pronouncements on treatment of derivatives and off-balance-sheet financing (Herwitz and Barrett 2001; Mark 2007). As with option expensing, industry groups and auditors were vocal in their opposition to these measures and sought to use their influence in Congress to defeat them. In all of these areas, the FASB ultimately adopted its proposed accounting treatments but only after prolonged conflict and delays (Herwitz and Barrett 2006; Mark 2007).

The Globalization of Financial Reporting Standards

Although GAAP has long been the standard for financial reporting for U.S. companies, its continued standing is open to question due to the widely perceived need to achieve convergence among competing accounting standards around the globe. Convergence proponents assert that uniformity in international financial accounting standards would broaden access to capital across borders and facilitate investors' ability to compare corporations from different countries, expanding their array of investment opportunities (Takor 2005).

Convergence efforts have focused primarily on encouraging countries to adopt International Financial Reporting Standards (IFRS), established by the International Accounting Standard Board (IASB), as the standard for financial reporting. Efforts to promote IFRS have been fairly successful and IFRS now governs in more than 100 nations and in the European Union. A second objective of convergence advocates is to reduce or eliminate differences between IFRS and U.S. GAAP. The FASB and the SEC have engaged with their foreign counterparts in these efforts. Under the Norwalk Agreement reached in 2002, the FASB and the IASB agreed to work to achieve compatibility among their respective accounting standards (Hanson 2006).

In 2007, the SEC embraced the convergence objective and moved to recognize IFRS for foreign issuers filing financial statements with the SEC, without reconciliation to U.S. GAAP (SEC 2007). The SEC took this step to reduce impediments to foreign issuers listing their securities on U.S. stock exchanges. In August 2008, the SEC went further and released a "road map" that proposed shifting the financial reporting standard for U.S. companies from GAAP to IFRS (SEC 2008b). The road map envisioned optional IFRS reporting for large issuers beginning in December 2009, with a transition to mandatory IFRS reporting for all issuers by 2014 (an earlier proposal had considered allowing optional IFRS reporting without an eventual mandate).

The proposed shift from GAAP to IFRS reflects a broader campaign to jettison a reporting system with rigorous, complex rules in favor of a principles-based system that would be more palatable to those who prepare financial statements. In the standard critique, GAAP's rules-based regime is maligned for being formulaic, complex, difficult to interpret, and easy to evade (formal compliance while evading the purpose of the rule). In contrast, IFRS's principles-based regime is deemed to be more flexible, substantively meaningful, and easier to apply (Cunningham 2008a).

Cunningham (2008a), Cox (2009), and Bratton and Cunningham (2009) have expressed skepticism regarding the SEC's haste to embrace IFRS. They point to gaps in expertise, conversion costs, and substantial treatment differences between GAAP and IFRS as reasons to tread cautiously on the march toward globalization. With the change in the presidential administration, the U.S. shift to IFRS is again in doubt. SEC chair Mary Schapiro is reevaluating the proposal. Schapiro has acknowledged critics' concerns with the road map's timetable and conversion costs. In the meantime, the FASB and the IASB continue to focus on convergence, seeking greater compatibility pending consensus on global accounting standards.

The Problem of Accounting Fraud

The SEC's financial reporting system and the accompanying liability threat form an important component of the corporate governance accountability system. The financial reporting regime creates at least two sources of discipline for managers. For companies that regularly access capital markets, reported financial results directly affect their ability to raise capital as well as the cost of capital. Therefore, managers are motivated to run their companies effectively so as to assure continued access to low-cost capital. In addition, many companies use equity to finance acquisitions. A higher stock price means that equity will go further in support of a company's acquisition strategy.

The financial reporting regime remains an important disciplinary device for companies that do not rely on capital market financing. For most corporations, executive compensation is linked closely with reported financial results, which means that managers of companies that report higher earnings can expect to earn more. These compensation schemes are designed to encourage managers to lead their companies in a manner that achieves earnings growth over the long term.

Management's Role

The effectiveness of financial reporting as a disciplinary tool depends on the accuracy and reliability of management's financial reports. Management prepares a company's financial reports subject to the oversight of the directors and an audit by a public accounting firm. Management's control over financial reporting creates a basic conundrum for our corporate governance system.

Managers face strong incentives to manipulate financial reports in order to present as rosy a picture as possible of a company's financial condition. In general, managers aim to present an impression of steady and predictable earnings growth over a sustained time period. However, the reality of a firm's financial performance rarely jibes with the smooth and steady growth profile most managers hope to achieve. This divergence between ideal financial results and the inevitable ups and downs of business performance can lead managers to smooth reported earnings (Levitt 1998).

Scholars describe income smoothing, or *earnings management*, as the practice of using discretionary accounting judgments to shape the level of reported earnings to meet management objectives or analyst expectations (Erickson, Hanlon, and Maydew 2006; Lev 2003). Managers can also manage earnings through manipulation of discretionary expenditures or purchases such as research and development or capital improvements (Cunningham 2008b). This form of earnings management, often termed *real earnings management*, may be objectionable, but it is legal.

Incentives to manage earnings intensify when the compensation of high-level executives is directly linked to a company's stock price. Stock option grants are the most common method that corporations use to align executive and shareholder interests. Stock options give executives the right to purchase company stock at the current price at some point in the future. As a company's stock price increases, options become more valuable. Thus, option grants create incentives to manage the company so that earnings and stock prices rise in a reliable fashion.

While stock options likely provide incentives for hard work and effective management, they also create incentives to manipulate reported earnings. Numerous studies have sought to establish a link between equity-based incentive pay and accounting fraud. Bergstresser and Philippon (2006), Elayan, Li, and Meyer (2008), and Zhang, Bartol, Smith, Pfarrer, and Khanin (2008) all find a positive correlation between earnings management and high levels of equity compensation. A study by Baker, Collins, and Reitenga (2003) suggests that managers are more likely to engage in earnings management when their total compensation depends heavily on financial performance, as through stock options. Johnson, Ryan, and Tian (2008) report that these effects are most pronounced when compensation consists of vested options or unrestricted stock, when managers would feel the effect of a drop in stock price most acutely.

In contrast, studies by Erickson et al. (2006) and Armstrong, Jagolinzer, and Larcker (2009) fail to demonstrate a conclusive link between compensation practices and accounting fraud. Laux and Laux (2009) theorize that one explanation for the lack of clarity on this issue is that although lucrative equity compensation increases incentives to manipulate earnings, it may also increase the audit committee's scrutiny of financial reporting, thereby reducing opportunities for fraud. A study by Cornett, McNutt, and Tehranian (2009) on governance and earnings management at bank holding companies lends support to this contention.

The Auditor's Role

A corporation's directors and its auditors form the front line for protecting investors and the public from management fraud in financial reporting. Although directors have oversight over a company's financial reports, they rely chiefly on auditors to assure that these reports are prepared in accordance with GAAP and fairly reflect the company's financial condition.

The securities laws require an independent audit of annual financial statements filed with the SEC. The purpose of the audit is to provide some assurance to those who use financial statements that management's assertions have a reasonable basis in fact. The audit firm seeks to verify enough of the information contained in the financial reports so that it can reasonably conclude that the company prepared these reports in accordance with GAAP.

During the 1990s, evidence began to mount that auditors were insufficiently rigorous in their review of corporate financial statements. Between 1997 and 2002, 10 percent of all listed companies restated their financial reports, indicating widespread audit failures (Klein and Coffee 2004). The number of SEC fraud enforcement actions also rose dramatically in this period (Beasley, Carcello, and Hermanson 1999). After a series of major audit failures, including at Enron and WorldCom, public officials grew wary of the auditing profession's ability to maintain proper auditing standards and oversee its members' compliance with such standards.

With SOX, Congress set out to overhaul the financial reporting process and reallocate responsibilities for establishing audit procedures and for the oversight of auditors. The centerpiece of the legislation was the creation of the Public Company Accounting Oversight Board (PCAOB), a new private nonprofit entity to oversee the accounting industry (Nagy 2005). SOX gave the PCAOB authority to establish generally accepted auditing standards (GAAS), stripping the AICPA of its traditional role. Congress also charged the PCAOB with maintaining standards for auditor independence and conducting inspections of audit firms on a regular basis.

The PCAOB first recognized extant GAAS on an interim basis. It also acted quickly to adopt standards for the audit of internal control procedures prescribed by SOX Section 404. Section 404 requires managers to annually assess and report on the quality and effectiveness of their firms' internal controls and requires the independent auditor to attest to management's report. Perhaps the most controversial provision of SOX, Section 404 imposed new costs on public companies. Critics maintain this provision has encouraged public companies to go private and has discouraged foreign listings on U.S. stock exchanges (Committee on Capital Markets Regulation 2006).

Assessing the costs and benefits of Section 404 is a challenging task. In a review of the empirical literature on Section 404's impact, Prentice (2007) concludes that the provision's costs have been exaggerated and that its benefits, while real, are hard to quantify. According to Prentice, estimates of the average Section 404 compliance costs in the initial implementation year were about $4 million per issuer. However, a major portion of these costs are properly attributed to improvements in internal controls that firms needed but had deferred. The initial costs also included significant nonrecurring ramp-up costs. After initial implementation, Section 404 compliance costs declined 40 percent for large companies and 30 percent for smaller firms.

Prentice (2007) concludes that the empirical literature supports the view that Section 404 has proffered concrete benefits by restoring investor confidence, contributing to better-quality financial reporting, and likely decreasing the incidence of fraud. First, SOX helped fuel a market recovery by restoring investor confidence in management's financial reports (Benoit 2006). Further, studies by Bedard (2006), Doyle, Ge, and McVay (2007), and Li, Rupley, and Johnstone (2009) suggest that Section 404 has improved the quality of financial reporting, reducing the incidence of abnormal accruals and restatements.

Finally, studies by DeFranco, Guan, and Lu (2005) and Doyle et al. (2007) show that companies reporting internal control deficiencies under Section 404 saw declines in their stock price. Ashbaugh-Skaife, Collins, Kinney, and LaFond (2009) show that after companies corrected reported deficiencies, their costs of capital declined. These studies suggest that the internal control audit conveys useful information to investors and improves the allocational efficiency of markets.

Still, many critics complain that the costs of Section 404 exceed its benefits, especially for small companies that lack economies of scale. Some argue for a Section 404 exemption for smaller firms (Butler and Ribstein 2006; Committee on Capital Markets Regulation 2006). A special SEC Advisory Committee (SEC 2006) recommended that the agency exempt smaller companies from Section 404 compliance. Thus far, the SEC has deferred the Section 404 compliance date for smaller companies multiple times, but has declined to provide a complete exemption from its requirements. In the absence of further delays, all companies must be fully compliant with Section 404 in their reports for the fiscal year ending on or after June 15, 2010 (SEC 2009).

The Audit Committee's Role

In addition to strengthening oversight of auditors, SOX sought to encourage greater director involvement in the financial reporting process. Congress looked to the audit committee of the board of directors to help insure the integrity of management financial reports. Section 301 of SOX instructed the SEC to require stock exchanges to adopt rules mandating that all members of the audit committee of listed companies be independent of management. Congress also called for increased accounting expertise on the audit committee. Section 407 requires issuers to disclose if the audit committee has at least one member who is a "financial expert." If no member of the audit committee is a financial expert, the issuer must disclose that fact and explain why not. Finally, Congress sought to enhance the resources and authority of the audit committee. SOX specifies that the audit committee (not management) has the authority to hire and fire the auditors and that auditors must report directly to the committee. SOX also makes clear that the audit committee can hire its own experts with the corporation bearing any costs related to such consultations.

Congress apparently believed that increasing the audit committee's independence and assuring expertise would encourage directors to take a more active role in the review of financial reports and oversight of the audit. Empirical research suggests that enhanced director independence and expertise does have a positive impact on the quality of financial reporting (Cunningham 2008b). Carcello and Neal (2000), Klein (2002), and Anderson, Mansi, and Reeb (2004) all report that the presence of independent directors and financial experts on audit committees appears to improve the quality of a firm's financial reporting.

Further research has shown a greater benefit from accounting expertise than from either independence or general financial expertise (Abbott, Parker, and Peters 2004; Dhaliwal, Naiker, and Navissi 2006). Thus, directors with experience preparing or auditing financial statements seem to contribute most significantly to constraining earnings management and other forms of financial fraud (Cunningham 2008b).

PROSPECTIVE REFORMS

The SOX provisions reviewed in this chapter are a stark example of Congress's direct regulation of corporate conduct, which disrupted the traditional understanding of the federal role in corporate governance (Bainbridge 2006). With Section 404, new audit committee rules, and other governance provisions, Congress delved deeply into the details of how management and the board conduct their affairs. SOX has also laid the groundwork for more intensive federal engagement in corporate governance.

The 2008 financial collapse and subsequent government bailouts have created an even more direct federal role in the oversight of major corporations. Massive federal funding of private corporations sets new precedents and raises important questions about government's role in business. Importantly, the bailouts shift the terms of the governance debate, as corporate law can no longer be viewed purely as a matter of balancing private interests.

Against the backdrop of the federal government as a partner in private enterprise, a new wave of regulatory reform looms on the horizon. President Barack Obama's financial reform proposals include enhanced federal oversight of systemically significant financial firms and a new financial regulator to focus on consumer protection. The President has also proposed legislation to provide for the regulation of hedge funds and derivatives, as well as measures to enhance shareholder power over executive compensation and the selection of directors.

Amidst calls for regulatory overhaul, the continued viability and authority of the SEC hangs in the balance. The SEC's reputation has suffered severely in the wake of the 2008–2009 financial crisis (Coffee and Sale 2009; Fisch 2009; Poser 2009). The agency's passivity during the collapse of Bear Stearns, its failure to detect Bernard Madoff's massive fraud, and the failure of the Consolidated Supervised Entity program for financial conglomerates have led to serious questions about the agency's competence and relevance.

Despite these recent missteps, sober analysis suggests that the SEC needs to be strengthened rather than weakened in response to recent crises. The SEC's rule-making authority and political independence equip it to respond more deftly to emerging problems than either Congress or the courts. The SEC's recent failures can be attributed in part to the erosion of its independence and authority at the hands of Congress and the courts (Jones 2009). Budgetary threats and adverse federal court decisions delayed or thwarted SEC initiatives to increase oversight of financial firms, hedge funds, mutual funds, and auditors. Perhaps more importantly, the SEC was led most recently by a chairman who appeared less than committed to the agency's mission (Scannell and Craig 2008). The regulatory dormancy engendered by his approach allowed problems in the financial markets to fester and worsen, eventually requiring urgent intervention by the Treasury and the Federal Reserve. If the agency can be reconstituted under competent leadership and its proper authority restored, the SEC can be expected to reprise its role as the bastion of investor protection that it has been during most of the past 75 years.

SUMMARY AND CONCLUSIONS

The structure of the U.S. corporate governance system has remained fairly stable since the time of the New Deal. The SEC has overseen a regulatory system that relies heavily on financial disclosure requirements to motivate responsible conduct by corporate officials. These rules are backed by a severe liability threat that encourages full and fair disclosure to shareholders and the public.

Congress has generally ceded specific conduct standards to the states, which developed common law fiduciary duties to govern the conduct of corporate officials. Over time the rigor of state regulation dissipated and the erosion of the fiduciary duty doctrine compelled Congress and the SEC to engage more directly in corporate governance issues, leading to SOX and likely more substantive governance reforms in the future.

Overall, the U.S. corporate governance system is sound in design but problems with enforcement, at both the state and federal level, mean that the performance of corporate executives and directors does not reflect the lofty standards embodied within state and federal law. The best hope for responsible management seems to be the broad inculcation of proper moral standards in the individuals who run our corporations. How the law can play a role in that endeavor is a question that has confounded corporate law and criminal law theorists for decades.

DISCUSSION QUESTIONS

1. Why do state courts generally defer to management's business judgment? What might be some dangers of imposing liability for breach of fiduciary duty more frequently?
2. If the SEC recognizes IFRS for U.S. issuers, the IASB, a foreign nongovernmental organization, would have authority over U.S. accounting standards. Is such

an arrangement consistent with SOX's requirement for a government-funded accounting standards setter? (See Sarbanes-Oxley § 109.) Does ceding power over U.S. accounting standards to a foreign body create accountability problems? How might such issues be resolved?

3. Numerous studies cited in the chapter support the view that incentive compensation contributes to financial fraud. Assuming this connection is well founded, how should compensation practices at public corporations be reformed?
4. The topics reviewed in the chapter suggest that each of the accountability mechanisms relied on for corporate governance is flawed in some way. What appear to be the most pressing problems in corporate governance? What are possible reforms to increase the accountability of corporate managers?

REFERENCES

Abbott, Lawrence J., Susan Parker, and Gary F. Peters. 2004. Audit committee characteristics and restatements. *Auditing: A Journal of Practice & Theory* 23 (1): 69–89.

Alexander, Janet Cooper. 1991. Do the merits matter? *Stanford Law Review* 43 (3): 497–598.

American Law Institute. 1994. *Principles of corporate governance: Analysis and recommendations*. St. Paul, MN: American Law Institute Publishers.

Anderson, Ronald C., Sattar A. Mansi, and David M. Reeb. 2004. Board characteristics, accounting report integrity, and the cost of debt. *Journal of Accounting & Economics* 37 (3): 315–342.

Armstrong, Chris S., Alan Jagolinzer, and David Larcker. 2009. Chief executive officer equity incentives and accounting irregularities. http://ssrn.com/abstract=1132411.

Ashbaugh-Skaife, Hollis, Daniel W. Collins, William R. Kinney, Jr., and Ryan LaFond. 2009. The effect of SOX internal control deficiencies on firm risk and the cost of equity. *Journal of Accounting Research* 47 (1): 1–43.

Bainbridge, Stephen. 2006. The creeping federalization of American corporate law. *Journal of Regulatory Economics* 26 (1): 26–32.

Baker, Terry, Denton Collins, and Austin Reitenga. 2003. Stock option compensation and earnings management incentives. *Journal of Accounting, Auditing, and Finance* 18 (4): 557–582.

Beasley, Mark S., Joseph V. Carcello, and Dana R. Hermanson. 1999. Fraudulent financial reporting 1987–1997: Trends in U.S. public companies. *Directorship* 25 (5): 14–17.

Bebchuk, Lucian. 2007. The myth of the shareholder franchise. *Virginia Law Review* 93 (3): 675–732.

Bedard, Jean. 2006. Sarbanes-Oxley internal control requirements and earnings quality. http://ssrn.com/abstract=926271.

Benoit, Robert. 2006. The Lord and Benoit report: Do the benefits of 404 exceed the cost? Worcester, MA: Lord and Benoit, LLC. http://www.section404.org/UserFiles/File/Lord%20_Benoit_Report%20_Benefits%20vs%20Cost.pdf.

Bergstresser, Daniel, and Thomas Philippon. 2006. CEO incentives and earnings management. *Journal of Financial Economics* 80 (3): 511–530.

Black, Bernard, Brian R. Cheffins, and Michael Klausner. 2006. Outside director liability. *Stanford Law Review* 58 (4): 1055–1159.

Bratton, William W. 2007. Private standards, public governance: A new look at the Financial Accounting Standards Board. *Boston College Law Review* 48 (1): 5–53.

Bratton, William W., and Lawrence A. Cunningham. 2009. Treatment differences and political realities in the GAAP-IFRS debate. *Virginia Law Review* 95 (4): 989–1022.

Butler, Henry N., and Larry E. Ribstein. 2006. *The Sarbanes-Oxley debacle: What went wrong, how to fix it*. Washington, DC: AEI Press.

Carcello, Joseph V., and Terry L. Neal. 2000. Audit committee composition and auditor reporting. *Accounting Review* 75 (4): 453–467.
Cary, William L. 1974. Federalism and corporate law: Reflections upon Delaware. *Yale Law Journal* 83 (4): 663–705.
Choi, Stephen J. 2007. Do the merits matter less after the Private Securities Litigation Reform Act. *Journal of Law, Economics & Organization* 23 (3): 598–626.
Clark, Robert C. 1986. *Corporate Law*. New York: Aspen Law and Business.
Coffee, John C., Jr. 2002. Understanding Enron: "It's the gatekeepers, stupid." *Business Lawyer* 57 (4): 1403–1420.
Coffee, John C., Jr., and Hillary A. Sale. 2009. Redesigning the SEC: Does the Treasury have a better idea. *Virginia Law Review* 95 (4): 707–83.
Committee on Capital Markets Regulation. 2006. *Interim report*. Cambridge, MA: Committee on Capital Markets Regulation. http://www.capmktsreg.org/research.html.
Cornett, Marcia Millon, Jamie John McNutt, and Hassan Tehranian. 2009. Corporate governance and earnings management at large U.S. bank holding companies. *Journal of Corporation Finance* 15 (4): 412–430.
Cox, James D. 2009. Coping in a global marketplace: Survival strategies for a 75-year-old SEC. *Virginia Law Review* 95 (4): 941–987.
Cox, James D., and Randall S. Thomas. 2003. Enforcement heuristics. *Duke Law Journal* 53 (2): 737–779.
———. 2009. Mapping the American shareholder litigation experience: A survey of empirical studies of the enforcement of U.S. securities law. http://ssrn.com/abstract=1370508.
Cunningham, Lawrence A. 2003. The Sarbanes-Oxley yawn: Heavy rhetoric, light reform (and it just might work). *Connecticut Law Review* 35 (3): 915–987.
———. 2008a. The SEC's global accounting vision: A realistic appraisal of a quixotic quest. *North Carolina Law Review* 87 (1): 1–82.
———. 2008b. Rediscovering board expertise: Legal implications of the empirical literature. *University of Cincinnati Law Review* 77 (2): 465–500.
De Franco, Gus, Yuyan Guan, and Hai Lu. 2005. The wealth change and redistribution effects of Sarbanes-Oxley internal control disclosures. http://ssrn.com/abstract=706701.
Dhaliwal, Dan, Vic Naiker, and Farshid Navissi. 2006. Audit committee financial expertise, corporate governance and accruals quality: An empirical analysis. http://www.ssrn.com/abstract=906690.
Doyle, Jeff, Weili Ge, and Sarah McVay. 2007. Accruals quality and internal control over financial reporting. *Accounting Review* 82 (5): 1141–1170.
Elayan, Fayez A., Jennifer Li, and Thomas O. Meyer. 2008. Accounting irregularities, management compensation structure and information asymmetry. *Accounting and Finance* 48 (5): 741–760.
Erickson, Merle, Michelle Hanlon, and Edward L. Maydew. 2006. Is there a link between executive equity incentives and accounting fraud? *Journal of Accounting Research* 44 (1): 113–143.
Fisch, Jill E. 2009. SEC: Top cop or regulatory flop? *Virginia Law Review* 95 (4): 785–823.
Griffith, Sean J. 2005. Good faith business judgment: A theory of rhetoric in corporate law. *Duke Law Journal* 55 (1): 1–73.
Grundfest, Joseph A. 1994. Disimplying private rights of action under the authority of the federal securities laws: The Commission's authority. *Harvard Law Review* 107 (5): 961–1022.
Hanson, Mark J. 2006. Becoming one: The SEC should join the world in adopting the International Financial Reporting Standards. *Loyola L.A. International and Comparative Law Review* 28 (3): 521–546.
Herwitz, David R., and Matthew J. Barrett. 2001. *Accounting for Lawyers*. New York: Foundation Press.

———. 2006. *Accounting for Lawyers*. New York: Foundation Press.

Iksander, Magdi R., and Nadereh Chamlou. 2000. *Corporate governance: A framework for implementation*. Washington, DC: World Bank.

Johnson, Marilyn F., Adam C. Pritchard, and Karen N. Nelson. 2006. Do the merits matter more? The impact of the Private Securities Litigation Reform Act. http://ssrn.com/abstract=883684.

Johnson, Shane A., Harley E. Ryan, and Yisong S. Tian. 2008. Managerial incentives and corporate fraud. http://ssrn.com/abstract=395960.

Jones, Renee M. 2004. Dynamic federalism: Competition, cooperation, and securities enforcement. *Connecticut Insurance Law Journal* 11 (1): 107–131.

———. 2006. Law, norms, and the breakdown of the board: Promoting accountability in corporate governance. *Iowa Law Review* 92 (1): 105–157.

———. 2009. Legitimacy and corporate law: The case for regulatory redundancy. *Washington University Law Review* 86 (6): 1273–1333.

Klein, April. 2002. Audit committee, board of director characteristics, and earnings management. *Journal of Accounting and Economics* 33 (3): 375–400.

Klein, William A., and John C. Coffee, Jr. 2004. *Business organizations and finance*. New York: Foundation Press.

Langevoort, Donald C. 2006. The SEC as lawmaker: Choices about investor protection in the face of uncertainty. *Washington University Law Review* 84 (7): 1591–1626.

Laux, Christian, and Volker Laux. 2009. Board committees, CEO compensation, and earnings management.

Lev, Baruch. 2003. Corporate earnings: Facts and fiction. *Journal of Economic Perspectives* 17 (2): 27–50.

Levitt, Arthur. 1998. The numbers game. Address as chairman, U.S. Securities and Exchange Commission, at the New York University Center for Law and Business, September 28. http://www.sec.gov/news/speech/speecharchive/1998/spch220.txt.

———. 2002. *Take on the Street*. New York: Random House.

Li, Chan, Kathleen Hertz Rupley, and Karla M. Johnstone. 2009. Changes in boards of directors, audit committees and management: Evidence on the remediation of internal control weaknesses. http://ssrn.com/abstract=1091685.

Macey, Jonathan R. 1994. Administrative agency obsolescence and interest group formation: A case study of the SEC at sixty. *Cardozo Law Review* 15 (4): 909–949.

———. 2004. Wall Street in turmoil: State-federal relations post Eliot Spitzer. *Brooklyn Law Review* 70 (1): 117–140.

Mark, Gideon. 2007. Accounting fraud: Pleading scienter of auditors under the PSLRA. *Connecticut Law Review* 39 (3): 1097–1209.

Monks, Robert A. G., and Nell Minow. 2004. *Corporate governance.* Malden, MA: Blackwell.

Nader, Ralph, Mark Green, and Joel Seligman. 1976. *Taming the giant corporation*. New York: Norton.

Nagy, Donna M. 2005. Playing peekaboo with Constitutional law: The PCAOB and its public/private status. *Notre Dame Law Review* 80 (3): 975–1071.

Nagy, Donna M., Richard Painter, and Margaret Sachs. 2008. *Securities litigation and enforcement*. 2nd ed. St. Paul, MN: Thomson/West.

Poser, Norman S. 2009. Why the SEC failed: Regulators against regulation. *Brooklyn Journal of Corporate, Financial, and Corporate Law* 3 (2): 289–324.

Prentice, Robert. 2006. The inevitability of a strong SEC. *Cornell Law Review* 91 (4): 775–839.

———. 2007. Sarbanes-Oxley: The evidence regarding the impact of SOX 404. *Cardozo Law Review* 29 (2): 703–764.

Pritchard, A. C. 2005. The SEC at 70: Time for retirement? *Notre Dame Law Review* 80 (3): 1073–1102.

———. 2008. Stoneridge Investment Partners, LLC v. Scientific Atlanta, Inc.: The political economy of securities class action reform. *Cato Supreme Court Review* 2007–2008, 217–255.

Rock, Edward B. 1997. Saints and sinners: How does Delaware corporate law work? *UCLA Law Review* 44 (4): 1009–1107.

Romano, Roberta. 1993. *The genius of American corporate law*. Washington, DC: AEI Press.

Ryan, Ellen M., and Laura E. Simmons. 2008. *Securities class action settlements: 2008 review and analysis*. Boston: Cornerstone Research. http://www.cornerstone.com/pubs/xprpubresultscornerstone.aspx?xpst=pubrecent.

Sale, Hillary A. 2004. Delaware's good faith. *Cornell Law Review* 89 (2): 456–497.

Scannell, Kara, and Susanne Craig. 2008. SEC chief under fire as Fed seeks bigger Wall Street role—Cox draws criticism; low-key leadership during Bear crisis. *Wall Street Journal*, June 23, A1.

Schapiro, Mary L. 2009a. Chairman, U.S. Securities and Exchange Commission Address to Practising Law Institute's "SEC Speaks in 2009" Program, February 6. www.sec.gov/news/speech.shtml.

———. 2009b. Chairman, U.S. Securities and Exchange Commission Testimony before the Subcommittee on Financial Services and General Government, June 2. www.sec.gov/news/testimony/2009/ts060209mls.htm.

Seligman, Joel. 2003. *The transformation of Wall Street*. New York: Aspen Publishers.

Stout, Lynn A. 2003. On the proper motives of corporate directors (or, why you don't want to invite homo economicus to join your board). *Delaware Journal of Corporate Law* 28 (1): 1–25.

Takor, Mary. 2005. Convergence and the implementation of a single set of global standards: The real life challenge. *Northwestern Journal International Law and Business* 25 (3): 687–688.

Thomsen, Steen. 2008. *An introduction to corporate governance*. Copenhagen: DJOF Publishers.

U.S. Government Accountability Office (GAO). 2009. *Securities and Exchange Commission: Greater attention needed to enhance communication and utilization of resources in the Division of Enforcement*. Washington, DC: United States Government Accountability Office.

Winter, Ralph K., Jr. 1977. State law, shareholder protection, and the theory of the corporation. *Journal of Legal Studies* 6 (2): 251–292.

Zhang, Xiomeng, Kathryn M. Bartol, Ken G. Smith, Michael D. Pfarrer, and Dmitry M. Khanin. 2008. CEOs on the edge: Earnings manipulation and stock-based incentive misalignment. *Academy of Management Journal* 51 (2): 241–258.

CASE LAW

Basic, Inc. v. Levinson, 485 U.S. 224 (1988).

Guth v. Loft, 5 A.2d 503 (Del. 1939).

Lyondell Chemical Co. v. Ryan, 970 A.2d 235 (Del. 2009).

Oberly v. Kirby, 592 A.2d 445 (Del. 1991).

Smith v. Van Gorkom, 488 A.2d 858 (Del. 1985).

Stone v. Ritter, 911 A.2d 362 (Del. 2006).

In re Walt Disney Co. Derivative Litigation, 906 A.2d 27 (Del. 2006).

STATUTES AND LEGISLATIVE MATERIALS

Delaware General Corporation Law, Delaware Code. 2002. (Annotated) tit. 8.

Private Securities Litigation Reform Act of 1995, Pub. L. 104-67, 109 Stat. 737 (codified in scattered sections of 15 United States Code).

Securities Act of 1933, 15 United States Code § 77a et seq.

Securities Exchange Act of 1934, 15 United States Code §78a et seq.
Sarbanes-Oxley Act of 2002, Pub. L. No. 107-204, 116 Stat. 745 (codified in scattered sections of 15, 18, 28, and 29 United States Code).
U.S. House of Representatives. 1995. Committee on Commerce Report 104-50 "Common Sense Legal Reforms Act of 1995." February 24.

SEC MATERIALS

Securities and Exchange Commission (SEC). 2000. Final rule: Selective disclosure and insider trading. 17 C.F.R. parts 240, 243, and 249, release nos. 33-7881, 34-43154, IC-24599 (July 15).
———. 2006. Exposure draft of final report of advisory committee on smaller public companies. Release no. 33-8666 (April 23). http://www.sec.gov/rules/other/33-8666.pdf.
———. 2007. Acceptance from foreign private issuers of financial statements prepared in accordance with International Financial Reporting Standards without reconciliation to U.S. GAAP. 17 C.F.R. Parts 210, 230, 239, 249. SEC release no. 33-8879. December 21.
———. 2008a. Office of Inspector General, Re-investigation of claims by Gary Aguirre of preferential treatment and improper termination. September 30. http://finance.senate.gov/press/Gpress/2008/prg100708.pdf.
———. 2008b. Roadmap for the potential use of financial statements prepared in accordance with International Financial Reporting Standards by U.S. issuers. 17 C.F.R. parts 210, 229, 230, 240, 244, 249. SEC release no. 33-8982. November 14.
———. 2009. Press release: Small public companies to begin providing audited assessment of internal controls over financial reporting in nine months. October 2. http://www.sec.gov/news/press/2009/2009-213.htm.

ABOUT THE AUTHOR

Renee M. Jones is an associate professor at Boston College Law School where she teaches corporate and securities law. Her scholarship focuses on corporate governance, corporate ethics, and the federal-state relationship in corporate regulation. Her articles have appeared in *Iowa Law Review*, *Washington University Law Review*, and the *Journal of Corporation Law*. Professor Jones is a graduate of Princeton University and Harvard Law School. She was a faculty fellow at Harvard University's Edmond J. Safra Foundation Center for Ethics in 2005–2006 and is a member of the American Law Institute. Before teaching law, she practiced for eight years at the law firm Hill & Barlow in Boston, Massachusetts.

CHAPTER 29

Corporate Governance Rules and Guidelines

ZABIHOLLAH REZAEE
Thompson-Hill Chair of Excellence and Professor of Accountancy, The University of Memphis

INTRODUCTION

Recent global financial crises and the resulting economic meltdown indicate that market-based correction mechanisms have failed not only to prevent financial crises, corporate malfeasances, and scandals but also to penalize corporate wrongdoers. Thus, governance rules and guidelines are necessary to establish a corporate environment and culture that enables effective corporate governance and reliable financial reporting to protect investors. The purpose of this chapter is to present corporate governance rules and guidelines including corporate laws, federal laws, and the Sarbanes-Oxley Act of 2002 (SOX). In addition, the chapter discusses best practices and global corporate governance principles and standards intended to strengthen corporate governance.

The remaining portion of this chapter consists of five sections. The next section discusses corporate governance rules followed by corporate governance drivers. Attention then turns to a discussion of the Sarbanes-Oxley Act of 2002 and its implications for corporate governance. The next section examines the convergence of corporate governance rules. The final section presents a summary and conclusions.

CORPORATE GOVERNANCE RULES

Corporate governance rules are intended to protect investors from corporate inefficiencies, malfeasances, and misleading financial information and, thus, to restore public trust and investor confidence in financial markets, corporations, and their financial statements. The rash of financial scandals at the turn of the twenty-first century in the United States and the inability of market mechanisms to prevent and detect scandals prompted Congress to pass the Sarbanes-Oxley Act in July 2002 to further hold public companies accountable for their financial reports.

Some argue that there is no need for corporate governance rules and regulations because market competition provides incentives for public companies to adopt the most efficient and effective corporate governance structure. Companies that do not adopt effective corporate governance are presumably nonsustainable and will ultimately be replaced. Nonetheless, the wave of financial scandals since the late 1990s indicates that market-based mechanisms alone cannot solve corporate governance problems.

The capital markets hit bottom in the early 2000s and again in early 2009 primarily because market correction mechanisms, lax regulations, and poorly developed disclosure standards failed to protect investors and thus diminished public trust and investor confidence in the capital markets. Market correction mechanisms may affect corporate governance after the destruction of substantial wealth, as evidenced by the recent subprime loan crises and the resulting economic meltdown. Market mechanisms failed to prevent the corporate debacles of companies such as Enron, WorldCom, and Global Crossing that devastated shareholders, employees, pensioners, and society and resulted in the destruction of almost all corporate wealth. To help prevent such problems, market participants expect corporate governance rules to create an environment that promotes strong marketplace integrity and efficiency as well as investor confidence in public information.

CORPORATE GOVERNANCE DRIVERS

According to Rezaee (2007), the primary sources of corporate governance rules and guidelines are corporate laws, federal securities laws, listing standards, and best practices.

Corporate Laws

State corporate laws establish standards of conduct for corporations and define the fiduciary duties, authorities, and responsibilities of shareholders, directors, and officers. State laws affect corporate governance by establishing guidance and requirements for companies' directors and officers. The goal of state laws is to protect shareholder rights by enabling investors to (1) elect directors; (2) inspect companies' ledgers, books, and records; (3) approve certain business transactions such as mergers and acquisitions; (4) receive proxy materials; and (5) receive disclosures for related-party transactions. No uniform body of corporate law exists in the United States as each state can establish its own model. The state of Delaware, however, has been prominent in influencing corporate law. State corporate laws often require:

- The corporate board of directors to be composed of at least one member.
- The board to designate new members if a current member is disqualified or resigns.
- The board to run the business and affairs of the corporation.
- The directors to receive protection while performing their fiduciary duties.
- The board to determine the compensation of directors and officers.

Federal Securities Laws

The overriding causes of the stock market collapse of 1929 were the lack of both reliable financial information and useful corporate disclosures in protecting investors. Congress responded by passing the Securities Act of 1933 and the

Securities Exchange Act of 1934 to improve investor confidence. The intention of these securities acts was to protect investors from false or misleading financial information, to maintain the integrity and efficiency of the capital markets, and to promote capital formation. Congress also established the Securities and Exchange Commission (SEC) to enforce provisions of the securities acts. These two securities acts are primarily disclosure-based statutes that require public companies to file a periodic report with the SEC and to disclose certain information to their shareholders, enabling shareholders to make investment and voting decisions. SOX expanded the role of federal laws in corporate governance by providing measures to improve corporate governance, financial reports, and audit activities.

The SEC is the federal agency in charge of administering and enforcing the federal laws governing securities markets in the United States. Its mission is to strengthen the integrity and soundness of securities markets by protecting investors; maintaining fair, orderly, and efficient markets; and facilitating capital formation. The SEC has four major goals. The first is to enforce compliance with federal securities laws by detecting problems in the markets, preventing and deterring violations of the laws, alerting investors to possible wrongdoing, sanctioning wrongdoers, and returning funds to harmed investors. The second goal is to promote healthy capital markets through an effective and flexible regulatory environment that facilitates innovation, competition, and capital formation, and by improving investor confidence in the capital markets. The SEC's third goal is to foster informed investment decision making by ensuring that investors receive complete, accurate, and transparent financial information and by implementing various investor education initiatives. The final goal is to maximize the use of SEC resources by improving its organizational and internal controls effectiveness and by making sound investments in human capital and new technologies. Achievement of these goals contributes to improvements in the governance of public companies, the integrity and efficiency of the securities markets, economic growth, and prosperity for the nation.

Listing Standards

Listing standards adopted by national stock exchanges (NYSE, NASDAQ, and AMEX) establish corporate governance standards for listing companies in order to promote high standards of shareholder democracy and corporate accountability to shareholders. Corporate governance listing standards address various governance issues of listed companies including uniform voting rights, mandatory audit committee formation, and shareholder approvals of executive compensation including broad-based option plans. Listing standards often go beyond the requirements of corporate and federal laws by providing specific definitions of, and criteria for, director independence and composition of board subcommittees. In the post-SOX era, all major national exchanges revised their listing standards to comply with the provisions of SOX. Exhibit 29.1 presents the listing standards of the New York Stock Exchange (NYSE) as approved by the SEC. Corporate governance rules of other stock exchanges are similar to those of NYSE.

National stock exchanges originally established criteria for the admission of stocks to their listings to ensure that investors would receive adequate information about listed companies. To properly and continuously monitor stocks, national

Exhibit 29.1 Corporate Governance Rules of the New York Stock Exchange

1. Listed companies must have a majority of independent directors.
2. In order to tighten the definition of *independent director* for purposes of these standards:
   a. No director qualifies as *independent* unless the board of directors affirmatively determines that the director has no material relationship with the listed company.
   b. In addition, a director is not independent if any of five additional tests are failed.
3. To empower nonmanagement directors to serve as a more effective check on management, the nonmanagement directors of each listed company must meet at regularly scheduled executive sessions without management.
4. Listed companies must have a nominating/corporate governance committee composed entirely of independent directors.
   a. The nominating/corporate governance committee must have a written charter that addresses:
      i. The committee's purpose and responsibilities.
      ii. An annual performance evaluation of the committee.
5. Listed companies must have a compensation committee composed entirely of independent directors.
   a. The compensation committee must have a written charter that addresses:
      i. The committee's purpose.
      ii. An annual performance evaluation of the compensation committee.
6. Listed companies must have an audit committee that satisfies the requirements of Rule 10A-3 under the Exchange Act.
7. The audit committee must have a minimum of three members.
   a. In addition to any requirement of Rule 10A-3(b)(1), all audit committee members must satisfy the requirements for independence set out in Section 303A.02.
   b. The audit committee must have a written charter that addresses:
      i. The committee's purpose.
      ii. An annual performance evaluation of the audit committee.
      iii. The duties and responsibilities of the audit committee.
   c. Each listed company must have an internal audit function.
8. Shareholders must be given the opportunity to vote on all equity-compensation plans and material revisions thereto, with limited exemptions.
9. Listed companies must adopt and disclose corporate governance guidelines.
10. Listed companies must adopt and disclose a code of business conduct and ethics for directors, officers, and employees, and promptly disclose any waivers of the code for directors or executive officers.
11. Listed foreign private issuers must disclose any significant ways in which their corporate governance practices differ from those followed by domestic companies under NYSE listing standards.
12. Each listed company chief executive office (CEO) must certify to the NYSE each year that he or she is not aware of any violation by the company of NYSE corporate governance listing standards, qualifying the certification to the extent necessary.
    a. Each listed company CEO must promptly notify the NYSE in writing after any executive officer of the listed company becomes aware of any material noncompliance with any applicable provisions of this Section 303A.
    b. Each listed company must submit an executed written affirmation annually to the NYSE.
13. The NYSE may issue a public reprimand letter to any listed company that violates a NYSE listing standard.

Source: New York Stock Exchange (2003).

stock exchanges require periodic disclosures of business activities, financial reports, and future plans of listed companies. Exchanges also establish corporate governance listing standards to ensure investors are protected from corporate malfeasance and abuse and to provide enforcement mechanisms to promote compliance with their standards. Furthermore, exchanges establish trading processes designed to enhance the efficiency of capital markets. While there are many similarities between the listing standards of the NYSE and NASDAQ, some differences remain. These listing standards should be consolidated with a keen focus on convergence toward more principles-based listing standards.

Best Practices

Public companies listed on stock exchanges are required to comply with state and federal laws as well as listing standards of national stock exchanges. However, mere compliance with corporate governance rules will not ensure effective corporate governance. Companies must integrate best practices into their governance structure. Best practices can serve as benchmarks to determine the ideal way to strengthen corporate governance effectiveness and can provide guidance for high achievement and excellent performance. In addition, investors may penalize companies if they fail to consider best practices. Corporate governance best practices suggested by professional organizations (e.g., The Conference Board and Business Roundtable) and investor activists (e.g., Council of Institutional Investors) are nonbinding guidelines intended to improve corporate governance policies and practices beyond state and federal governance rules and listing standards.

THE SARBANES-OXLEY ACT OF 2002 AND CORPORATE GOVERNANCE

The wave of high-profile financial scandals and the perceived ineffectiveness of market mechanisms at the turn of the twenty-first century paved the way for regulatory actions to rebuild investor confidence in corporate America, financial information, and capital markets. In July 2002 Congress acted by passing the Public Company Accounting Reform and Investor Protection Act, better known as the Sarbanes-Oxley Act (2002). Bumiller (2002, A1) notes that President George W. Bush, in signing SOX into law, praised it as "the most far-reaching reforms of American business practices since the time of Franklin Delano Roosevelt." SOX provisions are intended to address the conduct of boards of directors, audit committees, executives, internal and external auditors, financial analysts, legal counsel, investment banks, and other groups and individuals associated with financial reports of public companies.

Rezaee (2007) summarizes the key provisions of SOX under the following five categories: (1) corporate governance, (2) financial reporting, (3) audit functions, (4) federal securities law enforcement, and (5) other provisions such as legal counsel and financial analysts. Exhibits 29.2 through 29.6 summarize these provisions and related SOX sections, which are discussed later.

Exhibit 29.2 Corporate Governance Provisions of the Sarbanes-Oxley Act of 2002

Section	Provisions
202	**Audit Committee Preapproval of Audit Services** All auditing services and non-audit services provided to an issuer by the auditor shall be preapproved by the audit committee of the issuer.
205	**Amendments to the Securities Exchange Act 1934** Defines *audit committee* and registered *public accounting firm.*
301	**Public Company Audit Committees** Each member of the audit committee shall be an independent member of the board of directors. The audit committee shall be directly responsible for the appointment, compensation, and oversight of the work of any registered public accounting firm associated by the issuer. The audit committee shall establish procedures for the receipt, retention, and treatment of complaints received by the issuer regarding accounting, internal accounting controls, or auditing matters.
303	**Improper Influence on Conduct of Audits** It shall be unlawful for any officer or director of an issuer to take any action to fraudulently influence, coerce, manipulate, or mislead auditors in the performance of a financial audit of the financial statements.
304	**Forfeiture of Certain Bonuses and Profits** CEOs and CFOs who revise a company's financial statements for material noncompliance with any financial reporting requirements must pay back any bonuses or stock options awarded because of the misstatements.
305	**Amendments to the Securities Exchange Act of 1934** Alters the phrase *substantial unfitness* to read *unfitness.*
306	**Insider Trades During Pension Fund Blackout Periods** It shall be unlawful for any directors or executive officers directly or indirectly to purchase, sell, or otherwise acquire or transfer any equity security of the issuer during any blackout periods.
402	**Extended Conflict of Interest Provisions** It is unlawful for the issuer to extend credit or personal loans to any directors or executive officers.
403	**Disclosures of Transactions Involving Management and Principal Stockholders** Every person who is directly or indirectly the beneficial owner of more than 10 percent of any class of any equity security (other than an exempted security) that is registered pursuant to Section 12, or who is a director or an officer of the issuer of such security, shall file the statements required by this subsection with the commission.
406	**Code of Ethics for Senior Financial Officers** The SEC shall issue rules to require each issuer to disclose whether it has adopted a code of ethics for its senior financial officers and the nature and content of such a code.
407	**Disclosure of Audit Committee Financial Expert** The SEC shall issue rules to require each issuer to disclose whether at least one member of its audit committee is a "financial" expert.
705	**Study on Investment Banks** Directs the comptroller general to conduct a study and report the findings to Congress regarding the role of investment bankers and financial advisers assisting public companies in manipulating their earnings and obfuscating their true financial condition.

Exhibit 29.2 (*Continued*)

Section	Provisions
806	**Whistleblower Protection** Provide whistleblower protections for employees of any issuer who willingly provide evidence of fraud or violations of securities by that issuer.
1105	**Authority of the SEC** The commission may prohibit a person from serving as a director or officer of a publicly traded company if the person has committed securities fraud.
1106	**Criminal Penalties for Violations of the 1934 Exchange Act** Increases criminal penalties for violations of the 1934 Act from \$1 million to \$5 million for individuals; from 10 years to 20 years imprisonment for each violation; and from \$2.5 million to \$25 million for each entity.

Source: Rezaee (2007).

Corporate Governance Provisions

Several provisions of SOX influence corporate governance. First, SOX addresses roles and responsibilities of corporate governance gatekeepers including auditors, analysts, and legal counsel, who are now considered an integral component of corporate governance. Second, SOX strengthens the fiduciary duties and accountability of directors and officers, particularly the audit committee and chief executive officer (CEO). Third, SOX mitigates potential conflicts of interest between shareholders and their company directors and officers. Many provisions of SOX are intended to influence corporate governance and investor confidence in corporate America, its financial reports, and capital markets. Examples of these provisions are:

- Senior executive certification requirements disclosing the already mandated certifications under securities laws.
- Real-time disclosure of key information concerning material changes in financial condition or operations to signal potential business and financial risks, and a discussion of their probability and magnitude from management's perspective.
- Separation of audit and non-audit services, which can inform the markets of the objectivity and effectiveness of audit functions and resulting impacts on credibility of published audited financial statements.
- Improved corporate governance by signaling a more vigilant board of directors and audit committees (e.g., approval of audit and non-audit services, code of ethics, financial expertise, and loans to directors).
- Disclosure controls and procedures provision of SOX, requiring public reporting on management's assessment of control effectiveness and auditors' attestation and report on management's control assertions.
- Whistle-blowing protections for employees who lawfully provide information that they reasonably believe constitutes a violation of securities laws.

Exhibit 29.3 Financial Reporting Provisions of SOX

Section	Provisions
108	**Accounting Standards** 1. The SEC may recognized as "generally accepted" any accounting principles that are established by a standard-setting body that meets the Act's criteria. 2. The SEC shall conduct a study on the adoption of a principles-based accounting system.
302	**Corporate Responsibility for Financial Reports** The signing officers (e.g., CEO, CFO) shall certify in each annual or quarterly report filed with the SEC that (a) the report does not contain any untrue statement of a material fact or omitted material facts that cause the report to be misleading; and (b) financial statements and disclosures fairly present, in all material respects, the financial condition and results of operations of the issuer. The signing officers are responsible for establishing and maintaining adequate and effective controls to ensure reliability of financial statements and disclosures and periodic assessment of the disclosure of material deficiencies in internal controls to external auditors and the audit committee.
401	**Disclosures in Periodic Reports** Each financial report that is required to be prepared in accordance with GAAP shall reflect all material correcting adjustments that have been identified by the auditors.
404	***Management Assessments of Internal Controls*** 1. Each annual report filed with the SEC shall contain an internal control report, which shall (a) state the responsibility of management for establishing and maintaining an adequate internal control structure and procedures for financial reporting; and (b) contain an assessment of the effectiveness of the internal control structure and procedures as of the end of the issuer's fiscal year. 2. Auditors shall attest to, and report on, the assessment of the adequacy and effectiveness of the issuer internal control structure and procedures as part of an audit of financial reports in accordance with standards for attestation engagements.
405	**Exemptions** Nothing in Section 401, 402, or 404, the amendments made by those sections, or the rules of the commission under those sections shall apply to any investment company registered under Section 8 of the Investment Company Act of 1940.
408	The SEC must review disclosures made to the SEC on a regular and systematic basis for the protection of investors, including a review of the issuer's financial statements.
409	***Real-Time Issuer Disclosures*** Each issuer shall disclose information on material changes in the financial condition or operations of the issuer on a rapid and current basis.
1001	**Corporate Tax Returns** The federal income tax returns of public corporations should be signed by the CEO of the issuer.

Source: Rezaee (2007).

Exhibit 29.4 Audit Function Provisions of SOX

This table presents provisions of SOX relevant to public company audits, including creation of the PCAOB to regulate audits of public companies in order to ensure auditor independence and audit quality.

Section	Provisions
101	**Establishment of Public Company Accounting Oversight Board (PCAOB)** The PCAOB is an independent, nongovernmental accounting oversight board that oversees the audits of publicly traded companies.
102	**Registration with the PCAOB** Registration of public accounting firms (foreign and domestic) that prepare audit reports for issuers.
103	**Functions of the PCAOB** The board shall establish or adopt, by rule, auditing, quality control, ethics, independence, and other standards relating to the preparation of audit reports for issuers; conduct inspections of registered public accounting firms; conduct investigations and disciplinary proceedings and impose appropriate sanctions; enforce compliance with the Act; and establish the budget and manage the operations of the board and its staff.
104	**PCAOB Inspections of Registered Public Accounting Firms** The board shall conduct a continuing program of inspections to assess the degree of compliance of each registered public accounting firm and associated persons of that firm with this Act, the rules of the board, the rules of the commission, or professional standards, in connection with its performance of audits, issuance of audit reports, and related matters involving issuers.
105	**PCAOB Investigations and Disciplinary Proceedings** The board shall establish, by rule, subject to the requirements of this section, fair procedures for the investigation and disciplining of registered public accounting firms and associated persons of such firms.
106	**Regulations of Foreign Public Accounting Firms** Any foreign public accounting firm that prepares or furnishes an audit report with respect to any issuer shall be subject to this Act and the rules of the board and the commission issued under this Act, in the same manner and to the same extent as a public accounting firm that is organized and operates under the laws of the United States.
107	**Commission Oversight of the Board** The SEC shall have oversight and enforcement authority over the PCAOB.
109	**Funding of the PCAOB** The board shall establish, with the approval of the commission, a reasonable annual accounting support fee (or a formula for the computation thereof), as may be necessary or appropriate to establish and maintain the board.

(Continued)

Exhibit 29.4 Audit Function Provisions of SOX (*Continued*)

Section	Provisions
201	**Auditor Independence: Services outside the Scope of Practice of Auditors** Registered public accounting firms are prohibited from providing any non-audit services to an issuer contemporaneously with the audit, including but not limited to (a) bookkeeping or other services related to the accounting record or financial statement of the audit client; (b) financial information systems design and implementation; (c) appraisal or valuation services; (d) actuarial services; (e) internal audit outsourcing services; (f) management functions or human resources; (g) broker or dealer, investment adviser, or investment banking; (h) legal services and expert services unrelated to the audit; or (i) any other services that the PCAOB determines, by regulation, are impermissible.
203	**Audit Partner Rotation** The lead audit or coordinating partner and reviewing partner of the registered accounting firm must rotate off of the audit every five years.
204	**Auditor Reports to Audit Committees** The registered accounting firm must report to the audit committee all critical accounting policies and practices to be used; all alternative treatments of financial information within generally accepted accounting principles, ramifications of the use of such alternative disclosures and treatments, and the preferred treatment; other material written communication between the auditor and management.
206	**Conflicts of Interest** The registered accounting firm is prohibited from performing an audit for an issuer who is CEO, CFO, controller, chief accounting officer, or person in an equivalent position employed by the accounting firm during the one-year period preceding the audit.
207	**Study of Mandatory Rotation of Registered Public Accounting Firms** The Comptroller General of the United States will conduct a study on the potential effects of requiring the mandatory rotation of public accounting firms.
208	**Regulations and Independence Guidelines** The commission was given 180 days to implement final regulations regarding the Act. It shall be unlawful for any registered public accounting firm (or an associated person thereof, as applicable) to prepare or issue any audit report with respect to any issuer, if the firm or associated person engages in any activity with respect to that issuer prohibited by any of subsections (g) through (l) of Section 10A of the Securities Exchange Act of 1934, as added by this title, or any rule or regulation of the commission or of the board issued there under.
209	**Considerations by Appropriate State Regulatory Authorities** In supervising nonregistered public accounting firms and their associated persons, appropriate state regulatory authorities should make an independent determination of the proper standards applicable, particularly taking into consideration the size and nature of the business of the accounting firms they supervise and the size and nature of the business of the clients of those firms.
701	**GAO Study and Report Regarding Consolidation of Public Accounting Firms** The GAO shall conduct a study regarding consolidation of public accounting firms since 1989 and determine the consequences of the consolidation.

Source: Rezaee (2007).

Exhibit 29.5 Securities Law Violations of SOX

This table addresses roles of the SEC in protecting investors from receiving misstated financial statements as well as penalties for the violations of SEC rules.

Section	Provisions
601	**SEC Resource and Authority** SEC appropriations for 2003 are increased to $776 million from which $98 million shall be used to hire an additional 200 employees to provide enhanced oversight of audit services.
602	**Practice before the Commission** 1. The SEC may censure any person or temporarily bar or deny any person the right to appear or practice before the SEC if the person does not possess the requisite qualifications to represent others, has willfully violated federal securities laws, or lacks character or integrity. 2. The SEC shall conduct a study of "Securities of Professionals" (e.g., accountants, investment bankers, brokers, dealers, attorneys, and investment advisers) who have been found to have aided and abetted a violation of federal securities laws. 3. The SEC shall establish rules setting minimum standards for professional conduct for attorneys practicing before the commission.
603	**Federal Court Authority to Impose Penny Stock Bars** Amendment to the Securities Exchange Act of 1934 which allows the court to prohibit any person participating in, or, at the time of the alleged misconduct, who was participating in, an offering of penny stock, from participating in an offering of penny stock, conditionally or unconditionally, and permanently or for such period of time as the court shall determine.
703	**Study and Report on Violators and Violations** The SEC is directed to conduct a study and report its findings to Congress regarding the proliferation of violations of securities laws and associated penalties.
704	**Study of Enforcement Actions** The SEC is directed to analyze all enforcement actions over the prior five-year period involving violations of reporting requirements and restatements of financial statements to identify areas of reporting that are most susceptible to fraud.
802	**Criminal Penalties for Altering Documents** Criminal penalties for document destruction, alteration, or concealment with the intent to impede federal investigations or in a federal bankruptcy case include fines and maximum imprisonment of 20 years.
803	**No Discharge of Debts in a Bankruptcy Proceeding** Liability for securities law or fraud violations may not be discharged under the U.S. Bankruptcy Code.
804	**Statute of Limitations for Securities Fraud** Statute of limitations to recover for a private action for securities fraud is lengthened to the earlier of two years after the date of discovery or five years after the fraudulent activities.

(*Continued*)

Exhibit 29.5 Securities Law Violations of SOX (*Continued*)

Section	Provisions
807	**Criminal Penalties for Defrauding Shareholders of Publicly Traded Companies** Amends Chapter 63 of title 18, United States Code, by adding Sec. 1348. Securities fraud.
902	**Attempts and Conspiracies to Commit Criminal Fraud Offenses** Amends Chapter 63 of title 18, United States Code, by adding Sec. 1349. Attempt and conspiracy.
903 **904** **906**	**White Collar Crime Penalty Enhancements** 1. Maximum penalty for mail and wire fraud is 10 years. 2. The SEC may prohibit anyone convicted of securities fraud from being a director or officer of any public company. 3. Financial reports filed with the SEC (annual, quarterly) must be certified by the CEO and CFO of the issuer. The certification must state that the financial statements and disclosures fully comply with provisions of the Securities Acts and that they fairly present, in all material respects, financial results and conditions of the issuer. Maximum penalties for willful and knowing violations of these provisions of the Act are a fine of not more than $500,000 and/or imprisonment of up to five years.
1102	**Tampering with a Record or Otherwise Impeding an Official Proceeding** Whoever corruptly (1) alters, destroys, mutilates, or conceals a record, document, or other object, or attempts to do so, with the intent to impair the object's integrity or availability for use in an official proceeding; or (2) otherwise obstructs, influences, or impedes any official proceeding, or attempts to do so; shall be fined under this title or imprisoned not more than 10 years, or both.
1103	**Temporary Freeze Authority for the Securities and Exchange Commission** Whenever, during the course of a lawful investigation involving possible violations of the federal securities laws by an issuer of publicly traded securities or any of its directors, officers, partners, controlling persons, agents, or employees, it shall appear to the commission that it is likely that the issuer will make extraordinary payments (whether compensation or otherwise) to any of the foregoing persons, the commission may petition a federal district court for a temporary order requiring the issuer to escrow, subject to court supervision, those payments in an interest-bearing account for 45 days.
1107	**Retaliation against Informants** "Whoever knowingly, with the intent to retaliate, takes any action harmful to any person, including interference with the lawful employment or livelihood of any person, for providing to a law enforcement officer any truthful information relating to the commission or possible commission of any federal offense, shall be fined under this title or imprisoned not more than 10 years, or both."

Source: Rezaee (2007).

Exhibit 29.6 Other Provisions of SOX

This table summarizes responsibilities of corporate attorneys, security analysts, credit rating agencies, and other professionals associated with financial reporting.

Section	Provisions
307	**Rules of Professional Responsibility for Attorneys** Attorneys who appear or practice before the SEC are required to report violations of securities laws to the CEO or chief legal counsel and, if no action is taken, to the audit committee.
308	**Fair Funds for Investors** The SEC may impose civil penalties on disgorged executives for the compensation of victims.
501	**Treatment of Securities Analysts** Registered securities associations and national securities exchanges shall adopt rules designed to address conflicts of interest for research analysts who recommend equities in research reports.
604	**Qualifications of Associated Persons of Brokers and Dealers** Amends the Securities Exchange Act of 1934 and refines the Qualifications of Associated Persons of Brokers and Dealers.
702	**Credit Rating Study and Report** The SEC is directed to conduct a study and report its findings to Congress regarding the role, importance, and impact of rating agencies in the marketplace.
805 905 1104	**Review of Sentencing Guidelines** The U.S. Sentencing Commission is authorized to review the sentencing guidelines for fraud, obstruction of justice, and other white-collar crimes and to propose changes to existing guidelines.

Source: Rezaee (2007).

- Increased criminal penalties for violations of securities and other applicable laws and regulations.
- Creation of a public company accounting oversight board (PCAOB), which signals the improved changes needed in the self-regulatory structure in the auditing profession.

Financial Reporting Provisions

The primary focus of SOX is to improve the quality, reliability, and transparency of public financial reports. High-quality financial information can substantially contribute to the integrity and efficiency of the capital markets. Financial reporting provisions of SOX and SEC-related rules are as follows:

- Certification of financial statements and internal controls by CEOs and chief financial officers (CFOs) under Sections 302 and 906.
- Disclosure of off-balance-sheet transactions.
- Disclosure pertaining to the use of non-GAAP financial measures.
- Disclosure of material current events affecting companies.

- Requirement of mandatory internal control reporting by management in compliance with Section 404 of SOX.
- Study of principles-based accounting standards.
- Convergence of accounting standards.
- Recognition of adequate funding for the Financial Accounting Standards Board (FASB) as an accounting standard–setting body.
- Oversight functions of the FASB by the SEC.
- External auditor report on internal control over financial reporting.

Audit Function Provisions

The overriding objective of SOX is to improve audit quality and thus minimize audit failure in not discovering or not reporting financial misstatements. Provisions of SOX and SEC-related rules addressing audit functions are:

- Creation of the PCAOB to regulate public accounting firms' practice before the SEC.
- Adoption of new rules related to auditor independence.
- Inspection of audit quality by the PCAOB.
- Establishment of auditing standards in guiding auditors to improve audit quality.
- Issuance of new rules related to improper influence on auditors.
- Issuance of new rules pertaining to retention of records and audit evidence relevant to reviews and audits of financial statements.
- Establishment of quality-control standards to protect investors from receiving misleading financial information.
- Establishment of the oversight functions of the PCAOB by the SEC.
- Attestation of, and report on, internal control over financial reporting (ICFR).
- Promotion of integrated audit of both financial statements and ICFR.

Enforcement of Federal Securities Laws

SOX strengthens civil and criminal liabilities for corporate wrongdoers who violate securities laws by empowering the SEC to better enforce federal securities laws to improve public trust and investor confidence in the capital markets. The "Fair Funds" provision of SOX empowers the SEC to obtain civil penalties resulting from enforcement cases and adds them to disgorgement funds to compensate investors who suffer losses due to securities law violations. Before the passage of SOX, the U.S. Treasury received any collected civil penalties. Section 1103 of SOX authorizes the SEC to (1) obtain a temporary order to escrow extraordinary payments by the company to its directors, officers, partners, agents, controlling persons, or employees; and (2) prevent the payment of extraordinary rewards to executives and others while the company is under investigation by the commission.

Provisions Addressing Conduct of Other Individuals

Several provisions of SOX address the conduct of all corporate governance participants including the board of directors, the audit committee, management, internal auditors, external auditors, investment banks, legal counsel, and financial analysts. The following SEC-related rules address the conduct of gatekeepers other than directors, management, and auditors:

- Rules governing research analysts' potential conflicts of interest.
- Rules regarding standards of conduct for attorneys practicing before the SEC.
- Rules pertaining to rating agencies.
- Rules concerning mutual and hedge funds.
- Rules pertaining to investment banks.

Evaluation of the Sarbanes-Oxley Act

Market participants broadly view SOX as (1) reforms to identify, assess, manage, and mitigate potential conflicts of interest among different corporate governance participants (directors, officers, and auditors); (2) the mechanics of improving integrity, reliability, and quality of public financial reports (certifications of financial statements and internal controls); and (3) measures to promote professional accountability and personal integrity (director independence, audit committee financial expertise, and auditor independence).

Regulators, the business community, and the accounting profession have extensively debated the cost and benefits of compliance with provisions of SOX. According to Rezaee (2007), the benefits of compliance with SOX in order of importance are: (1) stronger internal controls; (2) improved accountability of individuals involved in operations and financial reports; (3) reduced risk of financial statement fraud and better fraud safeguards; (4) reduced errors in financial operations and financial statements; (5) improved accuracy of financial reports; (6) increased empowerment of boards of directors, particularly audit committees; (7) enhanced visibility of public companies by investors; (8) strengthened corporate accountability; (9) increased investor confidence; and (10) prevention of widespread financial scandals.

There are two opposing views held by those evaluating SOX. Some claim that SOX is an overly burdensome legislation that has imposed unneeded and costly obligations on public companies. According to the Committee on Capital Markets Regulation (2006), the high compliance costs of SOX have caused some U.S public companies to go private, discouraged companies from entering the public markets, and deterred non-U.S companies from raising capital and listing in U.S. capital markets. The initial compliance cost of Section 404 of SOX was higher than anticipated primarily because (1) the management and auditor reporting requirement was new; (2) the SEC guidance on management's assessment of the effectiveness of ICFR has been evolving; (3) auditing guidance set forth in PCAOB Auditing Standard (AS) No. 2 is consistently being improved and was subsequently refined in AS No. 5; and (4) companies usually did not have adequate and effective ICFR or their internal control system was not documented.

The perceived benefits of Section 404 compliance are (1) enhancement of management and audit committee awareness of the company's risks and controls; (2) improvements in the identification of risks and related controls; (3) documentation and testing of control processes as particularly related to ICFR; (4) improvements in the control environment resulting from more participation by the company's board of directors, audit committee, and management; (5) better acceptance and the recognition of control concepts within the company's organizational structure; (6) strengthening of the year-end closing process and recording of journal entries; (7) better use of information technology for assessing computer-related control risks; (8) improvements in the company's antifraud programs and procedures; (9) more reliable financial reports resulting from stronger internal control processes; and (10) improvements in operational efficiencies and compliance with applicable laws, rules, and regulations caused by strengthening the internal control process.

The debate over the possible impacts of new corporate governance reforms and their compliance costs on U.S. capital market global competitiveness centers around two key views. The first view is that SOX and its implementation costs have contributed substantially to the loss of U.S. capital markets' global competitiveness as the majority of initial public offerings (IPOs) have recently been listed on capital markets abroad. Those who support this view advocate revising some provisions of SOX and relaxing implementation rules, particularly for smaller companies. The other view is that SOX and its implementation rules have substantially improved the accountability of corporate America, the quality and reliability of its financial reporting, and the integrity and efficiency of its capital markets. Those who support the latter view believe that SOX rebuilt investor confidence in U.S. capital markets and investors are willing to pay a premium for the increased protection provided by tougher regulations.

CONVERGENCE IN GOVERNANCE RULES

A vital financial system and reliable financial information are essential for economic development. The persistence of differences in global financial systems necessitates a move toward convergence in corporate governance measures and regulatory reforms. The emerging global corporate governance reforms are shaping capital markets' structure worldwide and altering their competitiveness and the protection provided to investors. The globalization of capital markets and the demand for investor protection in response to financial scandals worldwide such as Enron, WorldCom, Parmalat, Ahold, and Satyam also require consistency and uniformity in regulatory reforms and corporate governance practices.

Corporate Governance Reforms and Best Practices

There are no globally accepted corporate governance reforms and best practices. Differences are mainly driven by a country's statutes, corporate structures, and culture. Country statutes could pose challenges for regulators in adopting corporate governance reforms and financial reporting disclosures for both home companies and multinational corporations. Both the United States and the United Kingdom, for example, operate under common law, which tends to give more antidirector privileges to minority shareholders compared to countries operating under code law (e.g., Germany), in which the primary purpose is to ensure that majority shareholders do not benefit at the expense of minority shareholders. Additionally, corporate governance rules in the United States are typically regulator-led, being established by the SEC to protect investors. Yet corporate governance reforms in the United Kingdom are normally shareholder-led, indicating that investors are responsible for safeguarding their own interests.

Corporate and capital structure can also influence corporate governance and financial disclosure requirements. One of the key differences in corporate structure involves ownership of the company. In the United States, ownership of shares is dispersed among the more than 110 million Americans who own company shares through direct investment and retirement plans. Comparative stock ownerships in Europe are more concentrated, and thus controlling shareholders are in a better position to influence corporate governance and business operations.

Corporate governance in a dispersed share ownership is designed to align interests of management with those of shareholders. That is, management may have incentives to engage in earnings management and focus on short-term considerations at the expense of sustainable shareholder value creation and long-term performance. Conversely, with concentrated ownership, corporate governance creates a balance between the interests of minority and majority shareholders. The primary purpose of corporate governance in the United States is to enhance shareholder value creation while protecting interests of other stakeholders (creditors, employees, suppliers, customers, and government), whereas in Germany, the focus is more on protecting creditors, as banks play an important role in financing companies.

The board of director system can also influence corporate governance. For example, with one-tier boards as in the United States, shareholders elect directors to oversee management in running the company. By contrast, in the two-tier board system as in Germany, the supervisory board advises, appoints, and supervises the management board in company operations. In Japan, however, a complex system of committees oversees and runs companies. Cultural and political differences can also influence corporate governance, as some cultures are more collective and risk averse than others, such as Germany compared to the United States.

An appropriate question is whether differences in corporate governance can be reconciled and whether convergence in corporate governance is possible. In 2004, the Organisation for Economic Co-operation and Development (OECD) attempted a move toward corporate governance integration. The OECD has established a set of corporate governance principles designed to protect all investors, particularly shareholders, which the International Corporate Governance Network (ICGN) later adopted.

The global reach of SOX underscores the need for convergence in corporate governance reforms. More emphasis on national regulations is not relevant to emerging global investment, capital markets, or the economy. The issues that need to be resolved are (1) what measures are considered good corporate governance practices; (2) how such practices can converge while maintaining domestic market confidence in both national and global regulations affected by differences in legal, political, and cultural environments; and (3) to what extent effective global regulatory cooperation can facilitate the emergence of global corporate governance.

Each country has its own corporate governance reforms that are shaped by economic, cultural, and legal circumstances. These factors influence the effectiveness of corporate governance, which typically is measured in terms of creating shareholder value and protecting interests of other stakeholders. Worldwide response to corporate scandals promotes convergence in corporate governance across borders. This convergence is particularly vital in the areas of investor rights and protections, board responsibilities, and financial disclosures. While total convergence in corporate governance reform may not be feasible, global corporate governance practices should be promoted to improve efficiency and liquidity in the global capital markets. Worldwide corporate scandals caused regulators to respond by implementing regulations designed to reinforce business integrity and restore market confidence. The enactment of SOX was in response to the financial scandals of Enron, WorldCom, and others. The United Kingdom responded to several high-profile scandals such as Parmalat and Ahold by strengthening the Combined Code on Corporate Governance.

Compared to the United States, the United Kingdom's approach to corporate governance reforms is more principles-based, which requires companies to comply or explain their deviations from compliance. This flexible approach to corporate governance, coupled with the fact that shareholders in the United Kingdom are in a much stronger position than their U.S. counterparts to nominate directors and forward their resolutions, have recently made the UK capital markets more attractive to global IPOs. Different types of corporate governance structures are susceptible to various forms of financial misconduct and scandal. For example, the dispersed ownership system of governance in the United States is prone to earnings management schemes (e.g., Enron and WorldCom) whereas a concentrated ownership system is more vulnerable to the appropriation of private benefits of control (e.g., Parmalat).

Differences in Corporate Governance

According to Coffee (2005), determination of differences in corporate governance in the United States and other countries centers on the following: (1) corporate ownership and control, (2) capital markets, (3) culture, and (4) the legal system.

Corporate Ownership and Control

Corporate ownership in countries other than the United States is much more highly concentrated through large banking institutions or family ownership. The concentration of corporate ownership and control and government ownership of a large portion of corporate shares can significantly influence corporate governance in those countries. Ownership structure is an important aspect of corporate governance, which determines the nature and extent of both internal (e.g., composition of the board) and external (e.g., rules and regulations) mechanisms needed to protect investors and minimize agency costs (e.g., information asymmetries and self-dealing by management). The ownership structure can be: (1) highly dispersed with substantial ownership by institutional investors (e.g., pension funds, mutual funds, and insurance companies), such as the United States and the United Kingdom, and usually open to cross-border portfolio holdings; or (2) concentrated ownership primarily in the hands of families, such as in Europe and Japan, with potential agency costs arising between controlling owners and minority shareholders.

Capital Markets

Public companies in the United States raise both equity and debt directly from the public through the capital markets, whereas banks in Europe and Asia are the primary source of capital for companies. Public companies' lending arrangements with banks and banks' ownership of large blocks of shares empower banks to monitor and control the companies' affairs and influence their corporate governance. Capital markets provide the means to alleviate scarce financial resources, which in turn facilitates access to global investments, and also provide the forum for global exchanges to list public companies. Capital markets facilitate the investment process through more efficient allocation of capital, by scrutinizing management, and by mitigating financial constraints.

Culture

Under the U.S. market-based corporate governance structure, shareholder value creation is the primary objective of public companies. In many other countries, corporations are responsible for protecting interests of various stakeholders including shareholders, employees, customers, suppliers, government, and the public. Thus, the need to balance the interests of all stakeholders drives such corporate governance structure. Compared with the open, social culture in the United States, the close familial culture prevalent in many countries also affects the corporate decision-making process.

Legal System

A country's legal system is a key factor that influences corporate responsibility and authority as well as the composition and fiduciary duties of its directors and officers. The extant literature in accounting and finance examines the relationship between legal protection of investors and the development of financial markets and corporate governance. This literature concludes that the legal system is an integral component of corporate governance. Thus, better legal systems contribute to market liquidity. Corporate governance listing standards do not normally exist outside of the United States. The legal system determines the nature and the degree of investor protection across countries due to differences in legal regime.

Organisation for Economic Co-operation and Development (OECD)

OECD principles of corporate governance were first introduced in 1999 and since then have become a benchmark example of the best industry practices. Principles have been regularly reviewed since 1999 in order to address the real-world experiences that OECD and non-OECD companies face. The last revision of these principles occurred in 2004 (OECD 2004). These principles do not offer a single ideal model of corporate governance for publicly traded companies. Instead, the principles suggest a path that could eventually lead to the formation of good corporate governance in any particular organization and consequently help the organization to operate more efficiently, lower the costs of the capital, and stimulate growth. The ultimate goals of the principles are (1) to ensure an adequate framework for corporate governance; (2) to promote and advocate shareholders' rights; (3) to treat all shareholders and stakeholders fairly; (4) to consider the interests of all parties involved including minority shareholders, foreign shareholders, and stakeholders;

(5) to disclose all material matters properly and in a timely fashion; and (6) to make the board accountable to the company and shareholders.

SUMMARY AND CONCLUSIONS

Both a vital financial system and reliable financial information are essential for economic development worldwide. The persistence of differences in global financial systems necessitates a move toward convergence in corporate governance rules and guidelines. The emerging global corporate governance rules are shaping capital market structure worldwide as well as informing competitiveness and the level of protection provided to investors. The globalization of capital markets and the demand for investor protection in response to financial scandals such as Enron, WorldCom, Parmalat, Ahold, and Satyam also require consistency and uniformity in corporate governance rules and guidelines. Cost-effective and efficient corporate governance rules and guidelines presented in this chapter can align the interests of directors, management, and shareholders in achieving sustainable performance, which in turn promotes market efficiency and economic prosperity.

The recent financial crisis and the resulting global economic meltdown are caused by various factors including ineffective corporate governance rules and guidelines. The global bailouts in the United States, the United Kingdom, and other countries have cost trillions of taxpayer dollars and have yet to energize or stimulate capital markets and the economy. The general perception is that subsidizing troubled companies and their executives does not serve the economy, whereas better accountability and corporate governance should improve the global economy. Bailing out these companies without effective accountability and corporate governance provides their executives with powerful economic incentives, such as excessive compensation, to make decisions that destroy shareholder value.

There are two general solutions that address the global financial crisis and the resulting economic meltdown. The first involves global market mechanisms that allow shareholders to vote on a company's legal jurisdiction in a country that has better investor protection laws and more corporate governance. The second solution is to develop effective and enforceable global corporate governance rules and guidelines, as presented in this chapter, to hold companies worldwide accountable to their shareholders.

DISCUSSION QUESTIONS

1. Discuss the feasibility of the global convergence in corporate governance, including conditions that can work in favor of convergence and those that potentially hinder the convergence process.
2. Discuss the key drivers of corporate governance.
3. Some contend that ineffective corporate governance is one of the key contributing factors to the recent financial crisis and the resulting global economic meltdown. Explain whether and how more effective corporate governance rules and guidelines could either prevent or mitigate the effects of the global financial crisis.
4. There has been extensive debate on the passage of the Sarbanes-Oxley Act (SOX) and its impact on corporate governance effectiveness. Discuss the future of SOX.

REFERENCES

Bumiller, Elizabeth. 2002. Bush bill aimed at fraud in corporations. *New York Times*, July 31, A1.

Coffee, John C., Jr. 2005. A theory of corporate scandals: Why the U.S. and Europe differ. Working paper, Columbia Law School. www.law.columbia.edu/center_program/law_economics.

Committee on Capital Markets Regulation. 2006. *Interim report of the committee on capital markets regulation*, November 30. www.capmktsreg.org/research.html.

International Corporate Governance Network. 1999. http://www.ecgi.org/codes/documents/icgn_principles.pdf.

New York Stock Exchange (NYSE). 2003. Section 303A, Corporate Governance Listing Standards. www.nyse.com/pdfs/section303A_final_rules.pdf.

Organisation for Economic Co-operation and Development (OECD). 2004. OECDPrinciples of Corporate Governance. 2004. http://www.oecd.org/dataoecd/32/18/31557724.pdf.

Rezaee, Zabihollah. 2007. *Corporate governance post-Sarbanes-Oxley Act: Regulations, requirements, and integrated processes*. Hoboken, NJ: John Wiley & Sons, Inc.

———. 2008. *Corporate governance and ethics*. Hoboken, NJ: John Wiley & Sons.

Sarbanes-Oxley Act (SOX). 2002. *Public Company Accounting Reform and Investor Protection Act*. Public Law No. 107-204, 116STAT.745. www.sec.gov/about/laws/soa2002.pdf.

ABOUT THE AUTHOR

Zabihollah Rezaee is the Thompson-Hill Chair of Excellence and professor of accountancy at the University of Memphis. He served a two-year term on the Standing Advisory Group (SAG) of the Public Company Accounting Oversight Board (PCAOB). He received his BS from the Iranian Institute of Advanced Accounting, his MBA from Tarleton State University in Texas, and his PhD from the University of Mississippi. Professor Rezaee holds several certifications (CPA, CMA, CIA, CFE, CGFM, CGOVP, CSOXP and CGRCP) and has published more than 180 articles in various accounting and business journals. He has also published six books: *Financial Institutions, Valuations, Mergers, and Acquisitions: The Fair Value Approach* (John Wiley & Sons, 2004); *Financial Statement Fraud: Prevention and Detection* (John Wiley & Sons, 2009); *U.S. Master Auditing Guide*, 3rd edition (Chicago: Commerce Clearing House, 2004); *Audit Committee Oversight Effectiveness Post-Sarbanes-Oxley Act* (BNA Tax & Accounting, 2006); *Corporate Governance Post-Sarbanes-Oxley: Regulations, Requirements, and Integrated Processes* (John Wiley & Sons, 2007); and *Corporate Governance and Business Ethics* (John Wiley & Sons, 2008).

CHAPTER 30

Economics Aspects of Corporate Governance and Regulation

VALENTINA BRUNO
Assistant Professor of Finance, American University

STIJN CLAESSENS
Assistant Director of the Research Department, International Monetary Fund

INTRODUCTION

Corporate governance failures in the past decade have spurred calls for worldwide regulatory reforms to prevent reoccurrences of situations such as Enron, Ahold, Parmalat, and the East Asian financial crisis of the 1990s. The recent developments in the U.S. markets and the subsequent global financial crisis have once again demonstrated how inadequate regulation and supervision can have negative financial and real effects that may spill from one economy into the world financial system. Academics, politicians, international organizations, and practitioners have fervently debated the mechanisms most appropriate to prevent these outcomes. Proposals often involve new, globally consistent corporate governance and regulatory standards aimed at greater monitoring and control of companies' decisions and investments. Also, over the past several years, there has been an increasing availability of indicators capturing the quality of country and company corporate governance, which in turn has further encouraged the search for uniformly valid standards.

This chapter provides a survey of the theoretical analyses and empirical evidence of the effects of corporate governance and regulation on performance at the country and company level. Much of the existing literature highlights the positive consequences of corporate governance rules for performance and economic growth. In fact, corporate governance and regulation, especially when providing a guarantee of better investor protection, should help solve agency problems and overcome incomplete contracting (Tirole 2001). The literature also indicates that any form of regulation may impose costs on companies and possible negative externalities on the general economy. Associated mostly with the Chicago School of Law and Economics, this view is that competition and private markets can lead to optimal contracting and outcomes without the need for regulation.

Hence, a theoretical question remains as to whether more regulation is always desirable. This is well illustrated by the differences in country responses to the corporate governance failures of the early 2000s. In the United States after Enron and several other corporate scandals, Congress adopted the Sarbanes Oxley Act of 2002 (SOX) to restore confidence in capital markets and the integrity of financial reporting. The various rules and provisions of SOX aim to guarantee a higher degree of monitoring by directors, a better alignment between managers' and shareholders' incentives, and a lower likelihood of corporate misconduct and fraud. At least theoretically, the impact and the consequences of greater monitoring through these laws and regulations are unclear and may differ across companies. In fact, companies' monitoring and advising needs likely depend on their size, business characteristics, and ownership structure (Burkart, Gromb, and Panunzi 1997; Raheja 2005; Adams and Ferreira 2007).

Consistent with this need to accommodate firm heterogeneity, other countries have opted for more flexible forms of regulation. The response to corporate governance failures in the United Kingdom such as the Maxwell Communications, Polly Peck, and BCCI scandals was the introduction of a set of recommendations on guiding commonly recognized principles of best practice in corporate governance. The main premise of this approach is that because of the differences in companies, imposing a strict and rigid regulation common to all is inappropriate. Instead, companies should have the freedom to choose the corporate governance structure that best suits them because higher corporate governance standards cannot be achieved by rules alone.

Given the theoretical ambiguity of the effects of regulation on heterogeneous companies, the consequences of stricter or different country and firm standards become an empirical question. Fortunately, countries' regulations and companies' corporate governance differ significantly, as first documented in the seminal work of La Porta, Lopez-de-Silanes, Shleifer, and Vishny (1998) on the legal aspects of investor protection. La Porta et al. pioneered the quantification of the quality of a country's legal systems by collecting information on the laws governing investor protection, enforcement strength, and legal origins. Their main findings are twofold: Legal origins matter particularly in common law countries which better guarantee investor protection rights; and a link exits between the legal system and economic development, thus supportive of the view that legal protection has positive effects. The La Porta et al. study not only had important policy consequences, but also encouraged the creation of other indicators to document and benchmark countries' institutional characteristics. For instance, using the same approach, the World Bank's Doing Business project provides objective indicators for understanding the regulatory environment for business in 181 countries. This allows ranking the ease of doing business based on 10 different indicators. Using these indicators, Singapore ranked first and the United States third in 2009.

The empirical literature also investigates the prevalence and effects of corporate governance practices at the company level. Led by the influential work by Gompers, Ishii, and Metrick (2003), studies have compiled indicators of corporate governance practices based on the specific provisions and practices implemented and then related these to company performance and valuation. Many commercial providers of corporate governance data such as Standard & Poor's (S&P), Investor Responsibility Research Center (IRRC), and RiskMetrics provide metrics and methodologies aimed at capturing the overall governance quality of companies, largely under the assumption that one uniform corporate governance model fits all companies.

Recent evidence challenges the view that one size fits all in terms of corporate governance. This evidence documents that different companies need different governance arrangements and, more importantly, that the optimal structure is endogenously determined for each firm (Hermalin and Weisbach 2003; Boone, Field, Karpoff, and Raheja 2007; Coles, Daniel, and Naveen 2008). The empirical literature finds varying effects on firms following the adoption of the Sarbanes-Oxley Act (SOX) of 2002. For example, the effects of more stringent regulation are less beneficial for some types of companies and may have pushed some companies to unnecessarily go private (Chhaochharia and Grinstein 2007; Engel, Hayes, and Wang 2007). This is consistent with the view that optimal governance arrangements are endogenous and that rules and regulations imposing a uniform corporate governance structure may generate negative effects.

Similarly, uniform country corporate governance standards may not be optimal. While the positive effects of better corporate governance and especially investor protection seem to be less doubtful in developing countries, studies suggest more mixed evidence on the effects of regulation in advanced economies. In a cross-country study, for example, Bruno and Claessens (2010) find the existence of a threshold level of country development and investor protection above which regulation has little or even negative effects on firm performance.

This chapter first discusses the theoretical foundations of corporate governance and regulation, focusing on the reasons for the need for flexible mechanisms and standards. It then reviews the empirical evidence on the effects of company- and country-level corporate governance and laws. The next section discusses some limitations of the existent corporate governance studies and of the methodology used to quantify and rank the overall quality of countries' regulations and companies' corporate governance. The last section summarizes and concludes.

THE REASONS FOR CORPORATE GOVERNANCE AND REGULATION

The following paragraphs discuss the theoretical foundations of corporate governance and regulation. Understanding the theory behind corporate governance and regulation provides insights into the governance and regulatory decisions and their economic consequences.

Agency Costs, Internal and External Corporate Governance

According to the Coase (1960) theorem and more generally the neoclassical view of economics, there is no need for government regulation of business activities. In a world with no transaction costs, parties will naturally achieve the most efficient outcome without any government intervention through taxes or regulations. In fact, regulation would impose costs, distort the markets, and generate other problems.

The basis of this strict Coasian view is the crucial assumption that all the contracting parties are equally informed. In reality, asymmetric information exists between the parties of a contract. Managers are typically more informed about the firm's future prospects than are shareholders. In addition, firms needing funds are more informed about project profitability than are outside investors. The degree of asymmetric information can be endogenous, as, for example, reflected in the quality of disclosure (see Leuz and Wysocki [2008] for an extensive review). Companies may decide not to disclose information because doing so is not in their best interest. In fact, the controlling shareholder may be reluctant to provide full disclosure as it would reduce the consumption of private benefits and the scope for expropriation (Leuz, Nanda, and Wysocki 2003; Lang, Lins, and Miller 2004; Anderson, Duru, and Reeb 2009). More generally, agency problems exist, which increase the difficulty for financiers to be sure that their funds are not wasted on unattractive projects and that they will ultimately earn an appropriate rate of return on their investment.

Investors and corporate insiders find overcoming these information and agency problems difficult. Contracts among parties are by nature often incomplete because envisioning and stipulating actions for every contingency becomes too costly. Thus, mechanisms are needed to make decisions that have not been specified in the original contract and that allocate residual rights of control (Hart 1995). Contracts also need to be enforced and an external party can be more suited and more economical. Therefore, a well-designed body of law and jurisprudence backed by clear enforcement mechanisms in case of disputes among the parties can facilitate contracting. Agency problems and enforcement issues can justify the need for public corporate governance rules.

The need for public corporate governance rules varies according to the specific corporate governance problem. One refinement of corporate governance problems distinguishes between two aspects: corporate governance internal to the firm and corporate governance external to the firm. Internal governance directly acts on the agents constituting the firm (shareholders, managers, and directors) and their incentives. These agents may not act in the best interest of the firm. For example, large shareholders may have incentives to expropriate minority shareholders. In addition, managers can inefficiently allocate company resources to enjoy private benefits or allocate to themselves compensation packages that are not linked to performance.

Solving the internal governance problems includes implementing specific board structures, using committees, or constructing compensation packages that align the incentives of managers and shareholders. For instance, independent directors and a large majority of nonexecutive directors in principle should lead to greater monitoring of managers, thus helping to guarantee a better allocation of resources and better firm performance. This assumes that independent directors will act in the shareholders' best interest and monitor the managers, thus preventing expropriation and private benefits of control. Regulations such as the SOX embody this view.

A counterargument highlights that external and independent directors may have neither appropriate advising skills nor sufficient firm-specific knowledge. Thus, the costs of monitoring insiders can be higher than the benefits. Along this line, recent theoretical papers challenge the view that one board fits all. For instance, Raheja (2005) finds that firms where the incentives of insiders are better aligned with shareholders require smaller-size boards and that monitoring from outside directors becomes less effective as the number of directors increases because of free-riding in acquiring information. Therefore, as the cost of monitoring increases, smaller boards with fewer outside directors are preferable. Similarly,

Adams and Ferreira (2007) find that to encourage the manager to share information, shareholders may optimally elect a less independent or friendlier board that does not monitor the chief executive officer (CEO) too intensively.

Burkart et al. (1997) show that requiring high levels of shareholder monitoring and intervention may undermine managerial initiatives to search for new, profitable investment projects and reduce managers' incentives to exert effort, hence lowering returns and worsening company valuation. Similarly, Boot, Gopalan, and Thakor (2006) argue that corporate governance controls may sometimes leave the manager with little autonomy. In addition, such controls may not facilitate decisions that the manager believes are value maximizing and may affect the company's ownership structure. These theoretical arguments indicate that whether rigid standards, such as the requirement of a uniform board structure, are optimal for all companies is an empirical question.

External corporate governance operates from outside the company through law and regulations of the legal system and financial markets, the market for corporate control, and competition (Becht, Bolton, and Roell 2003). This classification of corporate governance follows that of Shleifer and Vishny (1997, 737): "Corporate governance deals with the ways in which suppliers of finance to corporations assure themselves of getting a return on their investments." The rule of law is obviously important because it can help guarantee investor protection and a fair solution to the post-contracting conflicts that may arise. Takeovers matter as they provide a way to monitor and discipline managers by identifying poorly performing companies and rewarding those that identify such companies. However, takeovers may suffer from a free-rider problem because small shareholders may not have an incentive to tender to the raider, given that they will receive just a small fraction of the capital gains (Grossman and Hart 1980). Product market competition should solve the managerial slack by providing more incentives to managers to exercise effort.

Enforcement and Commitment Aspects

Enforcement is an important aspect of the effectiveness of corporate governance mechanisms and it is more likely to be a problem in less financially advanced countries where weak property rights and poor ex post resolution of conflicts often exist. For instance, the cost to enforce contracts in the 30 country members of the Organisation for Economic Co-operation and Development (OECD) is on average 19 percent of the claim face value. However, the percentage is much higher in most developing countries such as Indonesia (122.7 percent), Bangladesh (63.3 percent), or Venezuela (43.7 percent) (Djankov, La Porta, Lopez-de-Silanes, and Shleifer 2003). Similarly, shareholders' ability to sue officers and directors for misconduct and the strength of investor protection are best in OECD countries and worst in sub-Saharan African countries (Djankov, La Porta, Lopez-de-Silanes, and Shleifer 2008).

In the presence of weak property rights and enforcement, companies face the issue of how to solve the commitment problem and how to assure their investors that they will choose the right projects. Berglof and Claessens (2006) review the effectiveness of certain mechanisms that companies can use to solve the enforcement problem and some possible policy interventions (listed in Exhibit 30.1). The

Exhibit 30.1 Corporate Governance Mechanisms

This table shows the importance and effectiveness of various corporate governance mechanisms, and their different scope for policy intervention.

Corporate Governance Mechanism	Relative Importance in Less Developed Countries	Scope for Policy Intervention
Large blockholders	Likely to be the most important governance mechanism.	Strengthen rules protecting minority investors without removing incentives to hold controlling blocks.
Market for corporate control	Unlikely to be important when ownership is strongly concentrated; can still take place through debt contracts, but requires bankruptcy system.	Remove some managerial defenses; disclosure of ownership and control; develop banking system.
Proxy fights	Unlikely to be effective when ownership is strongly concentrated.	Technology improvements for communicating with and among shareholders; disclosure of ownership and control.
Board activity	Unlikely to be influential when controlling owner can hire and fire board members.	Introduce elements of independence of directors; training of directors; disclosure of voting; possibly cumulative voting.
Executive compensation	Less important when controlling owner can hire and fire and has private benefits.	Disclosure of compensation schemes, conflicts of interest rules.
Bank monitoring	Important, but depends on health of banking system and the regulatory environment.	Strengthen banking regulation and institutions; encourage accumulation of information on credit histories; develop supporting credit bureaus and other information intermediaries.
Shareholder activism	Potentially important, particularly in large firms with dispersed shareholders.	Encourage interaction among shareholders. Strengthen minority protection. Enhance governance of institutional investors.
Employee monitoring	Potentially very important, particularly in smaller companies with high-skilled human capital where threat of leaving is high.	Disclosure of information to employees; possibly require board representation; assure flexible labor markets.

Exhibit 30.1 (*Continued*)

Corporate Governance Mechanism	Relative Importance in Less Developed Countries	Scope for Policy Intervention
Litigation	Depends critically on quality of general enforcement environment, but can sometimes work.	Facilitate communication among shareholders; encourage class-action suits with safeguards against excessive litigation.
Media and social control	Potentially important, but depends on competition among and independence of media.	Encourage competition in and diverse control of media; active public campaigns can empower public.
Reputation and self-enforcement	Important when general enforcement is weak, but stronger when environment is stronger.	Depend on growth opportunities and scope for rent seeking. Encourage competition in factor markets.
Bilateral private enforcement mechanisms	Important, as they can be more specific, but do not benefit outsiders and can have downsides.	Require functioning civil/commercial courts.
Arbitration, auditors, other multilateral mechanisms	Potentially important, often the origin of public law; but the enforcement problem often remains; audits sometimes abused; watch conflicts of interest.	Facilitate the formation of private third-party mechanisms (sometimes avoid forming public alternatives); deal with conflicts of interest; ensure competition.
Competition	Determines scope for potential mistreatment of factors of production, including financing.	Open up all factor markets to competition including from abroad.

Source: Berglof and Claessens (2006).

most important mechanism to alleviate the commitment problem is concentrated ownership because the delegation of authority to a large shareholder can solve the free-riding involved in monitoring managers.

There are at least two main drawbacks to the presence of concentrated shareholdings. First, the dominant shareholder can expropriate minority investors, especially in the presence of poor legal protection. Second, large shareholders can have a negative impact on the market for corporate control because takeover bids and proxy fights are less likely to succeed with concentrated equity ownership. Similarly, other corporate governance mechanisms, such as competition or shareholder activism, may be limited by the same institutional, cultural, and political characteristics of a country that limit the quality of property rights and enforcement.

In light of the commitment problems of insiders, especially in developing countries, Doidge, Karolyi, and Stulz (2007) explain why country-level characteristics are vital for effective corporate governance. These characteristics matter because better governance reduces a firm's cost of funds only to the extent that the firm can make a credible commitment to higher governance standards. As a consequence, better country legal protection enables companies to more optimally invest in corporate governance and to gain better terms when accessing capital markets. On the contrary, this commitment to legal security would be prohibitively expensive in countries with poor investor protection. Firms in countries with poor financial and institutional development would subsequently invest less in governance.

A question arises as to whether this argument applies in all circumstances. Theoretical analysis suggests that country-level corporate governance can have ambiguous effects. John and Kedia (2006) model multiple mechanisms of corporate governance, study the interactions among them, and characterize the optimal combinations. They show that the optimal corporate governance system for a given economy depends on the country's financial and legal development. Because governance mechanisms interact with each other, improvements in the legal system can alter the effectiveness of different mechanisms and the combined effect can be complex. Acharya and Volpin (2010) argue that firms may choose inefficient levels of governance because they do not internalize the benefit that their own choice of governance has on competitors. However, setting appropriate regulatory standards requires understanding the nature of the rules and the externalities imposed on companies, and regulators may not be capable of acquiring such knowledge. Consequently, Acharya and Volpin contend that market-based mechanisms may be more effective than regulations.

In the context of disclosure, Hermalin and Weisbach (2008) show that on the one hand, better information allows the principal to make better decisions because it reduces information asymmetries. On the other hand, disclosure can harm agents and induce them to take actions that are not in the principals' interest. Similarly, disclosed information can be used by competitors and other agents and create externalities. By mandating the socially optimal level of disclosure, regulation could mitigate this problem. Yet determining the most advantageous level of regulatory disclosure is generally difficult (Leuz and Wysocki 2008). Combined, these theoretical analyses suggest that the effects and benefits of country regulation are empirical questions.

EMPIRICAL EVIDENCE ON CORPORATE GOVERNANCE AND REGULATION

The following paragraphs discuss recent evidence on the determinants, economic and financial effects of firm-level corporate governance and country-level regulation.

La Porta, Lopez-de-Silanes, Shleifer, and Vishny (1998) and Related Literature

La Porta et al.'s (1998) seminal contribution has inspired much of the cross-country work on law, finance, investor protection, and regulation. In their widely cited paper, La Porta et al. begin by recognizing that legal origins and traditions cause laws to vary across countries, with especially large differences between common and civil law countries. Based on a template, they assemble a data set for 49 countries covering legal rules pertaining to investors' rights (e.g., voting powers, ease of participation in corporate voting, and protection against expropriation) and the strength of enforcement. They find that common law countries have the highest legal protection, whereas the French civil law countries have the weakest protection. Importantly, their work also shows that legal origins and investor protection help explain ownership structure.

The La Porta et al. (1998) literature also investigates the consequences of better investor protection. For example, evidence shows that better protection helps reduce minority shareholder expropriation and mitigates diversion of corporate resources, thus leading to higher corporate valuations. Using data from 27 wealthy economies, La Porta et al. (2002) find a positive association between better investor protection and corporate asset valuations, confirming the importance of regulation in limiting expropriation. In another study, La Porta et al. (1997) show that the legal environment, defining both equity and creditor protection, affects the size and development of capital markets (both debt and equity) across countries. This explains why some countries such as the United States and the United Kingdom have larger and more developed capital markets and why other countries such as Germany and Japan have more developed banking systems. Overall, the work of La Porta et al. highlights the positive effects of legal and regulatory protections for investors and particularly for financial market development.

The La Porta et al. literature inspired the creation of numerous indicators capturing the role of regulation on various aspects of business including starting a business, obtaining credit, trading across countries, enforcing contracts, and regulating labor (see http://www.doingbusiness.org). For instance, Djankov, La Porta, Lopez-de-Silanes, and Shleifer (2002) describe the procedures governing the entry of new businesses. In principle, the role of regulation should be to screen new entrants and ensure that high-quality products are traded, thus improving social efficiency and generating fewer externalities. However, stricter regulation may also be associated with less competition and encouraging bribery among regulators, thereby providing little social benefit.

Documenting entry regulation for 85 countries, Djankov et al. (2002) find great variation. For instance, the number of procedures required to start up a firm varies from 2 (in Canada) to 21 (in the Dominican Republic). Importantly, in the cross-country analysis, the authors do not find significant evidence that stricter regulation is associated with higher-quality products or fewer environment or health externalities, but the analysis does indicate that stricter regulation is associated with more corruption and larger unofficial economies. Less democratic governments also more heavily regulate entry than do more democratic governments. Botero, Djankov, La Porta, Lopez-de-Silanes, and Shleifer (2004) find that the regulation of labor is more cumbersome in civil law origin countries and that more intensive regulation of labor has adverse consequences for labor force participation and unemployment. Overall, the preceding evidence sheds light on some possible negative effects of regulation.

Firm-Level Corporate Governance: One Size Does Not Fit All

Firm-level analyses complement the country-level research on corporate governance. Several studies analyze the consequences of firm-level corporate governance practices. Most studies find a positive association between better corporate governance practices and company performance. Gompers et al.'s (2003) seminal work studies the effect of antitakeover provisions on a company's performance. Their data source for corporate governance practices is the Investor Responsibility Research Center, which tracks 22 charter provisions, bylaws provisions, and takeover laws such as those related to the tactics for delaying hostile bidders or limiting voting rights. Gompers et al. find that companies adopting more antitakeover provisions have lower Tobin's q, lower sales growth, and are less profitable than other firms in their industry.

As in the case of the La Porta et al. studies, the Gompers et al. (2003) study has led to the great use and abuse of corporate governance indicators to capture companies' corporate governance quality. An increasing number of studies check compliance with an ever-growing list of corporate governance practices—the tick-box approach to measuring corporate governance. These studies implicitly assume that the more provisions a company has adopted, the better is its corporate governance, and that better governance is unconditionally associated with better investor protection and performance. Among the various rating providers, Credit Lyonnais Securities Asia (CLSA) has calculated a corporate governance index for 495 firms across 25 emerging markets and 18 sectors. Using this index, Klapper and Love (2004) and Durnev and Kim (2005) find that a higher index, indicating stronger company corporate governance, is associated with a higher Tobin's q and improved operating performance. Other studies using corporate governance indexes, such as the S&P measure of corporate disclosure practices or the RiskMetrics corporate governance scores, report similar results. This has led to the general conclusion that stricter corporate governance standards, in the form of stronger boards, independent directors, transparency, or fewer antitakeover laws, are desirable.

Subsequent studies challenge this view. For instance, Bebchuk, Cohen, and Ferrell (2009) find that not all corporate governance provisions matter and that the level of board entrenchment appears to be the most important factor. Core, Guay, and Rusticus (2006) do not find any support for the hypothesis that strong governance causes better stock returns. At best, evidence on the association between board structure (a key corporate governance feature in many indexes) and performance is mixed and inconclusive. Generally, recent studies question the notion that a single type of corporate governance should fit all.

Corporate governance practices vary greatly around the world, suggesting a need for differentiating practices from one country or region to another. Exhibit 30.2 provides summary statistics on various corporate governance arrangements for listed companies in 24 advanced countries from 2007. Notably, the analysis indicates that companies choose very different corporate governance practices from country to country. For instance, most American and Canadian firms have independent boards with nomination, compensation, and audit committees. In contrast, boards of Italian firms have large insider representation. Norwegian companies have small boards. Danish firms separate the role of CEO and chairman while American firms often unify the positions. In Sweden and the Netherlands, companies are likely to have a dual-class capital structure, which is rare in most other advanced countries.

Given the wide differences in corporate governance practices across countries, the issue arises about what factors influence firms to implement specific practices.

Exhibit 30.2 Corporate Governance Characteristics in 24 Countries

This table shows descriptive statistics of the following firm-level corporate governance practices in 23 advanced economies: majority of the board of directors is independent; existence of a nomination committee; existence of a compensation committee; existence of an audit committee; board of directors annually elected; board of directors comprising less than six members; CEO and chairman separation; absence of dual-class shares structures.

Country	Majority Board Independent	Nomination Committee	Compensation Committee	Audit Committee	Annually Elected Board	Small Board Size (< 6)	CEO/Chairman Separated	No Dual-Class Shares
	%	%	%	%	%	%	%	%
Australia	42.02	83.19	94.12	96.64	1.68	11.76	68.07	97.48
Austria	65.00	65.00	60.00	80.00	0.00	5.00	90.00	95.00
Belgium	25.93	81.48	88.89	88.89	0.00	0.00	85.19	100.00
Canada	92.35	98.98	100.00	100.00	95.92	1.53	58.16	79.59
Denmark	72.73	9.09	31.82	27.27	59.09	4.55	100.00	72.73
Finland	75.76	54.55	69.70	72.73	81.82	15.15	87.88	84.85
France	37.93	79.31	89.66	93.10	0.00	5.75	52.87	73.56
Germany	71.74	60.87	63.04	66.30	4.35	11.96	97.83	97.83
Greece	15.91	18.18	22.73	45.45	0.00	0.00	63.64	100.00
Hong Kong	9.17	36.70	96.33	99.08	1.83	0.92	66.06	100.00
Ireland	29.41	88.24	100.00	100.00	5.88	0.00	41.18	100.00
Italy	6.76	6.76	81.08	2.70	0.00	2.70	79.73	100.00
Japan	1.00	5.67	5.67	99.83	56.50	4.67	0.33	100.00
Netherlands	91.67	83.33	85.42	87.50	4.17	37.50	97.92	72.92
New Zealand	38.89	77.78	94.44	100.00	0.00	5.56	61.11	100.00
Norway	78.26	8.70	56.52	56.52	21.74	47.83	100.00	91.30
Portugal	21.43	21.43	28.57	50.00	0.00	0.00	57.14	92.86
Singapore	44.12	85.29	88.24	95.59	0.00	2.94	54.41	98.53
South Korea	92.86	92.86	78.57	100.00	0.00	0.00	14.29	100.00
Spain	15.79	94.74	96.49	98.25	0.00	0.00	50.88	98.25
Sweden	63.27	8.16	71.43	61.22	75.51	2.04	75.51	67.35
Switzerland	79.37	87.30	96.83	95.24	14.29	9.52	80.95	100.00
USA	92.14	83.62	96.31	98.72	50.23	16.66	54.18	94.31
United Kingdom	39.54	95.25	99.05	99.24	19.39	7.60	14.26	100.00

Source: Calculations by Bruno and Claessens Using Riskmetrics Data.

Doidge et al. (2007) study this issue for a large sample of firms from advanced and developing countries. They find that observable firm characteristics, such as investment opportunities, size, or ownership, explain only a small fraction of the variance in corporate governance practices. By contrast, country characteristics explain many firm-level corporate governance choices. Doidge et al. argue that country factors matter most as they influence the costs and benefits that firms incur to bond themselves to good governance. In fact, better governance reduces the cost of raising capital only if a company can credibly commit to higher-quality governance. Consequently, better country legal protection gives incentives to firms to spend more on corporate governance because firm-level governance and country regulation are complements.

Doidge et al. (2007), however, find that beyond some level of investor protection, firm-specific variables are significant in explaining the governance choices of firms from more developed countries. Similarly, Durnev, Errunza, and Molchanov (2009) find that the benefits of better firm-level corporate transparency are realized in an environment of strong property rights. Such evidence suggests that a threshold exists beyond which country regulation becomes a less important determinant for firms' corporate governance practices. Overall, these results show that regulation and legal protection are of great importance in less developed countries because they allow company-level corporate governance to be effective. In more advanced countries, where the level of legal protection and capital markets development is already elevated, companies have enough incentives to adopt better company-level corporate governance regardless of regulations.

The different impact of regulation across levels of country development relates to the question of whether uniform regulation and one-size-fits-all corporate governance approaches are beneficial to all companies. This question can be rephrased as the debate on the appropriateness of mandatory versus flexible regulation. Countries already differ in corporate governance regimes. Following recent corporate governance failures, country regulatory bodies have adopted different solutions. For instance, the United Kingdom has opted for a voluntary form of regulation called "Comply or Explain," consisting of a code of best practice that lists provisions of and recommendations for good governance (e.g., board structure, committees composition, and independence). The main premise of this approach is that raising standards of corporate governance should not be forced. Because companies are different, imposing strict regulations common to all is inappropriate. Instead, companies should choose the governance structure that best suits their needs.

Several studies provide empirical support for the notion that different companies need different corporate governance arrangements. Coles et al. (2008), for instance, find that complex firms with high advising needs have larger boards, whereas research and development (R&D) intensive firms have a larger fraction of insiders on their boards. Based on this evidence, the authors cast doubt on the suggestion that smaller and independent boards are optimal under any circumstance.

Similarly, Boone et al. (2007) find that board size and the proportion of independent directors relate to firm size and complexity. They also find that board size reflects a trade-off between the firm-specific benefits of increased monitoring and the cost of such monitoring. In particular, having strong boards in companies where the manager has firm-specific knowledge may not be optimal because of free-riding problems. Overall, these analyses suggest that board corporate governance varies by firms and is the endogenous result of different monitoring needs and firms' characteristics. This is a further confirmation that one-corporate-governance-fits-all is unlikely to be appropriate for all companies.

The Effects of Stringent Country-Level Regulation

Whether stronger and uniform rules are optimal for all companies and lead to better monitoring, more efficient allocation of the resources, and higher performance can also be investigated by analyzing changes in regulations. The financial scandals in the United States during 2001–2002 led to the introduction of more stringent regulations in the financial markets and to the implementation of the Sarbanes-Oxley Act of 2002. The new legislation set enhanced corporate governance standards for all U.S. public companies, consisting of 11 sections ranging from auditor independence to financial disclosures, fraud accountability, and individual responsibility. In particular, all company boards must have a majority of independent directors; and compensation, nominating, and audit committees must consist of independent directors. Following other financial scandals, similar calls have arisen in other countries for stronger corporate governance measures and better investor protection.

Supporters of these regulations argue that introducing new rules is necessary to guarantee efficient and prompt monitoring by boards and directors, given the failure of the existing mechanisms. They also refer to La Porta et al. type studies showing that stronger country legal protections are associated with better growth and performance. Opponents of SOX and similar types of regulation contend that the new legislation introduces an excessive burden, especially on small companies, and undermines the competitiveness of capital markets because the costs exceed the benefits.

Several studies analyze empirically the financial and economic consequences of the mandatory introduction of rules and regulations. Chhaochharia and Grinstein (2007), for instance, construct portfolios of firms based on compliance with the SOX rules and compare the returns of the portfolios during the rule announcement period. They find that following the announcement period, less compliant companies earn positive abnormal returns compared to more compliant firms. Yet only large firms attain positive abnormal returns. The authors also find evidence of abnormal negative returns in small firms. Similarly, Zhang (2007) finds that U.S. firms experience a negative cumulative abnormal return around key SOX events, consistent with the governance provisions imposing net costs.

Engel et al. (2007) examine the going-private decisions of firms and how the SOX legislation affected their choice. They find an increase in the number of firms undertaking going-private transactions in the post-SOX period compared to the pre-SOX period. In particular, their evidence suggests that smaller firms have higher going-private announcement returns, thus confirming that the compliance costs weigh more heavily on smaller firms. Also, Leuz, Triantis, and Wang (2008) find that many public companies deregister their securities from the SEC, but continue to trade publicly in the Pink Sheets, which do not require SEC registration. These going-dark activities are associated with the introduction of SOX. Overall, these studies show that the effects of introducing new regulation are mixed and that the costs exceed the benefits for some companies, especially small ones.

The preceding evidence comes from a regulatory setting where investor protection is already elevated. In such a framework, introducing stronger regulation may have negative effects on some categories of firms for which the benefits of more monitoring are offset by the implicit and explicit costs of less flexibility in company operations. Such evidence does not necessarily translate to an environment where the level of investor protection is poor or lower than in the United States. Companies from less-developed financial markets can still overcome the limitations of their home regulation and financial development by borrowing better regulation from more advanced financial systems such as the United States and the United Kingdom. An extensive literature shows that companies with more external financing needs bond themselves into more onerous regulation and financial disclosure rules to enhance their ability to raise capital (Coffee 1999; Stulz 1999). This bonding happens by cross-listing in stock exchanges that guarantee better investor protection and enforcement. By doing so, companies signal that they are less likely to expropriate from shareholders and are less costly to monitor than they would be in their own, more opaque regulatory system. Consistently, evidence shows that cross-listed companies in the United States can raise more external finance, enjoy a lower cost of capital, and have higher valuations than non-cross-listed ones (Doidge, Karolyi, and Stulz 2004; Hail and Leuz 2006).

Clearly, such evidence has biases as it is based on companies that choose to cross-list themselves in the United States, which reflects their incentives and choices. The regulatory system in which these companies decide to cross-list is optimal for them. This self-selection aspect may not apply to other companies. Related to this, a recent debate focuses on how SOX affects the decision to delist. Zingales (2007) finds some evidence of decreased cross-listing due to SOX, although other studies such as Doidge, Karolyi, and Stulz (2009) find contradicting results.

Another way to study the interaction effects for performance between country regulation and company corporate governance practices is by using firm corporate governance practices data in a cross-country setting. Using this approach, Bruno and Claessens (2010) limit their study to regulatory settings (advanced economies) where investor protection is less in doubt. However, they cover more than one country (unlike the studies on SOX) and do not focus solely on the impact of country regulation (as in the La Porta et al. and Djankov et al. literature), but also consider corporate governance practices. Bruno and Claessens find that companies with better corporate governance standards and which operate in more flexible legal environments garner a valuation premium relative to companies operating in more stringent legal environments. This is consistent with the hypothesis that overmonitoring and lack of flexibility may generate negative externalities, harm managerial initiative, and lead to lower returns.

The study by Bruno and Claessens (2010) suggests the existence of a threshold effect, where above some levels of country development and investor protection, regulation has little or even negative effects on firm performance. Moreover, because the level of investor protection is already high in these countries, companies can credibly commit themselves to better corporate governance practices and enjoy a lower cost of capital and better valuation. Bruno and Claessens' evidence suggests that the interaction between country regulation and company corporate governance is complex and not necessarily linear. More importantly, their results confirm that country regulation needs to be well designed for its benefits to exceed its cost.

LIMITS OF EMPIRICAL STUDIES ON CORPORATE GOVERNANCE AND REGULATION

The preceding review shows that designing a universal model of corporate governance is difficult. Differences in size, characteristics, and monitoring aspects of companies may justify different board structures, compensation arrangements, and divisions of powers. Also, different country institutional, cultural, political, and legal origins will alter the impact of regulations depending on complex interrelated aspects and externalities.

The research findings contrast with the recent policy debates and actions stressing convergence in corporate governance systems. The increasing worldwide adoption of codes of best practices modeled on the UK system and the importance and influence of cross-listing in the U.S. markets support the idea of a corporate governance convergence toward an Anglo-Saxon model. Although there has been an increase in the use and implementation of stronger corporate governance laws, the effectiveness of such laws may be limited by many aspects that keep agency costs higher, such as weak product market competition, opaque businesses, ineffective compensation incentives, or other cultural aspects (Roe 2002). More generally, academics argue that different institutional characteristics, political forces, and path dependence will limit convergence to only more formal aspects (Bebchuk and Roe 1999; Black 2001).

Methodologically, investigating governance aspects and the de facto impact of corporate governance and regulation for endogeneity and measurement reasons is difficult. A single set of criteria to judge corporate governance is highly questionable as firms differ. Among others, Bebchuk and Hamdani (2009) argue that the quest for a single global governance metric is misguided because it does not appropriately consider how governance problems differ in companies with or without a controlling shareholder. Bebchuk and Hamdani give the example of antitakeover defenses in the market for corporate control. Even though takeover defenses are consequential for outside investors in widely held firms, they are unimportant in companies controlled by a majority or dominant shareholder. Hence, a corporate governance metric will inappropriately measure the impact of antitakeover provisions on the majority-held company's corporate governance quality. Therefore, governance-rating methodologies that use a single metric for assessing worldwide corporate governance practices are likely to produce an inaccurate or even distorted picture. At the minimum, separate methodologies should be developed for assessing the governance of companies with and without a controlling shareholder.

A similar argument can be made for the La Porta et al. type indicators. In fact, many critics maintain that the La Porta et al. indicators of investor protection are proxies for something else and that the effects of investor protection should not be considered independently from other country characteristics. For instance, some studies suggest that culture and religion may be more fundamental determinants of legal rules governing creditor protection (Acemoglu, Johnson, and Robinson 2001; Stulz and Williamson 2003). Others claim that political developments within a country influence the expropriation of minority shareholders and the evolution of countries' corporate governance systems (Pagano and Volpin 2005). Still other studies maintain that historical events, such as civil law countries suffering greater destruction during World War II, have led to a greater use of laws and regulations (Roe 2006).

Specifically, Roe (2006) argues that modern corporate law and securities law are in both civil codes and common law. As an example, much American corporate law is codified in the 1933 Securities Act, the 1934 Securities Exchange Act, and in major legislative amendments such as SOX. In addition, much stockholder protection comes from the massive codification of securities rules by the SEC. According to Roe, what is vital is legislation and the extent to which that legislation protects property and shareholders' rights and supports the development of capital markets. In this sense, either legal style (civil or common) can protect investors.

More generally, Rajan and Zingales (2003) show that in contrast to the findings of La Porta et al. (1997) during the 1990s, countries with common law systems were not more financially developed in the 1910s. For instance, in 1913, France's stock market capitalization (a civil code country) was almost twice that of the United States. However, by 1980, the size of the French and U.S. stock markets had dramatically reversed. According to Rajan and Zingales, this evidence suggests that the superiority of common law over civil law suggested by La Porta et al. cannot entirely explain financial development and investor protection, but that the strength of political forces is a major factor. In fact, groups representing private interests, such as large incumbent industrialists and financiers, may have influenced the implementation of economic policies to protect their interests and be hostile to arm's-length markets. Because the incumbents' impact seems to be greater in civil law countries, this can spuriously lead to the conclusion of a causal relationship (instead of correlation) between legal origin and development. La Porta, Lopez-de-Silanes, and Shleifer (2008) argue the opposite: specifically, that legal origins are highly correlated with a broad range of legal rules and regulations, as well as with economic outcomes. Nonetheless, capturing in one indicator all the various country characteristics that complement or substitute more formal aspects of legal investor protection and impact the economic activity is challenging.

Pure measurement issues also arise. Spamann (2010), who recodes the La Porta et al. antidirector index of investor protection, finds no significant differences between common and civil law countries. He also finds that the index does not predict stock market outcomes. Spamann argues that the La Porta et al. index is subject to severe endogeneity concerns because it measures differences in standard practice between jurisdictions (for example, the choice of bearer over registered shares, or vice versa) rather than differences in the law.

Endogeneity is an equally serious problem when investigating company-level corporate governance practices. According to Hermalin and Weisbach (2003), many corporate governance variables, such as board composition and independence, and their dynamics, such as CEO turnover, are endogenously determined. For instance, firm performance is both a result of the actions of previous directors and a factor that potentially influences the choice of subsequent directors. Moreover, if companies endogenously choose their optimal corporate governance structure, there should be no relation to performance. Also, factors related to unique company characteristics, such as ownership structure or the industry environment, may affect corporate governance choices and generate spurious correlations with performance. Controlling for all these aspects is difficult when constructing country-level or company-level corporate governance indicators and studying their effects on performance. Consequently, many studies only represent a partial analysis and leave conclusions about the ultimate benefits and costs of regulation and corporate governance unresolved.

SUMMARY AND CONCLUSIONS

This chapter provided an overview of theoretical and empirical works on corporate governance and regulation. The chapter discussed some positive and negative effects of corporate governance practices and regulation on firm performance. On the positive side, corporate governance undoubtedly alleviates agency problems and contract incompleteness. Thus, corporate governance promotes better investor protection and an efficient allocation of the corporate resources, which translates into superior growth and performance. However, the interaction effects between the various corporate governance mechanisms (law, product market competition, institutional and ownership factors, and the market for corporate control) are not only complex but can also serve as complements or substitutes for each other. Consequently, inadequate regulation can have negative financial and real effects if its benefits are not designed to offset its costs.

The evidence on the negative regulatory effects does not mean that regulation is always ineffective or harmful. The outcome of regulations and corporate governance practices can differ between developing and developed countries. In the latter, the problems of expropriation, rule of law, and monitoring are fewer than in developing countries. Developed countries are more likely to meet a minimum threshold of legal protection and enforcement to solve the commitment problem and access external financing. Therefore, country-level regulation matters more where financial markets and institutions are less developed. Corporate governance choices made at the company-level seem more important in advanced economies. This is because companies are less concerned about committing to high corporate governance standards (as the country standards are already higher) and are more focused on a timely, flexible structure that responds to the dynamic business changes and evolving needs.

A key message of this chapter is that corporate governance and regulation cannot be considered in isolation. Without an understanding of other economic and institutional factors that complement and affect firm incentives, corporate governance and regulation may be only partially effective. As several academics have argued, the quest for a single metric of global corporate governance is surely misguided. Consequently, the analysis and implementation of corporate governance and regulation should differ across firms with the aim of identifying the dimensions that matter most given firm characteristics. Similarly, corporate governance regulation differs according to the country's development. A one-corporate-governance-fits-all approach can still be helpful for developing countries as they strive to reach minimum standards of de facto and de jure investor protection to overcome institutional barriers and solve the commitment problem. But one corporate governance does *not* fit all in advanced economies where minimum standards of de facto and de jure investor protection are met and company characteristics matters more. Here, firm ownership and industrial, size, and growth characteristics will be vital in determining the optimal corporate governance practices. For such companies, uniform corporate governance standards may be inappropriate.

There are many important issues still unexplored in the literature. These include the dynamics and architectures of corporate governance and the complementarities with the existing institutional framework. Endogeneity and data limitations are major obstacles in the analysis of the interrelated mechanisms that ultimately affect company decisions and performance. This could explain why there are only a few studies on the interactions and complementarities between regulation aspects and other country institutional characteristics. Also, in many cases of regulatory reforms, the objective function is not clearly defined between maximization of firm performance and the macro aspects of commonwealth and country growth. Future research will hopefully solve this puzzle of regulation with better-quality data and longer time series.

DISCUSSION QUESTIONS

1. Evaluate the arguments and the economic foundations of corporate governance and regulation. How might corporate governance practices and country regulations affect firms' behavior?
2. Why do country institutional and legal characteristics matter for effective corporate governance? Discuss the differences between developing and advanced economies.
3. The post-Enron reforms have introduced new rules and regulations especially for boards and director oversight. Worldwide, there have been calls for more rules and more stringent regulations. These calls for reform have shifted the attention to *checklist compliance* with the rules and have often ignored the heterogeneity of companies. How might introducing more stringent regulations strengthen investor protection and confidence? What do studies show about the economic effects post Sarbanes-Oxley?
4. According to Roe (2006, 462), "Legal origin—civil vs. common law—is said in much modern academic work to determine the strength of financial markets and the structure of corporate ownership, even in the world's richer nations. The main means are two: First, common law judges protect minority stockholders better than do civil law judges. Second, common law systems regulate markets less rigidly than civil law systems and protect property more, systematically promoting transparency and markets. But, while stockholder protection and property rights are important, legal origin is not their foundation." Critically discuss this statement.

REFERENCES

Acemoglu, Daron, Simon Johnson, and James A. Robinson. 2001. The colonial origins of comparative development: An empirical study. *American Economic Review* 91 (5): 1369–1401.

Acharya, Viral V., and Paolo F. Volpin. 2010. Corporate governance externalities. *Review of Finance* 14 (1): 1-33.

Adams, Renee B., and Daniel Ferreira. 2007. A theory of friendly boards. *Journal of Finance* 62 (1): 217–250.

Anderson, Ronald, Augustine Duru, and David Reeb. 2009. Family ownership and corporate opacity in the US. *Journal of Financial Economics* 92 (2): 205–222.
Bebchuk, Lucian A., Alma Cohen, and Allen Ferrell. 2009. What matters in corporate governance? *Review of Financial Studies* 22 (2): 783–827.
Bebchuk, Lucian A., and Assaf Hamdani. 2009. The elusive quest for global governance standards. *University of Pennsylvania Law Review* 157 (5): 1263–1317.
Bebchuk, Lucian A., and Mark J. Roe. 1999. A theory of path dependence in corporate ownership and governance. *Stanford Law Review* 52 (1): 127–170.
Becht, Marco, Patrick Bolton, and Ailsa Roell. 2003. Corporate governance and control. In *Handbook of the economics of finance*, Volume 1, ed. George M. Constantinides, Milton Harris, and René M. Stulz, 1–109. Amsterdam, Elsevier North Holland.
Berglof, Erik, and Stijn Claessens. 2006. Enforcement and good corporate governance in developing countries and transition economies. *The World Bank Research Observer* 21 (1): 123–150.
Black, Bernard S. 2001. The legal and institutional preconditions for strong securities markets. *UCLA Law Review* 48: 781–855.
Boone, Audra, Laura C. Field, Jonathan M. Karpoff, and Charu G. Raheja. 2007. The determinants of corporate board size and composition: An empirical analysis. *Journal of Financial Economics* 85 (1): 66–110.
Boot, Arnoud W. A., Radhakrishnan Gopalan, and Anjan V. Thakor. 2006. The entrepreneur's choice between private and public ownership. *Journal of Finance* 61 (2): 803–836.
Botero Julian, Simeon Djankov, Rafael La Porta, Florencio C. Lopez-de-Silanes, and Andrei Shleifer. 2004. The regulation of labor. *Quarterly Journal of Economics* 119 (4): 1339–1382.
Bruno, Valentina G., and Stijn Claessens. 2010. Corporate governance and regulation: Can there be too much of a good thing? *Journal of Financial Intermediation*, forthcoming.
Burkart, Mike, Denis Gromb, and Fausto Panunzi. 1997. Large shareholders, monitoring, and the value of the firm. *Quarterly Journal of Economics* 112 (3): 693–728.
Chhaochharia, Vidhi, and Yaniv Grinstein. 2007. Corporate governance and firm value: The impact of the 2002 governance rules. *Journal of Finance* 62 (4): 1789–1825.
Coase, Ronald H. 1960. The problem of social cost. *Journal of Law and Economics* 3 (October): 1–31.
Coffee, John, Jr. 1999. The future as history: The prospects for global convergence in corporate governance and its implications. *Northwestern University Law Review* 93 (3): 641–708.
Coles, Jeffrey L., Naveen D. Daniel, and Lalitha Naveen. 2008. Boards: Does one size fit all? *Journal of Financial Economics* 87 (2): 329–356.
Core, John E., Wayne R. Guay, and Tjomme O. Rusticus. 2006. Does weak governance cause weak stock returns? An examination of firm operating performance and investors expectations. *Journal of Finance* 61 (2): 655–687.
Djankov, Simeon, Rafael La Porta, Florencio Lopez-de-Silanes, and Andrei Shleifer. 2002. The regulation of entry. *Quarterly Journal of Economics* 117 (1): 1–37.
———. 2003. Courts. *Quarterly Journal of Economics* 118 (2): 453–517.
———. 2008. The law and economics of self-dealing. *Journal of Financial Economics* 88 (3): 430–465.
Doidge, Craig, Andrew G. Karolyi, and René M. Stulz. 2004. Why are foreign firms listed in the U.S. worth more? *Journal of Financial Economics* 71 (2): 205–238.
———. 2007. Why do countries matter so much for corporate governance? *Journal of Financial Economics* 86 (1): 1–39.
———. 2009. Has New York become less competitive than London in global markets? Evaluating foreign listing choices over time. *Journal of Financial Economics* 91 (3): 253–287.
Durnev, Art, Vihang Errunza, and Alexander Molchanov. 2009. Property rights protection, corporate transparency, and growth. *Journal of International Business Studies*, forthcoming.

Durnev, Art, and E. Han Kim. 2005. To steal or not to steal: Firm attributes, legal environment and valuation. *Journal of Finance* 60 (3): 1461–1493.

Engel, Ellen, Rachel M. Hayes, and Xue Wang. 2007. The Sarbanes–Oxley Act and firms' going-private decisions. *Journal of Accounting and Economics* 44 (1–2): 116–145.

Gompers, Paul A., Joy L. Ishii, and Andrew Metrick. 2003. Corporate governance and equity prices. *Quarterly Journal of Economics* 118 (1): 107–155.

Grossman, Sanford J., and Oliver D. Hart. 1980. Disclosure laws and takeover bids. *Journal of Finance* 35 (2): 323–334.

Hail, Luzi, and Christian Leuz. 2006. International differences in the cost of equity capital: Do legal institutions and securities regulation matter? *Journal of Accounting Research* 44 (3): 485–531.

Hart, Oliver. 1995. Corporate governance: Some theory and implications. *Economic Journal* 105 (430): 678–689.

Hermalin, Benjamin E., and Michael S. Weisbach. 2003. Boards of directors as an endogenously determined institution: A survey of the economic literature. *FRBNY Economic Policy Review* 9 (1): 7–26.

———. 2008. Information disclosure and corporate governance. Fisher College of Business working paper 2008-03-016, Ohio State University.

John, Kose, and Simi Kedia. 2006. Design of dorporate governance: Role of ownership structure, takeovers, and bank debt. NYU working paper No. CLB-06-023.

Klapper, Leora, and Inessa Love. 2004. Corporate governance, investor protection, and performance in emerging countries. *Journal of Corporate Finance* 10 (5): 703–728.

Lang, Mark H., Karl V. Lins, and Darius Miller. 2004. Concentrated control, analyst following, and valuation: Do analysts matter most when investors are protected least? *Journal of Accounting Research* 42 (3): 589–623.

La Porta, Rafael, Florencio Lopez-de-Silanes, and Andrei Shleifer. 2008. The economic consequences of legal origins. *Journal of Economic Literature* 46 (2): 285–332.

La Porta, Rafael, Florencio Lopez-de-Silanes, Andrei Shleifer, and Robert W. Vishny. 1997. Legal determinants of external finance. *Journal of Finance* 52 (3): 1131–1150.

———. 1998. Law and finance. *Journal of Political Economy* 106 (6): 1113–1155.

———. 2002. Investor protection and corporate valuation. *Journal of Finance* 57 (3): 1147–1170.

Leuz, Christian, Dhananjay Nanda, and Peter D. Wysocki. 2003. Earnings management and investor protection: An international comparison. *Journal of Financial Economics* 69 (3): 505–527.

Leuz, Christian, Alexander Triantis, and Tracy Wang. 2008. Why do firms go dark? Causes and economic consequences of voluntary SEC deregistrations. *Journal of Accounting and Economics* 45 (2–3): 181–208.

Leuz, Christian, and Peter D. Wysocki. 2008. Economic consequences of financial reporting and disclosure regulation: A review and suggestions for future research. Working paper, University of Chicago, Booth School of Business.

Pagano, Marco, and Paolo Volpin. 2005. The political economy of corporate governance. *American Economic Review* 95 (4): 1005–1030.

Raheja, G. Charu. 2005. Determinants of board size and composition: A theory of corporate boards. *Journal of Financial and Quantitative Analysis* 40 (2): 283–306.

Rajan, Raghuram G., and Luigi Zingales. 2003. The great reversals: The politics of financial development in the twentieth century. *Journal of Financial Economics* 69 (1): 5–50.

Roe, Mark. 2002. Corporate law's limits. *Journal of Legal Studies* 31 (2): 233–271.

———. 2006. Legal origins, politics, and modern stock markets. *Harvard Law Review* 120 (2): 462–527.

Shleifer, Andrei, and Robert W. Vishny. 1997. A survey of corporate governance. *Journal of Finance* 52 (2): 737–783.

Spamann, Holger. 2010. The "Antidirector Rights Index" revisited. *Review of Financial Studies* 23 (2): 467–486.
Stulz, René. 1999. Globalization, corporate finance, and the cost of capital. *Journal of Applied Corporate Finance* 12 (3): 8–25.
Stulz, René, and Rohan Williamson. 2003. Culture, openness, and finance. *Journal of Financial Economics* 70 (3): 313–349.
Tirole, Jean. 2001. Corporate governance. *Econometrica* 69 (1): 1–35.
Zhang, Ivi X. 2007. Economic consequences of the Sarbanes–Oxley Act of 2002. *Journal of Accounting and Economics* 44 (1–2): 74–115.
Zingales, Luigi. 2007. Is the U.S. capital market losing its competitive edge? ECGI Finance working paper 192/2007.

ABOUT THE AUTHORS

Valentina Bruno holds a master's degree in finance and economics and a PhD in finance from the London School of Economics. Before joining American University, she worked at the World Bank in the Financial Sector Strategy and Policy Group and in the International Finance Team (DECPG). She is a research associate at the Financial Markets Group (London School of Economics). Her research interests include corporate finance and governance, law and finance, and financial intermediation, with a special emphasis on international finance, performance, and growth.

Stijn Claessens is assistant director in the research department of the International Monetary Fund where he heads the Macro-Financial Linkages Unit and a CEPR Research Fellow. He started his career teaching at New York University Business School in 1987 and then worked at the World Bank in various positions between 1987 and 2001. He taught at the University of Amsterdam from 2001 to 2004, where he remains a professor of international finance policy. Before his current position, he was senior adviser to the financial and private sector vice president of the World Bank between 2004 and 2006. His policy and research interests are firm finance and corporate governance, financial globalization, and business and financial cycles. Over his career, Mr. Claessens has provided policy advice to emerging markets, transition economies, and advanced countries. His research has been widely published and he has edited several books. He is an editor of the *Journal of Financial Services Research* and an associate editor at other journals.

PART FOUR

Answers to Chapter Discussion Questions

Chapter 2 The Financial Determinants of American Corporate Governance: A Brief History

1. Businessmen's main concern at the turn of the twentieth century was ruinous competition that drove prices down and many businesses into bankruptcy. Unlike farmers and manufacturers who feared the large trusts, businessmen wanted to combine. States, with New Jersey at the helm, responded to these concerns by eliminating restrictions in their corporation laws that banned corporations from owning stock in other corporations, merging without the unanimous consent of their shareholders, or otherwise capitalizing their business as they saw fit. Corporations could incorporate for any lawful purpose and exist as holding companies solely to own other corporations. The giant business corporations of the turn of the twentieth century were created and financed by virtue of these changes.

   The new statutes allowed corporations to use their own stock to buy assets, including the stock of other companies, and New Jersey's went a step further, giving directors the sole power to determine the value of the assets to be purchased and thus the stock to be issued. This allowed directors to buy corporations for inflated prices and to use stock instead of cash for these purchases. Given the incentives of trust promoters who took their fees in stock, the stock was promptly sold to a newly rising and financially ambitious middle class. By the end of the first decade of the twentieth century, a class of public stockholders had been established as an important characteristic of the American economy.

2. The new corporate statutes ended the individual shareholder's ability to participate in corporate management. The erosion of the traditional ultra vires doctrine and the reintroduction of the idea that the board's power was original and undelegated helped to minimize shareholder control, as did changing voting rules. Proxy voting, the introduction of majority vote for the approval of mergers sales of corporate assets, pyramiding, and nonvoting stock all allowed large shareholders (and the financiers who supported them) to control the affairs of their corporations.

   While individual shareholders had little if any role in the management of their corporation's affairs, they could expect (and the new corporations offered them the promise of) large dividends as financiers and their clients demanded large multiples of earnings for the opportunity to share in the future profits of industry. This demand led to a bubble that ultimately left the new corporations with devastated stock prices and unhappy shareholders. In the years that followed, corporations repurchased their stock and retained their earnings to support their securities prices. By the 1930s, industrial corporations lived off their retained earnings and no longer needed their stockholders (who had largely deserted them following the crash anyway). Management's control was complete and unsupervised.

3. The main attempts to control corporate power in the 1930s and 1940s consisted of calls for imposing stricter fiduciary obligations on corporations and the control group and efforts to give public shareholders more access to their corporation's management. Corporate law scholars, such as Adolf A. Berle Jr. and William O. Douglas, described corporate powers as powers in trust for the community and the directors as representing the shareholders, themselves a proxy for community interests. At the same time, the SEC promulgated Rule 14a-8 requiring corporate management to include certain shareholder proposals in the corporation's annual proxy solicitation.

   Neither the idea that corporate powers were powers in trust nor the ideal of shareholder democracy that underlay Rule 14a-8 were successful or even vigilantly pursued. But the attempts to control corporate power or empower public shareholders were bound to fail because the financial structure of corporations in the 1930s and 1940s ensured management's free rein. The practice of retaining earnings to support stock prices kept corporations from returning to the public market and allowed them to finance primarily from within, protecting first control groups and later management from external scrutiny. Shareholders continued to receive dividends as the primary form of return on their investments at the discretion of the boards, and a continuous stream of dividends served a protective function against widespread stockholder activism or shareholder suits.

4. The monitoring model of the board was developed in the 1970s and 1980s in response to growing criticism of the role corporations played in crises such as Watergate, the foreign bribery scandals, the 1970 bankruptcy of Penn Central, and the dual oil crises. Focusing on the actual functions directors could fulfill, the legal and business communities converged on viewing directors, especially independent directors, as responsible for monitoring the executives (who, in turn, manage the corporation). While some scholars wanted to use the monitoring model to make directors' duties more substantial, mainstream legal academia and the Delaware courts focused on the monitoring role of independent directors. If a majority of independent, disinterested directors, following the courts' procedural requirements, approved the board's actions (including conflict-of-interest transactions), the courts declared such actions to be shielded from further judicial inquiry. Reducing the role of the board to a bare minimum, the Delaware courts also transformed the business judgment rule from a rule of deference to expert opinion to a rule of defense precluding judicial inquiry into the directors' challenged actions.

   By the mid-1980s, the Delaware courts made the power of the monitoring board absolute and unquestionable, including the power to prevent shareholders from selling their stock to a hostile bidder. The Delaware courts legitimated this absolute power by describing directors as agents of the shareholders and protecting the shareholder vote—a meaningless ritual at best—from impediment by directorial action. While the courts did not explicitly make the connection, the independent directors, presumably without other ties to the corporation, made the ideas that the shareholders elected directors and thus that the directors were their agents less fictitious. The rhetoric of agency legitimated the independent directors' power while the courts' reliance on the independent directors' opinions helped limit the liability imposed on the board as a whole.

Changes in the capital structure of the large public corporations supported the Delaware courts' particular interpretation of the monitoring model of the board. In the 1950s and 1960s, the New York Stock Exchange engaged in a deliberate campaign to encourage individuals to invest in stock. Its success was reflected in the explosive market development of the succeeding years with a marked turn to investing for capital gains. Shareholders' desires for dividends gave way to the demand for capital appreciation. Stock ownership and the stock market were rapidly growing and corporations were using their retained earnings and replacing them with debt to satisfy the shareholders' demand for profit and to avoid takeovers. From its highs of the mid-century, internal finance dropped steadily and consistently.

With internal finance at record lows, the stock market became the principal governor of corporate behavior and stock price appreciation became an end in and of itself. Demands on American corporations to demonstrate elevated stock prices were multiple and growing. Apathetic individual investors and institutional investors alike came to see stock price as the best measure of corporate success and the courts made their wishes real. Viewing the independent directors as best suited for the task of guaranteeing continued stock price appreciation, the decisions of the Delaware courts simply advised directors as the shareholders' agents to maximize shareholder profit so as not to trigger the ire of their principals.

Chapter 3 Corporate Governance Systems

1. Contrary to most of the classifications from finance and law, the *varieties of capitalism* (VOC) literature does not assume that one set of institutions is superior to all other sets. Instead, the VOC literature is based on the concept of complementarity. One institution acts as a complement to another one if it improves the efficiency or returns of the latter. In other words, the VOC literature argues that different sets of institutions and the complementarities they create may generate similar economic outcomes. For example, the social democracies of Northern Europe with their less developed stock markets and strong workers' rights have similar standards of living as the United Kingdom and the United States, which have highly developed capital markets but weak employee rights.
2. Holderness (2009) argues that former studies have suffered from at least three biases that may have understated the concentration of ownership. First, most empirical studies cover only the largest companies and ignore medium-sized

and small companies. For example, La Porta, Lopez-de-Silanes, Shleifer, and Vishny (1998) and Enriques and Volpin (2007) focus only on the 10 or 20 largest firms and such firms are not representative of the entire U.S. economy. Second, electronic data sources used in previous empirical studies, such as Becht (2001), have been of relatively poor quality. Third, even empirical studies based on hand-collected data sets tend to understate ownership concentration in the United States because they do not properly adjust for substantial disclosure inconsistencies in the directors' and officers' proxy statements.

3. The first type of criticism refers to the construction of La Porta, Lopez-de-Silanes, Shleifer, and Vishny's (1997a, 1998) investor-protection index—that is, the anti-director index. Graff (2008) argues that some of the legal rules that the index considers do not measure investor protection and that others which are clearly of relevance have not been included in the index. Further, according to Spamann (2008), the index suffers from a significant number of encoding errors, which are mainly due to La Porta et al.'s (1997a, 1998) reliance on secondary rather than primary sources of law. Both Graff and Spamann argue that, if their criticisms are addressed, La Porta et al.'s key result that common law countries provide stronger investor protection than civil law countries is no longer valid.

   The second type of criticism relates to La Porta et al.'s (1997a, 1998) central premise that law drives corporate governance. For example, Licht, Goldschmidt, and Schwartz (2005) argue that law is only a proxy for the real driver of corporate governance, which is culture. Their empirical data suggests that culture is much better than law at explaining differences in corporate governance across nations.

4. The recent bank failures such as Lehman Brothers, Northern Rock, HBOS, and Royal Bank of Scotland have all occurred in common law countries while banks from French law countries such as France and Spain have been much less affected by the subprime mortgage crisis. The concentration of bank failures in the United Kingdom and the United States raises doubts as to La Porta et al.'s (1997a, 1998) thesis that common law countries provide better investor protection against managerial excesses, including excessive risk taking, than civil law countries. Therefore, the lesson to draw from the most recent failures in common law countries and those of Ahold in the Netherlands and Parmalat in Italy is that no single corporate governance system is infallible and that they all suffer from shortcomings.

Chapter 4 Corporate Governance Best Practices

1. Although still contentious, the evidence supports the view that corporate boards should represent the interests of the corporation on behalf of society, not solely shareholders or any other stakeholders.
   - Corporate law clearly states that directors have fiduciary duties to be loyal to and care for the best interests of the corporation.
   - Corporations in the United Kingdom and Canada are expected to act as responsible citizens and serve the interests of society.
   - A corporation is a legal person that is entirely dependent on and vulnerable to the board of directors, which is a critical test for a fiduciary relationship.

- People, whether natural or legal persons, whose civil rights are protected constitutionally, cannot be owned as private property, because that would be slavery.
- Director's fiduciary duties are subject to public laws that govern the relationship between individuals and society.
- Governments grant corporations legal license to operate, presumably to serve public policy interests.
- Boards of directors would be redundant in firms that are owner-managed and with active, controlling shareholders (also in not-for-profit and government organizations without equity owners), if their primary role was to protect the interests of owners. Corporate governance should be defined and guided by a universal set of criteria that apply equally to all corporate varieties.

2. A viable theory must satisfy all conditions. Agency theory, which sees corporate governance as a regulatory mechanism for resolving the principal-agent conflict, fails to account for all the value that boards add through leadership to create a productive corporate environment. Agency theory is inconsistent not only with the notion that corporate boards should serve the interests of corporations on behalf of society, but also with the idea that management, as agents, can never be trusted to represent the best interests of the corporation (or shareholders or society). In fact, in jurisdictions where directors' fiduciary duties extend to shareholders, directors (executive and independent) are expected to act as trusted principals themselves (a higher standard than that for agents), not as their agents, which is inconsistent with the mistrusting, agency theory. Moreover, without a countervailing force, such as stewardship theory, on its own, agency theory sets a single trajectory for only one possible future, namely increasing mistrust and regulation, and therefore continual value sub-optimization. Agency theory also invalidates corporate boards for firms that are owner-managed and with active, controlling shareholders, as boards would not have a legitimate role resolving a nonexistent principal-agent conflict. Finally, agency theory fails to allow for corporate governance models that align with strategic business priorities and public policy objectives. Corporate governance is more complex than resolving principal-agent conflicts involving many important relationships.
3. Attempts to prescribe best practices tend to generalize and oversimplify the corporate governance function, reducing it to a box-ticking exercise rather than a thoughtful process of applying wise corporate judgment. Best practices are designed to address a specific set of governance issues and optimize for one outcome, without regard for other valid issues and corporate objectives. They are not equally applicable to all firms at all times, yet their popularity influences all boards. Moreover, best practices inhibit creativity and innovation, and precipitate homogeneity and the status quo.
4. ACG provides a universally applicable, formal framework and context to guide the activities of corporate boards toward self-governance. The ACG framework is based on foundational performance, sustainability, and adaptability principles, and designed for complex, uncertain corporate environments. ACG transcends governance theories, principles, and practices, and serves as both a diagnostic and design tool. ACG considers three measurable and comparable

aspirational, rather than prescriptive, criteria: requisite organization, requisite variety, and adaptive capacity. Beyond providing a self-regulating sense-and-respond system of governance, it also facilitates adaptation of governance structures and processes to support strategic business objectives. Therefore, ACG facilitates collaborative creativity and innovation in corporate governance of all types of corporate forms. It also provides analysts and policy makers with comparable criteria to guide the advancement of governance structures and practices.

5. The ACG framework is used to organize various corporate governance principles and practices according to their role in affecting each of the three ACG criteria: requisite organization, requisite variety, and adaptive capacity. This method facilitates a direct comparison using independent ACG criteria, rather than basing the comparison on any one set of principles or practices. The analysis reveals that there is considerable variance in emphasis between each of the guidance instruments. Findings support the aspirational nature of OECD principles and highlight opportunities for improvement in NACD principles and popular best practices.
6. Governance committees could begin by reviewing their board's governance practices against the ACG framework to identify opportunities for the board to assume a broader, more proactive role in creating an effective and aspirational corporate environment; by increasing the cognitive capacity of boards to consider the bigger picture of strategic and systemic considerations over a longer time horizon; and by equipping directors with the ability to deal with dilemmas, ambiguities, inconsistencies, and novelties.

Chapter 5 What's Wrong with Corporate Governance Best Practices?

1. Defining *good corporate governance* in terms of the ability of firms to be self-governing on a sustainable basis implies that:
   - Good corporate governance would enrich democracy at a micro level while reducing the cost, size, and intrusion of government and its regulators.
   - Good governance can be evaluated by the extent to which government laws, regulations, and regulators are reduced, together with the use of legal proceedings to protect and further the interests of corporate stakeholders and citizens in general.
   - The evaluation of good governance becomes based on outcomes, not on any particular practices, processes, policies, disclosure, and transparency or economic performance.
2. Several inherent limitations and problems arise from firms governed by a single board. For example, a single board provides directors with absolute power to manage their own conflicts of interest, which in turn can corrupt both its members and the business. In addition, complex organizations have an insufficient variety of communication channels to cross-check the accuracy of feedback information, control channels to regulate manifold variables that are not optimal, and decision-making centers to reduce data overload and inaccuracies in information processing. Finally, a single board concentrates power in a minority to

create a basis for a majority of employees to be exposed to exploitation, social alienation, subservience, and dependency to inhibit self-esteem, self-expression, quality of life, and the incentive to be productive, creative, and entrepreneurial. This concern explains the emergence of network governance in highly dynamic, complex, innovative industries such as biotechnology.

3. Audits in the United States serve an economic purpose while audits in the United Kingdom play a governance role. In the United States, only the financial statements of a publicly traded company are audited. The purpose is to verify the economic status of a corporation for investors making economic decisions. In the United Kingdom, both the financial statements and the accounts are audited whether or not the corporation is publicly traded or whether its liabilities are limited by shares or by the guarantee of its members. This approach is to provide shareholders or members information for voting on the appointment and remuneration of directors and confirming that dividends are only paid from profits. UK auditors report only to members/shareholders but not to the directors as they do in the United States. UK auditors must be approved by the members or shareholders while U.S. auditors are appointed without any reference to shareholders.

   In both the United States and the United Kingdom, the auditor judges the financial statements of the directors. In addition, the directors nominate, engage, and remunerate the auditor, which creates a conflict of interest for both parties. Because the directors are paying those who judge their financial statements, this could be interpreted as bribery in a court with the judge/auditor being a paid agent of those being judged. This statement is true whether or not directors of an audit committee are classified as independent. Audit committees cannot be a best practice because they establish closer relationships between directors and the auditor to diminish the ability of an auditor to possess an independence of mind from the directors who engage and remunerate them for their services.

4. The following are difficulties associated with boards appointing directors who are classified as independent.

   A basic problem is that there are many ways to classify independence. The classification scheme adopted may not be relevant to removing, preventing, or mitigating perceived conflicts of interest, wrongdoing, and noncompliance with laws, regulations, stock exchange listing requirements, and codes. For this reason, the Delaware Court concerns itself with *disinterested* directors relevant to action being litigated rather than to the classification of being *independent* (Clarke 2007).

   Directors classified as independent because they have not been associated with the business or industry may lack the knowledge and authority to carry out the core duty of a director to direct and monitor the business and its management. Empirical evidence supports the view that independent directors do not enhance performance (Bhagat and Black 2002).

   Directors represent the company as principals, not just as agents of the company, and cannot be fully independent of the company. Classifying some directors as independent, disinterested, nonmanagement, or nonexecutive does not remove their accountability to shareholders through the audited accounts and financial statements that they present to them.

Classifying directors as independent can provide false comfort when the position on the board of each director is at the grace and favor of dominant investors, as most commonly occurs around the world. Independent, noninterested, nonmanagement, and nonexecutive directors may comply with the desires of dominant investors to overlook unfair transactions with the company; to allow management control of the auditor; to provide excessive remuneration of executives; to permit the nomination of noncompliant or inappropriate directors; and to fail to protect minority shareholders and other stakeholders.

5. Network governance can reduce business risks by preventing directors from possessing absolute power and so power to corrupt themselves and the business; introducing checks and balances on decisions and judgments in managing the business; and reducing errors in communication, control, and decision making through cross checking.

   Network governance can provide competitive advantages in the following ways:
   - Improving decision making by introducing distributed intelligence to also reduce information overload, allowing ordinary people to manage extraordinary complexity.
   - Improving identification and control of suboptimal performance through multiple cross-checking communication and control channels.
   - Integrating strategic stakeholders into the governance architecture of the enterprise to provide a basis for improving operations such as just-in-time delivery of supplies, total quality control of goods and services, and product/service innovations.
   - Reducing exploitation, social alienation, subservience, and dependency that can inhibit self-esteem, self-expression, quality of life, incentive to be productive, creativity, and entrepreneurial flair.

6. Corporate law and regulators may be considered irresponsible for the following reasons:
   - Allowing corporations to become publicly traded with directors obtaining excessive and inappropriate powers to corrupt themselves and the business.
   - Allowing corporations to become too big or too complex to be reliably managed and controlled with a single board to creditably further and protect the interests of stakeholders.
   - Failing to recognize the impossibility of centrally controlled government regulators monitoring and/or controlling complex activities without establishing a requisite variety of co-regulators that large, complex corporations require internally to provide competitive advantages.
   - Failing to require corporations to share power with citizens whose governments establish regulators to protect so that citizens can participate in obtaining the information, knowledge, will, and capability to protect themselves.

Chapter 6 The Effect of Corporate Governance on Performance

1. At some level, almost all corporate finance variables, such as governance, capital structure, ownership structure, and performance, of interest to finance and corporate law students are interrelated. The system of equations that

characterizes these relationships can be large and unwieldy. In addition, identifying appropriate instrumental variables for estimating the simultaneous equations system is difficult.

2. Board-related corporate governance mechanisms, such as increasing the number of independent directors or requiring that all audit committee members be independent, are unlikely to lead to an increase in company performance. Ownership requirements by board members might have been more effective. Board members who own more stock in a company are likely to pay more attention to their tasks on that company's board.

3. The "comply or explain" approach assumes all companies have a similar optimal governance structure. The lists of best practices underlying a comply-or-explain regime are, in essence, governance indexes in which each item on the list is equivalent to one of the components in an equally weighted index. This is because the regulator expects firms to comply with all of the approved practices on its list, and full compliers are considered firms with the best governance (i.e., the import of requiring firms to explain a failure to comply). The presumption is that firms should comply. Otherwise, there would be no reason to require an explanation for nonconformance. Likewise, the constructor of an index considers as a desirable feature that all firms have all index components. Thus, the firm with the maximum sum (highest value of the index) is identified as the one with the highest quality governance.

   Because noncompliers in a comply-or-explain regime have the burden of explaining away their decisions, noncompliance can have a chilling effect, dissuading management from adopting governance mechanisms that would otherwise be beneficial (i.e., the requirement of an explanation for noncompliance could be taken to imply that something is awry).

4. Greater shareholder participation in firm governance could lead to strengthening of corporate democracy. It may also lead to greater transparency in management compensation because shareholders would have to vote on these proposals. However, greater shareholder participation in firm governance is not an unmitigated blessing. It is costly for shareholders to understand what policies are consistent with firm value maximization. There are examples when shareholders have voted against their best interests. For instance, most antitakeover charter provisions decrease shareholder wealth—yet most such proposals are approved by shareholders. Instead of focusing on management compensation packages, focusing on stock ownership of board members might be more effective.

Chapter 7 International Corporate Governance Research

1. The interactions of economic growth with other systems suggest that where growth is observed, despite weak legal and financial systems, attention should focus on political or cultural factors. Consistent with this, Allen, Qian, and Qian (2005) find that China's state-owned and publicly traded firms have not exhibited strong economic growth. This is consistent with the more typically observed negative relation between economic growth and the strength of legal and financial systems. Instead, they find that China's growth has been driven

by private firms, who raise funds through alternative networks of financial intermediaries based on the principles of social and family order and trust that are associated with the teachings of Confucius.

2. The ability of financial capital to move across national borders opens up several additional ways in which an individual firm can become subject to the laws of a stronger investor protection country. For example, the individual firm can list its shares on the stock exchange of the stronger country, thereby becoming subject to the laws of that country. Alternatively, institutional investors who purchase stakes in firms in weaker protection countries often push for governance reforms in that country. Finally, target firms in cross-border acquisitions typically adopt the governance standards of the acquiring firm. Thus, being acquired by a firm from a stronger protection country generally results in an improvement in governance standards.
3. A shareholder who holds an influential stake in a firm receives both the shared benefits of ownership and the private benefits of control. An improvement in governance quality increases access to and lowers the cost of raising external finance. If the firm has profitable investment opportunities, the funds raised will lead to an increase in the value of the firm and therefore the value of the shareholders' ownership stake. However, more stringent governance mechanisms are likely to reduce large shareholders' private benefits of control by creating greater difficulty for them to transfer assets from the firm to themselves.
4. Many possible examples could be presented. The U.S. government has taken ownership stakes in a number of large corporations such as General Motors (GM). Other GM shareholders have invested their own or their client's money in order to earn an appropriate financial return, but the government has invested taxpayer dollars and has multiple objectives. If a particular dealership is no longer expected to provide an appropriate return to GM, the nongovernment shareholder would prefer to see that dealership closed, thereby increasing the value of GM. The government may pressure GM to keep the dealership open if it is owned by constituents of an influential government official.

   A second example is U.S. government proposals to further limit the amount and/or form of compensation that firms can pay to their top executives. Executive compensation is an important governance mechanism. By reducing firms' ability to design appropriate compensation packages, the government limits firms' ability to hire good managers and their ability to compensate them in ways that optimally align their incentives with those of the shareholders.

Chapter 8 Agency Theory: Incomplete Contracting and Ownership Structure

1. Agency costs under diffuse ownership can be summarized into three distinct groups: monitoring costs, bonding costs, and residual loss. Monitoring costs are actions taken by shareholders to observe the actions of management. As a result of moral hazard, shareholders need to establish systems that can report on managerial actions. These include a wide range of systems such as audits, compensation contracts, and the costs of hiring and firing management. As a result of agents ultimately bearing the cost of monitoring, managers will create

structures such as increased information disclosure that allow them to be seen as working in the interests of shareholders. The costs of such structures are called bonding costs. Residual loss occurs because the goals of managers and shareholders are never perfectly aligned. Therefore, such losses are likely to occur as a result of agency conflicts.

2. Type II agency problems occur between controlling and noncontrolling shareholders rather than between managers and shareholders. In this situation, the agency costs occur as controlling shareholders expropriate wealth from noncontrolling shareholders. This can manifest itself in several ways. The most common form of expropriation is through related-party transactions and transfer pricing. This situation occurs when managers sell the assets of the firm or issue equity to another firm that they control at below market value. Another issue that may occur is excessive risk aversion. In many family firms, a considerable portion of family wealth can be tied to the firm and so the managers of the firm may not undertake optimal investments. A possible outcome is to have a suboptimal capital structure because the family wants to keep the risk of the firm low. Thus, the family fails to adopt an optimal capital structure and loses the potential benefit of a debt interest tax shield. Alternatively, the family may undertake unrelated diversification to lower the risk of the firm's cash flows. This is unlikely to benefit other investors as they may already have diversified portfolios.
3. Type I agency costs may not be as prevalent as Type II agency costs in family firms because such firms often do not hold diversified portfolios and so their wealth depends on the firm's success. Family owners have an incentive to closely scrutinize the actions of managers. This is not the case where an atomistic shareholder base exists. If all small shareholders are assumed to hold diversified portfolios, the cost of monitoring management will exceed the benefits accrued as a result of their small holdings. Family firms also have long-term investment horizons and so they are less likely to undertake short-term investments that may generate a short-term gain at the expense of longer term success.
4. Family firms are likely to have different investment goals from other shareholders, such as intergenerational ownership transfers. Thus, family firms may make suboptimal investment decisions as a result of excessive risk aversion in order to ensure succession. Family succession may also reduce value because keeping the firm within family management limits the pool of available labor. Evidence shows that succession is costly and reduces firm value (Pérez-González 2006; Villalonga and Amit 2006).

Chapter 9 Theories and Models of Corporate Governance

1. Many classes of claimants can make deserving claims on the corporation. *Ownership* is sometimes justified by exchange (usually payment), but this is difficult to distinguish from *contract*. Moreover, if someone justifies ownership of property on the ground that she paid for it, that simply begs the question of what justifies the person's ownership of the resources she used to pay for it. That is, using the notion of *property* to justify corporate governance begs the even deeper theoretical question of why property is legitimate in the first place.

The point is that ownership and contract claims reflect moral assumptions about who deserves the greater part of the corporate surplus. These are typically based on arguments about the parties' relative contributions to production. First, this inquiry makes the unexamined assumption that direct economic contribution to production defines claimant status. Second, the arguments about contributions tend to be theoretical rather than empirical. For example, some argue that shareholders take more risk than bondholders or workers, but this requires empirical proof. Furthermore, the contractarian and fiduciary models ignore noncontractual contributors to production, such as communities that absorb pollution and noise or provide tax breaks and subsidies, which suggests further normative assumptions about what constitutes a compensable contribution. Even though corporate governance, particularly director power, is defined in broad relational terms, contracts with communities and workers have been defined narrowly in order to justify denying claims that would seem to resonate in relational contract analysis.

2. As with the previous question, the point is to identify normative assumptions people take for granted. While the previous question focuses on assumptions about claims on the corporation, this question also implicates assumptions about the relative roles of the state, shareholders, society, and management.

   As for the role of models in answering the question, this raises the argument at the end of the chapter that models can help identify normative commitments. Here readers may ask whether they agree that models should be limited to this task or whether essentialism provides insight into the descriptive reality of the corporation, and whether such descriptive insight yields determinate normative prescriptions.

3. *Corporate democracy* turns on the formal similarities between political democracy and shareholder participation in corporate governance, particularly shareholder voting for directors and proposals. The corporate democracy model exerts a powerful legitimating force in corporate law. The model assumes that democracy is a positive political value and appeals to that notion without questioning it. As discussed in the chapter, shareholder power is extremely limited in practice. This is hardly a secret, but the model survives. Why might this be? Note that American political democracy retains its basic legitimacy despite similar skepticism about voter power. One explanation is simply that there is a categorical commitment to the ideal of democracy despite its failings, but this begs the question about the origin of such categorical commitments.

4. The agnostic nature of doctrine allows flexibility but also can be seen as opportunistic. That is, the law's expressed commitment to a model may be limiting but may have practical value in that it places some restraint on the kinds of rules state actors (judges, legislatures, and regulatory agencies) can make. Too much flexibility can lead to arbitrary results. This is undesirable as a matter of democratic principle and as a practical matter of stability and predictability.

   Dewey (1926), however, argued that models are normatively indeterminate such that commitment to a model would have no disciplining effect on law in any case. Yet Horwitz (1992) has responded that, in a given historical context, a model has determinate normative meaning.

Chapter 10 Unfettered Agents? The Role of Ethics in Corporate Governance

1. In several cases mentioned at the beginning of the chapter, shareholders lost their entire investments, but they were not the only victims. Unchecked, management can use the company's resources as though they were their own. This is the problem that Berle and Means (1932/1991) saw as inherent in the "modern corporation." Management could do so by conducting business with other companies, which the managers themselves controlled, or simply by paying themselves larger salaries and bonuses. Managers are often paid more compensation because they manage larger companies. This fact may well have spurred some to undertake acquisitions that contribute little to profitability of the company but enhance the status and income of the chief executive officer.

   Much of the corporate governance literature that centers on agency theory seeks to identify mechanisms through which management's incentives will be kept in line with those of shareholders. For example, Robert Maxwell used corporate funds to fuel his ambition to become a great publisher, raiding the pension funds of employees to keep the company afloat. WorldCom and Enron used the same auditing firm, Arthur Andersen, some of whose employees and partners seemed, in hindsight, to have been aware of the growing problems. With its reputation for careful and honest accounting ruined, Andersen imploded. WorldCom's failure was the proximate cause of the Sarbanes-Oxley legislation in the United States, which led to substantial compliance costs for major companies around the world and for the global accountancy industry.

2. The role of the board of directors is often described as having two main elements: (1) monitoring and controlling the executives who run the business, and (2) providing guidance, wisdom, contacts, and ideas to help shape the company's strategy. These elements are analogous to applying the brakes and stepping on the gas. An automotive journalist once remarked that the purpose of the brakes is to make the car go faster—to make sure someone can get around corners efficiently without hitting anything along the way. But stepping on the brakes all the time prohibits the car from going anywhere.

   The solutions offered in agency theory include ones aimed at keeping management motivated to keep the company moving forward in a way that contributes to shareholder value. Stock options, for example, came into prominent use as a way to let executives benefit from rising stock prices, much as shareholders would. But stock options have proved to be easy to manipulate. For example, executives can massage financial statements to look good when they are about to exercise their options and bad when they are about to receive grants of new options. Alternatives have been tried such as long-term incentives, profit-sharing, and restricted stock, but each presents problems. With each new problem case, the calls grow louder for changes in the way boards go about their business: a greater role for independent directors; stronger audit, compensation and nominations committees; more rights for shareholders to have a say on corporate policy. Reducing the discretion afforded to managers and to the boards that oversee their work can make the job less interesting.

Moreover, much of recent thinking on strategy has emphasized what is often called the resource-based view of the firm. If companies achieve competitive advantage by having superior access to resources including relationships with customers, regulators, suppliers, and strategic partners, and if boards can facilitate access to scarce and valuable resources, then the board's role in strategy may be larger than often thought. Tying down the board as well as management may take attention away from development of key resources.

3. Every decision of the board, however trivial, may be considered an ethical issue if the board is spending somebody else's money. In traditional shareholder value–based notions of corporate governance, any value in the company belongs to shareholders, not to the agents they hire to look after it. Knowing that they cannot each afford to monitor the expenses, shareholders may have to accept that management will inflate some expenses. Transaction cost economics points to thresholds where the cost of monitoring is just too great to be worth the bother. The difference between a $20 bottle of wine and a $200 bottle is just too small for the economist to worry about. But if it signifies a broader attitude toward the business that percolates from the board to senior and middle management, those costs can add up. The $200 bottle of wine may, therefore, be emblematic of the agent's ethical egoism, which needs to be redirected towards a utilitarian view of shareholder value. But it could as well be deontological: Stealing money (in effect) is just plain wrong.

   Some economists regard ethics as an anachronism in the history of intellectual thought. They see *homo economicus* as a bundle of preferences looking for efficient delivery of the sources of utility preferred. The role of business is to organize production to deliver that utility in an efficient way. In many ways, this line of thinking has its roots in ethics, though the words used by Jeremy Bentham, and indeed by the Greek philosophers, may have been different. What is *good* is measured by its consequences. What is *preferred* is assessed by the pleasure or happiness it brings.

4. Many writers on corporate governance speak about the need for a balance in the board's activities. Independent directors have to be watchful as well as contributing and supportive. They need to challenge senior executives but in a collegial way. Many executives and nonexecutive directors view the attention given to increasingly defining the role of the board, especially after the Enron and WorldCom cases in the United States, as having tipped the balance away from value creation towards monitoring and control. Codes of corporate governance, often voluntary in nature and based on the principle of "comply or explain," have proliferated around the world. Audit committees have become independent of the full board in some ways and risk containment has followed. The extent to which companies have suffered or benefited from all this attention is unclear. The crisis in global financial institutions that started in 2007 and came to a head a year later seemed to show that the agents in charge of day-to-day operations of many banks and insurance companies had not been fettered at all, despite decades of talk about corporate governance and monitoring and control.

   Some observers, among them activist shareholders, have begun to question the purpose of the board of directors, especially if it cannot control the executives and cannot contribute much to strategy formation and value creation.

The alternative sometime voiced, which is even stricter disclosure regulations combined with more careful monitoring by institutional investors, is equally fraught. Much investment now is run through index-tracking funds, designed to keep costs of portfolio management low and based on the evidence that attempts to outperform the indexes are futile. But if low cost is the selling point, what incentive does any fund—even a large one—have to engage in monitoring?

One solution would seem to lie in growing a new generation of ethical managers. But what ethical basis should be used? Another is to avoid mechanisms intended to induce behavior considered ethical that then seem to reward the practice of manipulating the rules of the game.

Chapter 11 Board Composition and Organization Issues

1. In the past decade, U.S. public companies have responded to pressures from regulators and shareholders by strengthening the independence and expanding the expertise of their boards of directors. In particular, the Sarbanes-Oxley Act of 2002, subsequent rules by the Securities and Exchange Commission, and securities exchange listing provisions have brought changes in corporate board composition and imposed new standards of integrity for the performance of its functions. Some organized investors, including large public and private pension funds as well as activist hedge funds, have been taking unprecedented steps to monitor the governance structure of their portfolio companies. Today, they urge boards to repeal bylaws on classification and depart from the default rule of plurality voting in directors' elections.
2. In the post-Enron business environment, a growing number of companies have found attracting and retaining qualified directors increasingly more difficult. This is partially due to strict director independence rules and the requirement that companies appoint a financial expert to their audit committee. Qualified directors may also be more reluctant to join new boards because of increased scrutiny by enforcement agencies and institutional investors. Other factors include a potential for greater liability and the time commitment that is now required by the job. Studies show a decreased propensity of active CEOs to join the boards of other companies. However, the prestige of the position, as well as the opportunity to gain knowledge, add value, and network, will continue to serve as important motivators for attracting new talent to the boardroom. As a practical matter, companies continue to successfully nominate individuals from the ranks of retired CEOs, CFOs, heads of large corporate operating divisions, academics, and leaders of prominent scientific, nonprofit, or governmental organizations.
3. In considering director independence, the company should focus not only on the formal review of the nominee's background, current professional activities, and economic and family relationships, but also on whether the prospective director can, in fact, perform her duties without being subject to the influence of management. As some of the recent corporate scandals suggest, even boards meeting formal qualification criteria may not act as a strong independent check on management. Qualitative aspects of director independence should comprise the will to interact with senior executives as well as the confidence and expertise

to ask the hard questions required to provide effective oversight. The chapter discusses both a formal independence assessment dictated by national securities exchange standards and a contextual evaluation, as prescribed under Delaware corporate law.

4. Traditionally, in U.S. public companies, the CEO heads the management team that the board oversees with the CEO also serving as a member of the board. Those who support the preservation of this traditional structure of duality argue that single leadership fosters greater operational efficiency, facilitates internal communication from and to the board, and ultimately enables better business performance. Conversely, detractors of this practice observe that separating the roles gives boards an organizational basis for acting independently of management and avoiding dangerous instances of CEO imperialism. Because companies decide upon this structural issue, today's boards are unquestionably expected to establish procedural safeguards necessary to avoid conflicts of interest and to ensure appropriate balances of power.
5. To encourage participation, companies tend to adopt formal meeting attendance policies for board members. The majority of public corporations surveyed by The Conference Board pay directors a fee for each of the board or committee meetings they attend, whereas only a small group of respondents report that they penalize low attendance (for example, by means of a policy requiring directors to forfeit a portion of their compensation if they miss more than a certain number of meetings). The inability to attend more than 75 percent of the board meetings is required to be publicly disclosed in the company's proxy statements.

Chapter 12 Board Diversity

1. The benefits of board diversity include improved decision making due to different perspectives coming from directors with different backgrounds. Board diversity also fosters creativity and helps to gain access to different resources including social and political connections. Board diversity helps to promote the career of minority top executives through signaling and monitoring and to improve public and investor relations. Finally, board diversity can help a firm acquire legitimacy in the view of the public, the media, and the government.

   The costs of board diversity include intensifying conflicts among board members, which can lead to a lack of cooperation and communication, and communication breakdowns between outside directors and executives. Other costs include selecting less experienced or busy directors and the possibility that director heterogeneity may create incentives for directors to pursue their personal agendas at the expense of the company.
2. The following are the major findings from the board diversity literature.
   - Director heterogeneity affects corporate policies and performance, but these effects differ according to firm and director characteristics.
   - Firms appear to choose directors for their characteristics; different types of firms choose different levels of director heterogeneity.
   - Firms choose directors as a means to deal with the external environment.

- CEOs and top executives appear to prefer directors who are similar to themselves.
- Social networks and commonality of backgrounds appear to affect director appointments and the dynamics of the board.
- Directors from minority groups perceive their minority status as a hindrance to their work as a director.
- Minority directors may serve interests other than those of shareholders.

3. Some industries have more diverse workforces. Boards naturally reflect the composition of an industry's workforce, both because industry experience is valuable in the boardroom and because board composition signals career opportunities for managers in the industry.

   Evidence suggests that female directors are more prevalent in consumer goods industries, which may be related to the composition of customers in such industries. Having a woman's perspective may be particularly valuable in such industries. Understanding customers' preferences is an important skill that could be useful to firms.

   Finally, social connections appear to be an important determinant of the composition of boards. Thus, some director characteristics naturally cluster by industries.

4. A few studies report statistical correlations between firm performance and board gender diversity. The sign of these correlations varies across studies, with some reporting positive while others show negative associations between board diversity and firm performance. These results could be explained by (1) board diversity affecting profitability, (2) profitability affecting the decision to select different directors, or (3) the existence of some unobserved factor that is correlated with both profits and board diversity.

   Determining the exact cause of such correlations is a difficult task. The issue is complicated further because the effects of board diversity on firm policies and outcomes are likely to be heterogeneous, as shown in some existing research. A few firms may benefit from the additional increase in monitoring intensity associated with more gender diversity in the boardroom, but excessive monitoring may become counterproductive in firms that are already well governed.

Chapter 13 Board Subcommittees for Corporate Governance

1. The three mandatory subcommittees that listed companies are obliged to form are audit, compensation, and nominating/governance. The audit committee is responsible for protecting investors by overseeing internal controls, financial statements risk assessment, and external and internal auditor's activities as well as ensuring that these described procedures and processes comply with existing laws and regulations. The compensation committee has the responsibility of evaluating executive and director performance and establishing top-management compensation and benefit programs. The nominating/governance committee is usually responsible for identifying, evaluating, and nominating new directors for the board, renominating existing directors, and facilitating the election of new directors by shareholders.

2. Traditionally, an audit committee acted like a middleman between management and external auditors, but several pre-SOX review committees (Treadway Commission 1987; Blue Ribbon Committee 1999; Public Oversight Board Panel on Audit Effectiveness 2000) broadened the role of the audit committee in the corporate governance process. However, the reports from these varied groups were introduced in more of a best practices form rather than mandatory rules. Section 363.5 of the FDIC Improvement Act 1991 was the first to require large financial institutions to establish audit committees consisting of outside nonexecutive board members. The passage of SOX in July 2002 set new requirements for public-company audit committees to oversee financial reports. SEC rules and stock exchange listing standards also provide guidance for the formation, structure, and responsibilities of audit committees. For example, these standards suggest that audit committees meet at least three times per year (SOX 2002). The national stock exchanges established their own requirements for the composition and standards of the audit committees, which became effective in 2003. The SEC also established several rules regarding audit committees.
3. Independent members of the compensation committee can potentially provide unbiased opinions concerning the amount the company executives are receiving in the form of compensation and facilitate pay-for-performance schemes rather than random compensation schemes. Thus, the compensation committee can improve the transparency of financial statement reporting and can reduce administrative expenses.
4. Structure encompasses the committee's size and composition, independence, qualifications, attributes, and resources. For example, corporate governance reforms require that an audit committee consists of at least three independent directors, while the average size of the committee ranges from three to five in practice. The major requirement for the audit committee is that its members should be independent. *Independence* means that committee members are not employed by the company; are not receiving any income from the company other than their board pay; are not employed as consultants to the company; and have not been a member of the immediate family of the company executives or its affiliates within the past five years. Laws and regulations require that at least one audit committee member be qualified as a financial expert and that the other members should be financially literate. Audit committees should meet at least four times a year to review quarterly financial and internal control reports.
5. Based on the survey findings (Spencer Stuart Board Index 2008), the audit committee members are compensated now more with the retainer compensation rather than with meeting fees. Stock grants are a popular means of compensation and have become much more common than options. For example, the average retainer amount paid to audit committee members by S&P 500 companies was $74,872 in 2007.
6. Special board committees are usually formed to help management deal with unusual matters and issues. The most common special committees are governance/strategic, litigation, executive committee, and special investigation committees comprising solely independent directors. For example, a governance/strategic committee typically establishes the agenda for the company's board of directors to determine what issues the board should discuss with management and

to what extent. The executive committee typically reviews managerial decisions and plans. Thus, an executive committee consisting of available independent directors can make decisions on behalf of the company's entire board of directors.

Chapter 14 Executive Compensation: Incentives and Externalities

1. The efficient market mechanism of pay is effective if it stimulates rational managerial decision making focused on creating shareholder value and is simultaneously preventing excessive rent extraction by executives.
2. The adoption of stock option programs for executives stimulates these executives to focus on long-term value creation and leads to increased risk taking. The use of the Black-Scholes formula in the context of management options has several limitations: (1) It overstates the value of the option, as it assumes that the option can only be exercised at the expiration date; (2) the formula may be, at best, a measure of the firm's cost of granting an option (Hall and Murphy 2000); (3) the formula assumes that there are no restrictions on short-selling, while executives are not allowed to trade or sell their options; (4) options are forfeited when executives leave the firm, which again reduces the cost associated with granting the option and overstates the Black-Scholes option value; and (5) the formula is developed for European options, whereas the executive options are American but are only exercisable after the vesting date. As a result, executive stock options are worth less than the Black-Scholes price. Moreover, risk-averse executives demand a premium for accepting risky options, rather than safe base pay (Murphy 1999).
3. There are several alternatives to option repricing. First, firms can cancel existing options and issue new options with an exercise price equal to the current market price. Second, firms may extend the maturity of the existing options. Lastly, options can be indexed—that is, linked to a relative performance measure.
4. Skimming, as introduced by Bertrand and Mullainathan (1999), describes the situation in which an entrenched CEO and executive directors are able to dominate the board and determine their own pay. Thus, profits, which should accrue to the shareholders, are now captured (skimmed) by the CEO and the executive directors.
5. Pay-for-performance (PPS) refers to performance-dependent compensation. The essential idea behind PPS is to reduce agency cost by aligning the interests of managers and shareholders. The compensation contracts of management should be related to performance improvement, measured by the share price returns (and maybe also accounting returns). However, management can manipulate accounting returns. Placing too narrow a focus on short-term share price increases could have unintended and negative consequences. Therefore, a relationship between compensation and long-term share price evolution is most appropriate. Firms can achieve this relation by using long-term options with a vesting period or with long-term incentive plans (LTIPS), which are based on (peer-related) performance benchmarks.

Chapter 15 Compensation Consultants and Executive Pay

1. Firms use pay consultants because consultants supply data, information, expertise, and analysis. They are experts in their field and provide a low-cost way for the firm to design compensation packages. Firms can also use compensation consultants to legitimize pay. If pay is high, the board can justify this by reference to expert consultants. Finally, self-serving chief executive officers (CEOs) might use pay to get excess rents.
2. The market contains six main consulting firms. The U.S. "big six" consulting firms are Towers Perrin, Mercer Human Resource Consulting, Frederick W. Cook & Co., Hewitt Associates, Watson Wyatt Worldwide, and Pearl Meyer and Partners. There are many boutique consultants, but the big six claim the largest number of client firms. In 2010 Towers Watson was created from a merger between Towers Perrin and Watson Wyatt.
3. The main consulting firms also supply noncompensation services to client firms, including actuarial and other benefit services. To the extent that the fees from these other services are substantial, consultants might not be sufficiently independent.
4. The available empirical evidence suggests that CEO pay is positively correlated with the presence of a consultant. However, there is mixed evidence on the relation between CEO pay and conflicted consultants. Conflicted consultants are consultants who supply other business services to the client firm. Moreover, some studies show that CEO pay is higher in firms using consultants but so, too, are CEO incentives. This finding suggests that consultants also align the interests of managers with owners. When interpreting the current empirical evidence, the analyst should consider the methods used to establish the results. More sophisticated statistical techniques may lead to a different pattern of results.
5. If CEO pay is higher when firms use consultants, controlling for other factors, then a temptation exists to be concerned about the role of consultants. Policy makers may want to change disclosure rules or to provide advice on the relation between consultants and compensation committees. One proposal is for consultants to be fully independent of management. Compensation committees could be made responsible for hiring consultants and setting their terms of reference. The United States, the United Kingdom, and Canada currently lead the way on disclosure. In making changes, policy makers should consider both the potential costs and benefits associated with more disclosure.

Chapter 16 Corporate Governance and Ownership Structure

1. The idea that who owns the shares can influence corporate value and performance has its origins in Berle and Means (1932), who contend that, in the modern large open or publicly traded corporation, ownership and control of the firm are separated. In this situation, they propose that those who control the firm have little incentive to direct the firm to use its resources efficiently. Thus, because management has little share in corporate profits, therefore, they lack the incentive to use the firm's resources most efficiently. Berle and Means view this as a potential deficiency of the large, open corporation.

2. Morck, Shleifer, and Vishny (1988) as well as McConnell and Servaes (1990) conduct cross-sectional regressions in which the dependent variable is a proxy for Tobin's q. The proxy is essentially the market value of the firm divided by the replacement value of assets. Morck et al. use 371 of the Fortune 500 companies from 1980 to conduct their analysis. McConnell and Servaes use approximately 1,000 NYSE and AMEX firms from 1976 and 1986 to conduct their analysis. Their key independent variable is the percentage of share owned by insiders (i.e., top executives and members of the board of directors). Both studies find a nonlinear relation between corporate value and performance, with value first increasing as managerial ownership increases and then declining above a certain level of inside share ownership. Both sets of authors cautiously interpret their results to lend support to the conjecture that who owns the shares of the firms influences their value and performance. They also discuss a stronger interpretation of the results. According to the stronger interpretation, there are two opposing forces at work with regard to managerial ownership of shares: an alignment-of-interests effect and an entrenchment effect. At low levels of managerial ownership, as managerial ownership increases, the alignment-of-interests effect dominates such that corporate value and performance increase as managerial ownership of shares increases. At higher levels of managerial share ownership, the entrenchment effect dominates such that corporate value actually declines as managerial ownership of shares increases.
3. Demsetz (1983) argues that the ownership structures that are observed across firms will be the endogenous outcome of a maximizing process among managers and firm owners. If so, the ownership structures that are observed will be the optimal structure for each firm. That is, Demsetz argues that the concerns raised by Berle and Means (1932) are moot. If large firms with ownership of shares dispersed across a broad set of largely uninvolved shareholders are observed, this is because such an ownership structure for that firm is optimal. By extension, all firms operate at or near their optimal ownership structures all the time. The empirical results of Morck, Shleifer, and Vishny (1988) and McConnell and Servaes (1990) imply that some firms are not operating at their optimal ownership structures, and for these firms, an adjustment to either more or less share ownership by management can increase value. The argument made by Demsetz implies that the cross-sectional relation indentified by Morck et al. and McConnell and Servaes is the accidental result of a misspecified regression analysis.
4. Aggrawal and Knoeber (1996) and Demsetz and Villalonga (2001) both use a simultaneous equations approach to deal with potential endogeneity between insider ownership and corporate value. Aggrawal and Knoeber estimate the impact of ownership structure jointly with several other governance mechanisms and find that the significant relationship between insider ownership and Tobin's q disappears in the simultaneous equations framework. Demsetz and Villalonga restudy a random sample of the firms analyzed in Demsetz and Lehn (1985), paying special attention to the measurement of ownership structure and q. Similar to Aggrawal and Knoeber, they find no significant relationship between ownership structure and value when estimated using a two stage least squares simultaneous equations methodology.

Himmelberg, Hubbard, and Palia (1999) use a firm fixed effects model to control for firm heterogeneity and suggest that unobservable firm characteristics explain a considerable amount of variation in managerial ownership. They find that variables which proxy for asymmetric information are positively and significantly related to the level of inside ownership, consistent with the notion that each firm optimizes its structure given its particular contracting environment.

Chapter 17 The Effects of Management Turnover on Firm Performance

1. The scapegoat theory suggests that managers are replaced even when boards know that the replacement will not be of higher quality. The termination of the outgoing CEO is required to provide appropriate incentives to provide effort. Under the scapegoat theory, termination solves a moral hazard problem (the supply of effort when actions are not perfectly observable). Terminations resulting from scapegoating will be followed by improvements in measured performance as scapegoats are removed following negative performance shocks. Because the shocks are transient, changes in performance are positive as performance reverts to its mean. The possibility of scapegoating behavior makes controlling for mean reversion an essential component of any analysis of the effects of management turnover on firm performance.
2. Event studies of turnover announcements suffer from the *mixed-signal* problem. A turnover announcement includes both information about expected performance changes and information about the quality of the incumbent. Any new information about the inferiority of the incumbent manager offsets positive effects of the expected performance changes associated with the successor.

   The mixed-signal problem does not make the results of event studies useless. Bonnier and Bruner (1989) carefully design their study so as to minimize the amount of information about the incumbent's quality revealed by the announcement. In their sample of turnovers at poorly performing firms they find evidence of positive and significant abnormal announcement returns. In addition, Bonnier and Bruner and Borokovich, Parrino, and Trapani (1996) examine cases involving the appointment of outsiders. Outside appointments are expected to be associated with greater improvements in CEO quality, which increases the likelihood that the real effects of better future management dominate the effect of information about the incumbent. Both papers report positive and significant stock price reactions to the appointment of outsiders. Finally, Huson, Malatesta, and Parrino (2004) present evidence that part of the announcement return reflects changes in future operating performance.
3. Hiring an outsider will result in higher disruption costs. Additionally, hiring an external candidate weakens the incentives provided to internal candidates. External hires are more likely to be observed following forced turnovers. Huson, Parrino, and Starks (2001) provide evidence that this is the case. The reasons for this include the following. First, managers who leave voluntarily are not likely to be of low quality. One of the projects in which they should have been engaged is the selection of their replacement. Baton passing usually involves an internal candidate. Another consequence of having a high-quality incumbent is that few

of this manager's policies will require substantial overhaul. There is less need for introducing a change agent when the existing policies are adequate or better. Alternatively, the policies of fired CEOs are likely to require substantial overhaul. In these cases, a change agent who is not invested in the failed strategies will be beneficial. The marginal costs associated with hiring an outsider are also lower in the case of forced turnover. Wholesale strategy changes will engender major business disruption. The board can also be less concerned about the incentives provided to junior managers associated with the failed strategies of the exiting CEO.

4. There are three pieces of evidence suggesting successor choice is an important determinant of CEO turnover. First, there is event study evidence. Bonnier and Bruner (1989) report that the stock price reaction to the appointment of an outsider to the position of chairman, CEO, or president is 1.99 percentage points higher than the reaction to appointment of an insider to one of those positions. Borokovich, Parrino, and Trapani (1996) report positive and significant average stock price reactions to the appointment of outsiders following forced CEO turnover (1.64 percent, p-value <0.01) and negative and significant average stock price reaction to the appointment of insiders following forced turnover (-0.85 percent, p-value < 0.01). Second, Huson, Malatesta, and Parrino (2004) show that changes in operating performance are higher when firms select outside replacements. Finally, Perez-Gonzalez (2006) finds evidence that the post-turnover performance of firms with family successions is worse than that of firms with nonfamily successions. Further, he presents evidence that post-turnover performance at firms with family successions is poorer when successors have weaker educational backgrounds. These results indicate that turnover-related performance improvements are not only predicated on the removal of poor performers but also require the board to identify and hire high-quality replacements.

Chapter 18 Corporate Monitoring by Blockholders

1. A shareholder who monitors management invests time and money in these activities. While he bears all the costs of monitoring, he will only benefit from potential performance improvements in direct proportion to his share stake. Thus, if a shareholder only holds 0.01 percent of the equity, he will only receive 0.01 percent of the potential gains (through capital gains or increased dividends) but will bear all the costs. All the other shareholders free-ride on his efforts. Therefore, only blockholders are expected to monitor whereas atomistic shareholders are unlikely to do so because coalitions are hard to form and maintain.

2. In the Anglophone countries, the ownership structure is rather dispersed; the largest share stake in the average U.S. firm is lower than 5 percent and the largest stake in the average UK listed firms is about 14 percent. In contrast, in Germany, the largest share stake in the average listed firm is more than 60 percent. Similar strong ownership concentration is found in other Continental European countries. Therefore, a takeover of a Continental European firm is impossible unless the largest blockholder who typically holds majority control wants to sell out.

3. In contrast to other outside shareholders, less corporate monitoring is expected from institutional investors. Institutions may be more passive shareholders because of the following reasons: (1) They lack the resources to be involved in the corporate strategies of all the companies in which they invest; (2) their share stakes in individual firms are frequently modest in size; and (3) due to insider trading regulations, they abstain from collecting private information to avoid immobilizing the liquidity of their portfolios.
4. Exhibit 18.1 shows how ownership pyramids are built. The reason for creating a pyramid is to *obtain power without money*, or to obtain strong control with a limited investment. The ultimate shareholder on top of the pyramid maintains majority control over all intermediate investment vehicles throughout the pyramid. Still, at every level, an investment from minority shareholders flows into the pyramid. Consequently, the ultimate shareholder has strong control rights but limited cash flow rights.

Chapter 19 The Governance of Family Firms

1. Ownership concentration is often a means to obtain sufficient control rights in corporations. Large ownership stakes may incentivize the family to monitor the firm's stakeholders, leading to a reduction in agency costs. Concentrated ownership positions also allow the family to influence firms' decisions according to their preferences. These benefits of control may be pecuniary or nonpecuniary. Nonpecuniary benefits include, for example, the social status of running a newspaper or the pride from having a relative manage the company that bears the family name.

   Ownership concentration, however, also introduces important costs. In terms of diversification, the family will be exposed to firm-specific risk. As a result, a firm's investment decisions may be distorted toward less risky and smaller-scale projects. Investments that are intensive in firm-specific risk put owners at a disadvantage relative to diversified shareholders. Similarly, larger investments increase risk exposure or threaten family control. Another cost resulting from ownership concentration is that the family may make decisions that favor the controlling group at the expense of other firm stakeholders. Examples include appointing relatives to positions of power even when they do not have the merits to be in such positions, and exploiting promising projects in a different firm in which the family holds a higher ownership stake.
2. Most family firms that sell securities to minority shareholders purposely design corporate governance institutions in a way that guarantees family control of decisions. Family control often translates into effective control of the board of directors and into the appointment of a member of the family as chief executive officer (CEO).

   The tight link of ownership and control that characterizes family firms suggests that small changes in corporate governance provisions are unlikely to translate into meaningful transfers of control from the family to minority shareholders. In practice, a board of directors tends to have difficulty disciplining a manager when the manager and her family control the firm. Similarly, disciplining a CEO via a takeover also may be difficult when the manager's family stake in the corporation is so large that it is critical for the success of the takeover. In widely held firms, in contrast, the only link between the CEO and the firm is often her labor contract. As a result, the board of directors, the market for corporate control, and other governance institutions may provide credible threats to CEO authority.

3. The arguments for the overlap of family and business structures often rely on market imperfections that make arm's-length contracts unattractive, or on private benefits that reduce family participation costs. One governance benefit unique to family firms is that family members have higher commitment to the firm. The reason underlying such higher commitment may be driven by the fact that they face higher separation costs than nonfamily workers because family members have both professional and personal relations at stake. Higher commitment leads to more effort provision, higher transmission of firm-specific knowledge across generations, and higher firm-specific investments. Another unique benefit is that family firms typically have long-term investment horizons. Family firms commonly have a preference for family succession in ownership and control positions. This long-term focus facilitates the development of strong reputations that lead to lower transaction costs in market interactions.

   Regarding costs, a common problem in family firms is using blood rather than merit considerations for both hiring and promoting decisions. Empirical evidence shows that the selection of the right CEO is crucial for firm performance. Also, this bias toward relatives has unintended consequences such as talented employees leaving the firm. Another problem with family firms is that family and business norms do not always coincide. Families tend to favor equality among members, while productive organizations base rewards on the value of marginal products of stakeholders.

4. Empirical corporate finance is plagued by endogeneity and omitted variable problems that create problems for a researcher to establish a causal connection between two variables of interest. Firms rarely make random decisions. Family firms, however, are an attractive laboratory for addressing research questions of general interest because variation in family firm decision making may result from family and not firm characteristics. Family traits can potentially be exogenous to a firm's prospects. Yet these family characteristics can affect governance and firm performance.

   As recent studies show, family characteristics can be used as plausible instrumental variables. Valid instrumental variables must be correlated with the key control variable of interest such as a governance characteristic, but they cannot be correlated with the error term in the outcome variable such as the performance equation. In other words, the instrumental variable should only affect performance through the effect of the key governance provision. In sum, family firms may be an attractive area of research because family traits can meet these two criteria.

Chapter 20 Institutional and Other Shareholders

1. In recent years, there has been substantial growth in institutional shareholder ownership in many countries. Given the large size of their shareholdings,

institutional investors have particular responsibilities as shareholders to act in the interest of their ultimate beneficiaries and to ensure that appropriate standards of corporate governance are developed or exist within their investee companies. Various corporate governance codes and guidelines emphasize the power and influence of institutional investors. For example, these include the Combined Code (2008) in the United Kingdom, the ISC Statement of Principles of the Responsibilities of Institutional Shareholders and Agents (2002, 2005, and 2007), the ISC (2009), and the ICGN Statement of Principles of Institutional Shareholders' Responsibilities (2007). These codes and guideline statements advocate that institutional investors have a responsibility to engage more with the companies in which they invest. Such engagement should help ensure that a sound system of corporate governance is in place, which should protect shareholder value.

The extent to which institutional investors can engage, or be activist, depends on a various factors including the economic cost. That is, do the costs of activism bring sufficient benefits? Studies including Becht, Franks, Mayer, and Rossi (2006) and Junkin and Toth (2009) indicate financial benefits associated with engagement.

2. Institutional investors have a responsibility to intervene under certain circumstances. For example, they should intervene if the company is underperforming in order to try and protect their investment. However, directors need to be able to undertake their role without too much interference, which might be detrimental and limit entrepreneurial flair. Many consider board succession and board remuneration as issues on which institutional shareholders should be involved. Board succession is an important but often overlooked area. The institutional investors should meet with the board and ensure that plans are in place for individuals to take over the roles of key directors both in a planned situation, such as retirement, but also under unforeseen circumstances such as an unexpected loss of life.

   Board remuneration is one of the hottest topics in corporate governance, and institutional investors should analyze companies' executive director remuneration packages in detail to assess whether pay is related to performance, whether the performance targets are appropriate, and whether the overall package is fair.

   Some contend that a firm's corporate social responsibility policies (CSR) are an area in which institutional investors should have less involvement. Others contend that issues involving CSR are increasingly mainstream to corporate governance and fall within the domain of institutional investors. CSR can encompass a wide range of areas including environmental issues, child labor, and the use of sweatshop factories. These are all areas that firms should consider, including the ethical and moral implications. For example, engaging in unfair practices may be detrimental to the reputation of the company and its long-term sustainability.

3. Tools of governance include constructive dialogue, voting, focus lists, and shareholder proposals (resolutions).
   - *Constructive dialogue.* This is a fundamental tool of governance. Institutional investors should engage in regular constructive dialogue with their investee companies. Meetings with the board of directors cover areas such as the

strategy of the company, succession planning, and executive remuneration packages. Many areas of potential conflict between institutional investors and boards can be resolved by dialogue. Although dialogue can be effective, it sometimes fails. For example, the directors may be unresponsive. In these instances, institutional investors may make use of one or more of the other tools of governance or possibly exit by selling their shares.

- *Voting.* Ordinary shares usually have one vote for each share. A generally accepted view is that institutional shareholders have rights and responsibilities including the responsibility to vote. Institutional shareholders should always vote in a considered fashion, not just box ticking. Thus, they should carefully consider individual resolutions and then cast their vote. Voting is an effective tool of governance and can result in directors not being elected (or reelected) or in remuneration packages not being approved (referred to as *say on pay*, although this is often advisory rather than mandatory). Voting may be ineffective as a tool of governance where there are barriers to voting, such as having to be physically present to vote (rather than proxy voting); where share blocking exists; where there is a lack of information on resolutions; where information on resolutions is provided in the foreign language of the home country and not translated into English; and where there is a short time between information being received and the deadline for votes to be cast.
- *Focus lists.* Focus lists highlight companies that are underperforming a benchmark index and that usually have not responded to institutional investors' requests to discuss and change their strategy or aspects of corporate governance. Therefore, focus lists target underperforming companies and put them under an unwelcome spotlight. CalPERS is one of the main proponents of focus lists, which seem to work well for CalPERS. The limitations are in terms of the resources needed to put companies on a focus list and then to carry through the engagement. Some institutional investors do not have the resources and they might want to avoid direct action against a company.
- *Shareholder proposals (resolutions).* Shareholder proposals are more widespread in the United States, where they are often put forward by church groups on CSR-related issues. In the United Kingdom, there are only a few shareholder proposals each year, which presently focus on executive compensation. This is because of the difficulty of meeting the criteria for putting forward a shareholder proposal in the United Kingdom, as the number of members necessary is either members having 5 percent of the voting power of the company, or 100 or more shareholders whose paid-up capital averages at least £100 each. The resolution may be circulated at the expense of the members making the request unless the company resolves otherwise. Shareholder proposals are an effective tool in the United States but are not much used in the United Kingdom for the reasons just given.

4. Sovereign funds and private equity funds have recently had a high profile as they involve powerful and influential types of investors. A *sovereign fund* is a fund owned by a government. These funds are often very large and influential. For example, Norway's sovereign fund has stakes in some 3,500 companies but is seen as being fairly transparent and relatively unthreatening. The sovereign funds of some Middle and Far Eastern countries, however, are seen as being

much more opaque. This can become a problem when these funds start to buy into strategic businesses and their motivation and long-term investment strategy is unknown.

A *private equity fund* is broadly defined as one in which investments in a company occur through a negotiated process. They typically involve a transformational, value-added, active management strategy and can be divided into the following categories: venture capital; buyout; acquisition of a large portion or a majority control in a more mature company; investment in a distressed company; or investment in a company where value can be unlocked as a result of a one-time opportunity such as changing industry trends and government regulations. Concerns exist about the lack of disclosure in relation to companies that private equity firms buy. So in the United Kingdom, for example, a review of the private equity sector, *Guidelines for Disclosure and Transparency in Private Equity*, chaired by Sir David Walker, the former Bank of England official, placed a much greater onus on private equity funds to provide more details of the financial performance of companies they acquire. The new rules required private equity companies to publish accounts for the larger companies they own no later than six months after financial year-ends.

Chapter 21 The Politics of Shareholder Activism

1. Shareholder stances can be classified as follows, using the framework suggested in this chapter:
   - The gadfly investors of the 1970s often had a *maintain* stance in the attitude dimension of the shareholder stance. They used their shareholdings at annual meetings to speak about company policy, which made them activists with typically a long-term horizon.
   - Index-tracking shareholders have an attitude of maintain for the shares in their portfolio, except when the index is reconstituted. Therefore, they operate universally on a long-term horizon. While many are docile in participation, some long-term holders such as CalPERS, Hermes, and the members of the Council of Institutional Investors take an activist approach because they believe they cannot otherwise improve the performance of their funds.
   - Traditional fund managers actively manage their portfolios by buying and selling shares in an attempt to outperform the market. Their attitude will be different with each stock they hold and it will change as they decide how to reshape the portfolios. They may be activist on the participation dimension but many are walkers, choosing to sell rather than incur the cost of engaging in a dialogue with companies about management's performance. Traditional fund managers often describe themselves as having a long-term horizon and do not see themselves as speculators. Interestingly, such managers in mutual funds, insurance funds, and even many pension funds have been taking a generally shorter-term orientation to their portfolios as they face growing pressure to meet ever more aggressive performance targets. Studies of U.S. actively managed funds suggest that the horizon of managers is growing shorter, with many trading so frequently that they turn over their entire portfolios within a year.

- Activist hedge funds are, by definition, activist along the participation dimension, seeking to agitate for change in corporate direction. They may quickly shift between accumulate and reduce as they assess the likelihood of success of their campaigns. The news media often describe hedge funds as short-term on horizon, but they have been known to maintain large stakes in a company for several years as they seek to influence policy. Their intention is to sell the position and realize a capital gain rather than to hold shares a long time. So short-term is perhaps still the best description of their orientation.
- Some index-tracking funds and other large investors can hold a *perverse* orientation as they lend stock to boost their fund's performance. By lending the shares, they receive a fee—that is, they benefit—from giving up claims of ownership of the company for a fixed period. As a result, they have a *maintain* stance on the attitude dimension. If that period falls over the point at which they are eligible to vote, their status as long-term investors and either docile, walker, or activist in participation turns perverse. These perverse investors stand to benefit over the longer term from good corporate performance, but they have signed away their rights to influence company policy.
- Normal short-sellers, often the counterparties of stock lending, are by definition perverse in that they hold the shares but stand to benefit from falling share prices. While often helpful in maintaining the liquidity of equity markets, short-selling can in extreme cases mean that value destruction is in the best interests of holders of a majority of a company's shares. Although short-sellers have an attitude that involves both accumulate and reduce, they will maintain their position for a short time. Their horizon is almost always short-term even though some may roll over their lending arrangements several times. Many are activist in participation. There are often reports that such perverse investors spread rumors of difficulties in the companies whose stock they hold. By contrast, naked short-sellers cannot participate as they do not hold shares at all. That does not prevent them from spreading false rumors in an effort to depress the share price.
- Individual retail investors may be inclined to buy, sell, or hold at any given time, but they tend to have a long-term horizon to their investments. Voting records suggests that many do not use their proxy statements and so can be considered docile in participation. As a result, some companies like to have a large number of retail investors on the share register even if they are expensive to maintain. Having many retail investors gives management and the board a freer hand to set policy without intervention from shareholders.

2. Most investors want to see a higher share price. Traditional fund managers can argue that their activism has, in effect, the tacit agreement of many docile investors even though those investors have never stated a preference. Indeed, some accuse docile investors as being *free-riders*, accepting the benefits that arise from the activism of others without having to contribute to its cost. Ironically, their docility often weighs against the cause of the activists when company managements and boards then claim that the activists control only a small proportion of the shares. Short-sellers will find support from would-be shareholders who do not yet own the stock but might like to accumulate at a lower price. These would-be shareholders may be those who believe the company has become

overvalued relative to its profit outlook but still represents a good investment over a longer time horizon.

3. The most obvious case is when one shareholder is inclined to reduce when another shareholder of similar orientation on participation and horizon is inclined to accumulate. These two shareholders' reasons for selling and buying are based on other factors such as one's need to book a capital gain for tax reasons. The private equity fund that brought a company to the stock market may be long-term in horizon, activist in participation, and required to maintain its investment for a period of time after the company floats shares on the stock exchange. But the private equity fund's interests rest in maximizing the value of the share price by the time it is free to sell its shares. The funds may thus advocate that management scale back research and development while concentrating efforts on sales. By contrast, an activist pension fund with long-term horizon that is inclined to maintain the position in the initial public offering (IPO) may want to build the business more gradually and build value through new product development. Some investors of identical orientation may prefer higher dividends while others seek capital gains. These differences often lie behind the practice of stock lending by allowing one fund to realize the dividends that another fund does not need.
4. The obvious way is to seek a vote of shareholders and go with the majority. In some countries, companies are required by law to seek shareholder approval for transactions that can transform the business: a merger, a major acquisition, and dissolution of the business. In many countries, shareholder votes bind the board; but in the United States, shareholder votes generally have only an advisory capacity and the board is free to ignore the vote.
5. Directors have long been wary of single-issue activist shareholders—those who buy the shares to agitate for specific changes in policy. Examples in the chapter include those who sought to use shareholdings to protest the Vietnam War or apartheid policies in South Africa. Following their advice might have been moral in some senses but equally unethical in other senses of a director's duties (see Chapter 10 of this book). Some companies, especially those in the United States, have been anxious about moves to make the task easier for investors to nominate directors and place resolutions on the agenda of the annual meeting. One reason is that companies fear trade unions might use their pension fund holdings as a means to influence company policy in ways that favor employment and employees rather than profitability. The justification of such approaches depends on one's view of justice and of the purpose of the company. Directors who believe they have a better understanding of the future prospects of the business might also ignore the expressed interest of shareholders. This could be in the long-term interest of shareholders.
6. Advocates of a strong view of stakeholder theory (see Chapter 10 for elaboration) often argue that shareholder value is the wrong basis for corporate decision making. A contention of this chapter is that shareholder value is fundamentally a difficult concept to judge, precisely because of the many different interests that shareholders can have at any given time with respect to any given decision. One alternative often discussed in the corporate governance literature is for directors to keep in mind the *long-term* interests of shareholders. This is problematic

because boards and management must keep in mind the interests of those long-term shareholders while ignoring the interests of short-term or perverse shareholders who may hold a majority of the shares. This is not a moot point for advocates of shareholder value.

For example, consider a recent IPO. Do directors decide to support the views of the mutual funds, which have just bought the shares? Or, alternatively, do directors take the view of the venture capitalist who helped to build the company and wants to realize the value of that work within a year or two? This dilemma underlines a problem with the concept of *shareholder value*. Another stance is to argue that the duty of the directors is to the business rather than to shareholders. Without a clear definition of *business*, directors may suffer from goal confusion.

Chapter 22 Executive Behavior: A Creditor Perspective on Managerial Ownership

1. Shareholders have a broad array of different governance devices or mechanisms that they can use to ensure that managers pursue shareholders' interests. One classification system breaks these different governance devices into those that are either internal or external to the firm. Internally, shareholders can use boards of directors, executive compensation systems, executive ownership, threat of termination or turnover, perquisite (*perks*) grants, and corporate bylaws. Externally, shareholders can sell their shares (i.e., walk), engage in proxy contests, use the market for corporate control (i.e., takeovers and acquisitions), and pursue legal action. Each of the internal and external mechanisms attempts to ensure that shareholders earn an appropriate rate of return on their investment.
2. Jensen and Meckling (1976) argue that supplying equity stakes to managers can alleviate the classic principal-agent conflict. Equity stakes potentially provide monetary incentives for managers to improve firm performance and increase firm cash flows, thereby benefiting investors. According to Jensen and Meckling's model, managers' incentives to expropriate firm resources depend on the cost that they bear from misbehaving relative to the benefits from misbehaving. Managers tend to incur greater costs from misconduct as their ownership stake in the firm rises. Misconduct becomes particularly costly as managers' human capital and wealth become increasingly undiversified in the firm. Agency theory specifies that equity ownership mitigates managerial incentives to waste and expropriate firm resources.
3. Stewardship theory centers on empowering managers and fostering commitment and identification with the firm. Specifically, stewardship focuses on the idea that managers can identify with the firm and internalize the organization's mission, leading to a collaborative management approach. In this context, managerial identification with the firm leads to a situation where managers incorporate firm well-being into their utility functions. Rousseau and Shperling (2003) argue that equity ownership plays a key role in developing managerial identification with the firm. Sundaramurthy and Lewis (2003) prescribe providing managers with an equity stake because it encourages firm identification and

assists in developing long-term relationships. Thus, stewardship theory suggests that equity stakes help managers be better stewards of corporate wealth.

4. Managerial fraud, misconduct, or incompetency can have a devastating effect on debtholder wealth. As an example, WorldCom executives in the late 1990s and early 2000s attempted to hide the company's poor performance by fraudulently manipulating accounting statements. If shareholders (or bondholders) had known about these fraudulent activities, they could have intervened to protect their interests and possibly prevented the complete collapse of the company and the destruction of so much wealth. Many analysts and researchers argue that WorldCom's governance systems abysmally failed in controlling the actions of Bernie Ebbers, WorldCom's CEO, and other top corporate executives. Consequently, debtholders show great concern toward governance systems because these devices protect their wealth as well as the wealth and well-being of the other stakeholders in the firm.

Chapter 23 Governance of Banking Institutions

1. Bank boards are larger than those of nonfinancial firms. Also, customer-directors (directors whose employers have lending relationships with the bank) and merger-directors (target directors who are added to the board following an acquisition) seem to play an important role in banks. Bank directors often sit on subsidiary boards and work in the vicinity of the bank. Statistics on the prevalence of customer-directors and merger-directors and information about employer distances for directors of nonfinancial firms are unavailable. Yet the fact that no study has examined the features of boards of nonfinancial firms may suggest they are relatively less important in nonfinancial firms.
2. Bank regulation and laws influence bank board governance both directly and indirectly. Regulators may impose specific restrictions on bank boards, such as size limits for national banks and residency requirements. Regulation may also affect bank boards because it was a factor leading banks to adopt the bank holding company organizational form. As documented in the chapter, organizational form plays a role in board composition. In the past, regulators and state laws restricted the market for corporate control, which affected bank boards.
3. A common problem in board-performance regressions is endogeneity biases in regression coefficients caused by omitted variables and reverse causality. To date, neither is there a clear understanding of the factors that shape bank boards nor are there good measures of them. If the factors that shape bank boards are related to performance, then performance regressions will be biased. For example, lending relationships may be important factors shaping bank board composition and lending relationships may affect bank performance. But controlling for lending relationships with directors' employers in performance regressions is difficult because of a lack of good measures.
4. Because regulation influences bank governance, the question often arises whether bank regulation substitutes for bank governance (by stepping in when bank governance is weak) or complements bank governance (by making current governance mechanisms more effective). This question may be both too

narrow, because it does not allow for the possibility that regulation may simply weaken bank corporate governance, and too broad because of various ways in which regulation affects governance. For example, while the literature on consolidation is inconclusive, much of the evidence suggests that regulatory restrictions on corporate control activity seem to have been value-decreasing. Brook, Hendershott, and Lee (1998) estimate that eliminating geographic banking restrictions through the Riegle-Neal Act increased the value of the banking industry by $85 billion. If regulation had been a substitute for weak bank governance caused by the absence of a market for corporate control, then why bank value rose after eliminating corporate control restrictions is unclear. Similarly, how restrictions on corporate control could have a complementary effect on bank governance is clear. While, on aggregate, regulation may have a substitution or complementarity effect, examining this issue is difficult due to the absence of variation in regulators in samples of public banking firms. Thus, finding few studies on this subject is not surprising.

Chapter 24 Corporate Governance: Nonequity Stakeholders

1. Rational incentive approaches often view shareholder and stakeholder rights as mutually exclusive. The reason is that, while other stakeholders have an interest in plowing back resources into the organization, shareholders will desire a return on their investment. Further, institutional features such as law or politics that favor one grouping will inevitably be detrimental to the other. For example, common law legal systems have traditionally privileged the rights of property owners. As legislation in such systems tends to be broad, the law is fleshed out by decisions made by the courts. Litigation naturally tends to favor the side with more legal resources at its disposal, while employees who resort to litigation against their employer risk undermining the entire basis of their employment relationship. In contrast, central to socioeconomic accounts is a notion of *complementarity*. Specifically, complementarity suggests that different rules and practices may work better together than on their own, building on strengths and compensating for weaknesses. Thus, potentially enough resources follow from a range of inputs for more than one side to win, moving shareholder-stakeholder relationships beyond the arena of a zero-sum game. Hence, in contexts where stakeholder rights are stronger, there is no reason firms should be any less successful in generating returns to their owners.
2. The Hall and Soskice model does not take into account all the different types of systems that operate in advanced societies (e.g., Mediterranean capitalism) and the major differences between dissimilar types of coordinated markets. For example, important differences exist between Continental European/Rhineland type economies and those of Scandinavia. Such differences include variations in the rights of individual employees—particularly with regard to job security—and the resources devoted to training. For example, in Scandinavia, there is less emphasis on vocational training and more on flexicurity-based add-on training for lifelong skills.
3. First, centralized collective bargaining may allow unions to cope with hostile governments. Second, what constitutes a stakeholder-friendly government may

vary. In many social democracies, trade union–social democratic party relations have weakened in recent years. Third, a focus on political ideologies may obscure broad underlying social consensus. This explains why right-wing governments in Scandinavia have been reluctant to implement the kind of radical anti-union reforms as those encountered, say, in Britain during the 1980s.

4. Rational hierarchical approaches suggest that a single dimension—relative private property rights—will affect all others. That is, the degree of property rights and how this is secured under the law will affect all other aspects of behavior. An assumption is that in contexts where property rights are the strongest, firms will perform best. In contrast, socioeconomic approaches see the firm as the center of a web of social relations. No single dimension is necessarily more important than others. Corporate governance represents a product not only of rights to property but also of the nature and quality of relations among owners, managers, and other stakeholders. This suggests that no specific institutional contexts will necessarily work better than others. In fact, firms may perform better in contexts where property rights are weak.

Chapter 25 Proxy Contests

1. Proxy contests received considerable attention in the 1980s and 1990s as an alternative to takeovers in replacing incumbent boards and management. This was bolstered by the fact that after a series of antitakeover laws and charter amendments following the 1980s hostile takeover wave, most firms became very well-protected against takeover threat. Nonetheless, hostile takeover activity and proxy contests exhibited similar cyclical patterns until the late 1990s, falling dramatically after 1988, and recovering somewhat for the mid-1990s. During this period, individual shareholders rather than corporate entities waged most proxy contests. These shareholders sought control of the board but were either unable or unwilling to launch a formal takeover bid due to resource constraints, the target firm's use of antitakeover devices, or other considerations. In the 2000s, hedge funds have come to dominate proxy contests. These investors rarely seek board control but instead pursue short-term governance arbitrage and more event-driven objectives such as takeovers, spin-offs, share repurchases, or dividend payouts.
2. The empirical literature shows that dissidents tend to win at least one directorship in both *control contests* waged for majority control of the board and *participation contests* for minority board representation. However, most control contests fail to achieve their actual objective of taking control of the board, presumably because they carry relatively high ex post risk from the perspective of the voting shareholders. Since 2001, hedge funds have won around two-thirds of their participation contests. The literature shows that contest success depends on a number of factors including the operating performance of the target firm, the resource commitment of the dissident, management's comparative advantage in proxy solicitation, the identity of the voting shareholders, and the voting rule in place for director elections.

   Evidence suggests that once a dissident challenge materializes, it imposes a greater threat to management than is implied by its immediate success. Several studies find that many firms are sold either during or immediately after a proxy contest, and observe significant management turnover and asset restructuring whether or not the dissident has taken control of the board. No evidence indicates that successful contests improve the operating or stock price performance of the target firm.

3. The 2000s wave of proxy contests has been attributed to two key factors. First, technological advances have made the task easier and cheaper for dissidents to start and publicly communicate proxy contests. The Internet has been particularly instrumental in disseminating information, getting more shareholders involved, and increasing general awareness about shareholder rights. Second, hedge funds have become formidable players in the activist arena and have been using proxy contests for short-term governance arbitrage. Hedge funds have been very successful in winning proxy contests, as they are mostly supported by proxy advisory firms as well as employ innovative campaign strategies such as *wolf-pack* coordination with other hedge funds and the use of derivatives to accumulate hidden voting power. Whether the wealth and performance effects of these contests are different has yet to be examined empirically.
4. The voting outcomes on proxy contests are likely to be boosted by the fact that as of the 2010 proxy season, the SEC is finally banning discretionary broker votes on uninstructed voting positions. Nonetheless, the majority voting rule is simultaneously becoming the norm in director elections, which also creates difficulties for dissidents to elect their own director nominees.

   The SEC's proposed revisions to proxy access rules are likely to affect the utility of proxy contests themselves as a means to contest director elections. The new rules would allow shareholders to include their own nominees in the firm's proxy materials for up to 25 percent of the available directorships, as well as permit shareholder-initiated proxy proposals to seek changes to nominating procedures. These amendments should clearly reduce the incentives of dissidents to distribute their own proxy materials for the purpose of director elections, and mirror similar changes already instituted in Delaware.

Chapter 26 Corporate Takeovers and Restructurings

1. The motives for takeovers are numerous, but include the following: capacity expansion, asset reallocation due to economic shocks, acquirer equity overvaluation, hubris, agency problems, market power, target mispricing, synergies, empire building, managerial entrenchment, and market discipline. The positive reasons (capacity expansion, asset reallocation due to economic shocks, target mispricing, synergies, and market discipline) are in conflict with the negative reasons (hubris, agency problems, empire building, and managerial entrenchment). Although these motives conflict, they are not mutually exclusive.
2. All four transactions involve a subsidiary operation within a firm. Spin-offs, equity carve-outs, and targeted shares create tradable shares of the subsidiary firm, but targeted shares do not have voting rights or a claim on the cash flows of the subsidiary. Subsidiary sales, spin-offs, and equity carve-outs separate the subsidiary from the parent, but equity carve-outs are often still under the control of the parent through majority ownership. Subsidiary sales, equity carve-outs,

and targeted shares raise cash for the parent, but this varies widely within equity carve-outs. Subsidiary sales are acquisitions while the other transactions are not.

3. The market for corporate control is the market in which managers compete for the right to oversee a firm's resources. This market has changed over time mainly in the manner by which managers compete and how they finance the transaction. In the 1980s, the competition for control was less friendly and more heavily financed with debt and cash. In the 1990s and into the first decade of the twenty-first century, the competition became friendlier and the transactions were more likely to be financed with the equity of the acquiring firm.
4. In an efficient market, prices reflect the discounted value of the firm's future cash flows. Therefore, the stock price conveys information to the manager about the firm's prospects based on all of the information available to the public. Thus, price is an important feedback mechanism in which managers can listen to the market with regard to a number of their investment decisions and respond appropriately or suffer an increase in the cost of their equity capital.
5. Because stockholders can diversify on their own, diversification within the firm is suboptimal unless the diversification produces some sort of efficiencies that the firm could not realize otherwise. This reason is the most basic one that relates firm value to firm-level diversification efforts. An additional reason is that intrafirm diversification increases the amount of informational asymmetries between managers and stockholders. The more sectors in which a firm operates, the greater the difficultly in correctly assessing the available information and the more easily managers can conceal value-destroying behavior (i.e., investing in pet projects with negative net present values). These asymmetries in information also dull the incentives of divisional managers because their compensation may not be highly correlated with firm performance.

Chapter 27 Corporate Takeovers and Wealth Creation

1. Disciplining takeovers are expected to target poorly performing firms and create value by improving the corporate governance of these firms (i.e., by replacing their management). In this type of takeover, the bidding firm typically bypasses the management of the target firm and makes a direct offer to the target firm's shareholders to buy their shares. If the offer is successful, the target's incumbent management team is replaced. Jensen (1988) defines this activity as the market for corporate control, where management teams compete with one another for the right to manage the assets owned by shareholders. The team that offers the highest value to the shareholders acquires the right to manage the assets until another management team that can realize a higher value of the assets comes along to replace existing management. Hostile takeovers are expected when the target firm performs poorly and its internal corporate governance mechanisms fail to discipline managers.

   Despite the expected gains from the improved corporate governance of target firms, hostile takeovers are frequently associated with lower wealth effects to the bidder's shareholders (see, for example, Franks and Mayer [1996]; Goergen and Renneboog [2004]; Martynova and Renneboog [2009]). Shareholders of bidding firms fear their firm will offer too high a premium if the target opposes the bid or if a bidder makes an offer directly to the target's shareholders. The anticipated upward revisions in the offer premium may erode the takeover gains accruing to the bidder's shareholders. Conversely, the higher wealth effects for the targets reflect the fact that opposition against the bid may be a profitable bargaining strategy to extract a higher offer price.

2. Recent empirical research documents the fact that better investor protection and a more shareholder-oriented corporate governance focus results in lower agency costs and higher company valuations and growth potential (Levine 1999). Extending these arguments to M&As, one should expect takeovers by firms from English legal origin countries (i.e., countries with better corporate governance regulation) to yield higher returns to the bidder's and target's shareholders than takeovers by Continental European firms (i.e., countries with weaker shareholder protection).

   Differences in laws and their subsequent enforcement also may affect the costs associated with completing a takeover transaction and may vary significantly across countries. For example, Goergen, Martynova, and Renneboog (2005) argue that strong protection of minority shareholders increases the bargaining power of the target firm's shareholders, enabling them to ask for a higher offer price. This reduces the returns to the bidder's shareholders and may also discourage some bidders from initiating a takeover if the expected synergies are not high enough.

3. Although diversifying or conglomerate acquisitions are expected to create operational and financial synergies, the creation of diversified firms is associated with various negative attributes such as rent-seeking behavior by divisional managers (Scharfstein and Stein 2000), bargaining problems within the firm (Rajan, Servaes, and Zingales 2000), or bureaucratic rigidity (Shin and Stulz 1998). These disadvantages of diversification may outweigh the alleged synergies and result in wealth destruction for the bidder's shareholders. Diversifying mergers may be an outgrowth of agency conflicts between managers and shareholders. As such, M&As between companies operating in unrelated industries are expected to trigger lower takeover returns to the bidder's shareholders than M&As between firms in related industries. Conversely, the wealth effects to the shareholders of the target firm are likely to be higher in diversifying M&As. The reason is that investors expect bidders pursuing diversification strategies to bid more aggressively and hence pay higher takeover premiums than bidders adhering to a focus strategy.

4. Analysis of takeover announcement returns hinges on the assumption that an M&A announcement brings new information about the bidding and target firms to the market such that investors update their expectations about the firms' future earnings, which is then reflected in the share price. An incremental change in the share price of the bidding and target firms on the day of the deal announcement is the expected net present value (NPV) of the takeover. The incremental share price change is measured by the abnormal returns, which is the difference between the realized return and a benchmark return. The latter is the return that would be generated if the takeover bid had not taken place. In this context, one should interpret negative abnormal returns at the M&A announcement as evidence that the market expects the takeover to be unprofitable.

However, in the context of equity-paid acquisitions, negative market reaction to the announcement of the takeover may be unrelated to the profitability of the takeover. This is because investors consider an equity offer as a signal that the bidder's shares are overpriced and hence adjust the share price downward. This is in line with the notion that managers attempt to time equity issues to coincide with surging stock markets or even with the peak of the stock market cycle.

Chapter 28 Corporate Governance and Accountability

1. The standard rationale for judicial deference to board decision making is the need to avoid deterring corporate officials from taking business risks. When corporations take risks, shareholders benefit from the innovation and profits that can result. A deferential approach to board decisions thus redounds to the benefit of shareholders. Further, a well-diversified investor should be shielded from the ill effects of aggressive risk taking, as losses resulting from bad bets at certain firms will be offset by gains made by other firms that are more successful.

   Another justification for judicial deference is recognition of the dangers of hindsight bias—the natural inclination to view a decision that turned out badly as unreasonable when the decision was originally made. Because judges are not business experts they hesitate to substitute their judgment for that of a corporation's leaders. Many also view ex post litigation as an inefficient method for resolving corporate disputes. Therefore, judges often assert that shareholders should sell their shares or elect new directors instead of looking to the courts to resolve disputes with management.

   Finally, there is the widely embraced belief that most shareholder lawsuits lack merit and are brought not to vindicate shareholder interests but to enrich plaintiff attorneys. In this view, the scant benefits shareholders derive from such litigation rarely justify the excessive costs to the corporation and its shareholders.

   One danger of increasing the risk of director liability is that fear of litigation might discourage qualified directors from serving. Fear of liability could also encourage officials to be excessively cautious in their management of corporate affairs. Finally, reducing the procedural burdens on shareholder litigation might encourage frivolous litigation and unduly strengthen plaintiff attorneys' hands as they seek quick settlements of their claims.

2. The SEC proposal to adopt IFRS seems inconsistent with the requirements of SOX § 109 because the IASB is funded through voluntary contributions by foreign governments and private firms. This conflict with the law might be resolved if the SEC or FASB recognize IFRS standards on a one-by-one basis—approving some standards and rejecting others, rather than adopting IFRS wholesale. Alternatively, the SEC could persuade Congress to amend the statute to recognize the legitimacy of IFRS.

   Perhaps of greater concern, the IASB is not subject to the control of the SEC or FASB and is instead controlled by a committee of private officials who come from a range of countries across the globe. Given this structure, U.S. citizens cannot easily hold the IASB accountable for its decisions. The only apparent accountability mechanism is a government's threat to withdraw or to reject IASB standards. Considering the significant conversion costs involved, once U.S. regulators adopt IFRS, this threat may lack credibility.

3. One possible reform is to reduce firms' reliance on stock options by reducing their size in proportion to total compensation. Option schemes could also be restructured by imposing longer holding periods for stock acquired under options, or by indexing options against industry averages in a way that rewards firm-specific performance rather than stock price movements tied to general economic trends. Companies could also include clawback provisions in employment contracts, requiring the forfeiture of incentive pay that turned out to be based on inflated earnings, regardless of an individual actor's culpability in the error.

   Another possible approach is to delay the payment of incentive-based compensation for several years so that any earnings manipulations might be detected in the interim. Firms could base incentive pay on a three- to five-year rolling average of annual income, and thereby encourage a longer-term perspective for all employees.

4. One of the most pressing problems in corporate governance seems to be a lack of individual accountability for mismanagement and fraud. Another problem is the persistence of powerful incentives for managers to manipulate financial reports. Finally, despite recent legal reforms, directors appear to lack sufficient authority and expertise to effectively oversee financial reporting.

   In light of these problems, reform options include revising incentive compensation schemes (see response to question 3), increasing SEC enforcement efforts, and the adoption of legislative and judicial reforms to reduce barriers to shareholder litigation at both the state and federal levels. Such steps should inspire greater vigilance by officers, directors, and auditors by reducing incentives for fraud while heightening consequences to individuals for engaging in or acquiescing to misconduct.

Chapter 29 Corporate Governance Rules and Guidelines

1. Global governance convergence recently became a hot topic. The 2009 G-20 meeting, which was conducted in London, was a remarkable milestone for the global governance conversion. G-20 is still a small group of countries but the global convergence of the governance standards is inevitable. Currently, there are many potential and real shortcomings that hinder the convergence process. First and foremost, corporate governance rules and guidelines are incompatible worldwide. Although some countries have made a move toward a convergence (e.g., moving from one-tier model to two-tier model), most remain secluded so the convergence process may take longer than advocates predict.

2. Various factors influence corporate governance including corporate laws, federal laws, listing standards, and best practices. Each of these drivers influences corporate governance by requiring compliance with its own rules and guidelines. State corporate laws mainly exist to protect shareholders rights. No universal standard for the state corporate laws exist, so each state can establish its own model.

The Securities Exchange Act of 1934 is the most illustrative example of the federal laws. The intention of this act is to protect investors from receiving false and misleading information, maintain efficient markets, and facilitate capital formation.

Listing standards usually narrow what corporate governance issues should be enforced. They provide clear definition of and criteria for director independence and composition of board subcommittees. All major national stock exchanges require compliance with SOX provisions.

Best practices, which are guidelines suggested by professional organizations such as the Council of Institutional Investors, are not mandatory to implement, unlike federal and state laws and stock exchange rules. Yet companies are more likely to follow these guidelines if they want to strengthen their corporate governance effectiveness.

3. The main reasons for the current crises are ineffective regulation and the greed and incompetence of executives of troubled financial institutions. Effective corporate governance plays an important role in addressing these crises by boosting investor confidence and developing effective global financial markets.
4. There are two contrary views involving SOX. Critics consider SOX as burdensome and expensive to implement. Further, SOX discourages companies from going public. In fact, the number of IPOs for both U.S. and non-U.S. companies has declined dramatically since the implementation of SOX. This legislation is especially inconvenient for international companies because they have no other choice but to comply with SOX if they want to be traded in the U.S. market. Burdensome compliance requirements impede the potential global growth by limiting the opportunities for the non-U.S. companies to raise capital.

   SOX advocates believe that the legislation substantially improved public trust and investor confidence in corporate America and its capital markets and financial reports. Proponents of SOX argue that the sustainable benefits of SOX are hard to quantify, but that its short-term costs are exaggerated and easy to measure. Sustainable benefits of SOX include the improvement in public trust and investor confidence in capital markets and the reduction of corporate malfeasance and auditing fraud. Nonetheless, the efficacy and sustainability of SOX depends on its cost efficiency and scalability of its implementation rules established by the second PCAOB. SOX will need to be more efficient and more cost-effective to reduce its compliance costs.

Chapter 30 Economic Aspects of Corporate Governance and Regulation

1. Corporate governance and regulation are mechanisms that help to alleviate agency problems between shareholders and managers and among shareholders. Typically, managers are more informed about their firm's situation, project profitability, and future prospects (asymmetric information) than are other outside investors. Managers can also misallocate corporate resources and extract private benefits of control (moral hazard). In addition, contracts are often incomplete as they cannot include all possible contingencies and need to be enforced.

All of these problems indicate that firms are not necessarily run for the best interests of shareholders and other stakeholders.

There are several ways to help solve these problems at the firm level. For example, board structures can be aimed at greater director monitoring. Companies can design compensation packages that link pay to performance. At the country level, laws and regulations to strengthen the legal system and the financial markets can help. Better corporate governance standards and more stringent regulations should prevent expropriation and fraud and ensure better allocation of resources and firm performance. In turn, these actions should promote confidence and investment in the financial markets. Regulations such as the Sarbanes-Oxley Act of 2002 in the United States embody this view.

2. Companies searching for external financing will try to bond themselves to high corporate governance standards to assure investors of an efficient allocation of the resources. Consequently, this will reduce the costs of funds (capital). This is why company characteristics such as financing needs and growth opportunities help to explain the variation in corporate governance choices of companies, as some companies have more to gain from bonding. Country characteristics such as legal protections and the level of economic and financial development affect the costs and benefits firms face in implementing such bonding mechanisms and more generally when improving their own governance. When property rights are weak and financial markets are less developed, verifying and enforcing the companies' corporate governance commitments are more difficult. Therefore, companies in countries with poor country-level investor protection have weaker incentives to invest in firm-level governance mechanisms as they will not get rewarded. By contrast, companies in countries with strong investor protection do not suffer from this commitment problem and will be willing to spend more on corporate governance.
3. The Sarbanes-Oxley Act of 2002 introduced more stringent rules to decrease the likelihood of corporate misconduct and fraud under the implicit assumption that better monitoring will positively affect all companies. However, several studies show that the introduction of new rules has generated negative externalities. This is especially evident for small companies for which the compliance costs are higher than the benefits of stronger regulation. Other evidence shows the existence of a threshold effect where, above some levels of country investor protection, regulation has little or even a negative effect on firm performance. These studies highlight the fact that the interaction effects between the various corporate governance mechanisms are complex and that introduction of new regulations has to take into consideration the economic and institutional factors of a country that complement and affect firm incentives. Similarly, evidence shows that one model of corporate governance is unlikely to be optimal because firms are heterogeneous, have different monitoring and advising needs, and vary in their ability to recover compliance costs through lower cost of capital. This evidence has important policy consequences because it shows that too stringent and single-type regulation can generate negative financial and real effects on companies and the overall economy.
4. La Porta, Lopez-de-Silanes, Shleifer, and Vishny (1998) show that laws vary across countries as a consequence of legal traditions. Specifically, they find that

common law countries have better investor protection, better capital markets development, and higher firm growth than civil law countries. However, several studies contend that the existence of other omitted and perhaps more important country characteristics determine laws and regulations as well as economic and financial outcomes. For instance, creditor rights are strongest in countries where the main religion is Protestant, regardless of legal origin. Historical events such as World War II and the Communism threat have led to frequent changes of laws with no change in legal origins. Political groups can lead to the implementation of protectionist country policies that are hostile to arm's-length markets and investor protections, regardless of legal origin. Consequently, highlighting the existence of *correlation* between legal origins and shareholder protection, rather than classifying it as a *causal* relationship, would be more appropriate.

Index